"Little Italy" Stanley, Bridgewater Massachusetts, USA

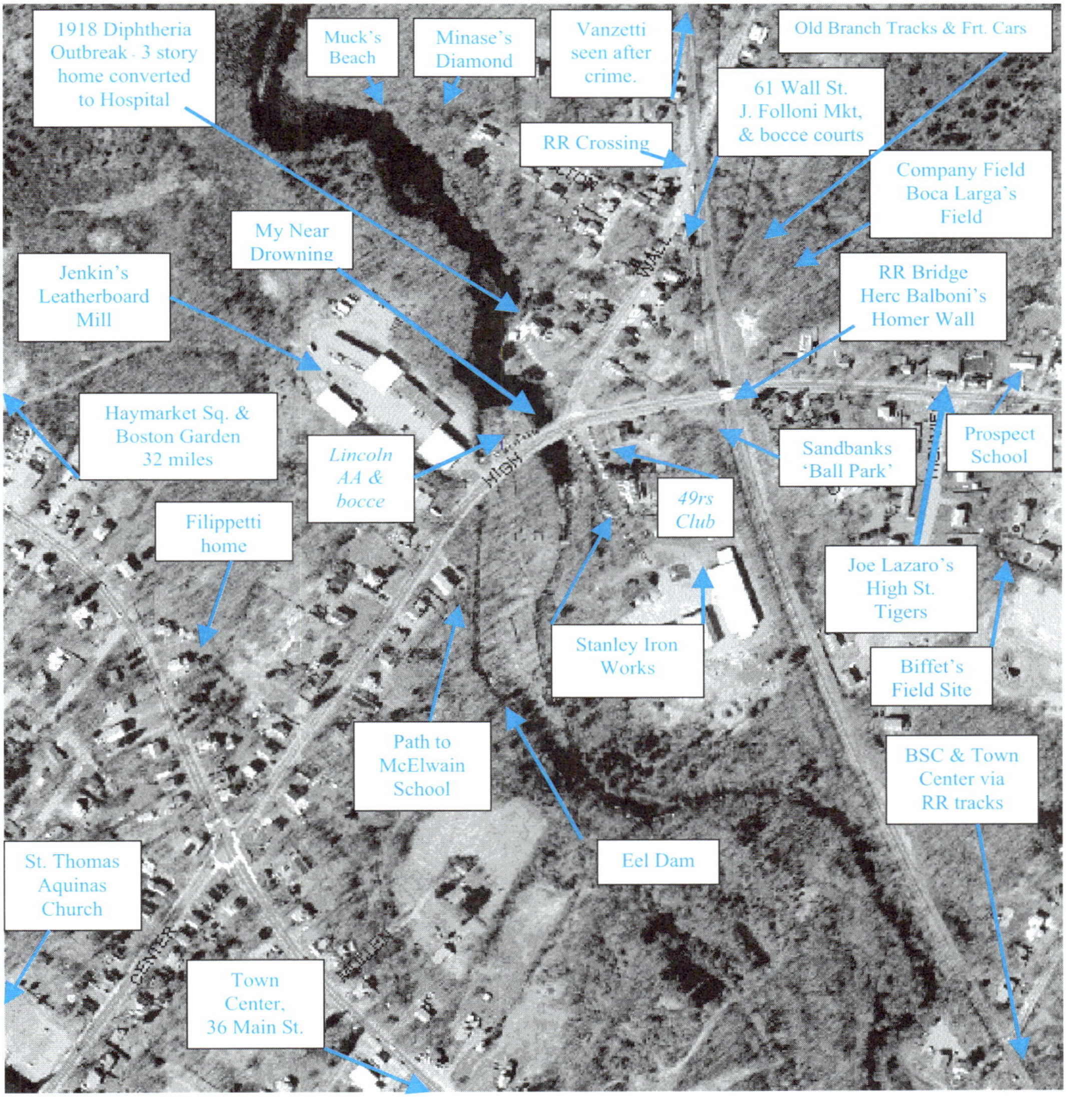

My Game of Life

- **Dedication & Introduction** …Warm Up & Tip Off
- **1st Quarter — Early Years** …Hope Springs Eternal
- **2nd Quarter — Service & Career** …Regular Season
- **Half Time** …A Funny Thing Happened
- **3rd Quarter — Family Life** …Playing Field Lights
- **4th Quarter — Twilight Years** …Crunch Time

My Way
The Memoirs of Coach Larry Folloni

*An All-American Success Story of one man's
Loving devotion to God, Family and Career*

Full of Love, Warmth, Humor, Tragedy & Nostalgia
This Classic includes Excellent Coaching and Business Tips
And a Delicious Slice of the History of 'The Greatest Generation'

COACH LARRY FOLLONI

A Moment in Time with The Coach in His Prime

Larry Folloni
With Michael E. Folloni

Illustrations by James McKelvy Walker, Cover by Richard Acosta and Michael Mata

A Light Energy Book

My Way   *The Early Years 4*

Bonus Shots

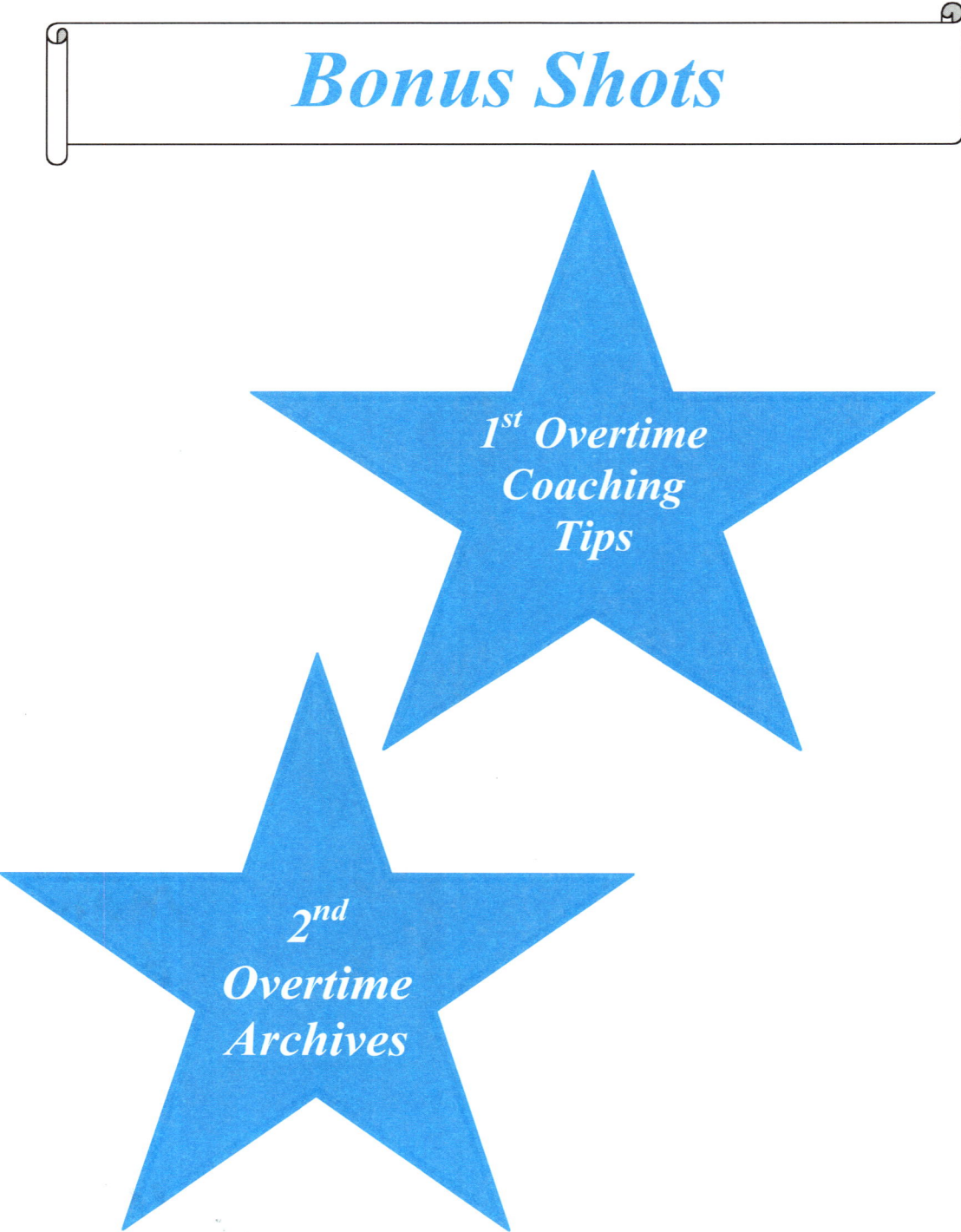

1st Overtime Coaching Tips

2nd Overtime Archives

"Extra Books" within this Book

WHAT PEOPLE ARE SAYING ABOUT COACH LARRY FOLLONI & 'MY WAY'
Cheering Section

"With all due respect to the amazing Mr. Bird, he wasn't the first 'Larry Legend'. Before "Fabulous Flutie" came 'Fabulous Folloni.' Alongside the 'Sultan Of Swat'and the 'Splendid Splinter' now stands the 'Stanley Slugger.' And on the Mt. Rushmore of true geniuses behind sport's most famous dynasties, adoring fans have carved the faces of Red Auerbach, Vince Lombardi, and John McGraw ... soon to be proudly joined by the "Old Coach!

Recently <u>Sports Illustrated</u> chose the *"Top 100 Sports Books Of All Time."* Wonder which one they'll have to bump to make room for MY WAY?" *Larry Jr.*

"I have read some of the excerpts from "My Way". It just can't miss; it sounds like it will be a huge success." *Ralph Sherman, one of Coach's 1st H.S. Athletes*

"The heirloom that I would choose to hand down is my grandfather's book that he is writing. This gift would tell my children about their ancestors. It would also help them learn about history through my grandfather's stories. I think reading this book will be a fun way for family members to learn." *Cameron Henry Leen, Age 8*

"I remember his work ethic, how he stressed the fundamentals and how he instilled his *Famous Folloni Special Press*. This press was devastating to our opponents, and his teachings have carried me on through life. I'll never forget those happy years playing Basketball for you. I'll never forget all that you did for us through our school years. Thanks!! *Paul Pallatroni, Co-Capt. '60-'61 Championship teams*

"You're a legend who was way ahead of your time and you created true Champions. Your foresight, concepts, creativity, skills as an innovator, ingenuity, and accomplishments, cast you in a legendary light." *Nate Thompson, The Gazette*

"I remember his teams in '60 and '61 and people went to the Garden to see them play. For younger coaches who wanted to be the best they went to see [Folloni], because he certainly was the best. But the thing that really sticks out in my mind was his caring for the kids," said Miller. "A lot of people have great records but he really cared for the individual." *Leo Miller, State Coaches Hall of Famer*

"Folloni is the conscience of school sports in the state". *Larry Ames, Boston Globe*

"Folloni's shoes may never be filled." *Tony Sirrico – Brockton Enterprise*

"Sacrifice for your teammates, how to win gracefully and how to lose with dignity. All traits a person needs to succeed in life. I learned all these things from my basketball coach. We're All Winners because of you**.** I can hardly wait to read your memoirs."   *Steve Pivacek, Co-Capt. on '60-'61 Championship teams*

No player stood above the others. All contributed equally. It was sacrifice and teamwork that you instilled upon us that made us Champs.
Steve Prophett, Co-Capt. on '60-'61 Championship teams

I never knew much about Larry Folloni, but I find it very gratifying to know that this is the man that coached my father. He seems like quite an amazing man and I look forward to the finished book.*Chris Ghelfi, Son of Championship Player Tony*

"He's been the heartbeat of Schoolboy athletics for a long, long time in the state of Massachusetts. On the town level, a dynamic leader who got the town moving recreationally for the youngsters. In every way, Larry Folloni has proven to be an extraordinary example to follow, for young and old alike. As a parent, as a peer, as a leader and as an organizer, Larry Folloni accomplished everything he set out to do and he did so with "Class". Not many come down the road like Larry Folloni. They are few and far between. Our lives have been a lot better and a lot brighter for having known him and having him touch our lives. I firmly believe that his readers will experience his warmth, humor and perspective in re-living the memories of a half-century in the sports world."   *Mike Silva, Sports writer, Taunton Gazette*

No one knows any more than I do of the impact that you have made on Schoolboy Athletics in our Great State. Your dedicated efforts on behalf of the kids will stand forever.   *Dick Neal, Executive Director of MIAA*

The MIAA Council at its meeting on June 2, 1970, voted to express commendation and appreciation to you as chairman of the MSSADA Rules Committee for a difficult job well done in revising and updating the rules for interscholastic sports in the state. The MIAC not only recognizes the high quality of the work done but also is aware of the amount of time and thought that went into this task.
Bertrum Holland, Executive Secretary of MIAC

"I remember how you praised the way I dove for a loose ball during one of our practice sessions. The things that I learned from you as a player, like pushing myself to my max, putting in extra time on the little things like faking, being aggressive, working on all the fundamentals, and generally the work ethic that you instilled in us, all of this lives on. And I have you to thank in large part for the success that I have had in life." *State Rep. Peter Flynn, 1956 Championship Team*

"Larry Folloni has built a farm system that is the envy of every coach in the state".
Fred Foye - Boston Herald Traveler

"You were the most fun father and my, and everybody's favorite famous Coach!"
Barbara Collins, A friend of my daughter Jean, who I called "My Little Girl"

"It has been an honor and a privilege to play under your tutelage; I owe much success that I have achieved to your teaching and coaching."
Attorney Bobby Seaver, Captain from early 50's Team

"Competing with you on the golf course is something that I treasured and I will always remember. A great competitor and a great guy who never quit. Your accomplishments and achievements on the golf course will never be equaled or forgotten."
Herc Phyllides, Golfing associate

I have often told my friends that there never was a more hardworking conscientious individual than Larry Folloni. The hours he gave to the B-R School System and the MIAA- "UNREAL"!
Will Cingolani – Friend, Administrator and Coach

Coach Folloni was a supreme tactician; a fundamentalist and disciplinarian, all rolled into one. He was a perfectionist, never took anything for granted. His practices were run with the precision of a fine tuned watch--no wasted time, every drill had a meaning. Any drill he designed was for the expressed purpose of being used in a game. "Teamwork always was and always will be his hallmark."
Dave Messaline – Capt. BHS '61 State Champs

"There'll never be another like Larry Folloni…He's been the heartbeat of schoolboy athletics for a long, long time in Mass.". "Not only a driving force in implementing new athletic programs at B-R and for the state, Coach Folloni is a true leader and a man who has excelled".
Mike Silva – Taunton Daily Gazette

"When I think of Larry, I remember sitting with my Dad at Legion Field watching the Lincoln AA baseball team. You were at 2nd base and Hank Pearson at 1st. I remember the pick-off play when you came in behind Hank as he came in from 1st to cover a bunt attempt. Dino pitched out, Bo fired the ball down to you at 1st for the out. It was executed perfectly. I knew before you did, that you were meant to be a coach. Lester Lane would have been proud of the play you called that day."
Ed Denton, former star pupil and athlete, later Superintendent Principal, boss.

"Re: Your Coaching Tips: I read everything over and it sounds great – just like a Coach should be. That only thing that I can add is that when I came to Bridgewater in 1962, Larry Folloni was a 'legend'. Now in 2003, he is even more of a legend with all of his accomplishments. Keep on going."
Don Prohovich

Don Prohovich was an All-American Baseball player at Holy Cross and a member of the 1954 National Invitational Tournament (NIT) Championship Team that included 2-time All American and Celtic Star Tom Heinson, Togo Palazzi, Joe Liebler, Dick Santaniello & (The Super Catholic Memorial H. S. Coach) Ronnie Perry.

MY WAY
The Memoirs of Coach Larry Folloni

Published by: **Light Energy Books**

All rights reserved. No part of this book may be reproduced or transmitted in any form or by any means, electronic or mechanical, including photocopying, recording or by any information storage and retrieval system, without written permission from the author, except for inclusion of brief quotations in a review.

All claims and opinions expressed herein are solely the responsibility of Lawrence F. Folloni Sr. Unattributed quotations are by Lawrence F. Folloni Sr.

Copyright 2003 by Lawrence F. Folloni Sr. & Light Energy Books

First Printing 2003

Printed in the United States of America

Library of Congress Cataloging-in-Publication Data

Library of Congress Control Number: 2003092602

Folloni, Lawrence F. 1919 –
     My Way: The Memoirs of Coach Larry Folloni
     [With assistance of] Michael E. Folloni
     1st Edition
     Illustrations by James McKelvy Walker.
     ISBN 0-9740480-0-3 (cl) $19.95

♦   Sports & Recreation. 2. Family & Relationships. 3. History.
     4. Autobiography 5. Business & Economics

Bowker Books in Print #6906549335

Cover Design & Graphics Donated by Richard Acosta & Michael T. Mata, L.A., CA

This book is available from:
Coach Larry Folloni
13 Ross Ave., Hampton Beach, N.H. 03842
1-800 425-7440
CoachFolloni@comcast.com

TABLE OF CONTENTS
Schedule

This book is an eclectic collection of a wide variety of topics written for an equally diverse group of readers. Parts are written for several very narrow audiences, but all in all it has some entertaining worth for a very wide audience. **"My Way"** is:

- A history book
- A coach's manual
- A cookbook
- An inspirational book
- A philosophy book
- A biography
- A family album
- A real estate business 'how-to' book
- A comedy with some tragedy, and
- A collection of a simple 20th century immigrant family's heirloom fotos & facts.

I didn't set out to make a book that was all things to everybody, but I'm sure that "My Way" does have at least some things in it for everybody to enjoy.

Few, perhaps, will enjoy every bit of this book, so I urge you pick and choose your way through it to find what suits your fancy.

And if you like "My Way", buy one for a friend or family member. A substantial amount of the profits will go to worthy youth recreation and scholarship programs.

I'd love to hear your feedback, good or bad, and any input that you might have for the 2nd edition.

"Little Italy" Stanley, Bridgewater Massachusetts, USA Aerial Photo		01
What People are Saying	*Cheering Section*	05
Table of Contents	*Schedule*	09
Acknowledgements	*Assistant Coaches & Roster*	14
Dedication	*Warm up*	17
Foreword	*Ringer*	19
Introduction	*Tip Off*	22
Legion Field Aerial Photo		24

1ST QUARTER, EARLY YEARS

MY FAMILY & ROOTS	*Team Try Outs*	25
NEAR ESCAPES FROM DEATH	*Almost Cut*	34

DIPHTHERIA OUTBREAK	*Conspiracy Theory*	41
GAMES WE PLAYED	*The Real Farm Leagues*	42
WHERE WE PLAYED	*Fields of Dreams*	43
IMPROVISED EQUIPMENT	*Before Spaulding, Reebok & Nike*	46
NEIGHBORS NICKNAMES	*Home League Handles*	49
PRE TEEN YEARS	*Little Leagues*	50
SPORTS VS FAMILY CHORES	*Workouts*	51
LIFE IN THE 20'S	*Team Depth*	53
DEPRESSION & THE '30'S	*When Things go Wrong…*	56
	Don't Quit	57
PROHIBITION ERA	*Bootleg Play*	58
EARLY TEEN YEARS	*Mickey Cochrane Hank Greenberg*	60
HOOP COURT DEDICATION	*Coach's Box Score*	63
BASEBALL IN 30' & 40'S	*4-Fingered Mitts & Negro Leaguers*	64
OLDER BROTHERS & SISTER	*Rock Solid Teammates, Varsity*	72
TWO HICKS MAKE IT BIG	*Rocky Marciano Tales*	79
YOUNGER FAMILY MEMBERS	*Rock Solid Teammates, J.V.*	83
MOM & POP STORE	*Teamwork*	89
BIRTH OF TOWN CREDIT UNION	*Credit where Credit is Due*	91
SCHOOL & 1ST CHAMPIONSHIPS	*Chalk Talk*	97
BHS '37 VARSITY TEAMS	*Lester Lane Era*	106
LIFE AFTER HIGH SCHOOL	*Detour to the Next Level*	109

2ND QUARTER, MARRIAGE SERVICE AND CAREER

COVER PAGE	*Regular Season – winners All*	112
WORLD WAR II YEARS	*Recruitment for War & Peace*	113
DATING AND SERVICE TRAINING	*Inspired Impactful Innovations*	116

Boston, Philadelphia, New Orleans, Texas Tech-Ellington Field, Santa Ana & Victorville, CA

WEDDING BELLS	*The Starting Bell*	124
ON TO VICTORVILLE	*Cal-is-then-ics*	127
B U YEARS – TERRIERS	*Go to College, Get Some Knowledge*	131
START OF TEACHING & COACHING	*Rookie Year*	136
END OF 1ST TEACHING & COACHING	*Released*	142
DREAM CAREER IN B'WATER	*Trading Up*	146
AVAILABLE EQUIPMENT/FIELDS	*Gear and There*	146
REVIEW OF RECREATION NEEDS	*Create a Home Field Advantage*	147
OVERCOMING OBSTACLES	*Eyes on the Prize*	148
PLAY TIME USA FILM	*Pro-motion*	149
RECREATION PROGRAM	*Enthusiastic Beginnings*	151
LOOKING BACK	*Post Game Post Mortem*	156
BUMPY ROAD TO SUCCESS	*No Pain No Gain*	159
OPENING OF NEW B.H.S.	*Start of New Season*	163
RELIVING CHAMPIONSHIP TEAMS	*Glory Days*	167

ON TO THE 1956 CHAMPIONSHIP YEAR	*One for the books*	169
STATE TOURNEY TIME	*Gut Check*	174
BUILDING NEXT TWO STATE CHAMPIONS	*Vital Rebuilding Years*	178
CORNERSTONE 1958 & 59 TEAMS	*Unsung Heroes*	179
THE 1960 STATE CHAMPIONSHIP TEAM	*Two for the Looks*	182
TESTIMONIAL FOR '60 STATE CHAMPIONS	*Playoff Payoff*	189
MY WAY CUT SHORT	*Abrupt Change in Life*	191
1961 STATE CHAMPIONSHIP TEAM	*Three for You and Me*	193
FIRST RETIREMENT FROM COACHING	*Going out on Top?*	197
THE KEYNOTE ARTICLE	*My Swan Song*	198
B-R REGIONAL HIGH SCHOOL YEARS	*New Team, League & Era*	204
MY LAST YEAR AS A COACH	*Saving the Best for Last*	209
TIME TO MOVE ON -- MIAA WORK	*Going Going Gone*	210
LIFE IN THE 70'S AT B-R	*And now the end is near ...*	212
EARLY GOLFING YEARS	*Fair Way*	217
TED WILLIAMS "RED LETTER DAY"	*Perfect Practice & Heroes*	226

HALF TIME ENTERTAINMENT

'MIRACULOUS' COMEBACK	*A Funny Thing Happened*	228
CLEAN-UP HITTER	*C. Cole, D. Bicknell, Celtics*	228
FIRST FENWAY FUN	*Agnes Yakavonis*	228
TITICUT FOLLIES	*James Folloni, Dave Flynn*	228
SPORTS TRIVIA	*Bill Prophett & J33958*	229
YOUR KIND OF PACE	*Ty Cobb, Jim Folloni & ?*	229
PRIDE BEFORE THE FALL	*Roberto Folloni*	230
COWHIDE	*D. Dowd, Hurricane Donna*	230
DECOY PLAYS	*Who Dung It?*	231
DISCIPLINE	*Tale of 2 Steve's & Johnnie*	231
SHOOTING FOR THE MOON	*Jack Falloni*	232
LARRY'S CRUNCH	*Willie Ferioli*	232
IT'S A SNAP	*Glenn Poole*	233
BRINGING THE FIRE TO THE FIREHOUSE	*The Best Day of the Year*	234
PAPA GOT LOST	*Milkman Jackie Mark*	235
	Travels with Taylor	236

3RD QUARTER, LIGHTS OF MY LIFE

COVER PAGE	*Family Enrichment*	237
REAL ESTATE & MARKET VENTURES	*SIDELIGHTS*	238
LIVING WITH THE MARK & FOLLONI FAMILIES		239
36 MAIN ST.	*1948*	244
91 BEDFORD ST.	*December 30, 1953*	253
DISASTER STRIKES THE FOLLONI TEAM	*Fire at Bedford St.*	257
20 SOUTH ST., BROCKTON, MA	*November 12, 1964*	262
13 ROSS AVE., HAMPTON BEACH, NH	*June 14, 1971*	270

6 STEVENS AVE., BROCKTON, MA	*October 22, 1974*	281
61-63 WALL ST., BRIDGEWATER, MA	*1983*	284
LANDLORD – TENANT EXPERIENCES	*Considered Adventures*	287
5880 SABAL PALM BLVD., TAMARAC, FL	*February, 1984*	291
OUT WITTING THE RIP OFF ARTIST	*Never Forget*	298
STOCK MARKET VENTURES	*What Goes Up…*	306
9 ROSS AVE, HAMPTON BEACH, NH	*June 12, 2001`*	311
WORK ETHIC & JOBS	*MOONLIGHTS*	314
VACATION, TRAVEL & GOLF MEMORIES	*FLIGHTS*	320
QUEBEC	*Changing Guard*	323
NEW YORK CITY	*4 Aces*	324
WASHINGTON D.C.	*Record Game*	326
ST. LOUIS, MO	*Busch Leagues*	328
CHERRY HILL, NJ	*Family Fulfillment*	329
NEW ORLEANS, LA.	*Bjorn Bjorg*	332
CALIFORNIA	*Big Mac Attack*	333
ITALIAN ROOTS TRIP	*When in Rome*	338
FLORIDA & STOPOVERS	*It's a Small World*	344
CHICAGO	*An Honest Friend*	347
OUR AUTOMOBILES	*Can you a Ford it?*	349
FOLLONI GOLFING TEAM	*Chips off the Old Block*	354
NH SENIOR'S GOLF ASSOCIATION	*Straight Shooters*	362
QUOTES FROM GOLFING ASSOCIATES	*Clubhouse Chatter*	364
A FEW OF MY FAVORITE THINGS	*DELIGHTS*	365

4TH QUARTER, TWILIGHT YEARS

COVER PAGE	*Crunch Time*	367
MY (NEAR) LAST HURRAH	*Severely Injured & Disabled*	368
ANOTHER SETBACK FOR THE TEAM	*Helen 'Knocked Down'*	382
ITALIAN SERENADERS	*'Down but not Out'*	388
SEACOAST / HAVEN HEALTH CENTER	*Home away from Home*	389
HAND ME DOWN FAMILY TRAITS	*Bad & Good*	399
WHY I BECAME A COACH	*Share the Enjoyment*	401
WHY SPORTS ARE SO IMPORTANT	*Common Sense is not Common*	401
HOW I'D LIKE TO BE REMEMBERED	*The Right Way for Kids*	401
WEALTH = ACCOMPLISHMENTS, NOT $	*Satisfaction*	402
CLOSING THOUGHTS	*Play & Stay Together*	403
'MY WAY' LYRICS	*Yes, it was My Way!*	405
POSTSCRIPT	*Yes, it was My Way!*	407

1ST OVERTIME, COACHING TIPS & ALL TIME ALLSTARS

COVER PAGE	*BONUS SHOTS*	408

HOW TO BECOME A SUCCESSFUL COACH	*Book Excerpts*	409
COMPARISON OF HOOPS IN VARIOUS ERAS	*'30's to the Present*	428
MY FAVORITE COACHING COLLEAGUES	*Honest, Loyal, Dedicated*	434
MY ALL TIME ALL STAR TEAMS	*'40's to Present*	450
BEST OF THE BEST MY TOP 8	*Dedication, Teamwork*	452
MY BEST COMEBACK TEAMS	*1957 & 1968*	455
BEST COMEBACK GAMES	*1954 & 1957*	456
BRRHS "PURE SHOOTERS"	*1950 – 2000*	457

2ND OVERTIME, ARCHIVES

COVER PAGE	*For You to Pick & Choose*	459
BHS, BRRHS SPORTS HISTORY	*Basketball*	460
BHS, BRRHS SPORTS HISTORY	*Football*	462
BRRHS SPORTS HISTORY	*Other Teams & Individuals*	463
BHS, BRRHS SPORTS HISTORY	*Basketball Captains*	464
ACHIEVEMENTS OF SOME STUDENTS	*A 1% only sampling*	465
MEMORABLE EVENTS & TEAMS	*The Ones that Got Away*	470
MEMORABLE EVENTS & TEAMS	*More 'Bests'*	470
SOME SCARY STORIES	*Lead Paint, Lead Shot*	471
REBOUNDS FROM THE PAST	*Guest Contributor*	472
A SECOND CHANCE IN LIFE	*Rebounds for the Future*	477
RECOLLECTIONS OF STANLEY	*Teen Games & Mischief*	478
RECOLLECTIONS OF STANLEY	*Neighbors, '20's –40's*	480
RECOLLECTIONS OF STANLEY	*Pre-Teen Games*	485
RECOLLECTIONS OF STANLEY	*'Stinkos', Jenkin's Mill*	488
RECOLLECTIONS OF STANLEY	*Sacco and Vanzetti*	489
FAMILY ATHLETIC CONNECTIONS	*From a Single Acorn*	491
MY CHILDREN'S ATHLETIC FEATS	*Chips off the Coach's Block*	493
TOM DENT'S AMAZING GOLF DAY	*An Ace's Ace & Every Base*	496
NEPHEW'S & NIECES & PIECES	*Extended Family Stars*	497
FAMILY ALBUM, 1ST EDITION		503
TED WILLIAMS RED LETTER DAY	*True American Heroes*	506
AWARDS & TESTIMONIALS	*Coaches Hall of Fame*	508
AWARDS & TESTIMONIALS	*"World's Greatest Coach"*	512
AWARDS & TESTIMONIALS	*BU Athletes Hall of Fame*	514
GREATEST FORTUNE & LOVE	*Helen Mary Louise Mark F.*	516
MY GREATEST TESTIMONIAL	*My Children & Theirs*	520
MORE GOOD THINGS IN LIFE	*Families & Friends*	531
OBSERVATIONS & CONTRIBUTIONS	*OWL & L; FLAP & A*	533
INVENTIONS & INSPIRATIONS	*For the Benefit of All*	534
FAVORITE & NOT FAVORITE THINGS	*Some Surprises in Here!*	537
HELP FROM THE BENCH & SIDELINES	*With Help from Friends*	548
FINAL FAMILY FEATURES & SAYINGS	*Rules, Pets, Ava, Exhortations*	556

SPECIAL ACKNOWLEDGEMENTS
Assistant Coaches

I'm especially grateful to my son Michael, for his organizational and editorial assistance, my champion player Dieter Stark for his strong help, and my sons Larry Jr., Bobby and Jimmy for their enthusiastic encouragement on this book and their assistance in bringing me into the computer age. Also to Jean (Folloni) Leen and Debbie (Folloni) Dent and their husbands and kids, who along with my sons have done so much to take care of, assist and brighten the lives of my wife Helen and me throughout the sunny and darker days of our twilight years.

Saysha the athletic Yorkie, Michael and 'The Old Coach'

Taylor Rose Leen, Victoria and Thomas Scott Lawrence Dent with Grandpa Lawrence

TaylorRose & Cameron Henry Leen, Ava Grace Folloni and Scottie and Victoria Helen Mary Dent With Grandma Helen Mary

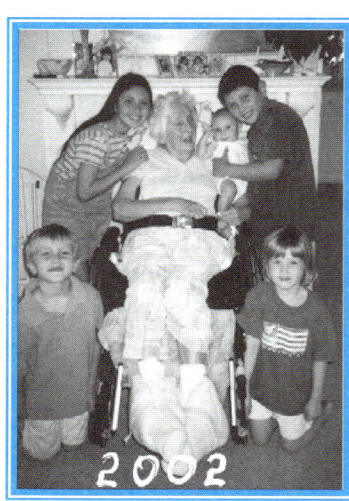

ADDITIONAL ACKNOWLEDGEMENTS
Roster

- Francis Morast, Donnie Strong, Peter Flynn, Larry Fisher, Charlie Simonds, Tommy Arrighi and the Bridgewater Playground Commission for their undying appreciation and ever enthusiastic promotion of memorials for The Old Coach, and more importantly for their work to improve youth recreation programs.

- Dr. Charles Ferguson and the MGH doctors, nurses and staff who rescued me from death's door for another 'overtime'. And Dr. Frank Fedele, Dr. John Novello, Dr. Constance Passas, Dr. Stephen Paul, Dr. Daniel Crowe, Dr. William Berry, Dr. Miles Scheffer, and Dr. Douglas McCullom for their efforts to keep me going in "overtime". As well as Dr. Edward Bromfield, and the entire staff at Brigham and Women's Hospital for their wonderful care during my recent stay there. Also to Dr. Hasan Basari, Dr. Galen Henderson, RN Greg Nuzzo-Mueller, Dr. Christopher Kwolek (MGH) for ongoing care.

- Jackie Mark, for helping me to not quit when things seemed worse.

- Jeff Cohen, who after watching a local cable TV broadcast of me advocating for the elderly, bicycled to my home and gave me Byran & Frances Sterling's "Will Rogers Speaks", from which I 've taken several quotations for this book.

- The Filippetti Princesses, and their families for their input and encouragement.

- DAV agents, Ron Reilly and the inspirational Ron Currier, who worked so diligently to assist me in securing Disabled Veterans medical benefits.

- The Media, (Radio, TV, & Newspapers) who have all been so kind and generous in their praise my teams and me over the years.

- My precious grandchildren, Taylor Rose, Cameron, Victoria, Scottie and Ava, whose unfettered love has provided inspiration to write this book for posterity.

- The entire town of Hampton staffs that have been helpful to us during our recent hardships. Including Chief William Wrenn, Chief Hank Lipe, John Hangen, James Barrington, the Selectman, the Police, Firemen, and EMT's.

- The Bridgewater and Raynham parents and Town Officials for their support throughout my career. They made it possible for me to carry out my dream to have the privilege to lead their children to have fun while growing up and to help in their development towards becoming great citizens of our society.

- All of the many teaching, coaching and athletic and golfing colleagues and boosters that I may have inadvertently forgotten to mention above.

- Tony and Joan Zonferelli, who supported our athletic programs at crucial times, and who's star athlete and student manager kids made the programs look good.

- David Moore and the Bridgewater Conservation, Historical and Recreation Commissions for their historical references and their contemporary efforts to preserve the rich heritage of our town and region through promotion of positive programs involving education, parks and athletics.

- Kevin Scanlon, for his selfless and helpful assistance.

- Eye (Cataract) Dr. Warren Goldblatt, Dr. Lucian Szmyd

- Thuy Vo, for her understanding and gracious support of my son Michael's participation in this project.

- Don Victor Robles, my son Michael's Compadre, for his strong moral support. Also Victor's friend Richard Acosta and his brother in law Michael T. Mata for donating their valuable professional time and skills to develop the design and graphics for the covers of this book. Richard's brother Frank and Victor are the management team for the rising welterweight boxing star **Panchito Bojado, *"The Baby Faced Assassin"*.**

- My wife Helen, for having steadfastly and assiduously chronicled my career and our lives together in her 'Baker's dozen' of scrapbooks. These records have been invaluable source material for this book. Helen, in turn, was an invaluable source for the material of my life.

- BRIDGEWATER TELEVISION (BTV), for their excellent research work, and their service to the community by keeping athletics and our rich athletic history in the forefront of town life.

- Harry Brown, the surfin' late night computer consultant, who very ably helped us over last minute manuscript technical preparation glitches.

- Printers **McNaughton & Gunn Inc.** and all of their extraordinarily competent, responsive and helpful employees and representatives.

DEDICATION
Warm Up

I would like to dedicate this book to my parents, my brothers and sisters, and my wife and children, 'The Folloni Team'. It couldn't have happened of course, without all of my former students and athletes whom I have been privileged to coach, and all my other mentors, friends and colleagues who have been an inspiration to me throughout my teaching and coaching career.

Back Row, l-r: Larry, Johnny, Mike, Al
Front Row: Virginia, Mother Maria, Father John, Angela

Of particular note, I want to show appreciation for my good friend Jim Buckley, who has been like a father to me throughout my career. Jim stuck with me through good times and bad, during my trip over that sometimes-bumpy road of success. Jim passed away in 2002 at the age of 96. He was a love filled, bright beacon to the end.

Jim ('Seamus') Buckley, pictured here with a loyal friend, personified his favorite values of Caring with Concern, Understanding with Patience, Acceptance with Trust, and Affection with Respect and Regard.

****

To all my dear friends and relatives whose stories are not included or not more complete herein: Please know that I could write a whole chapter with the fond memories that I have of each of you. Although the editorial constraints of a book prevent all the stories from being printed here, they will never abridge my great appreciation of your influence in my life or of the happy times I had with you.

FOREWORD
'Ringer'

There is no question in my mind that 'The Old Coach', Larry Folloni would make me run additional laps for not agreeing to write a foreword to his most interesting book "My Way." Fortunately, it is a pleasure and an honor for me to do so. The recollection of memories and sentiments expressed in this foreword have been, in part, recalled from many resources including readings, special occasions, and individual conversations about Coach Folloni. I wish to acknowledge with deep appreciation and gratitude all those who have contributed directly or indirectly to this foreword. I'm sure that readers will find the book to be as fascinating and creative as Coach Folloni is.

I know that Larry wrote the book in good part as a keepsake for his family and friends who he so vitally interacted with over the last 9 decades. He also wanted to make another contribution in wisdom and humor to his friends, other coaches and parents and readers of future generations. And I'm told that true to character, he plans to donate profits from the book to charity. Larry is so deservedly blessed to have such a great family and beautiful wife Helen. I was always so pleased to watch his children grow and mature and to be a small part of their lives at Bridgewater-Raynham.

Our super boss, Mr. Serge Bernard, Superintendent-Principal at BRRHS always told me that Larry was the greatest high school basketball coach he had ever seen. Mr. Bernard was no slouch as a basketball coach himself, being the head coach at Clark University. Larry was the master of the fast break and if I remember correctly the originator of the modern press and race-horse basketball style. Yet as a tactician, he might just as well throw in a carefully choreographed slow-down or 'freeze' offense just to gain the edge of surprise to prevail. I know that everyone (except his opponents) enjoyed watching his teams play. There is no question in my mind that Larry could have coached at any level and be on top of the league. Thank God he decided to stay at our high school level because he was so instrumental in developing character, sense of responsibility, and the sense of achievement for so many student athletes.

When Larry took over as Athletic Director we never had to worry about any of the programs. I know I am speaking for all the administrators during my years at our school when I say that Larry was the 'best'; a class act, and a credit to his family, himself and all the students athletes that had the privilege to be associated with him. To know Larry is to love him. I feel so fortunate to have him for a friend.

When we consider the important elements by which we measure lives, Larry stands out like a giant. He is truly a prince of a man, the salt of the earth, and a rare being who has inspired all who he has touched.

Over the course of his illustrious career, many articles in the local and Boston press called attention the kind of work that has characterized the career of Larry Folloni. These articles have revealed not only the diversity of Larry's concerns in the field of education and athletics, but also the enthusiasm, energy, and dedication with which he has pursued them. His contributions vary far and wide. He founded the town's youth recreation programs, including the farm, little and biddy leagues. The high school players he coached were champions both on and off the courts. He was a main driving force behind the rules and systems that govern scholastic athletics in the state. He helped to originate the present state-wide playoff systems in basketball and football. He always found ways to honor the achievements of others, ranging from organizing award banquets, varsity jackets and his unique 'Hall of Fame' wall at the school, to chairing a committee to erect a scoreboard in honor of an old, retired, and ailing teacher and coach in Bridgewater. After retirement from coaching, he supervised the growth of a school sports program that more than doubled in the size and number over his last decade of work. Not content with rewriting the regulations for sports in the state, he campaigned as far as Washington, D. C., for year round daylight savings time, to extend the sporting hours available not only to student athletes, but to all other amateur athletes outside of their school system as well.

The majority of people who have read the articles and this book have not met Larry Folloni and in all likelihood will never have the pleasure of doing so. They will, however, have obtained an impression of a man who combines devotion to what is best in the history of Massachusetts athletics with a commitment to the idea of making its future even better. Those who have known Larry personally and have worked with him on a day-to-day basis have a fuller idea of his many fine qualities. They know that Larry actually possesses a genuine respect for the youngsters who participate in the program under his direction, that he takes pride in their accomplishments and shows faith in their potential and possibilities. They also know that his enormous enthusiasm for sports has always been coupled with the insistence that academic development comes first and must continue to do so. Students responded warmly to this respect and enthusiasm; parents appreciated his sportsmanship, his fairness, and his sense of priorities. As a former professional colleague, I know I can say with confidence that Larry has the kind of good humor and realism that made the experience of working with him a pleasure rather than a burden.

Larry has enjoyed the most successful of careers, and a well deserved long retirement. Retirement for him, of course, is little more than a chance to win more (golf) championships, develop more projects and promote more public service causes. Major health setbacks to him and his wife over the past five years might have knocked others out of the game. To Larry and Helen, however, they were one more way to show how to make impossible comebacks and demonstrate to us how to be winners in the game of life and love. Can you imagine that in his eighth decade, shortly after doctors had all but pronounced him gone, he learned to use the computer and came up with one more phenomenal gem of a work? This 'My Way' book, and my friend Larry, are true gifts to be enjoyed.

Thirty two years ago Larry received a letter from a woman who wished to thank him for his efforts in leading a campaign to honor Lester Lane, a retired teacher and coach in Bridgewater who, at the age of 87, was then living out his last years in a retirement home. The woman's letter concluded: "I hope that in another quarter century or so one of your athletic stars will think to nominate you for a similar distinction in your field: I'm sure that it will be well-deserved." Of course Larry won many a testimonial and accolade even since that letter. And it is very fitting that his many contributions are to be commemorated by the naming of basketball courts in his honor at the very same 'Lester Lane' Legion Field / Mickey Cochrane Complex that he so well served us on.

Larry, may you be well, happy, and remember that you will always live in the hearts and minds of your fraternity of athletes, friends, and family.

May God bless you!

Chet Millett
Former Assistant Superintendent Principal,
Bridgewater Raynham Regional High School

INTRODUCTION
Tip Off

Now as I live in the twilight of my life enjoying my retirement, I am finally finding the time to recall the happy (and sometimes sad) days gone by. I will try to relive these days with you as best that I can with the help I've gotten from my loving family and friends.

I hope that you will enjoy sharing this trip down my memory lane that started in a little old shack by the railroad track in the close knit Stanley (Little Italy) community in Bridgewater, Massachusetts. *MY WAY* wound through countless rich depths and heights of individual, family and team experiences. Along the way I shared rewarding times with thousands of unforgettable students and friends. My encounters included working with many troubled and/or promising kids on their way up with a helping hand. They also included memorable moments with stars like Ted Williams, Hank Greenberg, Rocky Marciano, Bob Cousy, Bill Russell, Joe Lazaro, Rick Pitino, Mike Lynch and Bjorn Born, who extended their comradery with me while they were well on *THEIR WAY* to becoming cultural icons.

In a bonus section to this book I share my insights and innovations on coaching basketball. Maybe a future coach or teacher can glean a hint or two from it. There are also sections that discuss some inventions and business ventures that I had a hand in; a few, hopefully exemplary, stories of my exploits on the golf links, and a number of humorous stories that I trust you'll get a kick out of. I hope that my personalized slice of the history of one group of Italian immigrants in New England is of interest to you, and that my accounts of our Championship Teams and what it took to get there, are enjoyable. Most importantly, I hope that readers can take some inspiration from my story to help you with your own careers and family lives, whatever *YOUR WAY* may be.

To slightly paraphrase the lyrics that Elvis and Frank Sinatra so movingly sang: I've lived a life that's full, I've loved and laughed and cried; and had my fill, my share of losing, but I did what I had to do, and saw it through without exemption. The record shows, I took the blows, I faced it all, and I stood tall (all 5'7" of me), and did it *MY WAY*.

The essential question of this song was: *"What is a man, what has he got, if not himself?"*

And it's reply was: *"(So) then he has got to say the things he truly feels and not the words of one who kneels"* (except before God). This, I believe, is what I did when I was at my best in life; it's an attitude that I hope my young at heart readers will emulate, and one I shall endeavor to remain true to herein.

They say that nobody likes a braggart. Although I may be somewhat guilty of this foible, please know that it is done in an explanatory spirit: ***If a guy like me can succeed, imagine what you can do?!*** Besides, as my esteemed contemporary, the Great Satchel Page once said: *"If it's true it ain't braggin!"*

Like the song says, as the tears of joy and frustration of my life subside, I can now find it all somewhat amusing. And when I think back on all that I've done, *"I can say, not in a shy way, Oh no, Oh no not me, I did it My Way!"*

To add the humbling perspective that over 80 years in the game of life can afford, I can now see that 'My Way' wasn't always the best way. Indeed it more than occasionally caused others and me some unnecessary grief. Despite my mistakes though, I don't feel at all like a failure, because I believe that I've been pretty faithful in making a whole-hearted effort to learn from them, and to try to set things right. I think that both because of, and sometimes in spite of my reactions; but always as a result of my overriding innermost fervent intent to do good, that God and my Guardian Angel friends on earth and beyond did work to help guide things to the best. Thanks to them, 'My Way' managed to coincide with **'GOD'S WAY'**, **'THE RIGHT WAY'**, enough to have allowed me an overall very successful, fulfilling life. For this I am thankful indeed. *Coach Larry Folloni, June, 2003*

LEGION FIELD

Dedicated to: Cecil V. Hayes, Lester Lane, Mickey Cochrane, Paul Mahan, Joe Lazaro and Larry Folloni, with the Gino Guasconi Building

1st Quarter

The Early Years
"Hope Springs Eternal"

Brothers Albert & Michael, Larry seated. Sisters Angela and Virginia circa 1925

Parents Giovanni (John) and Maria (Mary) Folloni

MY FAMILY AND ROOTS
Team Try Outs

We were raised in a little shack by the railroad tracks that led to the Stanley Iron Works a couple of hundred yards down the road. This little village within the town of Bridgewater Massachusetts was called *'STANLEY'* and *'LITTLE ITALY'*.

This valley village name came from the Stanley Iron Works below the dam at the head of the central road, Wall St. The Stanley Tool company bought the plant from Lazell Perkins & Co. in 1898. It's earlier roots came shortly after Robert Perkins built a dam on the river in 1691 to harness it's power. This plant made cannon for The War of 1812, cannonballs for the Civil War, wagon wheel hoops, ship anchors and locomotives for the opening of the west and armor plating for ships. It gained some fame for casting the iron structures that went into making the renowned Union battle ship the 'Monitor', which won the historic battle with the Confederate ship 'The Merrimac', in March of 1862.

At that time Bridgewater earned the reputation as the "Bethlehem of the East." Stanley Tools closed it's operations in 1926, when I was 7. My father and many of the other residents of the Stanley area were employed at this foundry until then. By the time that the Great Depression hit after the stock market crash in 1929, most of the local residents had already lost their sole means of a livelihood. Times were real tough for all of us. Fortunately our parents were able to subsist on the meager necessities of life. They cultivated a little garden to raise the vegetables that we needed. To supplement the food requirements of our family of eight, my father built a chicken barn and a pigsty. The chickens gave us the eggs for our breakfasts. When their egg production days were over, my mother used them to make her delicious chicken dinners and broth. She would add some of her home made pasta and Italian cheese to the chicken broth and the result was *yummy*. I can still taste the delicious homemade soup to this day.

My father always raised a couple of pigs in the backyard pen. It was a tradition every year just before the Christmas season to slaughter one of them to supply us with meat for the winter months. I can still recall helping my father prepare the tasty sausages and salami, pork chops, blood pudding and many other delicacies from the pig's carcass.

My brothers and sisters and I would all pitch in with the work and chores that went with the raising of six children. My mom and dad also had a couple of goats to supply us with milk. I was quick to learn milking. It was tricky at first but once I got the knack of it; I could get the goats to produce as good as anyone in Stanley. I honestly believe that my early training of milking the goats was one of the reasons that I developed the strong wrists that were to be a great asset to me in my future career as a baseball and football player and golfer. I needed these strong wrists to slash quickly through the ball in baseball and golf, and to pass and defend well in team activities. And of course writer's or typer's cramp from working as a coach and Athletic Director, or from writing this book, was never a problem.

My Dad was born on August 5, 1881 in Italy, in a small shack in the mountains of Gigliana. His christening name of Giovanni was changed to John upon immigrating to the U.S.A. His parents were Michael Folloni and Rosalinda Leonardi.

My Paternal Grandparents Rose Leonardi & Michael Folloni, Italy, 1908

My Mom was also born in Italy on March 24, 1888 up in the mountains in a farm village by the name of Irola. Her maiden name was Maria Luisa (Mary Louise) Lombardi. Her parents were Giovanni and Angelina (Argenti) Lombardi. They were of German, Italian and possibly Asiatic heritage. After the Lombard Tribe of Mongolia overran Germany and Northern Italy around 570AD, they inter-married with the locals. It's not unlikely that my mom was descended from them.

According to verbal history collected by my brother Johnny during one of his trips back to the area of Italy where our folks are from, our maternal grandfather, Giovanni Lombardi, was a salesman who traveled for long time periods by ass. During one of his excursions he met our Bis-Nona (great-grandmother), Mrs. Argenti, who had 2 or 3 daughters. He asked her if he could marry one who he fancied, and she said 'Yes'. So Giovanni promised that he'd be back in 6 months for the wedding.

When our Nono (grandfather) Giovanni returned on schedule, Mrs. Argenti had some startling news for him. Local lore has it that she said:

My Mom's sister Fiora Linda with our Maternal Grandparents Giovanni Lombardi & Angelina (Argenti) Lombardi

"I'm so sorry Giovanni, but *another traveling salesman* came by a month ago and he married your favorite, but I have *another daughter,* Angelina, who is still available!" Not wanting to lose out twice, our Nono said "OK, then I'll marry Angelina." And they did just that quickly before another salesman came along!

The couple returned to Irola where Angelina lived with her in-laws, my paternal great-grandparents. Nono soon left for another 5-year journey, leaving his pregnant wife with his family up in the mountains. The baby (my mother) was born nine months later and named "Maria".

Giovanni Lombardi returned 5-years later and they had a second child. He again left for business returning 4-years later when they had their third child. Then the wonderful railroad was invented. Nono could then take the train *and sit on his ass rather than ride on his ass* on his business trips. That's progress. He then returned home more frequently and they had two more children only a year and a half apart! One of them, Fiora Linda, is pictured above with our grandparents.

When my Dad was a youngster, all of his family had to do every trade available to squeeze a living out of the mountainous terrain. They mastered stonemasonry, carpentry, vegetable, grapevine, olive tree and small animal farming, and the skills to process the goods into respective finished products of oil, cold cuts, cheeses, wine etc. to feed the family. These skills would all come in handy later in life when he had to face the New World in America. They did find some time to play however, and during one of these fun sessions as a preteen, one of his sisters accidentally poked a sharp stick into his eye. Without access to modern medical miracles of today, he ended up losing his eye completely, and was somewhat lucky to survive the trauma and infections.

Life became even more serious to him then, but he didn't wallow in self-pity, rather he counted his remaining blessings, and used his remaining eye to see a future far beyond the hills and shores of Italy. As a 17-year old, he took his first lonely trip to America in search of more opportunity. There he worked on enough grueling jobs to survive, to figure out that there just might be *A WAY for him* to carve out a future for himself and a new family there, and to save enough to head back to Italy to find a wife.

When my Dad started to court my Mom, he had to either hike or take a mule about 10 miles through the rugged mountain terrain in order to date her. Dad and Mom were married in Italy on August 24, 1910 when he was 29 and she was 22. Their first child, my oldest sister Virginia, was born a year later on July 29, 1911. Dad built a stone house for them in the valley between their two childhood towns.

1902 My Father Giovanni (John) Folloni

Shortly thereafter, my Dad acted on the greatest decision of his, and all of our lives, when he took the courageous step to migrate to America along with the huge wave of European immigrants who arrived here shortly after the turn of the 20th Century seeking freedom and opportunity. It is amazing to contemplate how many children, grandchildren, great grandchildren and great great grandchildren are enjoying the fruits of this land now because of his bold and enterprising move!

Partial Annual Clan Reunion, August 1951 & 2002 Nono & Nona have 6 children, 25 grandchildren, and countless great-grandchildren and other descendents.

I have often admired the courage and fortitude that such immigrants displayed in coming to an unknown land with little more than fare money (which was borrowed and later repaid), a prayer, and good health, to embark on a new life. It certainly was a long and tedious endeavor. I am very grateful and proud of their successful struggles and thankful that they chose to make their lives in America. When my Dad came to the U.S.A. for the second time he moved his wife and newly born daughter Virginia out of their valley home, and left them with her parents. He again sailed across the Atlantic with his meager belongings and magnificent hopes for a new and improved life for his family.

John Folloni, Hero

My Dad went to work for the Railroad Company that was building the new lines from Canada, all along the eastern seaboard of the USA. He earned the grand amount of $ 0.50 cents a day for his hard labor, out of which he had to pay his living expenses and save what he could to establish his new life. My brother Mike related the following story of my Dad's time on that job: On a cold New England day while working on a railroad bridge span over the Connecticut River, John Folloni spotted a youngster whom had fallen through the ice. Without any hesitation he jumped into the icy waters and rescued this 8-year-old boy from drowning.

Later when the boy's parents found out about the rescue they immediately sought out the hero among the workers to thank him and give him a reward for his bravery. When they found him they presented him with 200 shares of AT&T stock. Just think what those shares and all their subsequent splits would be worth on today's market!

That is not the end of the story. Remember the Grinch that Stole Christmas? Well here's a parallel story in real life. When my Dad's cranky old Irishman Boss got wind of the gifted shares, he stormed over to the chilly barracks with chillier tidings. He gave Dad hell for taking unauthorized time off of work (to heroically jump into the frigid waters at risk of life and limb), and told him that since he was on company time then, that the shares rightfully belonged to him and the railroad company, and he confiscated them. Of course, Nono, being ignorant of his legal rights to these shares, and not being able to afford loss of this job, meekly handed them over to his avaricious and heartless boss.

Despite the very harsh obstacles and paltry wages, he still managed to accumulate enough money for his wife and daughter's passage to come to join him in the U.S.A. They settled in Bridgewater, Massachusetts, and my dad secured work at the Stanley Works. After 25 years of hard tedious work under difficult conditions, my father managed to save enough money to build a small grocery store next to our home at 61 Wall Street that Dad had purchased from the Cleary's in the early 1920's. The Irish factory workers in the late 1800's built the St. Thomas Aquinas church up the hill on Center St. It's been said that the Cleary's home was a site for one of the first Catholic masses in Bridgewater before the church was built.

My Mother certainly carried on the religious tradition. To begin every day, despite the weather or work load, she trudged the 1. 5-mile round trip to the St. Thomas to pay her devotion and give thanks. As kids we'd joke to each other: "When it's dawn, she's gone." I'm sure that her prayers and meditations helped her to graciously weather the sometimes not so subtle exhortations of my Dad, and the mild chaos of a house full of exuberant kids. My Mom's example brought us to almost take it for granted that one needed to look to God first for guidance and support. It certainly pulled us along far enough to where we could discover for ourselves the value of this attitude. Imagine nowadays automatically walking to church at every daybreak! We may not think it practical, but I can assure you that after services, Mom worked as long a day as anyone I've met. I think that the results of how her children and theirs (and theirs) all succeeded against more than plenty of odds, speaks volumes as to the real world utility of her priorities. It also paid dividends in getting more than a few Guardian Angels recruited to our team!

Dad also encouraged his kids to go to church, but figured that Mom did enough of the formal worshipping for the both of them, so he only attended sporadically, and he sometimes gave Ma hell for giving too much money to the priests. He preferred to show his spirit by working for the good of the family and neighborhood and by sharing fun with them on the bocce courts, and sharing necessities with the needy on a person to person level. He never, however, missed going to church when it was time to bury a fellow immigrant to Stanley, and was always called upon to give the Eulogies. He became quite eloquent at it.

While the Stanley Iron Works employed Dad he had them withhold 25 cents of his pay each week to purchase shares of their stock. By the time he left there, he had accumulated the grand total of 33 shares which I later purchased. These same shares along with stock splits, my added purchases and the dividend payments that were reinvested grew by 1997 to a total in excess of 2,600 shares worth in excess of one hundred thousand dollars! Unfortunately the severe stock market plunge and my wife and my huge medical bills of the last few years have depleted these funds.

Successful and Content Patriach, John Folloni, who lived 93 years

MY NEAR ESCAPES FROM DEATH
Almost Cut

Somehow I feel that it is integral to my story of my good fortune to relate *my near escapes from death*. The Guardian Angel(s) that Mom endorsed must have been watching over me. If it wasn't for my Guardian Angel and God's help in pulling me through these near tragedies, I never would have been able to live my dream and accomplish the goals of my childhood dreams and go on to a very rewarding and successful athletic, teaching, and coaching career.

My first escape from death probably occurred at birth when I was delivered by one of the family neighbors; a midwife named "Tranquilla" Resmini who performed this service for most of the families in our 'Little Italy' in those years. In those days there were no Doctors or Hospitals available to assist in births. So it was because of minor miracles performed through Tranquilla that I, my mom and my brothers, sisters and neighbors did survive.

The first real escape that I can vaguely recall came when I was about 3 or 4 years of age. This is what happened as recounted to me by my brother Al. My older brother Mike had gone across the railroad tracks, which were located next to our house. I wanted to join him so I climbed up the small embankment to the tracks and tried to cross them. As I did so a train came around the bend just below the High Street Bridge. The engineer frantically hit his whistle when he saw me on the tracks.

I guess I must have panicked at the sight of the oncoming train and hearing the alarming whistle. As the train kept coming at me I kept tripping over the ties and the tracks with each step. My mother kept yelling and praying from our back yard as she saw the train approaching. Luckily my older brother Mike came running back to grab me by my arm and drag me across just as the train brushed by me. I've looked to Mike as a hero throughout life; only in hearing this story from Al do I realize that he was a superhero.

The next escape that I can vividly recall came when I was about 8 or 9 years of age. We were playing ice hockey on the Town River next to the Lincoln Club at the fork in the roads of Wall and High Streets. The ice was pretty thick and safe in most of the areas where we skated and played hockey.

There was, however, a stretch of open water just in front of the bridge next to the Lincoln Club. This was there because the current was running pretty fast as the water ran under the tunnels of the bridge and headed for the dangerous dam that was located just on the other side.

The older boys were playing their hockey game about 50 yards up the river on the safe ice. I was playing with the younger boys down river near the bridge. During the course of our game the hockey puck ended up very close to the edge of the open water near the tunnel under the bridge. As I approached the area to retrieve it, the ice suddenly gave way and I went down into the icy cold water.

I grasped for the solid ice that was still there and could feel the strong current pulling me toward the tunnel. I knew that I couldn't hold on for long. Fortunately, as I desperately hung on to the cold ice, two young girls, Esther Resmini and Mary Tassinari, were watching the games from the railing of the bridge above. They saw me fall through the ice and immediately yelled to the older boys. One of them, Vinnie Cassiani, came to the rescue. He laid down on the ice and stretched his hockey stick out as far as he could. My grasp on the ice was slowly losing its grip and just as the strong current was about to suck me under the bridge and certain death, I made one last desperate lunge for the stick.

The good Lord was with me as I managed to grasp it and Vinnie tried to pull me out. It was touch and go for awhile to see who would win the tug of war: - the strong current or Vinnie. After a tough battle, Vinnie succeeded. What made it increasingly difficult was the fact that my belt buckle was locked onto the edge of the ice as Vinnie was trying to pull me out. Luckily with one last tug, the buckle broke free and I was on my way to safety. This experience 75 years ago is still ingrained in my mind. How can one ever thank someone like Vinnie enough?

Maybe my Dad's heroics a decade earlier in saving another 8-year old from the icy Connecticut River earned some heavenly dividends afterall!

My fourth encounter with death came about when I was about 10 or 11. We were on our way up to a baseball game at 'Biffers Field' on High Street. As there were no sidewalks then, we were walking on the street in a line about 8 or 9 abreast. I was on the right side of the line at the very end, closest to the middle of the road. Suddenly we heard the beep of an automobile horn. Everyone in line went to the left to make way for the car and of course I, (doing it my way again), went to the right. With the car bearing down upon me I had no where to go. At the last second the driver of the car in trying to avoid hitting me veered off the road to the right and went down an embankment. In doing so he wrecked his car but he saved my life. Doing it 'My Way' didn't always work out the best for all involved in my younger days! I learned here that sometimes it makes sense to follow the leaders. After all, they say that to stand taller than others, one should avail any opportunity to stand on the shoulders of giants!

My next encounter with death happened at about the age of 14. While playing 2nd base in a baseball game I received a spike wound on my right wrist while tagging out a runner. As a safety precaution I was given a tetanus shot, from which I came up with a life threatening reaction. I can still recall the rash that appeared all over my body and the high fever and shakes that this caused.

Young Dr. Hector Douglas, God love him, remained at my bedside for 24 hours working feverishly to save my life. He succeeded and I am forever grateful to him for his dedication and his efforts to save my life. This was the beginning of a fond and lasting friendship with Dr. Douglas who later was to become the team physician at all our athletic events when I became coach and Athletic Director. Many years later we inducted him into the school's Athletic Hall of Fame for his many services.

Escape number six came after I had just turned 16. I had just received my driver's license and had borrowed my dad's car to go to Braves Field (Now BU's Nickerson Field) to see the Boston Braves, the Major League team that I idolized as a youngster. It was a great game and I had the opportunity to see all my favorite ball players, Wally Berger, Sibby Sisti, Tommy Holmes, and "Rabbit" Maranville to name a few.

After the ball game we hit the road to drive back to Bridgewater. I had promised my Dad that I would pick him up at 5 p.m. to drive him home after his workday. As luck would have it, the traffic was pretty heavy and time was creeping up on me to meet the time line to pick up my Dad. With this deadline on my mind, I foolishly tried to make up some time by speeding all the way home.

Everything went fine until we got within 3 miles of home when I chose to save more time by going 'the back way' in West Bridgewater. When I got to the intersection of East Street and Route 104, I kept up my speed to try to make the fast approaching deadline.

Just as we can contribute to our 'good luck', we can also set the stage for 'bad luck'. When I got to the intersection, lo and behold there was another car right smack in the middle of it heading toward West Bridgewater center.

Fortunately, the lady who was driving that car applied her brakes and stopped in the middle of the intersection. Due to my excessive speed, it was too late for me to stop so I swerved my car to the right. I just managed to clip the rear end of my car, which hooked on to her bumper and spun both of us around. If she had not stopped I would have hit her broadside and probably killed her and her two small children who were passengers in her car. And very likely my passenger, Eddie Chiocca and I would have also been killed due to my excessive speed.

This harrowing experience was a real learning experience for me at such an early age. Once again 'My Way' was sometimes the 'wrong way' in my early formative years. Since that near fatal experience I have been a very cautious driver and I try to never take foolish chances behind the wheel. I also try to never hurry with any project, because that's when mistakes happen that can waste more, if not all remaining time.

As a 25-year-old in 1944 while in the service, I nearly met my Maker when I was given tetanus shot for a wound in my thigh. An Army medical technician made an error by giving me the wrong shot. It was later found that I was given lcc of Tetanus Antitoxin instead of the Tetanus Toxin that was prescribed by my physician. This mistake nearly killed me. I clearly remember during the early morning of my ordeal, when I overheard the doctor asking if I had any family in the area. My brother Mike was notified. Mike's Navy ship had just returned from battle in the Pacific and he was in dock in San Francisco. My brother Al was in the European Theater. The rest of my family and my wife were far away in New England.

The doctor had given me up for dead and he wanted all of my family notified. A priest had given me the last rites of the Catholic Church. As I lay there very weak with severe abdominal cramps and on the verge of unconsciousness I could feel my life literally ebbing away when suddenly as daybreak rose around 5a.m, I began to feel my strength returning.

The crisis was over and I slowly began my recuperation from my journey towards death. A few weeks later when I was feeling much better my doctor came to see me. He reviewed what had transpired during the crisis and told me he never expected me to survive that night. He said it was a miracle that I made it.

Larry, just outside of death's door

Next in line of escapes from death came following my graduation from Boston University. During the summer months while waiting to start my coaching and teaching career at Dighton High School, which was to start in September, I hooked on with a Semipro Baseball Team, The Casey Club in the Boston Park League. It was an opportunity to earn a few dollars between semesters, plus it kept me in shape for a potential contract with the Brooklyn Dodgers Professional Baseball Team the following year.

We were in the Park League playoffs for the championship. I was the first batter as was my usual position in the batting order. A fellow by the name of Toye was pitching for the opposition. I had faced him a few times earlier in the regular season and had pretty good success in batting against him. He was their star pitcher who had a real major league fast ball in the 90-mile per hour zone. The very first pitch that he threw was a fast ball around 95-mph and it headed straight for my head. Like with the train coming at me as a toddler, I guess that I froze in my batting position and was not able to get out of the way. No brother could help me then.

The ball hit me high on the upper left cheekbone, missing my temple by a mere fraction of an inch. My cheekbone was crushed and reconstructive surgery was needed to mend the broken bone and facial injuries, (very similar to the injury that Tony Conigliaro of the Boston Red Sox suffered that led to his subsequent death) The surgeon who did the corrective work later told me that if the ball had hit me one inch higher to the left, I would have been killed by the impact to my brain. In those days we had no protective batting helmets. After all my close calls, I figure that the Great Manager of All must have my destiny well in order, and that he'll know when to bring me back to the Great Clubhouse in the sky.

There were a few other escapes from death to follow later in my lifetime. One of them was the result of what I now believe to have been caused by food poisoning. It happened at the end of our February school vacation in the 1970's. Helen and I went out for a Saturday night escape at a dinner and dance restaurant in Raynham. The Capiello Brothers, who were acquaintances of mine from our baseball playing days, owned the restaurant. They were nice guys and pretty good baseball players, who played for our archrivals from Brockton. I had a craving to have a nice Lobster Dinner.

As luck would have it, after we had ordered our lobster dinners the waitress came back in a few minutes to inform us that they were all out of lobsters but they did have one last Lobster Pie. Well Helen graciously allowed me to have the Lobster Pie and she ordered the chicken dinner.

When the dinners were served I offered Helen a portion of the lobster pie but she declined and I devoured the entire dish. After eating it I said to Helen, "That lobster was bad." Since I didn't want to embarrass my friends, the restaurant owners, I didn't make any fuss over it. After we finished our dinners we danced for a couple of hours then went back home.

About 3 a.m. I woke up with severe abdominal cramps. I went to the bathroom and vomited. Then I became very weak. I was shaking and very cold. I called to Helen and she called the EMT's who rushed me off the hospital. It was touch-and-go throughout the night. As I neglected to tell the Doctors who were attending to me about the Lobster Dinner, they were at a loss to know how to treat me. I remained in the hospital for three days and to this day the doctors never did diagnose this episode that nearly killed me.

I met the doctor about three weeks later and asked him what happened. His reply, "I don't know, do you know?" Well after giving it some thought I finally told him about the Lobster Pie that I had eaten the night before my attack. We then came to the conclusion that it was food poisoning. By the way, I understand that when I was a kid that Lobsters were considered sea floor scavengers and junk food in New England. So much so that Lobsters were common fare for the prisoners at the ancient Bridgewater State Prison of 'Titticut Folly' fame.

Yet another near escape from death occurred in 1995. My brother Al had the first of his many strokes that were to ensue before his death in 1997. My brother Mike, my sister Angie, and her daughter Linda accompanied me on a trip to New York to visit Al in the hospital. On the return trip to New England I was driving my new Honda. After driving about half way through Connecticut, I asked my brother Mike if he would take over the wheel, as I was feeling a little tired and drowsy. Mike took over the driving and I promptly fell asleep.

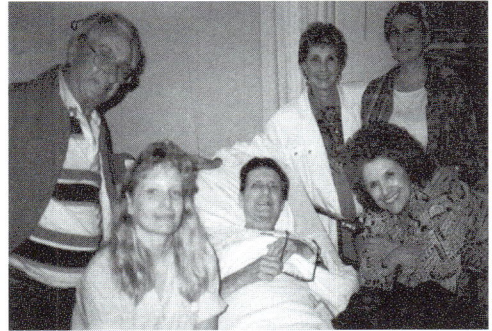

Mike, Barbara, Al & Connie Falloni, Angie & Linda Balboni

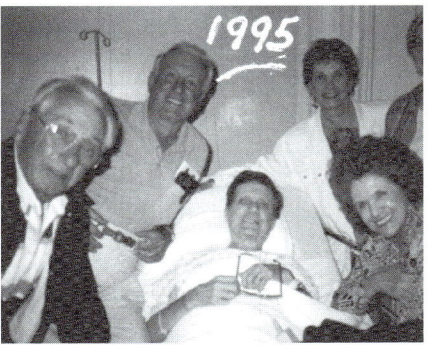

*I was there too!
Al was smiling & sweet to the end*

Somewhere just near the border of Connecticut and Rhode Island, a sickening grinding noise suddenly awakened me. The Honda was still careening along the side of the wire rails at the side of the road and it finally came to a screeching halt at a 90°-degree angle to the roadway.

I was still in a daze and I looked in the back to see if Angie and Linda were O.K. Then I turned to Mike who was white as a ghost and asked him what happened. He responded that we had a tire blow out, which pulled the car up against the side barriers. If it hadn't been for Mike's skillful handling of the careening car and those wire rails, we would have catapulted off the road and down a 200-foot steep embankment to an almost certain death. Once again Mike was the hero. Of course as dramatic as his heroics sometimes were, it was Mike's day to day consistency as a humble, hardworking and humor-filled leader of the family that impressed itself most on me. In the end, this is what most helped set the stage for me to catapult to my modest successes in my career and as a father.

Mike Makes Boss at Independent Nail Al, Larry, Mike & Young Johnnie Folloni

There were to be a couple more dramatic escapes from death much later in my life. Notably on Dec 7, 1998 and another in the summer of 2000. I'll explain this in detail later.

3 months out of it, and many experts said I'd never return. Thankfully God has given me another chance, which I'm using to enjoy my wife, family and friends, and to write these memoirs for you. May they help you in forging YOUR WAY!. May God Bless You. Larry

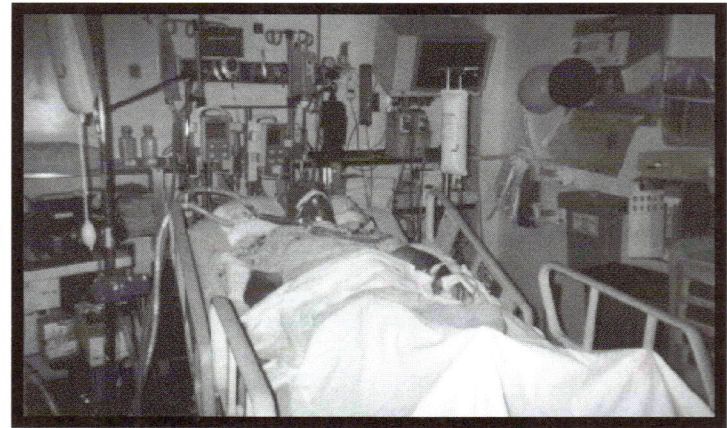

• • • • • • • • • • •

WWI ERA STANLEY DIPHTHERIA OUTBREAK
Conspiracy Theory

Based on an internet published interview confirmation by our neighbor Lena Cassani that was called to my attention by local historian and preservationist David Moore*, I can now confirm a report of a possible astute escape from the 'Grim Reaper' by my Dad in the year before my birth. There was an outbreak of diphtheria in Stanley in 1918 that was so bad that authorities converted the 3-story home by the river dam into a hospital. According to reports by Lena that match stories told by my father to me, when people went to the makeshift hospital, they "gave 'em a pill that made them spit up black stuff. And all the people that went there died! But the ones who stayed home and drank wine or whiskey *lived!*"

As my Dad (and Lena) told the story, these pills were given to everyone in the area who contracted this flu, and virtually everyone who went to the hospital, along with many who didn't who took the pill, died. My father said that he threw his down the outhouse hole and therefore lived. Conspiracy theorists would opine that the government tried to quash the epidemic by killing off all those immigrants who might spread it. Others would say that those who went to the hospital were the most sick and therefore the most likely to die anyway. In any case, this is an accurate and interesting account of common opinion from that era of this crisis in Stanley, where the immigrants were often distrusted and misunderstood by the established citizenry, and visa-versa.

It is interesting to note that many of the key events surrounding the infamous Sacco & Vanzetti case centered in Bridgewater, and that they began within weeks of my birth in 1919. Some historical background and my thoughts on this case can be found in the 'Archives' section at the end of this book.

•••••••••••••••••••••••••••••

David is the grandson of James Moore, pictured here, who became the Chief of Police in Bridgewater in the "Roaring '20's, shortly after the diphtheria outbreak and the Sacco & Vanzetti arrests.

Chief Moore faithfully performed his duties in many ways, including by arresting my mother for making wine during the Prohibition in 1928!

GAMES WE PLAYED DURING OUR PRE-TEEN YEARS
The Real Farm Leagues

As youngsters growing up we had some games we played as diversions from our family chores. These games entailed very little cost, which was necessary since we had no money to spend and no elaborate playing fields or gyms. Our playing areas included:

- the unpaved streets where the games were occasionally interrupted by passing horses and buggies;
- nearby open fields, from where we were often chased off by the owners with their axes;
- Or the sand bank, from where we returned home with a shoe full of sand to our mothers' dismay.

For equipment we scraped up left over junk that nowadays would be thrown into the trashcans. Here are some of the games we played:

PADDLE BASEBALL	**PEG**
DUCK ON THE ROCK	**BUCK BUCK**
KICK THE CAN	**HORSE AND RIDER**
CRICKET (Stanley Style)	

I've detailed the rules of these highly organized games in the appendix. As an example, here's how we played *'Duck on the Rock'*:

Each player found himself a rock about the size of a baseball. The rock was called the 'DUCK'. One player was chosen to be "IT". To start the game, all the players would toss their rock at the home base, which was a large stone that had a flat surface to hold the DUCK. The player whose DUCK was furthest from the home base was chosen to be "IT", and would place his rock (DUCK) on the home base.

The rest of the players stood behind the GOAL LINE, about 20 to 30 feet from the home base, and would now try to knock the "IT" player's DUCK off the rock. If any player's DUCK did not knock the "IT" player's DUCK off the rock, then he would try to retrieve his DUCK and return to the goal line before being tagged by the "IT" player. The "IT" player could tag another player trying to get back to his goal line only if his DUCK was still on the rock. In the meantime while the "IT" player was chasing one player, all the other players would be trying to knock the DUCK off of the rock to protect the player being chased. If the "IT" player was successful in tagging another player before he returned to the goal line, *and IF HIS ROCK WAS STILL ON THE ROCK*, then the player who was legally tagged, then became the new "IT". Confused? No wonder it was relatively easy for me to later master the baseball rules book to the point where as a Junior League player I could quote verse and line from any rule book to correct the umpires!

WHERE WE PLAYED AS KIDS
The Fields Where Dreams Were Born

"Wall Street": The first area of play was the dirt street. As this was the closest to our homes it was the logical place for us to play our games. The only problem was that we were restricted for space and our games were continually being interrupted by horse and buggy vehicles and later by the old Model T Fords. Also of course our parents disdain for our wearing out the soles of our shoes so fast by playing on the road didn't lend popularity to this site as a playground.

"The Diamond": Named thusly because it was a patch we cleared out in "Minase's woods that we shaped like a diamond. This was our off street baseball field on the riverbank. After a hot game of baseball in the summer we retreated to the swimming hole we called 'Muck's Beach' that was located a short distance away on the riverbank.

Young son James watches 'Minase' (wheelchair) sample some of Nono's post Prohibition home vintage from the grape vines seen behind Grandpa Nono and Uncle Mike.

"The Sand bank": Again named appropriately, as it was a patch of loose sand. It was located adjacent to railroad tracks and the Stanley Iron Works, next to The Smoky Hill Area. (It was called Smoky Hill because all the smoke from the foundry would blow up to the homes on the hill off of High Street.) The Sandbank playing area was smaller than the size of a present day Little League Field. The only difference was that we had no grass. It was all loose sand that filled our shoes in short order. I must confess that the Sandbank wasn't very popular with our mothers, who had to sweep up a shovel full of sand that we generally left on the floor after taking off our shoes. Rules were soon implemented throughout Stanley that when we arrived home from our sandbank ball games the first thing that we had to do was to take off our shoes and empty them.

Another difference is that the outfield fence was The High Street Hill, which was reminiscent of the Green Monster at Fenway Park. Anyone who hit the ball over this hill was considered a super star. Steve 'Bye Bye' Balboni's dad, Charlie, (we called him 'Hercules', or 'Herc') was one of the few who hit them over the Hill quite frequently. "Bye Bye" who played for the professional baseball teams, (New York Yankees, Kansas City Royals, Seattle Mariners, and Texas Rangers) must have inherited some of his Dad's power.

"Boca larga's Field": Was also called 'the Company Field' because the Stanley Iron Works, who called it that, first owned it. The Cassiani Family later purchased it. We then called it "The Boca Larga's Field". This was the huge hay field across the railroad tracks. It had plenty of grass and was large enough for all our activities. Many were the times that we ended up stepping on or sliding through some juicy cow flaps ('pasture patties', 'meadow muffins'). Our bigger problem, however was that "Boca larga" ('Big Mouth') Mr. Cassiani, was always chasing us off the property. This was just after Teddy Roosevelt, so Mr. Cassiani did 'carry a big stick', that he probably would have used on our backsides if he could have caught us. Unlike "T.R.", however, "B.L." did not *'speak softly'*. How ironic it would have been to be saved by his relative Vinnie Cassiani only to be brained later by Boca Larga! Of course no one would have really inflicted serious damage on us, but we could count on at least a bit of a spanking at the time if caught, and a bigger one when we got home if our Dad found out that we had disrespected an elder.

The old Stanley Iron Works and an adjacent field, as seen in 2002. These grassy areas are now being restored to pristine conditions of the days of our youth. (Perhaps better—no cows!)

Biffet's Field": This field was a step up in quality for our baseball games. It was located up on High Street across from the Prospect Elementary School. The field had a bowl setup. The level playing area of the baseball field extended out to left field towards Ricci's House on Oak Street. The right field area was very short, only about 30 yards beyond 2nd base, but it was set up on a hill with a stone wall bordering on the Balastracci's farmland.

At least we then had some grass on our baseball field and as we grew older and into baseball competition with other teams, Biffet's Field was the stadium for players and spectators alike. It was an annual rite of spring when we would set fire to the high dried out grass to get the ball field ready for our games. One year our grass fire got out of control as the high winds blew the flames right up to the Ricci House in deep left field. The firemen came just in the nick of time to save their home from going up in flames. To their credit, even after this, the Ricci's still let the neighborhood kids play there. I remembered this later in life whenever a kid made his first youthful transgression and I always tried to find a way to give them the same type of second chance that was afforded to us.

Other playing fields of note outside of Stanley were the home fields of our opponents. These included the field next to the St. Thomas Church, (now a parking lot next to Helen and My final resting plot), the Lumberyard Field, L. Q. White's Field on Spring Street and of course the Old Legion Field off of Bedford Street, next to the present Veterans Club.

These patches of grass, dirt and sand meant the world to us as 10-year old ball playing youngsters. Once we were involved in a game, time was irrelevant. My Dad always expected us to be home in time for dinner and when we were not home then we could always expect to be taken out to the wood shed for a spanking of our bottoms.

On one of these late arrivals after an extra inning game, I knew I was ticketed for the shed. So I came up with a brilliant scheme to place a wooden shingle in the seat of my pants to absorb the sting of the spanking. Sure enough when I entered the house, my Dad was waiting, and he promptly escorted me to the woodshed. My Dad put me over his knees and his first whack hit the wooden shingle with a loud thump. He let out with a screaming "Ouch". What was the result? My Dad ended up with a broken thumb and I was promptly grounded and not allowed to play baseball for a week. I never tried that trick again!

"When I was a boy...."

Many moons after our boyhood days I returned to the old Biffet's field with my son James to show him one of the 'Fields that Dreams were Born on'

HOW WE IMPROVISED EQUIPMENT FOR OUR GAMES
Before Wilson, Spaulding, McGregor Nike & Reebok

The above are only a few of the many games we played as youngsters. We did of course play the well-known games of Baseball, Football, and Hockey.

BASKETBALL was not a very popular game at the time of our youth, especially since we didn't have the warm and dry wood-floored gyms or the hoops to play the game as it is played today. However we did manage to adapt a game very similar by using the hoops from old wine barrels and nailing them to the electric posts on the street under the street lights so we could play at night. For a basketball we would use any rubber ball available.

The reason that I mention and explained the games we played as youngsters is to show how we improvised for the equipment needed for these games. The equipment did not cost anything except a little work on our part and being innovative to create the playing implements as needed. The following is a sample of how we improvised our equipment to play these games at no cost to our parents except the wear and tear of the leather soles on our shoes (which was still considered a significant cost factor in those days):

FOOTBALL: For footballs we would use old burlap bags, wrap them, then tie them with rubber bands cut from old tire inner tubes.

BASEBALL: For bats we took some solid limbs and carved and pared them with a hand knife to the shape of a bat. If we were lucky enough to recover an old broken bat from one of the Semipro baseball teams; we would nail or screw the bats together then tape over the nails and the splinters.

For baseballs, we would go to the Old Legion Field on days that the Semipro teams played and when they hit a foul ball into the woods we would scamper to the ball and depress the ball into the mud to cover it from sight. We'd mark the spot with a stick, then come back after the game when the teams had left to recover the baseball. After we played with that ball for awhile the cover would eventually fall off, which meant taping and re-taping the balls. Where did we get the tape? Of course this was during the depression days of the late 20's and early 30's and our parents had all they could do to feed and clothe us, never mind spare the nickel for the roll of tape.

The following was the course of action we took to get the much-needed tape. There was a street light right across the street from my house. We had some pretty good shooters with slingshots and some good pitchers who were pretty accurate at throwing rocks. It didn't take long for one of us to hit the light target.

The next step was to notify the electric company that a street light was out. Within a few days the electric linesman showed up in his truck to replace the bulb. The linesman was a kind old man, who had made the same light bulb replacement trip on many occasions during the summer months and he knew just what we needed to cover our baseballs.

When he climbed up the pole he conveniently left the door open on his truck to expose the rolls of tape for us to help ourselves. After he replaced the light bulb and returned to his truck, he would then wave good bye to us with a friendly smile and say, "Hit a home run for me". This may have been an early example of 'enlightened self interest', as the more tape he left, the fewer repair trips he had to make, and the more these poor kids could keep out of mischief on their way to becoming productive citizens.

For bases we used trees, posts, or rocks placed at what was presumed to be the correct distance apart, but many times the configuration of the diamond would have to be adjusted due to the limited area we were playing on.

ICE HOCKEY: For our Ice Hockey games we really had to improvise. For Hockey sticks we would cut out a curved stick from the woods. For the hockey pucks we would flatten tin cans and shape them like a puck. Very few of us could afford the old double runner clamp skates, so we would take tin cans and shape them to the insteps of our shoes. We quickly learned the art of securing the cans to our shoes so they would not fall off and they would act as grippers on the ice so we could maneuver without slipping and falling. We would use old logs or rocks to mark off our goals.

WATER SPORTS: Following our Baseball games we invariably ended up going for a swim (skinny-dipping) at Muck's Beach. That's the name we gave to an inlet on the Town River where we cut out all the brush and built diving boards for added fun.

I can still remember how we first managed the Dog Paddle to swim the 30 to 40 yards across the river to reach the mud banks on the other side. Many a time that we clung on to some huge turtle's back to get a free ride. As our swimming skills improved we would swim down to another beach created by the Main Street Gang, which was located about a half mile down stream on the other side of the river. When we accomplished this feat we were considered real big shots. Of course none of this was supervised or controlled, and it took some good luck along with our family instilled common sense to avert tragedy on these backwater forays.

Fishing was another recreational activity that we usually availed ourselves of on days when it was too hot to play baseball. For fishing poles we would cut out the straightest stick we could find from trees in the woods. For fishhooks we would use safety pins to tie on the end of our lines. Worms we gathered from our gardens were used as bait.

For a street game we played called "Peg Ball" we would use the ends of empty grape boxes to make wooden paddles and carve a peg out of another piece of wood to be used as the ball. Another popular game we played on the confines of the street with a bat and baseball utilized sets of tin cans with sticks placed on the top. This game was actually a derivative from the English game of Cricket, played *Stanley Style.*

Intermingled with all the games we played as youngsters, was the dangerous "Rock Fights" we held. I can recall one of these fights when I was the target. Our neighbor "Mickey" Ferioli and his brothers were throwing rocks at us from across the street. One of the pellets hit me squarely on the head and blood spurted from the gash. That incident ended the Rock Fights for awhile.

One other prank was our throwing rocks up and breaking street lights and breaking windows at the old McElwain Shoe Factory (later Jelco) on our way home from school.

The above are just a few of the pranks and mischief that we engaged in as youngsters. If we were to commit these pranks in today's climate, we would have been sent to reform schools or jails.

And I can't forget our "King of Stanley" competitions. Every week or so anywhere from a couple to several boys who were feeling their oats (or pasta) would spontaneously decide to challenge the reigning King to a fight for the title. Noses would be bloodied, bruises and scrapes acquired, until finally only one remained standing with no more willing challangers. Although I somehow managed to win the title once, Peter Resmini and Peter Mattie were the perennial "Kings of Stanley". The word 'Peter' in the Bible of course has come to mean: ***"Rock".*** Two trolley car stops up from us in Campello (old North Bridgewater) the neighborhood King at that time was a Rock named Marciano. Thankfully by the time we could afford the trolley to compete with his teams, the venue had shifted to baseball!

OUR NEIGHBORS IN STANLEY (LITTLE ITALY)
Our Home League

As youngsters growing up in the age of the great depression our only recreation was in the field of sports such as football, baseball, and hockey and in the games that we created. The Stanley area was pretty well congested with youngsters about my age and we had little trouble rounding up teams for our wide variety of games.

In an appendix of this book, I'll share with you who some of the neighbors and youngsters of Stanley were during those depression years, within which we were too busy creating fun games of ball to be depressed at all.

NICKNAMES WE GAVE TO OUR STANLEY & TOWN FRIENDS
Handles

It was a custom for all youngsters in the Stanley area to be given a nickname. Very few individuals escaped with being called by their real birth name. We weren't too 'politically correct' about naming people back in those simpler, more straightforward days when sticks and stones could and did break bones, but people didn't let names hurt them. Here are some of the nicknames that I recall:

Birth Name	Nickname	*Birth Name*	Nickname	*Birth Name*	Nickname
Renaldo Cassiani	Tack	*Quinto Cassiani*	Spike	*Nado Cassiani*	Nails
Angelo Cassiani	Muskrat	*Louis Cassiani*	Sacco	*Albert Chiocca*	Bud
Leo Pallatroni	Peko	*Peter Resmini*	King	*Mario Chiocca*	Speed
Paul Pallatroni	Bucky	*Valentino Morterelli*	Stovepipe	*Ernest Chiocca*	Ney
Ernest Valeri	Barber	*Albert Giovanini*	Skinny	*Romeo Campanini*	Roach
Ernest Valeri, Jr.	Sunny	*Leonard Tassinari*	Mutt	*Peter Mattie*	King
Tersine Moruzzi	Mayor	*Alphonse Moruzzi*	Shine	*William Ferioli*	Bo
Albert Folloni	Polack	*John Folloni*	One Eye Reilly	*Robert Pratti*	Pint
Frank Ferioli	Ceco	*Aldo Ferioli*	Mickey	*Nello Pratti*	Curly
Alfred Bertelli	Fredo	*Dino Bertelli*	Bert	*Etra Pratti*	Zeke
Andrew Ticchi	Mass	*Alex Santilli*	Sundruchie	*Erminio Abati*	Bo
John Resmini	Minasse	*Victor Messaline*	Turk	*Charles Balboni*	Herc
Julian Lucini	Jiggs	*Larry Campbell*	Digger	*Victor Martelli*	Lefty
Flurindo Balboni	Jake	Elmer Balboni	Mouchie	*Johnnie Folloni*	Junior
Paul Dellenegra	Blackie	Romeo Campanini	Roache	*William Rubeski*	Biscuits
Bresciani Twin	Fatty	*Bresciani Twin*	Skinny	Jerard Provost	Jiggs
Albert Piscatori	Goose	*Manuel Munise*	Bull	*Emilio Ticchi*	Sam
Mario Ferioli	Martin	*Elmer Balboni*	Mouchie	*Preston Balboni*	Press
Sylvio Cassiani	Boca Larga	*Larry Folloni*	Lodi	*Adolf Folloni*	Bing

MY PRE-TEEN YEARS
Little Leagues

The Stanley area was pretty well filled with youngsters about my age and we had little trouble rounding up teams for games of football, baseball, and hockey. As I look back upon my Pre-teen Years my first recollections revert to my love for sports. I can remember the many games we played I the fields and on the streets. Of all the sports that we played, baseball was my favorite and the game that I was best adapted to because of my size, speed and athletic reflexes.

I can recall how I cultivated these reflexes and the many hours of practice that I would endure. I'd use a rubber ball and throw it against the side of the cement steps in front of my Dad's store and retrieve it as it bounced back. This practice was really fun and was of great help to me in fielding ground balls and in developing my reflexes.

It was during these years, at the age of 10, that I organized and coached my first team. We named ourselves *"THE STANLEY STEAMERS"*. I remember how we raised money to buy our first uniforms for our team. We salvaged rags, old lead pipes, old newspapers, and anything that the Junk Collector would buy.

When we thought we had earned enough money for our Jerseys we thumbed rides into Boston and went to a McGregor Sporting Goods store. It was there that I met a kind young salesman by the name of Paul Moynihan. After perusing through the many sample jerseys that Mr. Moynihan showed us, we finally came up with the Jerseys we wanted. But alas as luck would have it we were going to be short about $25.00 to complete our purchase.

But luck was on our side as Mr. Moynihan seeing how heartbroken we were, gave us the Jerseys anyway and said, "Larry you can pay me when you make it to the Major Leagues". Well that was the beginning of a friendship that lasted a lifetime. When I became Athletic Director in the years ahead, I remembered Paul Moynihan's kind deed and whenever possible our athletic purchases went through him at his McGregor Sports Store. Mr. Moynihan went on to become a CEO for the McGregor Co. in Cincinnati, Ohio, and we never lost touch through the years.

I remember how proud we were when we first put on those colorful Royal Blue Jerseys with *"THE STANLEY STEAMERS"* emblazed on the front in bright yellow. Our Stanley Steamers baseball team went on for many years with great success. The experience that I gathered in those early years of coaching and managing the Stanley Steamers was very instrumental in my future career as a Coach and Athletic Director.

SPORTS VS. FAMILY CHORES
Workouts

In growing up during my pre-teen and teen years I would say that 70% of our out of school time was devoted to playing sports and recreational activities. The other 30% was spent at chores and work to help with supporting the family. In those days we had no TVs to watch, video games or computers to play with or cars to drive around in. Neither did we have the perils of drugs and alcohol to ruin our young lives. Oh, all the Italian families did have wine on the table to sip with their meals, but it was such a normal thing and the family and close-knit neighborhood group kept it in such check that it very rarely became a problem.

I can still recall when late in the fall season the trucks came into the Stanley area loaded with grapes for sale. These vendors knew better than to start with my Dad, as he would bargain with them literally to the end. Typically at about 10 or 11 p.m. after the vendors had gone to every house on the street, they would return to our home with what remained of their load. That is when my Dad would get the best bargain. Since the vendors did not want to take any product back with them, my Dad would purchase the remaining grapes for about 1/4 of their asking price of earlier in the day.

To unload the crates of grapes, my brothers and sisters formed a chain from the truck to the cellar as we passed them from one to another until we had all safely packed away. In the days that followed we would all help with the wine making process. I vividly recall how we first placed the grapes into large wooden tubs and took our shoes and stockings off in preparation for the fabulous frolics to begin.

Then my mother would scrub our feet in soap and water before we entered the tub and jumped up and down on the grapes to squeeze out all the juice. The juice was then screened out of the tubs and poured into wooden barrels to ferment into the fine tasting wine that was served at all of our meals throughout the year. The remains of what was left of the grapes, including the stems, skins and seeds, were fed to the pigs.

After many of these memorable years my Dad finally purchased a grinder to mash the grapes to a pulp. He also bought a press to squeeze out the remaining juice in the grapes. With the coming of the machine age we were deprived of the fun of our annual dancing on the grapes.

This was only one of the myriad chores that we experienced in our youth. Of course we dug the garden each year with hand spades; helped to plant all of our vegetables in the spring; weeded the gardens during the growing seasons; and finally reaped the rewards late in the summer. I'll never forget the gratification of going into the garden when we were hungry and sampling the delicious tomatoes, cucumbers and other tempting fruits of our labors. These vegetables along with the chickens and the pigs and milk from our goats sustained our growing family of six.

One of the beneficial by-products of our chores and work ethic was that we developed our bodies physically to a point that we had a distinct advantage over other youngsters our age when it came to athletic competition. Another was that although we valued our play time, we knew that there was a never ending trade-off between it, and the time that was needed to be dedicated for survival, so sports also took on a mantel of somewhat serious business.

OUR LIFE IN THE 1920'S
Team Depth

My memory of the Folloni household at 61 Wall St. in Little Italy in the 20's, was that of a very simple existence. We didn't have the luxuries of today's homes and we lived in pretty cramped quarters. My two sisters occupied one of the downstairs bedrooms and Mom and Dad occupied the other. The three boys slept in one of the small bedrooms upstairs. Boarders or other guests usually occupied the other small upstairs bedroom. Our home was always the stop off place for transients coming over from the old country to make it in the prosperous USA. My Dad was always there to lend a hand to anyone in need of a helping hand.

Bill Haley and the Comets may have introduced 'shake rattle and roll' in the 50's, but from the '20's onward our house, which was located on the cheapest angled lot available, just feet from the railroad tracks, would do all that and more several times a day whenever the train passed.

We had one large (12' x 15') room that was used as the living room and doubled as the dining room when we had large gatherings. The sink room next to the railroad tracks was a small area that had double slate tubs with a single faucet. One side was for washing dishes and the other was for washing clothes or kids in our Saturday night baths. We had no dedicated space or water heaters. I remember how my mother would fill a large copper boiler with water and place it on the kitchen stove to heat up to fill the tubs. All the boys took turns cutting wood for heat. This room also doubled as part of the kitchen where we ate most of our meals.

The center of home activities was not the modern day playroom or TV and multimedia center. It was the kitchen. Ours was not very big, but it contained all the necessities: A table, chairs, utensils, a well-organized pantry, and of course, the stove, which was used for cooking as well as for heating the whole house.

At first it was a wood stove for which we had to collect kindling wood and logs throughout the year in order to last through the long winter months. Later it was transformed to run on kerosene. Kerosene stoves are now banned because they are a fire hazard. (We did have a scare when ours once flared up. Fortunately my sister Angela saw the leaping flames and alerted my older brother Mike, who tore the kerosene jug from the stand and threw it out the door in time to save our home from disaster.) We all took turns going outside in all seasons including freezing weather to refill the kerosene jug. Our meals were typically quick, but we all gathered together around the small table to enjoy the warmth of the family closeness that outlasted that given off by the stove.

I can vividly recall how our mother would heat bricks in the oven of the kitchen stove, then wrap them up in newspapers and give each of us 'our brick' to take up to bed. That was our only heat for the night. We had no inside toilets. All we had were potties with a little water to dilute the urine odor.

Since we had no central heat, many was the night during our cold New England Winters that we woke up in the morning to find ice in the potties. Those of us who brought a glass of water to bed could count on having a glass of ice waiting for us in the morning. Dad had built an Outhouse between the home and the tracks where we went for our daily duties. In the summer the stench there was unbearable. During the winter it was so cold that we didn't linger any longer than was necessary. The old Montgomery Ward and Sears Roebuck's catalogs in the stall were not used just for reading! This old outhouse stills remains as a storage shed and a momento of days gone by.

The outhouse is back there!

In our close quarters we not only ran the family store, but we also maintained the rudiments and places of work for several sidelight businesses: My Dad's carpentry and shoe repair shops, as well as Mom and Dad's basement food and beverage processing plants, and the store warehouse. It's no wonder that we had to learn to become organized. To this day I regularly exhort to all my charges:

"A place for everything, and everything in its place!"

Refrigeration as we now know it was certainly not available. Many of our foods were either fresh or home dried or cured to preserve them. We were one of the first in the area to afford a small ice box, which was filled twice a week in the summer by 'the ice man' on his rounds in the ice truck. Bridgwater had a thriving regional ice cutting business on Carver's pond. The huge blocks that were cut from there during the winter months were stored in great warehouses and later sold in small pieces in the warmer months. Naturally no one in Stanley wasted money on ice during our cold winters. We could harvest our own.

Resources were scarce, but hard work, and just as importantly, smart work, was unlimited. And those who kept plugging as best they could with whatever they had available were the ones prepared to capitalize when opportunity presented itself. As the popular athletic saying goes:

"When preparation meets opportunity there is success."

In the good old days of 'the roaring twenty's' and during the great depression years of '30's which followed the stock market crash of 1929, we didn't have the luxuries of TV's, video games or fancy automobiles. We managed to have loads of fun in inexpensive ways. We also managed to scheme and work to generate a few luxuries that none of the other families in Stanley were able to afford.

Although a couple others had built unreliable radio tuners, our 'Poly Royal' cabinet style radio was the 1st day to day connection to the outside world in Stanley. I remember when my Dad installed the outside antenna, which was needed to get any reception in the railroad gully between hills that comprised Stanley. All the neighbors came over to lend a hand in hoisting the long pole that held the antenna.

As we ate our mom's scrumptious risotto dinners made from baked rice, chicken stock, egg and parmesan cheese, a cup of homemade wine was at every child's and adult's setting and the mellifluous sounds of the Italian station out of Boston would emanate from our precious radio.

Whenever there was a championship fight, such as Jack Dempsey vs. Gene Tunney, or a World Series Baseball game, the whole neighborhood would congregate outside the window of our living room to listen to the sporting events.

We were also one of the first two families in Stanley to own an automobile. (Tom Magistrate owned the other one.) I can still remember the Ford that my Dad bought from Lucini Motors for a grand total of $200.00. We all learned to drive it, as we had to share the duties of carrying groceries to customers of our Mom & Pop store. The line between business and pleasure was often razor thin. We learned to enjoy and master whatever our task.

Al, Angie and Mike, in 1943. By ten years after the depression our hard team work had earned a new car, a new storefront, and the chance to go serve the country that gave us the opportunity to strive to prosper.

OUR LIFE IN THE 1930'S AND DEPRESSION YEARS
When Things Go Wrong, As They Sometimes Will Or – Throwing a Brick

My Dad's thriftiness made our puritan descendant townsfolk seem like spendthrifts. When it came time for an important investment for the family, however, the saved resources were there. In the early 30's we built an addition to our home. With all of us children growing up and with the birth of our youngest brother Johnny in 1933, my Dad felt it was time. I can recall that during remodeling all of the children had to sleep across the street at the Ferioli's. My Dad rented space in their large home until the work was completed. It was a real treat for all of us to come home to the modern convenience of an indoor bathroom and a central heating system along with some added room space.

Though we were better off than our neighbors, we all felt the pangs of the great depression. Aside from the sweat equity and burgeoning family driven home improvement, even more than normal we made do with the meager material possessions that we had.

Our work ethic dating from our heritage and those times deserves some mention. All the kids had to chip in as they could, but the biggest burden fell upon the oldest. My sister Virginia, who was the first in the family of six, had the misfortune to have to give up her schooling at an early age to go out to work in the nail and shoe factories to help support the family. Its amazing that through hard work and an ever upbeat attitude, she was still able to forge a life that eventually included trips around the world and to visit her many very successful children and grandchildren.

My brother Mike was next in line to hit the labor market. He at least had the opportunity to complete his high school education before taking a full time job at the Independent Nail Factory. It was a big sacrifice and rough going for him, but he made the best of this experience, which eventually led him into establishing his own very successful Nail Packing Company.

All of us had our turn at finding part time jobs along with our chores in the Mom and Pop store. A few of these part time jobs bring a chuckle when I now think of them. It was customary for all of us to go to work for Tim Madden when he cut the hay in the Company Field across the railroad tracks. Our job was to turn the hay over to dry. When it was dried up enough we had to use pitchforks to throw the hay up on to the wagons. It wasn't an easy job for we pre-teen youngsters. Since there were no Child Labor Laws at this time, we were paid according to our age. I can vividly recall my first payday at the age of 8 when Mr. Madden gave me 8 cents. My brother Al, who was a year older than me, got 9 cents and my eldest Brother Mike got 10 cents for our day's work in the hot sun.

I also remember going to work for Eddie Dame's grandfather to clean bricks from dismantled buildings. We were paid by the number of bricks that we cleaned: One penny each. Mr. Dame would pick us up early in the morning and transport us to New Bedford in his truck. One day while we were clearing bricks from a second floor level Mr. Dame was directing us from below. After we cleaned up each brick we had to toss it down onto the truck nearby. Well I missed with one of my throws and the brick hit Mr. Dame squarely on his cue ball baldhead, giving him a gash that spurted blood and required several stitches.

They say that Jerry Rice became the world's greatest football receiver in part from his experience catching bricks thrown by his dad. My brickwork experience also strengthened my arms and more importantly my playing concentration. Mr. Dame taught me to take my time and be extra careful before making any sporting throw. It's a long lonely journey home after any loss, especially if one is walking and hitch hiking alone from New Bedford to Bridgewater!

I guess that the main lesson that I learned from the Great Depression and my family's response to it, is best summed up by this anonymously written poem that my good friend State Representative Dave Flynn reprinted for his constituents:

Don't Quit!

When things go wrong, as they sometimes will,
When the road you're trudging seems all uphill.
When the funds are low and the debts are high,
And you want to smile, but you have to sigh,
When care is pressing you down a bit -
Rest if you must, but don't you quit.

Life is queer with its twists and turns,
As every one of us sometimes learns,
And many a fellow turns about
When he might have won had he stuck it out.
Don't give up though the pace seems slow –
You may succeed with another blow.

Often the goal is nearer than
it seems to a faint and faltering man;
Often the struggler has given up
When he might have captured the victor's cup;
And he learned too late when the night came down,
How close he was to the golden crown.

Success is failure turned inside out –
The silver tint of the clouds of doubt,
And you never can tell how close you are,
It may be near when it seems afar;
So stick to the fight when you're hardest hit –
It's when things seem worst that you mustn't quit.

                                        Author unknown

PROHIBITION ERA
Bootleg Play

"You can pick an American bootlegger out of a crowd of Americans everytime. He will be the one that is sober."
-George Will, August 19, 1927

THE ENTERPRISE
BROCKTON, MASSACHUSETTS

TWO RAIDS IN BRIDGEWATER

Bridgewater, Sept. 15 (1928) -- Bridgewater police last night raided the home of John Folloni, 61 Wall St, and seized 128 quarts of beer, six quarts of cherry wine, 136 empty bottles and 200 gallons of mash.

They also raided the home of Philip Znortin, 306 North Street. This raid yielded two gallons of wine, 32 quart bottles of beer and 151 empty bottles.

The raiding party consisted of Chief James Moore and Officers O'Leary, Hunter and Shaw. The two raids last night made a total of four in three days.

Prohibition, the 18th Amendment to the US Constitution, was in effect from 1920 to 1933. Still, the period was known as the "Roaring 20's", as the age-old industry of 'Bootlegging' thrived.

My Dad and Mom (Nono and Nona) were among the many immigrant people of all nationalities who continued their traditional practice of making their own wine and brews during those days. Making and consuming home brew was legal, but selling it was not. My older brother Mike related several now-humorous stories about their bootlegging activities:

Although both my parents and our neighbors made the brew primarily for their family and friends, they wouldn't normally shrink from selling some to the rare Stanley family who didn't make their own, or to some persistent townies and the occasional outsider passing through. The other exception was during the weekly neighborhood bocce tournaments. To make the competition more interesting, there was some friendly betting, and the losers would have to pay for the drinks.

Although these transgressions were relatively mild, the repercussions could be troublesome, as was the case in the above noted raid, when my saintly mother landed in the 'pokey' for a day because my dad wasn't around when the police came. So prudence dictated that countermeasures be taken. My family subsequently decided that Mike would have the job of bringing a few bottles of each batch of our home made vintage to the new Irish Police Chief "to show gratitude for the Department's excellent service and protection."

Since most of the locals in Stanley eventually became well acquainted with this time-honored technique of influencing community affairs, the arrest rate in Little Italy became conspicuously low. This seemed a little odd to the state police, especially since so many truckloads of grapes from Haymarket Sq. in Boston seemed to find their way to the tiny area of Wall Street and Bolton Place in Bridgewater. So the state authorities decided to take aim at this 'target-rich' local immigrant community.

One day while a few of my dad's friend's were playing cards and having a few drinks at our village store, a shabbily dressed young man sporting a nice ring showed up asking for beer or wine. He explained that he was a construction worker on the new West Bridgewater to Brockton road, and that he just wanted a little hooch to help while away the hours after work so he wouldn't feel so lonely being away from his family. Nono was a very gracious host, inviting him to sit in on the card game and giving him as much to drink as he wanted while playing. When the guest offered him cash for it, Nono repeatedly refused, explaining that for such a nice guy, win or lose, all of it was 'on the house'.

Well, my Dad was not the only one solicited by a 'lonely construction worker' that afternoon. By early evening virtually every other 'bootlegger' in Stanley had been arrested and brought to the town jail by a team of undercover agents. Nono, of course, volunteered to come down and bail them all out. When he arrived at the lock-up he saw the "construction worker" who had tried to dupe him and his other set-up men. The out-witted agents of course wanted to find out why Nono wouldn't accept any money for the booze. When they asked, he told them:

"I may only have one eye, but I'm smarter and more observant than most people with two eyes. I know that a construction worker is not going to wear an expensive ring like this guy." (Nono had worked at his uncle's jewelry store in Italy and he immediately recognized its value.) The other undercover men laughed heartily and the embarrassed agent stalked off, exclaiming, "I guess you are smarter than me." Nono once again proved that: *"Common sense is not a common thing."*

The aware and visionary John Folloni Near "Boca Laga's field

MY EARLY TEEN YEARS
Mickey Cochrane-Hank Greenberg-American Legion Baseball

In the early 1930's fellow Boston University Hall of Famer; Gordon "Mickey" Cochrane was given a Testimonial by our hometown of Bridgewater. Cochrane and Harry Agganis were selected as the greatest athletes ever to have come out of BU. Mickey went on to become one of the greatest professional catchers of all time. He was immortalized in Cooperstown with the following tribute:

He started his Major League career with the Philadelphia Athletics under the tutelage of Connie Mack. After leading the Athletics to several World Championships in the late 20's, Cochrane went on to become the player-manager of the Champion Detroit Tigers.

The entire Detroit Tigers team was invited to take part in the ceremonies to honor Bridgewater's greatest athlete. This event to honor my childhood idol gave me the opportunity to experience the thrill of my young life. Preceding the testimonial, I went to see all of Mickey's teammates who had congregated at a staging area near the BSC campus before parading around the Town Common. Suddenly Hank Greenberg, the Tiger's giant first baseman, reached down, picked me up, put me on his shoulders and proceeded to carry me around the Common!

Literally & figuratively, the Great Hank Greenberg hoisted me above the common

On his shoulders I was on top of the world. How special I felt that he had singled me out for this experience. But why me? This moment seared into my consciousness the feeling of glory, and the belief that if I could come so close to those who had so deservedly earned theirs, that I could one day achieve it myself somewhere in the athletic world. And perhaps one day I could return to Bridgewater with the pride of having worked to fulfill this dream.

How coincidental that, of all the kids in town, this slugging star elevated the one who would someday join Mickey Cochrane as a member of the BU Hall of Fame? And who could believe that adjoining playing areas of Legion field would end up being named after Mickey and me! How fulfilling can a man's life get? I am truly honored and blessed by this remarkable course of events.

To this day I have never forgotten the great Hank Greenberg's kind and inspirational gesture. I think that acts like this made me a little extra mindful later in life of the positive impact of a simple kind gesture from a role model adult to an aspiring youth.

As exhilarating as my spirit-soaring ride on Hank Greenberg's shoulders was, I was to experience a down to earth disappointment just as great shortly thereafter. The local American Legion baseball team was having tryouts for the upcoming baseball season. Getting on this team was the ambition of all youngsters with any intentions of 'making it' in their baseball careers.

When it came time for me to bat during the tryout, the Legion coach, a fellow by the name of Ned Pickett, stopped me cold in my tracks. He approached me and would not let me even try to bat, saying, *"Hey Wop, you're too small! Go home and eat some spaghetti!"* If he had hit me over the head with the bat he couldn't have hurt me any more than with those stinging words and his refusal to let me tryout. Needless to say, never, ever in my subsequent coaching career would I deny any kid, regardless of skill level or appearance, the opportunity to test and prove him or herself competitively. This experience also contributed to my later conviction that I should never criticize a player in front of his peers.

I was so humiliated and shocked by this turn of events that I ran the mile and a half home crying all the way. I vowed that I would come back to the Legion Field someday and show that coach that I could indeed play the game of baseball better than any of the players he had selected for his team.

Did I come back to Legion Field? I sure did. When they dedicated the new Legion Field in 1936 I had the honor and distinction of making the first hit (a double down the right field line) in the first game played on that new baseball complex. This Legion Field was the best Baseball Park in the area for many years to come. I went on to play many more games on these beautiful grounds, both for my high school and later for Semipro teams.

Larry Folloni made the first hit at the new Legion Field in 1936

Sadly, like me, my idol Hank Greenberg also suffered much prejudice during his playing career. According to Nancy Camp of ICOM, 1930s Detroit was "a hotbed of anti-Semitism" where Father Charles Coughlin preached pro-Nazi sentiments on his popular radio show and Henry Ford, a frequent Tiger Stadium patron, published a tract warning against a vast Jewish conspiracy to destroy Christian civilization. 'Hammerin' Hank Greenberg's baseball feats rivaled those of Babe Ruth and Lou Gehrig. Yet as glorious a hitter as he was, time and again, my hero had to turn a deaf ear to the stands where even his own team's fans tossed slurs simply because he was a Jew who dared to set foot on the field. He just sucked it up, went out there and hit it out of the park. In the year that he hit 58 homeruns. Opposing teams stopped giving him anything to hit late in the season to prevent him from reaching Babe Ruth's Record.

Despite all of the adversity, my hero maintained a distinctive grace with which he accepted defeat and victory, both on and off the field.

Some say that the greatness of a man can be gauged by how he treats the 'little people'. This little guy can testify that Hank Greenberg was definitely one of the greatest.

What famous Harvard attorney Alan Dershowitz said about Hank Greenberg probably most aptly described the strong underlying motivation that Italian kids from Stanley had:

"He was what they all said we could never be. Baseball was our way of showing we were as American as anybody else."

THE BASKETBALL COURTS AT LEGION FIELD BY MICKEY CORCORAN COMPLEX WERE DEDICATED IN MY HONOR ON JULY 26, 2003

Larry Folloni 1919 – 20__
Married to Helen Mark Folloni

**Born, raised, and educated in Bridgewater • WWII Veteran • Father of 6
Founder Town's Youth Recreation, Basketball and Baseball Programs
Teacher, Coach, and Athletic Director, 33 years at BHS and BRRHS
Coached 3 State Champion Basketball Teams • Undefeated at Boston Garden
214-86 career coaching record • State Athletic Director of the Year, 1976
State Secondary School Athletics Rules Committee Chairman 13 years
Director of State Basketball Tournament • Co-founder of State Superbowl
State Coaches Hall of Fame • Boston University Athletic Hall of Fame NCAA
Baseball Record at BU for reaching base 17 consecutive at bats
First official base hit (a double) at WPA-renovated Legion Field in 1936
New Hampshire Senior Golf Champion, 1997 and 1998**

"Have Fun, Play Hard, Play Fair. Do Your Best & let God do the Rest!"
"If you win enjoy, if you lose, be gracious and congratulate the winner."

BASEBALL DAYS IN THE 30'S & 40'S
4 Fingered Mitts and A Satchel of Memories!

My earliest recollection of my baseball days was from my playing and coaching the Stanley Steamers team in the late 20's at the early age of 10! We organized this ballclub from our daily pickup games on the Streets, the Sandbank and the Diamond Fields as related earlier.

Next, I played for Coach Tom Tinsley's Knights of Columbus team during the summer months of the 1933 and 1934 seasons. It was a team made up of youngsters in the 12 to 15 years age levels who had been among the dominating players in the State in their age group. We won about 90% of our games. Many of the wins were against teams made up of players that were much older than we were. One victory that I well remember was when we challenged the adult Jenkins team that was the champion of their Mayflower League. It was a hard earned win for us youngsters and with the crowd cheering us on we won by a score of 5 to 3. We further stunned all by going on to win a 2 out of 3 series!

Tom Tinsley and his 1934 K of C Juniors Baseball Team

45th Reunion K of C Baseball Team, Sept. 1979 L to R Front Row: Larry Folloni, George Paleti, Joe Lazaro, Bill Broderick, Dan Roderique. Back Row: Coach Tom Tinsley, Jack Dowd, Bill 'Biscuits' Rubeski, Eddie Snarski, and Joe Tinsley, Mgr.

It was then on to my High School playing days lettering in 3 sports for Coach Lester Lane, where I was the Captain of the baseball team in my senior year. I can credit Coach Lane for teaching me the basic fundamentals of all of these sports. To this day his teaching me how to square away and bunt the ball properly stands out in my mind. I could still stand up as an old man and square away and lay down a bunt against any of the top pro pitchers in the game of baseball. I now get so frustrated as I watch the modern day, overpaid professional baseball players attempt to bunt a ball. They need a Coach like Coach Lane!

My next step was the Semipro Level. During the early and middle 30's, the local 49ers-baseball team was the dominant Semipro club in the South Shore area. It was loaded with Stanley kids, "Bo" Abati, Elmer Donati, Peter Donati, Andy Moruzzi, "Skinny" Giovanni, "Ceco" Ferioli, Mickey Ferioli, Harry Piscatori, and "Bud" Chiocca, to name a few. Elmer Donati, a fiery leader, coached the Team. It was Coach Donati who recruited George Paleti and me on to their roster in 1935, as we were the brightest young prospects on the very successful Bridgewater K of C team. We were only 14 years of age and still freshmen in H.S. at the time, and we never expected to see much action with the adult team. Midway through the summer season we had an unexpected introduction to Semipro Baseball, which turned out to create some of my fondest baseball memories:

My best boyhood baseball thrill came during a game against Whitman. Their team had a lopsided lead and Coach Donati became frustrated with the caliber of play of his starters. Half way through the game he inserted George Paleti and me into the lineup as the young keystone combination of the future. In my first at bat, with the bases loaded, on the very first pitch, I hit a line drive over left fielder, "Spike" Hennessy's head. The ball rolled all the way across the road in left field and I had a grand slam home run for the big team! Of the many hits that I made in my entire baseball career, none was as sweet or as memorable as that one. When I became a coach I often successfully employed the tactic of plugging in a fresh youngster from the bench during stale team moments, both to challenge his older teammates, as well as to inspire the newcomer.

After my High School days I spent two years working at menial jobs and playing baseball for several other Semipro Baseball Teams including the Lincoln AA coached by "Bo" Ferioli. I then went on to Bridgewater State College where I met Fred Meier, a Coach and extraordinary educator who was to become a dear friend for life.

Dr. Meier coached all three Sports; Soccer, Basketball and Baseball at the College during my two-year stay there. Fred later went on to become the President of Salem State College. While at Salem State he invited me up several times to be his golf playing partner in Member Guest Tournaments. Following his retirement, he returned to live in Bridgewater and we became golfing partners for many years, winning our share and in any case sharing time happily like winners. Fred passed away in 2000 at the age of 89 and his lovely wife Louise joined him inside the pearly gates shortly thereafter.

After Bridgewater State, I enrolled at Wentworth Institute in Boston for one year and played on the Baseball Team under Coach Joe Tansey. With the outbreak of World War II, I then enlisted in the Army Air Corps. While stationed at the Victorville Army Air Base in, California I played on the Baseball Team under Coach Reichle, a former Professional Baseball player and Coach of UCLA. We had many former Professional Baseball Players on this team that flew all over the West Coast of the Country to play other service teams to boost military comradery and moral.

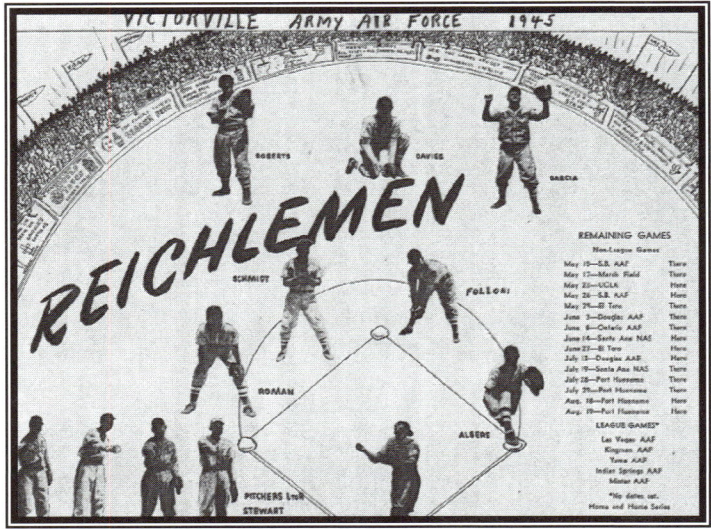

Larry's Victorville baseball squad (Named for Coach Reichle, not for the 3rd Reich who they were preparing to beat.)

2nd Baseman Larry 1944

Upon my discharge from the Air Corps in 1946 I headed for Boston University to complete my college education. It was here that I established a National Baseball Collegiate record feat that still stands. During one stretch of four games, I reached base 17 consecutive times. The streak consisted of 12 hits, 3 walks and 2 safe on errors, which could well have been ruled hits as the balls were hard hit. The streak ended when I lined out to the third baseman, who made a spectacular diving catch. Following that out, I went on for another 6 straight hits before making an out. But for the Brooks Robinson like catch by the third baseman, my record streak would have been 24 instead of 17. This record, that was established before the NCAA existed, has never been surpassed as of the date of this writing, although it was tied twice on the NCAA level. Ted Williams of the Red Sox has the major League record with 16.

My Baseball Coaches at BU were Mel Collard and Harry Cleverly. My last two years there were very productive on the diamonds. They included a career batting average of over .400 including against our major rivals Harvard, BC and Northeastern, and, thanks to my childhood reaction drills, several seasons with minimal fielding errors: All in all, good enough for me to be inducted into the BU Athletic Hall of Fame!

During the summer months of my college years I played for several Semipro Teams. Among them were the Lincoln AA coached by "Bo" Ferioli and the Casey Club in the Boston Park League, coached by none other than Dick Casey who was a prominent political figure in the State.

I remember the Lincoln AA venture for the grand finale we had in 1946, the year when most of the Stanley gang and the rest of our generation returned from World War II. (A few of our buddies never made it back, including Fredo Bertelli, Bob Pratti and Mario Chiocca, who made the supreme sacrifice losing their lives in overseas battles.)

Before their dutiful and courageous war efforts, (and for too much of an extent for too many years after) the kids from Stanley were considered to be low life, 'white trash' from 'the other side of the railroad tracks'. When it came to baseball and other sports, however, the Little Italy kids were the best in town by far Just to show how we dominated the sports scene let me go through the lineup for the Lincoln Club Baseball Team. This crew represented the entire town and was the top Semipro Team in the South Shore Area in the late 30's before World War II and in the late 40's following the war. At the catching position were "Bo" Ferioli and "Herk" Balboni, the pitchers were "Shine" Moruzzi, and brothers Dino and Fred Bertelli. (Fred was later killed in a bombing mission over Germany.) At first base we had Fred Valeri and Alec Dziergowski. Hank Pearson also came in after the war to play first base. I was the 2nd baseman; George Paleti was at shortstop. George left us in the later years to play professional ball in the Minor Leagues, and Johnny Roderick took his place at short. At third base we had Eddie Snarski, the only non-Stanley player on the team. In left field was "Mickey" Ferioli. In center field was Joe Lazaro, of Portuguese descent, who looked and played like Joe DiMaggio. Joe lived on High St. next to the house where I was born, and was the star on our childhood rivals the High St. Tigers. In right field and for pitcher we alternated with "Shine" Moruzzi and Elmer Balboni.

The 1946 Lincoln AA team was pitted up against St. Colmans of Brockton in what the Boston Papers named the "Little World Series of Semipro". The series was well attended with crowds of up to 5,000 at each Game. The classic lived up to advanced predictions by going down to the final game of the 4 out of 7 series.

Lincoln AA 1946 baseball squad

This great series was marred by the events that ended the last game. We had each won 3 games and the contest to determine the championship was played at the Legion Field in Bridgewater before the largest crowd ever to attend a Semipro game. With the score tied in the last of the seventh inning, I was on second base poised to score the series winner. "Bo" Ferioli hit a screeching ground ball that caromed off of the third base bag into the crowd and I scampered home with what should have been the winning run.

Would you believe that the Umpire ruled it a foul ball? All hell broke loose as players and fans swarmed onto the field to protest the horrendous call. A near riot ensued but all to no avail and the game went on with St. Colman's eventually winning out by a 4 to 3 score and a 4-3 series.

My experience with the Semi-pro Casey Club also had a disastrous ending during the playoffs for the League Championship, where I was the victim of an accident that sounded the death knell of my Professional Baseball aspirations. As the lead off batter I was hit in the face by one of ace pitcher Fred Toye's 95-MPH fast balls. I ended up in the hospital for two weeks with a broken cheekbone. The surgeon who operated to repair the damage said that if it had hit me another inch to the left that it would have been fatal.

Here are two more happy incidents that I fondly recall from my playing days with the Casey Club:

One occurred at a game at Roslindale. My normal position was at 2nd base, but due to the fact that I had suffered a shoulder injury in the previous game, Coach Casey started me in center field. In the last inning with the bases loaded and the game on the line, one of Roslindale's heavy hitters slammed a tremendous shot that was headed straight to center and well over my head. I took off at the crack of the bat, turned and ran full speed straight back. At the last instant I put my glove out as far as I could reach and the ball landed in my little 4-fingered mitt. As I headed back to the dugout the fans all stood up and gave me a standing ovation that I'll never forget. Years later Willie Mays of the New York Giants made what many call 'The Catch of the Century" in Game 1 of the 1954 World Series. Ten years after I made my over-the-head-basket-catch, some who were in attendance told me it was every bit as good as that made by Willie, 'The Say Hey Kid', Mays! Now that's a compliment!

The other incident occurred in 1946 when we played the Colored Giants, one of the renowned Negro League Teams that toured the world with their talented players. We played the game under the lights before a sell-out crowd. In over 400 inter-race, inter-league games between the Negro Leagues and the then segregated white Major League Baseball, the Negro league won almost 7 of every 10 games played. 'Cannonball' Will Jackman, who baseball historians consider to be in the top handful of Negro League pitchers ever, was on the mound for the opposition.

As usual, I was the lead off batter......... *When Jackman threw his first side arm pitch, it actually started out as though it was going to go behind me. By the time the ball reached home, I had hit the deck, and the ball curved over right in the middle of the plate! He then made two more similarly impossible pitches that I whiffed at, looking real foolish in striking out. It seems Cannonball learned a few tricks from his friendly rival, the legendary Leroy 'Satchel' Paige!*

My next two appearances at bat against Cannonball Jackman were quite different. I had made up my mind that no matter what; I would hang in the box and wait for the pitch to come up to the plate before reacting.

With all of my competitive juices flowing, I somehow succeeded in getting two hits off of this great athlete and man. The first hit was a hard grounder between the shortstop and the third baseman. The second one was a line drive to center field. Not too many can boast of hitting .667 against a top notch Negro League Pro in his prime!

Cannonball Will Jackman after his Hall of Fame Career

I was in good company with my difficulties batting against an all time all star Negro League Pitcher. Here's a quote by Major Leaguer Jerry Haiston to the Boston Globe about Cannonball Jackson's rival and friend Satchel Paige: "My grandfather caught Satchel Paige in an all-star game," Jerry Hairston said. "I remember him telling us that Joe DiMaggio struck out twice against him. DiMaggio turned to my grandfather and said, 'This is the best pitcher I've ever seen.' At the time, I was young and it was no big deal, but now as I look back at it, that's huge, my grandfather caught Satchel Paige."

And speaking of the 'Yankee Clipper', Joe DiMaggio, here's a quote from him that I can really relate to: "A ballplayer's got to be kept hungry to become a big leaguer. That's why no boy from a rich family ever made the big leagues." Of course this has changed somewhat these days, with modern TV coverage attracting wider audiences and with some of the better families still instilling the desire to excel in their children. Nonetheless as the common folk in our society make economic gains, we cannot afford to forget the DiMaggio attitude and rest on our laurels, be it in the sports, business, service or governmental fields.

My family, Coaches, teammates, Ted, 'Cannonball' and 'Rocky' certainly had a strong influence upon my athletic career. Another big influence I almost forgot to mention was a scout for the Brooklyn Dodgers, named Bill O'Connor. "Okie", as he was called, scouted me throughout my Semipro days and when I graduated from BU he offered me a contract to play in the Brooklyn Dodger Farm system.

As luck would have it I had just signed a contract with the Town of Dighton to teach and coach in their school district. It broke my heart to have to pass up this chance to accomplish my childhood dreams of becoming a professional baseball player. I thanked "Okie" for his kind offer and said that I would honor my contract with Dighton for the year and if things worked out I would contact him for the following year.

Of course my injury ended my dreams to go on to play professional baseball. With this dream dashed I threw myself into involvement with my next love, which was to become a Coach, and to help other youngsters to have the fun in life that I enjoyed so much growing up in the 'slums' of Stanley.

In retrospect it is interesting to me to ponder that had I not been hit by Toye's toss, and had I continued to progress as a solid 2nd baseman and hitter, that I may well have not only been drafted by the Dodgers, but I may have also made the 1947 team. And had I done so, my fellow rookie teammate under fabled owner Branch Rickey would have been none other than JACKIE ROBINSON, the 1st Black player to break the color barrier in the major leagues! Actually, since both of us played 2nd base, had I passed my injury hurdle, I'd have had a much taller one facing me in competing with Jackie to man the keystone sack.

I did make one small comeback in 1951 when I was asked to return to play for the Lincoln AA in the Championship playoffs. Some of their key players had gone back to college for the fall and they were shorthanded. How well I remember my last hurrah! I could still hit pretty well, averaging better than .600 for the series, but age and lack of conditioning was creeping up on me. In my last at bat I hit a long drive to right center field and tried to stretch a triple into a home run. I got hung up in a run down between third and home. By the time they finally tagged me out I was all pooped out and fell flat on my face. That was an emphatic end to any illusions of continuing a pro baseball career. I called it quits after that game.

"Ain't no man can avoid being born average, but there ain't no man got to be common."
-Leroy 'Satchel' Paige

MY OLDER BROTHERS AND SISTER
Rock Solid Teammates, Varsity Team

"They are able because they think they are able."
Virgil

My oldest Sister Virginia was born in Italy on July 29, 1911. On Thanksgiving Day in 1935 she married Caesar Filippetti. This is a date that I shall never forget. It just so happened that her wedding was at the same time that our High School football team was to be playing its traditional Thanksgiving Day football game. Since I was the quarterback it was a very difficult choice for me to make.

Should I attend my sister's wedding or play the football game? Being young and loyal to my teammates I chose to play in the football game then join in the wedding festivities later in the afternoon. My sister Virginia never let me forget that I missed the wedding ceremony. I of course I made it up for this slight by the many favors that I returned to her throughout her life while she was raising a beautiful family of 7 children.

Virginia was a woman who never attended high school due to depression challenges, and ended up working all her adulthood as a cleaning lady at the local State College, yet, who did a super job with her husband in raising a large and well educated and successful family. Despite their economic challenges of both being 'non-formally educated' immigrants, Virginia and Caesar established a very nice household on a large plot of Main St. land. Their biggest success came in the form of seven fantastic children, Mary, Louis, Rosalie, Helen, Francis, Nancy and Richard, and of course, their grandchildren and great grandchildren.

Louie, Caesar, Virginia, Mary, Nancy Helen, Francis, Rosalie. (Richard on way)

Just a small portion of the great grandchildren in 1987

[See the 'Family Album' in the appendix for more photos of Virginia & Caesar Filippetti's children and their families!]

With her children, her siblings, and by her own gumption, Virginia eventually managed to travel much of the USA and Europe, and once in a new place, she had a knack for quickly finding someone who knows or is related to someone else she has met! She consistently personally proved the axiom that within 3 steps of who knows who, everyone in the world is connected by somebody in common. Virginia taught me that being shy never got anyone anywhere. Her forthright manner may have put some off, but her warm almost childlike enthusiasm that she maintained throughout life was overwhelming, and would melt the hearts of most that she encountered. This trait, along with her unswerving persistence, got her astoundingly far in life.

With Helen in Holland   *At the Leaning Tower of Pisa*   *And the Eiffel Tower*

Like my mother, Virginia was also a lifelong devoted Catholic who daily followed my mom's trail to St. Thomas Aquinas church. She succumbed to cancer in 1987.

When Virginia was a little girl she once saw a New Orleans style parade of a funeral procession given for one of the more wealthy citizens of our town. From that time she vowed to have a similar happy celebration of life upon her demise. Sure enough, she provided for just such a parade in her honor through the streets where she spent much of her life walking from one humble job to another, with a brass band of a cheery greeting for all that she met.

Kindred spirits Virginia Filippetti and my son Robert summer, 1987

The oldest sacrificed to help the rest of us to succeed.

And they still succeeded greatly in their own right.

Virginia   *Mike*

• • • • • • • • • • • • • •

Next in line in my family was my oldest brother, Michael, always called "Mike". Mike was born on January 1916 in a home at the corner of Main and High Streets in Bridgewater. Mike married an astute girl named Helen Levy, whose brother at one time served as the Fire Chief in our town.

Mike and Helen met while both were employed at the Independent Nail Factory in town. When the Nail Company sold their holdings to an out of state organization, Mike and Helen set up their own Nail Packing Company. They started out working out of their home's garage and basement in East Bridgewater and later bought a plot of land up the street to build their factory. A tragic fire leveled their plant a few years later. With grit and determination they rebuilt another modern plant. With the assistance of other family members and the persistent hard work of their three children, **P**eter, **E**dward, and **M**ichelle **Fo**lloni they built their business into a very thriving business entity.

Whenever anyone in the family was in need, everyone chipped in to help out in a spirit of happy cooperation. Here we wished Mike & Helen "Bon voyage" on their rebuilding of PEMFO Packing Co., which we all happily gave back to Mike just a bit of the financial & moral support that he'd given to us.

Mike and Helen now reap the rewards of their hard labor by living in Florida for 6 months a year, then returning to their new home in Halifax, Massachusetts for the other 6 months. They enjoy their golf both in Florida and in Halifax. They live just off the 10th hole of the beautiful Halifax Country Club. Their children are still running the company, which from the start was named **PEMFO**, after their children, **P**eter, **E**ddie and **M**ichelle **FO**lloni.

Mike & Larry reflecting on legacies well established

Mike never had the opportunity that I did as a youngster to play sports, as he was the oldest boy in the family and the burden of working to help support the family fell upon him, Al and my older sister Virginia. Nonetheless, he was an excellent bowler (perhaps he developed his technique on my Dad's bocce courts).

In the late 50's Mike won a $5,000.00 prize when he scored a '193' with candlepins in a League Bowling competition. This is the equivalent of between a '290' and '298' in 'Big Pins'!

Mike and Helen used his bowling winnings to build a family swimming pool in his back yard. Their pool and large yard became the scene of many memorable 'Folloni Clan' reunions; complete with intergenerational ball games, hot dog & hamburger BBQs, sweet corn feasts, and bushels of pepper, onion and butter laden little neck 'steamer' clams.

Nono & Erminia enjoy the fun & family

All of my Father's children & grandchildren treasure the extended family memories that were created and shared at Mike & Helen's East Bridgewater compound.

I've always looked up to Mike, not just because he is older, but because of how remarkably strong of character, even-tempered and kind he has always been. He has always shouldered a tremendous load for his families, but never has he been self righteous or petty about his contributions. He seemed to do it all with a sense of joy and a healthy dose of lighthearted humor to go along with his sterling purpose.

True Blue Mike

Al, Larry, Nono, Mike & John late '50's

Helen & Mike's original PEMFO Michelle, Peter and Edward c. 1960 (Peter, Edward, Michelle, Folloni)

••••••••••••••

My brother Albert was born on April 28, 1918 at another home on High Street, and was educated in Bridgewater public schools. On October 19, 1952 he married a pretty and vivacious Sicilian American girl from Brooklyn, N.Y. named Connie Genova. They became the parents of Albert Jr., Marie and Barbara.

Marie McLure Falloni with 2 of her 3 children

Al & Connie

211-16 50th Ave, Bayside Hills Queens, New York. Al's home

Al & Connie raised their children in New York, where Al became a very successful real estate developer and the Business Manager for World Heavyweight Champion Rocky Maricano.

"Your Real Estate Supermarket"

Connie was a confirmed 'city girl' with a great sense of humor and a hearty laugh to go with it (which must have come in handy since she was a life long die-hard Mets fan!) She took good care of Al right up to the end of his life. Like their Dad, the children are all quite witty, creative and intelligent. Marie and Barbara are both 'Knock-Outs', and Jack can put you on the canvas with his understated and true tales of real-life humor. Al served in World War II as a Medical Technician. Following his tour of duty in Europe and England, he returned to New York and became Director of the Armed Forces Radio Services, with an office in Times Square.

Rocky Marciano – Al Falloni Enterprises were thriving before Rocky's tragedy.

Al's work as a recruiter and provider of celebrity entertainment for Armed Forces Radio earned him public acclaim on the occasion of his retirement in 1961.

Note the WABC station bus in the background at this Times Square Tribute.

Although his civic promotions often got the Mayor's goat (and results), New York City also recognized Al's talents and outstanding contributions by giving him a 'Man of the Year' award, as depicted on the right, below:

It was while Al worked in Times Square that I made arrangements for him to first meet with Rocky Marciano. This culminated in a friendship between Al and Rocky that led to their business associations following Rocky's retirement from the ring.

Prior to his enlisting in the U.S. Army for World War II, Al served as a Grand Knight and Executive Secretary of Bridgewater K of C Council. Al was the last survivor of the 13 Founding Members of the Bridgewater Credit Union. In addition to being Marciano's personal business manager, Al also served as a public relations agent and business manager for former heavyweight champion Jack Dempsey, and as a business agent for the New York Knicks legendary all-star Willis Reed.

After serving for 22 years in the U.S. Army, Al became a successful Realtor in Bayside Hills, New York where he made his home until his retirement in 1988. Following Rocky Marciano's death, Al re-devoted most of his time to his Real Estate business. He served as secretary of the Long Island Realtors Credit Union and corresponding secretary of the Queens North Shore Chapter of Labor. He also served as president of the Bayside Hills Civic Association and president of both the North Shore Council of Homeowners and the Queens Federation of Civic Councils.

Upon his retirement, Al and Connie took up residence in Margate, Florida, where his daughters Marie (McClure) of Coral Springs and Barbara of Miami often joined them, while his son would visit from CO. Al passed away on May 14, 1997 at his Florida home after a long tough battle with diabetes.
At Marie's home in Coral Springs, Winter, 1997

TWO SMALL TOWN HICKS MAKE IT BIG IN THE BIG APPLE
Road Games with Rocky

My brother Al wove words as smooth as silk. One of his favorite sayings was:

"A person can catch more flies with honey than with a swatter."

Al was a real charmer, but his professional presentation was not merely a façade. He was a genuine genius in business and public relations, who had a heart that dwarfed his substantial material holdings.

Al once told me this story: After Rocky's fighting days were over, he and Al were walking down 42nd Street in Times Square following a business session that had lasted well into the night. As they walked below the glaring lights of the city, Rocky put his arm around Al and poured out his soul. He said to Al, "You are the only true friend that I can trust. Here we are two hicks (from bordering small towns Bridgewater & 'North Bridgewater' {Brockton} making it big in the Big Apple." Rocky really opened up as he proceeded to reveal some of the troubles in his life. With tears streaming down his face he related his many battles with (his boxing manager) Al Weill throughout his fighting days and lamented how everyone back home expected him to bail them out of their money and other problems.

I also have many interesting memories about my pal and idol, "Rocky Marciano". They started with my playing against him in the baseball rivalry between his St. Coleman's team and our Lincoln A.A. just after World War II, and continued through his years with Al and right up to the time of his unfortunate fatal accident. Though neighboring town and team rivals, Rocky and I became quite friendly out of mutual respect for our 'take no prisoners' approach to semi-pro baseball, where he was a very good catcher. (He caught pitches better than he caught punches!) Our will to win was rarely withstood. In team sports that meant that mine often won. There's no way, however, that I would have risked challenging Rocky to an individual battle. I'd already cheated death more than my share! While he was still training out of Brockton for his earlier fights, Rocky would often run the 6 miles or so each way to Bridgewater and stop in to visit with my gym classes.

When Rocky started his journey to the boxing heights I made arrangements for him to live with Al and Connie in Bay Side Hills, NY. Rocky stayed with them throughout many of the days when he was financially broke while climbing the ladder to the world championship. He never forgot Al and Connie's kindness in helping him out financially or their constant encouragement and friendly guidance during his struggle to the championship.

I last saw Rocky just weeks before he died as we were playing in a tournament at the Thorny Lee Golf Course in his hometown of Brockton. By that time, long into his retirement, Rocky had become a real HEAVY weight, probably tipping the scales at half again that of his fighting form. As always, he was full of friendship, warmth, humor and good will toward his old friends and all around him. From just seeing his ferocity in the ring, no one would know what a nice gentleman Rocky really was.

Before his death Al related many stories about Rocky, which have never before been revealed to the public. One is that Rocky at times was in the habit of burying his money outside his beach home in Ft. Lauderdale, Florida. Apparently he did not have too much faith in conventional banks. I'm not sure how much was supposedly buried, but I understand that it was a fairly substantial amount. To this day the money has never been found. Another is that Al tried to locate Rocky on that Labor Day weekend when he was killed in the tragic plane crash. Al and his family were spending the holiday weekend at my summer home in Hampton

Beach, N.H. Al had lined up a TV commercial for Rocky on the following Tuesday and tried unsuccessfully for several days to make contact with him. If Al had been able to locate him, Rocky may never have been on that doomed plane.

While they were in Germany six weeks before the fatal crash, Al told Rocky Marciano about a bad premonition. " I dreamed that you were on top of a 15 Story building," Al said, "and that you fell off and got killed and everybody started giving me hell for letting you go up there." "What did they do that for?" Rocky laughed. "When my time comes, it'll come. There's nothing you'll be able to do about it." Rocky was right, as that time came quickly thereafter in a patch of weeds in Iowa. There was nothing Al could do about it. Nothing but grieve. Rocky had so much to live for, so many things he planned to do.

Al told me that Rocky had never been busier, never happier than he was in the weeks preceding his death. They had just finished a world tour that summer and everywhere they went the people came in droves to be around Rocky. His reception was unbelievable and Rocky himself said he was amazed that he was still so popular.

They visited troops in Hawaii, Japan and Vietnam for the USO, then went on to North Africa, England, Germany and Italy. It was Rocky's first time in Italy and the people treated him like a hero. They mobbed him every place that he went.

Rocky was able to do something he'd always wanted, which was to visit his Mother's hometown, Bruscia, which is about 20 miles outside of Naples. He was so thrilled that he and Al made plans to bring his mother and father there in November. This was one big thing that Rocky always wanted to do but couldn't before the Man Upstairs counted him down and out.

Just a few weeks before his tragic death, Al had finished preparing Rock's life story for television. Al was always telling Rocky something might happen to him someday and that he wanted him to pick out the things he wanted in his story.

Rocky chose six fights that he rated his most important--the two with 'Jersey Joe' Walcott and the ones with Joe Louis, Ezzard Charles, Don Cockell and Roland Lastarza. Al said that to the day that he died Rocky felt awful about beating Joe Louis. When he was a kid Rocky used to listen to Joe's fights on the radio and he worshiped the guy. He hated to knock him out.

The Brockton Bomber Rocky winning the Heavyweight Championship of the World Against Jersey Joe Walcott in Sept. 1952

Rocky deplored boxing's long decline. Al and Rocky had just formed the new American Boxing Association, to help the sport. He was also trying to get Congress to appoint a federal boxing czar to help save the boxing game.

Al and Rocky had so many other plans. The week that he was killed Rocky was supposed to make three TV commercials--for a shaving cream, a finance company and a heavy equipment firm. And he was always in demand for personal appearances. In fact, that's where he was heading when his plane went down.

Al had always admonished Rocky for taking flights in private planes. On that fateful weekend the hosts wanted to give him a birthday party and the only way he could get there was in a private plane. Rocky couldn't bring himself to refuse so now he is dead and Al could only helplessly grieve. Now I grieve for both of them.

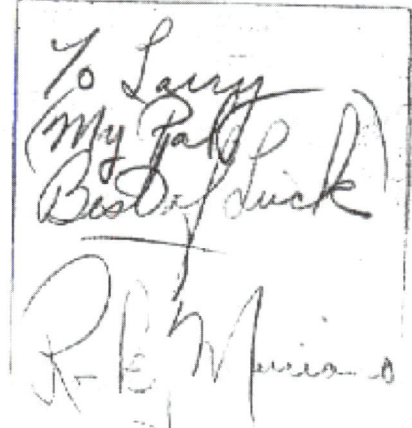

Billy O'Donnell, Rocky, Larry Jr., '50. Rocky was gracious in coming often to help get our recreation program get off to a walloping start.

Rocky returned as a referee to supervise this classic rematch between 'Lofty Larry Jr.' and 'Bobby the Bomber' Folloni. The fight was declared a "draw".

MY YOUNGER SISTER AND BROTHER AND ME
Rock Solid Teammates, Junior Varsity Team

Next in line after Virginia, Mike and Al came me. "Lawrence, Lori, Larry", three of the many names that have appeared on my records over the years. I was born on November 5th, 1919 at our old High Street home.

I married a lovely young girl from Arlington, Mass, by the name of Helen Mary Louise Mark, "Hollywood Helen", who presented me with 6 beautiful children.

From the day I married Helen, my world turned to living color!

Larry & Helen

Following me next in line was my young sister Angela. Properly named, as she was truly a living Angel who followed my mother's model as a loving and giving person. Angie was born on April 12, 1921. She was also delivered by the midwife Tranquila Resmini at our new home at 61 Wall Street that Nono moved into to accommodate his growing family.

Toward the end of World War II Angie married Elmer Balboni, one of my childhood friends who lived a few houses up the street. Their only child, Linda was a breech birth and Angie nearly died in the process. She survived but due to the birthing complications she was never able to have any more children.

Angie & Elmer's Wedding Day, '44   *Proud & Happy Angie with Baby Linda*

Cousins Linda Balboni & Larry Folloni Jr. go out on the town

Richard Balboni Bright Cheerful Teen

As a young child Elmer's nephew Richard spent his early years in rough conditions in New York. When his parents died Angie and Elmer legally adopted him. They raised Richard along with Linda as brother and sister in a very happy family.

Following the War Elmer along with his 3 brothers (Preston, Jake, and Charlie) went into business. They built their own Auto Wash on Main Street in Brockton. They all put in countless hours of back breaking work to build the business from the ground up.

Proud Papa Elmer with Linda. Uncles Jake & Larry approve.

Angie and Elmer always offered warm smiles

Their efforts were well rewarded and after building up their business in Brockton they branched out to Manchester, New Hampshire. Two of the Balboni brothers, Preston and Jake remained at the Brockton Wash and the other two, Elmer and Charlie went to New Hampshire to work the new branch. Elmer and Charlie purchased homes side by side on Celeste Street, in Manchester.

It didn't take them long to revitalize the New Hampshire Auto Wash. Within a few years they were rolling along with a very successful business. With their kids watching the shop, and Angie watching the books, Elmer and Charlie managed to sneak in a few rounds of golf in between hard work at the Wash. They would alternate playing days on the lean business days and when it rained the Wash closed down and both would go out and slosh through a round.

This was to be excellent training for them as they paired off in the club four-ball championship, which was held every Labor Day weekend. It just so happened that during that annual holiday weekend the weather was often rainy and since Elmer and Charlie were well practiced in working and playing golf under adverse conditions, they won the club four ball championship for 5 of 6 years at one stretch.

Their wives Gladys and Angie soon joined them on the golf course for Husband and Wife golf tournaments. Elmer and Angie have the distinction of being the only Husband and Wife to both have a hole-in-one in the same year at the Manchester Country Club.

Johnnie, Mike, Angie & Larry

Helen, 'Herc' Balboni, 'Bo' Ferioli, Elmer & Angie late '40's

After many years of hard work in New England's extreme weather conditions, working together with the troops in the wash line, Elmer and Charlie finally retired in 1982. After that they reaped the fruits of their hard labor by sharing their time on the golf courses and fishing holes between their homes Florida and New Hampshire. Angie and Elmer, of course were the greatest of grandparents for Linda and Paul Bardorf's five kids, and Richard's wonderful Wendy.

Angie and Elmer suffered the cruelest and most incomprehensible loss in December of 1997 when their shining star of a daughter Linda succumbed to cancer three months after Lady Diana of England and Mother Teresa of India passed. I'll never know how Angie and Elmer managed to maintain their warm and friendly demeanors after that.

Elmer passed away in of 1999. Angie has stayed active, upbeat and as concerned about others first as ever, although I know that she has to terribly miss Elmer and Linda, who along with Richard were the most precious loves in her life.

An interesting story about Linda: When she was in the midst of her courageous fight against cancer, she heard from her Goddaughter, my child Jeannie, that my son Michael was sponsoring a delegation to go see Mother Teresa in India. (This group included Michael's friend, Ernie Siravo, Director of The Star Alliance for peace organization, who was perhaps the last visiting male to see Mother Teresa alive.) Linda, who was extremely financially successful from an innovative educational system that she developed and marketed nationally, made a very generous donation for Michael to have delivered to Mother Teresa's Sisters of Charity. Linda asked Michael to ask Mother Teresa to kindly explain why it is that humans have to endure so much suffering. Michael (somewhat regrettably to him in retrospect), chose to stay in California to attend to business matters, but did have his sponsored representative relay Linda's question to the Saintly Nun. Mother Teresa's answer to Linda's question was simply:

"To bring us closer to God."

Unfortunately by the time the videotape and returned to Michael, both Mother Teresa and Linda had succumbed. Two great angels ascended that same season. I can't help but believe that Linda and Mother Teresa (who Linda already considered to be a saint) united in Heaven to muse over matters mundane, an continue their watch over us.

Linda with her beloved family, the Bardorf's.

By the way, Charlie ('Herc') and Glady's Balboni's son Steve starred as a Professional Baseball player for 16 years. Steve was called "Bye Bye" because when he hit the ball that's about all you could say to it as it sailed out of the park. In 1982 Steve cracked 32 round trippers and 86 RBI's in *half* a season for the Yankees AAA team, the Columbus Clippers. Steve played for the New York Yankees, the Seattle Mariners and the Kansas City Royals. (When the Royals won the World Championship in l985 he batted .321 in the series, and had a rally sustaining hit at a crucial juncture in a key game.) He also played for the Seattle Mariners and the Texas Rangers before his retirement from active ballplaying. Steve stayed in the business as a batting coach for several major league programs.

The last member of my family, Johnny was born at our home on Wall Street on Feb. 5, 1933. Johnny was still in his early teens when our mother passed away in 1948 and he was left to be raised through his teen and college years with the compassionate help of our older brother Mike. It surely must have been traumatic for him to go through these tough teen years without a mother. But with great determination Johnny went on to school to become an electrician. He later joined the Air Corp where he rose to the rank of Lieutenant Colonel before his retirement.

After his tour of duty in the Air Corps, Johnny went back to Boston University where he earned his degree in Aeronautical Engineering. That's where he met his pretty and witty wife Marie. They were married in Somerville, Mass. and moved to Rhode Island where Johnny commuted daily to his work as an aeronautical engineer for Pratt and Whitney in Hartford, Connecticut. Johnny & Marie are the parents of three charming and bright children, Lynn, Jack, and David. They have 3 grandchildren. Johnny has made many trips back to our roots in Italy, and he often regales us with fascinatingly detailed tales of our family history.

Young Johnny with accordion

Johnny was Commissioned as a Lieutenant in 1953

Lieutenant Johnny at the controls of A T-3 for the Strategic Air Command

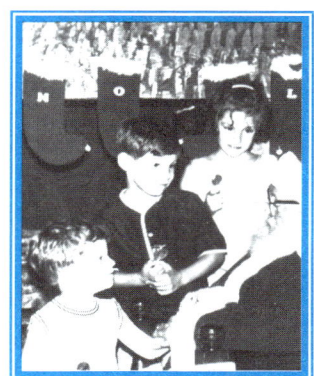

Marie & Johnny's gifts, c. '60's David, John & Lynn Folloni

FOLLONI FAMILY – BROTHERS & SISTERS
Team Photos

Folloni Family-1970's: -Al, Johnny, Larry, Virginia, Mike & Angie

Folloni Family-1987: - Angie, Johnny, Virginia, Al, Mike & Larry

THE FOLLONI MOM & POP STORE HISTORY
Teamwork

The building of the grocery store next to our childhood home was another memorable chapter in our young lives. Although my dad worked full time at the Stanley Works, his ambitions and initiative did not stop there. He managed to scrape together enough spare capital to buy the home on 61 Wall St., and the materials with which to build and stock a store to provide a second income to help his family to move up the socio-economic scale in the new country.

I vividly recall an accident that I caused during construction of the store. Although it now is humorous as I recall it, at the time it happened it wasn't so funny, especially to the unlucky individual who was the victim. The construction was at the stage where the crossbeam studs had already been installed but the flooring was not yet completed. I happened to be passing time in the area during a rare idle and unsupervised moment. As a curious youngster of about 10 years of age, I picked up a 5 lb. sledge hammer, grasping it by the wooden handle and began swinging it between the studs of the unfinished flooring like a pendulum of a grandfather clock. Suddenly I lost my grip and the sledgehammer headed south into the cellar, about 10 feet below. As chance would have it, one of our neighbors, Peter Rego was down there doing his 'sidewalk superintendent' "snooper-vising" of the work.

Peter, who was the victim of an earlier automobile accident, which resulted in his having a metal plate inserted into his skull, just happened to be in the wrong place at the time. You can guess the result. The hammer landed squarely on Peter's head and he dropped like a stone to the cement floor. I thought that I had killed him. Fortunately for everyone, he survived the accident. From that point on, during the rest of the construction process, both Peter and I were banned from any future ventures in the work area. (Which punishment, notwithstanding a paddled backside, had the distinct side benefit of freeing me to play sports.)

Our childhoods were quite centered on work and play activities around the store, and we all have many fond memories of those years before the supermarkets took over to drive most of the Mom and Pop stores out of existence. Although all of my brothers and sisters pitched in to help Mom and Pop in the daily chores of the running of the store, most of the burden fell on my brother Al. He was the one who went out on the road to take daily orders from families in the area then make the deliveries. The orders were everything from a loaf of bread for the Ferioli's to a full order from Suzi Balboni to feed her 5 fast growing youngsters. When Al was on the road the rest of us took turns at minding the store for walk-in customers, who came at all hours of the day and night. Many was the occasion when Delchesa Pratti would come knocking at our door at 10:00 p.m. to purchase a loaf of bread and a quarter-pound of salami.

The usual pattern for the local customers from the Stanley area was to come to our store when they didn't have cash and charge their groceries. When they *did* have cash, however, they walked more than a mile to the First National or A&P stores in town to save a penny on some of their purchases. The ledger of nonpaying customers, many of them freeloaders, was a burden to us, as we had to pay our bills in order to get materials to stock our store supplies. Since my parents were very charitable, however, they wrote off the debts of the really needy. For the majority who did have ability and goodwill, but who were temporarily unemployed and/or cash short, we had to come up with another solution.

Al, Angie and Mike in front of the J. Folloni Market, 1943

BIRTH OF THE BRIDGEWATER CREDIT UNION
& A TRADITION OF SHARING
Give Credit Where Credit Is Due

*John Folloni Market
Site of Birth of the
Bridgewater Credit Union*

This brings me to the story of how the Bridgewater Credit Union was born during the depression years in the middle 1930's. My brother Al was friendly with Bob King, who was the chief accountant and payroll manager of the Jenkins Mill, which was located down the end of Wall Street.

Everyday Bob would take his lunch break with Al on the porch of our store. It was during one of these lunch breaks that Al mentioned the problem of our debtors who couldn't pay their bills. Between the two of them they devised the scheme of getting about a dozen influential citizens and businessmen in town to contribute $100.00 each to use for assets to loan out to any individual needing money.

All of these contributors became charter members of the Board of Directors. Their $100.00 contributions may not seem like a substantial amount, but remember this was back in the middle of the 1930's during the depression years. That $100.00 dollars was the cash equivalent of about $1,000.00 today, and the value of that founder's stock in today's market could well be in the tens of thousands or more

With about $1,200.00 in assets as a starting point, my brother approached each of our debtors with the suggestion that they could borrow the money from the newly formed credit union to pay off their accounts with our family store. It didn't take too much convincing to sell them on the plan to rid their debts.

After all they would only have to pay 1% interest, and for collateral my brother Al co-signed for all of the loans. He had nothing to lose, since the debtor signed over the money to pay off their debt to our Mom & Pop store. If the debtor did not pay off his loan my brother would have been liable to repay the loan. But with the proud, honest and hardworking nature of these recent immigrants, most did manage to come up with the monthly payments to clear their debts with the Credit Union, and to establish their credit to help them to progress in the new world.

Thus the Bridgewater Credit Union had its beginning. After a few more years of successful loans it established an office on the third floor of the old Odd Fellows building in the center of town. Bob King gave up his position with the Jenkins Mill and went on the Credit Union payroll full time as their Secretary Treasurer. The Credit Union soon had enough assets to construct their own building at the corner of Union and Main Streets. After many years there they moved across the street to a real big time building that is a sight to behold.

They have also added branches to their Credit Union in Plymouth, Fairhaven and just recently in Quincy. My brother Al was the last surviving charter member of the original 13-person board of directors. Successful ventures like this one reinforced our family credos that *if you find a way to help another, they will be more likely to find a way to help you in return, directly or indirectly, and that when any one of us is helped along, we all progress.*

A few years following Mom's passing, Nono went back to Italy and met up with Erminia whose husband had just passed away. They were old friends from the same locality in Italy and they decided to get hitched. He took her back to America. Erminia of course could never pass off as our own beloved mother but she was very talented and helpful around the house and the store. She was an excellent cook and seamstress. After about 10 years with us she passed away in the early 1960's.

We prospered more than most in Stanley thanks in part to our hard and smart work at the J. Folloni Market. Here's Erminia & Angie by another of our new cars at the family store circa 1955

There were many other incidents that were part of the history of the Mom & Pop (and Brother & Sister) store that are clearly etched in my mind. I have many fond memories of all the neighborhood kids congregating on the porch of our store on a daily basis. The many games and sports that we played were initiated from here. This is where the teams were selected, the rules were made up and the childhood hijinks were hatched.

I recall so vividly the night that we played a prank on Shine Moruzzi during a game of "Kick the Can". When Shine wasn't looking, we substituted a brick in place of the can. Since it was dark out and the only illumination was the dim streetlight in front of our store, it was difficult to differentiate the can from the brick.

Well Shine came running down from an embankment to give the can a good kick. Kick it he did. But the brick didn't give, as the can would have. Shine let out a shrieking yell that was heard down the end of the street. Poor Shine ended up with a broken toe and hobbled around on crutches for a good while. Shine lost a bit of his luster for only a bit, though, and quickly emerged bright as ever, his sunny personality superceding his gimp and chagrin. Shine was one of our best pitchers on our baseball team.

There were many, many fun days for all of us, but one summer night lasting tragedy struck one of our comrades, Paris Martinelli. Paris had come over to this country from Italy with his parents and 4 brothers and sisters, one of them a young blind girl. When the Martinelli family first arrived they had no money or other assets. My Dad made provisions for their entire family to live with us until they were able to get settled and secure employment. I remember how all of us had to double up in our home to accommodate and feed them for several months. Like Rocky, my Dad fought fiercely for and was sometimes misunderstood by all, including his family and friends, but he was at heart, full of kindness and compassion.

A few years later the Martinelli's were well established and Paris had a job at the Local Fireworks factory where he managed to scrape up the materials needed to make some giant firecrackers for his friends. One night he, along with other members of the local teen gang were teasing my Dad by creating a disturbance out on the porch. They had set off a couple of the big blasters and Paris had just lit another one when my Dad came out of the store to chastise them. With the giant firecracker still clutched in his right hand, not realizing that the fuse was lit, Paris tried to hide it behind his back. It exploded, blowing off his thumb and all his fingers. About all that remained below his wrist was a stub. Here he was a young lad in his early teens that became handicapped for life. All because of a childish teasing prank.

There was a lot of irony in this accident. My Dad also had been permanently handicapped by a childhood accident, having lost his left eye. Kids being kids for time eternal, it was in good part due to this physical deformity that the teens sometimes teased him. Also, Paris' father, Ernest, who was a carpenter by trade, was the one who headed the project to build the store adjacent to our house where the incident happened. After my father befriended the Martinelli family by helping them to get settled, Ernest returned the favor by providing low cost professional help with the construction.

My Dad had built a Bocce Court out next to the store and this became a focal recreation area for the adults of 'Stanley'. They would hold many matches there, and usually the stakes were for the losers to buy the drinks. During one of these matches my cousin Adolph, "Bing", Folloni, became involved in a dispute with Victor, "Turk" Messaline who married my cousin Emma. One word led to another when finally, Bing bent over to pick up a bocce ball, and "Turk" let go with a haymaker. The sucker punch dropped "Bing" to the ground with a broken jaw. I guess it was retribution.

Bing had a reputation in his bachelor years of getting into trouble constantly because of his excessive drinking. I can recall many an altercation when we had to physically restrain him from assaulting others. One night after he had consumed a few drinks he began wrecking the furniture in our home and he actually tried to beat up my Dad until my brothers and I finally subdued him. Bing was my father's brother's son who had come over to this country as a teenager and lived with us for many years. *Bada Bing*

When Bing left his youth, he also left behind his drinking problem and settled down to become a loving and devoted parent. He sent for Clara, his childhood sweetheart in Italy and they married and had two lovely children, Lisa, who is one of the greatest and most beloved primary schoolteachers to ever practice in Bridgewater-Raynham and a son Danny, who now oversees computer systems operations for many Massachusetts State Departments. I'm delighted to hear that Danny now volunteers with his lovely wife in organizing school sporting events in their town of Mansfield.

Another tragic story that is seared in my mind happened one night before the 4th of July. Our home and store were located a few yards from the railroad tracks and about 35 yards from the railroad crossing over Wall St. We were all gathered on the steps of the store with the adults chatting away and I was bouncing a ball against the store steps, as was my daily exercise routine to sharpen my reflexes.

Suddenly a train headed south began blowing its whistle, which was the usual procedure when approaching a crossing.

On this occasion the engineer was blowing the whistle extremely longer and louder than usual. I looked up to the crossing just as the train made contact with an automobile. The train drove the car all the way down onto our property next to the Bocce Courts with parts of the vehicle nearly reaching us by the store. The trashing of the automobile was not the big casualty. Our neighbor, William Pincolini was. He was riding on the running board of the car when the train hit it and he was instantly killed. His body ended up on our lawn near the Bocce court. The victim, by the way was the father of my sister Angie's sister-in-law Gladys Balboni. He was also the maternal grandfather of the not yet born Charlene, Pauline and Steve Balboni.

After reading of the above tragic incidents associated with our family Mom & Pop store one might be led to believe that there was disproportionate sadness associated with the history of our home. The actuality of the majority of warm happy memories of our home and store, however, is really quite pleasant and life affirming.

First worthy of recall is the good that my Mom & Dad did for their friends and neighbors. As noted earlier, my parents were very generous and charitable to all that came to the store to purchase food or seek temporary shelter for their families.

During those depression days there was poverty all around and when these people came to get food without any money, my parents simply gave them the groceries they needed to survive. Sure they wrote it down in the ledger, but they knew full well that many would never be able to pay off their debts. My parents never received financial rewards for their charity but let me relate a couple of examples as to how some of the beneficiaries reacted many years later:

My brother Mike, who was a foreman at the Independent Nail Company, had hired my oldest son, Larry Jr. to work during the summer months. Larry's job was to lift kegs of nails onto the benches for the girls on the production line to package. As was his other summer job working at the Balboni's Brockton auto wash, this was a pretty tough and strenuous job for a youngster still in High School. It just so happened that there was a fellow named Louis Rego, who was working in the same department and for some unknown reason he took a liking to Larry Jr., befriended him and helped him at every turn. One day out of curiosity, Larry asked him why he was always so nice to him. Louis replied: "Many years ago, before you were born, during the depression years I was a little boy with 4 brothers and sisters and my father was out of work and had no money to feed us. Your grandfather gave us food whenever we needed it, no questions asked. I've never forgotten his kindness to my family."

My Dad often gave the outward appearance of being a mean grumpy man. Actually he was just the opposite, on the inside he would melt like butter. He was always very charitable and ready to help any of his neighbors in need. If anyone of them was ill or in need of help in any way, my Dad was always the first one to show up at their home to offer his assistance.

After bringing my mom and my sister over to this country, he worked real hard to earn enough money to support his growing family and secure a home for us. Through all of this, in the 20's, he managed to save enough to make a return trip to his homeland to revisit with his family.

On his return trip from Italy by boat, he encountered Mrs. Miastrangi, a dignified lady with 6 children on her way to America to start a new life in our land of opportunity. One day while conversing with her on the Atlantic crossing, she broke down and cried. She revealed to him that she was penniless and didn't know how she was going to survive in the New World with all her children and no money. Now mind you my dad didn't know this lady and never met her until this time on the boat trip. But he was so moved by her impassioned plea that he peeled out $600.00 for her to get started on her adventure in the USA. (At that day and age, $600.00 was an awful lot of money.) It was a 'loan' that he never expected to get back.

About 3 years later he was pleasantly surprised when this same lady appeared at our home with her six children and returned the $600.00 that he had loaned her! She wanted to pay him interest but my dad wouldn't take any. The Miastrangi's had settled in South Boston and started a knife sharpening business with the money that my dad had loaned them on the boat.

They worked hard and made a very successful venture, which to this day still thrives. They have branched out to other areas around Boston, with each of the children running their own successful business. The Miastrangi's never forgot my dad's kindness in helping them get their start in this country and for many a year thereafter they would return to our home in Bridgewater with gifts of appreciation for all of us.

My mother was the saintly one, who every morning, come rain, ice, snow or sunshine, would walk about a mile each way to go to church for the daily mass to offer prayers for all the needy. My dad and mom's charitable manner must have rubbed off on all of us children, because later in life as we all managed to have successful careers we continued these ways of our parents. I'm sure all of my children have also inherited these same qualities. Each one in turn followed suit. And from what I understand, this charitable streak runs through all of my parent's descendents.

MY SCHOOL DAYS AND 1ˢᵀ CHAMPIONSHIPS
Chalk Talk

My first recollection of my school days begins at the age of five when I started the first grade at the old Prospect School located on High Street across from Biffers Field. It was a two-story wooden building that had only the bare necessities. (I mean bare, outdoor toilet facilities, very limited heating and furnishings, negligible books and supplies etc.)

Many years later after this school was closed down due in part to lack of indoor and outdoor play facilities. The property was purchased by Jim Gabriel who converted it into apartments. There were 4 rooms and 4 grades there. I still recall my first grade teacher, Miss Sullivan. She was very pretty and really the first female outside of my family that I 'fell in love' with.

After one year I was transferred to the McElwain School on Main Street about a mile from our home. Yes, like the other old timers we had to walk to and from school daily, come rain, snow, sleet, prohibition or sunshine. School was never called off for weather and I can recall many a winter day when we had to battle the wind and blowing cold snow in our faces in our walk to and from classes. (I also remember how we wrapped ourselves in scarves and mittens that our mother made from yarn and cotton balls to protect us from the blistering wind and snow. They were crude but they did the trick in keeping us warm. Occasionally we would use them to wipe the moisture from our runny noses and the moisture would promptly freeze on them. To keep our feet dry we had rubbers on our shoes or wore rubber boots when the snow was real high.

When the weather would allow, we would take the short cut through woods and yards to the McElwain School. We would cut in behind Mrs. Mundle's property, then go on through the Mullin's and Battistini's properties on to Main Street next to Harry's garage. Mrs. Mundle's property was adjacent to the Stanley Iron works and ran along the Town River. These kind citizens never gave us any problems for using their right of way.

Along the short cut route there was a dam with a deep water hole just below the falls. We discovered by accident that there were many large eels harboring there. On our daily walk to school, it was our ritual to each drop a fishing line with worm bait into the hole and tie the other end to a tree. On the way home we would stop by the dam to see our luck.

Invariably we would be rewarded with a good-sized eel at the bottom of our line, which we would take home for our mothers to cook for our supper. (Note that at that time the fish were not yet contaminated by the effluents from the leather-board company which was later built about a couple hundred yards up-stream.) Those eels were real tasty. The idea of them being aesthetically unappealing never crossed our minds. The tangible rewards of reaping benefits from extra efforts sowed along the normal way did enter our minds in the most memorable of manners -- directly through our bellies.

My years at the McElwain School (1926 to 1931) were not very eventful. We enjoyed the usual training that most public elementary schools offered, and of course we always looked forward to our recess periods to go out on the playground to engage in our many athletic games.

My 2nd grade teacher was Miss Hennessy. I don't remember the name of my 3rd grade teacher. Miss Helen Powers was my 4th grade teacher. She stayed with the school system long enough to do an admirable job teaching 5 of my 6 children! Miss Veronica Freeman was my 5th grade teacher and Miss Hart (Collins) was my 6th grade teacher. Over 20 years later, when I first started my teaching career in Bridgewater, Miss Hart was still the teacher at the McElwain School when I went there as the Supervisor of Physical Education. Then the teacher became the pupil, as I instructed her in how to conduct 'modern' physical education classes, as I had learned while earning my Masters Degree in Boston University.

In the fall of 1931 I entered the Junior High School (now the Hunt School). I vividly remember those next three years. One lesson that I shall never forget came about, naturally enough, during a recess period. The Principal, Mr. Morton Seavey, had set up a rule that if any balls were hit into the neighboring yard of Atty. McMaster, we were not allowed to retrieve them. The playground behind the school was very small and we were very athletic, so of course many balls were "inadvertently" deposited onto Atty. McMaster's property. OK, maybe the thrill of powering a home run over the fence made us forget about the repercussions.

On one particular day after I had hit a ball into the forbidden area, I choose to go over the fence and retrieve it. Mr. Seavey observed me breaking his rule and he was waiting for me as I came around the wooden fence with the ball. He let go with a real roundhouse open hand to my face that spun me around like a top. He caught me with complete surprise and *boy did that slap sting!* I learned my lesson not to break any more of his rules. (Since a few balls lost meant no more playing, my friends and I became quite adept and smashing the low liner.) By the way, I didn't go home to complain to my parents about the whack that the principal gave me, because if I did my father would have given me another spanking for being disobedient. In my future years as a coach and teacher I never resorted to this sort of physical or 'corporal punishment', but I must admit that on more than a few occasions I substituted sharp and stinging verbal jabs to get the attention of wayward students.

My 7th grade teacher was Miss Alice Wood, who was a very strict disciplinarian. No one dared to get out of line in her classroom. In the next room to Miss Wood was a young teacher by the name of Miss Elsie McLoed (Holmes). Being new, she had not yet developed the skills to maintain control of her charges. Many were the days that Miss Wood had to go into Miss McLoed's classroom to discipline her unruly students and bring order back to her classes. Three decades later Miss Wood was still an intimidating figure to most of my children who she also taught. She was the only teacher to make students stand up in class to answer when she randomly called on them. Students knew that they had better be prepared at all times in her class! To her credit, Alice Woods did earn the respect of many subsequent generations of students, and was as effective an educator for them as she was for me.

Miss McLeod (Holmes) eventually learned her trade, and ended up being a very influential teacher for thousands of students, including my son Larry. She was the namesake of but I'm not sure if closely related to Stanford 'Bunky Holmes', who was a big affable and hardworking athlete and coach under me in later years. Mr. Holmes often encouraged fun in his classrooms; there was never ever any discipline problems.

Another teacher who had trouble with classroom discipline was a fellow by the name of Mr. Moss. I recall one incident when his wife had baked a beautifully decorated Christmas cake. While Mr. Moss was out of the room, some student dug into the cake with his hands and left a gaping unsightly hole in the middle of it.

When Mr. Moss returned to the classroom and saw the unsightly mess he let out with a bellow, "Who in the name of God is the rat who did this?" The class roared with laughter. To my knowledge he never found out the culprit. I vividly recall seeing another incident with Mr. Moss being chased down the corridor to the principal's office by a student stabbing away at him with a pen.

My Junior High geography teacher was a Miss Grace McElroy who everyone called 'Miss Nosey" or "Miss Busy Body". She would question every student to find out all the gossip of what was going on in his or her home life. Looking back I think that to some extent in those pre-social worker days, she was merely trying to find out more background on each of us to assist in her ability to discover special needs and tend to them. There were only a couple hundred of families in town then, so news and reactions had to travel fast 'the old fashioned way'. Then again, maybe she was just a plain old busy body!

Another incident that stands out involves a Miss Sirinossian, my 9th grade English teacher. My older brother Mike had preceded me as one of her pupils a few years earlier. Mike was chummy with a gang that included Walter Joyce, who was known as the wise guy of the class, and of course Mike was tagged as a troublemaker by association.

One day near the end of the school year of that last grade in Junior High School, Miss Sirinossian approached me to give me a commendation that I never forgot. She confessed that when I first entered her class in September, that she had prejudiced herself into thinking that I would be following in the footsteps of my brother as a troublemaker. Since my Jr. High days were nearly over she wanted to congratulate me on having such a successful year, ending up with all 'A's' in all subjects. She then said that I would be definite college material and that I would do well in my future. She said that she wanted to wish me the best of luck in my future career, which she accurately predicted would be in the teaching and coaching field. In my later career I tried to never prejudice my opinion of any student despite any real or perceived ill or extra good done earlier by *any* relative. Every kid got an equal chance on his or her own. Like Miss Sirinossian I also often made an effort to commend and encourage students when they worked to merit it. *The best thing a teacher can do is to catch a student doing something right, and to let him or her know that you expect great things from them. More often than not, a student will live up to the teacher's expectations, be they highly positive or very negative.*

The following September I entered the Senior High School at the Old Academy Building at the south end of the Bridgewater common. The Academy Building still stands as a historic landmark and now houses the Police station and other town offices. The Academy has also served as the town's children's library and home to countless civic groups, meetings and events. With the growth in town at the end of century, it became time for the Police Dept. to move on, but the Academy Building will always be a seat of civic activity and pride. I have many memories of my three years there, most of them from the Athletic Field and Gym. I also have some pleasant memories of the classes that I attended.

My English teacher, Miss. McFarland was another cutie who I liked very much. Maurice Walsh was the Faculty Manager of Athletics and a math teacher. He later went on to teach at Boston College and eventually became a member of the School Committee that hired me for my first teaching position in Bridgewater.

Miss Alice Cook was a stern Latin teacher who held her ground with any and all. When they finally opened our new High School, and I returned to Bridgewater as the Director of Athletics and Supervisor of Physical Education, she was still teaching Latin.

Miss Rich and Miss Margaret Gates taught me to type. To attend her class I actually had to fight a school policy that would not allow anyone in the College Program to take typing. Typing was allowed only for those in the Business Program. My older brother Al, who had majored in Business and was an excellent typist, urged me to pursue the course, so I applied for it as an elective and was turned down. I protested to the Administration and after a long discussion, I finally convinced the powers that ruled to allow me to take the course.

My struggle to be allowed to take typing as an elective resulted in opening the door for all future college program students to take it as part of their College Prep Curriculum. *I learned from this experience that with good reasoning, innovative thinking and some persistence, one could often work with the system to implement innovations*. With today's worldwide computer oriented environment, anyone who does not have knowledge of the keyboard will be lost. With it, they have a strong tool to help them to use their own gumption to initiate their own improvements in the world. I am so grateful to my brother Al for his advice to take that typing course and for his support of my protests and presentations until I got in. The ability to type was one of my greatest aids in my career as a Teacher, Coach, and Athletic Administrator. And of course, if it were not for my typing skills I would never have been able to compose this book!

Last but not least I warmly acknowledge my Athletic Coach and Social Studies and History Teacher, Mr. Lester Lane. I can thank Coach Lane for giving me the real basic fundamentals of all the team sports. Mr. Lane worked in the era when one man coached all the Sports teams in each High School.

The 'original' Coach Lane ushered in new coaching and teaching talent to help break the mold of how athletics were developed. Pictured here with Coaches Maurice Walsh and Joe Yuknis.

There were no such things as Assistant or one sport Coaches in those days. I was indeed fortunate that during my first year at Bridgewater High, the school committee led the way to the modern era by hiring Joe Yuknis as a Jayvee Football coach.

I can remember the days that we held our practices up at Walsh's Field, a hilly, bumpy cow pasture. Coach Yuknis, who was our chemistry teacher and who later became a very successful Superintendent of Schools in Connecticut, had a very great impact on my future career in Athletics. He was a real stickler on the fundamentals of the game and he worked hard to instill our confidence in ourselves and our knowledge of the finer aspects of the game. In retrospect *I learned from Coach Yuknis that of all the things that a Coach can impart to his charges, CONFIDENCE and ENTHUSIASM is probably the most important.* Mr. Yuknis was one of my best coaches and mentors.

I'll never forget the day that he came up to me after a real intense practice, put his hand on my shoulder and said, "Larry you're being promoted." And as he handed me a new jersey he said, *"Coach Lane needs a good quarterback on the Varsity. You've earned this promotion by your hard work. I have all the confidence in the world that you will go on to be a great success."* I never forgot those words and I thanked him for all the help he had given to enable me to move on to the next level of athletic competition. *I can only hope that I was able to so increase the confidence and bolster the dreams of even one other student during my long career.*

Many funny as well as serious incidents occurred during my 3 years of High School at the Academy Building. As noted, my first season as a sophomore was mostly spent with the Jayvee Football team until I was promoted to the Varsity to groom me for the starting quarterback position the next year. I could hardly wait for my Junior year to begin, and was so excited when practice sessions finally came around. Nothing eventful happened during the first game of the year, but in the second one against Scituate High School I had an afternoon to remember. I scrambled for 3 touchdowns and dropkicked 2 extra points to score 20 of our team's points in a 26 to 0 win. My first touchdown was on an 80 yard run after a pass interception. The second and third TDs were on runs up the middle of 25 and 10-yards respectively.

Actual hand-stitched reward 'pigskin' from 1935 BHS football game

That I can still remember so much detail about these events of so long ago just reinforces the importance that athletics has in the formative years of an individual; a concept that was not lost on me in my eventual choosing of a career.

I missed the next two games due to an injury I sustained during a scrimmage at our practice field. Since the Legion Field was being renovated, all of our games had to be played at our opponent's gridirons and we held our practices in back of the McElwain School, which was a pretty bumpy field, bordered by a stone wall. During one scrimmage, while I was trying to avoid being tackled as I ran around the left end, I put my right hand out to straight-arm the tackler. A boulder tripped me up and I landed against the stone wall badly bruising my shoulder.

When I returned to the lineup for the game against our archrivals, Abington High, I caught the opening kickoff and returned it about 50 yards to midfield. As I was tackled to the turf, one of the Abington player's knee caught me on the side of my head and gave me a pretty good concussion. In those days the helmets we wore were nothing more than a thick piece of leather that gave very little protection.

As I rose to me feet, my head was still spinning from the blow. I remember going back into the huddle and telling "Biscuits" Rubeski to call the plays as I had lost my memory. Well I played the rest of the game by pure instinct. I can remember twisting and spinning off of potential tacklers throughout the game, but that was the extent of my memory.

After the game I asked who won the game and was told that we won 7 to 0, that I was the star of the game and had played the best game of my High School career. It wasn't until our bus arrived back in Bridgewater that I finally began to get over the debilitating effects of the concussion.

Even though I may have played my best game ever by pure instinct, I now realize how dangerous it was for me to have continued playing after receiving that concussion on the opening kickoff. With today's knowledge of concussions, I would have been rushed to a hospital and then made to sit out a month before returning to action. Although this did not result in any permanent brain injury (even though my kids and my wife sometimes begged to differ), I can definitely say that this affected my future coaching. Whenever I saw anything vaguely resembling such a potentially serious injury to a player, I took immediate steps to care for his or her short and long term health, no matter what the game status. I also took pains to make sure that appropriate medical practitioners were on site or on call, and that emergency procedures were in place.

A kid's entire future is far too valuable to mortgage for a game at this level. We later instituted a number of secondary school rules statewide to contemplate the serious reality that kids sometimes get hurt playing sports, and that everything reasonable must be done to mitigate the risks, and to care for students when accidents happen.

We finished the season with 4 wins, 4 losses and one tie (2 of the losses came while I was on the injured list). Actually it was a disappointing season for us as we were expected to have a great year. The middle of our (offensive and defensive) line was comparatively small with Nelson Houlberg at center and George Sweeney and Fred Valeri as the guards. The rest of the team, however, was 'enormous' by the standards of those days. Al Lanzekos and Dino Bertelli at the Tackle slots were both about 250 lbs. At the ends were Fred Kondrotos and Wilfred Bois, both well over 6 foot tall and 200 lbs. In the backfield, I was the Quarterback; all of 135 lbs. soaking wet. Elmer Balboni was the Fullback, and "Biscuits" Rubeski and Teddy Bois were the Halfbacks. Buttressing lessons from my family life, *I learned from these guys that there never has been nor ever will be anything so effective or rewarding as TEAMWORK.*

My Basketball memories begin in my junior year. I had never played the game, but Coach Lane did a good job of recruiting to convince me to come out for the team. Having played on the Football and Baseball Varsity teams the previous couple of years, Coach Lane felt that I had the necessary speed and reflexes to help out the Basketball team. I'll never forget my first venture into this game: in my initial outing with the Jayvees, I managed to pick up four fouls in less than 5 minutes of playing time and soon after fouled out!

I was ready to give up basketball because I really didn't know the rules or have the fundamentals to properly play. Again a coaxing Coach Lane talked me into sticking it out. With each succeeding game and practice I continued to improve and by the end of the season I was promoted to the Varsity Squad as a sub. I remember sitting on the bench when Bridgewater High School won the South Shore Basketball Tournament at the old YMCA in Brockton, defeating Class "A" Weymouth in the 1936 finals. Even from my position on the bench, the thrill of that success was something that I could never imagine, and that I wanted others to share. Never in my fondest dreams at that time could I have imagined how richly that dream would come true later s as a player and a coach.

The next year I was promoted to the starting guard position on the Varsity. This was the first year that the rules makers had eliminated the Jump Ball at center court after every basket. This was one of the major rule changes that improved Basketball to make it one of the most exciting and attractive games in the world.

Later innovations like the 24 and 3-second *rules (and the allowing of blacks to play in the mainstream!)* helped to complete the advancement.

We had another outstanding year on the basketball court, going all the way to the Finals of the South Shore Tournament before losing to Attleboro 22 to 20 in front of an overflow crowd at the YMCA. It was especially noteworthy to me, since one of the spectators was my Dad.

This was the first and probably the last time that he ever saw me take part in any athletic event. To my Dad, a hard working immigrant from Italy, sports were a waste of time and shoe leather. Among the many skills he acquired to survive and prosper in the New World, he was the cobbler who would replace the soles of our worn out shoes. I still remember his workshop in the cellar where he had the cobbler and carpenter tools that he used in doing the maintenance work around the house and neighborhood. As a spectator at the game he didn't understand any of the rules, but he did recognize me out on the court and every time I had the ball in my hands he would yell out, *"That's Ah-My Boy"!*

Dad certainly taught me to be enthusiastically supportive of the family and "our team's dreams", no matter what the immediately apparent value!

*Good Sport 'Pa' playing ball
Ray & Jean Resmini watch*

*Before Ted William's batting lessons
with him, Jimmie practiced with Nono*

BRIDGEWATER H.S. BASKETBALL TEAM
1937 South Shore Tourney Finalists

Being the Champs in l936 and the runner-ups in l937 was really an outstanding accomplishment for us when you consider that we did not have a gym of our own. Our practice sessions were held at the old Brotherhood Church Annex near the center of town, a very poor excuse for a gym compared to the modern facilities that are in existence today.

Lester Lane and his 1936-37 Hoop Finalists

The Brotherhood gym was nothing more than a barn band box about 30' X 40' with beams running across the ceiling about 15 feet from the floor. In order to shoot a basket from any distance more that 20 feet you had to shoot *over* the metal cross wires. Since the baskets were flush with the end walls, if you went in for a lay up shot, you would have to brace your feet up against the wall to avoid colliding with it. Besides the college, this was the only gym in Bridgewater. Now we have at least 5 beautiful spacious gyms in our town. We also have the beautiful outdoor "Larry Folloni Basketball Courts" at Legion Field. I am very grateful to Town Officials for so remembering me I, in turn, was also very appreciative of all that Coach Lane had done for me, and so it was my pleasure to spearhead the organization of several events and memorials for him near the end of his career and again near the end of his life.

Coach Lane's retirement party at the old BHS. We gave him the huge cricket stick /paddle only after we knew he wouldn't use it to discipline us.

Bridgewater State College allowed us the use of their old Boyden Gym for one hour, 2 nights a week. On those days we had to walk about one and a half miles each way from our home in Stanley to go to school in the morning, then walk one and a half miles home to have lunch after school. Then we'd walk back to the Brotherhood gym for an hour of practice. Then we'd go back home for supper and make a return trip of another mile and a half to practice for another hour at night at the Boyden Gym. That was a total of about 9 miles walking distance if we took the shortcut down the railroad tracks. If we went via Main Street that added another mile for each trip.

The many miles of walking and running along with our chores around the house may have been a reason that the Stanley area youngsters were the top athletes in the town. *The desire to participate and achieve that this demonstrated was probably even more telling.* We didn't have the Weight Training Programs that the modern day youngsters have but our chores and work ethic kept us in great physical shape. *This dedication proved to be a great advantage when we competed in athletics and the lessons of determination and persistence served us even better later in our careers.*

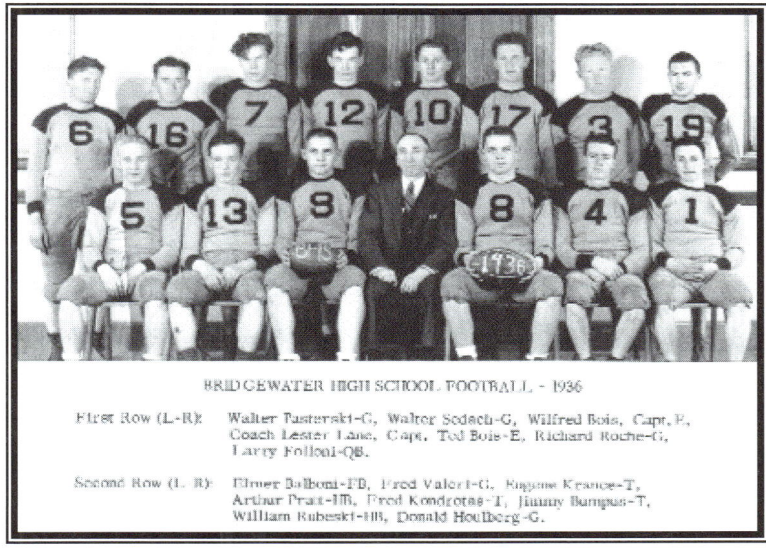

Coach Lane and his 1936 football team

Speaking of "Biscuits" Rubeski brings to mind the game we played against a heavily favored Dedham High School Team, which went undefeated that year. We were pinned back on our own 5-yard line and had to punt. With the aid of the wind at his back and a good roll, "Biscuits" got off a tremendous kick. The ball ended up on the Dedham 5-yard line, 90 yards from the line of scrimmage! Dedham was called for a 5-yard offside penalty on the play, and would you believe this, our captain chose to take the 5-yard penalty before anyone could correct him! Dedham blocked the repeat punt and scored a touchdown by falling on it, thus blowing our chance to score a big upset.

Watching such costly lame brained decisions by trusted supposed leaders helped me to realize that even though I was deemed a second class citizen by many, that perhaps 'my way' was something that I should consider asserting more in the future. Attention readers – be true and trusting to thine own instincts and beliefs!

One more incident that stands out vividly in my High School memory bank was during our game with Fairhaven. Being the quarterback in the old Notre Dame box formation I frequently had the chore of being the blocking back for one of my running mates. Mind you there I was about 5' 5" and 135 lbs., trying to be a blocking back. Fairhaven had a huge tackle towering about 6' 6" tall and weighing close to 300 lbs. We ran a play that was supposed to go through this tackle's territory. As I was leading the interference, how well I remember putting my head down as I met this giant at the line of scrimmage. My head hit him squarely in the midsection and I bounced back off like a rubber ball off of a cement wall. My head was spinning like a top and all that I saw were stars and sparkles. I didn't call that play again the rest of that game. Hitting one stone wall was enough.

One of my more pleasant memories happened on the Baseball front. The Legion Field was closed for a complete renovation during my first two years of high school. Finally in my senior year, during the spring of 1937, the new Field was baptized, and our team played the first game on the new baseball diamond. I had the proud honor of making the first hit on the new Legion Field - a double down the right field line. This was the first of many hits to follow in the next decade of my ball playing days in Bridgewater, both while in High School and later at the Semipro level.

Front Row, left to right: - Leo Provost, Elmer Balboni, Eddie Snarski, Captain Larry Folloni, Gerard "Jiggs" Provost, Renaldo Resmini Bill "Biscuits" Rubeski, "Bud" Farrell, and Ernie Giovanini.

Back Row, left to right: - Coach Lester Lane, Alfred Valeri, Arthur Pratt, Jack Campbell, Richard Roache, Edmund Rudis, William Nordberg, Mgr. Vic Staknus.

BRIDGEWATER HIGH SCHOOL BASEBALL TEAM 1937
*Pictured in front of Historic Academy School Building
(First team to play on new Legion Field.)*

LIFE AFTER HIGH SCHOOL –
DETOUR FROM MY SCHOOL DAYS
The Next Level

Upon graduation from High School it was time for decision making. At the very young age of seventeen, I had not yet matured, mentally or physically. Due, however, to my athletic skills and accomplishments, along with my good grades in High School, I was offered a scholarship to the University of New Hampshire.

Matriculating at a small college where I could participate in sports that would be at my level appeared to be the logical route for me. After all I was only 5'6" tall and my weight never went over 135 lbs. Although I would later prove to myself and all others that I could indeed compete at any level, at that time I felt that due to my diminutive size I could not have been of the caliber to make it in a Big Time College or University Athletic Program.

Well as we all know the best-laid plans of mice and men oft go astray and so it was with my plans to go to UNH. Upon my graduation from High School, my brother Mike got me into the Independent Nail Company for summer time employment until I was to go on to college in September. As luck or fate would have it, just before I finished up this temporary job, Mike had an attack of appendicitis, which meant that he would be out of work for several months. This presented a great financial hardship on my family as they depended upon Mike's income to survive. It appeared that it was my turn to give a little bit back to those who had given me so much, and so that was the end of my plans to go to UNH. I stayed with my job at the Nail Company for the rest of that year and part of the next. Although slightly disappointing at the time, in retrospect, *this was one of many critical life junctures in which what I perceived to have been a 'set back', was actually a 're-set' towards a better direction!*

> *By doing 'the right thing' in trying to help my family, a whole new series of rewarding opportunities later arose which I never would have dreamed of.*

Before those unfolded, however, a lot more of the mundane had to be traversed. The following Spring I hooked on with the Corcoran Shoe Company baseball team. One of the provisions of playing for them was that they would secure me employment in their shoe factory. This really proved to be a key turning point in my life. As much as I loved to play baseball, I hated the work in the shoe factory. I had a very successful year with the company Baseball team but not so successful in my work. It was pure drudgery and monotony. My first job was as a heel trimmer. After a few weeks they added the job of sole trimming. Well I just wasn't up to this kind of work. My mind was never on my job, I was always day dreaming of being out on the baseball field and as a result the racks of shoes from the rest of the line kept piling up by my station. As hard a worker as I generally was, and as quick as my reflexes were, my heart and soul just wasn't in this, and I couldn't bring myself to maintain the pace to keep the production line moving.

It was only a matter of time before the inevitable happened. At the end of our baseball season in late summer, I came in to my work station on a Monday morning and there to greet me was my boss, Mr. Morrison. Without any warning or fanfare he said coldly, *"You're Fired."* I was stunned by the manner that I was dismissed but as I look back on this day it was a very positive turning point in my life.

That morning I left the Corcoran Shoe Company, which was located in Stoughton, MA, about 15 miles from Bridgewater. I had no means of transportation to get home so I hiked the entire distance. As I trudged along the highway and some railroad track shortcuts many thoughts went through my mind. I was in turmoil.

Here I was 19 years of age, with the pressures of wanting to care for my family's immediate concerns yet wondering in which direction I should be going in my life. I felt that I was letting my family down because I was contributing most of my meager pay to my parents to help with the support of my 3 brothers and 2 sisters. On the other hand, I was able to reason that Dad was currently taking care of my family's basic needs, and that in the long run I'd best serve myself, my family, my future family and my town by making something more of my God given talents. By the time that I arrived back in Bridgewater about 5 hours later, I had made up my mind that I would go back to college.

In September I enrolled as a freshman at Bridgewater State College. There I had the great pleasure of meeting my excellent coach and teacher and eventual life long friend, the distinguished Dr. Fred Meier

Fred & Louise Meier & son Fred Jr.

With the great public school education I received in town I had little trouble with any of the academic curriculum. Although at times in my life I've been lauded for being quite charming, no one would ever confuse my overall record in this realm with 'Mr. Manners' or 'Eddie-Quette'. The BSC curriculum included courses in Music, Speech and Etiquette to help future teachers to become adept in the arts and social graces. Being a rugged athlete who was raised across the tracks in Little Italy made these courses the most challenging, and sometimes the most humiliating for me.

The gender ratio of Teacher-Trainees at that time was about 10 girls to every boy. I was a bit like a kid in a candy store, or maybe more accurately, a playful young bull in a China Shop when I first arrived. It didn't take long for Miss Pope, our Dean of Women and our Etiquette Teacher, to decide that I needed supplementary 'one on one' training. She covered everything from proper manners, to proper eating techniques and things that we should be aware of in dealing with the opposite sex. I guess she succeeded to some extent, as my natural and newfound charm techniques soon thereafter helped to win the hand of my lovely wife for life.

Our Music course was under the direction of Miss Graves, a real vivacious teacher who went to many extremes in sharing her enthusiasm for music. I vividly remember that we each had to take a turn to lead the class with the baton. When my day to lead came I was about petrified but as soon as I started to wave the baton I overcame my fears. If the reaction from the class was any indication I actually performed pretty well, as when I finished everyone gave me a great standing ovation! Sometimes you've just got to get going with something to really find out if you can it. Oftentimes you'll be surprised. God seldom gives us challenges we can't overcome, or at least learn from.

> *Whether you think that you can, or that you can't, you are usually right."*
> Henry Ford (1863-1947)

I always had dreaded the thoughts of ever getting up in front of any group to speak. I hated it so much that when it was my turn to get up on the stage of the auditorium to speak before the class; I just refused to do it. As a result, the speech teacher, Miss Hill, dealt me out the only failing grade that I ever got in all my years of schooling. There is some irony to this story because later in my career as Director of Athletics and Chairman of the MIAA Athletic Rules Committee, I was always very vocal in speaking out before many large audiences throughout the State.

Soon came the outbreak of World War II, and the government offered a free pilot training program to college students in the hopes of later recruiting them into the armed service. I signed up for the program and on my indoctrination flight I had an experience that my Instructor and I will never forget. The Instructor's name was Captain Schofield and the flight schooling took place from the Hanover Airport. It was a cool autumn day when we took off in a Piper Cub Trainer.

During our initial flight that covered most of the South Shore Area, Captain Schofield ad-libbed with comments about flying and procedures to follow during flights. He then proceeded to give me a taste of the feel of the plane during different maneuvers. He put the plane into loops and turns and finally into the dreaded stall that left my stomach still far up in the air while our bodies and plane plummeted straight down toward the ground.

He went on with these maneuvers for about 15 minutes and finally headed back to the Airport for a landing. By this time my stomach had been churned to a fare-thee-well and my face had turned green.

As we were making our approach for the landing, Captain Schofield turned back to me in my seat directly in back of his and blurted out, "Well how did you like your flight"? When I opened my mouth to answer I couldn't hold it any longer and I proceeded to puke out my guts right down the back of his neck. Well you should have heard him yell, "You Son of a Bitch"!

We landed shortly after and with my vomit still down his neck as he climbed out of the plane, he told me off in no uncertain language to clean up the puke mess that remained. Well you can well imagine my embarrassment at the time.

Several months later Captain Schofield made the headlines in the newspapers for being a expert flying Hero in making a forced landing in rugged terrain that saved the lives of his crew and passengers. I can think of at least one training mission that wasn't very helpful in preparing him for that day.

After 2 years at BSC and one more at Wentworth Institute I joined the war effort and did 4 years in the military. After my discharge from the service I finally returned to complete my college education at Boston University. Little did I know that all this was hardly the beginning of my many challenges and critical junctures through life.

BHS Class of 1937 20th Reunion

2nd Quarter

MARRIAGE, SERVICE & CAREER
"Regular Season" - Champions All

THE WORLD WAR II YEARS
Recruitment for War and Peace

On Dec. 7, 1941, one day after their attack on Pearl Harbor, Japan declared war on the USA and only 4 days later Germany followed suit. By late in the fall of 1942, my older brothers and all of my buddies had already gone into the service of our country to defeat these aggressive war countries. My oldest brother Mike was the first from my family to enlist in the Navy shortly after the start of World War II. My brother Al, who enlisted in the Army, soon followed him.

At the start of the War, if two members of a family were in the service, other members were exempt from the draft. This meant that I was the sole remaining son of age at home to help with the support of the family and help run the family Mom & Pop Store. My younger sister Angie took a job at the Quincy Shipyard as a "Rosie The Riveter" helping to build battleships to defeat the Axis.

With all of my buddies off to the Wars, it got to be a pretty boring and lonely existence to be left home alone. It finally got to me and even though I was exempt from the draft, I signed up with the Army Signal Corps. My program called for called for six months of school training, the first three months of which took place at the Boston State College.

It was during this training period that I met and 'recruited' the Love of my life, 'Hollywood Helen', who would become my partner in marriage for life, and I prayerfully expect in the Hereafter.

WOW!

I met Helen at a dance held at the Raymor-Playmor Dance Hall, a very popular Boston Nightclub during the War Years. Actually I had met her several years before while on a Cruise Outing held by the Corcoran Shoe Co. *(Remember what I said about rewarding opportunities arising from trying to do the right thing? The second part of that lesson is that it helps to develop an 'expectant awareness' to be ready to seize the opportunities that God gives us. I wasn't so alert on that first night! Luckily I had 'Guardian Angels' or destiny on my side.)* The cruise was from Boston to Provincetown on Cape Cod. I danced with her on the boat that evening, but little did I realize that she would become the future Mrs. Larry Folloni.

The fact is that I didn't remember this meeting when we first met at the Raymor-Playmor. One day later in our courtship while we were talking about different happenings in our past lives the subject came up about the Provincetown boat cruise. We pieced together the date and our friends who were on the cruise and we finally realized that it was us who had danced together on that enchanting evening! What a strange but a happy coincidence! More impactfully than ever before or since, God presented me with just who and what I needed to complete my life. He had to make the coincidence happen several times before I really 'got it', but although sometimes slow, even I could finally grasp a great thing when it reappeared!

Fate has a strange method to its madness. As unlikely as this chance meeting on the cruise and our re-connection at the Boston Hotel was, what happened following our first meeting there was a real Hollywood cliffhanger. While at the Raymor-Playmor I danced with Helen for a couple of songs and before the night ended I had her phone number to line up a future date. A few days later, I called her to set it up. We were to meet on Saturday night at 7:30pm in the lobby of the Hotel Torraine, which was the favorite meeting place for the men in the service and their dates. Saturday night came and I was there in the Lobby at 7:30pm sharp. I waited and waited for my date to show up. By 8:15 I became a little impatient and figured that I was going to be stood up.

I then left the lobby to see if she might be waiting outside, but no luck. Always ready with play options, I opened up my handy 'little 'black book', and went to a nearby phone booth to call another girl for a new date. After setting one up, *something inside made me decide* to take one last look back in the lobby of the Hotel Torraine.

There in all her shining beauty, covered with a black fur stole, stood Helen. *WOW!* You will never imagine the happiness that spread throughout my body. This was the start of a great love affair. We went to the Cave, a popular nightclub within Steuben's on Boylston St. and had a wonderful time. We had our picture taken there, which Helen still has in her memory scrapbooks. As for the girl who I in turn left 'high and dry', I can only hope and pray that with all of the single and eager servicemen at the Hotel that night, that she had somewhere near the good fortune that I did!

Doing it right!

Larry & Helen, 1943

*There are only two ways to live your life.
One is as though nothing is a miracle.
The other is as though everything is a miracle."*

-Albert Einstein (1879-1955)

DATING AND SERVICE TRAINING
Inspired Innovations & Impactful Presentations

Helen and I dated quite frequently during the next quarter year before I was shipped to Philadelphia for the last three months of our Signal Corp Training Program. The program at Boston State involved classes in the morning in Math, English, and Engineering, and during the afternoon we had our lab sessions.

I'd like to relate a couple of incidents that occurred during this initial training program. The first one happened in one of my math classes. My mother had taught me a trick on how to check out a multiplication problem to confirm its accuracy. Somehow I was bold enough to tell my instructor, Jack Morrison, that I could double-check a complicated math solution with my mother's method as quickly as he could with his. With a little urging from my classmates the instructor took up the challenge and we both went to the blackboard with the same problem and worked out the check for accuracy. Lo and behold to the cheers of my classmates, I won the contest hands down with my mother's European method. To my consternation, I found out the hard way that it's not a great idea to show up your instructor. From that time on, the relationship between him and me was very strained to say the least. *This incident also helped to reinforce in me the corollary rule that as an instructor, I'd try to never embarrass a student or a player in front of his classmates.*

One other noteworthy incident occurred during one of our lab assignments. We had been given a schematic diagram to build our own radios. The entire class had the same project and the same schematic diagram. After several days of work when most of the class had assembled their radios by following the provided plans, no one could get theirs to work.

I went back to my apartment that night and reviewed the schematic diagram. After a couple of hours of frustration and many calculations, I noticed a resistor in the diagram that appeared not to be needed. The next day at our lab I mentioned this to the instructor and he "pooh-poohed-it', saying that the schematic drawing that we had was correct and not to fool around with it. Well being the obstinate guy that I am, and doing things "My Way" as usual, I decided to cut out the resistor from the unplayable radio set that I had built. The moment of truth was now at hand. I turned up the volume to its highest point, and then I hit the power switch. The sound blast from my radio shook the entire lab. An equally loud roar came up from my classmates; *"Folloni has his radio working!"*

A humbled and distraught instructor then conceded that I was right in my contention that the resistor was blocking out the sound. He told the rest of the class to remove the unnecessary resistor and sure enough all the radios were back on track and working. I thought that just by solving the problem at hand, that all would put their egos aside and be happy that something has been improved for everyone. Counter to what I expected, an ensuing cool relationship developed between the instructor and me that lasted for the rest of the term. I guess that like when I just *had* to blast the ball over the schoolyard fence into the prohibited yard, I too let my ego slip a bit by choosing to blast the sound to top percussion to announce my triumph. Then again, there's something extremely sweet about about following one's instincts and succeeding in the face of detractors. Just maybe some in authority need to be jarred out of their tendencies to kill the aspirations of youth.

"It's kind of fun to do the impossible." - Walt Disney (1901-1966)

The balance between hurting a few feelings and being disliked by some on the one hand, as opposed to doing the right thing for the greater good and enjoyment of more people, is a difficult one to maintain. Perhaps I've bucked authority a bit too much in my day, but darn it, sometimes for the benefit of the majority you just have to assert yourself against stubbornly wrong people and policies in power. I suppose that in many cases of conflict, 'win-win' situations can be crafted to make everybody happy, but typically in my life, after getting nowhere with a little good faith negotiating, I was ready to go ahead and show the way. And my way usually worked out OK. I guess, nonetheless, that if there was one thing that I wish I'd learned better from the manners of my siblings Virginia, Mike, Al, Johnny and Angie, it might have been an alternative to my quick-draw 'sonic boom diplomacy'.

When our training at Boston State was over, we were given a week furlough which I spent dating Helen. I'd borrow my Dad's car to take the daily trip up from Bridgewater to Arlington to see her, and then I'd sleepily drive back home after midnight. It was a two-hour ride each way then, as route 24; the highway to Boston was not yet built. We had to travel the old route 28, which went through Brockton, Randolph, Mattapan, etc.

On one of those trips home, I was so exhausted that I fell asleep momentarily at about 2 a.m. while going through the Campello section of Brockton on Main St. when I suddenly woke up I was heading straight toward a parked car and I swerved just in time to avoid what could have been a fatal accident for yours truly.

For the last 3 months of training program we were assigned quarters at the Hotel Walton in the heart of Philadelphia. These were great accommodations and on the warm summer nights with the windows wide open we could hear the music blasting from the Hotel Penthouse. I can still hear the refrains of the performing girl singing some of my favorite tunes made famous by Harry James and his orchestra: *"You'll Never Know Just How Much I Love You"* and *"You Made Me Love You"*, which were two of the most popular songs of this time. Naturally being fervently involved with my courtship of Helen, and having to be away from her, these songs were especially poignant.

This stage of our training was held at the Philco* Radio Complex in downtown Philly. It was during one of my classes there that I revealed one of my many ideas and inventions that were later to become household items that greatly improved the lifestyle of everyone in America and beyond.

I mentioned to one of the chief engineers at Philco that I would like to have a gadget that would work like an alarm clock, but that when it was time for the alert, it would open a circuit to operate the on/off switch to the radio. Lo and behold this Managing Engineer was sharp enough to grasp my idea and soon thereafter Philco led the way with development of these household devices. We now see clock radios, clock TVs clock stoves, clock microwaves, timed safes, timed recorders and a wide panorama of other similar devices. Unfortunately there were no royalties for me for any of these innovations, but it does feel great to have perhaps played a small part in launching a big innovation that could provide a more pleasant timed alert or electronic function start *without an alarming clang!*

* During the 1930's Philco was the number one radiomaker in the country. During World War II, Philco (as well as other American industries) converted to 100% war work for the U.S. Government. It was during this time, in 1943, that the Philco International Corporation was formed to handle the export of Philco products around the world. After the Second World War, Philco concentrated on radios and home appliances. Philco eventually became part of Philips Consumer Electronics Corporation, known today for their Philips Magnavox line of consumer electronics products. Today, the name "Philco" can be found in Kmart stores on a line of value-priced televisions, boom boxes, and of course, clock radios.

My training period in Philly was most noteworthy for several other reasons. The most important one of course was the fact that Helen took a 1-week vacation to come down there to visit during that summer of 1943. We culminated our long beautiful courtship then by becoming engaged to be married. I can still recall so vividly when we went to see Judy Garland sing at Robin Hood Dell. Her booming voice was exquisitely beautiful and to this day she remains my favorite female vocalist.

Cupid, Robin Hood, Judy Garland,
City of Brotherly Love – Trick Photography
Whatever it takes, I've just got to get that girl!

My Valentine for Life, Helen

The other event that still remains fresh in my mind was my last visit with my boyhood buddy, Bob Pratti. Bob was stationed in New Jersey, the takeoff point for all the Army men headed for battle in Europe. Bob spent the weekend before he left with me and I treated him to a great dinner at a nice Italian Restaurant in downtown Philly. Little did I realize as we parted that Sunday night that it would be the last time that I or any of his other hometown family and friends would ever see him alive. Bob was killed on a beach during the invasion of France in June of 1944. It breaks my heart to think of all that he and those like him have missed in order to preserve freedom for us, and for so many others who just have no idea of the debt they owe. *If I live my life with a bit of extra fervor, it is in no small part in honor and appreciation of those who did so much for the rest of us by making the ultimate sacrifice in war. Out of respect for carrying on for them, as I know that they would wish, along with the knowledge that but for the Grace of God, I would not have this chance to use as I can, that I do.*

With the conclusion of my training in Philly I had another week furlough that I mostly spent seeing Helen. I put in daily trips from Bridgewater to Boston and we were able to squeeze in a few days at the beach at Brant Rock, where Helen's family vacationed every year, and where Helen and my future family would later pass many a memorable extended excursions.

After that pleasant week, I headed for Fort Devens, Massachusetts to report for my indoctrination into the U.S. Army Air Corps Signal Corps. After a few days there I was shipped down to the Lake Ponchetrain Army Air Base in New Orleans Louisiana. We'll see later how the fact that I was assigned to this Group proved to be of significant importance to my future.

My days at this Air Base were relatively enjoyable and enlightening for me. We went through all the basic training rituals of Army life including many hikes with backpacks and other important conditioning and training regimens that went with getting ready for combat overseas.

We young recruits experienced our first major psyche-shaking experience while on Bivouac out in the swamps of Lake Ponchetrain. Waking up one morning we discovered one of our tent-mates to be stone dead. Upon trying to revive him we found a colorful coral snake curled up on his stomach. It had bitten him and he apparently never knew what struck. This was scary to say the least.

New Orleans was a great city to be stationed near. The weather at that time of the year was great, with temperatures in the 70's and 80's everyday. We spent our weekends in the city, enjoying the French quarters and the many other activities that went on in this great quaint and historical French / 'Creole' City.

I can remember my first trip to the City from our Air Base, which was located about 15 miles away. We traveled in open streetcars and when we arrived we were greeted by some "Pick-A-Ninnies" as we called little black youngsters. These 7 or 8-year-old kids were pimping for their older sisters. Their greeting was: "Man, you got a date yet? My sister can do you much better for 25 cents!"

The food in New Orleans was out of this world and the prices were right. I had a favorite restaurant that had a delicious cinnamon glazed Apple Pie. *"Umm" was it ever delicious!* I would order two extra pieces of pie each time I had dinner there. In fact the pie was so good that I would have one piece for an appetizer before the main course, *then* I requested the two more for dessert! The cost of this delicious treat was a grand total of 10 cents per piece. Oh how I wish I could find the replica of that pie again.

Since our Air Base was located on Lake Ponchetrain, there were many nights when the fog would set in so thick that you couldn't see your hand in front of your face. On one of those nights, we were caught in town with no streetcars running due to the prevailing pea soup atmosphere. Since we had to be back early the next day to prepare for the weekly review parade, we had to walk the entire distance back to our base. Not being able to see the road or sidewalks in front of us, we formed a human chain holding hands with the man on the end guiding us to keep abreast of the curbing. After three hours of trudging we finally made it back.

Put me in Uncle Sam, I'm ready!

With the American Forces overseas getting ready for the invasion of Europe, I again began to get stir crazy from lack of serious action. After a few months that I felt were nonproductive to the War Effort, I finally signed up with the Air Corps for flying duty, which was the big need at that time. My new class in the Air Corps was sent to Shepard Field in Texas for preflight training screening. Then followed our preflight training, held at Texas Tech in Lubbock.

Our commanding officer at Lubbock was none other than Don Budge, the famous Pro Tennis player who in 1938 became 1st player to win the Grand Slam— the French, Wimbledon, U.S. and Australian titles in 1 year.

Don also led the U.S. to 2 Davis Cup victories (1937-38); and turned pro in late '38 before leaving competition to join the service like the other icon we've met herein, Ted Williams. Don passed away at the age of 84 in January of 2000 while I was writing this book.

By the way, my fellow veterans of WWII – as Tom Brokaw puts it –*'The Greatest Generation'*, are now dying off at a rate of 1,100 per day. I hope to not join them soon. If God allows, I'd like to serve (and volley) for another 83 years or so.

My remembrances of my time in Texas were mostly of the weather. It was hot and windy every day. We were up at 5:30 every morning. We had a hardy breakfast, (The Air Corp Cadets were always supplied with the best of everything, notably the food. My kids think that this was the reason that I selected this service!) Following breakfast we went out on the field for our daily calisthenics. They were tough in and of themselves, but the roughest part of our exercise period was from swallowing all the dust that the wind would blow up every day. This might have been better training for the modern conflicts in the Arab deserts or the then contemporary fight against Rommel in Africa than for the European Theater for which we were ostensibly bound. In any case the demanding regimen certainly taught us discipline, and how to push ourselves beyond our preconceived limits.

In the middle of our preflight training, about 75% of our class was taken out of the flying program and transferred back to their original Army Units. Most of them were sent to the Infantry and Motorized Divisions. The reason for this drastic transfer was that there was a great need for reinforcements and replacements for the troops who had invaded Europe. Men were needed immediately for the push through France, Germany and Italy. Fortunately for me, since I had been assigned to an Air Force Base as my original unit, I was allowed to remain in the Flying Program. All of the unfortunate ones who were pulled out of the flying program were sent to a three-week rigorous pre-battle training program and quickly sent over to the battlefronts. They really were not sufficiently trained for the task ahead, which was horrendous regardless of preparation. We later learned that about 80% of these men ended up as battle casualties.

Following our weekend leaves we had to get back to the Air Base for the Sunday afternoon parade reviews and inspections by the Generals. The ceremonies were supposed to start at 2 p.m. However it was usually about 4 p.m. before the Generals arrived. We had to stand at attention or parade rest for about two hours waiting for the top commanders to arrive, and between the heat, the standing and the lack of sleep (and the post leave hangovers sported by some), many of the cadets would pass out on those afternoons.

Following our Preflight Training at Texas Tech it was then time to move on to our Flight training at the Air Cadets Training Base in Santa Ana, California. We spent 4 more months of extensive training there. Again the weather in Southern California was beautiful as we were stationed right next to Los Angeles. On our weekend leaves we had the opportunity to spend time in and about Hollywood, Santa Monica and many of the other fine beaches on the southern California coast. I can still see the huge 10 feet waves that we battled for fun on many occasions. I don't remember any bathing beauties though, possibly because most were serving our country as 'Rosie the Riveters', and certainly because by then I only had eyes for and thoughts of my beloved fiancee, Helen Mary Louis Mark.

Here's Helen and I having fun in LA with our friend Ruth Ramirez, whose husband Fred took this picture, and who was shortly thereafter killed in action. War is hell.

I was still at Santa Ana when my older brother Mike, whose ship had just returned from battle in the Pacific, stopped by to pay me a visit. We had not seen each other for about 3 years and when he first spotted me he nearly didn't recognize me. He said that I had put on a lot of weight from the scrawny kid that I was when he first left home in Bridgewater to join the Navy. I guess it was the great food that they supplied to the Air Cadets that did the trick. (Some cadets often joked that they were fattening us up for the slaughter ahead.)

Next, it was back to Texas for the last stage of our Air Corps training at Ellington Field, a few miles southeast of Houston. Due to my demonstrated math skills and other test results, I was assigned to the Navigation Unit. The unit that I was in was broken down into groups of four for flight training purposes. My group consisted of John Foley, Robert Fox, Bob Durgin and myself. John Foley became one of my trusted friends throughout our training.

Our 4-month training period was nearly over when I had an accident that was to change the direction of my future in the Air Corps and my life after the service. During a football game, I was tripped up, landed on my shoulder and dislocated it. I was in a quandary. I didn't want to miss graduation from the Class of 45N, so I didn't reveal my injury to my superiors. I went through the remaining weeks of the training in great pain but I did manage to graduate at the scheduled time in January of 1945. This shoulder injury, along with another more serious injury I suffered later while playing semi-pro ball, contributed to the eventual end of my promising career as a professional baseball player

Football helmet,
Baseball helmet
Flying helmet,
Shoulder pads
Shoulder harness
Shoulder Injury
Whatever the challenge,
Bring it on!

WEDDING BELLS
The Starting Bell

Next came the big day in our lives. Helen and I had made plans to be married upon my receiving my wings. The happy day was February 4, l945, exactly 58 years and a day ago from the time of this writing. The wedding was performed at the Immaculate Conception Church on the Alewife Brook Parkway on the Arlington-Cambridge line. This was next to the Camel Lounge, where I used to drive Helen's Father James every Friday night for a treat. He would have one beer and one shot of Irish Whiskey. After he gulped it down he would say, *"OK Larri, let's go."*

Helen and Larry's Wedding Day

Best Woman, Agnes Mark
Best Man, Primo Resmini

Papa & Mama Mark, Helen
Larry, Nona & Nono

The weather was cold and snowy. All of my relatives drove up from Bridgewater and the conditions were horrible. Their cars spun around on the slippery highways several times on the trip.

The reception was held at the Continental Hotel in Cambridge. Our Honeymoon didn't last long. We spent the first night at the Continental Hotel. Then followed two more days with our families; one night in Bridgewater at the Folloni homestead and the next night at Helen's sister Teresa's home on Park Avenue in Arlington. Before we knew it, it was time to head back to Ellington Field in Texas to await my new assignment. Helen and I traveled by train and had Pullman sleeper accommodations for the cross-country trip. It was a slow tiring ride over bumpy railroad tracks. There was no traveling by plane in those days as all available flights were strictly for military use. To break the monotony, we made one overnight stop in St. Louis along the way. We arrived in Houston a few days later and immediately began the search for living quarters.

Apartments and rooms were a scarcity throughout the country, especially in areas near any Army or Navy Bases. We spent the entire day going up and down every street in Houston, knocking on doors and checking any possible leads that might have the slightest chance to give us sleeping accommodations.

Near the end of the day when we were completely exhausted we finally hit pay dirt. A kind old lady named Maude took pity on us, and allowed us to sleep in a hallway of her tiny home. She placed an old door on top of two chairs and gave us a sheet and blanket to sleep on. That was our honeymoon suite. As humble as it was, it beat being beat on the street, and the extraordinarily caring effort of the property owner warmed our hearts. This experience, along with the generous humanitarian habits and values of our parents, was to help shape the 'go the extra mile as you can for your tenants' attitude that became a hallmark of our later successful ventures as landlords.

ON TO VICTORVILLE
Cal-is-then-ics

Helen and I spent the next few days waiting for the orders for our new assignment. By the end of the week we heard that were going to the Victorville Army Air Base in California. Victorville is located in the desert west of the Sierra Mountains, about 50 miles east of San Bernardino and 100 miles east of Los Angeles. It was a necessary stopping off oasis on the famous Route 66 where cross-country travelers would refill boiling radiators. And of course thousands of Army Airmen converged there to train under its abundant blue skies for the invasion of North Africa and Europe. Like the rest of them before us, once again we were packing and on our way by train to another post. Our train left Houston about 3 a.m. for the four day and night trip to Victorville. After our last accommodations, the pullman sleeper and bumpy tracks felt like the Ritz!

Upon our arrival four days later, again at about 3 a.m., we were greeted by an unusual sight. The Victorville Army Air Base was noted for its good cloud free flying weather. They had never-ever had any snowfall on their hallowed turf. As if to give a special New England welcome to Helen and me, as we pulled in to the station, we were greeted by six inches of the cold wet white stuff piled up on the ground! Everyone was shocked to say the least. That was the first flying morning ever missed at the Victorville Army Air Base! By 12 noon all the snow had disappeared due to the resurgence of the normal heat in the sandy desert. This was our initiation to Victorville, which was to be our station for the rest of my stay in the Service.

Again we began the search for living quarters off the Air Base. It was the same old story that we went through while looking for living quarters in Houston. The only difference was that we were then in the small cow-town country around Victorville, whereas in Houston we were searching in a crowded metropolitan city.

Our repeated difficulty with finding housing further bolstered my compassion for those just starting out or otherwise with less than average resources who needed a break in getting decent shelter. It also increased my appreciation of those who invest their time and resources to develop rental housing for those who need it.

Our search finally led us to a little 3-room ranch house on the edge of town. A chubby lady who had a set of 8-year-old twins and a live-in boy friend made these living quarters that we were so fortunate to acquire, available. They gave up their bedroom to us, while they utilized the couches in an anteroom off the kitchen for sleeping.

We stayed with this living arrangement for about 2 months while I was going through my Navigator-Bombardier Training. Helen eventually took a job as a secretary at the Air Base to keep herself occupied while I was on my training missions. She was a good score for the service, as her typing, shorthand, spelling and organizational skills, as well as her warm friendly demeanor, were all top notch.

Navigator Larry

After a short while, due to my accelerated flying schedules at all hours of the day and night, and the fact that we were given orders that all Officers had to be quartered on the Base in case of any emergency, we had to move closer to the action. Also with Helen's new job, she too had to get living quarters nearer the Base so that she could meet her work schedule.

We were fortunate to find a place for Helen just outside the gates of the Air Base in a motel that was run by an ex-convict and his wife. Helen's living quarters were pretty comfortable compared to what she had previously, and her accommodations included three pretty good meals each day. Helen was usually my guest for the typically excellent dinners served at the Officer's Club. During the weekends we would take trips out to the Los Angeles and Hollywood areas, and we spent much time on the lovely beaches in Santa Monica.

"Handsome" Larry at Disneyland
Sweetheart Wife Helen at the Beach

On one of our rare days off, one of my flying buddies invited me to go fishing up in the mountain streams above Victorville. On our trip up the narrow winding one-lane country road, lo and behold as we sped around a curb we encountered a cow standing in mid road. As good a pilot as my driver was, there was nothing he could do to avoid hitting it and sending it flying up and over the hood and onto the roof. While we were considering whether or not to posthumously award this bovine its wings, out ran the owner screaming, "You killed my prize heifer!" Army pay not being the greatest, we courteously suggested that he send the bill and the hamburgers to Uncle Sam!

Italy surrendered in September of 1943, and their Axis partner Germany followed suit in early May of 1945. With the war effort in Europe winding down by the summer of 1945, our great country turned its entire focus toward ending the war on the Pacific Front. Our particular group went through 3 more months of intensive Bombardier and Navigation Training on B17's and B-24's. We found out later that this was to prepare us for our next stage, which was to be training on the B-29's that were soon to drop the deadly Atom Bombs on Japan.

Soon the day arrived that so many both hoped for and in some ways dreaded*. An Atom Bomb nicknamed 'Little Boy' was dropped on Nagasaki on August 6, 1945, and a few days later another named 'Fat Man' was dropped on Hiroshima. The destruction was unbelievable, and over a quarter of a million Japanese citizens and subjugated Korean factory workers were killed. It brought the Japanese to their knees begging for surrender, which was formally signed on September 14. As heartbreaking and as devastating a death toll that these Atom Bombs created, it was truly a life saver for a far greater number of Japanese and American soldiers and citizens, including quite possibly myself, who would have been sacrificed if the war were to have continued.

With the war coming to an end on both the European and Asian fronts it was time to concentrate on getting back to civilian life again. Shortly after the Japanese surrendered, Helen went back home to Arlington, as she was pregnant with our first child.

"A bright light filled the plane," wrote Lt. Col. Paul Tibbets, the pilot of the Enola Gay, the B-29 that dropped the first atomic bomb. "We turned back to look at Hiroshima. The city was hidden by that awful cloud...boiling up, mushrooming." For a moment, no one spoke. Then everyone was talking. "Look at that! Look at that! Look at that!" exclaimed the co-pilot, Robert Lewis, pounding on Tibbets's shoulder. Lewis said he could taste atomic fission; it tasted like lead. Then he turned away to write in his journal. "My God," he asked himself, "what have we done?"

-Special report, "Hiroshima: August 6, 1945

Once that the war was over we were given a few more liberties including being allowed to play on the Victorville Air Force Baseball Team under Coach Reichle, a former Professional Baseball player and Coach of UCLA.. I played second base on a team that was studded with former professional baseball players. We traveled by small planes to play games all over the West Coast. We played one game in Las Vegas when the temperature was 125 degrees in the shade.

Also during this post-war period, sometime in the month of October while doing routine training, I suffered the thigh piercing accident that resulted in me getting the wrong medication and once again almost dying as a result of the reaction.

I never did tell my wife of this near miss until much later after I returned to New England. On the 19th day of the very next month of November, Helen gave birth to our first son, Larry Jr. I just couldn't wait to get home to see Helen and my new son. I was discharged from the Air Corps just in time to arrive home for Christmas. Following a happy reunion with my new family for the Christmas holidays it was time to get on with the rest of my life. As scary as the world's problems were, with Helen and Larry Jr. in my life, I felt all the confidence in the world about the future.

BOSTON UNIVERSITY YEARS
Go to College, Get Some Knowledge

"Go to College, get some knowledge, Stay in there till you're through. If they can make penicillin out of moldy bread, they can make something out of you!"
-Muhammad Ali

Not wasting any time, I enrolled at Boston University to begin the second semester that started in January of 1946. I only needed three more semesters to receive my Bachelor's degree in Physical Education and Athletics, and with my fine preparation from public schools in Bridgewater, along with my intensive military training, college studies were a breeze. Dr. Harmon was the the chairman of the Physical Education Department, and his relations through marriage, Baseball Coaches Mel Collard, and Harry Cleverly rounded out the true family atmosphere there.

Dr. Irwin taught a pretty tough course in Physiology, a subject that not too many of us could master. A very revolting incident occurred during this course when Dr. Irwin's secretary gave one student a copy of a test in advance. Practically the entire class got hold of a copy of the test to learn the answers in advance. Well you can imagine Dr. Irwin's chagrin when almost the entire class ended up with A's on this test. He violently blasted everyone and voided the test scores. He did however offer to give anyone in the class the opportunity to take a head to head verbal test with him to prove their knowledge. I took him up on it and even though I did not answer 100% of the questions correctly, I did well enough for him to honor my high mark.

"Always do right. This will gratify some and astonish the rest"
- Mark Twain (1835-1910)

One of my first stops upon entering BU was to pay a visit to the gym on Stuart St. where their Terrier basketball team was practicing. I was given an introduction to Coach Russ Peterson by a common acquaintance that knew of my athletic exploits, and the Coach immediately invited me to come out to practice.

It wasn't long before I got into the swing of things and became a member of the BU Varsity Basketball team which went on to a record of 11 wins and 2 loses. This was the best winning percentage (.846) of any Terrier Team to date and far beyond. The only two loses that we suffered were both to Harvard College, who went on to represent the area in the NCAA Basketball Tournament. Our winning record was to last another 50 years until Coach Dennis Wolfe's team of 1997, which compiled an .862 percentage with 25 wins and 4 loses.

BU Basketball Team, 1946

Larry's Basketball & Baseball exploits helped earn him a Hall of Fame Career at BU

One game that stands out in my memory is our second battle against Harvard. We were all pepped up for this return meeting which was crucial to get us an invitation to the NCAA Tournament.

I guess that we were overly pumped up as we got off to a very slow start. Nothing was going right for us and we fell behind by about 10 points early in the second period. Suddenly I got hot and hit four quick baskets with some driving lay-ups, a couple of outside bombs, and a foul shot mixed in to close the gap to one point. Harvard called time out to stop the run. During the time out, the Harvard Coach gave Saul Maraschian instructions to stick to me wherever I went on the court. Saul was a Harvard All-American, who was to go on to a career in Professional Basketball.

Saul was a streetwise kid from New York, and an excellent defensive player who knew all the tricks of the game. He certainly used them against me. He stuck to me like glue for the rest of the contest and was continually holding on to my trunks to make sure that I didn't get away from him. I kept complaining to the officials about his holding tactics, to no avail. I didn't score another point the rest of the way and of course we lost.

With the end of the Basketball Season it was time for Baseball. Coaches Collard and Cleverly immediately inserted me into the lineup at second base as the leadoff batter. This was the season when I was fortunate enough to establish a National Collegiate Record for reaching base consecutively that to this day still stands. *

This streak over four games included 12 hits, 3 walks and 2 errors. The 2 errors could well have been ruled hits as the balls were hit pretty hard. The streak ended when the opponents 3rd baseman made a diving catch of a line drive to rob me of another hit and from there on I had 6 more consecutive hits which would have extended my streak to 24.

I was also tutored by football coaches "Buff" Donelli and Steve Sinko. My two seasons as an overall athlete at BU were productive enough for me to be inducted into the Boston University Athletic Hall of Fame.

*Editor's note: During the final editing process in 2002, Shaun Larkin of Cal St. Northridge finally eclipsed this NCAA Div. 1 record by extending the streak to 18. It is fitting that Larry Folloni's record had held for **56** years. Only Joe DiMaggio's major league streak of **56** consecutive games with a hit has had similar longevity. And you'll soon read how Larry's BHS team was '**56** *champs!*

With my college career and my GI Bill Educational benefits at an end, and with toddler Larry Jr's life at its beginning, I quickly sought out and secured a teaching and coaching position at Dighton High School to start in September.

New Grad and New Dad Larry Forging ahead with Full support of Wonderful Wife for Life Helen.

A short time after I signed the contract with Dighton, along came Bill "Okie" O'Connor, the Dodgers Scout in the New England area, with another proposition. Bill had followed my collegiate athletic career, and *lo and behold he too offered me a contract – to join the Brooklyn Dodger professional baseball organization!*

I was really in a quandary, as sports were my first love and since I was a youngster I had always dreamed of becoming a professional baseball player. What made the decision even more difficult was the fact that I now had obligations to support my new love, Helen and our $1^{1/2}$-year old son Larry. Playing 'catch or fetch the ball' with my already aspiring athlete son while mulling over my dilemma sealed a compromise concept in my mind. I knew that I had to establish my professional reputation by sticking to my agreements and, more importantly, that it was also time to be more concerned with the next generation of athletes. I reasoned, nonetheless, that if I could continue to hone my baseball skills in my spare time, maybe I could increase my market value as a major leaguer and later on achieve both goals.

I thanked Bill O'Conner for his offer, but told him that I felt I had an obligation to fulfill my one-year contract commitment to teach and coach in Dighton. I told him that I would complete my 1-year contract and that if everything worked out that I would consider his offer for the following year.

After my graduation from BU in May I signed on to play Semipro Baseball in the Boston Park League with the Club owned and managed by Dick Casey. The Casey Club was noted for having the best team in the league for many years, mainly due to Dick signing on the better prospects in the Boston Area. I enjoyed a pretty good season that summer, until fate stepped in to stop my 'toying' around, and to definitively seal my future career direction.

During a playoff game for the league championship I faced fastballer Fred Toye, who's 95mph rocket delivery crushed my cheekbone. Doctors told me that I was lucky to escape with my life. This incident gave my young bride and me a fairly gruesome taste of the dangers of the sport at big league levels. This was before the days of large contracts, insured body parts and pensions for professional players. With our priority desire being to raise a large family with a safe and secure home life, my hard decision of a few months earlier suddenly became quite easy. *I would attempt no comeback.* While my dreams for a professional baseball career were shattered, the door opened wide for me to completely dedicate myself to my career in teaching and coaching.

I have often regretted the fact that I never gave myself the chance to make it in Professional Baseball but I have never regretted my ultimate career choice. In spite of all the bumps along the way, I have had a wonderful career in coaching and in the athletic world. I enjoyed working with the many youngsters under my tutelage and I have many pleasant memories of my dealings with my professional associates. I wouldn't change this life for all the money or fame in the world.

*Flanked by the two strongest steadiest and most beautiful supports in my life,
my wife Helen Mary Louise
and my mother Maria Luisa
my Stars are aligned and
I'm ready to take on the world!*

START OF MY TEACHING & COACHING JOB IN DIGHTON
Rookie Year

I shall never forget the first day of my three-year stay at Dighton High School. My head was completely shaven during the operation to repair the broken cheekbone that Toye's fastball smashed and I was still pretty bald a few weeks later when I walked in to teach my first class, so I wore a jungle hat to cover it. My first joking comment upon introducing myself was that I was just returning from a Safari in Africa and that I became so attached to the jungle hat that I wanted to wear it everywhere. The comment drew a good laugh and broke the ice with my first class of students. A little humor almost never hurts. (OK, in this case 'laughing in stitches' did hurt a little, but as always, it removed more pain than it occasioned.)

My homeroom class was a freshman group. So it meant that we had rookie students and a rookie teacher, both of us just starting out on a new venture. Seated in my class of about 20 pupils were 4 girls who had the same last name, "Rose". It was quite a coincidence and I nicknamed them the 'Four Roses'. The students and I loved each other from the start.

"DHS Rockettes" pranksters on the playground

Three of the four Roses

My first principal was Dana Webber, a kind individual who had the dubious job of being the in between of a virulent superintendent and his teaching staff. As I was a rookie teacher and coach, Mr. Webber nursed me along and protected me from the unwarranted demands of the superintendent. Mr. Webber was liked by all of the teaching staff, and I count him among the top few of the best bosses in my career.

I really enjoyed my first year at Dighton. I was the backfield coach in football, working under Head Coach Leo DeMarco. Coach DeMarco was a huge, jolly fellow who had played tackle at Fordham University. I couldn't have had a better Teacher-Coach to work under in my first Coaching job. He didn't know too much about backfield play, but he was well versed in line play, which made for a good coaching team with me concentrating on my specialty of the backfield and Leo focussing primarily on his linemen.

Coach DeMarco was not only a good fundamentalist but he was also a great psychologist. I learned many good tricks about coaching as I observed his tactics.

One excellent lesson that I learned from him was from his method of installing his running and passing plays. He would always explain the play first. Then he would walk the players through their patterns. Then he would have them go through the play in slow motion. Then they'd jog through the play.

He would do this over and over until he felt that the players knew the play by rote memory (to train positive instinct reactions). Then and only then would he allow the players to run the plays at full speed. The technique of using repetition of a subject through different modalities is something that later scientific studies have proven to be most effective in learning, especially when hand / eye coordination and motor skills are involved. Look at the great Jerry Rice. Even he still repeats his pass receiving routes virtually endlessly until surgical precision in their execution is automatic. Years later Ted Williams told me that it was his philosophy to repetitively practice moves that he did right and forget those that he did wrong.

This approach to coaching may have appeared boring and tedious, but it sure paid off in the results we obtained. Coach DeMarco didn't have many plays, maybe a half dozen or so, but the ones he did install were drilled and drilled. He was a stickler on fundamentals and would not leave a play until it was perfected. He really got down to the level of the players. The first two football seasons were uneventful as we were only a bit above average, but the third year, in 1949, we went through an undefeated season and ended up as State Champs in our Class! This was quite a valuable way for me to start my career as a Coach.

I understand that perennial #1 rated high school team in the nation today, De LaSalle out of Walnut Creek, California has now won 135 straight games based to a good extent on the very same philosophy that Coach DeMarco espoused of instilling a few plays to perfection.

"Perfect Practice Makes Perfect."

In addition to my duties as backfield coach, I did most of the scouting of our future opponents. I remember one of my scouting trips that took me to the Islands of Martha's Vineyard and Nantucket. Since the Ferryboats only took one run a day during the Fall Season we had to stay overnight. I took my wife Helen along on this trip and except for the fact that I managed to get seasick en route we had a very enjoyable weekend on the Islands. It's a good thing that I didn't join the navy!

A couple of the games stood out during the undefeated championship season: One was with our archrival Somerset, the perennial powerhouse in our league. We won that game 6 to 0 on a touchdown that was scored in a bizarre manner. On the opening kickoff, our kicker blasted the ball into the Somerset end zone. The pigskin laid there for sometime as none of the players realized that it was a live ball. I yelled and screamed for someone on our team to fall on it until one of them finally heard me and did. When the Referee put up his hands to indicate a touchdown the other players of both teams were flabbergasted.

The other game that stood out for me was the one we played on my birthday, Nov. 5, 1949 against Bridgewater. The game was highly publicized in the local papers with stories of my return as a coach to my hometown. The game was a rout, as we defeated BHS by a score of 49 to 0. After the game the players handed me the game ball as a birthday gift. That, however, was not the end of the celebration.

The players asked my wife and I to come to be chaperons at a dance that night. Helen and I went to the dance thinking that we were to be supervising the kid's fun, but to our surprise as we walked into the hall we were greeted with a "Happy Birthday" chant! In the middle of the head table there was a large cake decorated with the gridiron lines of the football field and the inscription,

"HAPPY BIRTHDAY COACH -- D.H.S. 49 -- B.H.S. 0.

Some of the players from that Dighton area are still fresh in my mind including notably the four Dutra brothers. Jimmy played halfback on the football team; and was a state all scholastic who led it in scoring in 1947. He was our captain and truly a great leader and all around athlete.

His brother Johnny as the other halfback was not as flashy as Jimmy, but he was a good blocking back. Johnny was later to pay the supreme sacrifice when he was killed blocking a bullet during the Korean War in 1951. The youngest of the Dutra brothers was George, who played halfback on our 1949 State Championship team. The last brother was Larry. He couldn't play due to a crippling defect but he was our team student manager in all sports and a great inspiration to our teams.

A few other players of note: Billy Baxter Greene, a scrappy and wiry athlete, was the quarterback on the football team, a guard on the basketball team and the shortstop on the baseball team. Carl Spratt, who later became the Chief of Police in Dighton, played end on the football team, center on the basketball team, and first base on the baseball team. Both of them died in the 1990's due to heart attacks.

George Amaral, a speedy halfback on the 1949 State Championship team, was the leading scorer in the state. Following that championship season the townspeople gave us a great testimonial.

Here's an interesting sidelight: One of my star players on all of our Dighton sports teams was a boy by the name of Edgar Standring who was a star in all three major sports. In 1997, as I was heading to the first tee while playing in a Profile Seniors Golf Tournament at the Lake Sunapee Golf Course in New Hampshire, I bumped into a middle-aged man, who greeted me with a warm, "Hi Coach". I stared at him for a moment and he realized that I did not recognize him. Then he blurted out; "Do you remember Edgar Standring, one of your athletes at Dighton High?" Upon his calling out his name to me it all came back. Here was one of my first student athletes now eligible to play in the Seniors Leagues! Although my body felt great as a very young 78-year-old, this made me begin to realize how old I really was.

Larry's Dighton High School Hoop team, 1947-1948

Following my first Season coaching football in 1947, I was then on my own to coach my first basketball team. Prospects were not too bright but we had one big plus going for us. Jimmy Dutra was returning from the previous year and he, being the great athlete that he was, proved to be a great nucleus to start with.

After 3 intensive weeks of practice in which we worked mostly on conditioning and the fundamentals to establish our pressing defense and fast break, we were ready to test our skills against a heavily favored Diamon Voke team from Fall River.

For the first time in my athletic career I really felt the jitters. I was like a nervous little tiger, pacing up and down in front of our bench. My fears were ill founded as my players really came through for us. Our defense was superb and even though our offense had not yet jelled, it was good enough to pull out a hard-earned upset victory.

We won our next two games, which set up a meeting with our always-powerful archrivals from Somerset. Emotions on both sides were still really fresh from our shocking victory on the gridiron just a couple of months before. Once again, we were both undefeated going into this game that was to be played before a packed house in our home gym. Our team was really up for it and we defeated them by over 20 points. Our trapping press defense, which really upset the Somerset, team's offense and our fast breaking offense, were the keys to this highly cherished victory.

I vividly recall when after the game, our Superintendent met me in the middle of the gym to congratulate me on the win. A member of the school committee accompanied him. As the Superintendent introduced me to him he said, "Mr. French, meet Coach Folloni. Last Spring during our search for a Basketball Coach we came up with this guy who was the best Coaching prospect in Massachusetts." We'll soon see how quickly the superintendent forgot those rare kind words.

After winning our first six games we traveled to Dartmouth, where we suffered the first loss of my coaching career. We had a cold shooting night and Dartmouth had a good night both offensively and defensively. I was disappointed, but all the more determined to go on to future successes.

We hit a cold spell halfway through the season and lost a couple more games, but we were still in first place late in the season when what to us was a tragedy struck our team. It happened during one of our physical education classes when we were preparing for our annual gym show. Our star forward, Bobby Booth, broke his wrist while doing a dive over a Swedish Box.

We lost the next night and the following week we played Somerset in a game that would decide the League Championship. The game was at the Somerset gym, which is long and very narrow. The loss of our high scoring forward was a little too much of a handicap for us, as Somerset beat us by 2 points.

This was the same Somerset team that we handily defeated by 20 points in our previous meeting when Bobby Booth was in the lineup. Somerset went on to win the State Championship at the Boston Garden by defeating Oliver Ames by some 30 points. If Bobby Booth had not suffered his unfortunate injury that could well have been Dighton as State Champs.

Next on the coaching agenda was the baseball team. Up to that year Dighton had always been the doormats of the League in baseball, as they never even had a 500% or better winning team. Our first year we hit the 500% mark. The second year we were at 600% and the third year we hit the 800% winning mark for the best baseball record that Dighton ever had. We went from the cellar to the top in three years!

I felt as if there were an aura of inspiration pushing this team and me on to great achievement

THE END OF MY FIRST TEACHING & COACHING POSITION
Released

In addition to my coaching of Football, Basketball and Baseball, I had the added duties of coaching the Track Team as a sidelight. For all my Coaching duties, Athletic Director work and Physical Education Supervising for all the Elementary and Junior High Schools in town I was paid the grand total of $200.00 per year!

Additionally, of course, I was paid $2,500.00 for my teaching salary, which by the way was the highest pay any of my BU classmates for their first teaching jobs. After my first year I went to my Superintendent and asked for a raise for my extracurricular duties. As he rejected my request, he looked at me as though I were asking for the Moon. (If I had known how this clown would handle me in the future, and if I had had some of my sons' inclinations, I might have given him a moon of my own!) When a journalist asked Babe Ruth around the end of the depression if it was unseemly that he was earning more than President Herbert Hoover, he replied: *"Why not? I had a better year than he did!"*

I remained on my job at Dighton for three years after which the same Supt. who gushed so glowingly about me after my initial success against Somerset, *unceremoniously fired me!* I first learned of my firing in April, when I read in the sports pages of the Taunton Gazette that I had a successor, Walter Scanlon. The Superintendent didn't have the guts to fire me face to face. He later sent me a letter of notification that my contract was not to be renewed for my tenure year. When I later confronted him his official justification was that my Basketball Team, (which was 'King in Dighton'), did not win the League title in three years. This at least was the surface explanation, but I am well aware that the real reason was that I did not fit in socially with his click of teachers, who catered to him with drinking parties after all athletic contests.

Well here I was as a "Lame Duck Coach", guiding the Baseball Team to the best winning record ever for any Dighton Team. I could very well have gone through the motions, but that was not my nature. I felt it my duty and obligation to give it my best for these kids who were very loyal to me during my watch. Besides, it felt right to do right

While my first teaching job in Dighton lasted only 3 years, they were memorable ones for me for many reasons. It was my first venture into the teaching and coaching field. At long last, my boyhood dreams were being realized. Too bad, I thought for awhile, that the dreams had turned into nightmares when after so much real dedicated work on my part, my self-centered Superintendent refused to grant me tenure.

Believe me, I loved Coaching and the Athletic Director work, and I loved and admired most of my bosses, but I did not relish the ordeals that I had to go through with a few egotistical and dictatorial Administrators that I worked for. In my humble opinion, professional jealousy and personal envy too often tainted the actions of these bureaucrats. I really feel that the success and publicity I gained in coaching overshadowed them and that they felt the need to put me down to compensate for their own inadequacies.

You really don't know what pressure is until you have undergone the type of stress that they so pettily applied. In the case of Dighton, there I was with a wife and two children to support and I had no job. Well if you think that you have pressure, just think what I was going through.

Larry Jr. feeds Bobby

If any of you think that you are stressed out and bored with your job, I urge you to think twice before just chucking it. There were many, many days when I felt unbearably strained and unmotivated, but I NEVER QUIT, and I continued on to do it *MY WAY, BECAUSE IT WAS THE RIGHT WAY FOR MY STUDENTS.*

I found that if I could calm myself by having a little talk with The Man Upstairs, and in any other way manage to persist a little more, soon enough new inspiration and motivation would come along to boost me. And more often than not, the generative power came from counting my blessings, the biggest of them being my own fabulous family. As my esteemed contemporary Satchel Paige said:

"Never let your head hang down.
Never give up and sit down and grieve.
Find another way.
And don't pray when it rains,
If you don't pray when the sun shines."

MY WAY WAS ALSO THE RIGHT WAY FOR MY CAREER AND FOR MY FAMILY. It was my duty and responsibility to see to it that my children were properly clothed and fed, and that they had the opportunity to get an education. In order to accomplish this, I sometimes I had to work three or four different jobs along with my teaching and coaching duties. It wasn't easy and to do so I had to sacrifice time that I would have loved to share with my children when they were growing up. Not having more time to spend with my youngsters is the one thing that I most regret. Although I often included one or more of my kids in my professional activities, which did, after all center on youth, their loving mother was still left to do much of the legwork for them in their growing years.

For all of Helen's sacrifices, my children and I have always been forever grateful to her. Now that I am in my retirement years, I am so thankful to the Good Lord for giving her and me the opportunity to have a little more time to enjoy our grandchildren, Taylor & Cammy who live with us in NH. God willing, we'll have more of the same to share with our other grandchildren Vicky & Scott of Chicago and Ava Grace of Pittsburgh.

My career as a Coach and Athletic Administrator was truly a rewarding and enjoyable one for me. There were many bumps along the highway but as the song 'My Way' states, *"Regrets I've had but few."* Contrary to the lyrics, however, which state that they are too few too mention; I *shall* mention some regrets and regrettable characters later. Fortunately, in any case, throughout my career I also encountered some loving and caring administrators who helped me to maintain my sanity and self esteem by encouraging me to continue to apply my unique skills to excel. That type of caring consideration contributed considerably to my carrying on with my successful career. I will also mention a few of these sterling characters later.

For now I want to thank and acknowledge a gentleman by the name of Dana Webber, who was my Principal at Dighton High School. Mr. Webber was the catalyst that kept me going and guided me through the rough times of my early learning experiences. I really enjoyed my three years at Dighton. With the exception of the aforementioned Superintendent, the rest of my associates were very compatible. The students were very lovable and a joy to teach and coach. What little contacts that I had with the townspeople were of a positive nature.

Principal Dana Webber far left, really nurtured my budding career. Dighton H.S. Boys & Girls League Champions, 1948, Coaches Miss Campbell & Mr. Folloni

Teaching jobs in the early 1950's were still very scarce, as the baby boom kids were just beginning to enter 1st grade then. There I was with a growing family to support, and with no job on the horizon. For some time I was really depressed. *And once again, even though I was down in the dumps over losing my job, as I look back, this was really a kick upstairs for me.* It led me to my chosen dream of coaching and teaching in my hometown of Bridgewater; a heaven sent job that was to be offered to me after what seemed like the longest 2 months of my life

I was extremely fortunate to get the assistance a couple of true friends in my hometown that were on the School Committee: Jim Buckley, a lifelong 'Guardian Angel in town' and Maurice Walsh, my former High School Teacher at the Old Academy building. These two led the fight to land me my first job in Bridgewater.

They were building a new High School. (The first state of the art school building the town ever had.) The building was not to be completed until the fall of 1952. This meant that I had one year to wait before I could start at my new teaching and coaching position.

In the interim I enrolled at BU for credits additional to my Master's Degree in physical education and administration. Luckily I had assistance from the GI Bill which paid me the grand sum of $75.00 a month. And of course the most encouraging thing that I had was the support of my caring brothers, sisters and parents who helped us out financially and morally until I could begin my career in Bridgewater.

3 Generations of Good Sports, Larry, Michael & Nono

START OF MY DREAM CAREER IN BRIDGEWATER
Trading Up

A few weeks before I finished at Dighton I got the great news that I'd have a job teaching and coaching at the new Bridgewater High School. I normally had one free period a week from teaching at Dighton, and in it during one of those last weeks I sat down in my little 4x6 cubbyhole of a Physical Education Office and suddenly found myself daydreaming about my upcoming job.

I'd normally spend this one free period in planning my work for the following week. However since this was to be my last year in Dighton, I suppose I could hardly be blamed if my thoughts began to stray from my usual routine.

Many thoughts went through my mind during that one short 45-minute free interlude. The first question that I asked myself was: "What can I do for my home town that would make it a happier place for the youngsters to live and grow?"

To answer this, I asked myself another question. "What things did I enjoy when I was a youngster growing up in the poor 'Little Italy' section of town known as Stanley?" The answer to this was easy, since the happiest days of my life were spent in the sandlots, muddy streets and cow pastures of our neighborhood playing baseball, football and any outdoor games that such very limited facilities and equipment would allow.

OUR ATHLETIC EQUIPMENT AND FIELDS
Gear and There

Our facilities and equipment were very limited indeed since we grew up in the days of the depression and our hard working parents had all they could do to put the food on the table and to keep us clothed. As I detailed in the earlier section called 'The Fields Where Dreams Were Born', *our playing conditions were far less than safe, sanitary, suited for purpose, or consistently available.* And, as I detailed in the section called 'Before Wilson, Spaulding, McGregor and Reebok', *our equipment consisted mostly of self-made items available on a haphazard and sometimes less than conventionally acquired basis.* Stanley wasn't the only area of town in the depression and post depression eras where the kids had to overcome substantial challenges in securing playground space and equipment. In fact, all of the kids faced the same challenges. It just wasn't right in my mind that kids would have to go through so much before being able to get down playing organized sports.

REVIEW OF RECREATION NEEDS OF THE TOWN OF BRIDGEWATER
Turning Home Field Disadvantage to an Advantage

With these memories of my childhood days as a background, it was easy for me to see what the youngsters needed. In my mind the need for a better Recreation Program in the Town of Bridgewater was obvious, and the basic elements required to meet that need were threefold:

1.) Facilities: New updated gyms and playground areas for all sports.

2.) Equipment: Proper equipment and supplies.

3.) Organization: Proper supervision and coaching to organize play for the youngsters. This had to be buttressed with community participation for program support and authoritative legitimacy.

One of the first of these needs, a playground, was very well provided for in the middle thirties when the Lions Club and American Legion working together, secured the land at the old Legion Field and donated it to the town. A 'W.P.A. Project' soon turned this swampland into one of the finest playground sites in the South Shore area. For those of you too young to remember, the WPA stands for Work Project Administration, which was a federal program of President Franklin D. Roosevelt's administration from 1936 to 1943. It was designed to use Federal Funds to put millions of depression era unemployed and relief (welfare) recipients back to work doing useful public works projects. WPA's building program included the construction of 116,000 buildings, 78,000 bridges, and 651,000 miles of road and the improvement of 800 airports. Special projects ranged in scope from the building of the Hoover Dam to the renovation of Legion Field. Even though we subsequently had an excellent site for a playground, the grounds had not received much maintenance attention or use by the youngsters for about a dozen years. The baseball field, which was by far one of the best in the state, was only used by the local Semipro teams in the summer and by the High School and State College teams during the Spring. Aside from that, this beautiful playground was getting very little use by the youngsters of our town. The reason for this of course was the lack of proper organization, supervision, equipment and supplies.

OVERCOMING OBSTACLES TO CARRY OUT DREAMS
Eyes on the Prize

All throughout my daydreaming I was trying to project ways to surmount these obstacles. After mulling over them during the next few weeks, I decided upon a plan of action.

After dutifully completing my contract at Dighton, I got right to work on *my life's big project*. The first thing that I did was to contact a group of influential individuals in our town to come to a meeting, which I had set up at the old Academy Building. I borrowed a movie projector from the local High School and rented two films from my Alma Mater Boston University's Physical Education Department.

The annual 'sack' races at the Rec. Program are treasured memories for many town youth. Overcoming adversity and testing ourselves in competition is natural.

"Make no little plans. Make the biggest one you can think of
and spend the rest of your life carrying it out."
-President Harry S. Truman

Films – 'Playtime USA' & 'Leaders for Leisure'
Pro-motion

The titles of the films were 'Playtime U.S.A.' and 'Leaders for Leisure'. I dug the $10.00 for the films rental fees out of my own pocket, and this proved to be the best little investment of my life. Most of the group that I invited to see these films were men who belonged to the Lions Club, which was one of the organizations in town that had aided in securing and developing the old Legion Field.

After a real enthusiastic and spirited meeting this group was easily convinced of the need for a supervised play program in our town and also of the fact that we needed to promote the maximum use of the facilities by our youngsters.

Even though I had convinced them of the need for this supervised play program, the problem of raising the necessary funds to get it started was something else. As supportive as they were and as much as they would have liked to, the Lions Club budget was already committed to other projects, and they were not able to contribute financially at that time. (In later years, of course, the Lions were one of our best financial supporters, and additionally, many of their members directly dedicated their time and talents in a variety of ways.)

The next step was to find a means of financing the project. I called upon my good friend George Stone, President of the Independent Nail Co. and outlined my plans for the project. George was always a willing contributor to any worthwhile projects that would benefit youngsters.
George Stone, President of the Independent Nail Co

Not only did Mr. Stone contribute $100.00 to the fund, but he also contacted the other major industrialists in town; Al McIntyre of the John E. Lucy Co., George Jenkins of the Jenkins Mill Company and Edward McHugh of the Eastern Grain Company. The total contributed by the Industrial Organizations, plus a sizable donation by my good friend Judge Robert E. Clark, brought the amount of the initial fund to $450.00.

I then went door to door and solicited from the merchants and other organizations in town, including the K of C., The Lincoln Club, The 49ers Club, The Veterans Club, The Polish Club, and a few individuals to bring the total of the fund to over $900.00. The money raised for this project was then turned over to the Lions Club to act as custodian for the Supervised Play project. This was pretty big money in those days!

I'd be remiss at this point, if I didn't remember the many contributions of my cousin, my best friend, the best man at my wedding, and the BEST ORIGINAL BOOSTER FOR KIDS RECREATION IN TOWN, Primo Resmini!

It was Primo who volunteered his time and substantial skills to spearhead the original 'behind the scenes' work with the K of C, the Lions Club, and many other civic organizations in town to foster our youth recreation and athletic programs. It was also Primo who anyone in need could count on for help, and know that it would be done with a warm smile, with no questions asked, and no repayment expected. He did all of this with a true enthusiastic attitude, and without any affectations of self-righteousness.

Primo died of a heart attack in 1967 at the ridiculously early age of 45. The world lost a truly great man on that day. My son, who idolized Primo, asked me if anyone ever disliked the man. The closest I could come up with was the initial reaction of those who he would boldly walk up to and say, "Gimme a buck". No one would refuse because they knew it would be for a great cause, and that Primo himself had already donated $10 of his own money and much of his free time to it. Everyone respected Primo.

Primo Resmini was truly #1.

RESPONSE TO 1ST SUPERVISED PLAY PROJECT
Enthusiastic Beginnings - Hope Springs Eternal

The response of the youngsters to the first year of the recreation program was amazing. That program consisted of organized baseball and softball, tennis, and other supervised play for the youngsters. It was a huge success from the start.

Primo's son Louie watches my son Mike whiff while still making a mighty stride forward during the first year of the town's recreation program. Since that first year, thousands of Bridgewater kids have stepped forth forcefully on their own quests having tested themselves in these youth programs and playgrounds of dreams.

The interest was so great from the townspeople that the Lions Club sponsored an article in the town warrant having the town raise and appropriate the funds for the Recreation Program for the following year. Each year since, the town has sponsored the Recreation program under the direction of the Playground Commission.

The town recreation program was a real hit. Here my friend Rocky Marciano, fresh from another of his 49 winning heavyweight fights, volunteers his time to show young Billy O'Connell and my son Larry how to be sporting champions in life. To my great pride, joy and satisfaction, Billy, Larry and so many others grew up to fit very well into whoever's shoe's (if not gloves) that they aspired to fill.

The program has grown with more and more youngsters taking part each year. During the first two decades of my involvement and beyond, the amount of mainstream sports, along with simpler games like 'kick-ball' 'checkers' and 'tidily winks' that were organized is countless. The weekly weenie roasts that we held at the tall stone grill in the grove by the old stream at Legion Field are legendary. Old participants still tell me how special those programs were in their formative years. In subsequent years we added to our staff of supervisors and developed other recreation programs at other sites in town to accommodate youngsters from every age and every neighborhood, without charge.

Put us in Coach, we're ready!

No sad sacks at the Recreation Program

As offshoots to this original Recreation Program the following youth programs have been established in town:

- Little League Farm League, and subsequent T-ball and Babe Ruth Baseball
- Biddy League Basketball
- Pop Warner Football, and
- Youth Soccer

He's small, but he's on the ball! Little hustler helping Krueger Auto over Rexall's in Biddy League action.

NAILERS, LITTLE LEAGUE CHAMPS
L-R, Front: Larry Folloni Jr., Mascot; Thomas Alfieri, Batboy; Seated: David McGinn, Philip Skillings, Douglas Bromley, Wilfred Preti, Jimmy Denton, Jimmy Ellis, Billy O'Brien, Standing: Allan Stone of Independent Nail Co., Roddy Walsh, Paul Benton, Robert Bevis, David Krukonis, richard Amber, Charles Doyle, Larry Folloni, Manager. Absent when photo was taken: Robert Cirelli, Albert Ghelfi, George Paleti & Ronnie Hogg, and George, James and Leo Stone, Sponsors

In those days we organized healthy sporting recreation programs for kids from ages 5 to 50, including adult basketball and baseball leagues. Besides the town, our sponsors then for all of these sports included Kruger Auto, Rexall Drugs, Independent Nail Co. (Nailers), Jenkin's Mills, Lucey Shoe (Jelco) Lincoln A.A., Lion's Club, K.of C. Club and Woronicz Hardware. Now, of course the world is progressing and so are the programs, with inclusion of more women's sports like softball, and a myriad of other activities, mostly with public funding.

We got the whole community involved right from the beginning. Locals will recognize many of the participant's names from this 1951 Father & Son Game. Everyone will recognize at least one of the Umpires. Can't knock that guy!

By 1954 our Playground Baseball leagues alone had over 200 players, included (41) Mity Mites playing for the 'Red Sox' and the 'Indians', (78) Juniors, (38) Pony Division players and (47) girls playing for the "Crazy Legs" and the "Puddy Tats"!

This did not include more female and male participants in our many other sports and games activities. When you consider that our town's population then was less than a quarter of what it is today (50 yrs. later), that would be like having around a 1000 kids now just playing baseball! Not a bad start!

MITY MITES FATHER & SON GAME
AUGUST 16, 1951

LEGION FIELD   6:15 P.M.

The Line ups:

LINCOLN AA		RED SOX	
Name	No.	Name	No.
Larry Folloni	1N	Robert LaCrosse	4J
Tom Alfieri	12N	William Panza	10L
Paul Attacki	5N	Richard LaCrosse	9J
Phil Skillings	12J	Mike Crowley	3J
Albie Ghelfi	4N	David Carreira	11J
Paul Pallatroni	11N	Stephen Prophett	2J
John Ferrari	7N	Freeman Perry	5J
Connie Thibault	2J	David Bowker	4L
David Messalini	3N	Jackie Cerci	1J
Gordon Ross	4J	Robert Marzelli	10J
Bill Ferioli	6N	Richard Costa	1L
Fred Filippini	5J	Steve Bonfiglioli	6J
Eddie Hill	9N	Jim Cowgill	7J
Bill Cowgill	6J	Bill Podielsky	8J
Ronald Ferioli	7J	Robert Wood	5L
Francis Ferioli	8N	Richard Hill	8L
Ronnie Hill	1J	David Lambert	3L
Ray Calabrese	9J	Kenneth Merrey	9L
Russell Braddock	2N	Peter Duif	12J
		Ronald Wagman	11L

Uniform Letter Code: J, Jenkins   N, Nailers   Uniform Letter Code: J, Jelco   L, Lions

UMPIRES
"Rocky" Marciano   Judge Robert G. Clark, Jr.   George C. Stone

---

Playground Baseball League, 1953-54
Playground Commission: Chairman, Russell Cowgill, Clerk, Cecil V. Hayes

Mity Mites, *age 5-8 (later the farm league) Indians, Red Sox*

Junior Division, *age 9-12 (later the little league) Dodgers, Cubs, Cards, Giants*

Pony Division, *age 13-5 (later Babe Ruth) Reds, Browns, Panthers, Wildcats*

Girl's Division, *Puddy Tats, Crazy Legs, Hepcats, Be-Bops*

My first love, the Mity Mites of '51   *My night flights - Lincoln AA champs*

Bridgewater can now boast of having one of the finest youth programs and facilities in the State. And the successes of the School's Athletic Programs as one of the best in the State can well be attributed to the start of this Recreation Program in the early '50's, and the great job of those who kept it growing and improving.

I can't tell you how satisfying it is now to drive by the new "Mickey Cochrane Complex" / Legion Field to see how well developed and groomed it is, with the new Town Recreation Commission Building on site. The field and the modern programs just burst with activity. Those who succeeded me in the service of youth recreation in Bridgewater, along with all of those who helped build it along the way, have a lot to be proud of. I'll always place my family 1st, but if after my passing I'm allowed to scout over any geographical area for **'The Ultimate Manager'**, I'll request duty on these fields.

Ralph and Marian Simonds were among the early faithful supporters of our programs. Ralph coached the Jenkins little league team, and Marian, who for many years taught Sunday School along with my wife Helen, would often host barbecues for the kids and their parents.

Another of those who was consistently giving his time as a volunteer coach and overall supporter of youth programs was my older friend since childhood Gino Guasconi, who the town named the Legion Field recreational equipment building after. Gino was a ubiquitous presence around our programs. He was the epitome of good-humored support and set a prime example for other volunteers to follow. When he wasn't coaching or working behind the scenes, he was a loyal fan for the kids, from the little and biddy leagues, all the way through to the State Championships. You could always count on Gino to be there on his own time rooting the kids on. Like the building named in his honor, Gino's presence was sometimes unnoticed but it always served as a crucial mainstay for the youth and their recreation programs. It is pleasing and somehow fitting to see that his daughter Gina is now a key player on the Recreation Commission. While she continues Gino's tradition, she looks out from her work post at the new commission building on site over some of the same fields and facilities that were so graced by the presence of her Dad.

After his family, Gino's first and enduring love was coaching the Rexall Biddy League Basketball. Gino led this 'Dynasty' through generations of players. The kids loved to play for Gino. Gino was serious about having the kids learn to play well, and he was even more serious about making sure that they had good clean FUN!! His sometimes-serious visage could never mask the warm glow of his caring for kids. Dennis Ferioli, Dave Santilli & 2-yr. old James Folloni cheer Rexall on to another championship.

Gino Guasconi

LOOKING BACK
Post Game Post Mortem

Now as I look back to that day 53 years ago that I spent daydreaming in my little cubbyhole office in Dighton, I beam all over when I see how much we have progressed and grown with our Recreation Programs for the youngsters in Bridgewater. I realize that there are many things that we still need, but I know that it is now in the capable hands of a new generation of public servants like Gina Guasconi, Tommy Arrighi, Charlie Simmons, George Rogers, Angelo Mattie and Jim Campbell from the 2003 Town Recreation Commission. I understand that the Legion Field is now not only one of the largest and nicest facilities in the state, but that it is also the most utilized! The work done by the sporting generation that succeeded mine in town completely thrills me!

What did we oldtimers accomplish and set the foundation for? Well I can demonstrate a few of the concrete results of our programs by looking at the accomplishments of the youngsters who have benefited from them. So many of those went on to very successful careers in business, law, medicine, agriculture, public service and other worthy vocations. Many of them have come back and thanked me for the many happy memories of their childhood spent on the playgrounds and gyms in Bridgewater. League or State champions or not, thousands have become good sports in life and great citizens due in part to the influence of our athletic programs.

One of the more immediate concrete results of our programs was the winning of the State Championships by our High School Basketball Teams 1956, 1960, and 1961.

Our High School Baseball teams have had more than their share of success over the years, winning the State Championship in the '70's, and being top contenders for many years in between. And we've sent more than our share of Little Leaguers off to the Major Leagues, including Glen Tufts, Richard Dubee, George Stanley, Sam Leclair and Brian Warren. Mickey Pina played at BRRHS before joining the Boston Red Sox.

There have been many other noteworthy accomplishments of the local High School Teams over the years, such as the Girls State Champion Basketball Team (25 - 0) in 1990. Under the tutelage of 400 game winner Coach Gerry Cunniff BR's girl's hoopers are perennially dominant. The Boys Basketball Teams have recently made resurgence to their prominence of the late '50's-60's era, *and then some*. Many of our Boys and Girls Soccer teams have gone on to high rankings in State play. Joan Cassabian, our field hockey director, has been named state coach of the year as a result of her team's performances. Bunky Holmes is a state and national Hall of Famer for the amazing exploits of his wrestling teams.

The Football program, after a relatively slow start in the '60's & part of the '70's, has now come back to reach and perhaps surpass the heights of the other sports. Under the superb direction of Coach Danny Buron, Bridgewater-Raynham has had a few undefeated years. We won the league championship six out of seven at a stretch and made many trips to the State Super Bowl Game, several of which we won. Coach Buron has created a true dynasty. Big Marc Columbo, who starred on BR's football and basketball teams, went on to shine at BC and from there was drafted in the first round by the Chicago Bears where he started at offensive tackle as a rookie. Marc has excellent potential to become an NFL great. Marc, the son of Ed Columbo, Gayle McCann and stepson of Steve Arrighi, is also related to Alie Columbo, Rocky Marciano's brother in law and fight manager. Marc's cousin Steve Marciano also starred in college football in Boston.

Not only have we been dominant in the team sports but we have done very well in individual competitions as well, including Kevin Flynn the State Golf Champion in l983. As detailed earlier, Larry Folloni Jr. was one of the elite high school golfers in New England. Lee Beane was a 2 time state wrestling champ, a 2 time New England Champ, and was 6th in High School Nationals! Toby Wyman was a state champ, as was Neil Zonferelli. Our cross country running teams have often excelled winning many league championships under coach Larry Tufts, and several of the individual runners, including the late Keith Deane and my son Michael set many still standing course records all around the south shore.

B-R soccer whiz Philip Sheridan is ranked 6th ***ALL TIME NATIONALLY*** for scoring 176 during his high school career (1983-1986). Coach George Pacheco certainly had something to do with Phillip tallying this astounding record.

Chrissy Hall, who went on to play at Yale, was the career field hockey assists leader at Bridgewater-Raynham High School and was a two-time league all-star. She took part in the 2000 Bay State Games and the 1999 Junior Olympics.

These highlights of course are just the tip of a very substantial iceberg in Bridgewater of which we are very proud indeed. However, I personally feel the greatest accomplishments of our programs can be seen daily during the playground seasons as the youngsters come and go year after year, enjoying themselves at the many activities still offered to them.

From what I understand, all of the fields and courts at Legion Field are filled to the maximum, all weather permitting days. Folks who have seen our Recreation Program and others around the state and country (and world) say that ours is in the very top echelon. And many of those who made and keep it that way are people who had been involved as players and/or parents and/or volunteers in our programs over the years. And the newcomers in town who are so admirably competing came to our town because of it's great historical heritage and quality of life, of which our athletic and recreation legacies play a not insignificant part.

It is my sincere wish that this program will continue to grow and flourish in the years ahead. The youngsters are with us for such a short time. Isn't it appropriate that we should give them the opportunity to grow up with happy times to remember their childhood days? By keeping them off the streets and keeping their minds and bodies clean and healthy we are helping them to mature to become good citizens. And maybe we'll help to keep them off of drugs or other bad habits that youngsters can very easily get into in their growing years, especially during these risky times.

*"Victory has a hundred fathers,
But defeat is an orphan."*
-Galeazzo Pavese (Mussolini's son-in law, executed in 1943)

Note to Readers:

Please see the "1ˢᵗ Overtime" "Coaching" Chapter and the "2ⁿᵈ Overtime" "Archives" Chapter for a far more detailed review of Bridgewater and Bridgewater Raynham team and individual achievements over the 20ᵗʰ Century.

BUMPY ROAD TO SUCCESS IN BRIDGEWATER
No Pain No Gain

All was not always rosy with my career in Bridgewater indeed, like with most successful people, I encountered somewhat of a Bumpy Road along the Way. My difficulties started right from when I first applied for the position of Director of Physical Education and Athletics at the new High School. Since I was leaving my job in Dighton as of June of 1950 and the new High School would not be completed until September of 1951, it meant that in addition to returning to BU for graduate studies, I would have to find some interim employment to support my family. Fortunately, due in large part to Jim Buckley and Maurice Walsh of the School Committee, a temporary position was created for me in the elementary schools for that one year. I am forever grateful to these two gentlemen for how much they did for me then and during every other major hurdle along the way as my career progressed. 'My Way' would have been far different if it hadn't have been for *'THEIR CARING & LOVING WAY'.*

The struggle to land me the position as Director of Athletics and Physical Education was, I found out, not an easy one. Unbeknown to me, the Superintendent at the time had promised the position to the football coach. There was an in-house battle for several months between the Superintendent and the School Committee on their way to their final decision to hire me.

Jim Buckley and Maurice Walsh eventually convinced the other members of the School Committee to vote to give me the job. The vote was not unanimous, but it was 4 to 2 in my favor. One of the votes against me came from a member, who was a renowned 'YES MAN' for everything that the Superintendent would propose, regardless of merit. The other came from Committeeman George Durgin, who was one of my math professors at the State College.

Later, to his credit, George revealed to me why I didn't get his vote. He explained that he did not want to subject me to the criticism that he was sure would come from over-exuberant sports fans whenever the Teams did not win. His quote was: "Larry, I think too much of you to expose you to the type of criticism you'll be subjected to, win or lose. Even Jesus was not well received as an adult in his hometown. Naturally your home townspeople will never appreciate anything that you accomplish no matter how successful you are." (How prophetic he was with regard to some townsfolk, but thankfully, how wrong he was with regard to so many more!) Even though Professor Durgin did not vote for me, I really admire him for his honesty and his somewhat accurate predictions, which often haunted me throughout my career in Bridgewater.

The decisive third vote that insured my election to my position came from a totally unexpected source: Mrs. Alice Holmes. Her maiden name was Alice McLoed, remember her? She was the former Junior High School teacher who had trouble in keeping discipline in her classroom during her 1st professional years. She went on to become a highly respected educator and public servant, eventually working on the school board to make so many decisions that had such a great impact on the future of children from our town! Jim Buckley and Maurice Walsh somehow managed to convince her that I was the man for the position. Maybe it also helped that I was not counted among the kids who had tormented her during her rookie year as a teacher!

*"Be careful how you treat people on the way up,
you're likely to meet them again on the way down."*
- Jimmy Durante, Comedian

I have a feeling too, that one of the factors in her decision making came from her past relationship with my older brother Al, who she taught in Junior High School. Al was really a knowledgeable and bright guy in the business field in which he was to become a huge success later in life. As bright as he was, however, for some reason he was only an average 'C' student in school. Miss McLoed, nonetheless, somehow recognized his talents and consistently encouraged him to develop them.

When Al later made it big in Real Estate in the Big Apple, he remembered this teacher who believed in him even though his grades were low. He sent Miss Alice McLoed a nice letter thanking her for her kind assistance during his school days and he offered to set up a scholarship in her name. This award was to go to a student who had low to average grades, but who showed some future potential in any particular chosen field.

The fourth vote in my favor came from Gordon Hall; a member of the Lions Club who had been instrumental in helping me to get the Recreation Program started. I can recall vividly a conversation that cropped up between us while the school committee was thrashing about my job status. Gordon and I were both members of the Town Bowling League, and following a match one cold winter night, he offered me a ride home.

On the way home we discussed the future possibilities of the changes in the Athletic Programs that I had proposed if I were to get the job. The topic of Basketball Tournaments came up and Gordon said to me. "As long as we have our present coach we will never get to any State Tournaments. He is a nice guy but he has no knowledge of the modern game." I didn't want to be disparaging about any former coach, but I do remember saying to Gordon that if I were to be fortunate enough to get the Basketball Coaching job, I predicted that I would have the Basketball Team in the Boston Garden in 5 years. I was close; we made it in 4!

Although Gordon Hall would cast a crucial vote to decide whether or not I'd get my dream job in Bridgewater, I definitely didn't compromise my integrity and try to 'suck-up to him by letting him beat me or my team in bowling!

The 1950 Metro Bowl Champs: Fred Reed, Nido Cassani, Mike Folloni, Larry Folloni, Bo Ferioli and Bo Abati

Well even though we won the first battle in my being hired, the War was still ahead of us, with many turbulent years ahead. Per plan, my transition period for the 1950-51 year involved going to classes at Boston University. Schooling was intermingled with part time hourly work with the Elementary and Junior High School children. Since, however, the new school building was not completed on time, I was faced with another year delay. Whereas I was hired by the town for the 1951-52 school year, it meant that starting then, I had to continue to work, but fulltime, at the Elementary and Junior High Schools. At first I was very disappointed at the delay, *but I quickly forgot about the apparent misfortune and decided to make the best of it.*

Even though we had no facilities to work with, it proved to be a very fruitful year in preparing me to plan my work for the future. Our facilities consisted of empty classrooms and hallways and in some cases the assembly hall at the Junior High School. I still recall having to move the chairs in the assembly hall to make room for our Physical Education classes. I also heard the complaints from the teachers who said we were making too much noise that interfered with their classroom teaching. I could well empathize with their feelings and we tried to keep the noise level down with quiet, yet still vigorous activities. Try to be successful at that trick with pre-teens without rapidly becoming *an enthusiastic leader with strict disciplinary tendencies!*

It was also quite an experience to go back to the Schools to train and supervise the classroom teachers on how to conduct Physical Education Activities. Part of my job was to prepare them so that they could conduct their PE classes on their own starting the next year when I would be at the new High School. One of those who I taught then was Mrs. Hart (Collins) who was my teacher when I attended the McElwain School as a youngster! Experiences like this helped to remind me that my career was really on the move, that it was then my turn, and that I'd better make the most of it. Of course I also had to do good because I still didn't want to get scolded in front of *my students* by my 6th grade teacher!

One other benefit from this start later bore fruit with our State Championship Basketball Teams in the 50's. I had basketball hoops installed outside at all the schools. I can still recall the youngsters who were to become the nuclei of our Championship Teams, including Paul Pallatroni (who passed away in January, 2003) Mikey Crowley, Dave Messaline, Connie Thibeault, Willie Ferioli (who was later to become Chief of Police in our town), and many other promising youngsters. That early interest that we created with the new Basketball and Baseball Youth Programs was to carry on throughout my teaching and coaching career in Bridgewater. This was the start of our multi-sport 'Farm System' that became the envy of schools throughout the State.

"When life gives you lemons, make lemonade."

Or

"I can hardly wait to see what good comes of this!"
—Star Mohle, inventor & artist

OPENING OF THE NEW SCHOOL IN BRIDGEWATER
Start of a New Season

Finally the Big Day of the opening of our new High School arrived in September of 1952. Also arriving on September 4, 1952, was my third son Michael. As was often the case, I was busy at school and away from Helen's side for the important family moment. No sooner had I returned to work at 8:30 am after dropping Helen at the hospital, than I was called back to greet this mighty mite. Then of course, it was right back to work to support him, his brothers and his mom.

Bridgewater High School was the first built-for-purpose modern school building in the town. It was located adjacent to the top-grade outdoors Athletic Facilities of Legion Field. The new building had a beautiful large gym, the first ever in the public schools of Bridgewater. It also had a nice auditorium and a complete shop for vocational students. Additionally it boasted a new cafeteria to serve hot lunches, excellent teaching facilities, science and language labs and a nice library.

Along with the great new facilities we had new teaching and administrative staffs. Most of the teachers from the old Junior and Senior High Schools came over to our new school. Mr. Winston Keck, who was recruited from the Boston University School of Education, headed the new administrative staff. Mr. John McGovern, who was the principal at the old Junior High School, became the Assistant Principal. When Mr. Keck left a few years later, Mr. McGovern took over as our Headmaster. He proved to be a very popular and capable administrator who brought back the morale of what was by then a somewhat demoralized teaching staff. Mr. McGovern was a kind individual who was well liked by all. His primary concern was always for the best interest of the teachers and the students. He treated all with respect and dignity, and is one the superiors who I most respected and admired. Mr. McGovern left a couple of years later to take a position with the Massachusetts Department of Education. His departure left a big void in our staff, and faculty and students alike sorely missed him. Following his departure Mr. Herbert DeVeber took over as our Principal for four years and Mr. Paul Zdanowicz followed him.

Mr. Meredith Williams, the principal at the old High School, came down to the new school as a teacher to finish off an illustrious career in education. This new school was later to be named in his honor for his many years of dedicated and capable service to the community. Mr. Williams was the principal at the old High School when I was a student back in the middle 1930's.

Perhaps the greatest shakeup of all came in the Athletic Department that I was to head up. We hired Henry "Hank" Woronicz to be the new Head Football Coach. I served as his assistant for a year to help get our new football program started. I also became the new Head Basketball Coach, with Bernie Chestna as my assistant. Billy Sullivan became our Freshman Coach in both Football and Basketball. Coach Sullivan later became the Superintendent of Schools in our neighboring town of Raynham.

Larry Folloni, Billy Sullivan, Henry Worinicz, Charley Varney and Moe Rucker. 1952 Coaches.

In Baseball, the only carry over was Mr. Lester Lane, the veteran coach of all sports for about 25 years. Mr. Knute Anderson, a former Basketball Coach, coached the Track Teams. In addition to teaching Physical Education and being the Cheerleader Advisor, Miss Dorothy Moore took over the coaching of all girls' sports.

All in all, it was a great staff and we got right off to a great start in Football. After going through a string of 22 straight losses in the previous three seasons with the old regime, we managed to drum up some great school spirit and citizen fan support and began the new era with three straight wins. I can still recall the great rally that I organized to start our new athletic program off.

The night before our first game we had a great parade, replete with floats and fire engines blaring proudly through downtown, around the common, and ending up at the Legion Field for a pep rally.

The pep rally at Legion field was full of enthusiasm and we capped the festivities off with a huge bonfire. This was the first of many annual bonfires that we held over the next 35 years, until pollution and safety issues drew that memorable town tradition to a close.

Our first game was against a heavily favored Plymouth High School. I'll never forget the joy and happiness that rang out from the players and the student body after we, the underdogs, defeated them to break our school's long losing streak. We ended up our first year with the first winning football season in several years. Having successfully completed our first hurdle, it was then time for me to venture into my new career as the Head Coach of the Basketball Team.

On the last football game of the year, Eddie Denton, our star quarterback and the captain and leading scorer on our basketball team, suffered a torn ligament in his knee. Needless to say this was a severe blow to our hopes for a successful year in basketball. Eddie courageously tried to come back late in the season to play the last few games of that losing year. Push himself as he might, he hobbled around on one leg and just couldn't come up to the form of his previous years. What was left of the team of seniors without Eddie Denton was not enough to compete with the other teams on our schedule. (Hard working and doggedly determined Eddie, my first captain, later became my boss as the Superintendent at the Bridgewater-Raynham Regional School.)

The remaining Seniors tried hard at first to adapt to a new system but they really didn't have the basic fundamentals or the ability to carry on the load without Eddie to lead them. I had made up my mind soon after the start of the season that without Denton; it was going to be a hopeless year. So I therefore decided to concentrate on the underclassmen to teach them the fundamentals that would be needed to implement my style of Fast Breaking and Pressing Defense.

As the losing year went on I could sense the players harboring the resentment that I was spending more and more time developing my underclassmen. A few of the players quit the team and of course they tried to spread the venom around to the other players and the student body. They succeeded to some degree, and as a result I wasn't the most popular teacher or coach in their minds at this time. *I was too strict and demanded too much from my students and athletes without enough immediately tangible results for their taste.* At least that was their perception at the time. *Many years later some of these same athletes and students came back to me and thanked me for being so tough with them, saying that it was the best preparation that they had in the transition to the work ethic required in the real world.*

I am very grateful to the few players who stuck it out and struggled through this disastrous season. It was players like Eddie Denton, Ted Gilmartin, John Scheffler, Skippy Poole, and Bobby Seaver who were to be the catalysts of the teams to come.

Some of our 2 & 3 sport players from '52-53 during football season.
l. Coach Woronicz & Varsity stars Skip Poole & John Scheffler
r. Coach Sullivan & Frosh

We went through that losing basketball season (1952-53) in my rebuilding program with high hopes for the future. That first year we won about 5 games and we earned a lot of hoots from the fans.

'53 Coaching Staffs included Billy Sullivan Henry Worinicz, Moe Rucker, Larry Folloni, and Charley Varney (left)
And Dot Moore and Bernie Chestna (right)

The second year (1953-54) we were up to a 500% record. with the help of Captain Bob Seaver (left and far right), Skip Poole and John Scheffler

The third year (1954-55), with a 10 and 4 record, we qualified for the State Tournament for the first time in the School's History. The fourth year, 1956, we had a record of 20 and 3, the best ever for a Bridgewater High School Team. Oh, and did I mention that we won the State Championship at the Boston Garden? And that we then followed that up with a repeat State Championship in 1960 and another in 1961?

For High School teams that have played in the Boston Garden more than one year, we have the honored distinction of being the only one that never lost a game there. In fact we were probably the only team at any level to go undefeated over a whole group of playoff games. Our 1956 team scored a record 92 points in the semifinal game at the Boston Garden against Newburyport. These records are still intact, and now that the Old Boston Garden has been torn down and replaced by the Fleet Center, for that hallowed hall, these records will stand forever.

RELIVING THOSE CHAMPIONSHIP TOURNAMENT TEAMS
Glory Days

I guess that the best way to relive those championship years would be to take a look at the clippings from the scrapbook that my lovely wife Helen had compiled during those happy times. I will start with the 1954-55 Basketball Teams, because they were the basis of our Championship Team of 1956.

Actually the real start was the rebuilding process that I had started earlier with the 1953-54 teams. Those were the crucial years when I spent the time with the underclassmen to teach them the fundamentals of the Fast Break and the Pressing Defense that was to be the key to our future success.

It was a slow and tedious teaching process, but as time went on the players began to grasp the system that I was trying so hard to convey to them. With each day I could see the improvement and the growing confidence in all of the players. The more the success, the greater their self-assuredness.

I think the turning point came during a game against Cohasset early in the 1954-55 season. We got off to a horrible start and found ourselves down at the end of the first period by a score of 29 to 4. In between periods I tried to calm them down and told them that I wanted them to go into the original "Folloni Press" also known as the "Special Press".

They went out on the floor and started the second period like possessed demons. The Cohasset players were completely surprised, quickly becoming befuddled and disorganized by our Press. Before the end of the second period we had caught them and we soon went ahead to lead at half time. We kept the pressure on them the rest of the game and went on to win handily. From that day on whenever I yelled out "Special!" they knew what to do and it all became gravy!

The 1955 team that qualified for the State Tournament at 10-4, lost out in the first round of the Playoffs to a veteran Hanover Team. The Tournament experience that we gathered, however, was to be invaluable to the success of the Championship Team which was to come a year later.

Our Season didn't end with the Tourney loss in 1955. In those days there were very few restrictions on time allotted for Sports Seasons. (The MIAA would later adopt strict time limits for each Sport Season.) After being eliminated from the Tournament in late February, we still had the whole month of March when the weather in New England was still not very conducive to outdoor Spring Sports. I dreamed up the novel idea to have a Post Season Tournament for our returning underclassmen to give them added experience for the next year.

I called my friend, Al Farley, the Basketball Coach at Middleboro High School, and explained my idea to him. He was very enthusiastic about the plan, so we set up the dates for a two out of three series. We gave the Tourney the name of "Award Bowl Tournament". I also contacted my good friend Jim Goldrick, of the Pierce Hardware Company for help, and he donated the huge trophy that was to be awarded to the winner. The first team to win the Tourney for three years would retire the trophy.

Since neighboring Middleboro was a natural rival, we packed the gyms for all of the games, with the money we raised going to a scholarship for one of our worthy athletes. As added attractions, we had our freshman teams play one of the preliminary games, and the other involved only the senior boys of both schools. In another short novelty preliminary game, the boys playing with boxing gloves, competed against the girls teams.

Faculty games and student faculty games were other enduring fun and spirit building traditions that we initiated. The money we raised with our wide variety of 'non-tradtional' events helped with school programs and scholarship funds. In terms of creativity, promotions and moving towards equality of access by the sexes, we were way ahead of Bobby Riggs and Billie Jean King! Winning ways are fun!

We won the first leg of the 'Award Bowl' trophy by winning two straight games. In the first game we defeated them on our home court by a score of 61 to 37. We won the second game at Middleboro by a much closer score of 78 to 63.

All in all it was a very successful promotion. We raised a good sum of money for a very worthy scholarship. We kept the students and athletes occupied for another two weeks in early March before starting their Spring Sports Season. We raised community spirit and backing for the aspiring champs and we began to showcase girls sports both as entertainment as well as for plain healthy and fun competition. And of most importance, our basketball players gained the experience that was to be so valuable to us in the upcoming Championship year.

ON TO THE 1956 CHAMPIONSHIP YEAR
One for the Books

With the start of a New Year we were looking forward to the stiff competition ahead. The perennial Mayflower League champs, East Bridgewater, having lost only one player from the previous year's championship team, was coming back looking for a repeat with their veterans. Avon was also loaded with a veteran team.

We were the underdogs going in to start that season, especially since we had lost 5 players to graduation. We would miss our captain, Herman Fries, along with Eddie Dziergowski, Phil Prophett, Art Noles, and Richie Clark. On the plus side, we were returning a real good crop of players who had gained the experience of Tournament play from the previous year. They now had three years of drilling on our Fast Breaking Offense and the "Folloni Pressing Defense". Despite the tough opposition that Easties and Avon would provide, we had high hopes of winning the Mayflower League title and a repeat performance to qualify for the State Tournament and hopefully more...

We started the season with two small backcourt men. Lou Filippetti and Don Pittsley, who each stood all of 5 foot 7 inches, but they were both talented playmakers and good shooters. Filippetti was the leading scorer on the previous year's team. He had the knack of being in the right place at the right time. He was excellent on our pressing defense and good at driving to the basket at the slightest opening. *(Remember it was his mother Virginia who so deftly demonstrated that being shy of approach never got one to the goal!)* Don Pittsley was also great on our pressing game and an excellent outside shooter. His value to us would have been even greater if they had the 3-point rule in at that time.

At the forward positions we had Stan Smudin and Ronnie Hogg. Stan Smudin at 6'3" was the tallest player on our relatively small team. Stan was the Johnny-come-lately who had never played basketball prior to his Junior Year. I recruited him out of one of our Physical Education Classes. I saw the potential in him and since we needed some height I instructed our J.V. Coach, Bernie Chestna to utilize him heavily on the J.V. team to help him gather the experience needed to help us out in his Senior year. Coach Chestna did an excellent job in bringing him along, as Stan was invaluable to us in our Championship year. (Stan later took over his Dad's grocery business and did very well with it.) Recently at our 42nd Reunion, Stan thanked me for inviting him out to play on the Team, telling me that his experiences on the Basketball court were of great help to him in carrying on his business and community duties.

Ronnie Hogg at the other forward was probably one of the greatest 3-sport players ever to come out of Bridgewater. In my mind he ranks up there with Mickey Cochrane, the Major League Hall of Famer, and John "Az" Spirida who played for the Washington Redskins professional football team. Hogg at only 5'-11", had great reflexes; was an excellent rebounder, had great speed and was excellent at stealing off the dribble and interceptions in our pressing defense. The fact that Ronnie was raised on a farm, doing all the attendant chores, was definitely an asset to him in developing his excellent physical body and concentration skills. Nowadays the athletes have to go to the weight rooms and mind-focussing gurus to gain similar results.

Ronnie suffered an injury late in the season and his loss down the stretch cost us a chance to win the League Title. Thankfully Ronnie did manage to come back for the final two Championship games at the Boston Garden and was very instrumental in our glorious victories there.

Ronnie went on to play professional baseball. He rose all the way to Triple A Ball before an injury ended his career. He then took over his Dad's Farm business in a very successful tenure. He recently sold the Farmstead to the town of Bridgewater and has retired to Florida. The town is now building a state of the art Police Station and other offices on this site.

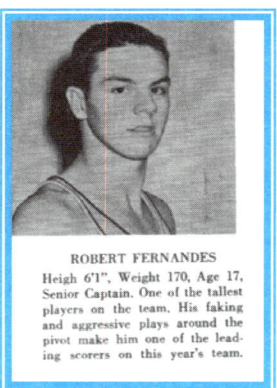

Coach Folloni

The center spot went to our Captain Bob Fernandes, who proved to be a great leader for our Champs. Bob at 6'2" was very rugged and held his own against many much taller opponents throughout the season. At our 42nd reunion in 1998, Bob thanked me for my help in developing his abilities that led to his very successful career as a State Trooper. Bob became the stepfather to and a primary developer of the baseball skills of Glenn Tufts, who sportswriters proclaimed to be the greatest natural country hitter available in the draft since Ted Williams!

As a high school senior in 1973 Glenn picked up on his step-dad's champion ways and was drafted 3rd in the nation for that year's Major League Baseball class. (Robin Yount was drafted 1st out of college that year.) Only a tragically debilitating car accident while he was prepping for the majors kept him from eventually becoming a major league all-star. Peter Gammons said that one of the longest homeruns that he had ever seen at any level of play, was a blast hit by Glenn in the State High School Tourney.

We were also very fortunate to pick up Dick Cornwall, *(pictured at left,)* a 5'9", a transfer from Randolph. After Ronnie Hogg suffered his injury, Dick filled in very nicely in his spot as an excellent outside shooter. The other players who filled in at very opportune times included juniors James Buckley, Peter Flynn and Donald Strong, and Sophomores, Melvin Crest, Peter DeVeber and Tony Ghelfi. All of the players on this team went on to very successful careers in their chosen fields.

State Champions
Lou Filippetti 31,
Ronnie Hogg 12,
Bob Fernandez 34,
Stan Smuden 32,
Don Pittsley 13
Herbert DeVeber
Coach Joe Lazaro
Faclty Mo Rucker
Dick Cornwall 41
Tony Ghelfi 15

Coach C. Varney
Coach L. Folloni
Jim Buckley 43
Peter Flynn 51
Donnie Strong 23

Peter DeVeber 14

Lou Filippetti was a very successful Insurance executive, rising up to vice-president of a very well known Insurance Company. Both he and Donnie Pittsley also went on to be very successful Sports Officials. Lou was recently elected to the prestigious position of President of the C.B.O.A (National Basketball Official's Organization). In April of 2003 the IAABO (International Basketball Official's Organization) awarded Lou with it's Life Member Dedicated Service Award.

Other players who went on to successful careers include Peter Flynn, who served in the State Legislature for many years then went on to serve several years as the Sheriff of Plymouth County and as head of the Plymouth County Correctional Institution before his eventual retirement to Cape Cod.

Peter's comments at our recent 42nd reunion are worthy of note. He stated that the work ethic that I stressed during our practice sessions that helped him achieve his success later in life. He recalled an incident during a practice session when he and Richard McFadden dove on to the floor to retrieve a loose ball. I blew the whistle to stop play and I immediately praised both of them for their aggressiveness. My message to the whole team was, "That's the way to go after the ball. That's the kind of aggressiveness and determination that wins ball games." *Such discipline and focused desire helped in no small way to lead Peter and many of my other charges to great success later in life.*

Donnie Strong has become a successful photographer/writer and has his own publishing firm. He has succeeded in spite of a long battle with Multiple Sclerosis. He showed a lot of courage in his battle against this disease and he credits his experiences on the basketball court in part for his comeback against heavy odds. Donnie went on from school to become a Vietnam-era Naval Aviator serving with carrier squadron "VAW-33" on board the U.S.S. "Wasp".

Tony Ghelfi and his lovely wife Rosalie (who as a freshman was a scorekeeper for the champs), established a pair of Home-Made Candy Stores on Cape Cod, and have nurtured a wonderful large family that now includes 4 grandchildren. Their son Michael is now a very successful golf pro, and Christopher is a star actor and athletic dancer on Broadway. Scott & his wife now help run the stores, and Sharon has been supportive in her attorney husband's career in radio broadcasting.

Jim Buckley, Jr. went on to become a policeman in our neighboring town of East Bridgewater.

Now back to the story of our Championship Team. We started the season off with a bang, winning our first four games. The winning streak came to an end on our fifth game when the veteran Avon team defeated us by a score of 64 to 58. This game showed us that we had more to do to become the best. We then redoubled our practice efforts, and vowed to improve on the little things that cost us our loss. We also realized that we could play with anyone, and that with a little improvement, we could prevail. We then went on a ten game winning streak, which included two wins over our archrivals East Bridgewater, the perennial champs and theretofore favorites to repeat as same.

Despite our redoubled efforts it was the Avon team that again broke our win streak when they defeated us handily on the next to last game of the season to end our hopes of winning the League Championship. We were at a great disadvantage in that game as Ronnie Hogg saw only limited action due to the knee injury that he suffered late in the season. Although we both won our last regular season games, Avon won the League title and we finished up as the runner-ups. The previous year's champ, East Bridgewater finished in third place.

It was then time for the annual South Shore Tourney. We defeated Holbrook in the first round and were matched up to play East Bridgewater in the Semifinal round. We had already defeated Easties twice during the regular season but the third time around proved disastrous. We were again without the services of Ronnie Hogg and the rest of the team had an off night as East Bridgewater belted us by a score of 65 to 46. We then defeated West Bridgewater 80 to 66 for the Consolation Title. East Bridgewater went on win the South Shore Tournament by defeating the Mayflower League regular season Champions Avon. Since we knew that when healthy and sharp that we could beat the Easties, and that they defeated Avon, we figured that if and when Hogg came back, we could finally overtake Avon in the upcoming State Tourney. If the Easties could finally figure them out, then we'd be ready for them too.

The power of positive thinking was definitely with us.

STATE TOURNAMENT TIME
Gut Check

When it came time for the State Tournament we were not in any way ready to lie down like sheep because of our earlier setbacks. *We believed that we could always improve, and we had long ago set our minds above all on the ultimate prize of the State Championship.* Just like I never scrimmaged to win, I saw in-season games as important too, but only preparatory for the STATE TITLE. It finally became time for us to 'bring it all together' to avenge our earlier disappointments in not winning the League Title or the South Shore Tournament. The State Tournament was the real goal for all teams and a successful trip to the Old Boston Garden was the ultimate goal of all schools. Bridgewater, along with Avon and East Bridgewater from our powerful regional league had qualified for the State Tournament.

In the first round we were paired against Oak Bluffs in a game played at the Wareham High School gym. We defeated them in a hard fought battle by a score of 67 to 63. The Oak Bluffs game was the toughest and closest game we were to experience in that State Tourney. Victory was clinched by a very key play made in the last few minutes by my 7th player, Donnie Strong, who made a great rebound and followed it with a great pass to Captain Bobby Fernandes who scored the decisive basket. Without that heads-up and heart-out play by Donnie we may never have advanced. One never knows where the essential help is going to come from in crunch time, so all players in the game of life should always be treated with respect.

East Bridgewater was paired off with Avon again in a first round game played at the Quincy High School Gym. The Easties again defeated Avon in a close game by a score of 60 to 57. They were coming on strong, but we knew that if we had to play them again, we had their number. In a way we were also relieved that Avon was out, and we'll never know how things might have transpired had they stayed in. I'm confident; however, that with this group of champions the third time against Avon would have been a charm for us.

In any case, we were then off to the Boston Garden for the semifinals. It was Bridgewater vs. Immaculate Conception of Newburyport and East Bridgewater vs. Wayland in the other bracket. Everyone was hoping for a rematch of Bridgewater and East Bridgewater for the State Championship. This was not to be. Both East Bridgewater and Bridgewater were the underdogs with Joe Morey's Easties given the best chance to make the finals. Newburyport was heavily favored to defeat Bridgewater.

Wayland defeated East Bridgewater in the first game by a score of 60 to 49. In a way this was fairly intimidating, but we couldn't dwell on that, because we had other business at hand. We were then the only team remaining from the South Shore area. Happily Ronnie Hogg returned for the first time in several games, and even though he was not fully recovered from his knee injury, our team was spurred on by his presence in the lineup. We went on to defeat the heavily favored Newburyport team by a Boston Garden Schoolboy team scoring record of 92 points to their 69.

The outstanding Fast Breaking play and our Special Pressing defense were the talk of the Garden and the Media. The comments from Coaches, Garden Personnel and News Media were all superlative accolades. One well known Sports writer stated that he had never seen a better High School team performance at the Garden.

It was then on to the Finals against Wayland. Once again we were the underdogs to the heavily favored Wayland team, led by 6 foot 1 inch Fred Tassinari; their high scoring all scholastic star. After our last outing, however, we were not intimidated by the entire advance hype about this star studded Wayland team. We had worked harder than hard, and we knew what it meant to succeed as an underdog. Besides, we had just dominated like no other in our previous game. We were on a righteous roll!

With a large following from Bridgewater in attendance we delivered an outstanding team performance. It was a good balanced attack with all of our starters scoring in double figures. *There was no individual star; it was a coach's dream of a team effort.* Don Pittsley and Dick Cornwall hit some key outside shots to bring the Wayland zone defense out, which opened up the middle for Lou Filippetti to score many spectacular driving lay-up shots. Assistant Coach Joe Lazaro had always trained the boys to penetrate as far as possible with the intent to score. but that if the defense converged and that goal was not likely, to turn and pass back out to or dish off to the side to what would have to be the open man. This technique also made for some critical scores.

Our two big guys, Stan Smudin and Captain Bob Fernandes were immense on both ends of the court, controlling both offensive and defensive rebounds. Ronnie Hogg, our injured hero came through late in the game with some driving lay-up shots to help put the game on ice, before he had to put more ice on his swollen knee.

As good as our Semifinal victory over Newburyport was, our team played equally as well against the very talented Wayland team (even though we didn't match the point total). Our Fast Breaking Offense and our Full Court Special Press broke their backs. It was a well-deserved State Championship for a gang of kids who never gave up. Even after key injuries and 3 losses during the season, they came back and worked extremely hard to earn this State Championship. I am real proud of all of them from the starting five on to all the reserves, whose dedication and work throughout our practices during the season enabled the starting players to go on to this Championship. Our overall tally of 20 wins and 3 losses was the best ever record in the history of Bridgewater High School, and this was to be our First of Three State Championships over a span of 5 years.

Our big little men Lou Filippetti and Don Pittsley on the Shoulders of Giants Boston Garden, 1956

1956 State Championship Team

Left to right: Don Pittsley, Capt. Bob Fernandes, Stan Smudin, Ronnie Hogg, Larry Folloni Jr., Coach Folloni, Mascot Robert Folloni, Dick Cornwall, Don Strong, Asst. Coach Bernie Chestna, Lou Filippetti, Fac.Mgr. Maurice Rucker, Asst. Coach Joe Lazaro, Melvin Crest. Others on Championship team not in view: Jimmy Buckley, Peter Flynn, Pete Deveber and Tony Ghelfi.

Coach Folloni, and son Bobby, carried off Boston Garden Floor by jubilant players following triumph over Wayland for State Championship in 1956.

1956 State Championship Hoop Team 42nd Reunion 1998

BUILDING OF THE NEXT TWO STATE CHAMPIONS
Vital Rebuilding Years

THE 1957 TEAM

With one State Championship under our belts it was time to begin to rebuild for another. With the loss through graduation of practically the entire team, we had a tough job ahead to excel in our highly competitive league. Of the returning players the only real bright star was Dick Cornwall, our fill-in replacement for the injured Ronnie Hogg on the '56 Championship Team. He along with Donnie Strong, an excellent rebounder at about 6'1", constituted the backbone of this team. The rest of the players were real good kids and athletes, but of mediocre caliber compared to what we would be facing from our tough League opponents.

In spite of the fact that they were over-matched in ability and size by the likes of the veteran East and West Bridgewater teams, this 1957 team exceeded my expectations and came up with another winning season, once again qualifying for State Tournament play. We ended up with ten wins against five losses during regular season play. The scrappy and aggressive players on this team included Francis 'Slugger' McFadden, Peter DeVeber, Melvin Crest, Ray Gomm, Pete Flynn, Jim Buckley, Tony Ghelfi, 'Skipper' Doyle, Donnie Strong and the Captain, Dickie Cornwell. In the 'Archives' section of this book I'll share Donnie Strong's write-up about the grittiness and determination of this team in a great comeback attempt against the then mighty Holbrook squad.

THE 1958 TEAM

With the exodus of all of the remaining players from the 1956 and 1957 winning teams, it was rebuilding time again. I was left with another tough decision. Should I go with the reserves left over from the 1957 team, or with the talented incoming underclassmen that had been developed through our Biddy League Farm System?

Being the soft hearted and sentimental guy that I was, (even though most thought I was just grumpy and mean), I chose to go with the returning upperclassmen players who were the subs from the 1957 team. We went through a mediocre season, with an average team in our tough League competition, and failed to qualify for the State Tournament for the first time since 1955. Throughout the season, nonetheless, whenever the occasion would present itself, I would devote much of my time to developing our talented underclassmen, teaching them our innovative Fast Break and Pressing fundamentals.

The players on the 1958 team included Seniors Peter DeVeber and Tony Ghelfi as Captains, along with Melvin Crest and Francis McFadden. The Juniors were Armand Bena, Bobby Ghelfi, Richard Carter and Dave Krukonis. Sophomore Michael Crowley rounded out the group.

THE CORNERSTONE 1958 & 1959 TEAMS
Unsung Heroes

Then came the 1959 season. The Freshman Teams of the previous 1957 and 1958 teams both had undefeated seasons. And Mikey Crowley, who was a real good prospect as a Sophomore, was now as a Junior ready to make his move with the Varsity. I had another tough decision to make. Should I go with the returning J.V.'s or with Mikey Crowley and the talented Freshmen and Sophomores? Once again being the sentimentalist that I am, I chose to start the season with the Juniors and Seniors. I went with the Senior group for the early part of the 1959 season and of course we had our share of bumps.

I tried to work in my talented underclassmen as much as possible to give them varsity game experience. By the middle of the year it was quite obvious to everyone that the underclassmen were much superior to the Junior / Senior group. As I increased the playing time of the underclassmen during the second half of the season, I could once again sense the resentment of some of the upperclassmen players. Like in my first year, a couple of them quit the team. The rest of them, to their credit, hung on for the balance of the year.

It was from this group of Upperclassmen players who hung on when the going got tough, along with several spirited upper and underclassmen subs from the subsequent year, who taught me one of the greatest lessons of my coaching career. They were the ones who I credit for the refining of the "Folloni Special Press". My experience with them led to the solidification of my dedication to full development and utilization of this technique, which had befuddled our opponents in the past, and which was to raise havoc with them for many years to come. I had some good pressing teams in the past, but what I learned from these kids made me look like a genius.

Let me explain. One day, my talented underclassmen, who were the starters in the last half of 1959 and onto the 1960 Championship team, were scrimmaging against the 2nd squad, consisting largely of our demoted upperclassmen from both years. Well these 2nd teamers, who didn't have anywhere near the talent of my 1st team players, were doing a great defensive job against my starters. It got so bad that I called off practice early that day. Now I'm sure that there was some noble elder pride from the Seniors and some assertiveness to show they belonged. Or maybe they and the non-starter underclassmen just wanted to show the Coach that he made a mistake. I think mostly however, that they sensed that we had something special growing, and they wanted to give their all to making the TEAM as strong as possible. In any case the impact of their *will-based* extemporaneous clobbering of their younger prodigies has created a real legacy.

That night after practice I went home and mulled over what had happened. Here were these scrubs playing helter-skelter, swarming all over the ball and my starters just couldn't move it up the court. I kept saying to myself, if these guys could do this to my more talented players, then why can't my top players do the same and more to our opponents? I watched and gleaned a valuable lesson. *"You can learn from anyone, if you can humble yourself to appreciate meaningful contributions as they arise!"* I stayed up into the early morning hours, and devised some drills that would incorporate and systematize what I witnessed that day. *Thus was born the 'Folloni Special Press'* The *'Special'* came from the heart and soul of those who inspired it. Before then we had the 'Folloni Press' and the 'Special', but these guys helped bring it all together. Most memorably among them were: Gordon Ross, Roy Litzen, Charlie Devine, John Ferrari and Mickey Flammia.

I am very grateful to these real nice kids who hung on in spite of the fact that they were upperclassmen who had lost their starting roles to my super-talented underclassmen. Without their efforts my signature 'Folloni Special Press' would never have been born. Just who were these players from the classes of '59 & '60 that inspired this lesson and the enormous contribution to BHS and BRRHS basketball? As I remember the Varsity and Jayvees that year included: *1959 Senior Co-Captains Bobby Ghelfi, Bobby Bumpus, Armand Bena, Richard Carter, David Krukonis, Robert Bishop, Doug Bromley and Edmund Burke. Juniors Michael Crowley and Michael Flammia along with Sophomores Shawn Burke, Dave Messaline, Paul Pallatroni, and Steve Pivacek, with Freshman Steve Prophett completed the varsity. 1960 Captain Mike Crowley, Charlie Devine, Roy Litzen, Gordon Ross, Juniors Shaun Burke, Dave Messaline, Paul Pallatroni, Steve Pivacek, John Ferrari, Michael Flammia, Sophomores Steve Prophett and Artie Hoke and Freshmen Charlie Costa & Larry Folloni Jr. completed this squad. My best ever Student Manager Chris Lee was an integral part of both teams.* To this day, the 2nd teamers probably don't even realize how much they contributed to the future successes of BHS and BRRHS on the court. *Men, we thank you.*

Junior Mikey Crowley of the 1959 Team, Captain of the 1960 squad

Our 1959 team went through a bit better than mediocre season as I expected. The one highlight came about in the South Shore Tourney when we nearly pulled a great upset. We barely qualified for the tournament and were bracketed to play the number 1 seed, Norwell. Since I knew that we could not match their talented

League Title winning players, I tried an innovative approach that was contrary to my basic philosophy of a fast breaking and pressing game. We totally surprised everyone by playing a game of keep away! We held the ball as long as we could on each possession to keep the score down and hoped for a few breaks to keep the game close. We succeeded in slowing down the game and our ball holding tactics frustrated Norwell to where we nearly pulled the upset of the year. We lost the game by a 22 to 20 score. That was probably the lowest scoring game of the last 20 years. (Back in 1937 when I played against Attleboro in the South Shore Tourney finals we lost to them by a 24 to 22 score.)

As Mohammed Ali would later bring to an art form, we were prepared to implement **'whatever it took within the rules'** *to get the 'W'.*

THE 1960 STATE CHAMPIONSHIP TEAM
Two for the Looks

FRONT ROW: Larry Folloni (Coach), Paul Pallatroni (24), Steve Pivacek (32), Mike Crowley (15 Captain), Steve Prophett (21), Dave Messaline (25), Shawn Burke (51). SECOND ROW: Larry Folloni, Jr., (13), John Ferrari (14), Charlie Devine (22), Roy Litzen (42), Mickey Flammia (35), Gordon Ross (43), Charlie Costa (12), Chris Lee (Student Manager). BACK ROW: Charlie Varney & Bernie Chestna (Asst.)

1960 State Championship Hoop Team

With the coming of the 1960 Season, I had great expectations from the crop that had matured through our Farm System: Biddy League, Junior High School, Freshmen, J.V's, and finally the Varsity Team.

Our high scoring & playmaking guard, Captain Mike Crowley, led our starting lineup. Mike was the only starting senior on the team. The other guard slot went to junior, Paul "Pekoe" Pallatroni, a cool and excellent outside shooter with the ability to drive to the hoop when the defense came out to stop his outside shooting. He was the best foul shooter on the team with a conversion rate well above 90%.

At the forward positions we had Dave Messaline, a junior, and the most underrated player on the team. Dave at only 5 foot 9 inches was one of our power forwards with the speed of lightning. He was the key to our Fast Break with his anticipation of events and acceleration down the floor. The other forward was Steve Pivacek, another junior, who was a very intelligent and very coachable, quick learning athlete. He was excellent at driving the base line and a proficient rebounder.

L. Steve 'Froggie' Prophett with the rebound, Steve Pivacek blocking out.

R. Dave Messaline driving for two.

A strange coincidence for those days, both of our forwards, Dave Messaline and Steve Pivacek wore glasses when they played. It didn't hurt their performances on the basketball court nor did it hurt them in their future careers. Both of them went on to become very successful in the once again coincidentally, the same business field! Dave went on to become Vice President of a very well known stock firm and Steve also ended up with his own lucrative market related venture.

The last spot went to a Sophomore, Steve "Froggy" Prophett. Here was a guy who if you asked him to jump across the Mississippi River would answer, "O.K. Coach, where is it?" Loyalty, aggressiveness and determination were his credentials. At one time during a half time of a game I was giving a pep talk to the team. I pleaded with them to "get ferocious". Steve in all earnestness, yelled out, *"Coach, what number is Ferocious, I'll get him!"*

Steve was so aggressive out on the court that there were many times I had to get him out of the game for a minute to get him to calm down to prevent him from fouling out. Steve gave us many happy memories by his contributions to our team.

Steve Prophett with rake, surrounded by friends and neighbors Bobby and Larry Folloni, and his father Phil. Steve and Bill both tragically passed away not long after this photo was taken.

There was a very sad ending in the Steve Prophett story. Unbeknown to anyone, Steve had a heart problem that was never diagnosed in his youth. He had passed all the physical exams that were required of all athletes. Later in life this problem was finally detected and at the young age of 44 he died while undergoing heart surgery. It was a tragic loss for all of us.

Pivacek & Prophett Team Up Again!

The other 'Extra Special' quick and aggressive supportive players on this 1960 Championship Team were Seniors, Charkie Devine, Roy Litzen, and Gordon Ross; Juniors, Shawn Burke, Mickey Flammia, John Ferrari and Peter Zahr; Sophomore, Artie Hoke; and Freshmen, Charles Costa and Larry Folloni Jr.

Preseason predictions favored the Westies, Holbrook, Marshfield, and Bridgewater as the teams to be in contention for the League crowns. We started the season off with impressive wins in our first two games over Hull and Holbrook. The Hull game was fairly close for three periods. Our press and fast break offense finally broke the game open in the final quarter.

In the Holbrook game our fast breaking got us off to a good start and we led by a score of 21 to 15 at the end of the first period. In the second period Holbrook switched from a man to man to a zone defense in the hopes of stopping our fast breaking offense. I immediately called a time out and counteracted this zone defense with a 'semi-freeze' slow down tactic. Our variety of extreme tactics, coupled with our solid training in the fundamentals to allow us to take advantage of openings these moves created, was usually just too much for the competition.

We held on to a 33 to 24 half time lead. In the third period we went to the 'Folloni Special Press'. This completely befuddled the Holbrook team as we held them to a mere 3 points in the period. I played the reserves for the final period as we handed Holbrook its first loss of the season after they had started with 4 straight wins. The final score was 56 to 39.

Now with one of the top teams out of the way we were to tangle with another undefeated team, our neighboring archrivals and nemesis West Bridgewater. We were not so fortunate in this third game of the season, which was played at West Bridgewater before a packed house. The game was nip and tuck throughout. We led 14 to 11 after the first period.

At the half, The Westies went ahead by a score of 32 to 30. We went ahead again after the third period 49 to 48. In the fourth period we built a 9-point lead before our two key players, Captain Mike Crowley and Steve Prophet, both fouled out. The scrappy Westies fought back to overtake us in the final 10 seconds when Jon Churchill was fouled as he drove in for a lay-up. He made the foul shot for the 3-pointer to seal the win for West Bridgewater.

This was really a heartbreaking loss for us, as we had outplayed The Westies up to the time that our two key players fouled out. Our kids really never quit afer this letdown though, and they then went on a 14 game winning streak to complete the regular season with a 15 and 1 record and the League Title. The real key game during this win streak was our overtime victory over a previously undefeated Marshfield team. Dave Messaline made a steal and drove in for a lay-up shot to give us a hard earned, real tough win.

Now it was on to the annual South Shore Principal's Tournament. We won our first game by defeating East Bridgewater handily by a score of 70 to 41. In the semifinals we were pitted against a good Norwell team that we had beaten during the regular season by a score of 64 to 59. I think that our kids were looking ahead to a rematch with West Bridgewater in the finals and as a result Norwell turned the tables on us and defeated us by a score of 69 to 63! West Bridgewater, who we knew we could beat, went on to win that Tournament.

We now had to put this loss behind us and concentrate on the big one, the State Tournament. The four teams from the South Shore League to qualify for the State Tourney were West Bridgewater, Marshfield, Norwell and Bridgewater. Norwell and Bridgewater were in opposite brackets of Westies and Marshfield so there was a good possibility that we could meet Westies in the Finals.

We won our first round game against Bedford by a score of 70 to 56. Norwell was defeated by Bourne in overtime by a score of 54 to 53. We then played Bourne in the quarterfinals, which we won handily by a score of 59 to 42. In the other bracket The Westies and Marshfield both won their games. They met in the quarterfinals and Marshfield came up a surprise winner. The Marshfield team then defeated Wayland in the semifinal game at the Boston Garden.

We then went on to handily defeat a previously undefeated Norton team in our semifinal game at the Boston Garden, by a score of 67 to 50. It was a cherished victory over a team that came in heavily favored to win. A little side light to this win: Early in the season we had a scrimmage with this Norton team. They kept score and were victors in the scoring department. With this "victory" in mind, the Norton team came into the game at the Garden with an overconfident cocky attitude that they could handily beat us.

What the Norton team did not realize was the fact that I used my early season scrimmages for teaching and experimenting purposes and not for the purpose of "winning" a game that was only a practice session that did not count on our records. In this scrimmage I really didn't show the Norton team all our stuff. They were really taken by surprise and were completely befuddled when we threw our Special Press and Fast Break against them at the Boston Garden.

It was then Marshfield vs. Bridgewater in the Finals at the Boston Garden. We had played Marshfield twice during the regular season. We won the first game 56 to 55 in overtime at their court and we won the second game at home by a score of 70 to 69. Both games were closely contested right to the very end. This was to be a classic matchup. In both games it was their star Eddie Fonseca who was the thorn in our side. Eddie had an average of better than 25 points per game. We knew that we would have to stop him if we were going to win the Championship.

I studied the game films of our previous two games, and after staying up nearly the whole night watching every move that Fonseca made, I finally came up with a plan to counter him. I noticed in the films that every time that Fonseca had the ball his first move was to his left to draw his defensive man in that direction. Then he would come back the other way and either drive or shoot to his right.

Anxious moments at the Boston Garden knowing that Marshfield was always tough to beat.

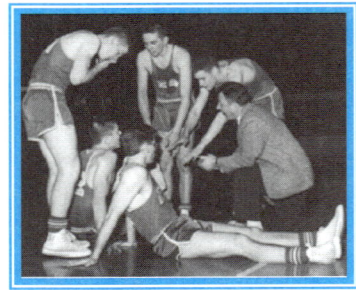

I gave the job of covering Fonseca to Paul Pallatroni. I instructed Paul to NOT follow Fonseca's first move to his left, but to wait and cover him closely on his right side. Paul followed my instructions to near perfection, as he stuck to Fonseca's right side like glue. Fonseca was so frustrated that he only had one basket and 7 points in the first three periods. We built up a commanding lead by that time and against our reserves in the final period Fonseca was able to add another 10 points to his total, but to no real avail. The final score of the Championship game was Bridgewater 64 Marshfield 57.

Helen Filippetti leading the way with soaring spirit

We're going to win this Championship!

I put the reserves in the final quarter in for four reasons:

- To not run up the score and embarrass the opposition (who deserved respect and who would likely challenge us again in the future);
- To give my starters the chance to be pulled off the court individually to get their deserved applause from a Garden crowd;
- To give our Senior reserve players the opportunity to experience the thrill of Garden play;
- To give our underclassmen the experience that would be needed when it was their turn to lead the charge to more titles. They too, deserved some of the limelight for having spearheaded the development of the definitive 'Folloni Special Press'.

One other sidelight of this game, Steve Pivacek our star forward, suffered a shoulder separation just before the end of the first half and we had to go all out in the third quarter to compensate for his being out of the game.

Larry carried off Boston Garden floor by the victors after 1960 State Championship victory against Marshfield

1960 Coaching Staff

Hank Walmsley, Charlie Varney

Larry Folloni, Bernard Chestna, Mo Rucker

TESTIMONIAL FOR OUR 1960 STATE CHAMPIONS
Playoff Payoff

Following our championship success, the Bridgewater Knights of Columbus, with Primo Resmini as the energetic Chairman and with the help of the local manufacturers and merchants, gave us a heartwarming Testimonial. The events of that evening in honoring our State Champions were duly recorded on audiotape and summarized in a testimonial booklet. *[Note to Readers: Coach Folloni has copied this tape, and has added other recorded features on his teams and career to it. For a copy of this audiocassette or a photocopy of the testimonial booklet, contact the Old Coach or his family.]*

Items on the tape include:

0 - 60	Fred Foye, Radio Station WEEZ Boston - Message to 1960 Champs.
60-90	Dom Valentino, Station WBET - Exciting Team commentary
90-115	Judge Robert Clark, Tribute to Coach Larry Folloni
115-350	Coach Larry Folloni's Congratulatory and Thank you speech
380-410	Dick Bradley, Bridgewater School Committee resolution
410-630	Dom Valentino, WBET Sports Announcer Tribute to Coach Larry Folloni on his retirement. (May 24, 1961)
630-664	Larry Folloni radio interview after Wayland Championship game at the Boston Garden. (March 9, 1956)
664-700	Larry Folloni radio interview after Marshfield Championship game at Boston Garden. (March 7, 1960)
700-End	Larry Folloni radio interview after Weston Championship game at the Boston Garden. (March 10, 1961)

The following items are taken from an article written in the Brockton Daily Enterprise on March 28, 1960:

TOAST TO TITLISTS...

**BRIDGEWATER IN TRIBUTE TO STATE CHAMPIONS
LARGE TURNOUT HONORS HIGH SCHOOL HOOP TEAM;
FINE AWARDS AND SPEAKING PROGRAM.**

In one of the best organized and most complete testimonials ever accorded a High School Team, the town of Bridgewater, led by the sponsorship of Bridgewater

Council 488 Knights of Columbus, honored the Bridgewater High School Basketball team and its coaches last Saturday night at the High School.

Primo Resmini, a leader and organizer of Bridgewater sports, was the Chairman of the committee which made the plans, including a complete brochure, with names of sponsors, congratulation messages from individuals and business concerns, and pictures of the team, coaches and cheerleaders.

Toastmaster, Judge Robert G. Clark, Jr., put the program into action and kept things moving much to the enjoyment of a crowded auditorium.

The assembly to honor this championship team…

****

Editor's note: --- Due to a series of emergency surgeries on Coach Folloni beginning on December 7, 1998, his *'My Way'* story was abruptly cut short at this point and put on hold for about 2 years while he was recuperating from the misfortunes that complications from the first surgery caused. Many of us close to The Old Coach, who knew the medical prognoses, thought it likely that he'd never make it back at all. All hoped and prayed, but few were able to believe that he'd rebound like he did to become a computer whiz at age 80^+ and finish this book! Although he never made it back to the golf links, the 'Old Coach' eventually also picked up where he left off in real estate ventures, and in caring for his family and friends. Of course he also got back into prominent community participation, including occasionally 'reading the riot act' to wayward public servants! Some of us didn't yet fully appreciate the power of *'Larry's Way'*, as he says was achieved with the help of God and His Guardian Angels. Perhaps they just couldn't ignore his unique determination to *NOT QUIT UNTIL COMPLETE SUCCESS OF HIS LIFE'S PLANS WERE ACHIEVED*.

****

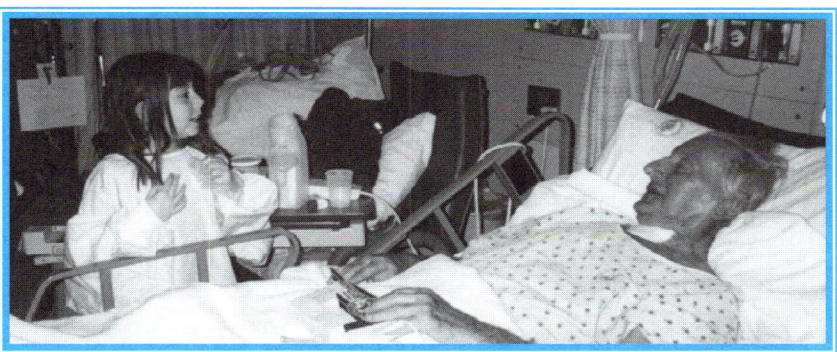

Grandaughter Taylor Leen providing powerful personal prayer for 'Papa', 1999

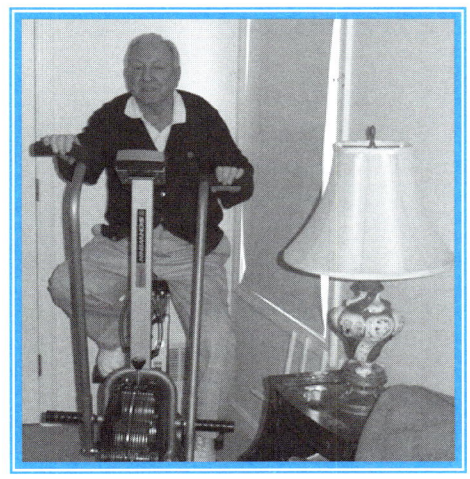

The Old Coach, May, 2003

Illegitimum Non Carborundum

[Background music: Theme from 'Rocky']

> *Author's note*
>
> At this time I would like to pick up on my memoirs of "My Way", which were put on hold for over two years due to circumstances largely beyond my control. Please forgive that I abruptly interrupted the narrative on my teams, just as 'my chartered course' was so abruptly interrupted (and almost ended) at the time that I was writing it. Sometimes the ACE UPSTAIRS can throw us a curve that makes Satchel's best look like a farm leaguer tot's toss! And all we can do then is to trust enough to hang in there, and go along as optimistically as we can, with the faith that in "His Way", God will help to bring something Extra Good out of it. Through His Mercy, and with the help of my family, friends, medical professionals, and I'm satisfied to say, more than a bit of 'My Way', I think there's yet a Champion's ending to this story in the works!

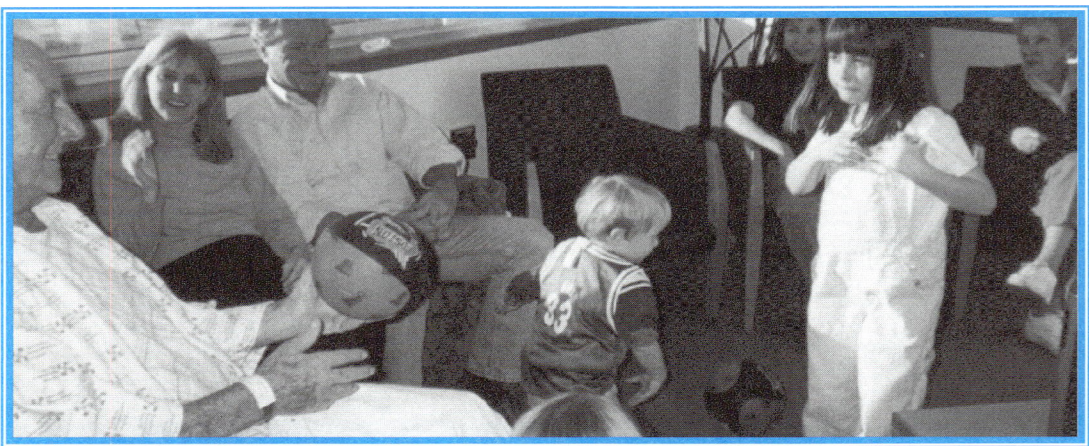

'The Old Coach' giving it another Go! 1999, above in Rehab with Grandchildren Scottie Dent (#33 'Larry' Bird), Debbie & Tom Dent. Taylor's mom Jean and Helen.

2000, below at home with Taylor Rose Leen Victoria & Scottie Dent.

1st basic health, then back to work!

"Work to be done a War to be Won!"

THE 1961 STATE CHAMPIONSHIP TEAM
Three for You and Me

From our starting five of the previous year's 1960 Championship Team, we were without our captain, Mike Crowley, who had graduated. To fill in his spot we had Shawn Burke, a Senior who we platooned with Larry Folloni, Jr., a very promising sophomore, to round out the starting five in battle.

The other veterans, Seniors, Paul Pallatroni, Steve Pivacek, David Messaline and Junior Steve Prophett, were all back and ready to go. Other important contributing players on this team included: Peter Zahr, Mike DeGregory, Jay Gauthier, Charlie Costa, Fran Cloutier, Peter Liberman, Leon Hoke and Ralph Lawson.

With our nucleus of returning veterans, we were finally the favorites, (and heavily at that) to win our League title and go on to defend our State Championship. Fortunately, we were able to accomplish this cherished task and after winning the League, we went on to defeat a good Weston Team in the finals to keep Bridgewater's undefeated streak at the Boston Garden intact.

Coach Larry Folloni and Mascot son Michael being carried off the Boston Garden floor by jubilant players after victory over Weston for State Championship in '61.

I guess this year could be considered anti-climatic to the previous two championship years but believe me when I say that winning any State Championship is truly rewarding and the continued record of never having lost a game at the Boston Garden remains a treasured accomplishment.

Looks like we're going to win the Championship!

Wonder if I can score a date with a cheerleader?

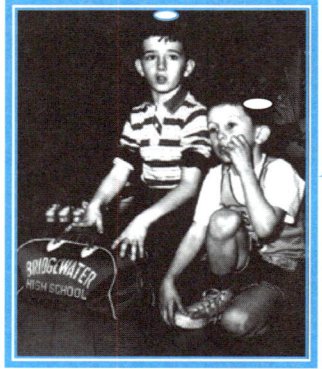

Lou Resmini and Michael ponder post victory celebrations.

Wonder if I'll hit my head on the rim while riding on my Dad's shoulders? Maybe I can dunk one!

There were many notable happenings during this Championship run. On the good side, the kids didn't let the fact that we were favored go to their heads, and that helped us to win our League Championship. During the run we had a string of 25 successive wins before we were defeated by our rival nemesis, West Bridgewater aka: our "Jinx Team". We had one of our poorest shooting games that night as we converted only 20 % while Westies were real hot shooting 56 %. By the end of the year, our win total extended to 41 out of our last 42 and 48 out of our last 52. And once again we failed to win the South Shore Tournament as had been the case in the 1956 and 1960 years. Fortunately, however we did bounce back all three times to win the more important State Championship.

We Won!

Larry Jr. cuts off the baseline at the Garden

If you looked up the word **"Team"** in the dictionary, I wouldn't be surprised if you saw a photo of this group. As Boston Globe Sportswriter Ernest Dalton wrote midway through our season on February 6, 1961:

Togetherness Pays
Five Co-Captains
Lead Bridgewater

Byline: Ernie Dalton: They have five cocaptains; they have been together since ninth grade; the front line is called the "Pea-Shooters", and they have girl scorekeepers. That's the story on Bridgewater's unbeaten basketball team, winner of 12-straight this year; winner of the last 25 league games, loser of only one in the last 40 league starts.

A year ago, with a 'six man' team made up of one senior and five juniors, Bridewater built for 1961. But that gang went out and won the Class D championship at the Tech Tournament.

When it came time to elect a captain for 1961, none of the five seniors-to-be wanted the job, none wanted to be rated above the others.

They said: "Let all of us be captains, let's all pitch in and win in 1961." Thus the five cocaptains.

The nickname "Pea-Shooters" came naturally for the three front men, the trio who do most of the scoring, all have names beginning with "P". There is Paul Pallatroni, 5'10", good outside shot, good driver, and Steve Pivacek and Steve Prophett, both 6'2", both good scorers, both good under the boards.

Of this trio, Pivacek is gradually shaking off the effects of a shoulder dislocation, first suffered in the Tech final last year, and all over again in football.

Back of the Pea-shooters" are Shawn Burke, 5'11, and Dave Messaline, 5'11, who not only get their points, but when the going is rough, play key roles in the "Folloni Special", a unique pressing defense set up by Coach Larry Folloni.

And the defense must be something special, for the other day verses Holbrook, after a close first half, on went the "special press" defense to hold Holbrook to two baskets in the last 14 minutes of play.

This year Bridgewater is a 'seven man' team, for spares Pete Zahr and Larry Folloni Jr. see as much action as the cocaptains. Folloni is the assist man when he gets out there, Zahr, 6'4", is the rebounder.

The gal scorekeepers? They are Irene Feeley and Merri Jones. Others in the Bridgewater cast, and head coach Folloni takes pains to spell out their worth are Junior High coach Joe Lazzaro, unpaid volunteer who starts the kids off; freshman coach Charles Varney, who gets them next, and Bernie Chestna, jayvee coach who polishes them up for Folloni

1961 State Championship Team Pallatroni, Pivacek, Messaline, Burke, Peter Zahr, Mike DeGregory, Jrs. Steve Prophett, Jay Gauthier, Soph. Larry Jr., Charlie Costa, Fran Cloutier, Peter Liberman, Leon Hoke and Ralph Lawson

MY FIRST RETIREMENT FROM COACHING
GOING OUT ON TOP?

Following our successful defense of our State Title, it was time for me to make a big decision. This was to be the last year of the existence of Bridgewater High School. Starting in September we were to be opening the new Regional High School with neighboring Raynham. After much deliberation and many consultations with our new Superintendent, Mr. Serge Bernard, I finally made up my mind to relinquish my coaching duties and devote my full time to become the Athletic Director and Physical Education Supervisor at the new Bridgewater-Raynham Regional High School.

It was not an easy decision for me, but now as I look back, I can see that I made the right move. After 13 years of dedicated work to rejuvenate the Athletic Teams and establish Physical Education Facilities and Programs, I found myself physically and mentally exhausted. Even though I enjoyed every minute of my 15 to 16 hour workdays, the grind finally caught up to me. I just had to get away from the pressure cooker of coaching. True, I placed most of the pressure upon myself, but being a perfectionist and wanting to get the best out of my athletes, I over-extended myself.

"Yes there were times, I'm sure you knew, when I bit off, more than I could chew" –My Way

In the end I saw my exhaustion and the opening offered by Serge Bernard as signs that I could stay responsible to my career and town, and still satisfy my desire to dedicate more time directly to my family.

Dad, please stay home and play catch with me more. Nono likes playing bocce and doing bricklaying better than playing baseball." Jimmie

I think that the best way to express my feelings on this retirement is to review this article that appeared in the *BRIDGEWATER KEYNOTE* Newspaper on March 23, 1961, four days before Helen gave birth to our last son James:

THE KEYNOTE

"Larry Folloni, who piloted Bridgewater High School basketball teams to 3 State Tournament titles in the last 5 years, announced today that he is leaving the coaching ranks at the end of the school year.

Folloni will devote his full time to the duties of Athletic Director and head of the Physical Education Department at the new Bridgewater-Raynham Regional School, slated to open in September.

He has served as Athletic Director and Basketball Coach at BHS since 1952. During that span his teams won 145 games and lost 57. They have won 48 out of their last 52 games.

A graduate of BHS and BU, Folloni has also served as President of the Massachusetts Secondary Schools Athletic Directors Association.

Folloni issued the following statement on his retirement from the coaching ranks:

"Just how does one start a letter like this? How does a person say he is going to give up his right arm and not feel it? Coaching has been near and dear to me starting from when as a 10-year-old youngster, I organized and coached my first team. We called ourselves the "Stanley Steamers", and our big rivals were known as the "High Street Tigers". Since that time, many nice things have happened to me both as a player and as a coach.

With the end of this school year I am retiring as a Coach to devote my full time as Athletic Director and Head of the Physical Education Department at the new Bridgewater-Raynham Regional High School.

This has not been an easy decision for me, and I have had many sleepless nights pondering it. I talked it over with my wife and my family, and after discussing every angle, including the pros & cons of whether to coach my talented son

Larry in his Senior year, they left it to me. As my wife, Helen, finally put it:

> "Do as you've always done, whatever you believe to be best for the family and your career. Whatever your decision is we know it will be the right one, and as long as you are happy, the children and I will also be happy."

I made my decision known to the Superintendent-Principal of the Regional School, Mr. Serge Bernard, approximately five weeks before our basketball team wrapped up our most recent State Championship. At the time I asked him to kindly hold off any announcement until the season was completed, as I did not want to cause any disruptions to our team. Mr. Bernard has been very cooperative and understanding, and has given much helpful guidance to me during the past three months as I painstakingly pondered my predicament.

You may wonder why I arrived at my decision to retire from coaching at a peak of my achievements. True, I am still young, and God willing, I could have many more years of fruitful coaching. There are many other considerations, however. Some are personal, like my wanting to reduce the general pressures of the extra job. I must confess, however that one of the greatest factors for leaving is so that I may devote more time to my growing family at home. We have three boys and two girls, with another addition expected any day now.

As I look back over the past 14 years, I suddenly realize the meaning of "TEMPUS FUGIT" (TIME FLIES). I'm afraid that if I don't take the time now to enjoy my children while they are still young, that they will be grown and gone before I realize it.

Even though our teams rarely lost over the past few years, I know that even in defeat they gained a great deal of stature. I was very pleased at the way our boys have taken our defeats in stride, especially after our 25 game winning streak was broken. They always congratulated the winners, and had no sour grapes or alibis. They were disappointed, yes, but they were not discouraged.

Exemplary of the heart of my teams over the years, my three championship teams all came back after defeats at crucial stages during their seasons. They responded to setbacks the way real champions do. And hopefully each team member will experience the self-confidence and satisfaction of these accomplishments forever. As, I hope will the unsung non-starting members of the practice squads and losing teams who helped me to develop my coaching abilities.

As those of us who have been fortunate enough to take part in sports can really appreciate, the life of an athlete is a charmed one. In spite of the knocks and bruises he absorbs, the punishment he takes, and the sacrifices that he makes, *LUCKY IS THE BOY OR GIRL, WHO BY THE GIFT OF GOD HAS BEEN GIVEN THE FINE PHYSICAL BODY, DESIRE AND COORDINATION NECESSARY TO TAKE PART IN THEM. LUCKY TOO IS THE CHILD WHO HAS BEEN ABLE TO TASTE DEFEAT AND LEARNED TO BOUNCE BACK TO THE VICTORY TRAIL, FOR WHAT IS LIFE BUT A SERIES OF DEFEATS AND VICTORIES?*

I too have had my share of setbacks and defeats in life and I am certain that without my experiences of athletic competition in my younger days, I would not have been able to bounce back with victories later in life. I feel sorry for the youngsters who go through their school days never having learned how to bounce back to the victory path. How unfortunate it is that some youngsters must wait until they are out of school, then suddenly find when they meet their first setback in life that they do not know how to cope with defeat. Since their first venture in life may have been a failure, they often retire into their shell and in some cases never come out of it for the rest of their lives. This is not to say that those who are more artistically, intellectually or otherwise inclined are less blessed or less likely to succeed, but the record shows that participation in athletics is one of the most prevalent avenues to successful development in schools and careers.

The responsibilities of athletes are great and justly, their advantages are many; the lessons that athletes learn by competition are priceless; the memories of their athletic contests are indelible. How, for example, can the memories of our State Champs of 1956, '60. and '61, and their record feats at the Boston Garden ever be erased from the minds of the players who participated? How can the memories be forgotten by the student body members, parents and town supporters that joined the bus and car caravans to the Garden to cheer the team on to victory?

The friendships that the athlete makes with coaches, teammates and even some opponents will last a lifetime. Don't the 'Slendid Splinter' Ted Williams, and the 'Yankee Clipper', Joe Dimaggio; hold one another in the highest of esteem? The influence and example that the athlete sets for the younger generation will be the mold that the youth will try to pattern. It sure beats the example of others whose habits can drag a youth down.

When an athlete has earned his letter by participation in sports, he has earned a great accreditation to go forward with greater skill and confidence in the *Great Game of Life*. This is one of the reasons that I always have always have made and always will make such an effort to organize elaborate award ceremonies with letters, team jackets and testimonials. If student athletes play the game of life fair and square; and if they play by the same rules and standards that they have played their athletic contests; I am sure that the final tally will be much better for all.

Now that my days of coaching are over I would like to pay tribute to my colleagues in the coaching field. There are not many, except for those who have the experience who realize that the lot of a coach is not an easy one. Oh sure, all coaches love to teach youngsters how to play the different sports, and they are proud and thrilled to see young awkward kids develop into well coordinated and confident young men.

And all coaches realize that among the many requirements during their career, they must be: a teacher; a guidance counselor; a psychologist; a trainer; a judge; an attorney; a big brother or big sister; and a father or mother; and they must be also be firm disciplinarians! Yet they must be kind, understanding, and sympathetic; they must have self-control; they must keep up good relations with other teachers, with spectators, with the general public, and with parents. In other words, to do it right, they must be a jack of all trades and something of a SUPERMAN OR SUPERWOMAN.

A common perception of the public is that if 'their' team wins, the players are great and the coach was along for the ride, but if the team loses, the coaches are considered to be at fault for stomping on the potential of his players. As a coach, one must be ready to take these slings and arrows, and win or lose, appreciated or not; and know how to rely on the intrinsic satisfaction of having made progress in helping to develop young lives.

Not many people realize the sacrifices that coaches make for their athletes, or appreciate the close formative relationships that are forged between coaches and their players. Nor do many people realize the time and effort coaches put into their work. If only the public would realize that coaches are trying to serve the best interests of their athletes. If instead of being critical of a coach because their team loses a game, fans would only pitch in and be helpful in the cooperative way that they could, it would take a great deal of tension and strain off the coach. No one wants to win any more than the coach. But let's face it both teams can't win. Does that mean that half the coaches in every game are bad?

It has been my privilege during the past year to work with Mr. Serge Bernard, one of the finest administrators that any coach or teacher could ask for. Mr. Bernard provides a great example of how to help staff, student and townsfolk alike by recognizing the potential in his staff, and diplomatically coaxing the most out of them. He never looks to tear down people, only to build them up.

I have also had the privilege of meeting with the State Principal's Standing Committee on Athletics several times during the past few years. You will not find a more capable or more cooperative group anywhere. The primary purpose of this committee is to see that the athletic programs of all schools in the state will be carried on at the high level that all educators are striving for. Most of these administrators are former athletes and coaches who understand the problems and the great value of athletic programs in our High Schools. They have spent many hours working out these problems. I believe that all the recommendations and decisions that they make are in the best interests of the youngsters and overall athletic programs for all schools.

Even though coaching is not the most financially rewarding profession, I treasure my coaching experiences, because to me all the money in the world couldn't replace the cherished memories that came from them. What could be more rewarding than to have one of your former athletes come back to you and say, "Thanks Coach for everything you did for me back in high school, I'll never forget it."

Whenever any youngster calls me "Coach" it carries a special connotation that to me sounds just as distinguished as "Mr. President" or "Your Honor". It makes me feel that I am the richest guy in the world.

Of course I've been thrilled and proud of the accomplishments and success of my teams. However some of my greatest satisfaction will come from watching the progress and success of my pupils after they leave my courts. I will be repaid a thousand times over by the future successes of such boys as Bobby Seaver, the Clark brothers, Ronnie Hogg, Bob Fernandes, Lou Filippetti, Steve Pivacek, Dave Messaline and others that I have been privileged to coach.

If I were to list all of the organizations and people who have contributed to our success, I wouldn't find the space on this paper to list them all, but to all of my friends who have helped in any way, may I express to you my sincere thanks. My thanks also to the Media; who have been so kind to my teams and me throughout the years. It has been a pleasure working with you. And last but not least my sincere thanks to all the parents who allowed me the privilege to guide their youngsters through their school years."

Coach Larry Folloni

THE BRIDGEWATER-RAYNHAM REGIONAL HIGH SCHOOL YEARS
New Team, New League, New Era

The opening of the Regional School in September of 1961 marked the beginning of a new era in my Athletic career. I would no longer have the pressures of coaching, but I would have the responsibilities of building an Athletic Program.

It all started in 1960 with the hiring of Mr. Serge Bernard as the new Superintendent. He was hired one year before the opening of the new school with the mandate to get the best teachers and coaches available to staff it.

Our School Committee, headed by Walter Murray and Jim Buckley, had the prudent foresight to adjust the Regional School pay schedule to 20% above the going rate in the State. This and other perks including the use of state of the art facilities and the prospect of working under a great administration were effective incentives to getting the best teachers and coaches available.

The best knew how to get dressed for the 1963 faculty – student game. l-r including: Ed Cassabian, Tony Zonferelli, Serge Bernard, Larry Folloni and Don Prohovich

Mr. Bernard was up to the task of recruiting the best, and together we built a great school with a great tradition. Our reputation soon spread throughout the State and before long many new and influential people from surrounding towns moved into the Bridgewater-Raynham area because of the EXCELLENT EDUCATIONAL AND ATHLETIC OFFERINGS IN OUR HIGH SCHOOL, in addition to the town's other fine schools. Other area schools then tried to emulate our success.

Progress in our Athletic Program was slow in starting, especially our Football and Basketball programs, which were very hard hit by losses of many Jr. High School Stars to Cardinal Spellman High. Our Baseball teams continued the success of the old High School teams with "Hank" Pearson at the helm. The other sports teams, Track, Tennis, Golf, Gymnastics, and Hockey all were mediocre.

Between 1961 and 1975 our programs grew from having only six coaches for four boy's and one girl's sport to having 42 teams, 48 coaches and 880 participants out of a student body of 1,400. We also grew to scheduling 513 yearly events compared to 127 events in 1961. I'm happy and proud to say that the quantity of girl's sport teams became the equal to those of the boys' teams under our system!

'62 Basketball team with Coach Hill   The 1963 BRRHS Lettermen

Following the loss of our head coaches in Football and Basketball after the first couple of years, Mr. Bernard asked me if I would be interested in coming back to coach the Basketball team. I was hesitant at first, but I shared Mr. Bernard's view that we should redouble our efforts and plant the seeds to get the program back to its peak levels of the '50's and early '60's. Plus I had so much respect for Mr. Bernard, who had done so much for me and the town, that I just had to follow his lead. In 1965 I agreed to take over for a few years to help out. Also it gave me the opportunity to coach my son Bobby, who was following in the footsteps of his older brother Larry as a top notch Basketball player. (I still had some pangs of regret about not staying to coach Larry Jr. in his senior year to help him and his teammates excel further, and this helped to influence my decision to come back to coach my second son.)

Bobby was only a sophomore when I took over and his playing skills were good enough to help out the varsity. Bobby asked that he not play ahead of some seniors. I went along with Bobby's request, just gradually working him into the lineup throughout the season. My sons Bobby and Larry Jr. both feared that I might show favoritism towards them. If anything the opposite was true. The record shows that I held them back more than I had other underclassmen with similar skills and promise that I coached over the years.

We had a mediocre record that first year ('1964-'65), but the underclassmen got a lot of valuable playing time and were groomed for the following season.

The '65-'66 squad was led by Captains Barney Ross and Ron Dziergowski and David Alden. This was the last year that we competed in the South Shore League, and we tied with Hull for the League Championship and qualified for the State Tournament. Unfortunately, after winning our 1st tourney game we were matched up to play Hull in the quarter-finals and they eliminated us. Our team had been progressing nicely toward the end of the regular season and we thought that we could take Hull in any venue, but our entire team seemed to come out flat on that judgement day.

l-r, rear: Coach Jim Swan Bob Folloni, Ricky Warren, Tom Balboni, Frank Barstow Dave Alden Fran Yanuskiewicz, and Peter Murray, student manager.

front: Captain Barney Ross Coach Larry Folloni, Captain Ron Dziergowski

Even our explosive star and hustling leader Barney Ross had an untypical off game that day, especially in the first half when we dug an enormous hole for ourselves. We almost caught Hull in the 2nd half, but it was too late. Barney was going for the rare achievement of scoring 1000th high school career point that day. Everybody knew he was close, but only our statistician, my eighth grade son Michael and I knew just how close.

Barney broke the 1000 point mark in the first half, but we never mentioned it to him until after the game, at which point he plaintively asked Michael: *"Why didn't you tell me?"* I don't know whether or not telling Barney when he made the milestone bucket would have bolstered his confidence and relaxed him enough to have gotten him back on his game a few crucial minutes sooner. That's one thing about coaching. Sometimes you never know what the best thing to do is, but you always have to live with your decisions…

Barney Ross was one of my 'All-Time, All-Stars'

The next year we began playing in the Old Colony League, which was much stronger than the South Shore League. We had a good year, finishing in second place and qualifying for the State Tournament. This '66-'67 team included Tommy Balboni, Bobby Rego, Bobby Doyle, Ricky Warren, Ricky Lankalis, Buddy White, Frank Barstow, 'Lance' Cogliano, Richard Filippetti, Bobby Folloni, Bobby Morgan, Teddy Geppner and Mike Tokarsky.

Up front we had a tall and still somewhat gangly but ever-improving underclassman Frank Barstow, and Tommy Balboni who like Charles Barkley was way undersized vertically but who more than carried his weight underneath. Besides them, we basically had a team of *'miracle making midgets'* (four of whom were named Bobby, which made my exhortations to hustle more efficiently personal) who racked up countless heads-up and hustling steals and fast break conversion points game after game. Their defense was our best offense. This is the crew of giant killers that defeated the supposedly unbeatable Franklin High School team in an exciting interleague matchup. They appropriately dubbed themselves 'The Hondo Boys' after their Celtic 6th man hero John Havlicek, a team player who consistently came off the bench to act as a team sparkplug.

Ricky Warren and Bob Folloni-
Two of the terrific talents
we had on the court in 1967.

"It's not the size of the dog in the fight,
it's the size of the fight in the dog."
-Mark Twain (1835-1910)

Even though some of my other teams over the years had better winning records, in many ways this group represented the epitome of our fast paced pressing squads. This team might have had less raw physical ability than many, but they also might have had more spunk and enthusiasm than any did. I remember a conversation with Jim Buckley's wife Mary, who taught many of this group of characters in the 2nd grade. She said that of her 40 or so years in teaching, they were the biggest 'wiseguys', but that they were also the smartest and essentially nicest group of children that she'd ever taught. I agree. They were just so sharp that the school work bored them. They weren't only bright 'pranksters', but they were also aggressive and highly team oriented competitors, and with a break or two might they have become the most unlikely State Champions ever from our town.

"Some criticize today's youth, but I think that that criticism is unwarrented.
Youth must have it's fling, we must be tolerant with those that are flinging."
- Will Rogers, December, 1928

We lost one of this team's brightest stars early in the season for non-school related disciplinary reasons that would have been ignored in today's world. This might have been the crucial difference in how far we went, but then again, who knows? In our first game of the State Tourney against a strong Xaverian team from Westwood we once again came out real flat. About the only highlight of the game that I recall was a 3/4 court shot taken by my son Bobby from the opponent's foul circle at the buzzer ending the first half. It swished in, and for at least a bit our fading hopes soared as that shot did! Although a point and spirit lifter, alas, this feat and a valiant last quarter 'Folloni Special Press' weren't quite enough to overcome our horrible start, and so passed what might have been.

"We didn't lose the game, we just ran out of time." -Vince Lombardi

FRONT ROW (L to R): *Coach* Larry Folloni, 21 Bob Doyle, 23 Tom Balboni, 13 *Capt.* Bob Folloni, 33 Frank Barstow, 42 Mike Tokarsky, *Mgr.* Jim Malone. BACK ROW: 35 Scott Donaldson, 31 Richard Filippetti, 22 Ted Geppner, 24 Ronald Cogliano, 41 Glenn Meixner, 15 Richard Lankalis, 25 Billy White, 14 Bobby Morgan, 51 Andy Fruzzetti.

My Last Year as a High School Basketball Coach
Saving the Best for Last

I stayed on as Basketball Coach for one more year. Our team in 1967-68 had only one returning starting letterman, Captain Frank Barstow. Few thought when we recruited Frank to the Varsity as a Sophomore 'Project' that he would ever excel, but excel he certainly did. Frank worked hard, he listened well, and he patented some very special 'Kevin McCale-ish' inside moves that earned him League All-Star status. Although this was not one of the top teams that I had coached, it turned out to be one of the most satisfying coaching seasons of my career.F Preseason forecasts had us to finish in the lower half of the strong Old Colony League. We started off very slow, and due to inexperience we lost 7 out of our first 8 games, but by the middle of the year we were giving the top teams a battle right down to the last buzzer.

In terms of job satisfaction, the experience of guiding my last team from being the losingest' to becoming the 'winningest' within the same season was the best!

l-r, rear: Coach Folloni, Bruce Maclay, Richard Filippetti, Peter Daley, Doug Wiggins, Louie Resmini, Scott Donaldson Dino Battestini, student mgr.
l-r, front: Bobby Morgan, Paul Yanuskiewicz, Ronnie Cogliano, Frank Barstow, Tony Belolli, Bobby Rego, Glen Meixner. Not shown: Wesley Morris

Bobby Morgan, who at times replaced the star lost in our previous season, used the opportunity to make himself a seasoned star contributor. *Once again the downs of one year in a way helped give rise to the successes of the next.* We won 7 out of our last 8 games and missed out in qualifying for the State Tournament by only one game. As I've said, you never know. Or as they say: *Man proposes and God disposes."* And yes, it is all for the best.

TIME TO MOVE ON – WORK WITH MIAA
Going Going Gone

It was then time to move on to other challenges in the Athletic Field. I had always taken an active part in the State Coaches Associations and the State Athletic Director's Association, and my final retirement from coaching gave me the time to get more involved on this higher level.

Mel Wenner of Belmont High, Emory Loud of Lexington High, and I were the original founders of the Mass State Basketball Coaches Association in the late 50's. I was also among the founders and charter members of the Mass State Athletic Directors Association. Over the years I went the entire route of officership, Secretary, Treasure, Vice-President and finally President of the MSSADA in the early 60's.

The 60's were a time of major upheavals and changes throughout our country, and Athletics was no exception. So much turmoil had evolved in High School Sports, that the MSSADA saw the need to update the MIAA (Massachusetts Interscholastic Athletic Association) Rules that governed them. They selected me to be the Chairman of the State Rules Committee. This was perhaps one of the most important jobs that I ever volunteered for.

I proceeded to gather a committee that consisted of Coaches, Athletic Directors, Principals, Superintendents, and School Committee members of great character and good will. We worked hard for several years and finally came up with an updated Rules Book that expanded the old 10-page version to over 60 pages. Although it did not solve all the problems, it was a great step in unifying all groups and setting the groundwork for future rules changes and amendments as needed.

I feel very proud that I was instrumental in the many rule changes, which today benefit high school youngsters throughout the State. One rule that I proposed and am especially proud of states that any group, individual, or coach has the right to petition to change or amend present rules for the benefit of high school youngsters.

All rules and amendments that were submitted prior to November 1st of each year were then sent on through the channels of each of the following State groups for their recommendations: The first step was the Coaches Organization of each Sport. Next came the Athletic Directors Association, then on to the Headmasters Association. Followed by the MICA (Superintendents and Pricipals Association), which voted, on final approval or disapproval of the rule or amendment as submitted. To this day this same procedure that we set up back in the 60's is still in effect. And as Dr. Bertram Holland so aptly expressed, *"We in Massachusetts have the most democratic process for athletic rules in the whole United States".*

"The candidates were 'high-type gentlemen' till the contest got close, then the brutes came out in 'em. What started out to be a nice fight, wound up in a street brawl. But it all comes under the heading of democracy, and as bad as it is, it's the best scheme we can think of."
-Will Rogers, November 13, 1932

Larry Folloni: the conscience of school sports in state

By Larry Ames
Globe Staff

When Larry Folloni hangs up his athletic director's spikes at the end of the school year, the interscholastic athletic family at Bridgewater-Raynham and the state will be losing more than a dear friend and worker.

Larry Folloni will be remembered as a teacher, coach, physical educator, athletic director and many other titles. But he will also be recalled as the conscience of school sports.

"Larry Folloni is the elder statesmen among athletic directors as far as we're concerned," said Massachusetts Interscholastic Athletic Assn. executive director Dick Neal. "He's always involved in the critical issues."

Folloni was past chairman of the MIAA Rules Committee and one of the principal contributors to the Blue Book.

The biggest hat Folloni wears is as South boys' basketball tournament director. He's headed the tourney for three years, but he's been involved since the late '60's and was one of the main people responsible for the expansion of the old Tech Tourney in the '50's.

He's always been an independent sort of guy but Folloni has always been respected for his integrity and his fortitude. "I think the song 'My Way' was written for me, particularly the words, 'Regrets I have but few, along the by-ways, I've done things my way' I've always been a scrapper and a fighter, but everything always came from my heart. I may be gruff on the outside, but I melt on the inside."

Folloni, a founder of the athletic director's association and a former AD of the year, played baseball, basketball and football at Bridgewater High. He played basketball and baseball at Boston University and holds the BU baseball record of reaching base 17 consecutive times. After serving as a navigator in the Army Air Corps, he finished school and began his career in Dighton from 1947-50.

"I got paid $200 for coaching four sports, and when I asked the superintendent for a raise, he was insulted," laughed Folloni. "Boy, how times have changed."

At Bridgewater, Folloni coached basketball (three states titles) and baseball and directed a program that has grown from six programs in 1952 to 42 teams, 48 coaches, 880 athletes and 513 events.

"Larry's been very involved," said Silver Lake athletic director Tony Sirico, a veteran colleague. "We've been lucky to have him"

Steve Sarantopolous, the former Brockton star who succeeded Folloni 15 years ago as basketball coach, said, "Larry has been a steadying influence at the school. His is a father's image. He's there when you need him."

(March 3, 1983)

LIFE IN THE '70'S AT BRRHS
"And now the end is near, I'll state my case, of which I'm certain"

There comes a time when all good things come to an end. Mr. Serge Bernard, after 10 years of dedicated work in establishing one of the finest educational programs in the state, decided to retire as the Superintendent at Bridgewater Raynham Regional High School. To the detriment of the town, his incomparable assistant Chet Millet, also left to eventually take on Principal and Superintendent duties at Raynham and Abington schools. Filling Mr. Bernard's shoes would be the tallest of orders for anyone. Remembering life under Mr. Bernard, naturally students and teacher's weren't so happy for awhile after his departure. Serge's style of helping others to make things happen, and then letting them take the credit for the success, was a rarely followed secret to true success. It is little wonder that his children have gone on to such success in their various fields of endeavor.

Dr. Ed Denton took over as the new Superintendent in the early 70's. Eddie was my first basketball captain back in 1952 when I started my coaching career in Bridgewater. Incidentally his mother was a distant relative of my mother. Eddie was a hard worker and full of ambition. He had more than his share of difficulties in growing up, but Eddie worked his way through college and after a few years of teaching experience he earned his way up to become the Superintendent of the Bridgewater School system. He was later deservedly elevated to the BRRHS Superintendent position, where he did an excellent job in our town then he went to Wareham and later on to warmer climates to complete his career.

I enjoyed working for Eddie, who, like me and other successful members of the town's educational establishment, was mentored and championed by Jim Buckley. Although Ed matured into a top-notch all around educational administrator, in my opinion his only weakness in his early years was in falling sway to the influences of at least one elder in his administration.

I had some unpleasant encounters with this administrator, just two of which I'll touch on here. Once he decided to add to my full Athletic Director's duties and physical education teaching schedule by assigning me to take on a health science class. I was tipped off to this by one of my coaches who informed me that during one of the summer school chit chats at a coffee break, this boss came in and boasted how he was going to saddle me with extra work outside of my area. He then purportedly said, "I'd like to see the expression on Folloni's face when he sees this added assignment."

Well he was right: when I heard of this plan I was infuriated. Adding this class to my already overburdened workload was contrary to the teaching contract that I had worked out with Mr. Bernard back in 1961. That contract called for me to teach two physical education classes at the start of the school day, then the rest of the day was to be used by me to carry out my duties as Athletic Director and Physical Education Supervisor.

As previously stated my workload as Athletic Director had increased five to tenfold over those years. Our programs grew from 1961, when we had only six coaches, four boys' sports and one girl's sport to 42 teams, 48 coaches and 880 participants out of a student body of 1,400. And they included the scheduling of a total of 513 yearly events compared to 127 in 1961, a fourfold increase!

I'm happy to say that we carried forth some aspirations of the 'Hep Cat's and the 'Puddy Tats' girls teams of our '50's recreation program, during my years as the AD at BRRHS. The number of girl's sport teams and participants and the number of their events, became the equal of those of the boys' teams.

Nancy says "We bucked the trend!"

Every year I kept accurate records of the Athletic Programs, which included all of this data. When I learned of the attempt to load me with another teaching class, I contacted the State Teachers Association to get help in resolving the issue. They assigned an Attorney to help me fight the case. During the negotiating period that followed, the story leaked out in the local newspapers and it became headline material. After several weeks of talks we finally went before the School Committee to present our case.

I was well prepared and presented all my evidence to substantiate my position. As I was making my presentation to the School Committee, my friend Jim Buckley later informed me of the conversation that went on between representatives of the administration. He said that they at first snickered at me, but soon became dumbfounded to hear me spiel off all the data that I had accumulated over the years.

We won our case and the School Committee instructed the Administration to return my schedule to as originally contracted. It wasn't long, however, before our Superintendent was influenced to make another attack on our Athletic Program.

Our football team won the League Championship in 1971. This exciting team was led by captains Michael Lyford & Tommy Bois, quarterback Jack Levy and future Brown University star lineman Billy Kairit. It also featured future L.A. police officer and national police motivational speaker Tony Ginewicz as well as the fan favorite Jose Soares from Portugal, a tremendously effective field goal and extra point kicker, which was a rarity in those days.

During the next few years, however, the football program went downhill. After a couple of coaching changes, the team still was taking its bumps. Once again, my esteemed top boss was steered to a hasty, and in my opinion, ill-advised direction: The administration became convinced that the only solution would be to withdraw from the Old Colony League and try to gain entrance to the Hockomock League.

Without my knowledge my superiors made visits to many of the schools in the Hockomock League to try to convince them to admit B-R. One of my good friends, Val Muscato, the Athletic Director and highly successful coach at Oliver Ames High School in Easton, called me on the phone one day to tip me off of the underground operation of our administrators in seeking to withdraw from the OCL.

I let Val know that I agreed with him that such a move would have undermined the tenets of fairness for South Shore Athletics that we involved AD's had all worked so hard to create, and that it would not be in the interest of any of the kids. Val got the word around to the other schools in the Hockomock League and they unanimously denied B-R's application to enter it. Having failed in this direction, the next step for the administration was to ask for withdrawal from the OCL, with the idea that we could play other schools on an independent basis.

This was the last straw. I vehemently opposed this action, as it would have been the death knell to our athletic program. Just about every team in the State was affiliated in a league. It would be almost impossible to schedule any games. Not only would it affect our football program, but also all of our sports teams and their players would suffer.

Reporters from the local newspapers called me for my opinions and I expressed them frankly in the hopes that the parents of the students would come to our rescue. The stories made the headlines of the sports pages. Within days of this information reaching the public, parents demanded an open meeting to discuss the situation. It was quite apparent from the reaction of the parents at the open meeting that they did not want the whole athletic program to be hurt because of the failure of the football program. The School Committee finally withdrew its request to withdraw from the OCL.

To his credit, Ed Denton then took control and embarked on a new road to solve the football program problem. His first step was to hire an Olympian Hammer-thrower named Boris Djerassi (who finished 6th ahead of Brian Olmstead in the '78 World's Strongest Man Competition) to be our weight-training instructor and to spearhead and expand our varsity athlete fitness program. We then went out and hired one of the most successful football coaches in the area, Paul Urban.

The football program redeveloped quickly and within three years it took off to great heights highlighted by a League Championship with the school's first undefeated season ever. From the '80's on, B-R Football teams have been the scourges of competition in Massachusetts. In the past 20 years they have risen to 'Class A' status, and have won the OCL title six out of the last seven years. They have been state Superbowl finalists for a number of years, and in 1998 under (BR grad) coach Dan Buron, they won the top honors over the mighty Brockton Team. (By the way, remember that yours truly helped to found the state Superbowl, and note that Armand Columbo, the state's winningest coach and also Rocky Marciano's brother-in-law, coached Brockton. It's a small world, afterall.)

In conjunction with the above successes, Ed was instrumental in securing the funds necessary to build our athletic facilities into one of the finest High School Athletic Plants in the State. He also continued on to admirably mature in all other aspects of his job for the ultimate betterment of the community. By the late '70's all of my children had graduated under my watchful eye, and I had had enough years and petty aggravations under my belt to decide that it was time to let a younger generation take over my tasks. Shortly before my retirement departure in 1983, Superintendent Ed Denton was very gracious in getting me a job as golf coach to allow me to coach this sport which I had developed a passion for.

Ed went on to become superintendent in Wareham, then later to a school district in San Luis Obisbo, CA, from where he retired from full time work. The last that I heard, Ed is now happily retired, spending a lot of time on the golf courses of Las Vegas, NV., and doing some part-time consulting work in construction management.

I would be remiss if I didn't remember three of my most loyal coaches two of who were also my teammates during our boyhood athletic days.

Joe Lazaro was my right hand man in getting the youth recreation and athletic programs organized. He was humble, competent and caring as they come. I don't know of anyone who knew Joe who didn't like him. Some did not sufficiently respect him, but that didn't seem to bother Joe. He just kept giving his all for the kids and athletics in our town.

"Hank" Pearson served as the most loyal (and successful) coach in my reign as Coach and Athletic Director at BRRHS. There's more about Hank and Joe in my 'Favorite Coaches' section towards the end of this book.

The other loyal coach was my assistant in the late 60's, Larry Fisher who is now the head basketball coach at B-R. He is doing an excellent job in carrying on the "Folloni Special Press" as a part of his coaching system. Larry is a mild mannered soft-spoken individual, and he genuinely cares about the kids enough to learn and teach them what is best for them, and to this they respond. Larry's teams have been extraordinarily successful over the years, winning several OCL Titles and taking his 1999 team to the Div. 1 Eastern MA final game at the Fleet Center.

I am glad to have had Larry's fine assistance and also to have passed on some of my basketball knowledge to such an eager learner. The kids and the town are very fortunate to have his services. I am very fortunate to have his friendship. Some of my greatest joys in retirement have come from watching the ongoing successes of the programs and philosophies that my friends and staffs have championed since 1950.

Coaches Larry Fisher & Dan Buron with me at 2003 B-R Baseball EMass Final

EARLY GOLFING YEARS (1956 – 1983)
Fair Way

"I guess there is nothing that will get your mind off everything like golf will. I have never been depressed enough to take up the game, but they say you can get so sore at yourself that you forget to hate your enemies." —Will Rogers, Dec. 2, 1928

My golfing life began back in the middle 50's. It was the last day of school and our football coach, Charlie Varney, asked me to go golfing with him. Charley had a friend by the name of Bob Sullivan, who was the pro at the Brockton Country Club and he was certain that he would get us a tee time.

After we checked out of our closing year duties at school, I went home to get a set of starter golf clubs that my wife Helen had bought me for Christmas. Charlie and I made our way out for what was to become an important part of my recreational life from that day on. Being a baseball fanatic all of my life, I just loved the national pastime. There was no greater feeling than having a bat in my hands and hitting a baseball. Now I had found a sport that has you at bat all the time with no outside help or hindrance from anyone to hit that ball.

I will never forget that first round of golf at BCC with Charlie Varney. The first nine I had 63 strokes and the second nine by the time we reached the 17th hole I already had about 60 strokes. We were exhausted, but I was HOOKED ON THIS GAME. I joined the Pine Valley Golf Club, a public course, and played there the rest of that summer.

I liked the game so much that I felt it was time to join the private Brockton Country Club. My brother-in-law Elmer Balboni was a member there and we made up a close knit 'made in Stanley' foursome that included Elmer's brother Charlie and Lou Marzelli.

I spent the next 20 years at the BCC and enjoyed every minute of my membership there. I made many friends (and a few not so friendly golfing adversaries) during those 20 years. Most memorable among my golfing buddies during the 60's were

Al Saccocia, my partner for most of the tournaments, our local jeweler Henry Cormier, who was a real nice guy, on and off the golf course; and Dave Flynn. Dave became an influential State Representative and subsequent charismatic heavyweight in State and regional Politics. Dave has been a real good friend of mine any many others for life.

I could write a book about the greatness of Dave alone. This progressive and enthusiastic player in the game of life actually had a regulation practice golf hole built in his back yard. This was probably the only place Dave could get away from the masses who looked to him for assistance, which he gladly dispensed from his positions of power.

It was State Representative Dave Flynn who originally found and printed up the inspirational "Don't Quit" poem that I reprinted earlier in this book. I kept a copy on my desk and whenever I got down in the dumps I would read this classic poem. Believe me, it helped get me out of many rough spots.

Dave Flynn, 2003

In the early 60's my good friend from my college days at Boston University, Warren "Red" Meacham moved to Brockton to become a principal at one of the schools in Brockton.

Red and Eleanor Meacham

Red soon joined the BCC and as a team we became the scourge of the club. The easy going and warm hearted Red and I paired off as partners and won the four-ball Club Championship three times, a feat never before accomplished there.

In one of those championship rounds we played against Bob McCann and Vic Renzo in the finals. We were tied in regulation and on the first overtime hole I knocked in a 20-foot back and forth breaking 'snake' putt for a birdie and the championship.

The next year in one of the playoff rounds to the championship I had my first hole-in-one. It was on the par 3-second hole, where I hit a 7 iron into the cup. Actually I never saw the ball roll into the hole since the shade of a nearby tree blocked our view from the tee. The only indication that I had was from the roar of the players ahead of us who were on the green at the time.

I ended up with six career holes-in-one, which I'm proud to say was a complement to the three that my sister Angie had in her (ongoing) golf career! Actually our official tally is tied, as only three of my Aces came in competition. The other three were unofficial since they came while I was playing alone without the benefit of a witness.

Angie shows off her championship form.

One of my unofficial hole-in-ones happened one year on the opening day of the season of the BCC. I was so anxious to get out on golf course that I started playing from the par 3 seventh hole, which is the nearest one to the parking lot. I pulled out my driver no less, and the very first ball that I had hit in about six months rolled right into the hole! I turned around to see if anyone was around to witness the shot. No one was in sight except for one car passing by. I think that Bob Jardine was the driver. I frantically waved for him to stop to verify the hole-in-one. Since he did not realize why I was waving, he didn't stop but waved back at me and said, "Hi Larry" and kept right on going.

Another one of my hole-in-ones came while I was playing at the Sabal Palm Golf Course in Florida. While walking down the first hole I witnessed a golfer playing the adjacent 9th hole par 3 hit his tee shot into the hole for a hole-in-one. I walked over to him and congratulated him on his shot and said that maybe this will rub off on me. Sure enough two holes later on the 170 par 3, third hole I scored an 'ace' by hitting a 5 iron into the cup on my tee shot!

It was on this same Sabal Palm course that I first shot my age. When I was 77, I invited my golfing friend Bill Snow, from Portsmouth Country Club, to come over for a round. Bill was at nearby West Palm Beach for the winter. We were coming in on the 17th hole when I realized that I had a chance to score a tally equal to my years.

I needed a birdie on one of the last two holes to reach this long-awaited cherished goal. I had about a 4-foot putt for birdie on the 17th but I missed it. We then came to the last hole. I hit a six iron onto the 160-yard par 3 and I was left with about a 7-foot uphill putt for my birdie. I knocked it right in the middle of the cup! Later that same year when I returned to New England I shot my age once again. We were playing in the Brockton Seniors Championship at my former home course when I shot another 77. Not being one to rest while life still coursed in my veins, I established new goals and high hopes of matching the feat of shooting my age for years to come. My catastrophic illness changed that. My brother Mike who only took up golf in his later years, has won several tournaments and is still shooting at the age of 88. *(News Flash! Guess what? Mike shot his age of 87 this past year. Remarkable!)*

During the summer time school vacation days, I managed to tie in with a golfing group called the 'Gang Busters'. We assembled daily at 12:30 and teams would be made up for tournaments. Guys like Charlie Maurea, Harold "Butch" Ware, and Dave Breen, Bob James, area Coaches, Dick Morey, Tom Divol, Paul Sargent, and Bob Reagan were a few of this 'Gang' that come to my mind. Butch Ware was a jolly fellow who wore the same wide smile whether he scored an 'ace' or hit two in a row out of bounds! And each of the others was a genuine character in their own right. I was happy to have had the opportunity to bring my kids around the club to learn a bit about life from this upright collection of fairway and all weather friends.

Our Wednesday afternoon gang consisted of "Doc" Carr, Henry Cormier, Harold MacLauglin, Bruno Malinowski, Paul Giamperoli, Paul Sargent, and Paul and Maynard Stetson. I really enjoyed playing with this amicable group. We often played medal tournaments: One dollar for each nine and one dollar for total. Players were paid a quarter for each birdie and a dollar from each of the other players for an eagle. The long third hole at BCC was the most difficult on the course, so if you birdied that, it was also worth one dollar.

There were many humorous events worth relating that happened on the golf course. The first that comes to mind was the day that Paul "temperamental" Stetson missed a short putt on the second hole. He became so infuriated that he threw his putter high up in the air. It never came down, having been firmly lodged in the branches of a nearby tree. Paul and Maynard spent the next 10 minutes throwing rocks up into the tree to try to dislodge the putter, but to no avail.

My good friend Paul Stetson

They finally gave up when the foursome of ladies behind us kept yelling for us to move on. Paul played the rest of the round putting with his 2 iron. A few holes later when he was putting the ball jumped as he stroked it. I casually made the remark, "Hey Paul that ball jumped." He turned to me and sneered, "What do you expect when you are using a 2 iron to putt?" After the match was over, it was so funny to see Paul and Maynard walking down the first fairway carrying a ladder to fetch his putter.

I had many, many matches with Paul. Every Thursday night Paul and I would engage in a friendly 9-hole match. The loser had to buy the pizzas at the Cape Cod Cafe, (HOME OF THE BEST PIZZAS IN THE WORLD). When we first started these matches, nine out of ten times it would be Paul picking up the tab. As time went on Paul and Maynard improved greatly, so the odds of the matches eventually evened out, to where it about became 'dutch treat' at the Cape Cod Café. Paul competed fiercely on the course, and his friendship off of it was equally intense.

I recall one of my matches with Paul Stetson. Frannie Mansfield and I were paired off in a nine-hole match against Paul and "Jiggs" Lucini, the owner of the local Ford franchise. Fran Mansfield was an outstanding athlete in High School until he was hit with the devastating Polio disease. It left him severely handicapped for the rest of his life. Fran did fight back though, and with the use of crutches he played a pretty good game of golf. He would swing with one hand while he supported himself with the crutch in his other hand.

In this match, I had one of those magical rounds when everything went my way. Paul Stetson shot an even par 36 and I shot a one under par 35. I had 8 1-putt greens and a chip-in for a birdie on the 4th hole. When we completed the match, Fran Mansfield gleefully remarked, "Stetson hit every green in regulation with two putts for a par 36 and Folloni doesn't hit a single green in regulation but he still beats Stetson!"

I can still visualize Maynard Stetson's favorite 'SHANKING HOLES'. The 2nd, 6th, and 7th. He would go along playing par golf for 5 holes, then on his second or third shot on the short par 5 sixth hole; he would promptly shank one out of bounds. Maynard's cousin Paul owned a successful exotic fish farm and store, and had a bit more time to practice than he did, but except for the occasional lurking melt-downs, Maynard did more than hold his own, and was a good partner and foe.

Every year, the last Wednesday of September, "Doc" Carr would make the arrangements to go to a golf course down the Cape to play the ""Doc" Carr Tournament." During one of these tourneys at the Wianno Country Club while playing the par 3 third hole, Maynard hit one of his famous shanks that ended up through the window of a cottage off the fairway. Paul stepped up with a big smile on his face and emulated Maynard by shanking his ball in the lower half of the same window that Maynard had hit! Talk about the closeness of cousins!

Maynard eventually got over his shanking days. He took a few lessons and turned out to be a low handicapper. He also did all right for himself as he first took over running the restaurant at the Halifax Country Club and later became the owner of the entire club. He eventually sold it for a hefty price and is now spending his retirement in Florida.

One of my favorite golf stories comes from when Dave Flynn and I were paired off as partners for the club four-ball championship. We were in the semifinals playing against the formidable team of Eddie Mahoney and Roger Boucher. We were all even at the end of 13 holes.

Dave was first to tee off on the 14th hole. As he came down from his back swing he suddenly "broke wind", which distracted his golf swing and he proceeded to hit the tee shot out of bounds way into the woods. Needless to say there was pandemonium on the tee. We all broke out in laughter. Talk about a windy politician!

Next it was my turn to tee-off. Well would you believe it, I was so shook up with laughter that I hit under the ball and popped (pooped?) it straight up in the air. Needless to say we lost that hole, the only hole that was won by either team, and Mahoney and Boucher went on to win the match 1 up. They also went on to win the Club Four-Ball Championship in the Finals. I guess you could say that we *really* blew that one!

One year later, fate had the same two twosomes paired against each other again in the semifinals for the Club Championship. This time we were more careful about what we ate for breakfast, but nonetheless after the same 14th hole we found ourselves down by 4 holes with only 4 holes remaining. We were "dormie", which means that we couldn't win in regulation, but with a great comeback we could tie and push the match into extra holes. As we walked off of the 14 green I put my arm around Dave's shoulder and said, "Dave we ain't dead yet, *Let's Go*". ("We can still blow these guys out!")

I then birdied the 15th with a 6-foot putt, and birdied the 16th with a long putt. On the 17th I came up with my 3rd straight birdie. We were then only one down going into the last hole. Just to prove that I was human, (and to let Dave have the pleasure of chipping in?) I proceeded to dump my tee shot into the rough a few yards in front of the tee. Dave came through like a champ with a birdie on the last hole to even up the match.

The rest was almost anti-climatic. We went on to win the match on the 21st hole. On our way back to the clubhouse, Dave gave me the greatest compliment ever. He said, *"Larry you have just got to be the best 10 handicapper in the world."* I knew what he meant. I was never a great golfer; my style was mechanical, with a grooved short back swing and a great short game. My handicap ranged between 8 and 10 for most of my golfing career. One year as the 'Pro' in our Pro-Am Tourney group, I shot a 3 under par 69 on my own ball. The handicap committee immediately cut my handicap down to two.

When I accomplished this fabulous round of 69, an interesting sidelight occurred. When we reached the first green, I had about a 3-foot putt remaining for my par.

As I looked in my bag for the putter it was nowhere to be found. One of my youngsters had borrowed it the day before and didn't replace it in my bag. I now had to run back to the clubhouse and retrieve my putter from my locker. After running back to the green, still puffing and out of breath, I proceeded to miss the short putt. I managed to recover after this start to shoot the 69, which included 4 birdies, 13 pars and one bogie. Only in retrospect can I thank my son for allowing me to avoid a '1' handicap!

The week after the committee cut my handicap down to 2; I was scheduled to play in the annual Member Guest Tournament up at the Manchester Country Club with my brother-in-law, Elmer Balboni. In our first round match we were paired off to play against a pair of 6 handicappers. And Manchester is a much longer course than BCC, which was more suited to my close-in game.

After watching one of these 6-handicappers whack his drives about 250 to 275 yards on every hole, I asked him how he carried his handicap. Here I was giving away 4 strokes to someone who out drove me by 50 to 75 yards. He responded that he only turned in his scores when he played the longest 'Blue' Tees. Well in spite of this mismatch of handicaps, Elmer and I still went on to defeat this team.

Year after year Elmer and I finished in the top three in the Manchester Country Club Member Guest Tourney. I learned a valuable lesson from Elmer during one of those Member Guest Tourneys. That year we both started out by taking double bogies on the first hole.

On our way to the second tee, Elmer said to me, "Don't let those two double bogies worry you. Remember we are only amateurs and we are going to get 6 or 7 bogies in a round of golf. So if we get them in the first hole we won't get them later on. With this reassurance in mind we went on to finish the round in a flourish. I birdied the tough 17th hole then knocked in about a 30-foot curler for another birdie on the 18th.

It was a medal play tourney and this ending surge gave us a tie for first place. We went on to a sudden death play-off. The first overtime hole was halved with pars. Then on the next hole, a par 5, I had hit my second shot into the woods and was out of the hole. Elmer hit his second shot into the rough in a deep gully in front of the green. One of our opponents hit his second shot up on to the fringe of the green with a putt of about 20 feet remaining for an eagle. It looked pretty bad for our team. Elmer went down into the deep gully with a wedge and a prayer. God must have answered, as he put his shot about a foot from the pin and an easy tap-in bird. Meanwhile our shaken opponent three putted from the fringe and we walked off with another Member Guest Championship. My sister Angie told me that son Michael, who was our caddie, showed off his flair for the dramatic joke that day as he hurried back, two bags as big as he was in tow, to the waiting throngs at the clubhouse. Angie asked him how we did, and Michael just kept a straight face and walked in silent, feigned dejection to a quiet corner to tend to the clubs. There he listened as rumors abounded about the demise of the Balboni – Folloni dynasty, only to allow us to come in minutes later with the surprising true results!

I have met and played with a variety of people and made many lasting friendships. The notable people that I played with included Boston Celtics Basketball Hall of Famers Bob Cousy and Bill Russell. And of course Boston Red Sox Hall of Famer Ted Williams, who was probably the best hitter in the history of baseball.

I was thrilled to be able to compete on the golf course with these well known personalities but the greatest thrill that I had was the privilege of playing with the noted blind golfer, Joe Lazzaro* who played with a caddie who described playing conditions to him. Joe lost his sight while in the service when a landmine exploded in front of him. This guy was simply amazing. For the 9 holes we played he had a score of 43, ending up with a birdie 2 on the last hole. After watching such an unbelievable feat by this blind golfer, I made up my mind to never again complain about a missed golf shot.

* Not to be confused with my lifelong buddy, Joe Lazaro of Bridgewater.

I'd also be remiss to not mention one of the Greatest Champions in the *'Game of Life'* who I've had the pleasure to know: Dr. William Cohen. Doctor Cohen was a successful Orthodontist who bought a house for his family right near the ritzy Thorny Lea Private Golf Club. He somehow noticed my success in golfing, and approached me to ask if I could give him a few pointers. Here he was an esteemed Doctor, and he was treating this simple teacher like I was really some kind of pro whose opinions mattered. Our sessions grew into a friendship and we eventually became partners in some member-guest tourneys at Thorny Lea and later at BCC.

Although we never won, we did more than respectably, and most importantly we had respect for one another. Perhaps this respect grew in part from both of us having come from what at those times were considered minority groups, and from both of us having struggled to achieve success in our fields. Dr. Cohen not only treated all he met with dignity and class, but he also he took it upon himself to give free orthodontic treatment to many, including the children of this teacher who was raising 6 kids on a $12,000. annual salary when our house burned down in 1963. Will passed away far too early, but while he lived, he never mentioned to anyone this, or any of his other countless acts of charity. For this I call *Dr. William Cohen an All Time All Star Champion in Life!*

> *"That's the trouble with our charities:*
> *we are always saving somebody away off,*
> *when the fellow next to us ain't eating."*
> Will Rogers, March 22, 1932

TED WILLIAMS 'RED LETTER DAY'
Perfect Practice Makes Perfect (Heroes)

I learned another valuable lesson during a golf match with Ted Williams in 1968. Fellow area coaches and friends of mine Al Palmieri and Joe Comache, worked summers at the Ted Williams Baseball Camp in Lakeville. They called me up one day to arrange for Ted to play with us at the Brockton Country Club.

Ted arrived at my home on Bedford Street with Al and Joe at about 12 noon. After greetings and introductions we went into the house for a cold drink and a snack. My 12-year old daughter Jean had whipped up a batch of Chocolate Chip cookies which she left on the counter to get ready to pack up and ship to her cousin Richard Balboni, who was in a hospital in Vietnam after being seriously injured in battle. Richard was the only surviving member of his platoon. He was listed as Killed-In-Action but miraculously had survived and was returned to the base hospital. Jean had left a note to our family to save the cookies for mailing to Richard. This was unbeknown to Ted as he sampled one of them.

The first cookie tasted so good that he kept on picking away at the plate until very few remained. He finally spotted the note that Jean had written and placed beside the plate, which read: "Please do not touch these cookies, they are for Richard in Vietnam." After reading it Ted was embarrassed and said, "I goofed". Jean, who as always was as sweet as her sweets, told him, "Don't worry about it, I'll bake another batch of cookies for my cousin. Maybe you could just write a little message on the back of this note for him." Ted did and the gracious note and cookies were sent to Vietnam. Later when Richard returned home he told us about receiving the cookies with the note from Ted. He said that he became a hero among the heroes in the hospital for having received a personal message from the one and only Ted Williams!

Well that was the start of a very pleasant day. My youngest son Jimmy posed for some pictures with Ted Williams instructing him how to hold and swing the baseball bat. Undaunted by any pressure, Jim whacked a solid liner straight up the middle!

Ted tips Jim hits.

I had a chance to show Ted my golf machine and he tried it out and had very favorable comments about it. We had some discussions about baseball and hitting. Would you believe, here was the greatest hitter in the history of baseball asking me for some tips on hitting? I found out later that his astounding success as a hitter was due in good part to him always trying to learn something new from any source, even from a mere high school coach.

Well it was then time to go on to the golf course, where my son Michael gained valuable life experience by being Ted's competent caddie, and I learned one of the greatest lessons of my life. Ted was paired off as my partner in a friendly match against Al and Joe. A crowd of on-lookers from the club followed us around the course to watch him hit some towering drives that were reminiscent of the awesome home runs he hit for the Red Sox.

Not that there should be any doubt, but let's be clear: The four of us were all playing to *win*. We had played 12 holes in a pretty close match when on the 13th, Ted hit a wedge from about 90 yards and put it about a foot from the pin. After making this great shot, Ted remained at the spot and practiced his swing. When he finally arrived at the green I gave him a 'high-five' and said, " Nice shot Ted, but tell me why you stood there and practiced after making such a great shot". His classic reply has stayed with me throughout the rest of my playing, coaching and moonlight business career:

Ted placed his arm around my shoulder, and said:

> *"LARRY, WHENEVER I DO SOMETHING RIGHT,*
> *I WANT TO REMEMBER WHAT I DID AND PRACTICE <u>THAT</u>.*
>
> *WHEN I DO SOMETHING WRONG I WANT TO FORGET IT*
> *AND GO BACK TO PRACTICE WHAT I DID RIGHT."*
> - Ted Williams

If Ted Williams batted .406, and he ate 72 of my mom's cookies, maybe I can be an all star if I eat a gillion of them!

Cameron Hank attempts to re-enact Ted William's cookie chowing feat.

HALFTIME ENTERTAINMENT
A Funny Thing Happened on the Way to the Fields

'MIRACULOUS' COMEBACK

'Chauncey' Cole and Denny Bicknell were two Bridgewater H.S. grads who were allowed free court side charity wheelchair seating for a year or more by the Celtics for their Boston Garden games. This arrangement came to a dramatic halt during the final championship game in 1969, when as described by the Boston Globe: "At the game's end a young wheelchair occupant was exposed as an imposter as he was seen running and jumping about the parquet floor."

CLEAN-UP HITTER

Agnes Yakavonis was a kind old maintenance lady at B-R High who handled all of the cleaning and laundry needs of the Athletes. She was a native of Eastern Europe, who settled in Bridgewater with her family. Although she did not have complete mastery of the English language, she was ever so obliging and helpful and loved by all of us.

Following one of our annual athletic awards banquets, my picture appeared in the local papers with some of my athletes. The next morning as I entered the gym lobby, I was greeted by Agnes with her usual cheery greeting. Then she blurted out in her broken English, *"Mr. Folloni, I saw your picture in the paper last night. YOU LOOK MORE BETTER THAN YOU ARE!"*

FIRST FENWAY FUN

Being a central leader in the State Legislature and in our town, I don't know how he found the time, but Dave Flynn would also sometimes bring kids to see professional games in Boston. When my son Jimmy was about 7 years old, Dave brought him to see his first Red Sox Game. Jimmy sat forward in his seat with rapt attention through to the seventh inning stretch when Dave asked him how he liked being at a major league game. Without removing his eyes from the field Jimmy said that it was great. When Dave asked him why Jimmy responded,

"There are No Commercials!"

TITICUT FOLLIES

In 1967 Fredrick Wiseman made what is acclaimed by many to be the greatest documentary film of all time, called "Titicut Follies" which is about the horrendous living conditions at the notoriously archaic and decrepit Mass Correctional Institute for the Criminally Insane in Bridgewater. In his unending quest to be of assistance to all who lived in his district, State Representative Dave Flynn was a frequent visitor to the prison, where administrators, doctors, guards and inmates alike were on a friendly first name basis with him.

Like The Rev. Bob Mayhew and others after him, Dave often arranged special activities to help rehabilitate inmates and to ease their torturously monotonous existence. On occasion Dave would arrange for our High School Varsity Squad to get tougher on the court and softer in social consciousness by playing hoop games against the more sane and athletic of the prisoners.

During one of those contests around 1960, Steve Prophett's Dad Bill was at the scorer and timekeepers table when a prisoner went to him to check into the game as a substitute. Bill asked him: "What's your number?" Without skipping a beat he replied, "J33958"!

SPORTS TRIVIA

*What does the legendary Ty Cobb, who had a lifetime batting average of .366 in his Major League Career from 1905 to 1928, have in common with Larry Folloni's youngest son James?

 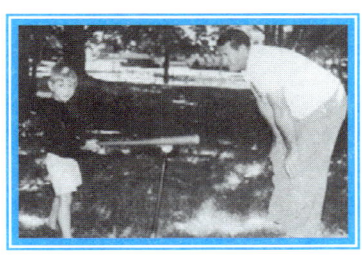 

Ty Cobb in his Prime   Jimmie with Ted Williams   &   Ty's contemporary, Nono

[*Trivia Answer: They both participated in batting lessons with the also legendary Ted Williams.]

Your Kind of Pace

My son Bobby has always found creative and comical ways of lightening up a scene for the pleasure of those around him. One of these stunts was caught on CNN International News, and replayed repeatedly around the world for a day and a half. One day while he was teaching and coaching at the Overseas School of Rome he played hooky along with some of his senior students to attend the grand opening of the first MacDonald's restaurant in Italy. As the CNN announcer stated: "All was quite on the trendy Piazza di Spagna when suddenly…" And the camera panned to Robert leading his crew thundering in dribbling basketballs!

It was back in Bridgewater a few years before that when Bobby first learned that it was customary for the first customer through the door at a new MacDonalds to get free burgers for a year. I'm sure that Bobby made at least of few of these grand openings, bottle of tabasco sauce in hand.

Pride Before the Fall

On September 29, 1960 Hurricane Donna struck New England with 130mph winds. By early morning it had already dropped a large maple tree onto our garage and a few branches on our car, causing moderate damage to the roofs. A little later, Dick Dowd, one of our friendly neighbors, came over to ring our doorbell. When we answered he gave condolences, then smiled and gloated that unlike the rest of us on Maple Avenue, he had wisely taken the precaution to park his new station wagon close to the side of his house away from any trees.

No sooner than the words had left his mouth that a resounding rumble rocked the air followed by the sound of crumbling steel and shattering glass. As we looked past Dick who was turning ash white, we observed the last vestiges of the brick chimney at the side of his roof cascading down to finish off what was left of his new car. To his credit, after getting over the shock, Dick led the laughter at the irony.

COWHIDE

Bridgewater Raynham High School was adjacent to the Hogg's farm that was owned by Ronnie Hogg of my 1956 Championship team. The Class of 1979 included a number of students who's parents worked in one or another capacity for the school, including Danny Buron, Mike Parker, James Folloni, Brian Cabral and Scott Denton. All of these young men went on to successful careers. The names of the perpetrators of the 'Cow-hide' incident may forever be unknown. What is certain is that some Seniors got hold of the keys to the school or propped a door open after-hours days before graduation, and that they led a herd of cows from Hogg's farm into the corridors to spend a night. The custodians were not amused at having to clean up the cow droppings that were left.

DECOY PLAYS

One night while Helen and I were away visiting relatives for the holidays, my son Bobby invited his gang over and his buddy Steve 'Degoberto' Crowley came up with a brilliant idea. He spotted a bottle of vodka that I had won golfing that summer neatly wrapped and ready to be given out as a Christmas gift. Steve emptied the alcohol from the bottle and filled it with water before he very neatly replaced it in the Christmas wrapped box.

Steven & Slim at 30th Reunion of "The Fabulous Cassottos"

The next day, not realizing what Steve had done, I delivered the gift to Brockton H.S. & Providence College Basketball star and B-R Coach Steve Sarantopolous. A few days later when I ran into the Coach he greeted me rather coldly and said, "What kind of a joke did you play on me. We expected to entertain our holiday guests with that. If I wanted a drink of water I could have gone to my water tap!" It took me only a little while to figure out that *at least one Steve* had a real party!

That incident brings to mind "The Stretcher Case". My brother Johnny is a retired Air Corps Colonel, who not so long ago was still in the Air Corps Reserves flying many training missions all over the world. When they went to Puerto Rico it was a common practice for his crew to load up on rum to bring to their Stateside buddies duty free.

On one particular flight as they were headed back to New York they got a tip from friends back at the base that the revenue agents were checking on every arriving flight to catch liquor smugglers at the base.

Johnny and his crew were in a quandary as to how to overcome this sudden obstacle. Meanwhile his cohorts on the ground concocted a quick plan: As their plane taxied up the runway to a stop, an ambulance greeted them. Two of their buddies hopped out of the ambulance and came up to the door of the plane with a stretcher. They started to yell, "Get the Litter Case out to us quickly!"

Johnny was dumbfounded at first. Then he grasped the situation and handed over the cases of liquor, which were placed on the stretcher, covered with a blanket, and then whisked away in the ambulance.

DISCIPLINE

Speaking of military hijinks, my older brother's son Jack was a highly intelligent army recruit who came to find the tedium of his peacetime tasks to be too tiresome, so he decided to give the army some of their own business. His Sargent had asked Jack to drive one of the trucks loaded with thrash down to the dump. Jack respectfully followed his orders to a "T". About an hour later when he returned to his barracks, the Sargent asked Jack why he didn't return the truck to the car pool. Jack's compliant reply: "I drove the truck down the dump as per your order Sir. You didn't ask me to drive it back."

SHOOTING FOR THE MOON

A humorous incident from many moons ago involved my cousin's boy, Willie Ferioli, who later was to become the Police Chief in the town of Bridgewater. Willie was a member of the BHS football team. One day following his gym class he took a shower and since he had some of his clothing left in his football locker which was in the adjoining Team Room, he entered it stark naked.

There was one little item that Willie didn't know at the time. It just so happened that the Football team room was equipped as a dark room and was used by both the boys and girls classes for visual aids teaching. As you may guess, when Willie paraded into the dark room whistling away, the girl's gym class was occupying it. As he turned on the lights he was shocked to suddenly hear the girls all screaming at the sight of him in his birthday suit.

You can well imagine Willie's embareassment. He quickly stormed out of there leaving an image of his scampering backside seared into the memories of the girls. Back in the gym locker room he dressed hastily and in the middle of the school day he left the grounds and headed for home. I never knew what had happened until about an hour later when I received a phone call from Willie's Mom to inform me that he was so upset about the incident that he was never going to be able to face his classmates again.

After several minutes of discussing the embarrassing incident, I convinced his mother to bring him back to the school that same day to take part in his team's football practice. Willie arrived back to my office just before the end of the regular school day. As he entered my office, my assistant Coach, Bernie Chestna was present and as Willie entered with a shy grin, we all burst out into a loud laughter. Well that broke the ice and after a few jokes about the incident we convinced Willie that he could resume his normal school activities without any guilt feelings. To this day every time that I have had the opportunity to meet up with Willie, he always relates this story with laughter.

LARRY'S CRUNCH

Skip Poole, one of my first basketball and football players at Bridgewater High, was a very likeable fellow, who looked a bit more like a sumo wrestler than a basketball player. Despite his size, Skip was a pretty good guard who was very coachable and a great asset to our team.

For decades **Larry's Lunch** was the favorite hamburger restaurant and youth hangout in the center of town. One Friday night Skip's just of age son Glenn stopped into **Larry's** to have a few beers after a long hot week of work on his family's farm. Since he was dehydrated, the brews went down quickly and took effect fast. As was his oft called upon duty, 'George the Greek', a perennial fixture behind the bar and at the grill, shut Glenn off from any more drinks. And as was often the next step, George felt that he had to show him to the door.

While the full house inside **Larry's** was returning to it's normal chatter, Glenn staggered to a nearby construction site, found a bulldozer, and hot wired it on. The patrons were soon stunned by the impact of the bulldozer crashing full speed directly into the brick wall front of **Larry's**. As they scurried for safety, Glenn backed up and with a 2nd thrust broke the wall down. He then backed up a third time and came roaring right at the bar. Fortunately John Kosboski, who was familiar with heavy equipment, was in the bar. John heroically leaped onto the moving menace and quickly disabled it.

Fortunately no one was injured but there was considerable damage done to the restaurant. The incident gained great publicity nationwide including mention on the Paul Harvey and Johnny Carson shows.

Needless to say Glenn had to wait awhile to get his next drink. It's not known whether or not anyone bought one for George or John.

IT'S A SNAP

The world's first Department Store Santa Claus was James Edgar in 1880. He was the owner of Edgar's Department store on Main St. in Brockton (originally North Bridgewater). Of course this tradition caught on big internationally, and it carried on at Edgar's for about 100 years until they closed their doors forever. Weeks before Christmas Edgar's would convert the corner of their top floor warehouse just in front of the attendant-operated elevator into a Santa visiting spot. Helen brought all of our children there for a yearly December pilgrimage. She did that is, until 1958, the year of our story.

Now this was a real big experience for the young children, what with the adventure of the scary ride on the 'old fashioned' elevator with the collapsible iron gating, where passengers could see the floors zooming past as they ascended. Children knew that if their hands roamed outside the cage that they could lose them and that the support cables to the cab might break. It was also scary because the operator almost never stopped the cab right at floor level, and little feet could conceivably misstep sending their owners tumbling down the shaft. Plenty for a child to worry about, but with the reward of seeing Santa at the end was worth the risk.

Naturally big brothers were always close by to whisper reminders of treacherous hazards to little brothers. Once these were survived, big brothers could be counted on to provide further guidance of how to navigate more new experiences. In this case, 9-year old Bobby whispered to 5-year old Michael that when he got on to the lap of the fat man in the red suit, that he should *pull hard on his beard to make sure that it was the real Santa.* Michael did and it wasn't.

Not all the words coming from the not so jolly fat man with the growing welt under his chin were understandable, but Mom explained to Michael that they probably had something to do with a delivery of coal that was expected on Christmas Day.

....

As an 8 year old, Michael was the only one in his class to memorize the long poem "THE BEST DAY OF THE YEAR" for their Christmas play. He was the star of the production. Santa's helper is shown here reheasing with Nono, cousin Linda Balboni, and Uncle Johnny's mother and father in law. I guess that young Michael felt some pressure to even the score with Santa. His gem of a performance transformed prospects of coal in his stocking. He said that it was a snap.

JACKIE THE FIRE / MILK MAN
Bringing the Fire to the Firehouse

Many little boys at one time or another talk about some day becoming a milkman or a fireman. How many of them can say they did both in one day? While driving a milk truck on Mass. Ave. in Arlington one day, Jackie Mark noticed smoke through the rear view mirror. The smoke rapidly turned into a full-scale fire in the back of his truck. Jackie thought quickly. Knowing that the Arlington Fire Department was nearby, he headed full throttle towards it. As he approached the entrance at a good clip, Jackie realized that the brakes had burned out with the fire. That didn't scare Jackie. He proceeded to drive the truck right through the fire station's front door!

A fireman was sliding down the pole yelling 'Where's the fire?' as his colleague responded, 'Right here!' The Fire Chief scolded Jackie, "You're drunk." Jackie fired back, "What are you, crazy? It's Ten O'clock in the morning!"

The fire was put out and the milk truck saved thanks to Jackie's quick thinking. Jackie was probably popular with the milk company though I don't think he ever went on to finally join the Arlington Fire Department. I wonder if they truck-proofed the firehouse door when they fixed it.

PAPA GOT LOST

One day in the early 90's when Jean and her 3-year-old daughter Taylor were vacationing with us in Florida, we went shopping at the upscale Galleria Mall in Ft. Lauderdale. While Helen and Jean went on a shopping spree, they left the babysitting chore to Papa. Well of course I had to entertain little Taylor and the best place I could find happened to be at the Disney World Store.

After about a half-hour roaming around and perusing all of the Goofy offerings, Taylor finally became engrossed watching the large screen with animated Disney Characters. I decided to play a little prank on Taylor so I hid myself out of her sight while she preoccupied with the Disney Characters.

After she had her fill of the screen, she looked around to join her Papa who was no where to be found. She walked around a couple of isles looking for me as I 'Larry Ducked' around staying just out of sight behind her. Finally out of frustration in not finding Papa, Taylor approached a female store attendant for help. Her approach and appeal was a classic. She tugged upon the attendant's pants and said, "Will you please help me find my Grandpa, I think he's lost"

Taylor Rose showing Papa a few dance moves before he got lost.

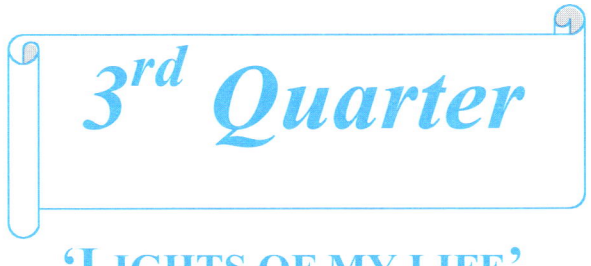

3rd Quarter

'LIGHTS OF MY LIFE'

"Don't stay in bed, unless you can make money in bed."
George Burns (1896-1996)

- ***Real Estate and Stock Market Ventures***   SIDELIGHTS
- ***Work Ethic***   MOONLIGHTS
- ***More Golfing & Vacations***   FLIGHTS
- ***Favorite Things***   HIGHLIGHTS

When Love and skill work together, expect a Masterpiece!

The Folloni Team Enjoying the Fruits of Labor & Love circa 1984

REAL ESTATE AND STOCK MARKET (AD)VENTURES
Sidelights

REAL ESTATE & STOCK MARKET (AD)VENTURES
In Support and Enrichment of our Family Life

LIVING WITH THE MARK FAMILY

After my discharge from the Army Air Corps in 1946 while I was attending Boston University, we were very fortunate to have Helen's family take us in to live with them at 12 Henderson Street, in Arlington, MA. We were sheltered in one of their large bedrooms on the 2nd floor that was big enough to place our bed and dresser and a crib for Larry Jr.

When Helen's brother Paul married his beautiful neighbor from across the street, Frances Mary Quattrocchi, (the sister of Richard Quattrochi, who married Helen's sister Teresa) we were in need of more space to house us all. Fortunately for us, Paul then purchased a two family home on Chandler Street.

Papa & Mama Mark, with children, grandchildren, & friends in 1950

Paul and his family occupied the first floor and the rest of the Mark family moved in up to the 2nd floor. Again it was a crowded situation. In order to make room for us while I was completing my education at BU we had to do a rough remodel of the unfinished attic on the 3rd floor.

With the help of Paul, who did the electrical work and my brother Mike, who drove up from Bridgewater on the weekends, we finally managed to complete making a livable space to accommodate us.

Our stay at Chandler Street is remembered for a number of reasons. Mainly I got to know the Mark clan as a true fun and loving family. I can recall many happy occasions during our short stay with them.

Paul Mark in the Navy

Papa and Mama Mark, all smiles

The Marks were great tea drinkers and it was traditional to have the nightly tea and doughnuts that Helen's sister Milly's boyfriend would bring without fail. Another ritual that I recall was that every Friday night I would take Papa Mark down to the Camel Lounge, near the Cambridge line for a quick treat. Within minutes he would drink a shot of whiskey, then gulp down a beer chaser and say in his English accent, "O.K. Larrie Let's Go."

Helen, Paul, Eddie & Jackie

Like my family, the matriach of the Mark clan was very religious, and the patriach was devout in his own dignified work-a-day way. Since Mama Mark emigrated from Ireland alone to the USA at the tender age of 8, and since she didn't carry any official birth records, we always celebrated her birthday on St. Patrick's day.

Larry Jr. & Jackie Mark, leaders of the new generation play at the beach. 50 years later both would later play key roles in saving my life!

Who knows, maybe Nellie helped too.

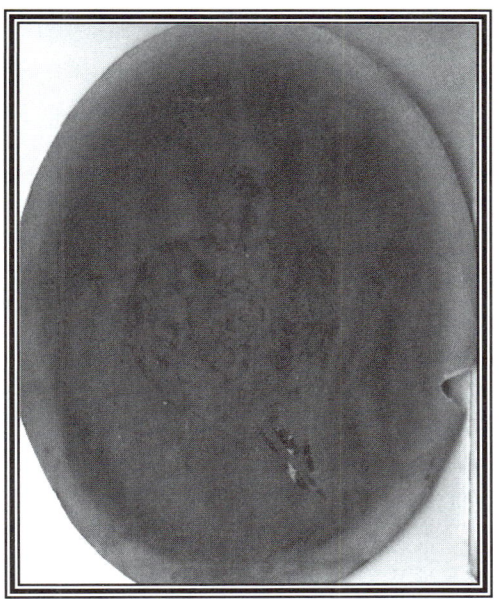

And every year on Christmas she would bake a great cake and all of the extended family would stop by to sing "Happy Birthday to Jesus"! Naturally Helen grew up going to Catholic school. Helen's Godmother was a close friend of her dad's who her family called 'Aunt Nellie', who frequently had the mysterious experience of the 'Stigmata'. This is a phenomenon of spontaneous bleeding from the same areas of one's body where Christ' body was pierced during his crucifixion. When Nellie would bleed onto a paper it would often create an image of a (sacred) heart, sometimes even with the visage of Christ inside. Helen framed and has kept a couple of these cherished relics all her life.

My mundane daily routine while staying with the Marks was hectic to say the least. During the week I would be up at 6am and grab a couple of Mama Mark's heavenly home cooked muffins.* With my school books in my green bag slung over my shoulder and with the muffins in my other hand, I would make the dash 1/2 mile up the street to catch the street car to head for my day at BU.

The recipe for Mama Mark's delicious muffins has been carried down to my wife Helen and then down to daughter Jean, who now makes those delicious blueberry, cranberry & cinnamon delights every Sunday. Mama's great granddaughter Taylor says that she will carry on the tradition.

My day at BU started with me reporting at 7am to BU's head maintenance man, Sylvio, who would line up my work for the next two hours. One of my chores was the landscaping work around the new buildings on Commonwealth Ave. To this day every time that I go by this area I take pride in the fact that I had a part in cultivating the nice green grass that grows there.

From 9am to 3pm I would attend classes. Then I would head out to Nickerson Baseball Field for practice or games. After practice I had another of the many jobs that BU made available to help support me through college. I worked for about one hour handling the athlete's laundry items.

"If things seem under control you're not going fast enough." Mario Andretti

I then headed back in town to work another 2 hours as a lifeguard at the BU swimming pool. At around 9pm I would head for my 4th job of the day, which was a four-hour stint at the Postal Annex at the South Station.

Then it was time to take the trip back via the streetcar to our home on Chandler Street in Arlington. I would get back to the house at about 1:30am and wake up Larry Jr. for a half-hour just to relax and finally enjoy my first baby son. I kept up with this schedule throughout my school days at BU.

Larry's 1st spring in Cambridge with Helen, 1946

Here's one incident from those days that makes me chuckle now, but which seemed pretty serious at the time: During the early spring, when I was getting myself in good running condition for the baseball season, it was my custom to do as much running as I could sneak in. This included my post midnight habit of running with my green book bag slung over my shoulder from the street car stop at the Capital Theater and cutting across the Hardy School yard playground to home. One night as I exited the schoolyard, a police patrol car cut me off and two officers came out to confront me with their guns drawn. I was bewildered and frightened to say the least. Thinking that they had apprehended a thief, they instructed me to put my hands in the air. They asked me why I was running across the schoolyard at that hour and demanded to know what I had in the green bag.

I tried to explain to them that I lived in the house across the street; that I had my schoolbooks in the bag and that I was running to get in shape for the upcoming baseball season at BU. This explanation didn't satisfy them and they asked me to show them my identification. I pulled out my license and the address on it showed that I was a Bridgewater resident. Then I was really in trouble. After much pleading, I finally convinced them to ring the doorbell at the house to get my wife Helen to identify me.

When Helen came to the door to claim me, they were finally convinced that I was not a thief. The story does not end here. The police wrote the incident up on their blotter and the word got around the town about my escapade with the police. Gerry Hern, the Sports writer for the now defunct Boston Post Newspaper was a resident of Arlington and got wind of the incident.

A few days later this story was the feature of his daily sports column. After relating the story to his readers he stated: "From now on when Larry Folloni, the stellar 2nd baseman for the Boston University baseball team, does his Spring training, he will restrict his running to Nickerson Field."

We remained at Chandler Street until I graduated from Boston University. In the fall of 1947 I took my first teaching job in Dighton. Once again it took the benevolence of family to see us through. This time it was the Folloni's on Wall Street in Bridgewater who were gracious and kind enough to make room for us until we were able to get our own home.

Larry Jr., Nono, Bobby and Helen at Wall Street in 1951.

Note Helen's warm coat from the Newberry St. fur shop of her sister Teresa's husband Richard Quatrochhi

5 years later, in 1956, the extended clan was still, as ever, welcoming.

l-r: Brother Mike, Bobby, Erminia, son Michael held by Larry Jr., daughter Jean held by Helen, Al, Nono, Sia and Angie in Back, with Richard and Linda Balboni in front with Connie.

From early childhood my son Michael liked to show the way. Here he stands at the entrance of the also ever-welcoming Mark home on Chandler St. in Arlington. "Grandma lives up there!"

36 MAIN STREET, BRIDGEWATER, MA,
PURCHASED 1948

Our Real Estate Adventures began with the purchase of the property at 36 Main Street, in the town center of Bridgewater, MA.

The very successful Dr. Belmore, who specialized in delivering babies during the post WWII *Baby Boom*, owned this two-home complex. He delivered more than 3,000 babies during his career! More than a few of them became my students. He became a great philanthropist to the local communities and he also made a huge contribution to the St. Ann's Catholic Church that was named in memory of his wife.

When he purchased this property on Main Street, it was his intent to make it a center for Nuns with the idea of building a convent at the rear of the complex. In addition to the three-family home at the entrance, there was a 5-room bungalow behind it, and he had already built the cement foundation for the convent.

For reasons unknown to me his plans for the religious center never materialized. The property had become a bit run down and was up for sale. It was in an excellent location, right in the center of the town. My dad and my brother Al, a New York real estate broker, immediately sized it up as a great investment opportunity, and they encouraged us to go for it.

So it became time for negotiating the sale. The asking price was $15,000. We took little Larry along with us to our first meeting with Dr. Belmore and he immediately took a liking to Helen and Jr. We explained to the good Doctor that I had just started my first teaching job and that since the pay was minimal, at his asking price it would be very difficult for us to come up with the necessary down payment to secure a mortgage. Several days went by and we finally got a call from the philanthropist. He informed us that he was sympathetic with our plight and that he would let us have the property for $10,000.! *What a blessing and a bargain this turned out to be!*

With the help of my Dad and my brother Mike, we came up with the down payment needed to secure the mortgage. There's an interesting sidelight story to our receiving this loan.

We applied for the mortgage at the Bridgewater Savings Bank that just so happened to be adjacent to this Main Street property. A few years later when the bank wanted to expand their facilities, they needed some extra land that then belonged to me. The shoe was suddenly on the other foot and they had to come begging to us for the land that they had earlier refused us a mortgage on!

At long last, we finally had the first home of our own! We had many happy experiences living in the 36 Main St. complex.

It was here that we began to raise our first three children, Larry, Bobby, and Michael. We had a nice back yard that my Dad and his neighbor 'Poleti' had cleared for the children to play in. This was a nice area for family get-togethers and cookouts, and we've always treasured the moving pictures that we kept from that era.

Larry showing Bob the way.

I set up a tire swing and one of my many innovative ideas and inventions: a *baseball batting tee* in this area for all the children in the neighborhood to use. This was the place that the Little League All Stars gathered to warm up before loading onto Sam Alfieri's truck to head out to their games.

36 Main was the home where 'Uncle Mike' brought us our first pet who we named "DUKE". Duke was a joy to the family for the next 6 years until someone broke our hearts by "Dognapping" him.

I always loved pets, but I hated that we out-live them. And I hated that when they grew too old to go on, the final ride to the vet was with me.

"And now, as tears subside, I find it all so amusing" —My Way

It was at 36 Main St. that Larry and Bobby would gang up with our young neighbor Kevin Chiocca and others in friendly jousts. It was also where they teamed up one night to pull an all time classic prank on their baby-sitter, George Zenaletto. Shortly after we left for the evening the kids engaged George in a game of 'Hide & Go Seek' and tricked him into going into a closet where they promptly locked him in for the entire time until we arrived home later that night! Poor George was too embarrassed to admit what had happened until years later. God knows what other schemes Larry and Bobby dreamed up while their keeper was kept!

Angelic Pride & Joy, Larry

Sweet but deceptively sly and definitely rambunctious Bobby & Larry were the scourge of babysitters.

Helen and I were preparing to leave this house one day for a birthday party at Mama Mark's when we had a humorous catastrophe. Helen had baked a beautiful cake with all the trimmings on it and she asked me to bring it out to the car. Well as I came out into the hallway onto the stairwell, I tripped on the first step. The cake flew out of my hands and fell the entire flight where it landed perfectly upside down an on the first floor! Helen's face dropped at the sight of seeing this disaster. Incredibly the cake itself was not damaged too badly, except for the decorations on the top. Helen went to work to patch and redecorate it and an hour later we were on our way to the party in Arlington.

Every Christmas season I would hook up a loud speaker on the porch and with my home made amplifier system we would pipe out Christmas Songs for the entire neighborhood to listen to. One time, however, I inadvertently shared a little too much of the stress of the holiday season. On this particular day, the children were getting more rambunctious than usual and I took a fit of screaming at them. Our back door neighbor Donnie Strong (who was to become one of my players on our 1956 Championship team), came knocking on our door and said, "Coach, your speaker is carrying your voice all over town." *Talk about voices we have heard on high!* Boy, was I ever embarrassed. And what's worse, *Larry and Bobby, who started the ruckus were able to get in a good laugh at me!* I then knew how George Zenaletto felt.

These are but a few of the precious memories of our happy times at 36 Main St.

Dad must be babysitting

Tired of barley breakfasts, Bob breaks open a 6lb pack of wheat

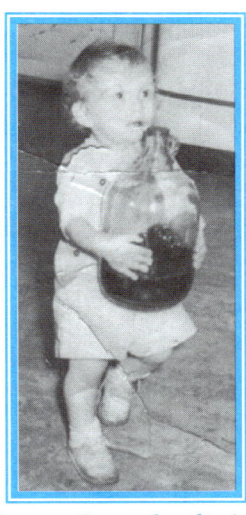

Lug a Jug of cider!

I can still recall the day that Bobby as a 2 year old youngster, went out in the back of the kitchen and got hold of a box of *'Softasilk'* flour and tipped the contents all over himself and onto the floor. *Smooth move, Bob.* Larry Jr., always there to help his siblings, was tugging his arm to pull him away from the mess.

Always the 'salt of the earth', Larry honed his sterling character early.

At left learning to think outside the box.

At right encouraging Bobby to eat his Quaker.

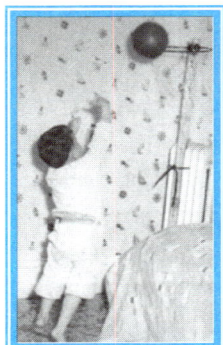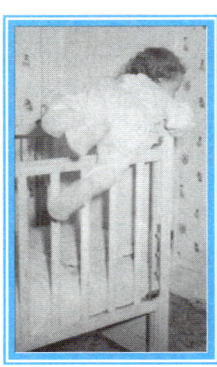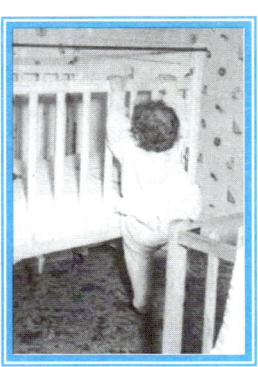

The always mobile Bob was making fast breaks from his baby crib, so I spent an hour 'escape-proofing' it with an extra barrier. This 'prevent defense' stopped Bob for about 10 seconds.

Larry perfecting his form early. *Bob making an easy escape.* *No defense could contain Bob's moves!*

From birth Bobby was extremely determined in whatever he set out to do. This photo essay of his perseverance in getting up onto the bathroom sink via the toilet bowl to grab his toothbrush is demonstrative of this trait.

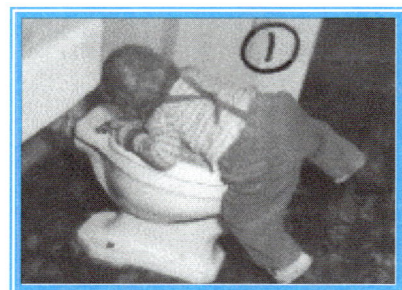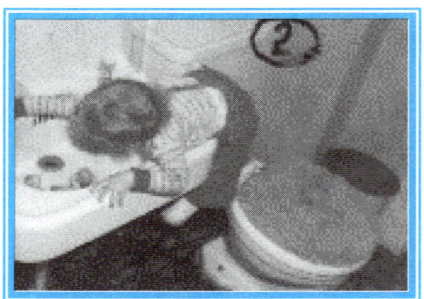

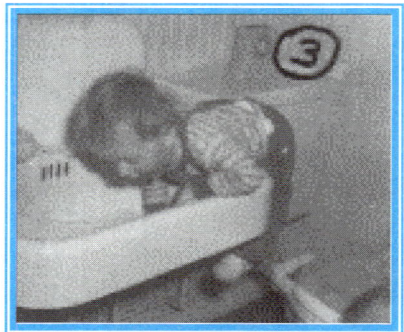

Mission Accomplished!

"Obstacles are those frightful things you see when you take your eyes off your goal"
Henry Ford (1863-1947)

Larry's 5th Birthday Party

Larry, Bobby & Cousin Linda Balboni Main St. Christmas '49

Bobby's first of several lifetime splashes onto the national media scene came at the tender age of 13 days!! We occupied the second floor of the complex and it was here in 1948 that we had the joyful experience of watching our *less than 2-Week old* son Bobby shock the country by walking! He was called *"The Amazing Walking Baby"* and he made the headlines in newspapers through out the USA. As a result of the extensive publicity he was the recipient of many baby toys from manufacturers from all over the country. He has continued to amaze people his entire life.

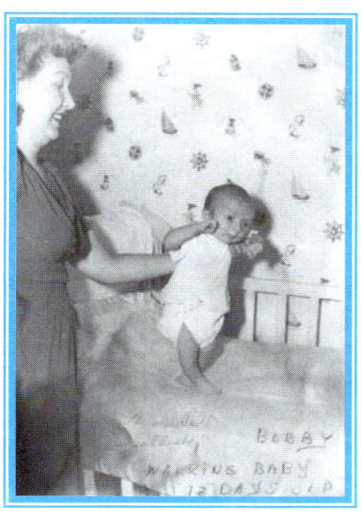

Bobby always on the move

We rented out the first and third floor apartments and the rear bungalow. The rental incomes, though not high, (about $30 per month each), helped us with our necessary expenses and the mortgage payments.

Interestingly, one of our renters from this time period was the DuLong family, from which came son Arthur, who turned out to be a premier distance runner. Like the Amazing Walking Infant Bobby, *Art also astounded the country by covering the mile run in 4:01 in high school, a*nd he later became an accomplished international steeplechase champion. And of course my son 'Baby Michael' also became a record breaking long distance runner in high school. *Whatever was in the water at that place should have been patented, bottled and sold!*

A big opportunity for us arrived one day when a Shell Oil Company agent came knocking at our door. He informed us that his company was interested in a piece of my land to build a gas station. This set in motion a series of deals that was be fascinating to say the least. There was another vacant lot between my land and the bank that Shell also needed to complete their gas station project. This lot belonged to a Greek gentleman from Whitman, who had hopes of setting his son up with a restaurant there. For reasons unknown, the son did not follow through with this project and the land remained unused for several years.

So I approached the owner of this lot and took out an option to purchase it, pending the deal with Shell. In our negotiating sessions with the Shell representative, we came up with the possibility of me building and owning the gas station. The offer appeared to be a very lucrative one. Shell would give us a 15-year lease at a sum that would more than pay for the monthly mortgage payments plus a little extra. We mulled the offer over and over and finally agreed to accept it.

A few days went by when the Shell agent came back to inform us that his Headquarters Office could not give out any deal that exceeded a total of $39,000. He then rewrote the deal for 11 years to bring the total amount under that cap.

We then had to make a crucial decision. Should we sell the land and take the money, or go for the lease deal that was offered by Shell? We went to our lawyer, Mr. MacMaster, who was a shrewd, but conservative man, for his expertise and advice. His counsel was to take the money and run. I'll never forget him saying, *"A bird in the hand is worth two in the bush."* (A key to applying axioms is to know when to and when not to do so. For the correct answer, buy my next book.)

We took his advice and sold our portion of the land, along with the vacant lot that I had the option to purchase for $3,000. We accepted the $15,000 from Shell and with the $12,000 profit we paid off our mortgage on the 36 Main Street complex.

This was a decision that I was later to regret. Even though the money seemed lucrative at the time, in the long run we would have been far better off financially if we had accepted the lease arrangement that was offered to us.

Two years later we had another great opportunity. We had a call from a young dentist named Dr. Ivan Rifkin, who was interested in setting up his dental practice on the first floor. All that he needed was the large front room, which he would remodel at his own expense.

Since the DuLong family rented the first floor we had to do some more 'finagling'. We offered Mrs. DuLong a reduction in her rent if she would give up the front room. She jumped at the offer. We then had an additional rental income from the dental office.

All went well for the next few years as I made my transition from my teaching position in Dighton to my new position in the Bridgewater School system as explained earlier.

At this house we added Michael and Jean to the clan. We then had sons 'Skipper' (Larry), 'Skeeter' (Bobby) and 'Scooter' (Mikey), and daughter, Princess Jean, who would grow up to become 'Jean the Queen'.

We had Bobby practicing his basketball & limbo dancing moves from an early age.

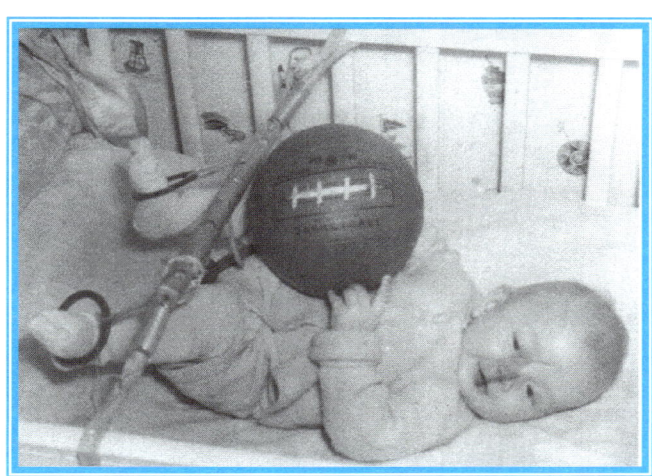

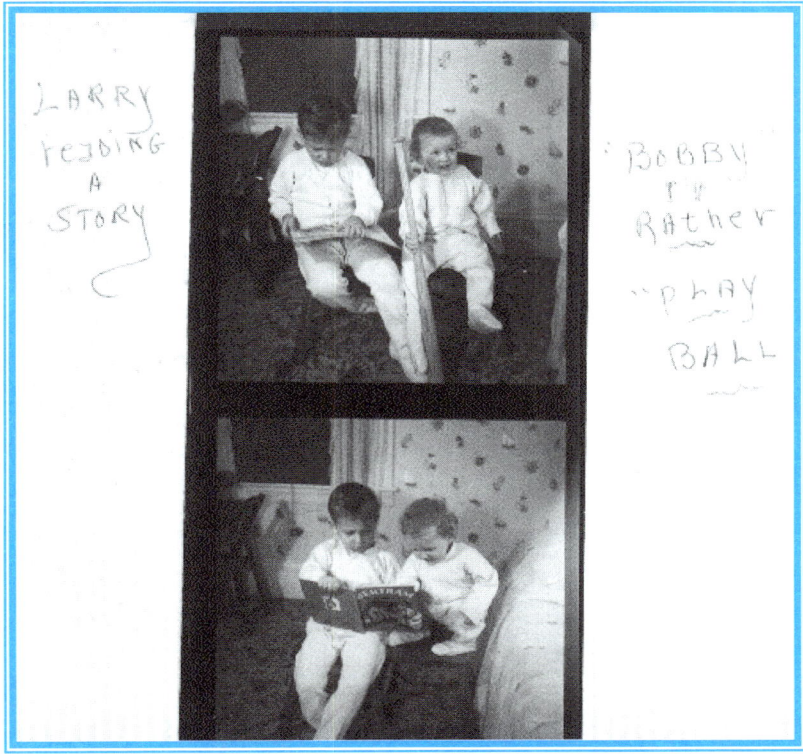

Helen's prodigious scrapbooks include her colorful and very motherly descriptions.

Helen's handwriting was perfect. It appears rough in this page due to the corrugated cardboard back surface that she wrote on.

Bobby & Larry playing on 36 Main land. Main St. in backround.

We would have had smooth financial sledding today had we held on to it.

The 3 income properties at 36 Main St. are now worth millions.

How I wish that I had found a way to hang on to them.

We'd have been back on easy street!

Dad, Michael, Mom & Jean, c. 1954

91 BEDFORD ST., BRIDGEWATER
PURCHASED DECEMBER 30, 1953

"A girl at last!" "Let's start buying & decorating."

With the boys getting bigger and Helen pregnant with the soon to be born Jeannie, we were a bit crowded for space to accommodate our growing family. As would happen again in the future, Little Miss Jean was a key catalyst in the next house acquisition. Her impending appearance let us know that it was time to start looking for more spacious and private housing accommodations.

Newborn Jean in her finery, with Godmother Angie & Mom

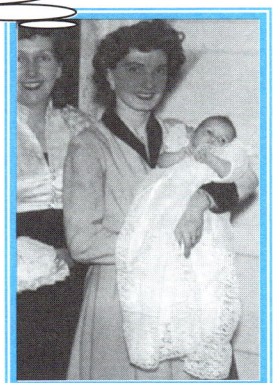

So began the next venture to find the home that was to be our living quarters and the center of our universe for many years. It is a story that only happens in Hollywood (Helen) scripts.

Helen's daily ritual of taking her children down to the playground at Legion Field led to our luck in finding this new home. Helen had to pass the house at 91 Bedford Street, across the street from the Prophett Funeral Home on her way to the playground. It was on one of these many trips that she saw Mr. McLain out in his front yard at the corner of Bedford Street and Maple Avenue and she struck up a conversation with him.

He expressed to her that he had seen her on her daily trips and said, "How would you like to live in this house and avoid the long walks across the busy intersections?" She immediately replied, "I'd just love that!"

Mr. McLain, an MIT grad, explained that since he was retired from his position as CEO of the Gin Works Company, his house was a little too big for him and his wife and that they were building a small bungalow for their retirement years. He asked Helen to go back home and talk it over with her husband and maybe a deal could be made for the home at 91 Bedford St.

Just that indeed we did. As always, we first had to overcome a couple of obstacles. Mr. McLain offered us this beautiful 8-room home in a wonderful location near the Legion Field and near all the schools for the amount of $15,000. Even though at this amount it was a great bargain, we had to inform him that it was out of our price range at that time. An added complication was the fact that in our search for more space for our growing family, we had just contracted with Mr. Brouliard to remodel and enlarge the cottage in behind our home on Main Street.

A few days went by and Mr. McLain came to our house on Main Street with an offer that we couldn't refuse. He said that because he liked Helen and the children so much, that he was going to sell us the house for the unbelievable price of $10,000. Helen's Guardian Angel God Mother 'Nellie', who she would often appeal to for divine intercession, apparently came through for us once more!

On the 30th of December 1953 we passed papers on our dream house, which was to give us many thousands of happy and a few tragic days over the next decades. The house was well built with many extra amenities. Mr. McLain had nothing but the best in his home and as a welcome bonus he left some of his antique furniture, which if we had saved would now be worth a lot of money. Two dresser chests that we did save are still in 'mint condition', and could be sold today for more than we paid for the house!

The only area that needed any updating was the kitchen. We hired Sam Alfieri, one of the best cabinetmakers around to remodel it. He did an excellent job for us and we were then ready to enjoy our new home. The years at 91 Bedford Street were where Jeannie, Debbie and Jimmie were born, and they constituted the prime of the richly rewarding formative family life for Helen, our six children and me. The stories from this epic are myriad and well seared into the memories of all of us and all those who had occasion to share a slice of it.

The regulation sized hoop that I mounted at about 5' high in our 8' tall cellar was the court of dreams for my kids and their friends.

James can too dunk!

Jean, Bobby, Debbie, Mike at QB. Get Set, Get Down, Go Go!

Sharpies Bob Folloni & Bob Baker

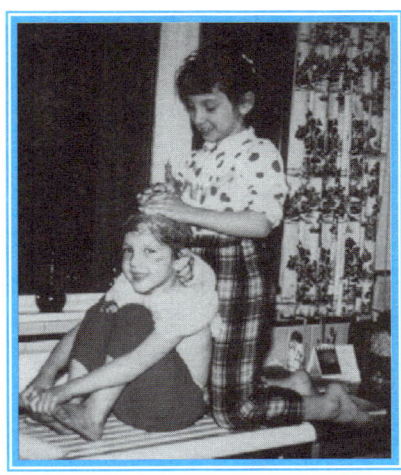

Jean fixing Deb's hair 1960.

"Groucho Mike" with Debbie & Jean Bobby's sign: "Well that's ridiculous!"

Cowgirls Jeannie and Debbie. Cute!

Folloni boys and girls who had been good all year always had all of their dreams come true on Christ' birthday, Christmas.

Pool 'Shark' Debbie practicing to become a lawyer in our cellar before Bobby remodeled the space to make a rental unit. Larry Jr. bought the 7' Brunswick table for his brothers and sisters from his hard earned wages at the local brickyard and auto wash. Larry also generously bought a swingset and many other toys of the time for his brothers and sisters. Educated during the time of 'Sputnik' and the ensuing scientific revolution in this country, Larry developed both brains, and a very charitible heart.

Jean, Debbie, Jimmy and Dutchess skating on Carver's pond in the early 1960's. Note that Carver's pond is where they carved ice in the winter to sell to citizens of town up to the 1940's in order to refrigerate our food.

DISASTER STRIKES THE FOLLONI TEAM

All went very well for us for several years, until one day in September of 1963, when minor tragedy struck. It was a Friday afternoon in the school gym where I was conducting a rally for our first football game of the season. I had just introduced the football coach to the student body and moved over to the end of the gym near the exit when Mr. Serge Bernard our wonderful Superintendent, came up to me and tugged on my coat and said, "Larry come with me. Hurry!"

Not knowing what the urgency was, I obediently followed his instructions and we headed out to his car and off we went. As we drove down Mt. Prospect Street in the direction of my home, I suddenly became panicky and grabbed his arm and asked him, "What is going on, did something happen to someone in my family?" He hesitated at first, then he blurted out, "Larry, your house is on fire."

As we came on to Maple Avenue I saw one of the most heart-breaking sights of my life to date. There were fire trucks lined up on the street and fire ladders hoisted to the upstairs rooms. The smoke and flames were pouring out the windows as the firemen trained the fire hoses on the fire. It was sickening.

My first reaction was of concern for the safety of my family. At the time of the fire Larry Jr. was at home baby-sitting with my youngest child Jimmy, while his mother was out shopping. I soon was able to breathe the biggest sigh of relief of my life and put the scope of the tragedy into perspective when I learned that my children and my wife (and our dog) were safe. Jimmy was around the corner with our friends the Haskells and Larry had made a heroic rescue of our second beloved Cocker Spaniel Dog, Duchess.

Larry had crawled back into the smoke filled hallway that exited the house and found Duchess curled up in a corner. He crawled back out on his hands and knees with the dog safely in his grasp. It was a dangerous rescue. If Larry had raised his head another foot higher, the poisonous fumes that came from the burning plastic tiles and other modern building materials would have killed him.

A few minutes later Helen arrived back home. As she came running into my arms she was hysterical and kept screaming, "My babies, my babies, where are they?" I embraced her and quickly reassured her that they were all safe. Then she kept crying, "My home, my beautiful home, it's gone!" It took some time for me to calm her down and to assure her that we would work things out.

The days that followed were glum indeed. As stressful and difficult a time that we had to struggle through, it was through this stressful period that we were to find the real meaning of charity and community as shared by our families and friends.

Let me recall just a tiny few of the events that followed this tragic fire. Our first step was to move our family back to the Folloni homestead on Wall Street. Early on that next Sunday morning, my good friend, Chet Millett, the principal of our school and a former All American football player at Holy Cross, came knocking at the door of my father's home.

He said, "Larry, come on out to my car and help me." I followed him out and as I looked in the back seat of his car there was a huge Turkey dinner with all the trimmings. Chet had cooked the entire dinner all by himself because his wife was soon to deliver one of their 8 children. God Love that guy and his wonderful wife Mary.

Sergius J. Bernard, 1971 *Chet Millett, 1971*

On that Monday morning when I returned to school, my caring superintendent, Mr. Sergius J. Bernard, called me into his office to console me on our loss. He then said and I'll quote: "Larry take as much time as you need to work out your problems. You can come and go as often as the need calls for your presence at your home."

This kind gesture and offer was a blessing and a great aid to me in getting our home back to living condition. I never abused the use of this offer. For every hour that I took off during the school day to oversee the work at my home, I gave back two or three hours later that night to make up for it.

That same week many offers of help came from my family and friends. The very first was from Fran Mansfield, the owner of the Bridgewater Brick Yard. Fran's son was the quarterback on our football team at the time.

Fran drove up to my home one day and he gave me a blank check and said, "Larry fill in any amount that you need to get you back on your feet." This offer came from his heart and I was grateful to him for the assistance to help tide us over until we were able to re-mortgage the house.

The next major act of charity on our behalf came from Dr. Wilfred Cohen, an orthodontist and a frequent member guest partner of mine at the Brockton Country Club and Thorny Lea golf courses. Two of my youngsters were undergoing orthodontic work with him. When he heard of our misfortune he promptly credited the entire balance on our amount that was owed, which was substantial.

In the next few weeks following the fire, the students and teachers at the B-R Regional School conducted a collection and a good sum of money was given to us to help in our home rejuvenation project.

There were many other offers of aid from members of our community but the greatest help, of course came from Helen's and my immediate families. Fortunately, due to the excellent work of the firemen, the main damage was contained to the kitchen, living room and bathroom areas, which were the most expensive rooms. The rest of the house sustained mostly smoke and water damage.

The Insurance Company was very slow in making restitution consistent with the coverage that we carried with our fire policy. In fact we had to go to arbitration in order to reach a settlement. After a few weeks of haggling we finally came to a settlement, which did not begin to cover our loss. We had to re-mortgage the house to pay for the necessary repairs and replacement of furniture, equipment and possessions that was needed.

As soon as we made the settlement, both the Folloni and Mark families with some help from our neighbors all pitched in to tackle the messy cleanup of the burned debris. It was backbreaking work for all of us. Many were the nights that I was up until midnight and 1am working to get us back into our home. The project took the better part of the next six months.

Again we secured Sam Alfieri and his son Tom to reconstruct key portions of the kitchen and home. Tom had been one of the first players that I had coached in the Little League about 10 years earlier, and he was then working with his dad in carpentry and cabinetwork.

Helen and Jean successfully lobbied for a new 'bay window' in the living room to round out the modernized and 'affluent' look. Taking on extra debt to install this window was a big step for us. Our confidence in looking out to the future became reflected there.

91 Bedford St. in 1983

A good part of the house took on a very 'modern' look for a modern family of the late 20th century. Eddie Cruz did the plumbing work. Jimmy Denton, another one of the players on my youth teams, along with Alex Gedutis did the masonry work including tiling the kitchen counters and building a beautiful white brick fireplace in our new living room. Helen had us save the beautiful white antique mantel that was there. We kept it in the garage for years, until we found a nice use for it in 1975.

Helen's brother Paul, who eventually became the Chief Electrician at Harvard, traveled down from Arlington every weekend to do the electrical work. My brother Mike also pitched in and helped me with much of the work. After 6 months of dedicated work by all of us it became springtime and in early April we were ready to get back into our newly rebuilt and refurnished home.

We were finally back to normal family living in the Folloni household at 91 Bedford Street where we were to enjoy the next decade in relative peace and enjoyment.

In the '70's Bobby took on the project of remodeling our front porch and making our cellar space into livable quarters for himself while he was completing his college studies in Bridgewater. (We had already been renting out Larry and Bobby's old bedroom for years.)

Bobby had the help of several of his friends, some of who were players on the many youth teams that I had organized and coached, and they did an excellent job. After Bobby completed his college and left to go over to Italy to teach and coach, we then had another room to rent out to college students. It was the income from these rentals that enabled us to help pay off the mortgage on our dream (vacation) home at 13 Ross Avenue in Hampton Beach, NH.

Two Christmas Dreams Come-true! Jeannie & Debbie. Helen's note in Scrapbook says that they just returned from skating. At birth each Folloni child was given a custom made stocking to hang on the fireplace mantel for Santa to fill. The kids still have and cherish these family heirlooms.

CHRISTMAS, EASTER & 4TH OF JULY AT 91 BEDFORD ST.

20 SOUTH STREET, BROCKTON, MA
NOV. 12, 1964 TO OCT. 2, 1996

After we had overcome our first fire setback at Bedford Street, in 1963, it was time to move on to our next real estate venture. At the urging of my brother Al to get into this field as a sidelight, we decided to have Helen quietly go about the task of inquiring about properties in the Brockton area. She contacted a real estate agent, and we soon found an interesting opportunity for 20 South St., in Brockton, MA.

20 South St., Brockton, MA in 1964 left, and 1984, right

We didn't have any available cash at the time but at the suggestion of my very successful realtor brother Al, we secured an 'OPM' (Other People's Money) loan of $1,000. from my father as a down payment. With that we were able to secure a 20-year mortgage in November of 1964. This $1,000 investment grew to the price of $85,000 when we finally sold the property in 1996. Of course, there were repair and commission costs out of the sale price, but in the end, at least my time, risk, expertise and headaches were somewhat compensated. It is hard to lose out with real estate investments if you can manage to maintain the property and have good relationships with good tenants.

There were, however, many twists, turns and bumps during the 32 years that we owned 20 South St. The first 10 years or so we were fortunate enough to have pretty good tenants. A Mrs. McGovern and her teen-age son occupied the first floor. The Young family whose rent was being subsidized by the Section 8 program, occupied the second floor with their 3 small children.

The only big problem was that I had to pay for the utilities. Since there was only one central heating system that fed both apartments, I had no way to control the escalating costs for heating. And since the tenants were not paying the fuel bills, when it got excessively warm inside their apartments, instead of going to the thermostat and turning down the heat, they would open the windows and let the heat into the cold outdoors.

In desperation, I finally installed two separate heating systems. Then I lowered the rent and had the tenants begin to pay their own utilities. Once they were paying for their own heat, they went to the thermostat to control it and left the windows closed. Next to home ownership, the best thing to help insure personal responsibility is 'ownership' of whether or not the house could be heated the next month in New England's winter. The McGoverns left after 5 years, and the new tenants, a hard working Vietnamese family with 4 young children, came in. The lady of the house kept it immaculately clean. They stayed about 4 years, and finally bought their own home. I was sorry to see them leave, as they were great tenants, *but I was delighted for their success, because they worked hard and truly earned their slice of the American Dream.*

For the first 15 or so years, we managed to break even and even showed a little profit from our venture at South Street. Then in the late 70's and 80's we had a series of costly problems there. Brockton was a city of positive renown, and a great place to live up to that time. Then with the influx of poor minorities from the Boston area and overseas, and the proliferation of excessive dependency-creating government give-away programs, Brockton became infested with drug addicts, deadbeats, and the low-life culture that accompanied them.

Now I have nothing against minorities, immigrants, or poor people. My family was all of those things. I do, however, have a problem with individual irresponsibility and those who foster it. And I have a greater problem with those who don't work to add productivity to our economy, but who do blame the hard working producers who pour their time, expertise and money into developing it. The rapid growth of this destructive culture, combined with misguided state legislation (including counter productive regulations and laws to protect tenants from lead paint, asbestos, and other supposed 'landlord abuses'), proved to be the death-knell for quality of life in that city. Of course, I don't advocate ignoring the poor and their problems, but we shouldn't approach it in a manner whereby, in trying to solve one problem, we end up creating more problems.

> *"Some people regard enterprise as a predatory tiger to be shot.*
> *Others look on it as a cow they can milk.*
> *Not enough people see it as a healthy horse pulling a sturdy wagon."*
> Sir Winston Churchill

This was a time when the tenants' rights movement really got out of hand. The new rules and regulations made it a nightmare for landlords. *Not only was this governmental intervention an albatross to the property owners, but also the intent of the laws actually backfired, and the tenants who were supposed to be protected often ended up becoming the victims.* The landlords, who did not knowingly purchase faulty property, and who could not afford the overwhelmingly high cost of de-leading, would not rent their units to any families with children. Due to a lack of de-leaded housing, families with children were not able to find living accommodations.

The following experience I had is an example of a nightmare scenario from the landlord's point of view. After the Youngs left the 2nd floor apartment, in came the 'Smith' (not their real name) family, a single mother with two children and on the Section 8 subsidized housing program with additional welfare assistance. Ms. Smith was an alcoholic who had not one but several drug addicted boyfriends who would regularly visit. And I later discovered that she had without authorization, sublet the attic rooms to some disreputable individuals. This was the incubator for a lawsuit that was brought against me later. On the first floor we rented to a "Mr. Jones" (again, not his real name), a self-employed painter who was later to be a witness in this suit. He too was addicted to drugs, and was very friendly with Ms. Smith and her associates.

On a summer day in 1991, Ms. Smith left her apartment to do some shopping. While she was away one of her boyfriends (I'll call him 'Mr. Hudson') was beaten up, apparently over a drug deal that had gone wrong. His assailant beat him with a hammer and left him in critical condition. Thanks to taxpayer and medical help, including insertion of a metal plate into his skull, Mr. Hudson managed to survive to become even more hardheaded.

Several months later, I received a registered letter informing me that this fellow was suing me with the claim that, because there was a defective lock on the entrance door, his attacker was able to get in to beat him up. I was furious at receiving this news. Ordinarily, if this was a legitimate claim, I would have gone along with it and had my liability insurance cover the damages. However, since it was a false fabricated claim, and since he had no business being in the apartment in the first place, I was determined to fight the case to the maximum of my ability.

One year later, in May of 1992, (just before my induction to the BU Athletic Hall of Fame) the case was heard in the Dedham Courthouse. The trial went on for one week. The insurance company's lawyer, who was representing me, did an excellent job in defending the case. His efforts, along with my compelling testimony, led to my being absolved of any liability by the jury.

In the courtroom the plaintiff once again asserted his claim for damages on the basis that the lock was defective and that therefore the intruder was able to access the apartment to inflict the injuries on him. He had Mr Jones, the downstairs tenant, testify that the lock had not been functional for some time before the break-in. It just so happened that one week prior to the reported incident, I had made an appearance at the property and upon entering the driveway, I observed Ms. Smith's son hammering away at the bulkhead door lock. I asked him why he was doing this, and he replied that the door to the apartment was locked and he didn't have a key to get in. Now why would he have to break this lock on the cellar bulkhead door if the apartment lock in question was not operating properly?

One other incriminating testimony that I revealed to the jury was the incident when Ms. Smith's daughter, by her own written admission, came home one day and couldn't get in because the door was locked. She proceeded to break the glass on the door to reach in and release the lock so that she could enter the apartment. Mr. Jones verified this by testifying that he installed a piece of plywood to cover the broken window.

It was quite evident that, in these two instances, the lock was effective in its security. After hearing this evidence, the jury saw things our way and dismissed the case. It's just too bad that the only ones who lose in such fraudulent cases are the unjustly accused.

With this problem out of the way, it was then time for new tenants to occupy the apartment. Ms. Smith finally left. A few years later, her son made the headlines in the Enterprise for several robberies that landed him in prison. I had Mr. Jones evicted for nonpayment of rent.

We didn't have much better luck with tenants during the next few years. With the City of Brockton's culture deteriorating rapidly, and with the severe restrictions and exhorbitant regulatory demands, the hardships for landlords went from bad to worse. Here's a letter that I sent to the City of Brockton Board of Health Department on November 16, 1990 as a follow up to their order of ten days prior.

Mr. Winfred Romans, Sanitary Inspector November 16, 1990
City of Brockton, Board of Health
City Hall
Brockton, MA 02401
Re: Premises Violations at 20 South Street First Floor, (Margaret Stevenson)

Dear Mr. Romans:

May I respectfully request a personal hearing to have the Board of Health order of 11-6-90 withdrawn?

There are many extenuating circumstances that you should be aware of before you make any final decision relating to the violations you have listed in your letter of 11-6-1990.

I am not a "Slumlord" and I am very willing, and will do all that is reasonably possible to meet with the minimum Health and Safety Codes of the Commonwealth of Massachusetts. However in all fairness you must realize that the tenants have some responsibilities to maintain the property and should be held accountable for their lack of proper maintenance and care of the property they are living in.

Over the past several years, I have spent over $20,000. on this property to improve the living conditions for my tenants. Including: supplying and installing new modern tile baths, new electric service, new heating and hot water systems, new storm windows and screens, new rugs and linoleum. I also sanded and finished the hardwood floors, redecorated the entire inside, made repairs to outside porch, railings, and gutters, and painted the outside twice. Additionally the cellar and yard have been cleaned up by myself and by some paid help every spring and fall to little avail.

This house is in better shape than most of the rented homes in Brockton. Why are you picking on me? Look at the condition of other houses on South Street. (This is supposed to be a Historical District.) There is no house anywhere that is in 100% condition at all times, including my own home and probably your own home. The house at South Street is livable and clean. (Except for finishing off the molding work in the back room, which the tenants agreed to complete so they could move in sooner, the house was immaculate the day they moved in.)

I just can't afford all the repairs that you demand. I am retired and on a fixed income. Where do I get any help to make these repairs? For all of my efforts to maintain this house and keep it in good livable condition, this Board of Health violation order is what I get in return!

Over the past 7 years or more, I have received from my first floor tenants very little rent including practically "ZERO" rent for the past 2 years. My new tenant has paid me a grand total of $100 plus $650 that I received from the Welfare Department for the first months rent, plus a $650 security deposit, which I cannot use. The lease calls for first and last month's rent payable in advance. This means that as of Nov. 7, 1990 they are in ARREARS $1950, less the $100 paid.

As a housekeeper, this tenant leaves much to be desired. Dirt, garbage and accumulated refuse are what bring 'mice and cockroaches" into the apartment. I don't bring them in. (We never had this problem before she moved in.) Who does the police work on checking the tenants cleanliness and other maintenance responsibilities? The tenants created most of the violations you cite, not me.

Please don't tell me that I have recourse through the courts. I am well aware of the legal process, which protects the tenants. I pay for my own legal protection and *through my payment of taxes, I also pay for the 'FREE LEGAL HELP' that my tenant gets, so that he can cheat me out of my rent. That is real "JUSTICE". I AM PAYING HIGH TAXES AND FEES TO THE CITY, STATE AND FEDERAL GOVERNMENTS. I AM THE ONE WHO IS PAYING THE BILLS FOR THE UPKEEP; I AM PAYING THE TAXES AND FEES. WHERE ARE MY RIGHTS? Where is my police protection from the hoodlums, who break the windows, kick in doors, and damage my property? Where is my Board of Health recourse to these tenants who live like pigs, ruin my property and live "Rent Free" while the courts procrastinate by delay upon delay for frivolous reasons.*

Please don't tell me that these violations that you have listed are due to normal wear and tear on the property. My wife and I have raised 6 children, (4 boys and 2 girls, as rough and tough and athletically orientated as any All-American boy and girl.). We have lived in our home in Bridgewater for more that 30 years, and the same screen, doors, windows, and railings are all still intact and in GOOD WORKING ORDER! Why can't these tenants be made accountable and responsible for doing the same with their families. THE TENANTS ARE THE ONES WHO CREATED THE VIOLATIONS IN ORDER TO GET FREE RENT. The courts and your bureaucracy are too busy protecting the rights of these 'CHEATS' instead of seeing to it that "JUSTICE IS SERVED FOR ALL'.

My wife and I have worked very hard to raise our family in a responsible manner. It certainly wasn't an easy task, but we worked at it. At times, while I was teaching and coaching, I worked at 3 or 4 jobs, moonlighting in order to pay my bills and honor my commitments to society. What have some of these scofflaw tenants contributed to help themselves? They manage to find the money to buy cigarettes and their 6-packs, and they spend anywhere from $40. to $50. per week on junk food, but they can't find the money to pay their rent so that I could afford to keep the houses in better repair.

Don't get me wrong. I am not a mean old SLUMLORD. I have never evicted a tenant for nonpayment of rent. I do realize that there are some people out there, who through no fault of their own are in dire need of assistance and my heart goes out to them. I have, over the years carried many a tenant with free rent in hardship cases, even though I could ill afford to do so.

We have raised all of our children to be charitable and to respect the rights of others. My oldest son's favorite charities are The Globe Santa and the Ouimet Caddie Scholarship Funds. He accepts no gifts from us for his birthday or Christmas. He insists instead that any gift to him be made to his favorite charities.

My third son gave up 6 months of his education time while a junior at Harvard University to go to Guatemala to work for 'FREE' to install a clean water system to help the poor unfortunates living there. When in the United States he organized a series of "Walks for Development", which raised over $300,000 for needy families. Upon his graduation at Harvard, he was given the "Ames Award" for Character and Leadership for his unselfish contributions to his fellowman.

My two daughters and my youngest son have followed in the footsteps of their older brothers. Each has in turn taken over the leadership of the "Hike for Hunger" and 'Project SOUL' in the years that followed to raise a considerable amount of money for the needy. My wife, in between raising 6 beautiful children, found the time to donate her services to teaching Sunday school classes and donated her time as a volunteer worker for many years at the Goddard Hospital. I have recently retired after 38 wonderful years as a teacher and coach and have given many, many, hours of service to my community.

For all the charitable things my family and I have given to the real needy it hurts that society shows it's appreciation by blaming me for the irresponsibility of others.

I recently came out of the hospital from an extensive operation, which will require 3 to 6 months of rehabilitation, and today I have been greeted with this "Court Action Threat". I received this notice, today, Nov. 16 with orders to correct the defects, (which are tenant made violations to avoid payment of rent) by Nov. 20. This gives me a grand total of 4 days (two of which are on a weekend) to correct said violations. DO YOU HONESTLY FEEL THAT THIS IS A REASONABLE TIMETABLE? Didn't someone have the common courtesy to get in touch with me to discuss the problems, if any did exist?

Right now I have exhausted all of my funds in trying to keep my head above water. The City has "milked the landlords dry", what with exorbitant water, sewage, and refuse fees and taxes that are assessed at MUCH BEYOND THE FAIR MARKET VALUE. It is no wonder that the City of Brockton is going to "POT". You are driving out your entire tax basis. What will happen if I don't rent out my apartment and leave the place vacant then abandon the property, which many landlords in Brockton are now doing? The city will now lose more taxable property--Right! Property in Brockton is tough enough to rent without adding any more obstacles.

I would also respectfully request that the Mayor, your City Councilors, Chief of Police, Tax Assessors, and anyone else who is interested in the salvation of the City of Brockton, to be in attendance at this personal hearing that I am requesting.

You can reach me at this number if you wish to discuss this matter or to set up a meeting date. I am looking forward to a meeting with all the people mentioned above to discuss this matter in a rational manner.

Thank you for your time and patience in reading this long letter.

Sincerely,

Larry Folloni
13 Ross Avenue
Hampton, NH 03842

I never got any response to this letter from any representative of the City. They did not drop the order and I had no choice but to borrow more money to comply. The sanitary inspector and his support bureaucracy, who saw no need to engage in dialogue with me, still got their paychecks. The tenants still paid no rent, and continued on their self-dignity and potential-robbing slide down to becoming even greater burdens on society. And the one person who actually did things that could have improved the quality of the tenants' lives was punished.

The string of tenants that followed were also one problem after another. The final blow came when I took in a middle-aged couple with an older child to occupy the first floor apartment. They were a hard-working couple living just above poverty level. Very seldom did they have enough money to meet the monthly rental payments. Being the charitable guy that I am, I carried them for about 3 years. Then the roof caved in on me.

Unbeknown to me, they had taken in one of their grandchildren to stay with them during the summer months. Late in the summer, the child had a cold and the grandparents took him to a doctor. During the routine physical examination, the doctor found traces of lead in the child's blood. By law, the doctor had to look for this problem and report his finding to the Board of Health. Now mind you, this child had only been at South Street for a few weeks, and could very well have picked up the lead poisoning from drinking water, or from his prior residence. Due to the fact that he was then living in my apartment at the time, however, it became my problem to correct and I was also vulnerable to a possible lawsuit by the parents. (Even though he was living there without my knowledge or permission.)

Independent of this problem, by this time we were already very eager to sell this property due to the decline in values, and the other problems mentioned above. A few years earlier, in 1989, we were offered $150,000. for the house. Unfortunately, just prior to the lead paint episode, we had agreed to sell the property for only $85,000 due to market decline. We were scheduled to pass final papers on the sale on a Wednesday, late that summer. Almost everything was in order to complete the sale. All that was needed was the original copy of the Trust Agreement of April 16, 1990. I had called my lawyer who held the original trust copy and requested it so I could culminate the deal. She happened to be out of her office at the time of my call and I informed her secretary that it was URGENT that she get back to me. She never did. Of course, without the documentation, we had to postpone the closing.

As luck would have it, the very next day after we were supposed to close the sale, I received a registered letter in the mail from the Board of Health with the news of the lead paint problem described above. I was flabbergasted and furious at my attorney for not following through on my request. If she had only followed my instructions, we would have completed the sale and I would have been off the hook regarding the de-leading process. And since the home became owner-occupied, they too would have been off the hook. If anyone should have borne the cost of de-leading it should have been the paint companies, or better the government that initially allowed them to sell their product to unwitting consumers.

I not only lost out on the sale, but I was also saddled with a $25,000 expense to de-lead the unit. Two months later, after we completed the de-leading we finally made the sale to a Vietnamese family.

Thus, on Oct. 2, 1996, ended the saga of our adventure at 20 South St.

Sadly, I just recently read in the Enterprise that a tragic fire demolished the house at 20 South Street. There were no fatalities, but the house was totaled.

13 ROSS AVE, HAMPTON BEACH, NH
JUNE 14, 1971 TO PRESENT

This became our 2nd home that the entire family could share and enjoy. How did we ever get involved with Hampton Beach? It's a long story but let me begin. Back in about 1951 we started out on our annual two week family vacation trips that took us all the way up to Quebec, Canada, back to Niagara Falls and upper N.Y., then ending our stop with a few days visit at my brother Al's home in N.Y.

Virginia, Helen and all the kids in Times Sq.

Our first stop over on these trips was always at Hampton Beach, NH. We became very attached to the family beach area and each year we would spend more time there, until it became almost our only vacation get-away.

Helen and the children just loved the annual vacations here and after almost 25 years we finally decided to look for a place to buy at Hampton Beach.

Again it was Helen's aggressive follow-up that led us to 13 Ross Avenue. During the 1970 vacation trip to Hampton Beach we stayed in a rooming house near the corner of Ocean Blvd. and Ross Avenue. One day as we took a stroll we noticed that the home at 13 Ross Avenue was vacant. We inquired with the neighbors across the street for any possible leads. They were very reluctant to give out any information, as they wanted to maintain privacy and security for the neighborhood. Well we didn't give up our search. I should say that Helen didn't give up, since she was the main catalyst. One day the next year in late March of 1971, Helen called me at school on a Friday morning and asked if I would like to take a ride to NH. After a hectic week at school I was all for getting away for the weekend to relax.

After the close of school on that day we bundled up and headed north. We left the children at home in the care of Larry Jr. and Bobby. Not knowing the intent of Helen's venture I headed up toward NH just thinking that we were going to visit my sister Angie in Manchester. When we came to the crossroad that branched to either Manchester or Hampton Beach, Helen said, "take a right toward Hampton Beach". I was flabbergasted to say the least, but there was some special calm authority in her voice that made me obey.

Well we arrived at Hampton Beach at about 7pm and rented a cabin. I can still recall that night we spent there as the weather was still pretty cool and the room did not have any heat. We just about froze! The next morning after defrosting and breakfast Helen led me into Ernest's Real Estate Office to inquire about the home at 13 Ross Avenue. After learning the details we were given a showing of the home. We immediately fell in love with the place. It had the 4 tiny bedrooms upstairs and another little bedroom downstairs. Ross Ave is a quiet dead end street. There was also a nice back yard for the children. It was still a summer cottage and needed a lot of work, but we could visualize the future potential of this home, which was in an ideal location on a quiet dead end street and only 100 yards walking distance to the beautiful beach. The hourly musical chimes from the Catholic church 100 yards in the opposite direction seemed to calm and beckon us.

We found out from our Real Estate Agent Ernest that the home was in the hands of lawyers who were handling the estate. The asking price was $15,000. *(This, remember was also the magic asking price for our Main St. and Bedford Street Homes!)* This was a lot of money at this time in our life. With 6 children to support on my teaching pay I was already doing 'moonlight' work on several fronts to keep ahead of the bill collectors.

All the way home Helen and I discussed the pros and cons. We both agreed that it would be a great financial hardship but Helen didn't quit. The following week unbeknown to me, Helen took Jean with her and made the trip to Hampton Beach to talk with Ernest and show Jean the home at 13 Ross Avenue.

Helen talked Ernest into seeking a reduction in the price. Ernest took a liking to Jean and asked her if she liked the home. Jean blurted out, "I just love the place!" That was all he needed to hear and he said he would do his best. As with Bedford St., once again Jean was a key facilitator in acquiring a home of our dreams.

A few days later we had a phone call from Ernest with the good news that the owners would come down to $13,000. We immediately signed a purchase & sales agreement and on June 14, 1971 we (the Folloni Team and the bank) became the proud owners of a beach home. Speaking of 'magic numbers, my boys wore #13 as basketball players in high school! Since convention said that "13" was unlucky, we liked to prove it wrong!

It was then time for planning our future in this new venture. We had to figure out how would we raise the money to make the downpayment and the monthly mortgage payments. The first answer came when my sister Angie and my father lent us the money for the downpayment. Then to make the monthly mortgage payments Helen came up with another great idea.

With our two oldest children away at College, we had a vacant room at our home in Bridgewater. The local priest at our parish had called Helen and asked if we could do a favor to friends of his who were seeking a place to room while going to Bridgewater State College. Everything just fell into place for all concerned. We would be helping out two lovely college girls and at the same time we could use their room rentals to help pay off our mortgage.

For the next 10 years we kept on taking in college girls in our vacant rooms in Bridgewater as the means of paying off the Hampton mortgage. This rental income along with all of our children working summer jobs at Hampton Beach helped us out considerably. Jean and Debbie took on waitress jobs at Hudon's Restaurant and Michael, Jean and Jimmy worked at the Tastee Tower of Pizza. Larry Jr. would also send home periodic checks from his work as a chemical engineer. For a number of years we also abandoned the cottage for a couple of weeks in mid-summer to rent it out at peak season rates.

Larry Jr. with two Miss Hampton's

Jean, Michael & Carlo Madonnini- TASTEE TOWER

Remember the beautiful white antique mantel that we removed and stored after the fire at Bedford St? It became an heirloom centerpiece at the cottage in Hampton; our magical bridge between the two homes that our whole family has shared. Since there is no fireplace at our Happy Hampton Home, the mantel appears to frame nothing. To those of us who know, however, it frames and bridges everything. Soon the moving mantel will be passed again, but it will always keep us connected.

Mike, Deb Jim, Jean, '63   *The Roaring '80's*   *2002*

Following the cottage purchase we then had the task of remodeling it. Each year we took on a new project. Our very first was to upgrade the kitchen. We hired a carpenter from Canada who was then living in North Hampton, to build a new counter and install some cabinets. We supplied all the materials. His price for labor for 3 days of work, hold on to your hat, was $35.00! What a bargain! And he did a great job.

Out of necessity to afford the upkeep and upgrades at all of our properties I relied almost exclusively on 'do-it-yourself' work. Through these experiences I gained the necessary expertise to do most of the remodeling at the cottage, including the electrical and plumbing work which was once again done with help from my brothers Mike and Johnny and my brother-in-law Paul.

One memorable incident occurred during one of our early weekend remodeling projects. We were replacing all the old iron plumbing with new copper tubing. I had worked all day long on this particular Saturday with no assistants around except for Helen to hold a pipe occasionally while I soldered the joints. Around 9pm Helen said she was getting hungry. So was I, as we hadn't eaten anything since breakfast. I told Helen that if she'd help me out in holding one last piece of pipe to the upstairs bath I would take her for a great meal at the Ashworth Hotel.

Helen obediently went to work and from the room below she maintained her vigil by holding the last piece of pipe in place while I was soldering the connection from above. Then the 'fun' or should I say the 'disaster' began. As I was making the connection, a bit of the hot solder broke loose and fell onto Helen's hand. The hot burning metal caused poor Helen to instinctively let go of the pipe she was holding and it and all the other adjacent pipes fell crashing to the floor.

That was the end of anything like an early exit from our work. It took about an hour to clean up the mess and start the soldering process all over again. This time we put a towel on Helen's hand while she held the pipe. Finally, successful in our venture but *really* hungry, we cleaned up and headed for the Ashworth. Luck was still against us. When we arrived there we found that they had stopped serving at 10pm. We then had to take a ride 3 miles into town to settle for a cheeseburger and fries, which was our crowning reward for a hard day's work.

Of course our real reward, which we have no regrets in having sacrificed for, was the many happy days that our family has been able to share at this home.

Stanford Students Jimmy & Debbie, Dad, Bob from Italy & Mom on beach

Jean's Wedding

Another of our yearly cottage improvement projects was to install a large Sliding-Glass Door in our living room to lead out to the side porch. Our neighbor's brother-in-law did the installation. *By the way, our neighbors, Maury and Mary Fama and Bob and Lucille Lambert are the greatest that one could ever have. They have been very helpful, tolerant and friendly and almost like family. We have been blessed and fortunate to know them.*

A few years after I had rewired most of the electrical circuits in the cottage we had it insulated and winterized. This allowed us to start coming to Hampton Beach for year round living. One of the greatest remodeling projects came about in 1983, the year that I retired from coaching and teaching. We hired a contractor named Jim McIlveen, to lift the house and install new cement and cinder blocks to replace the foundation, which was puny and sagging. It cost us $8,000. for this project, and it was well worth it. Jimmy did an excellent job.

In addition I designed a new layout for adding a sun deck on the side and back. The design was unique and it gave us the opportunity to utilize the side porch to a greater degree of access from both the living room and from the back door entrances. This, along with the sliding doors came into great usage for our family cookouts, and later to allow us to move my disabled wife in and out of the house.

The year after the foundation work was competed, I decided to excavate the cellar and convert it into needed storage space. I should have had the excavation done while the foundation work was being done but I didn't and as a result I had to dig out the whole area shovel by shovel and bucket by bucket. It took my 'slave labor' kids and me the entire

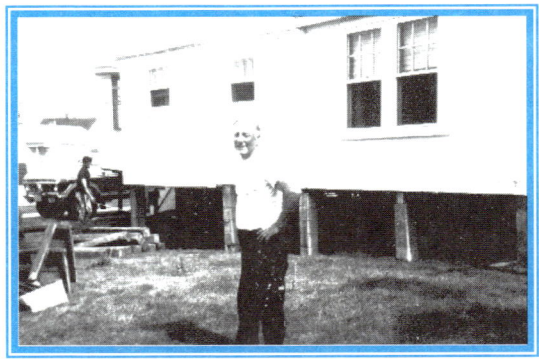

summer to complete the backbreaking job. A nice side benefit was that it also took off about 20lbs. of the excess weight that I had accumulated over the years. I believe that such pushing myself and staying active in my earlier years, helped me to survive the severe physical challenge that I ended up facing as a 79 year old.

After digging out the cellar I had cement poured over the area where I had the heating furnace and hot water tank installed. In the remaining portion of the cellar, I laid down a plastic canvas covering and then went up to the beach to get some nice dry beach sand and rocks to lay on top of it to keep the cellar area dry. Again this was a bucket brigade, container by container loaded into the trunk of my car and re-deposited back into the cellar. It was a backbreaking project but it kept me in great physical shape-the best I had been in since my ball playing days.

After that project it was time to create more space for all my office supplies that we kept on bringing up from our home in Bridgewater. Following my retirement we were spending more and more time at the cottage in Hampton and we were accumulating more and more of our family possessions with no room for them. 13 Ross Ave. is far smaller than the Bedford St. house, and as a result I've had an ongoing battle juggling my desire to use our things with my wife and daughter's desire to maintain a neat, uncluttered home.

We contracted with Rob Roy McGregor to build the present cubby-hole office and to renovate the front porch with new modern windows and paneling. Rob Roy was very reasonable and did a good job. The cost of the entire project was near $10,000., almost the equal of the original purchase price of the cottage. My major regret in this project is that I did not go far enough in preparing for the future expansion. For another 4 or 5 thousand bucks I could have added on the space to the upstairs bedrooms and added another 4 feet to my office to make it more functional.

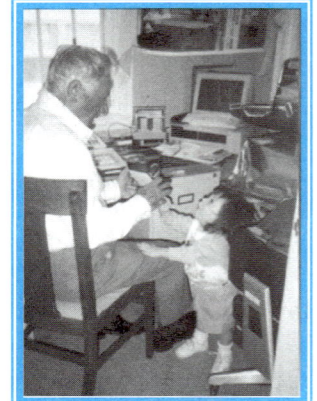

With Taylor a toddler, there was still room in the office for her to help Papa get ready for his BU Hall of Fame induction.

Not withstanding these mistakes, we now have one of the best homes on the street. With Helen and Jean as the decorators on the inside and with Jean's magic touch with the landscaping around the cottage we created a home of which we are proud. Our cottage is admired by all the walking traffic that passes from the church parking lot to the beach. There have been many, many compliments of Jean's flowers that blossom every year.

Jean and her husband Kevin, along with their children, Taylor and Cammy have been living with us through the years. It's a lot of people in tight quarters, but they've been real good about adapting, and have been an indescribable joy to us. We have been very fortunate and thankful for the support and help they've given to us, particularly during the last few years when severe health problems hit both Helen and me.

Taylor, Kevin, Jean & Cameron Leen. 1998

Finally time for that well deserved treat!

Note Grandma Leen in the background tending to Cammy.

Precocious 2 year old Cammy learned well from his sister. Here he climbed on his own up to the computer and loaded an educational game. With Leen genes and Folloni schemes, this boy will go a long way! And you should see him play!!!

Hampton Beach Beauties

Millenium Helen Chats on cell phone

Deb & Godmom Teresa

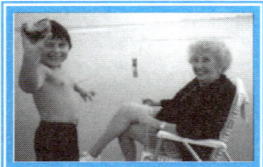

Can you see Saysha?

Even Saysha can play all like a Folloni!

Helen and James show that it is a good thing we winterized the cottage!

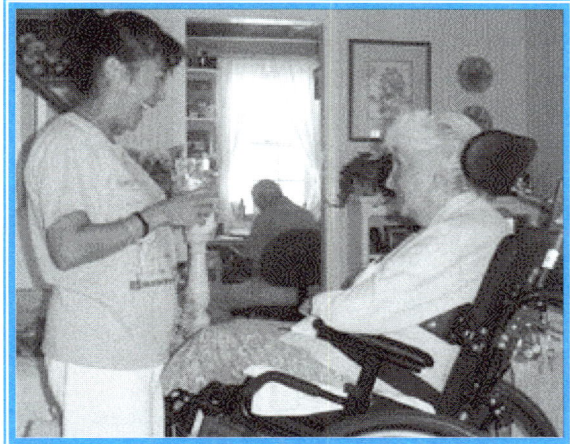

Thuy Vo brings much joy and laughter and two pretty Yorkies when she visits us in NH and in Florida. Everybody loves Thuy, who, along with her family in CA have been true family to Michael for 20 years. We hope that she soon becomes Thuy "Vo-lloni".

Helen says that lobster rolls & life are good indeed in 1998!

We're doing OK on Our Way!

Have I ever got plans for us!

6 Stevens Avenue, Brockton, MA
Oct. 22, 1974 to July, 1994

After a few years of experience managing the property at South Street we began taking in a small profit from the rentals. We then decided to look for more investment properties and Helen once again took the initiative to do the searching while I was off working at school. She found one at 6 Stevens Avenue, a short distance from our South Street apartment building. The price was right, $13,000. and the owner was willing to take over the mortgage.

It was a cute but small 2-apartment building that didn't need much work done initially. However as the years went by and the city of Brockton's deterioration spiral was accelerating, this place quickly turned into another nightmare.

We started out with good success in rentals as we had a single fellow, Bob Higgins occupying the first floor unit and his niece Cheryl Higgins living in the second floor apartment. They remained there for about 10 years until the welfare / drug culture permeated the area. Then it was one series of drug addicts and welfare families after another that took over and dismantled the property. It became one hassle after another in trying to maintain the property while maintaining my sanity, what with all of the disgusting incidents that were going on all around this area.

Not realizing that she was a front for a drug group to inhabit it, we rented out one of the apartments out to a young girl. One month later we read in the newspaper that she was a murder victim! Little did either of us know that having been caught up in that life, the poor thing was actually doomed by the time we encountered her.

There were drug raids on a daily basis in this area. My apartments were broken into with doors and windows being smashed with regularity. I was constantly replacing the broken windows and doors and making plumbing repairs. Once when a plumber repaired a sink blockage he found in the trap a solid chunk of rice with a crack pipe imbedded in it. Another time in clearing up a toilet blockage he found a screwdriver wedged in it.

If you have seen the movie "Pacific Heights", detailing the horrific tale of events that led to a landlord losing his home to his crazed tenant you may understand what we had to endure in this venture as rental property owners. We went through many of the horrors shown in the movie and then some.

To add to the hassles and insults that we endure as landlords we also had to suffer the indignity of being sued by one of these free loaders. The plaintiff was a 6'6" weight lifting buff and a drudge at best, who claimed that he broke his wrist when he fell off the stairs at 6 Stevens Avenue. He claimed that he could no longer earn money from fitness competitions.

As luck would have it, my insurance agent, who was a good golfing buddy of mine, had neglected to add liability insurance to my policy. That meant that I had to retain a lawyer at my own cost to fight the case. The lawyer that I hired was the widely esteemed Judge Robert Clark's son, Bobby, who had been one of my star athlete's back when I was coaching.

Bobby, very successful in his own right, was reluctant to take the case since he was well aware that at this time the courts and the judicial system were heavily prejudiced against landlords and that any disputes between them and tenants were predominately ruled in favor of the latter.

Bobby was pretty busy in his thriving law practice and really didn't have the time to chase down the true facts in this case. That meant that I had to do some real sleuth work to prove myself innocent of the charges brought against me. I knew from the start that this was another case of a someone trying to get some freebees at the expense of the supposedly 'wealthy' landlords.

"For what is a man, what has he got? If not himself?"
–My Way

My first approach was to find out where this character came from. After a few phone calls I found out that his family residence was in the Montello section of Brockton. I took a ride up there one day. He was not at home but I found one of his younger brothers out in the yard. I struck up a conversation with him and during it I found out some very revealing information that eventually won over the case for me.

The plaintiff's brother revealed to me that he was away at a weightlifting event. He boasted to me that his older brother had won many weightlifting contests in the past. This gave me an idea. I secured a copy of the regional weight lifting magazine to follow up on his activities. Lo and behold I discovered an article that contained the results of a contest held up in Maine where he was a winner. It listed the dates of his accomplishments and sure enough proved that he participated in competitive form just one week after he supposedly had broken his hand at my apartment!

I had also learned from my conversation with his brother that within the past year he had slipped on a ramp while coming off a pleasure boat and was injured from the fall. (In my opinion this was another fake fall in another attempt to steal a freebee from a 'rich' boat owner.)

I then went back to Attorney Bob Clark and presented the evidence that I had gathered. With these revelations his attorney immediately dropped the case. I escaped with only the costs of my thankfully limited legal fees.

Another harrowing experience with one of my last tenants at Stevens Avenue proved to be the death knell of our owning this property. I had rented the upstairs apartment to a Cuban lady who was on welfare. She had two boys ages 12 and 10. She also took in her boyfriend, who some have said was faking a back injury and receiving compensation for it from his former employer. They spoke very little English but they knew how to beat the welfare system.

They were a very unkempt group who left the yard and the house a filthy mess. They also had a dog and instead of walking it outside they would open the window of one of their rooms to let it go out onto the roof deck to do his business. The roof was a health hazard, loaded with feces and urine. They also constantly left the windows open day and night to let the heat out while I was paying the fuel bill.

I continually cleaned up the mess they left in the yard only to come back in a few days and find the place cluttered up again. I tried to convince the children to keep the yard picked up and offered them a couple of dollars for their efforts. Here they were on welfare and would you believe they refused, saying that it was not enough compensation. When we were youngsters growing up we didn't get one nickel to pick up and keep our play and living areas clean. We had pride and values instilled in us by our parents and communities. I feel sorry for children who weren't afforded this by theirs. I feel more sorry, however, for those of us upright citizens who have to foot the bill and headaches that these societal leeches create.

Finally the inevitable happened. Someone called in the Board of Health who immediately posted a sign on the door, condemning the property. I had to practically give it away. I called my real estate agent and luckily she found someone who was willing to take over the property for the sum of $10,000. A few years earlier, I had turned down an offer of $40,000. for this same place.

Thus, on June 20, 1994, we ended our adventure at Stevens Avenue.

61-63 WALL STREET, BRIDGEWATER, MA.
1983 TO 2001

Two of our last ventures were the result of the division of the Folloni family holdings of my father's property.

Earlier I explained our living conditions and the remodeling process that we went through at this property in the 1930's. In the late 50's when all of our family had finally left the old homestead, only my father and my brother Mike and his new wife Helen were left living in this sprawling home at 61 Wall Street. Mike had converted the upstairs into an apartment for himself and Helen and my Dad remained in the downstairs unit with a newly added bathroom.

Mike & Helen on Wedding Day

Johnny, Nono, Mike, Larry Jr. and Bobby circa 1950

One day during one of our annual family gatherings, my brother Al made the suggestion that we capitalize on the rental market and convert the house into 4 apartments. We all thought he was crazy with this idea. Being the consummate salesman that he was, however, he laid out a floor plan and proceeded to convince us that it could and should be done. His plan was a stroke of genius that inspired what turned out to be a very profitable remodeling project.

The old store was made into an apartment for Mike and his wife Helen and the house was transformed into 4 small apartments, which we were readily able to rent.

61 –63 Wall Street before the additions were made.

Our brother Johnny suggested that the family incorporate for the purposes of managing the business property and he had a neighbor friend of his in Rhode Island draw up the documents. We were then officially in business as the 'New York Development Corporation'.

Up until that time in order to keep up with the expenses of maintaining the home and supporting my father, all of us children who could afford it kicked in the sum of $20. per month. They appointed me to be the Treasurer to pay all the bills and to manage all of the rental and business transactions. I did all of the legwork involved and did not take any compensation for any of my time and work. At one of our meetings they voted to give me the sum of $2,000. per year for my efforts, but I never did take any of this stipend that was offered.

This new corporation and the rental dealings worked out very well for the next decade. Our annual meetings usually coincided with my father's birthday on August 4. It was a wonderful time to get all the Folloni families together.

61 –63 Wall Street after the additions were made.

Sometime in the 1970's my brother Al purchased an apartment complex in New York as a family investment and we called that the 'Mass. Realty Company'. With rent control still in effect in New York City, that complex turned out to be a 'White Elephant' as my brother Johnny named it. Al was continually digging into his own pocket to bail us out of debt in this venture.

Finally in the early 80's, once again at the suggestion of my brother Johnny, we discussed the breakup of the New York Development Corporation and the Mass Realty Corp. Angie was well set from her astute management of finances at the Auto Wash, Mike had a growing Nail Packing business and Johnny had a nice secure position working with the Pratt & Whitney Aircraft Company, which had many lucrative dealings with the Federal government. Johnny and Mike brought up the concern about possible tax consequences of the dissolution.

l-r seated: Mike, Angie, Johnny's wife Marie, Al, Virginia, Zartar & Helen, Larry and Johnny. l-r standing: Daughters Jean & Debbie and Mike's wife Helen.

After much discussion of the pros and cons, we finally agreed to dissolve the Corporations and to divide our family property holdings. In addition to the N.Y. Development and the Mass. Realty properties, in 1978 our brother Al had secured a condominium in Ft. Lauderdale, Florida. The intent of this transaction was for any of us in the family then nearing retirement age to have a footing into a retirement home in sunny Florida. To pay off the monthly mortgage for the Florida condominium we used funds from the rentals of the N.Y. Development property, which had finally started to turn a small profit.

Then to make an equitable division of the property holdings, Mike suggested that the three properties involved be valued at $40,000. each. We would then apportion whatever contributions were made by each of us over the years as credits toward the distribution. Mike, Virginia and Johnnie chose to take cash*, Angie took over the Florida Condo, Al took over the N.Y. property and I took over the Wall Street property. Everyone seemed to be in agreement with the split as a fair settlement and plans were drawn up and executed for the distribution of the family assets.

*Johnnie chose to donate his share to his older brother Mike, for the many contributions that he had made to the family. I, in turn, also donated the Poleti land on Oak St. to Mike.

MORE LANDLORD – TENANT EXPERIENCES

*"An inconvenience is only an adventure wrongly considered;
An adventure is an inconvenience rightly considered."*
Gilbert Keith Chesterton, (1874-1936)

With the distribution of the Folloni properties completed it became time for me to go on with the management of the Wall Street property. I have many tales of strange incidents that happened with the tenants at the Wall Street complex over the years. Naturally we had some good tenants along with some real bad ones. I have always tried to be a good landlord and as long as the tenants were cooperative I always bent over backwards to be of assistance whenever possible. If anything, I think that I have been overly charitable in trying to help out deserving (and some not so deserving) renters.

I had one standing rule with all my tenants. In spite of the rising cost of living with the passing of time, once a tenant agreed upon a lease with me, I never, ever raised the rent in any succeeding year, no matter how long they stayed! Although I'm generally against government mandated rent control, as I believe it to be a counterproductive attempt to assist tenants, I have steadfastly established and adhered to my own rent control policy. With one exception, I have never evicted anyone for nonpayment of rent.

These policies have probably cost me over $100,000. over the years in forgiveness of rental payments due, but I have the personal satisfaction of having helped some people in need. *Just as when the property was my Dad's home and store, neighborly assistance remained a hallmark of the sidelight business that thrived on 61-63 Wall St.*

I'm also perhaps one of the minority of landlords who would send Christmas cards and often even Christmas gifts (and can you believe it, sometimes even cash gifts for the tenants!). And if an emergency repair was needed, tenants could count on either me (sometimes with my kids) going right over to fix it.

I should point out that through my way of personalized management, I believe that I have made back a substantial amount of what was lost in rents.

One way I saved was by allowing some skilled tenants who were out of work to do maintenance and repair work at my properties for a price somewhat below what I could have gotten at market value. This sometimes meant doing a job a little before or a little after schedule, but I always made sure that the work was done right, and in the long run it paid. Of course since the tenants were going to stay there, I had a 'built in' labor warranty.

The risks that more bad tenants will come in increase with the number of changes in occupants, and the rate of turnover by tenants generally diminishes in proportion to the quality of the landlord tenant relationship that is invested in. Unless they happily graduate to become homeowners, my tenants tend to remain as my tenants. The savings in apartment cleaning and upgrade costs and tenant searches are tremendous. The aggravations associated with constant tenant turnover are substantial. What does a landlord really profit to charge more rent and not be flexible enough to work to prevent more frequent tenant turnover?

The mutual appreciation and loyalty that I endeavored to build also paid big dividends in reduction of vandalism and abuse of the property by my long-term tenants. Even if there was an occasional bad tenant, the others who cared about me because I cared about them, would step in to self-police the matter or they would alert me. I believe that in the long run this factor alone may have saved me as much as I've lost. And so what if it didn't? Things have worked out OK or better for me, and the intangibles of how my tenants' and my lives were enriched made the way as meaningful as the more transitory profit goal. The more commonly accepted impersonal management techniques employed today may collect more, but at what costs and what net gain?

Most of my tenants that didn't pay were deserving of help. Many, of course were scofflaws and freeloaders who went from place to place and stuck their landlords for the rents due. And upon leaving, these creeps would also typically leave the apartment in shambles and in need of costly repairs.

> *"You've got to accentuate the positive*
> *Eliminate the negative*
> *Latch on to the affirmative (and)*
> *Don't mess with Mister In-Between!"*
> Johnny Mercer, 1944

➢ ***You don't eliminate the negative by ignoring the positive potential.*** *Simply eliminating a perceived problem without building a solution just invites another, possibly bigger problem.*

➢ ***You can't be half-hearted in your commitment to building positive relationships.*** *Failing to move a business relationship from neutral to committed during their crunch time will cost you more at yours.*

Joe Struck is an example of a worthy renter who just needed an occasional break in life. One day the doorbell rang at my home and as we opened the door, there appeared Joe with his long hair and shabby clothing. As soon as we opened the door to let him in, he threw his hands up in despair and blurted out, *"Sorry Mr.*

Folloni, I have no money for this month's rent!" Several of my children observed this pathetic but sincere gesture by poor Joe. To this day some of the boys will tease hapless behavior of another by calling him 'Joe Struck'. Of course Joe honorably worked his way out of his temporary predicament, and we were happy to welcome him into our extended family of friendly and helpful tenants. The 'Joe Struck' nickname that is passed around by and between my boys is one of distinct appreciation and affection.

Warm memories from the likes of Joe Struck and many other grateful tenants over the years have done more than money to add to the richness of satisfaction that our family enjoys. Here are just a few examples of treasured correspondences that I maintained with some tenants over the years.

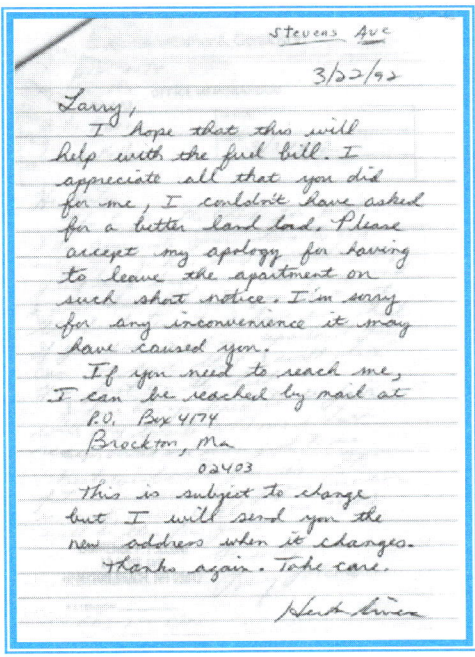

The first was a letter from Hector Rivera, a tenant at Stevens Ave., Brockton, MA. Hector had to leave the apartment on short notice, yet he showed the stuff of champions by taking the initiative to track me down and pay a past due fuel bill.

"I hope that this will help with the fuel bill. I appreciate all that you did for me. Please accept my apology for having to leave the apartment on such short notice. I'm sorry for any inconvenience it may have caused you. I couldn't have asked for a better landlord. Thanks again. Take care." – Hector Rivera

Naturally I responded to this nice note:

4/6/02

Hector: Thanks for the check for the fuel. I appreciate your honesty and integrity. I have had many tenants in the past and I will have to rate you as one of the best.

If you are ever in need of an apartment, you can be sure that I will place you first on the list. I have always tried to be fair with my tenants and most have reciprocated and been good to me.

Best wishes to you in the future and remember if you are ever in need, please call on me and I will be there for you."
Sincerely, Larry Folloni

While Kathy Murphy's husband was still a student at state college,

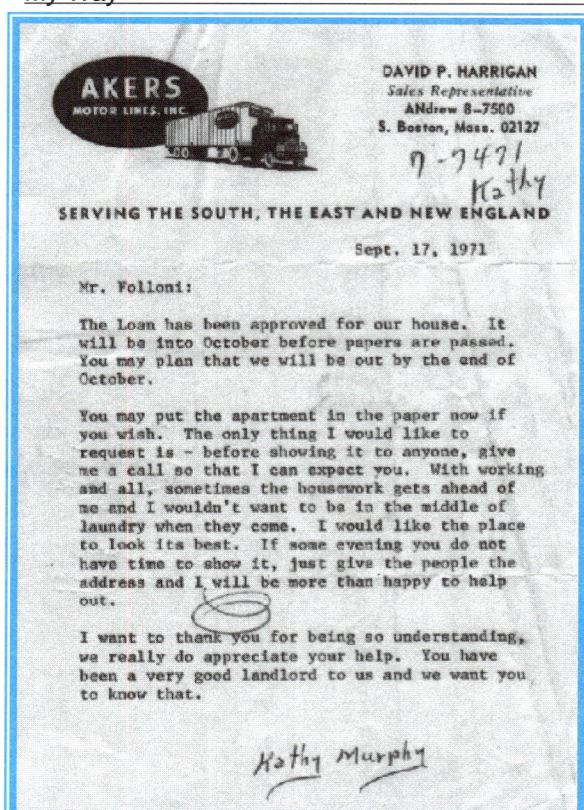

she was out working to help support her family until they could become financially secure enough to purchase their own home. The rent I charged them was well below the going rate but I knew they were good people and struggling so I was more than happy to help out.

She wrote this nice letter on her employer's letterhead. Kathy and her note very well exemplify my points. She is considerate and grateful and she proves it in her willingness to help the landlord. I not only appreciate her reciprocal acts, but also seeing that Helen and I were able to help someone to help themselves along on *Their Way* means the world to us.

These are copies of other glowing letters from a few of our many grateful tenants.

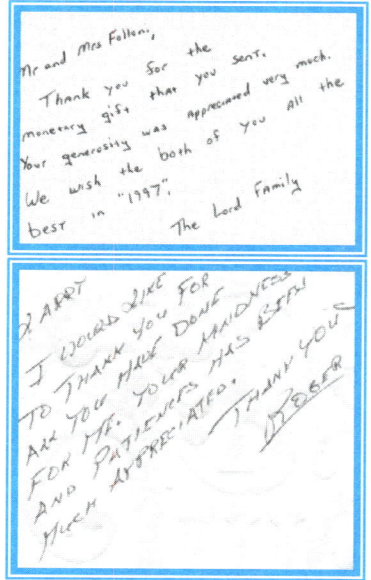

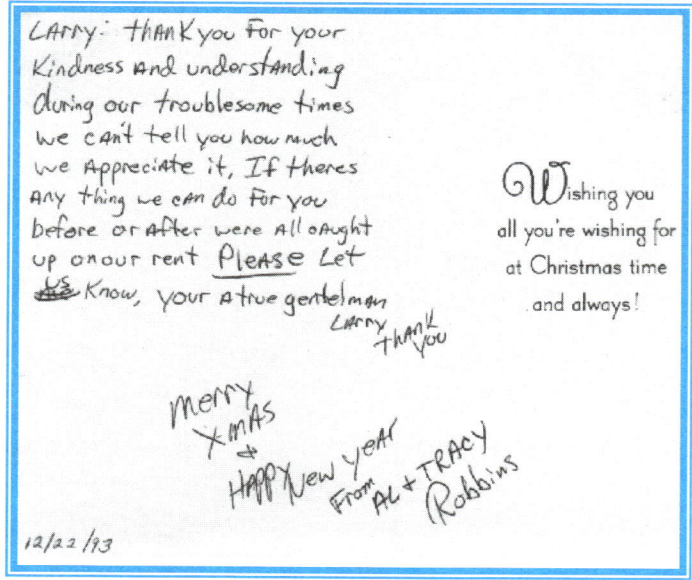

5880 Sabal Palm Blvd., Tamarac, Florida
February 1984 through January, 2001

The Folloni Family acquired this Florida Condo at Sabal Palm in 1978. My brother Al had purchased it for us from a New York client of his for a price of $28,000. including all the furniture. Al procured it to give all members of the Folloni Family a time-share type vacation opportunity and to give us an introduction to a future of living in the warm climate in our retirement years.

My sister Angie and her husband Elmer and my brother Mike and his wife Helen were the first to take advantage of this arrangement. After being down there for one year, Uncle Mike purchased his own Condo in the same complex. Angie and Elmer, then retired, stayed at Sabal Palm until 1982 when they purchased a mobile home in Val Rico, which is located about 30 miles N. east of Tampa on the quieter western part of Florida. In 1983, the first year of my retirement, Helen and I made our first trip to the Condo for the winter months. Since Angie and Mike had their own places, we in turn purchased the condo in Building 1 #123, from Angie in 1984. Mike sold his place in Building 2 and he followed Angie and purchased a home up in Val Rico.

The Sabal Palm Condo was a nice unit with two large bedrooms, two baths, a very large living room and a small kitchen. Al had the foresight to have one end of the living room fitted with a mirror, which gave the effect of a double room. We also added roll-up safety blinds out on the back porch. In addition I later had new expensive wall to wall carpeting installed.

Al made another very practical and smart choice in purchasing his retirement home a mile away in Margate. His Condo was located about 200 yards away from a great Shopping Center. Since his wife Connie did not drive, he wanted a place within walking distance to shopping. With Al being disabled over the last few years of his life, and even more importantly since his death, it has been very good for Aunt Connie to have this handy shopping plaza nearby.

For the next 15 years Helen and I made the annual trek driving down to Florida. We made it a leisurely trip, taking 3 days to get there. While our daughter Debbie was living as a young attorney in Washington D.C., we would break up the journey by staying a few days at her beautiful 6th floor condominium in the Atrium building.

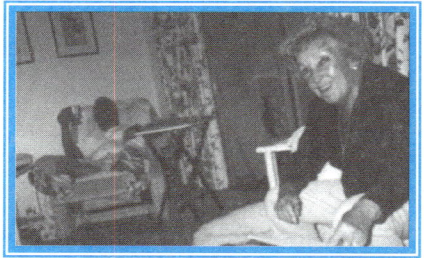

Our stay at Sabal Palm was a mixture of good and mediocre. The good part of course was the weather, since we got away from frigid New England beginning in November through to about April 1st each year.

Another plus for us was that Jeannie, who was the constant helping companion for Helen and me throughout our retirement years, also spent considerable time with us in Florida until she married Kevin Leen in 1988. Words cannot describe how selfless and kind Jean has always been to us. After Kevin and Jean brought grandchildren into our world we wouldn't leave New Hampshire until after the Christmas Holidays, as Helen wanted to spend Christmas at home with them.

Dad with two dolls

The Sabal Palm adult complex was inhabited by many of the Jewish people who migrated from the New York area. As my stories about Hank Greenberg and Dr. Will Cohen demonstrate, I have huge respect and fondness for the great majority of Jews, as I do with all other groups. This particular collection, however, had more than its share of jerks. Many of them never owned a place in N.Y. and when they acquired their own Condos, they were not shy about letting you know that it, and all around it was theirs. They were very possessive. Among their common expressions were, "Our grass", "Our pool", "Our house" "Our....!"

When we first arrived there about 75% of the owners were Jewish, about 20% of Italian descent and about 5% of other mixed nationalities. Over the years that ratio changed greatly and by last count there were almost as many of Italian descent as there were of Jewish. Again, don't get me wrong, I am not a racist or against any religion. Some of my best friends over the years are of the Jewish faith, but it grated me to see some of the intimidating rules that were initiated by this particular group of people. These archaic and obtrusive rules were posted on a sign just at the entrance to the pool.

A few of the rules drawn up by the Board of Directors really drew my ire, especially in how they were enforced. One of them was that you were supposed to shower before entering the pool. This rule was a standing joke. Since the majority of the owners were always trying to save a penny, they never had the hot water on for the showers by the pool. And since the water from the shower was always very cold, everyone would pretend that they were obeying the rules by going over to the shower, turning it on, and sticking one foot under the cold shower, then giving out a yell and stepping away. They all thereby felt that they were abiding by the rule of showering before entering the pool. Of course I realized that the intent of the rule was for health reasons so I always took a thorough hot shower back in my Condo before going to the pool. Even more than the universal superficial compliance, what bothered me most, was the selective enforcement of this rule against those outside of the clique of the majority in power. Often upon entering the pool others and I got grief from them because they didn't observe us going through their silly simulated showering sham.

Another rule that really frosted me was the requirement that everyone wear "tags" when coming to the pool. As a matter of principle I would never wear mine. One day one of the pool monitors berated me for not doing so. I asked him, "Why do I have to wear a tag?" His reply was, "So that we know who you are." I promptly extended my hand for a handshake and shot back, "My name is Larry Folloni, Building 1, #123. Now you know who I am so why do I have to wear this tag? I had my fill of wearing "Dog Tags" while I was in the Service for 4 years during the war and I don't intend to repeat that ordeal again." From that time on I was never again approached by anyone with that demand. I suppose that the WWII connection might have aroused their common sense indignation against the crass objectification of any people.

The third and most frosting rule that irritated me was the one that required that we purchase tags for any guest that we took to the pool. The cost of the tag was only a dollar, but it was very inconvenient to have to run over to the office to get the tag every time that a guest arrived. Occasionally people would come to the pool with their guests and not have had the time to get to the office while it was open.

Cammy & Taylor Leen were our two favorite guests

One day I witnessed one of the pool monitors loudly admonish a condo owner who had brought in some guests and had not picked up the guest tags. This was done in front of his guests and other people nearby at the pool. It was humiliating and embarrassing to say the least. I was really upset to watch this person being so treated, so I did a little investigating of the background of these archaic rules. I went to the annual meeting well prepared to speak. I made an impassioned plea to get rid of this and other obnoxious rules for the benefit of all the owners.

Helen's friend Jean, and our daughter Debbie

Bobbie visting from Italy.

I had found out that the original purpose of the Guest Fee charges was to supplement the cost of pool maintenance. The average income from these fees was about $800. per year. I therefore proposed to remove this bureaucratic hassle and add this amount to the monthly maintenance fee.

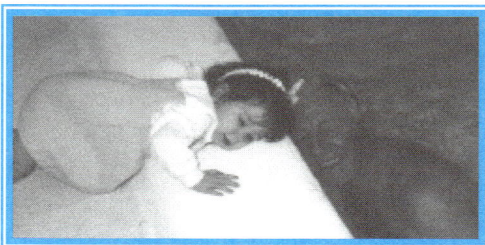

This amounted to about $4. per year or about 33 cents/month for each unit owner.

After much deliberation, my plan was finally approved. We then didn't have to go through the hassle of securing tags for our guests and we could avoid anymore humiliating and embarrassing experiences like so many of us had had in the past. They also removed the sign that posted the archaic and obnoxious rules.

When we came back to our Condos the next year we were dumbfounded to find out that without any prior notice to the rest of the owners, that they had rescinded the vote taken that previous year to eliminate the Guest Fees. The year-round residents reasoned that they were being charged $4. per year to cover these fees and they were not using the pool so why should they have to pay to maintain it?

Since there were none of us *'Snowbirds'* from up north around during the summer, the year round residents were able to rescind the Guest Fee motion and we were back to square one. I was furious when I found out what happened and I let them know my feelings. Here we were paying the full maintenance fee for all the residents to take care of their thrash removal, lawn and other maintenance work needed *year-round,* yet we *'Snowbirds'* were only there for 3 or 4 months of the year. And we live on the first floor, yet we pay for the elevator services even though we do not use the elevator. Etc. etc. etc. It's funny how many of the year-round residents had trouble keeping consistency in their logic.

Incidents such as these turned me sour about our stay at Sabal Palm. In spite of these, we did meet up with some very nice people there. The ever-affable Helen in particular made some lasting friends there including the Albas, the Weinbergs and the Brams. Some of the neighbors were very nice. Henry and Zelda Bram, for example, took a liking to Jean, who sent them Valentines Day cards and they were very appreciative of her thoughtfulness. Another friend was Jean Weinberg, an Irish girl, who had married a nice Jewish fellow. Jean's husband passed away in the early '90's and she remained a very good friend of Helen's for years.

Helen with friends

Helen with Glee Club friends

Of course I still had my share of fun!

Practicing to break par at the Breakers, Palm Beach.

Since I enjoyed golfing, one of the reasons for going south was to be able to play year round. There was a golf course right out the back door of the condo, but it was fairly crowded and not so well kept up as the greens fees might indicate. So for the first few years, while my daughter was with us there, I joined a better value golf club about 3 miles from our Condo. Jean would drop me off daily and then take her mother for an outing around Ft. Lauderdale and the surrounding areas of Boca Raton, etc.

Godmother Angie relaxing on a visit watches Jean scoot by on a golf cart.

This routine went on for several years until Jean got married in 1988. Then it was just Helen and I alone at the condo. We then socialized very frequently with 'Uncle' Al and 'Aunt' Connie, including many excursions to area restaurants. Once I was alone with Helen I practically gave up my winter golf in order to be with her throughout the day. We would go swimming in the pool in the morning on a daily basis. Then we would go to visit with Al and Connie later in the day. Al's first daughter Marie and her husband Phil were our frequent hosts.

Uncle Al had his stroke in the middle 90's. With Uncle Al disabled we spent most of our time taking him to doctors and hospitals for his dialysis treatment. In March of 1997 when we left Florida, we waved goodbye to Al for the last time.

I can still remember how Al waved good bye to us from his wheel chair with tears streaming down his eyes. He knew it would be the last time that we would see each other. Al passed away two months later, on May 14, 1997.

We returned once more to Florida the following year. It wasn't the same without Uncle Al around. We still kept Aunt Connie company and frequently took her out to dinner and then would take her for visits to Al's final resting-place.

When we left Florida in March of 1998, I sensed that it would be our last trip there. Even though we had made plans to return in January of 1999 our plans were drastically changed due to my botched surgery in December of 1998, which almost had me joining Al in the hereafter earlier than I had planned. I'm happy to say that we had many happy times in Florida both with my family, and with Al, who was responsible for getting us there.

Always the life of the party Al trips the light fantastic with his niece Helen

Always extending an uplifting hand

Linda (Balboni) Bardoff talking with Connie. Al at right, Mike & Johnny rear

Inside our condo, planning tomorrows SUPER FAST & LOUD JETBOAT RIDE!!!

Helen, Saysha & Cam   *We even found my buddy Paul Stetson in Florida!*

OUT WITTING THE RUG RIP-OFF ARTIST

"He who does not open his eyes, must open his purse."
Old German Proverb

When we took over the condo from Aunt Angie everything was in pretty good shape except for the old carpeting, which was worn and shaggy looking. Helen and I went shopping one day and we ended up at a rug outlet in Pompano. We looked at the display and finally found a carpet that we liked very much. We asked the salesperson to come up to our condo to take the necessary measurements and to complete the deal.

Later that night one of the owners came to our condo to take the measurements. As we conversed, it became known that he and his brother had come down to Florida from Middleboro, Massachusetts. This was the neighboring town to Bridgewater and he claimed to be friendly with my good friend, Joe Masi, their Athletic Director, and of several other aquaintances that I knew from there.

I felt that if he was a friend of these people, he could be trusted in any business deals that I would make with him. This of course set me up for the scam that was soon to follow. After he had measured the condo he drew up the contract and asked for 50% of the cost in advance to complete the transaction and order the carpeting.

Since he had gained my trust, I was foolish enough to go along with his request and gave him a check for $2,000. This was a move that I was to soon regret. The scammer had promised that he would have the carpeting in before the end of March, when we had made plans to leave to enjoy Easter at Debbie's.

Then came the kicker. With our departure date drawing nearer, we patiently awaited the arrival of the new rug. We gave him a phone call and he apologized for the delay saying that the rug was being shipped in from North Carolina and that since it was a special order, it would take a little longer to deliver.

He then suggested that we leave the keys to our apartment with a neighbor and that he would take care of everything from that point on. We left the keys with our friend Sally Bravo and took off north for Debbie's and home.

A few weeks after returning home I called Sally to inquire if the rug had been installed. She had heard no word from the Rug Company, so I put in a call to the store to ask them why there was still a delay. Again they came up with the story of it being a special order that would take a little time.

I kept calling them back every two weeks and kept getting the same excuses. I finally began to get very suspicious. I had Debbie call the Better Business Bureau and the Attorney General's office to inquire about this outfit. She also called the Rug Company and threatened to bring suit against them.

Finally, one morning in early June, I was able to contact the owner of the Rug Company by phone. He said everything was finally in order and that if I called him back after 12 noon that he would have more details on the installation.

At noon when I made the call the operator came on and said; "This number has been disconnected." I finally realized that I had been the victim of a scam. I learned that they declared bankruptcy and that my $2,000. was down the drain.

> *"Once is happenstance. Twice is coincidence. Three times is enemy action"*
> Auric Goldfinger, in "Goldfinger", by Ian L. Flemming (1908-1964)

> *"Three strikes and you're out!"*
> Abner Doubleday

Well the story does not end here and you'll see that like against 'Cannonball Jackman in by baseball days, my persistence and determination finally paid off.

The next trip down to Florida in the month of November, we made a return trip down to Pompano and went to the location of the Rug Store. Lo and behold they were still in business at the same place, but under a different name.

> *"Forgive your enemies, but never forget their names."*
> President John F. Kennedy (1917-1963)

Now it was time for me to do some scheming of my own. I had Helen and Jean look over the display of rugs and asked them to pick out one that was comparable to the one that we had selected back in the spring. They soon found the rug we wanted and I asked to see the owner.

This owner was the brother of the one I dealt with back in the spring and he had never seen me in person. (We had been in contact via phone conversations only.) Not realizing who he was dealing with, he worked out a deal with me for the new carpet. When asked me when I wanted it delivered, my response was, "Like yesterday." He said, "No problem I'll have it down by the end of the week. How do you want to pay for it?" He wanted my Visa Card number but I said no, I would rather pay by check. He was hesitant, since my checking account was back in Massachusetts, and he was afraid that it might bounce for insufficient funds.

I finally convinced him to take the check by calling the bank back in Bridgewater and having him talk to the President, who vouched for my credentials and that I had sufficient funds in my account to cover the check of $2,000 for the downpayment.

With the check deposit in his hands we made the agreement that the remainder of the amount due on the carpet, another $2,000., would be payable upon installation. He assured me that he would have the carpet picked up from his warehouse in Hollywood, Florida and delivered to my condo by 8pm that Friday. The installer was slated to be there on Saturday to install the carpet. We immediately headed home and I got on the phone to call my bank back in Bridgewater and told them to put a stop payment on the 'downpayment' check.

Come Friday evening at 8pm there was no show. I thought that I had been taken again. At 8:30, however, our doorbell rang. I hurried to the building entrance where I saw a large truck and two shaggy looking young fellows, who appeared to be on drugs or intoxicated. They said they were there to deliver the rug, which was great, but then a problem arose. How were they going to get the large rug in with all the corridor turns and narrow doors leading from the front entrance to our unit? I finally came up with the idea that they could drive the truck around in back and bring it in through the porch, as it was a direct path to the inside of our condo.

Front of condo. Note large tree front and center that I planted from a sprout when we 1st moved in.

Rear of condo unit

They followed my directions and when it was time to move the heavy rug off the truck another problem arose. One of the deliverymen just happened to have a bad back and could not do much lifting. So I volunteered to help. We finally maneuvered the rug halfway through the door where it became wedged!

We hugged and tugged it to no avail. Finally with one last pull by all of us the rug became un-wedged from the door, but another disaster was thusly caused. The force we had exerted to get the rug through the door had much more momentum than we bargained for. The rug careened across the living room and on through the wallboard on the opposite wall leaving a huge gaping hole.

Well we at least had the rug in the condo and we awaited the installer the next day. When he arrived he insisted that we give him a check for the remainder of the $2,000. owed on the rug before he would start the installing. This gentleman was a pretty good fellow who seemed to be honest. We explained to him that we would have to deduct the cost of the repairs to the living room wall and that we would write out a check to him for the amount due him only for his installation work. He finally agreed and we gave him his check of $500 for his services, which were excellent.

Then came Sunday night, and the owner of the Rug Company, who had just returned from a weekend safari, called me on the phone and wanted to know why I didn't give the installer the full amount due on the job.

I finally revealed to him that I was one of his (likely many) victims from the year before. Then I said, *"Now we're even, I have my rug and you have the money you fleeced me out of last spring."*

Hearing this he became furious. He said that the company that I dealt with last spring was bankrupt and defunct. He then threatened to have his 'Black Mafia' come up and rip the carpet out of the condo. Helen and Jean were very scared by this new threat and wanted to leave the condo and go to a hotel. I calmed them down by calling the police to inform them of the threat. The police assured me that they would be on the lookout for any trouble.

A few days went by with no further threats, then the Carpet Store owner called me again and this time very apologetically informed me that he would like to make a deal for the repayment of the money he fleeced me out of previously. He agreed to sign a statement stipulating that he owed me the money and that he would repay me on a weekly basis.

We agreed to meet the next day at my brother Al's bank in Margate, in the office of the President, who would be a witness to the signing of the agreement, which my daughter Debbie had faxed to me. I had explained to the bank official the situation and the threats that the scam artist made and to be on the alert if anything went wrong in. The bank President said, "Don't worry, if any problem does arise, all I have to do is push a button and the security police will be here in seconds."

Early the next day we arrived at the bank. Shortly thereafter, up pulls a Rolls Royce with our friend, the owner of the 'new' Rug Company. After we both signed the agreement, he asked me for a $3,500. check to complete payment for the rug. I gave him $1,500. which left a $2,000. balance on this year's carpet. I then informed him that he was to take the weekly payments that he had agreed to pay me and to use that money to pay off the debt. At my request, Debbie had written the agreement in a way that legally allowed me this flexibility, and the greedy character was in such a hurry to grab at another chance to rip off a *'Snowbird'*, that he didn't read the contract carefully.

He was really furious to find out that he was outfoxed at his own game. He spun off on his Rolls Royce, shouting profanity and fuming to the hilt. To this day we never again heard from this Con Artist who was treated to some of his own medicine!

Thus ended our Florida adventure. With the subsequent calamitous health problems suffered by Helen and me we put the condo up for sale. We had paid $42,500. to Aunt Angie to acquire this property that she had from the earlier settlement with our brothers and sisters. If this unit were located in our New Hampshire area, it would be worth around $200,000. With the glut of Condos in Florida, we weren't even able to get $25,000 for it, furnishings and all.

As with all our other homes, however, money didn't tell the entire story, because

More, what's more than this, I did it My Way!
-My Way

Helen at Palm Beach

Papa & Cammy share a warm Florida greeting

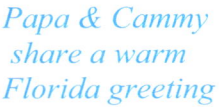

Papa teaching Taylor Computer at the Sabal Palm Condo

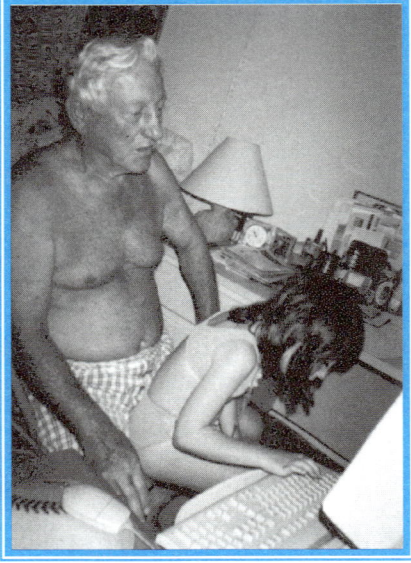

Jimmy, Jean, Cammy, Papa, Taylor, Helen Victoria and Debbie Folloni Dent

ANOTHER SETBACK FOR THE FOLLONI TEAM AT BEDFORD ST.

"Good fences make good neighbors."
Robert Frost, Poet Laureat of New England

After my retirement in 1983 we began spending very little time at our home on Bedford Street in Bridgewater.

Early in December of 1990, before leaving Hampton Beach for Florida I made a visit to our home at Bedford Street. While doing some paper work I noticed that the key to my desk had been removed and placed in a different location than where I had always left it. I became a little suspicious that someone was snooping around and I later realized that I should have followed up on this and taken some action.

Up to that year we had been leaving for Florida around the first of November and not returning until the following April. That year, however, Helen didn't want to leave until after the Christmas Holidays. The son of one of our neighbors had previously been in trouble with the law and he and his family were aware that we usually left for Florida in November. It's my firm belief, bolstered by hearsay that this young man, believing that we had already left for Florida, felt that he was free to go on a rampage. We believe that he did so sometime or times during the holidays.

On January 3rd, 1991, Helen and I were almost all packed at Hampton Beach and ready to head for Florida. We had a few items to pick up from our home on Bedford Street and made the stop off there. As we entered our home and stepped into our kitchen we were greeted with a scene of complete disarray, with empty beer cans strew all over the floor. Helen's first words as she looked into the glass cabinet, "My beautiful set of antique China is gone!"

I immediately went to my office and sure enough all the drawers were torn open and all my valuable coin collections were missing. We then went from room to room and found that the thief or thieves had turned every draw upside down in the hunt for valuables. The entire house was in shambles; nothing was left untouched. Included in our losses were thousands of pristine condition baseball cards that my kids had been collecting and carefully preserving over the decades.

We called the police who came down to take fingerprints and investigate the robbery, but nothing ever came of it. We stayed overnight at Bedford Street and the next morning we took off for Florida with great sadness. We left the place just as we had found it for the insurance company to view at a later date. Unfortunately this intriguing story didn't end there.

We were in Florida for about a month when early in February we received a call from one of our neighbors with more bad news. She said that she viewed some icicles on the inside of the kitchen window and upon investigating she found that someone had broken into the home *again*, and this time there was damage galore to the entire house.

Perhaps following a scene from the movie *'Home Alone'*, the perpetrator(s) had cut the water pipes leading to the upstairs bathroom and the water poured down through our lovely kitchen, saturating the entire first floor and leaving a 2-foot pond in the cellar that Bobby had remodeled. The kitchen was completely ruined and the damage to the rest of the house was beyond comprehension.

Water damaged kitchen ceiling

We had little doubt in our minds that it was one of our neighbors who was responsible for the theft and vandalism. The local police, however, were not able to make a case against him.

When we arrived back from Florida in the spring we went to work to repair the damage. Once again it took us a long hassle with the insurance company to settle the loss. Even with a substantial settlement, it was no where near enough to cover damages.

This setback couldn't have come at a worse time. We were already in the process of making an addition to the house on Wall Street and I was exhausted from trying to go from one place (and one state) to the other. Nonetheless, I came down from New Hampshire every day to supervise the work at both locations.

The contractor that we had hired to do the work at Wall Street quit half way through the project. We then had to hire another. Normally I would have had his credentials checked out but since he was the son of a police officer at the college I felt that he would be reliable and trustworthy. Wrong again!

He completed the work at Wall Street by the end of the summer and then turned his attention to the work at Bedford Street. We needed a lot of tile work in the kitchen and the bathroom. He recommended a friend of his, who presented me with falsified documents stating that he was a licensed contractor.

I was later heard that they were both hooked on drugs and we ended up suffering the consequences of their destructive acts. The tile man kept delaying his work and never appeared to be making any progress in completing his task, using one excuse after another.

With the rest of the house refurbished and in excellent shape, I finally got tired of hearing his excuses and gave him a deadline to complete the work by Columbus Day. On that holiday, I came down to Bridgewater, and as I tried to put my key into the doorknob, it wouldn't go in. I finally discovered that the keyhole was plugged with 'Crazy Glue'. I checked the other doors and they were all likewise sabotaged.

I finally gained entrance to the house through the cellar door. Upon climbing up the basement stairs and entering the kitchen, I met a sight that made me sick to my stomach. *Once again* a vandal or vandals had struck and they spray painted on the floor the message, "Ha Ha, We got you again." They had poured the crazy glue on to every draw and every appliance in the kitchen, and spray painted all the walls in the newly renovated house. The house was once again in complete ruin.

The police were called in again and again they had no success in finding the culprits. I later managed to get a confession from the first contractor as to who this most recent vandal was. It seems that he had a falling out with his friend the tile man and so he came to me with the whole story, which I have on tape.

He revealed that the reason that this tile man was delaying his work was that he was coming back every night to steal any valuable items that were left in the house. He had personally witnessed this creep loading some of my antiques and belongings on to his truck. I went to the police with this information and they told me that unless I had seen him in the act there was no way they could charge him with theft.

> *"But through it all, when there was doubt, I ate it up, and spit it out"*
> —My Way

Once more we had to start all over again. After hiring a reputable contractor we finally had our home back in shape before we were to leave for Florida the next winter. This time we took the key away from our neighbor and had one of my nephews live in at our home for protection. Thus ended another sad chapter in the otherwise mostly happy history of 91 Bedford Street

STOCK MARKET VENTURES

"Don't gamble! Take all your savings and buy some good stock and hold it till it goes up, then sell it. If it don't go up, don't buy it."
— Will Rogers, October 31, 1929

My stock market ventures began in earnest in January of 1997. My 'bookend' boys (oldest and youngest), Larry Jr. and Jimmy, were both heavily involved in stock trading and had done very well at it. After years of coaxing, they finally talked me into investing in the market. For me, this was a completely new ball game. I didn't have the slightest idea what it was all about. I didn't know what NASDAQ or Dow stood for, nor did I understand any of the terminology that was used in the trading. I was just a rookie playing in a new game.

Actually, my first taste of the market came as a spin-off of the earlier described Folloni Family property settlement. Starting back in 1923, my Dad had invested 50 cents per week from his meager earnings as a Stanley Iron Works employee to buy stock shares in the company. Over the years of his employment, he managed to accumulate a grand total of 33 shares of this 'SWK' Stock.

The SWK shares paid dividends on a quarterly basis. I can still remember as a child how my Dad would look forward to receiving the quarterly dividend in the mail. Each dividend check would amount to the grand sum of about $2.00. That was a *huge* amount in those days, and it really came in handy for family expenses. Years later, when the family income had increased, Dad began to reinvest the quarterly dividends into more SWK stock.

The original 33 shares, along with dividend reinvestments and later stock splits, had grown to about 55 shares by May, 1969. And by 1983, they had grown to about 171 shares, worth a total of approximately $3,600. In January of that year, I worked out an agreement with my brothers and sisters to purchase these shares, and to donate the proceeds for new furniture for our deserving brother Mike, who had just built a new home in Halifax.

With these stocks in hand, I made an additional investment of $10,000 to purchase more SWK shares. Through further reinvested dividends and stock splits, and through appreciation of the company's shares, this SWK investment grew to become worth $100,000 in 1998!

The stock took less of a beating than many of my other stocks, but still has dropped considerably from its highs. Nonetheless, this has still been a terrific investment from its modest beginnings when my Dad was investing 25 cents per week! Whatever else happens in the market, I have a pretty good feeling about Stanley

Works, and, if for no other than sentimental reasons, I intend to continue to honor my Dad and hold onto it.

> *"Success usually comes to those who are too busy to be looking for it."*
>
> - Henry David Thoreau (1817-1862)

My foray into the stock market, which began with my successful investment in the Stanley Works, was about to get much more involved. I took out a $100,000 mortgage on my Bedford Street home in Bridgewater so I could use some of the proceeds for my new market investments. Then it was time to decide how to make the stock selections.

My son Larry had been bragging about how well his leading computer manufacturer employer and other technology companies were doing. Meanwhile, I read an article in the business section, which stated that the NASDAQ was doing so well due to the activity of four companies that accounted for 80% of that exchange's trading. The companies were Microsoft, Cisco, Dell and Intel. So I proceeded to invest heavily in these four stocks. With some help from Jimmy, I invested in several other stocks along the way that first year.

In late 1996, I completed the sale of my property at 20 South Street, in Brockton, for $84,000. With Jimmy and Larry's help, I used some of this money to make other investments. Within a year, my portfolio (not counting SWK) was worth about $112,000, with a cost to me of about $85,000. My gain was about $27,000.

This $27,000 net gain in 10 months was more than I had made in any whole year of teaching before my retirement! It was also more than my retirement pension for the year. With continued advice and help from my boys, the next few years were even more fruitful. And by April of 2000, my portfolio had grown to the *unbelievable* amount of $860,000! Those were pretty heady days. I had made far more money in four years in the market than I had in 40 years of teaching and coaching!

YAHOO!

The most astonishing thing that happened in our stock dealings is the Yahoo story, which turned out to be another case of 'the luck of the Irish.'

As a noteworthy aside, Helen had a "Godmother Nellie," who was a great friend of Helen's father, and who had the mysterious gift of the "stigmata," a spontaneous bleeding from the wrist said to come from closeness to Christ and a sharing in his suffering. We still have several authentic photos and letters that were stained from these bleedings. They are in the shape of a heart, and in at least one, you can clearly make out an image of the face of Jesus. These are prized keepsakes to say the least.

Anyway, throughout life, Helen would pray to Nellie for many an important cause, whether it was for somebody to recover from illness, or for one of our kids to get accepted to a good college, or for the purchase of one of our dream houses to go through. It seems like every time Helen would pray to Nellie, her prayers would be answered. Whenever we needed a favor from the heavens, we would summon Helen by calling *her* Nellie, and she would take care of the rest.

Well, when I had begun to become an active stock trader, I would make trades by calling them in to a broker at NDB (National Discount Brokers). Then, in the summer of 1997, Jimmy came home from California for a visit, and decided to teach me how to save time and money by placing trades over the Internet. We were working on my computer one night, and Jimmy suggested that it would be appropriate to buy shares of an internet-related company with my first online trade. And why not take a stab at a company with a fun name like Yahoo!?

Jimmy walked me through the procedure, typing in the stock symbol and the number of shares, etc. I quickly realized how fast and convenient this method of trading would be, and I was racing toward the finish line to complete my first order. When I got to the last step, which was "click here to execute this trade," Jimmy grabbed my wrist and pulled my hand off of the computer mouse.

I was taken aback by this, and I said to Jimmy: "What's wrong?" He then said to me: "You're forgetting the most important step." Jimmy then looked across the living room at Helen, who was minding her own business, reading her Good Housekeeping magazine. When he said "Hey, Nellie," I knew exactly what was going on.

So Helen gets out of her chair and shuffles over to my little office where we were working, and she says: "What am I doing?" Well, what she was about to do, with one innocent click of the mouse, was to make over $100,000 in the first and only trade of her investing career!

First thing the next morning, we got 100 shares at $42.75, and by the end of the day, the stock had finished at $47. The next day, the stock hit 50. And the rest was history. It seemed like every day for the next three years, Yahoo's shares would go up or split, or both. It was always good news, and when we saw the YHOO stock symbol flashing across the TV screen, we would all shout out "Yahoo!"

Helen might have known more about the supermarket than the stock market, but it turns out she had the most sense of all of us. When we would explain to her on any given day how much money she made on her Yahoo shares, she would always say: "How do I get it?" We always explained to her that we didn't want to get rid of 'The Goose that was laying the golden eggs,' but in retrospect, we should have listened to Helen and cashed out when the going was good. Immediately after her massive stroke, almost as if in sympathy, Yahoo's shares plummeted in value.

MARKET MADNESS (And Some Personal Ironies)

Good things in this world never seem to last forever, and the stock market isn't any different. From its highs in March 2000 until the end of that year, the value of my portfolio dwindled to $300,000, and in the two years since that time, it has continued to erode at a dreadfully consistent pace. At the time of this writing, however, the stock market is beginning to show some signs of life again, so maybe all will not be lost. I still hold many of my former high-flying stocks, and I hope that some day they will be on top again.

As I reflect on the ups and downs that Helen and I have experienced in recent years, I can't help but to notice a number of ironies associated with our investments in the stock market.

During the time when my stock portfolio value was going up and up, I was actually incapacitated, spending three months generally out of it at Mass General Hospital, and another three months recovering at MGH and at Spaulding Rehab Center. I was making more money being flat on my back sick and doing nothing than I had ever made by breaking my back working!

I am a perpetually active person. To think that this money was flowing when I just couldn't 'get up and go' boggles my mind. Luckily, I bounced back somewhat and was able to enjoy some financial rewards for all of the years of sacrifice and hard work. Making it extra rewarding, we were successful in the stock market thanks to the skills and helpfulness of our sons - the same skills and helpfulness that Helen and I had worked so hard to instill in all of our children.

And how could I ever have thought that, as a poor young boy from Wall Street in Bridgewater, I'd end up making it pretty good on Wall Street in New York during my retirement years? Perhaps I should have known it was possible since my older brother Al paved the way, first as the chief Army Recruiter at the bustling Times Square office, then as a New York financial genius in his own right.

There is a sad irony to our stock market saga, as well. Shortly after our investments went to the top, my dear wife Helen hit rock bottom, with her own devastating health problems added to mine. I'll relate more details on that later. For now, all that I can say is that the cost for her care and my medical bills have consumed what little was left of our windfall, and we are now back to square one financially, and struggling to meet our monthy bills.

> *"I've loved and laughed and cried, and had my fill, my share of losing..."*
>
> - Frank Sinatra, "My Way"

Knowing what I do now, even if I was still at the top with my stock market and real estate investments, I'd give it all up in an instant if I could only have Helen back and well, enjoying life with us. Yet, I suppose that God has his grand plan, and I know that, in the end, none of us is left with anything material. In any case, the love that Helen and I still share with each other and our family has always been more important to us than all the money in the world.

This overriding value of family cooperation and closeness keeps me going right to my finish line in the game of life. In autumn of 2000, I began to plan an addition to our cottage home at 13 Ross Avenue. The purposes of this project were make the house handicap-accessible for my Helen's daily visits and for our dream that we could someday care for her at home and to add more space upstairs for Jean and her family. As enthusiastic as I was about doing this project, I didn't proceed with it due to the financial ramifications and my health. My children did not want me to be burdened with such an expensive and stressful building project at such a late stage in my life, particularly given my continuing health problems due to prior operations.

As it turns out, we did ourselves a big favor by shelving this project. Just a few months later, I was presented with a golden opportunity to make my next, and possibly final, real estate acquisition…

9 ROSS AVE., HAMPTON BEACH, NH
JUNE 12, 2001

With the help of my daughter Debbie and her husband Tom Dent, in June of 2001 we purchased the Kelty property at 9 Ross Avenue, two doors up towards the beach from #13.

Deb and Tom Dent, with Scottie & Victoria, have helped keep the Magic in my Kingdom

9 Ross under reconstruction, 13 Ross, foreground

John and Virginia Kelty had remodeled the house from the ground up about seven years prior and it was practically a new home. Getting this place would allow me to move from #13 to give Jean and her family more breathing and growing room, and with modifications #9 could afford larger space for Helen to spend more time with us in her cumbersome wheelchair.

The only immediately apparent problem was that there were no ramps to the house and no bedrooms downstairs. We added a ramp immediately. Since I was no longer able to climb stairs on a regular basis, however, we decided to add a downstairs bedroom and expand the kitchen and the office space for our computers. The plan was to also add rooms upstairs over the new addition, planning for the eventuality that my health problems might some day require a live-in caretaker. While waiting for the remodel, Larry Jr. and Bob moved in temporarily to assist Helen and I with our almost daily medical concerns, and they also generously pitched in to help make the mortgage payments.

In the winter of 2002-3 my kids and I took on the extensive planning and supervision of the ambitious remodeling project. My hands-on involvement in this adventure has done a lot to keep me interested in life and out of the bad-health induced doldrums during my 84th year. This and my many other projects help keep my mind off the fact that my body has been failing me, and I don't doubt that my positive attitude has affected my system on the physical cellular level, thus both prolonging my life and making it more satisfactory.

> *"As man thinketh in his heart, so he is."*
> James Allen – As Man Thinketh 1906

> *"What the mind of man can conceive **and believe**, man can achieve."*
> -Napoleon Hill

Larry Jr. mastered computerized room layout design software to assist me in development of my many dozens of conceptual ideas. Jean, Debbie and Jimmy have also been in almost daily touch with me on design details for the project. Bobby has added valuable practical building insights and substantial hands-on labor, as well as on site management assistance. With so many creative thinkers giving input, the scope of the project has steadily evolved. Jimmy and Debbie in particular are thinking ahead to build a place that can be used as a shared vacation spot near the rest of the clan that can be used by both of their growing families, as well as by their other out of state based siblings.

None of our kids have been immune from the adverse financial ramifications of the nation's recent economic slump. All of them still face substantial challenges in their middle age. Yet all are confident that they'll emerge on the plus side. Their willingness to all get involved in this project demonstrates their faith both in future in general, and also in the family. In fact they've gotten behind a plan to prepare a structurally sound supersized 3rd story attic suitable for possible future occupation. Helen and I may not be around for much longer, but the Folloni Team will carry on and still feel together and at home at Hampton Beach.

Our many change orders have caused more than a little understandable frustration on behalf project of the contractors, John Hart and John Castro and their crew. In the end, however, I think we'll all remember more how good the project came out than how long it took. And hopefully we'll want to give a great recommendation of their services to others.

To their credit, our neighbors have been gracious in bearing with the temporary congestion on the street and unsightliness of the house. Ross Ave. was once a sleepy little path with 1-story summer-only cottages. One by one people have been winterizing and expanding the size of their Hampton Beach getaways. And bit by bit, the beach side has been getting more commercialized. It seems that with each project most of us tend to grouse a bit about the other guy ruining the quaint character of the road, but we also tend to forget that we too have and/or may soon want to effect progress on our own properties. And in the end, among people of good will that we all really are, things do tend to work out for the better.

It has also been a joy to work so closely with my kids on this true family project. As I approach the publication deadline for this book I find myself as involved as ever with my family in productive, albeit non-physical, activities. The day that this manuscript leaves my temporary offices at #13 and #9 Ross Ave. to go to the printer, I leave to go to MGH for kidney surgery. The kids are around to assist, but no one is just hanging around waiting for things to happen.

"Don't wait for your ship to come in, swim out to it."

I feel like the CEO of a 'Fortune 500 Firm' with all my talented kids volunteering to do so much skilled work under my supervision for the Folloni Team. Along with construction management and taking the lead on pitching in with daily elderly care-giver errands on days when he is in town, Bobby has remained a major family breadwinner with his independent sales business and constantly imports new electronic gadgets for family betterment. In addition to managing the household that includes her husband and kids, Jean continues to shop for, feed, shuttle to and fro and give TLC to her parents. She selects and procures materials for the 9 Ross Ave. project and completely manages ongoing renovations at #13, including new floors that are going in as I write. Debbie stays up with property management and family legal issues, and Jimmy & Larry tackle a variety of complex special family projects while still helping me to manage what's left of my portfolio. Meanwhile Michael came from California for two months to help with the final editing of this book and in the preparations for the basketball court dedication program this summer.

Of their own volition, all of my kids execute their tasks faithfully, without self-righteousness and with a certain palpable sense of joy to be a contributing member of the team. Yes I still keep them running, and believe me they keep me going. And thankfully at the end of most of these full days, I still get to see Helen's warm smile and hold her hand for a spell in our TV room before the kids bring her back to the health center for the night. I'm so happy with and proud of my family! And I'm so confident that the growing edifice at 9 Ross Ave. will be a living testimonial to the Folloni Team.

After my (hopefully high) numbered days this house will hopefully end up being used by my family for many Folloni reunions to come. In any case, as with our other ventures, no matter the apparent outcome, our fortune has been largely in the doing!

"Chop your own wood and it will warm you twice."
Henry Ford 1st.

WORK ETHIC
Moonlights
MY WORK ETHIC AND JOBS

"I find that the harder I work, the more luck I seem to have."
Thomas Jefferson (1743-1826)

It's amazing how much Wall St. New York has affected this guy from Wall St. Bridgewater from childhood through my aged years. No matter the ebb and flow of fortune though, thank God that I've lived in this Great Land of Opportunity. To place things into some perspective in relating income to work done, let me go back again to my early childhood. *Grateful Moonlighter Nono*

We were raised in the days of the Depression that hit following the Stock Market crash in 1928. We didn't know the meaning of the word 'allowance'. Our struggling parents had all they could do to merely feed and clothe us. The only money that we received, we earned the hard way. We scraped up old pieces of lead pipe, copper tubing, rags, and old papers to sell to the Junk Man, who made weekly trips to our neighborhood. On a rare good week we were lucky to get a nickel from him for our efforts. We considered a nickel was a lot in those days--enough to pay our way into the Saturday morning movie cowboy serial thrillers. Since the government had not yet been doing surveys to determine that we lived in a 'ghetto', we were quite happy with our lot, and looked upon only the truly needy as worthy of help.

My first recollection of a real job was turning over hay and loading the hay wagons in the Company Field. We were paid according to our age, not by our production, and the rate was 1 cent per day per year of age. Mike got 10 cents, Al got 8 cents and I got 7!

My next paying job was cleaning bricks for one penny each. It was hard work for a 10-year-old, but I felt that I was really moving up then, as I could clean far more than 10 bricks in a day! We had to hammer away at the old cement attached to each brick that had come from a demolished building. We ended up with many a scarred knuckle and bruises from this toil.

My first *real* job with a bona-fide employer came when I was 14 years old. My brother Mike got me employment during the summer months at the Independent Nail Factory. This job entailed the loading of kegs of nails on to the workbenches for the girls to package. With Mike's appendicitis causing a drop in family income, I delayed college and continued full time for awhile at the Nail Factory.

I then switched over to working for the Jenkins Leather Board Company. This was another backbreaking job where I had to lift sheets of pressed leather onto trucks. I wasn't very happy there and finally in the spring of 1939 I hooked on to play baseball with the Corcoran Shoe Baseball team and to work in their factory. The history of that job, which was a pivotal turning point in my life, is told elsewhere herein.

While spending two years at Bridgewater State and another at Wentworth College, I continued to work in our family store and at other odd jobs to pay for my schooling. One day while thumbing a ride home from school Mr. Perkins, the owner of the Perkins Foundry picked me up. Upon learning that I was working my way through college, he offered me this job to work weekends at his Foundry. This job was noteworthy for two reasons:

➢ I began a fond lifetime friendship with his son Dave, who was my supervisor at work. (As I researched the history of Stanley it was interesting to find out that Dave is a direct descendent of Robert Perkins who built the dam on the river in 1691 to harness it's power for a foundry that later became the Stanley Iron Works.)

➢ On Sunday, December 7, 1941, while I was working making some foundry pattern molds, the news broke about the infamous attack on Pearl Harbor. This event changed my life dramatically for the next four years and beyond. As noted elsewhere, even though I was exempt from the military due to the fact that my two older brothers were already in the Service, I volunteered for my tour of duty.

Following the Service I enrolled at Boston University under the GI Bill. While there I held down several jobs to support my wife and first child Larry, Jr. Among them were: A couple of hours each morning of maintenance and landscaping work on campus, followed by class and athletic competition, then I'd work in the equipment room for another hour. After all that it was back to the BU swimming pool to work as life guard for a couple of hours, and from there I went over to the Postal Annex at the South Station to work for another three or four hours! Those were hectic days indeed!

Following my graduation from BU, I took my first teaching job at Dighton. The $2,400. pay plus $300. for coaching, though not that great to support a growing family, was the highest that any in my graduating class received for their first teaching positions. This relatively meager pay (compared to $180./yr. for my father when he started out!) meant that I had to scramble in order to properly raise and support our family. As the years went on, my teaching, coaching and administrative salaries increased, but never to near the levels that I could have commanded for similar efforts in the private business sector. So for me *moonlighting* became a career-long normality.

One of my first and ongoing 'moonlighting' jobs was to work as a sports official; another was giving after school lessons to athletes. (Most of the lessons were gratis if they couldn't afford to pay.) Pete Millikan of the Mt. Hope Finishing Company in North Dighton hired me during the summer months to run a baseball program for the youngsters in town.

After leaving Dighton, in the interim year before taking my Athletic Director position in Bridgewater, I attended graduate school to secure my Master's Degree. I got a very high mark in the Civil Service Exam for Post Service Work and was placed at the top of the list for positions, which I turned down several times to pursue my career. I still did moonlight work in the Postal Service for several years.

One of my favorite extra jobs was the one that I secured through the generosity of George Carney, working as a ticket seller at the Raynham Dog Track. My first meeting with Mr. Carney was very interesting. Bob Reagan, a fellow teacher who worked for him in running the Horse Races at the Brockton Fair secured a job for me at the Race Track as the gate security man. While on my job one afternoon, a nice looking young gentleman came to my gate to gain entrance. I promptly stopped him and asked him for his identification. He replied that he was George Carney. I blurted back to him, "I don't care who you are, you don't get by me without proper identification."

Since I had never met him before, little did I realize that he was the President and Owner of the racing facilities. Mr. Carney was so impressed with my tight security work that he told Bob Reagan that he wanted to hire me to work for him at the Raynham Dog Track, which I did for several seasons for their summer night races.

George Carney

As related earlier, for many years I directed the Summer Recreational Program for the town of Bridgewater.

During the summer months I also worked as the Golf Pro at Buncey's Golf Course. This job of teaching many males and females the basics of the golf grip, swing and chipping was a boon to my own game. By teaching others, I really improved my own short game tremendously and this was a great factor in my future successes on the golf circuits.

"The best way to learn something is to teach it."

Along with all of my moonlighting jobs throughout the 60's and 70's I volunteered many hours to working with the Massachusetts Interscholastic Athletic Association. There I served as Chairman of the State Athletic Rules Committee, as State Basketball Tournament Director and on many other Committees, including the State Baseball Tournament and the Football Super Bowl Committee. Except for the satisfaction of doing the right thing for the student athletes of the state, and the enjoyment of the meals we had after meetings, these were all non-paying jobs.

Oh! There is one area of work that I failed to mention. I was the chief maintenance man for all of our properties. With the help of my Dad, my brother Mike, and by my brother-in-law Paul, I managed to become proficient as an all-around handy man. I learned to do carpentry, electrical work, concrete work and lots more as needed. Application of these skills was necessary in order to afford to maintain the real estate that we acquired. No way could I have paid the going rate. And by sometimes dragging my kids along with me on these missions they learned valuable lessons in industriousness. Of course one of the lessons that they learned was that they preferred to excel in school to gain less rigorous work as adults! We also often managed to sneak out to the Cape Cod café for an after moonlighting for a pizza as a reward for work well done.

"A pint of sweat saves a gallon of blood."
General George S. Patton (1885-1945)

Not only was *'Do it ourselves'* a given in our family, but we also made thriftiness a source of wealth in its own right. I've always said *"a penny saved is worth two pennies earned"*. Since there are no taxes on non-spent money, and you don't have to work as hard to have that amount ready in your wallet for when more essential needs arise, I was scrupulously thrifty. Establishing and maintaining these habits in the family was another job in itself.

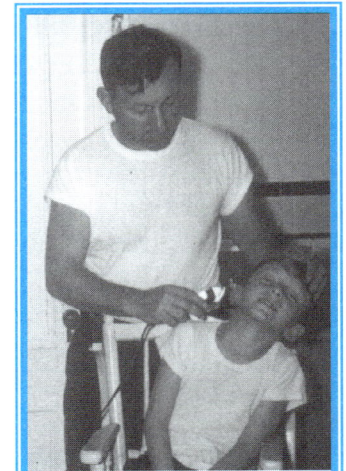

My kids hated that I gave them haircuts at home and made them do maintenance and yard work. We always ate all leftovers but the kids ate well. The kids wore hand-me-downs, but Helen dressed them the best. I wouldn't let them buy individual sodas, but we bought cases at a time wholesale for special treats. The lights and heat had to be off when not in use, but they were always available when needed. Jackie Mark said recently that I still have the first nickel I ever earned. In a way he's right, as I've recycled my earnings into lasting wealth.

Bobby endures another cut. Other kids on deck.

My conservative ways actually allowed me to be extravagant in other areas of life. Our kids may have been surprised that we even had resources to provide deserved fulfillment of their dreams at Christmas and to help them out on their own ventures.

A family legend about my extreme frugality has it that one day when the kids were begging me to let them go on the rocking horse and 'choo-choo' rides, that I made three of them get on the same car to stretch the nickel fee. When they wanted a second ride, I was said to have simply shaken the ride to give them the same effect! As you know kid's memories can be exaggerated. I can tell you without doubt that this family legend is fictional, as I never actually put the first nickel in!

"The best things in life are free."

I have never complained of my workload but the one thing that I have regretted was the fact that I had very little time left to spend with my growing family. Luckily I could at least watch over them closely within the school system where I worked and they studied. And I thank the Good Lord for my lovely, intelligent, creative and caring wife Helen, who took a strong home front lead in raising our children. *Helen & kids at D.W. Fields Park*

My working several jobs at a time both supported our children through high school and helped with their higher education expenses. Fortunately, all of my kids worked hard at their studies and earned scholarships to go along with loans and our support to help complete their education. And our assistance and insistence on their achieving excellent grades translated in all getting college degrees, including four of them graduating with honors from Harvard, Stanford and other leading schools. How valuable is that? All my work away from home, all of Helen's work in support of me at home, all the investments, all the extra 'two for one' efforts, have always been all about our true lasting wealth; our children and now theirs.

Now as I look back, I wonder how I managed to do all of this work in addition to putting in my many hours Coaching and Directing Athletics. My regular jobs alone often stretched into 15-hour workdays. My kids remind me that my work and moonlighting sometimes came at the expense of my resting or spending enough time with them in evenings, weekends and holidays other than Christmas.

Debbie says that I was often so wrapped up in my school duties that I'd pass her in the corridor and respond to her greeting by saying *"Hi Dear"*, not really recognizing that I was speaking to my daughter. Of course on many levels it was for their own benefit that I scrupulously feigned distance from them at school activities. Any hint of favoritism could possibly have proliferated preponderantly pre-existing pernicious peer pressure in that regard, and worse, it may have given my kids the idea that they could slack off in any way. On many occasions the only way that I could practically embrace my kids was to embrace my work, which was ultimately on their behalf. I know that my kids definitely suffered in a way from my absence while serving the kids of town who I also loved. I believed then and I believe now that I was doing the right thing, and that the Man upstairs helped me to make things right for my children for having done right by the others in my career. *The Big Playmaker in the Sky is, I'm quite sure, all for creating nothing but "Win-Win" situations. It's only up to us to endeavor to follow our individually unique heart's desire that surely God Himself must have planted in us.*

My kids do acknowledge that my creating programs and leagues in which they could participate did wonders for them. And they know that they did get some 'special' treatment in areas where their peers were not of age to notice. As children I included them on bus rides to my team's games and on scouting missions, and I involved them as cheerleaders, mascots, statisticians, and utility helpers around the gyms and playgrounds. All of these activities gave them some real quality time with me doing productive things for the benefit of the community at large, and they got a leg up on mastering many important life work and interpersonal relationship skills. They were able to learn that by truly helping others, they could, indeed help themselves.

"To think, I did all that,
And may I say, not in a shy way,
Oh no, Oh no not me, I DID IT MY WAY"

VACATION, TRAVEL AND GOLF MEMORIES
Flights

"I took the road less traveled on and that has made all the difference." Robert Frost

All work and no play definitely makes for a dull and less than fruitful life. That's part of why I chose sports and recreation as my 1st profession. I've always worked and played with vigorous enthusiasm, and by mixing the two I've been able to squeeze more into each day, maximizing my enjoyment of both.

It's not that I always consciously tried to find play in work or profit in play, but years of efficiency oriented habits ingrained in me an always ready openness to seize any such 'two for one' opportunities. For example, I'd say that my winnings of cash and merchandise while playing on the golf course over the years have paid for all of my membership dues. Also that my work as a teaching golf pro improved my game and the better I played the more fun I had. While vacationing, we grabbed at the chance to purchase the beach cottage that with our improvements is now worth 20 times the original price. My time at Hampton has in turn helped me to relax and be more peacefully productive. When I've traveled, I've often made it a point to stay with family. It saves money on meals and motels (which I more than spend on them), but more importantly, it cements and enhances these elemental life relationships.

I've also been a big believer in providing horizon-broadening recreation and family bonding adventures for my children. Sure we had to live frugally during my teaching and coaching career, but by eliminating wasteful consumption of forgettable junk by my family for fifty weeks each year, we were able to save-up enough for quality basics and have enough left over for an unforgettable two-week vacation trip each summer. These *'flights from the ordinary'* would usually come late in August at the end of the Playground Season and just before the start of school in September.

Larry's got Bobby, Jean has Debbie. Why can't mom & dad give me a brother too?!

The 'almost complete' Folloni Team in Bryant Rock in 1957 4 years before the addition of our last son James.

We often rented cottages on Cape Cod and Brant Rock, but our favorite annual vacation spot was Hampton Beach. I can still remember our first trip there back in the early '50's just before I started my teaching career in Bridgewater. We rented the McDonald cottage just across the Blvd. from the Boar's Head area of the beach.

New Hampshire Dreaming, 1959

The calm before the storm..unpacking at Olde McDonald's Cabins between the Salt marshes and Boar's Head Beach

After enjoying a few sunny days on the beach we were hit with a late summer hurricane. The tides were unusually high and the waves were constantly crashing over the seawall and across Ocean Boulevard. The great salt marshes behind us were also overflowing leaving us surrounded at high tide with rapidly rising water, which came precariously close to our elevated first floor, threatening to sweep us away. We had been given radio and police warnings throughout the day to evacuate the beach area, but having decided to ride out the storm, we ignored them for too long.

Larry Folloni Jr. running at Ocean Blvd. Hampton Beach by Boar's Head before construction of the seawall, circa 1950

We were scared at times, but luckily the storm subsided and by the next morning the terrible tease of the tides had receded. Like being *'Snowbound'* initiates one as a New Englander, the tides that blustery September day showed us guys the Hampton Way. (And starkly peopled, came so soon, a gladder bright real-estate boom!)

Year after year we returned to Hampton Beach for our vacations, until the day 20 years after our 'perfect initiation storm' (another 30 years before today), when we purchased the home at 13 Ross Avenue from which I now write.

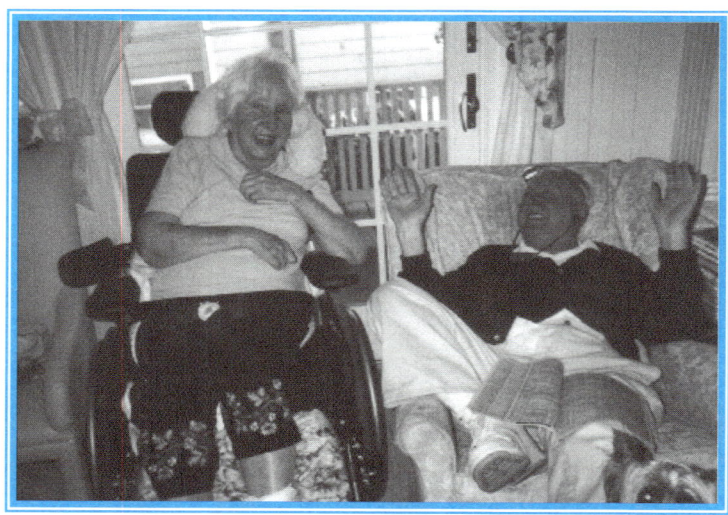

Despite many bleak waning days in the December of our lives, with the extraordinary help of our family, wheelchair bound Helen and I still manage an occasional hearty laugh at our Hampton Beach Home.

My daughter Debbie just wrote to tell me that just before her tragic medical problems, one night while sitting around the dinner table at Hampton, one of our children asked Helen why, out of all of her suitors and proposals, she picked their Dad to marry. Her response was*:*

"I knew he was going places."

QUEBEC

On many occasions during our short-term rental years at Hampton Beach Helen and I would take off after a few days there and head to other areas for a change of venue. We often traveled throughout New Hampshire and Maine and in 1953 we went up to Quebec, for a really enjoyable visit in Canada.

> *[This trip to Eastern Canada paved the way for another that we took there around 1960 with all of the children. It was this later family excursion that son Michael stills calls one of his favorites, probably in good part because of the reinforcement and thrill he experienced when I came to his grade school class during one of my teaching breaks to show slides of Canada to his classmates. I can still recall the beautifully choreographed 'Changing of the Guard' ceremonies in Quebec. And I recall how once back in Bridgewater, interchanging my duties as an educator and as a Guardian; as a worker and a vacationer, I was able to choreograph a memorable lesson for my son and his junior high school classmates.]*

I've lived a life that's full, I've travelled each and every highway, And more, much more than this, I DID IT MY WAY

After a few days stay on our original foray to Quebec, Helen and I went down to Montreal for a day, then on to the Niagara Falls and to Howe's Taverns in upper New York.

Michael Helen Bobby and Larry, Aug. 1953

All was going great until we spent a harrowing night at a disgustingly bad motel that was recommended by someone we met along the highway. Helen refused to even pull back the bed covers. We were so exhausted from driving all day that we just laid down on top of them to get a few hours of needed rest. As Groucho Marx once said: *"I've had a wonderful time, but this wasn't it."*

NEW YORK CITY

We left early the next morning and headed down to NYC to spend some time with Uncle Al and Aunt Connie. On this as well as other trips to visit them, Al and Connie were great hosts. Al of course showed us the many sights of the Big Apple, from the Statue of Liberty and tall skyscrapers to life in the heart of the city, Times Square.

During this first visit Al was still in the service working in the Armed Forces Radio Network and his office was located right in the heart of Times Square. We had the pleasure of going to see the famous Rockettes and to many theaters on Broadway. Little did we know that 40 years later our sister Virginia's grandson Chris Ghelfi would be starring in many productions there!

On one of our trips to New York we took a ride to visit Renaldo Resmini, a boyhood chum from Stanley who lived in a small suburb of Philadelphia. He was married to a girl whose cousin was one of the famous "Four Aces", and they took us out to dinner at the nightclub where the group was performing. After the show Renaldo introduced us to these 'ACE' gentlemen from 'The City of Brotherly Love': Al Alberts Dave Mahoney, Lou Silvestri and Sol Vaccaro. They weren't exactly John Paul George & Ringo, but for the decade of the 50's they were the top pop vocalists in the country.

At the time of our first meeting they were just starting out on their road to fame. I was very impressed with their performance and when I went back to New York, I told Al to sign them up as they were great singers and I knew they would make it big some day.

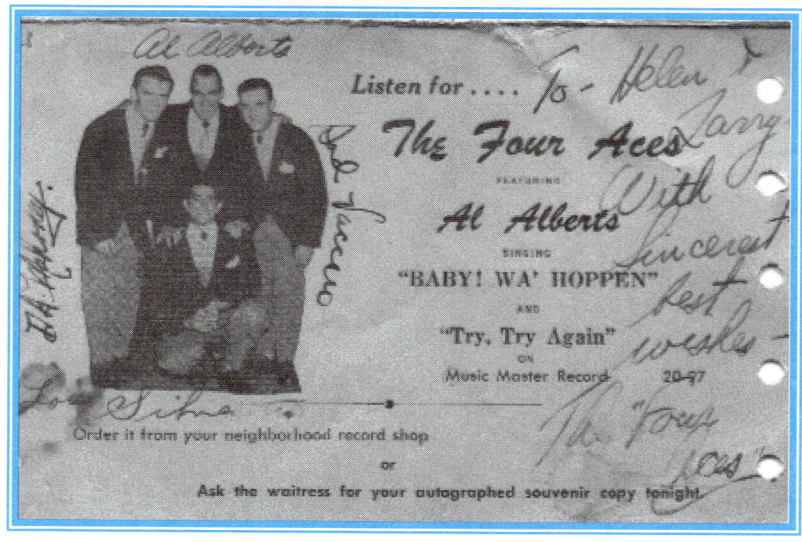

Al took my recommendation with a grain of salt, saying that New York was loaded with talented vocalists who were trying to cash in on the NYC network programs. Well a few years later on one of our visits with Al, Helen and I took in a movie in Times Square. After the movie we went to a theater club where we were treated to the pleasant experience of again seeing 'The Four Aces' on Stage.

When we entered this theater we didn't pay much attention to the Marquee that had blazed on it the name of the "Four Aces" as the featured performers. As soon as the curtain opened and they appeared on stage singing their then famous rendition of 'Sin' I recognized them as the group that Renaldo had introduced us to a few years earlier in Philadelphia. During their break we went back stage to visit with them again. They well remembered our first meeting back in Philadelphia and were very cordial to us. They spent most of the time between shows with us and before we left they gave us several autographed photos.

When we went back to Al's place and informed him of our chance meeting with the then famous Four Aces, he had to eat a little crow for not signing them up when we first mentioned them a few years earlier. He missed out on managing one of the Premier Pop Singing Groups of this pre-rock & rock era. Remember the song *'Mr. Sandman'* in the *'Back to the Future'* movie? That was one of the Four Ace's million seller gold records, to go along with *'Sin', 'Perfidia', 'Tell me Why', 'Love is a Many Splendored Thing'* and *'Three Coins In The Fountain'*. They also did *'Rock and Roll Rhapsody'*, and one of Taylor Rose's favorites, *'Bahama Mama'*.

Although Al missed out on this recommendation, he did follow up, as told earlier, on my introducing him to Rocky Marciano, who became the undefeated heavy weight-boxing champion of the world and Al's business partner.

Connie with son Jack and baby Marie. Barbara will make 3. Note picture of Rocky on shelf behind.

AD Conference Trips

Having given many hours of service to the Massachusetts State Athletic Directors Association I had the benefit of several all expenses paid trips to their Conferences throughout the country. Of course there was a lot of work and reporting associated with all of them, but I also managed to enjoy the nearby scenery and the quality people I met on these missions. The most memorable of these business trips were to Washington D.C. (1964), St. Louis (1972), Cherry Hill, NJ (1977) and New Orleans (1979).

Washington, D.C.

I made my first trip to our Nation's Capital Washington D.C. back during the early WWII years when I went to visit my brother Mike, who was stationed there in the Navy. My return visit as an AD in the early '60's brought back some of those memories.

Mike first showed me the many historical areas in the District, including the Capitol, the White House, the Washington Monument, the Lincoln Memorial, and the Arlington National Cemetery. It was very exciting for me to actually see the many national landmarks that I had read about in my history classes.

In addition to taking in the sights of D.C. with Mike I was fortunate to visit with some of our buddies from our hometown who were stationed nearby. One of them was Mario Chiocca, shown with me at right, who was to make the supreme sacrifice a short time later on the battlefields in Germany.

Mike also took me to see the NFL Championship game between the Washington Redskins and the Chicago Bears. (These were the days before the the AFL and the Superbowl, so this was *the* prize clash.) Washington, under Quarterback Sammy Baugh, was heavily favored to defeat the Bears and Quarterback Sid Lockman. ust a month earlier the Redskins had prevailed over the Bears in a 7-3 defensive battle. The result in the championship game, however, was a lop-sided victory for the Bears, as their head coach George Halas refined his "T" formation and it proved to be unstoppable. To this day the 73 to 0 win by the Bears remains the largest victory margin ever in a title game. There were only 12 footballs allocated to this game, and after each touchdown extra point kick the fan that caught it would be allowed to take home the souvenir. Running out of game balls, the NFL made the Bears run two-point conversions on their last two touchdowns!

My second trip to Washington in the middle '60's as a representative of the MSADA was made in Joe Hogue's automobile. Our good friends Henry Knowlton of Winchester and Earle Crompton of Wakefield accompanied us and we all shared rooms at a downtown hotel. During breaks from our conference work sessions we found the time to revisit the many sites of Washington D.C. It was a very enjoyable time and I miss my companions who have all since departed from this earth. Only I remain. And I hope to remain much longer yet, but as the great world leader and frequent visitor to D.C., Sir Winston Churchill said before dying around the time of our trip in 1965:

"I am ready to meet my Maker.
Whether my Maker is prepared for the ordeal of meeting me is another matter!"

In the early 60's when we bundled up the whole family and took along my sister Virginia to Washington. My kids remind me that we had 9 people in the sedan for the 18 hours of round trip driving! The poor kids were "sardined" into every nook and cranny of the vehicle. We made our first stop to exhale and visit Al in New York then we drove down to Virginia's daughter Mary's place in Laurel, Maryland. From there we went on another hour ride to give the kids their first taste of the marvels of Washington D.C. Extracting themselves from their corners of the car when we arrived after the ride from N.Y.C., seared into the kids minds an association of D.C. with **'The Land of the Free'**!

By the way, when we arrived unannounced at Mary Markey's house in Maryland, Mary and Steve were out, so we sent the baby sitter home and went to bed before they returned. Before going to bed we carefully laid out 9 pairs of shoes at the bottom of the steps to announce our presence.

When Debbie finished law school at Georgetown in the early '80's she signed on as an associate attorney with the Seyfarth, Shaw, Fairweather & Geraldson Law Firm located across from the White House and she purchased a Condo at the prestigious Atrium Complex in Arlington, VA.

By then I had become pretty well acquainted with the area and was able to maneuver around the Capital with ease. This became our stop off place for a few days during our early retirement era annual driving trips to Florida. Keeping with family tradition, in addition to resting and painting the town (and her Condo) a bit, I found time there while Debbie was working to install new electrical service in a basement room she converted to living space in her unit.

St. Louis

I attended the Annual Athletic Director's Conference in St. Louis, Missouri in 1972. This stands out since it was the first year that the now famous Gateway Arch was opened. We were among the first to cross the mighty Mississippi River on this extravagant architectural wonder that at 630 feet tall is our Nation's tallest monument. It was designed in the form of the arching supports of a Covered Wagon. This is appropriate, as St. Louis was the central connecting place and final major civilization outpost for travelers who pioneered on their Covered Wagons on their way to conquer the West. And remember the arches for the original westward wagons were forged at the Stanley Iron Works!

Conference attendees were given a tour of the Cardinal's new Baseball Stadium built by Anheiser Busch. The ballpark tour also included a beer-drinking bash for those who indulged. Of course being a nonalcoholic drinker, my beverage was a Coke, and I had a ball! Travelling is a great way to learn about history as well as about different moods and standards of present day people in various locales.

All in all it was a great experience as we attended the many conference sessions during the day and at night we had the opportunity to enjoy some Riverboat excursions and have several fabulous St. Louis Steaks and Prime Rib meals. St. Louis is called the *'Show Me'* State, and they sure showed me a great time.

St. Louis is also the boyhood home of the great American Writer Samuel Clemens, a.k.a. Mark Twain, the great grandfather of Environmental Sciences Professor Bruce Clemens, who was my son Michael's associate in a community development project in Guatemala and his roommate for a time during Graduate School at Harvard. It was Bruce's famous relative who passed along this valuable travel tip:

Bruce Clemens, 1973

"Don't let school interfere with your education."

1835-1910 Under the pen name Mark Twain, Samuel L. Clemens published over 30 works of literature including:

The Adventures of Huckleberry Finn,
The Adventures of Tom Sawyer,
The Prince and the Pauper,
A Connecticut Yankee In King Arthur's Court.

CHERRY HILL, NEW JERSEY

The Cherry Hill Conference in 1977 was noteworthy because it was there that I was honored as the recipient of the Eastern Seaboard Athletic Director of the Year Award. My lovely wife Helen, along with the four boys, Larry, Jr., Bobby, Michael, and Jimmy came down to attend the affair.

Son Michael stole the show when he unexpectedly interrupted the Master of Ceremonies and approached the stage to give an impromptu speech to introduce his Dad. It was a very touching moment as he quickly summed upon the memorable events in my career and recalled the vital supporting role played by my wife Helen. He finished by citing the inspirational quote posted above my AD office: *"When Preparation Meets Opportunity there is Success"* and noted the more essential meaning that his parents had demonstrated in lives of the Folloni Team, and that is:

"When Love Meets a Moment in Destiny, There is Fulfillment."

There was electricity in the air and hardly a dry eye in the house as we came together for an embrace. Michael and the Team were given a standing ovation from the gathering, and we were treated like celebrities for the weekend. Speaking of celebrities, *The Spinners* R&B musical group was in town, and son James convinced us all to take in their show, where we found fabulously fulfilling family fun. [The Spinners are famous for the songs *"Could It be I'm Falling In Love"*, "I'll Be Around", "Working My Way Back to You", *"Rubber Band Man"*, and of course the also appropriate *"Games People Play"*.

Michael, Larry Jr., Jimmy, Bobby, Helen and I enjoy cozy quarters in Cherry Hill.

The day after the Conference ceremonies, we all took a ride to Philadelphia, which was just over the bridge across the river. It was a nice reminder of the days there when I became engaged to *"Hollywood Helen"*.

Ever adventurous and ready to play ball, my boys engaged some Philly Ghetto kids in a 'hoop' game, or shall I say a 'box' game, as the goal was a bottomless milk crate nailed 6' up on a post. The boys never tire of teasing Bobby for getting **'Dr. J. Jammed on'** there by a pint size pre-teen. No one caught his name, but Bobby swears it had to have been some budding pro!

James, far right, is amused.

The ride home was also memorable. Upon nearing the Massachusetts border we encountered a real Northeast Snow Blizzard. My way apparently wasn't the right way that day, as we missed an exit in Hartford that would have led us to the southern route through Connecticut where we would have missed this storm and arrived home safely in a few hours. Instead we just managed to reach the northern border of Connecticut on Route 84 before the brunt of the storm hit us. By that time the roads had become very slick and on several occasions the boys had to get out of the car to push us up the slippery hills. After about an hour of mostly pushing to make the last mile into Massachusetts and with the storm steadily increasing in force, we finally gave up and decided to seek shelter in a cabin in the quaint town of Sturbridge.

We were all settled in for the night when suddenly the storm knocked out all the power in the area. The Sturbridge Village Theme park down the road features authentic 18th Century New England living. Unfortunately this cabin did not come equipped with an authentic wood stove or candles, so we were left exhausted and without any lights or heat. We all huddled close in our street clothes trying to keep warm while overcoming fears of any further damage that the storm might do.

Being **snowbound** really gave us the opportunity to call a 'time out' of our hustle and bustle routines. We spent the next several hours sharing happy stories of days gone by, relating and creating family history until the warmth in our hearts gave us rest and rejuvenation.

*If we're open to squeezing lemonade from lemons,
the Guy Upstairs offers The Best Way of Making Things Right!*

So we survived the ordeal and prospered as a family. By morning the storm subsided, leaving us with 2 feet of snow but also renewed for the still challenging drive back to the comforts of our lovely home in Bridgewater*.

Jimmy & Larry Jr. enjoying the comforts of home at 91 Bedford St.

*Where I promptly put them to work shoveling out the driveway and walkways.

NEW ORLEANS

I was able to take Helen along to New Orleans in 1972, to really combine the AD Conference with a marvelous vacation trip. In between work sessions we toured the French Quarters and took in the many sights that New Orleans had to offer. One of the most pleasant memories was our Boat Trip up the Mississippi.

One of the unpleasant memories came about from a restaurant in the French Quarters. I ate a salad that gave me a stomach infection that lasted for several months after our return home. Fortunately the infection hit me near the end of our vacation and we were able to enjoy most of our trip.

Our hotel had an inside tennis court and I stopped by to watch some of the players. Out of a clear blue sky along came a young man with a tennis racket in his hand and he asked me if I would like to volley some shots with him.

Unbeknown to me at the time, it was none other than the famous Professional Tennis Star, Bjorn Borg, just a few years before he started to dominate the Grand Slam Tournaments. Borg won the French Open in '74, '75, '78, '79, '80, & '81. He won Wimbledon in '76, '77, '78, '79, & '80. And he was the Runner-up in the U.S Open in '76, '78, '80, & '81.

"The true measure of a man is how he treats someone who can do him absolutely no good." Samuel Johnson, 1709-1874

I was really thrilled at this unexpected meeting with this nice man & star, who's charming personality was a precise counterpoint to the sometimes abrasive and combative John McEnroe with whom he had many an epic match.

Now I suppose that in a way maybe I could have given Bjorn some preparatory help there…

CALIFORNIA

In addition to our trips to California while I was in the service, we took two other vacations there. The first was in 1976 to visit Debbie during spring break at Stanford University. Following our visit to Stanford, we went on a tour of California and down to the border of Mexico.

Our first stop was in San Francisco, where we ran into one of their 1st 'Gay Pride Parades'. Helen was happy as ever freely chatting to all the free souls on the street, oblivious to the far out eccentricity of some of their outfits (and in some shocking cases, of the lack-thereof). We toured the city on Frisco's famous cable car system that goes from the Bay on up to the high steep hills and back down into the financial and shopping districts. We toured Fisherman's Wharf and stopped in at the restaurant owned by Joe DiMaggio's Family (where we ate 56-straight gamey crab and oyster au-devoirs) before we embarked on a shopping tour of Ghiradelli Square.

Between San Francisco's 'Little Italy' (North Beach) and Fisherman's Wharf is is Lombard St., known as the 'Crookedest Street in The World' named perhaps for the circuitous route that my relatives the Lombardi's took to get to Italy? Mann, was it ever fun driving up Lombard St.! The long & winding road..

All in all it was a very fascinating tour of one of the world's great cities. By the way, the summer fog blowing through the Golden Gate can bring summer temperatures down into the 40's in a hurry, much to the displeasure of tourists and to the delight of sweatshirt vendors. As author and humorist Mark Twain also said:

"The coldest winter I ever spent was one summer in San Francisco!" -Mark Twain

We then went down the California coastline for the famous 17 Mile Drive. We hit Monterey, the *'Canning City'* of John Steinbeck fame. This fishing town's factories packed tunas, sardines, oysters, tomatos, garlic and every fruit and vegetable imaginable from California's fertile valleys. Nowadays they mostly just pack in tourists. The bordering town of Carmel is a ritzy shopping area and hide-away for the rich and famous, including movie and TV stars. (It's also the scene of Helen's own famous 'soap story' – when a street bum asked her for a handout to buy some soap and Helen offered him a 'Palmolive' bar that she had in her purse!)

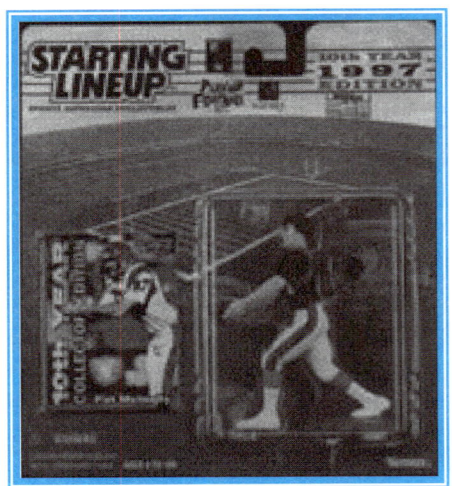

After the drive down the coastline we stopped in at Los Angeles and on to Santa Monica to visit with Pat McInally, the 6'7" stingbean leaper, College All-American receiver and NFL Pro-Bowl punter who was my son Michael's roommate for 3 years at Harvard. 10 years later, Patrick, who is now a motivational speaker and a nationally syndicated columnist specializing in youth sports issues, came up with the idea for Hasbro's 'Starting Lineup' Sports Action figures. Hasbro recently made an action figure to commemorate Pat's pro days and creative ways.

Pat is still famous for being the only NFL player to ever make a perfect score on the 'Wonderlik' IQ test that the league administers to all draftees. Big Mac took us out to a ritzy nightclub up in the mountains for dinner. I can still taste the delicious bean soup that was served as an entree to our meal. Although we were greatly entertained by this charming and successful record breaker, since all good things come to an end, we said goodbye to Pat and continued to blow south without him that night.

Speaking of 'jumping beans', we then went on down to Tijuana Mexico, planning to spend a few days there. After seeing the lousy conditions and lifestyle of those poor border tourist town Mexicans, we quickly hightailed it back to California to spend time in beautiful San Diego, the city that has perhaps the most comfortable climate in the world - between 50 and 80 degrees F. everyday!

Our next stop was an hour north at the Torrey Pines Golf Course area in La Jolla, where we went around with a Real Estate Agent, who showed us a beautiful 3-bedroom house right off the Golf Course that was selling for only 75 Thousand Dollars. That place now is probably worth Three Million Dollars.

*We missed out on seizing that opportunity, but you can't win em all.
And you can't seize the present if you obsess in fretting about the past.*

From there we went back to LA to catch our plane flight back to Boston. All in all it was a nice vacation trip for us.

We had a repeat vacation trip to California upon the year of my retirement and Jimmy's graduation from Stanford in 1983.

Following the commencement exercises Jimmy took over as tour guide and we went in a different direction. After stopping in to visit Michael and his budding "Energy Planning & Design" Power conservation business, we went to see the enormous old redwood trees in Muir Woods, just north of San Francisco. Some of these giants were on earth 200 years *before* Christ was born!

Michael endeavored to help people make efficient use of the lights of the world.

After another cable car tour of San Francisco we headed 3-hours east by rental car to Yosemite National Park. Jimmy had to make reservations 6-months in advance so we could stay in a cabin on the valley floor for a few days and enjoy this great resort area up close. Upon our arrival we were escorted to our cabin and after unpacking we went off to the park restaurant for dinner.

We had a very harrowing surprise upon our return to our cabin after eating. We arrived at Yosemite at the peak of the snow-melting season. It just so happened that during the hour or so that we were gone, the icy run-off water from the surrounding mountains flooded the area where our cabin was located. The water cascaded up over our hip level and there was no way we could get back into our belongings. After a long aggravating wait, the management finally found us another cabin on higher ground. With all of our luggage in the flooded cabin we had to make do with the clothes on our back for a few days until the flood tide receded.

Determined to make the best of it, and encouraged by our spectacularly awesome surroundings, we just 'went with the flow.' While on our stay at Yosemite we took daily trips to see the beautiful waterfalls, wildlife and mountain and valley scenery. We even climbed up the Mauro Mountain on foot. It was a tiring walk up to the peak, but we finally managed to reach it. We were a bit concerned about Helen's ability to make the climb as she had her heart attack just a few years prior to this adventure. When we reached the top, Helen put her hands up to the sky and said, *"Thank God, I made it and I feel great!"*

Next on the tour was the long ride through the high and low deserts of California and Nevada on the way to Las Vegas. The last time that I had been to Las Vegas was during the WWII years when I was stationed in Victorville and a member of the Air Force Baseball Team. At that time we flew there for a baseball game that we played with the thermometer peaking at about 120 degrees. The heat was *"no problem"*, however, because as they like to rationalize there, it was a *'dry heat'*, and this of course, is my best rendition of Larry Jr's. *'dry humor'*.

It was warm this time around, but not the scorching heat that we experienced as ballplayers. Helen, Jim and I spent several days in Vegas and we enjoyed the great inexpensive buffet meals. Everything else, however, was costly. We played some slot machines, 'investing' mostly on nickel slots but Helen had a hunch and she put in a silver dollar in one of the 'one arm bandits' and hit for a $50 dollar "bonanza".

I accumulated a tray full of nickels on my machine but before I finished playing I had put back all of my winnings. It was fun while it lasted, but the house's bank will always outlast that of the players. *The best bet really is to only play as much as you are ready to lose, and to make it a point to NEVER re-invest anything that the house 'gives' back to you in winnings.* The fact that most people keep feeding their 'winnings' back is how these phenomenal corporate casinos make their gargantuan profits. Sure the slots return 98% of what's put in on average, and sure, sometimes you make a quick bonanza. *The secret here, however, is that the casino's bank, relative to the reserves of the individual players, is unlimited. This allows them the staying power to weather the peak high and low points of the natural up and down cycles determined by the computer fixed odds, where the player's funds at some inevitable point, cannot withstand the low point.* If one keeps putting their jackpots back in, eventually they'll hit a (temporary) bottom that due to lack of reserves eliminates them before they can climb back up on the curve. So the players always end up going out big losers, leaving the house as the big winner.

Although we fell into the trap of 'reinvesting our winnings', we were at least wise enough not to toss in more than we could afford. And we were able to continue our trip content with having enjoyed the time in 'Sin City' while leaving with our souls and our wallets intact. We took the southern route over the Sierras and through the high desert back to CA. We made a few short stops along the way to see how the cowboys of long ago traveled and Jimmy had us stop in at some modern day 'honky-tonk' taverns to get the full hysterical effect of local historical development.

Our first stop was in Victorville to see the old Air Force Base that I was stationed at during the War. There was no way that I could recognize the Town. It was completely remodeled with new buildings and new roads. We then went on to the Air Force Base itself, which was still under tight security. We explained to the guard that I had been stationed there during the war and wanted to revisit my former home. This being the pre "9-11-01" era, we soon convinced him to let us go in for a tour of the Base.

Once inside we found that my old barracks had disappeared. In its place were lovely apartments to house the military personnel. The barren desert grounds that we knew were replaced with nice irrigated lawns and newly paved streets that were named after each state in the union. The crowning touch was a beautiful golf course right on the base.

We spent the better part of the day on base then took off for a ride up over the mountains to San Bernardino. Every Saturday night of our wartime weekend furloughs started at this city's Mama Mia's Restaurant for a delicious Spaghetti and Ravioli meal before going down to LA. We tried unsuccessfully to find Mama Mia's and were eventually told that the Restaurant site had been paved over by one of the many new highways. Disappointed, we drove on through the bumper to bumper traffic of Pasadena and the other suburbs of LA to finally catch our plane for the long flight home.

"In most cities they use cars to drive, but in Los Angeles they just park 'em. Some men leave their cars there all night in order to hold the space for the next day."
                                Will Rogers, 1920

Italian 'Roots' Trip

In l979 my son Bobby, who was coaching in Rome, Italy sent us two TWA airline tickets to come visit him in Rome, Italy.

Our first stop was a trip to the *Spanish Steps*, which were filled with flowers (and tourists) for the spring season. At the bottom of the steps is a fountain with a boat, which pours refreshing drinking water from both ends. You have to walk almost into the fountain and lean over to get a cool drink. Getting to the top of the Spanish Steps will get you in shape, and the climb is worth it. At this vantage point is the entrance to Villa Borghese, which offers a beautiful roof-level view of the city. You can see the Vatican, the top of Piazza Venezia, the Pantheon and many cupola church tops and colorful pergola stone capped buildings.

We did a lot of walking in Rome. On the way from place to place we'd stop to get a fresh squeezed spremuta di limone (lemonade) or a frulato di frutta (a sweet drink of blended fresh fruit, ice and 'top secret recipe' sweet syrup). Piazza Navona is Bob's and our favorite plaza with the three Bernini fountains, artists, minstrel singers and of course pretty Italian girls. The piazza's colorful buildings arrayed in an oval shape were actually constructed on top of a stadium used in Roman times. We saw part of the entrance to this ancient stadium from one end of the piazza.

We ate nearby at a very popular pizzeria, 'da Baffetto' (At the Mustache) where Romans don't mind the wait outside to get the fabulous thin crusted pizza inside. They served my favorite bruschetta, which is sliced and toasted Roman 'cassarecia' bread, meshed with garlic and oil or with sliced or diced tomatoes, oil and basil.

We attended the Vatican on Easter Sunday and got to see the Pope waiving from his window in the Square. We had reserved an 'audience' with Il Papa for the previous Wednesday. Unfortunately, Bob, who had gotten the tickets in advance, was planning on the winter audience schedule, which was at 5 p.m. Poor Helen's face dropped when Bob discovered on Wednesday afternoon that they had shifted the Pope's audience to 11am for the summer schedule. The one consolation is that although they call them 'private audiences', sometimes up to 5,000 people are there, so it is not all that intimate.

We also walked to the Trevi Fountain, which was especially Romantic for Helen and me as it was made famous by the 'Three coins in a Fountain' song that the Four Aces used to play. (The original song was obviously the Italian ballad 'Fontana di Trevi', from the score for a movie where a young Anita Ekburg took Rome by storm in her famous swim in the fountain.)

As always the Trevi Fountain is a place for romance, or, more crudely spoken, a 'pickup spot'. An immense amount of coins are thrown into the fountain. It is said that there is a lot of local politicking in determining who gets to retrieve those 'good luck' offerings, which add up to a tidy sum over time. Legend has it that if you throw a coin over your shoulder into the fountain, that you will return to Rome (albeit a little lighter in the pocket). All things considered, I think that the odds of making out at the fountain are little better than in Las Vegas!

"When in Rome, do as the Romans do" holds especially true for eating. A sure-fire rule of thumb for good eating is look for a restaurant, trattoria or osteria crowded with locals. This was the simple but valuable suggestion from Flavia De Stefanis, one of Bob's students at the American Overseas School of Rome.

Flavia's case was certainly proven at "l'Ambasciata di Abbruzzo", a well-known eatery where you 'walk in and roll out'. To start, we had to wait outside in a line. It was not so unpleasant however, as Jean and 'Slim' (Bob) sipped on the house red wine and we all snacked on some olives and other antipasti left in dishes on the windowsill or any place that would accommodate them.

This place must have invented the word 'appetizer', because once seated, the waiters brought us dozens of plates including peppers in oil, fried zucchini flowers, stuffed mushrooms, clams and mussels in various sauces, mozzarella di buffalo, and on and on. Then, (just before the wheelbarrow) came the pastas...many of them.

I had a very special surprise when I began eating the ravioli. They were just like the special homemade ones that my mom used to make. They sure were delicious, full of spinach and ricotta with butter, oil, sage and a sprinkle of parmigiano cheese. Italians sure can cook and they know how to eat!

Larry, ("Colombo") Folloni standing in front of the Rome Coliseum (April, 1979)

Bobby gave us an exciting 'Real Tour' of Italy. Following our extensive adverturing all around Rome we went down to Naples. While there we had the misfortune to run into some of the thievery for which Napoli is noted. The first episode occurred as we were getting on to a real crowded streetcar. As I was the last one to squeeze into the car, I felt someone tugging at my wallet in my rear pant pocket. I immediately reached back to grab hold of my wallet and it became a tug of war between the thief and me. I won out with one last pull as the door on the streetcar slammed shut on the creep's face.

The second episode came about shortly thereafter as we awaited the train for our next destination. I had placed my camera bag down on the floor and while we were gabbing one thief tried to distract us while an accomplice made an attempt to steal it. Luckily, Bobby, who was street wise to their tricks, spotted the thieves and scared them away.

We were not as fortunate in the next encounter with the local riff raff. As we got in line to board the train for Sorrento, a thief brushed by us pretending he was in a hurry to catch the train. While passing he managed to pilfer Jean's wallet out of her bag.

From there we went on to Sorrento where we spent a couple of days admiring the beautiful scenery with the wonderful pervasive scent of Orange and Lemon trees. We left Sorrento by boat to ride over to the Isle of Capri. Up to then this magical Isle existed for us only in an old song. Seeing the real Isle of Capri put us all in seventh heaven. Disembarking, we boarded the funicular (tram), which took us up to a mountain perched village named Anacapri. Helen and Jean really went on a shopping spree, while Bobby and I just spent the day soaking up the rich atmosphere.

On the boat back to Sorrento we encountered a group of Italians who were having a gala reunion of their war days. Among the group was a Captain, with a beautiful singing voice, who singled out Helen, to serenade her with the beautiful Italian Ballad "Parla mi d'amore Mariu". This event was a lovely lasting memory for Helen and she always treasured the glory of that island to mainland passage.

After leaving Sorrento we went up North of Rome to the West Coast stopping off at the seaport town of La Spezia. I remember my father often speaking about his many visits to this town. From there we went to Porto Venere. Bobby insisted that we take the boat ride into the bay and go through its many caves. It proved to be a memorable ride as we glided through the beautiful greenish blue water. It was a bit scary as we entered the caves at low tide. If we were to have lingered we would have become trapped and engulfed by the high tide.

Venturing further North we headed for the home of my relatives in the mountains of Comano. First we visited the home of my mother's sister, Fiora Linda. She lived in the rear of the church where our Cousin, Father Don Guiseppe was the parish priest. From this home we had a beautiful view of the flower filled hills in springtime and we could see the white caps of snow on some of the higher peaks.

Father Don Guiseppe took us on a tour of the area and the villages of Irola and Gigliana where my parents were born and lived before coming to America. We drove down the mountainside in his little car and as he rounded each treacherous curve he would blast away on his horn as the only warning to any oncoming traffic. Deaf drivers don't last long there. On the way down, he pointed out the mountain path that my Dad used to navigate to get to Mom's village during their courtship. It was a rugged two-mile hike, but his efforts were rewarded with the prize he got.

On our first stop as we walked up the street (actually a cow path) in the village where my Dad lived, we went by a shack where two elderly ladies were seated in front of their shacks. As we approached them, one of the ladies looked at me and said, "Tu sei il figlio di Giovanni Folloni!" Interpreted to say, "You are the son of Giovanni Folloni." Now here I was at the age of 60 and this lady had not seen my Dad in about 30 years and she was able to pick me out as the clone of him. I was truly amazed at her memory and of my apparent resemblance to my Dad.

We then drove by my Dad's birthplace and home. Don Guiseppe pointed out the remains of the house about 200 yards down an embankment. It was built of stone masonry with a tin roof. Since no one had occupied it for many years, all that remained was a pile of rocks with the tin roof collapsed on top.

We then drove over to my Mom's former abode. It was a home sitting across the street from the village church. The living conditions were crude to say the least. The cows, chickens, pigs and goats that they housed were located directly under the main floor and the stench of animals was quite evident.

Before we left, Helen and I got to renew our wedding vows with Father Don Guiseppe in the same church that my Mom and Dad were married in! What a wonderful treasured memory that is!

We then returned to Comano where a couple of humorous incidents happened. The bathroom at Aunt Fiora Linda's home still had the old fashioned flushing system with a tank of water located 6' high on the back wall, connected by a long pipe to the toilet. For some reason the toilet itself was set up on a platform about 6 inches above the regular floor level. I was looking out the window at the beautiful mountainside when I first approached this elevated throne. I didn't notice the platform until I tripped on it. As I fell forward the only thing that I could grasp onto to keep from taking a dive into the bowl was the pipe from the water tank. The force of my momentum pulled the toilet out from it's stoop and broke it into several pieces.

I was petrified at the sudden turn of events and went back into the living room to give them the bad news of my accident. The response and the actions of Aunt Fiore Linda that followed were hilarious to say the least. She calmly went into the bathroom and picked up the pieces of the broken toilet and fired them out the window. We all roared with laughter (until we realized that we still had duties to attend to). Before we left, I gave Don Guiseppe $100 to have the damage repaired.

We stayed up the street at an Inn owned by a friend of our cousin Maria. On the way up to our accommodations Helen asked me how long we were going to stay in Comano as she really wanted to get going to see more of Italy. I fired back saying to her, "Look these are my relatives and I will stay awhile and enjoy them." Well I was soon to change my tune. Our room was a little on the shaggy side and there was no heat. About 3 in the morning, I woke up freezing, I said to Helen, "Let's pack up and go. When is the next bus out of here?"

Proceeding further North, we stopped off at a small village for a few hours to visit a cousin of my Dad. He came from a very well to do family, that owned a couple Jewelry stores, one of which gave my Dad the knowledge of jewelry that later served him so well with the Prohibition Enforcement Agent as related earlier.

We then boarded a train over to Florence, a beautiful City with a beautiful domed cathedral and many other interesting sights. We stayed overnight and the next day Helen and Jean again went on a shopping spree.

From Florence we continued on up to the canalled city of Venice. This was one of the highlights of our country tour. We stayed there for a few days, taking in all the beautiful sights the only way possible, via gondola boats. We went to several glass blowing factories and purchased many souvenirs.

At last we came to the end of a fabulous vacation, thanks to Bobby. We took a sleeper train for the last long leg of our journey back to Rome to pack up and head back to the USA. Jean decided to stay on with Bobby for a few extra days and this led to a harrowing series of events.

We were scheduled to pick up Jean at Logan Airport in Boston on Friday at 4pm. She never showed. We tried all weekend to confirm if she had gotten on the plane and what happened, all to no avail due to the lousy and inconsiderate service of the now (deservedly) defunct TWA. In Rome Bobby finally confirmed that Jean had boarded, but still no one could explain where she was or why.

You can never imagine our anxiety and concern for our precious daughter's safety, as we waited three days to know if she was dead or alive. We continually pleaded and begged with them for help, all to no avail. The State Police and Red Cross also couldn't help.

On Monday morning we finally got a call from Bobby in Rome to notify us that Jean had been bumped off in France and was to come home on a later flight. The TWA officials in France were supposed to have notified us back in the States of this change in flight plans for Jean. Somehow, someone goofed, and no one did the right thing. This was an exhausting letdown to an exuberant voyage.

"Airplane travel is nature's way of making you look like your passport photo."
Al Gore

FLORIDA TRIPS AND STOPOVERS

After my retirement in 1983, Helen and I would take annual winter vacation trips down to our Condominium near Fort Lauderdale, Florida. We'd normally leave about the 1st of November and stay until April. It was an opportunity to get away from the harsh New England Winters and to enjoy the warm climate in Florida.

The first few years we were accompanied by Jean, who shared the driving ordeal with us. Along the way we'd make several stops to break up the trip. We'd stop for a short visit with my brother Al and his family in New York and the next stop would be in Washington D.C. to stay with Debbie for a few days.

Leaving D.C. the ride through Virginia was typically very uneventful. When we reached North Carolina the speed of traffic really picked up in accordance with higher posted speed limits and custom. I firmly believe that the 55-MPH limit, which was instituted to save energy and ostensibly to save lives, was actually responsible for many accidents. This is because too many motorists would be held up by a few who adhered to the slower limit. The other drivers in the slowpoke's lanes would get impatient and cut in and out of traffic more frequently than if everyone was moving along at 65-MPH. I think that they call this phenomenon of an act that causes the opposite result from that intended, *"The law of unintended consequences"*. I call it *"The expected consequences of employing 'Lilliputian' bureaucrats who let too much book learning get in the way of common sense"*. A few years later when some of the states increased the speed limits the accident rates magically decreased considerably.

An 8-hour drive from Debbie's is Manning, South Carolina, home of the Central Coffee Shop and restaurant where we met some very friendly regular patrons, including a Doctor and his family who we would visit with there year after year. I sent the café owners a copy of my retirement booklet and they promptly posted it along with their collection of famous athlete customers.

Passing though Georgia we were exposed to the stench of putrid rotten gas from the decaying trees in the swamps. Helen could never get over the odor and she would open the windows of the car, and blamed me for passing the gas. Of course by opening the windows, the smell would become more unbearable. Nonetheless, I could never convince Helen that I was pacifistic in passing through the Peach state.

Blasting through "smeller-rooskie Georgia", we'd finally arrive in Sunny Florida. We always looked forward to stopping at the State Welcome Center to enjoy their refreshing cool Florida *real* orange juice. After 3 full days of travel, we'd settle down for our stay for the winter at our Condo in Tamarac.

Travelling back through South Carolina one year we came to a town that displayed a large sign advertising the Milliken Cotton Fabric Plant. Curious, we pulled up in the town to see if this was the same Pete Milliken who ran the plant back in Dighton when I started up teaching. Sure enough it was. The family moved their manufacturing South to take advantage of cheaper labor. We spent a few hours there with Pete reminiscing of the days back in Dighton when he had hired me to run the Summer Recreation Program for the town.

Milliken's has more than 1,600 patents, more than 38,000 different products and the the largest textile research center in the world. Milliken makes a variety of fabric, yarn and chemical products including those that make comfortable uniforms for major league baseball players, and that give tennis balls their soft texture. To show what a small world it is, son Michael lived on the 1st floor of the Matthews House Freshman Dormitory at Harvard with Roger Milliken, namesake of the current C.E.O., and a man who is very involved with responsible management of vast tracts of the family's timberland in Maine.

A striking memory crossing through Georgia was witnessing the renowned shackled Prisoner Chain Gangs in action marching and picking up debris along the road.

Helen Preti-Wallace, Helen & Mike Folloni, Angie & Elmer Balboni, 1996

Highlights of our stays in Florida included time spent with Mike & Helen and Aunt Angie and Uncle Elmer in Val Rico. We'd then head down highway 75 through Tampa / St. Pete and on to Fort Meyers where we'd visit with my good friend from Brockton, Matey Piesco, and ride over to Sanibel Island and walk the shores, picking up many souvenir sea shells. After that it was down to Bonita Springs to see Angie's friend, Lorraine Paquette, who treated us to some delicious shrimp, fresh out of the Gulf.

Then we'd complete the loop through 'alligator alley' and back to the Miami / Ft. Lauderdale / Tamarac area, where we'd have a great time going to the beaches.

One year we secured a three-day all expense paid trip to a new resort development area up in the mountains, about 100 miles west of Augusta. We spent three wonderful days at this resort. The meals were fabulous and the entertainment was great. As part of the deal we were required to visit the new development. The tour consisted of a trip around a beautiful new Championship Golf Course.

Baby Victoria Helen Mary Dent with her mother, her Aunt Jean and her two grandmothers, Lynn and Helen

We were shown one of the newly built 3 bedroom homes just off of the 6th Tee. It was a beautiful home and the price was $125,000, which included a lifetime membership to the Golf Course. Little did we realize what a bargain that would become a few years down the road. As with Torrey Pines in La Jolla, CA, we again passed up a very lucrative deal on a golf course. I guess you've got to always be prepared for when you might bump into a good investment.

> *"Good fortune is what happens when opportunity meets with planning."*
> -Thomas Edison
> or
> *"He who hesitates is a damned fool."*
> -Mae West

I learned on these trips that bad fortune also happens. I can't tell you how many injury and death-laden car and truck accidents we saw, and how many near misses that we had. And in some cases there was not a thing that the driver could have done to prevent the tragedy. I still maintain, however, that if you do the right things, like stay rested and sober, and don't tailgate or allow tailgaters, that the odds are more in your favor that bad things won't happen. A good coach can't control a game of sports or the final results in the game of life, but he can increase the likelihood of good things happening, and decrease the chances of disaster. With good preparation, confidence and the will to achieve, making the right moves becomes almost automatic.

Chicago

After about 10 years working as an attorney in D.C., Debbie, by then a partner in her law firm, transferred to her firm's Chicago office. Here she was courted by and later married another partner in the firm, Tom Dent. They now have two beautiful children, Victoria and Scott. Debbie's first residence in Chicago was at Lake Point Towers, which is an architectural marvel located right across the street from Lake Michigan and the historic Navy Pier. Movies, including "While You Were Sleeping" have been filmed in Lake Point Towers, and many famous people have owned condos in the building, including Goldie Hawn, Scottie Pippen and Oprah Winfrey. Debbie's unit was on the 36th floor with a grand view of the Lake, downtown Chicago and the entertainment complex below.

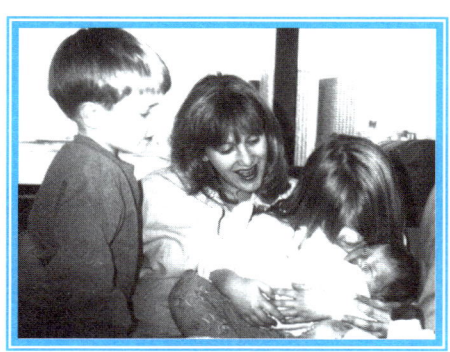

Michael & Jennifer Dent & Debbie look over newborn sister Victoria and the Chicago city skyline

We visited Chicago, the 'Windy City', one horribly hot and humid week in the summer. During that trip, we had a few travel mishaps that weren't terribly pleasant, but at least the company of Tom, Debbie and newborn Victoria was. The next trip to visit them was a few years later after they purchased a lovely home in Lake Forest, an affluent suburb about 20 miles Northwest of Chicago. (When Michael Jordan was leading the Chicago Bulls to several Championship years he had his residence in Lake Forest. The actor "Mr. T" also resided there.)

Laden with two toddlers, no babysitter, and still doing legal work out of her home, Debbie had her hands full. She sent out an "SOS" to her Mom and Dad, pleading for them to come to Chicago to help her unpack and take care of her children. Once again it was time to help Debbie get her new home in order. There were many chores that had to be done. Little odds and ends, unpacking of boxes, installing a hook here and a rack there, a gate at the foot of the stairs to keep the children from falling down the stairs, etc. I also did some wiring for the TV and audio systems and added some phone lines. In between chores we took some trips around the town and I played some golf with Tom. Helen, meanwhile, had the time of her life doting on her little namesake, Victoria Helen Mary.

Well that about sums up most of the vacation trips that we were lucky enough to enjoy. Some parts of my narrative here may seem a bit mundane, but worldly is what we must be on this earth. Life as "just a bowl of cherries" is for Hollywood movies. The sometimes tough and tedious moments of the journey in between destinations are part and parcel of the stuff that brings together the highlights of life's flights. The biggest highlights for me were the rare quiet times driving along contemplating God's influence in my life, and any and all moments along the way with my family and friends. As the writer Robert Lewis Stevenson, who's Gulliver's Travels told of Gargantuans, Lilliputians and all other manner of fantastic sights said:

"We are all travelers in the wilderness of this world, and the best we can find in our travels is an honest friend."

And as Dorothy said: "There's no place like home!"

OUR AUTOMOBILES

"The automobile has changed the mode of living and the habits of more people than Caesar or Mussolini or Chaplin or Daniel Webster or Amos 'n' Andy or Bernard Shaw. Why they have run over more people in one month than either Washington or Lincoln disposed of in their wars"
-Will Rogers June 1, 1930

The first prototype of the Model T Ford was made in 1908, a mere decade before my birth. By 1927 the 15th million Model T came off the production line. The automobile came of age when I did. We take cars for granted now, but our modern life wouldn't be too feasible if we didn't have the use of these relatively recently developed wonders to get us around. So I think it is appropriate to get a tiny glimpse of the history of this machine as seen through my rear view mirror recollections of the vehicles that we had access to over the years.

The family's first car was the Ford that my Dad purchased from Lucini Motor Sales in the early 1930's. It cost a grand total of $200.00. Ford's utilization of 'mass production' techniques made the advance of the auto accessible to the common man. Of course the first generation immigrant families in Stanley were not yet integrated into the common mainstream. Tom Magistrate, who married one of the Moruzzi girls and my Dad were the only ones in Stanley who owned an automobile at that time.

The family used this Ford to deliver groceries to our Mom & Pop Store customers. Business was revolutionized as we could obtain and distribute more goods to more people in shorter time. This was a benefit to our customers and us alike. There were some bumps on this technological road though. One day while Dad was driving his sister Louise and her daughter Gelmeida to the bank in East Bridgewater, his car was run off the road by another one. My Dad and Gelmeida escaped with minor injuries, but my Aunt Louise was not so fortunate, as she suffered severe injuries that left her incapacitated for many years to follow.

In the middle 30's we bought another Ford from Lucini's to replace our wrecked vehicle. This car lasted for quite some time. By the early 40's our enterprising family was able to afford another car for the family to share.

A traffic jam at the John Folloni market in 1946

"My customers can have any color car they want, as long as it's black."
- Henry Ford, on his low cost, mass produced Model T

I used the family car when they could spare it until 1947 when I got my first teaching job in Dighton and Helen and I purchased our first car, a little two-door coupe. From then on it was a case of purchasing second hand cars because we couldn't afford the cost of a new vehicle. In the early '50's we bought a 'used' Dodge from a private party. *That was before they invented*

"previously owned" vehicles.

Our first Dodge carried us through a couple of years, then we picked up another second hand car from my good friend Wally Krueger. This was the start of several deals that Wally Krueger was kind enough to work out with me. He always gave me cars at the lowest possible price.

I can remember one very comical trade-in deal that we made in the 50's: I called Wally and told him to wait for me, as I'd be right down to trade in my old car for another. Among our clunker's many other defects, the transmission wouldn't go forward, so I had to put it in reverse and back it about 3/4 mile down Route 28 to Krueger's Garage. When we got there, Wally greeted us by saying, *"You're going the wrong direction, Perry's Junk Yard is back that way!"*

Wally had a good sense of humor and was a real nice fellow who did a lot of charitable work for the youngsters in our town. Also, **Krueger Motors** always sponsored a biddy league basketball team. He took a liking to Helen and the kids and went out of his way to accommodate us when we were in need. I can still remember us bargaining with him for our first *brand new* car in the early 60's. It was *a Green Dodge with white wall tires*. It was a really classy looking car and lasted us several years.

Although I am a very 'hands-on' do-it-yourselfer, I never did find too much time to repair cars. Maybe that's also part of why I ended up buying so many used ones. Of course Wally Krueger saw how much I was helping the kid's in town, and being as civic minded and benevolent as he was, he pitched in with super bargain cars to help afford me the mobility to do my jobs as a teacher, coach and a dad.

"Mr. Ford is a good friend of mine, and I was at his home. I happened to ask him in the case of stiff competition, how cheap he could sell his car. He said, "Why Will, by controlling the selling of the parts, I could give the cars away. Why those things shake off enough bolts in a year to pay for themselves, and the second year, that's just pure profit." - Will Rogers, 1930

Mr. Ford was a great one for pre-planning a model's demise in several years. He'd go to the junk yard to see what car parts still worked. *Then he'd cut the quality and the cost of these 'over-engineered' parts so that all components would fail more or less at the same time.* Actually this **'reverse engineering'** was not all bad, as it was one of his many strokes of genius to make and keep new cars affordable to the common man. Sadly it also made car ownership for the non-well off who couldn't always afford new ones a game of 'musical chairs', with some nasty sounding parting notes often struck by the failing pieces.

Late in the '60's we picked up a used compact Mazda as a second family vehicle. Regretfully this car didn't last very long as Bobby loaned it to one of his friends who totaled it.

We also had a white 8 cylinder 4-door Dodge that like most of that make at that time was difficult to start, but once it got going you had to mind the accelerator or you could be approaching triple digits on the speedometer before you knew what you hit.

In the early 70's my brother Al from New York donated his old Chrysler to us. This car had a renowned history, as Al had driven many VIP's in it as part of his USO and community service work, among them, fabled entertainer Bob Hope, NYC Mayor John Lindsay and of course Rocky Marciano.

The ancient 'BobHopemobile' & other cars, c1988.

In the late 70's Larry Jr. purchased a Ford Mustang for Michael to help in his paralegal outreach work for migrant farm workers in Pennsylvania. Not being able to afford the many parking tickets it attracted when he returned to Graduate School in Cambridge, he brought the Mustang home to store. Months later he asked me to sell it, which I did for about $400. Returning one weekend Michael asked for the proceeds, which I told him were already spent for family needs. When he protested I simply agreed with his perspective and presented him with a bill for the family's share of his next semester's tuition. *Funny how he suddenly began to see things My Way!*

It was a big jump for us to switch from gas guzzling American made to Japanese cars. We were as patriotic as the next family, but we had just gotten to know all too well the sickening sound of any Dodge's ignition churning on freezing mornings without the engine turning over. Between the customary maintenance burdens and the skyrocketing fuel costs that accompanied the early 70's OPEC oil embargo, we simply had to find alternatives. The Japanese cars were just far less expensive and at least for a time appeared to be more reliable and economical. And besides, my good friend and Dodge Dealer Wally Krueger was by then retired.

Upon my retirement in the early '80's we purchased a new Mazda, which lasted about a decade. We had very good luck with this car until its final demise. It was due for an oil change and I went down to the garage to have it serviced. The line was too long and I told the mechanic I would stop back later as I had to pick up my daughter Debbie at the Airport. Well this proved to be a costly mistake. Just after leaving the airport, the engine froze up and that was the end of the Mazda. At the time we had a second car as we had purchased a grey Honda a few years earlier.

In the early 90's we purchased another Honda, a nice white one, which we loved very much. It was Helen's favorite. We had this car for only a short time when another accident happened. As related earlier, my brother Al had been hospitalized in New York and my brother Mike, my sister Angie and her daughter Linda and I went out to visit him. On the return trip we had a tire blow out. It was only the skill of Mike holding control of the car and the fact that the wire railing was there to keep up from plunging into a deep gully that saved our lives. Fortunately no one was injured but the car was totaled.

With this scare my daughter Jean convinced us to purchase a Volvo for safety reasons. We had already become convinced of the superiority and value of foreign cars, but we then wanted to go to something sturdier than the Japanese offerings. We still have this white Volvo and it has given us excellent service. We also picked up a used 1989 Grey Volvo for a second car. It was in pretty good shape and only had about 60,000 miles. With it Jean was able to maneuver better as a caregiver to us and as a chauffeur to her kids.

Our latest acquisition came about due to necessity in dealing with Helen's disability. With domestic manufacturers having largely caught back up to the competition by the '90's, and with the need for local customization in this case, we happily came back to US made. (Although with the internationalization of so many things, even this car has probably been built with half the components from overseas.) This new 2000 Town and Country Chrysler, which has been converted into a Handicapped Van, has been most worthwhile to transport Helen on an almost daily basis.

Nono, Louie Filippetti & Nona by the new '42

THE FOLLONI GOLFING TEAM
Chips off the Old Block

"Golf is the only game where practicing it and playing it is the same thing."
Will Rogers, January 24, 1926

After taking up membership at the Brockton Country Club, I enjoyed the game so much that I felt it was time to get my family involved. I invested in a family membership and soon my three sons, Larry, Bobby, and Michael were spending much of their summers on the golf course. In spite of the regrettable fact that they never had any professional lessons, they enjoyed themselves and turned out to be pretty good golfers.

Of course one might not have predicted this simply from seeing young Michael's 1st record breaking performance, which occurred on the very short par 4 fifth hole at BCC. In a mighty attempt to reach the green with one swing from the spot where his drive landed, he ended up hitting 18 in a row out of bounds! *And I thought that my 17 in a row record in baseball was unbeatable!* I think that the persistent personal style that he patented here served him much better later in life.

Michael developed and demonstrated other sterling traits while hanging around this *'gentleman's game'*: While playing in the final round of the annual John Loftus youth tournament at the Thorney Lea Course in Brockton, this 8-year old encountered a 30 yard long pond in front of the last tee. Playing with cut-off taped-up clubs and a scrawny 45lb body that could only loft a drive 25 yards, he took the creative yet practical approach of simply putting his ball off the tee and then up the narrow dirt pathway ten feet at a time till he reached the fairway. Arriving at the clubhouse Tourney Director Miles O'Connell asked Michael how he scored, to which Michael replied '36'. Miles said, "Now come on Michael, you're too young to shoot par for 9 holes." Michael responded: "Oh I thought you were talking about the last hole." Sure enough every stroke was dutifully counted and registered in its proper place on his scorecard.

The next day we were all delighted to read that Miles had placed a special recognition of Michael's honesty (and math skills) in the Brockton Enterprise newspaper, thus reinforcing another important lesson for life.

Michael showing Jimmy how it's done.
Poor Jimmy.

Larry, Bobby, Michael and Jimmy all played well for the High School golf team, and once every few years through adulthood they would still venture out on the links to surprise their friends and themselves.

James ended up pretty good once he got into the swing of things.

Mike blasts out of a big sand trap in Maui. I think he sometimes likes going out of bounds

Bob is more on target with his clubs in Maui.

Larry Jr. became one of the best young golfing prospects in New England. He won the Brockton Jr. City Open in his class for at least 4 straight years. Larry reached the Semi-Finals in State Jr. Championship, where he lost by a shot to the winner. Larry was also a medalist in Hearst New England Championship.

Larry Jr. won dozens of trophies & media accolades. Flanked in photo by brother Bob & Richard Balboni

Larry's best golfing achievement probably came at playing in a South Shore Jr. League match where he shot a BCC record 6-under par

66. This was only beaten by PGA Pro Tony Lema's 64, scored at Wallaston Country Club for that year's lowest competitive round of golf in New England. On that occasion Tony Lema defeated Arnold Palmer in the charity golf match. Lema, who won the British Open in 1964, was a favorite with the press. Every time that he won a Tournament he would tell the bartenders to 'set them up' for the media, the drinks were on him. With all the matches he won, no wonder he once quipped: *"Let's see, I think right now I'm third in money-winning and first in money-spending."* Lema died in a tragic plane crash on his way to play in a Tournament in 1966. He was one of the most charitable contributors to the sick and needy of all professional sportsmen of his era.

One other highlight of Larry's and my golfing careers was a play-off match we had for the BCC Championship. The 54 hole Tourney had ended up in a three-way tie between my son Larry Jr., my golfing buddy Al Saccocia, and myself. It took quite a dramatic ending to reach this impasse. For starters, Al Saccocia made a Hole-In-One on the very difficult last hole, which has a blind view of the green over a steep hill from the tee. After Al made this miraculous comeback shot, the pressure was on me to make a par to tie. Fortunately, I put my tee shot on this hard to hit green and two putted to catch Al. The high drama, however, was just beginning!

Meanwhile, in the group behind us, Larry Jr. had broken his putter on the 16th, and had to play the remaining two holes using his driver as a putter! On the 17th hole he had about a 4-footer for an eagle but stuck with having to use a driver, he missed the putt that would have given him the Championship. After 'blaster-tapping' in his birdie on the 17th, he made a par on the 18, driver for putter and all, to create the three-way tie, and set the stage for a play-off the next weekend.

Larry Jr. and I wanted to have a 36-hole play-off, but Al Saccocia wanted only an 18-hole match. After much deliberation with the Tournament Committee we finally reached the following agreement: If Larry Jr. or I were ahead after the first 18 holes, we would make it a 36-hole match, and if Al was ahead after 18 holes he would be the Champ. After the first 18-hole match, I ended up with an even par 72. Larry Jr. had a 74 and Al Saccocia ended up with a 77, which, per agreement, eliminated him from the competition. Larry Jr. and I went out the next weekend for the Championship. I had my usual mid 70's round, it really was no match, however as Larry burned up the course with a sub-par round to soundly defeat his Dad.

Following a brilliant teen-age golfing career, Larry's golfing buddy, Ross Pearson's Grandfather, the owner of the Knight Golf Shoe Company and Paul Fireman Sr., President of Kroyden Golf, two of the area's wealthy golf enthusiasts, were going to sponsor Larry on the Pro tour. Unfortunately, Paul Fireman, Sr., died of a massive heart attack before he could carry out his promise. His son, Paul Fireman, Jr., is now the president of the Reebok Shoe Company. Paul was also one of Larry Jr's golfing contemporaries. Paul recently built his own golf course down on Cape Cod and every year he has some of the world's best Pros take part in a charity tournament there.

After leading his High School class in athletics and academics, Larry went off to get his degree in Chemical Engineering. While at college, he played on the golf team. Following his graduation, he accepted a position as a Chemical Engineer at a major pharmaceutical firm, where in his first year he made more pay than his Dad ever had to date as a teacher and coach!

Larry went to a leading technology college at the time of the post sputnik scientific boom which motivated the best and the brightest to compete at top schools. Being as competitive and conscientious as he is, and wanting to succeed to help his family and others, Larry sacrificed tremendously to stay at the top in school and at work. Concentrating thus on his Engineering profession, his golf game went into the background and a very promising golf career was ended. Perhaps even more than his Dad, Larry was a perfectionist and since he could not devote the time needed to be a great golfer, he eventually gave up the game to devote his full time to his profession. If only I had had the foresight to continue to invest my limited time and money for lessons in Larry like Earl Woods did with his son Tiger; the world would likely have seen a 'Lion' Larry Folloni Jr. prowling the PGA.

Shortly after the computer revolution took hold, Larry left the pharmaceutical company to join the world's premier computer manufacturing company. There he designed and oversaw the construction of a 6 million-dollar QA & QC chemical lab. Larry's work in solving computer chip quality and production problems saved his company countless millions of dollars over the years. He was eventually elevated to their highest-ranking engineering position. Larry retired from engineering at the young age of 54, and has spent his time dabbling in the stock market, where he has done better than most even through the crash of 2002. His choosing to once again sacrifice his other dreams to stay close to and assist Helen and me through our senior days has been a selfless and invaluable contribution. Sometimes as Larry and I sit together in the cottage or at Helen's nursing home watching the Pro Golfers lay them up stiff to the pin, we still wonder, *what if? Yes, regrets I've had a few.*

As for my pre-retirement tournament golfing successes, I have also had at least a few. I cherished winning many tournaments at the Brockton and Manchester Country Clubs, as I do the memory of losing the epic Championship duel with my teenage son Larry Jr. Particularly memorable was the year when I won both the Medal and the Match-Play Club Championships, I was also very fortunate to have won the Bridgewater Open Championship twice.

After more than 20 memorable years at the Brockton Country Club I shifted my golfing scene to New Hampshire. In 1971 my wife Helen convinced me to purchase a home up on Ross Ave. in Hampton Beach. This turned out to be one of the best ventures in our family life. We could then spend our summer vacations at a beautiful beach resort.

I joined the 9-Hole Course Exeter Country Club, the oldest golf club in New England. I played at Exeter for a couple of years while I waited for my number to come up for membership at the Championship Portsmouth Country Club course. When I applied for membership there was a waiting list of 1100. They held a lottery for positions to be accepted upon openings. I was 111 on the list and it took three years before I was accepted for membership in 1978.

The PCC is a beautiful golf course, winding along a scenic bay. It has a nice layout, but with me being a short ball hitter, the 7050-yard course was a big challenge. This naturally caused my 7 or 8 handicap to shoot up to about 12 -13.

In spite of this distance factor disadvantage, I managed to take advantage of my great short game to successfully compete against much better golfers than me. Year after year I would win or end up in the finals of the Club Championship in my class.

I used every opportunity and conjured up many a fun method to help me to perfect my short game

Once again I became the golfer with the reputation that "He only scores when he needs to." True, I will confess that I probably didn't buckle down and completely concentrate on my game when I was out playing a casual round of golf. Maybe I would have been better served if I had taken Ted William's perfect practice preaching a little more to heart. Then again, I wasn't on the pro tour, and having to maintain my extreme competition intensity levels day in and day out would have worn at my enjoyment of the game. One thing I will say, however is that I never cheated anyone on the golf course. I played by the rules, counted every stroke and never, ever took 'gimme' putts.

There are many golfers who have a false pride about their handicaps, and this gets them into trouble. They take lots of 'gimme' putts, many of which they would probably have missed if they putted them out. As a result they end up playing with an inaccurately *deflated* handicap. Often when they get into a golf match in which they are under-handicapped, problems arise, the pressure soon gets to them and they choke. *Most matches that I won came with my opponents scoring significantly higher than their handicap!* If they played to their true handicaps they would often have beaten me. Contrary to that scenario, when I play in tournaments I never let a bad shot get me down. I always managed to find a way to recover with my straight woods and short game and my playoff intensity, and as a result I usually ended up on the winning side.

One of my most fondly remembered winning streaks at PCC came during the 1988 Club Championship. I had a miserable qualifying round, shooting in the 80's. As bad as it was, I still managed to end up in the last qualifying position. I was paired in the first round with the medallist, who had shot a par 72 in the qualifying round, almost a stroke a hole better than me.

We went out the next week on Labor Day weekend to play our matches. I had an excellent round and defeated the medallist by closing him out on the 14th hole! The next day, in the semifinal round, I defeated a good friend of mine, Angelo Boy. Again the match was ended on the 14th hole.

The next day I was scheduled to meet Jimmy Donahue in the Finals of the Division One Club Championship. We had a Northeaster storm, which canceled all events, and the match was rescheduled for the following weekend. Jimmy was an excellent golfer, and a fellow Athletic Director at a nearby town. During the summer months he was the dauntlessly diplomatic Supervisor of the large group of Hampton Beach lifeguards.

Typical for PCC on the Bay, it was still quite windy on the day of the match. On the very first hole, a par 4, Jim put his second shot about 6 feet from the cup. My second shot was about 20 feet in the back of the green. I hit my putt, which looked like it was going to miss the cup on the right. Suddenly a gust of wind came up and blew the putt in the side door for a birdie! Jimmy was so shook up that he missed his birdie putt. Sometimes I'd rather be lucky than good! Then again, one has to practice enough to be prepared to get close enough to where luck can kick in!

On the next hole, a difficult par 4, Jimmy hit his tee shot into the woods and ended up with a 7. I didn't play the hole much better than Jimmy did, but I did manage to end up with a 6 to go two up. From there on in, my short game took over. On the next hole, I chipped one about six inches from the cup for a tap-in to go three up.

The beautiful and windy 4th hole at PCC

I won the par 5 fourth hole with a birdie to go 4 up. We played pretty even for the next 8 holes. Then on the 12th hole, probably the most difficult par 4 in the State, I knocked in 10 footer for par and went 5 up.

Once again on my favorite hole, the par 5 fourteenth, I closed out Jimmy with a birdie. I had consecutively completed three of my finest rounds of golf ever at PCC, to once again win the Division One Club Championship. I'm sure that that string of performances left plenty of people muttering. I doubt, however, that anyone remembered that I played as hard as I could to barely qualify to play at all. I'd mutter about me too if I didn't know better. *Did I mention my guardian angels?*

Ten years later in 1998, at the tender age of 77, in what was to be my final year of golf, I again won the Division One Championship. Once again playing as the underdog, I defeated Charlie Johnson in the first round. He had me 4 down after the first nine holes. I fought back, winning 5 of the next 8 holes to win on the 17th.

In the semifinal round I was matched to play Bill Berriman, the fellow who had knocked off the qualifying medallist. He was a long ball hitter and a pretty good golfer. I was two down going into the 12th hole where I dumped my tee shot in the rough in front of the tee. My opponent hit his drive about 250 yards down the middle.

Things looked pretty bleak for me. As I was leaving the tee to go to hit my second shot, I saw my friend George McConnaughey. George is the only African American member of our club and for some reason whenever I played with him I would play like a scratch golfer. George came up to me and asked me how I was doing. I replied, "Not so good George, I need help." He shook my hand, patted me on the back and said, "Larry, I know you can do it. You're going to beat him."

With that encouragement I went on to hit my ball out of the rough. Bill, now trying for the kill and trying to reach the difficult 12th green in two, over swung and hit his shot into the ocean on the left.

This left me an opening, which I took advantage of by making a chip up close to the cup for an easy tap-in to win the hole. I won the next hole, the par 3 thirteenth, with a birdie to even the match. I won my favorite 14th hole with another birdie to go one up.

We halved the next two holes but I lost the 17th and the match is all even going into the 18th. The last hole is a long difficult par 4. We both were on the green in three. I was about 6 feet from the cup and Bill was about 20 feet away. He proceeded to knock his long putt in! Now I had the pressure on me to knock in my putt for a half. I took a couple of deep breaths and then plunked the six-footer right in the middle to send the match into extra holes.

On the first extra hole Bill was on the Par 4 in two, with a chance to win the match with two putts. I missed my 7 footer leaving me with a bogie. After Bill's first putt, he left himself with about a 3 footer to win. He missed it and we went on to play the second extra hole, which is one of the toughest on the course.

Bill was so shook up at missing his golden opportunity to win, that he knocked his next drive into the woods, ending up with an almost unplayable lie. I hit my tee shot about 200 yards down the middle. I then played a safe shot down the middle, leaving me about 50 yards from the green.

Bill then hit his second shot from the cluster of bushes. He made a miraculous shot to get the ball out onto the fairway. He reached the green in three and two putted for a bogie. My excellent short game came into play, however, as I hit a wedge shot up onto the green and made the 4-foot putt for a par and the victory.

As we walked back to the clubhouse, the Pro, Joel St. Laurent, who had been following our match, came over to congratulate me on the win and paid me a nice compliment. He said, "Larry, I don't know how you do it, but no matter what the odds are against you, you still manage to always find a way and do whatever it takes to win".

The finals the next day felt anti-climatic as I defeated my opponent with a 2 and 1 victory. Later in the month, in the swan song of my golfing career, I had my final glory day when I won the State of New Hampshire Seniors Championship for the 75 and older division at the New Hampshire Country Club for the second year in a row.

NEW HAMPSHIRE PROFILE SENIORS GOLF ASSOCIATION
Straight Shooters

With my retirement in 1983 I became involved with the Profile Seniors Golf Association. The PSGA is a statewide group dedicated to camaraderie and friendly golf for Seniors. They hold about 10 Tournaments each year at prestigious Golf Courses throughout New Hampshire.

It didn't take long for the good friend of my brother-in-law Elmer Balboni, Gerry Gauthier, to get me to be a member of the PSGA Board of Directors. At first I was reluctant to accept this position. I said to Gerry, "Look I just retired from my Athletic Director's job and I have served my time as a volunteer contributor to many Athletic Associations in Massachusetts. Now I would like to relax and just have some enjoyment on the golf courses." Gerry put his arm around me and said, "Larry you won't have any work to do. You'll be just a figurehead."

True, it was Gerry who carried practically the whole load in running the PSGA for many years. How ironical it turned out though. About 10 years later, when it was my turn to take over as President of the PSGA, Gerry fell dead of a heart attack while getting ready to come to a Board of Directors meeting. Here I was left shocked and in mourning over another good friend who was lost, but realizing that as the new President, I couldn't let Gerry down, and that I had to get on with the complex duties to carry on our organization.

We had our first tourney of the year scheduled for the very next day at the Portsmouth Country Club. Following the tourney, I called an emergency meeting of the Board of Directors right there at PCC. As an interim measure I appointed Ray Roberts as Secretary Treasurer to take over Gerry's duties.

I immediately set up committees and assigned each Director to take over the Chairmanship of one committee. I then sent a letter to all 350 members of our association to inform them of our new organizational setup. In it I beseeched them for their cooperation and prayers that we would successfully carry on the great traditions that were started by Gerry.

The response from our membership was overwhelming. There was immediate cooperation and many offers from the membership to help out if needed. We managed to get through the rest of the year in pretty good fashion. Indeed it went much smoother than I had expected. This was thanks in good part to the dedicated work of Ray Roberts, Roger Godin, and the other Board members, Andy Richer, Chip Moody, Soc Makris, Ed Butler, Andy Forti, Don Lavallee, Vin Roukey, Tom Tenda, Russ Wilkins, Paul Dorais, Foster Boardman, Tony Farmer, Hank Richardson and Frank Pickard.

With the end of the golf season in September it became time to get a new slate of officers. The By-Laws called for a one year of tenure-ship for all officers including the President. The board felt that I had done such an excellent job in bringing the organization together after Gerry's demise that I should remain as President for another year. I agreed to take on these duties for one more year in order to help the organization to gel during that year of transition. I became the first President of the PSGA to serve for two terms.

I had many enjoyable years in my association with the PSGA highlighted by making many lasting friendships and several very successful golfing campaigns. I was selected as the golfer of the year in my age group in three different years.

At the end of each year the State of New Hampshire held its annual Championship for all golfers in the entire state. The Tournament was always held at The Country Club of New Hampshire, a very popular golf course up in the mountains. I guess it was only fitting that I should end my golfing career by twice winning the State of New Hampshire Golf Championship in the age group of 75 years and up. Not bad for a hacker, who didn't start playing the game until he reached the age of 40 and who never had a golf lesson from a Pro.

I take that back. Way back after the end of my baseball career, after I caught the golf bug and had played a couple of years, the Pro at BCC suggested that I take a few lessons. I finally gave in and after a short lecture period on how to properly grip the club and how to lengthen my back swing, he had me swinging a club.

Try as I might, I didn't have much success in hitting my drives in the middle of the fairway. One drive would slice, the next one would hook, and then I'd dribble one down the middle. This went on for about 10 minutes when the Pro said to me, "Did you ever have any trouble hitting the golf ball down the middle?" I sheepishly replied, "No, I never had any trouble with my short swing." With this the Pro said, "I give up, go back to your own way of swinging." From that day on I went on to my own patterned short swing and had pretty good success without any help from any Pro.

FAVORITE QUOTES FROM MY GOLFING ASSOCIATES
Clubhouse Chatter

From Dave Flynn, after we had defeated Eddie Mahoney and Roger Boucher in the overtime in a rematch for the Club four ball Championship which we had 'blown' the year before: *"Larry, you just have to be the best 10 handicapper in the world."*

From, George Mcconnaughey, an amicable PCC member, on my short game: *"From 100 yards in, there is no one in this club who can beat Folloni."*

From, Joe LaCroix, who was one of my playing partners in PSGA Tournaments as he defended me in the chitchats that went on in the clubhouse after Tournaments: *"If Folloni was half a good as his reputation, he'd be playing on the Pro Circuit."*

From one of my golfing partners in many weekend matches, "Hank" Richardson following a string of my shots downs the middle of the fairway. *"After every good shot by a golfer, it's customary to say, "Nice Shot".* Hank said, *"I'm tired of repeating those words after Folloni hits every shot down the middle. From now on I am going to just say, "Press the Button for Mr. Automatic."*

From Angelo Boy after I defeated him in the semifinal round of the Division One, Club Championship: *"The only time Folloni leaves the fairway is to go into the woods to take a pee or to look for someone else's ball."* (Note: I once had a string of 43 consecutive holes in keeping my ball in the fairway. The string was broken on the PCC 8th hole when my drive ended up one foot in the rough off the fairway. I then went on for 13 more holes before going off the fairway. Coincidentally, that totals 56, the number of consecutive games that the incredible Joe DiMaggio hit in. *Of course my ball was standing still and his was coming at him at 90MPH!)*

From, Ray Roberts, one of the better golfers in the PSGA, after I had made a difficult 20 foot side hill putt to put our team in the money in the annual Rochester C.C. Tournament: *"Folloni is the best Money Player in the State of New Hampshire."*

From Fran Mansfield: Folloni doesn't hit a single green in regulation. He has 8-one putt greens and a chip in for a '35'. Stetson hits every green in regulation, and has two putts on every green for a '36'.

From Eddie Matta, member at Manchester C.C. on my short game, following my sensational round at the Rochester C.C. when he was Captain of our team. *"Folloni's short game is the envy of all golfers in the State of New Hampshire."*

Special note: All quotes from those with sour grapes over my golfing triumphs have been deleted, expletives and all!

DELIGHTS
A Few of My Favorite Things

*"We cannot do great things in this world.
We can only do small things with Great Love" - Mother Teresa*

Growing old can be real tough, heck, all of life can be tough. When the going gets tough, the tough get going, but sometimes even for a tough guy to get going, it helps, as Julie Andrews sang, to *"simply remember my favorite things, and then I don't feel so bad."*

So here are a few of my favorites. A more detailed account of these and other favorites can be found in the Appendix.

Bands	Glenn Miller, Harry James, Electric Bubblegums (James & Andy)
Male & Female Vocalists	Frank Sinatra, Bing Crosby Dean Martin, Mario Lanza, Luciano Pavaroti, Helmut Lotti, Judy Garland.
Singing Groups	The 4 Aces, The Beatles, The Fabulous Cassotos (Bob & Steve Crowley)
Recorded Songs	*My Way, With a Song in my Heart, Ave Maria, White Christmas.*
Movie	*Its a Wonderful Life*
Actor	Jimmy Stewart, Gregory Peck, John Wayne
Actress	Bette Davis, Linda Darnell, Audrey Hepburn
TV Show	All in the Family
TV Actor	Archie Bunker (Carroll O'Conner)
TV Actress	Edith Bunker (Maureen Stapelton)
<u>ATHLETES</u>	***My very favorites were those I coached, after them…***
Baseball	Ted Williams, Joe DiMaggio, Babe Ruth, Lou Gehrig
Basketball	Larry Bird, Michael Jordan, Bill Russell
Football	Doug Flutie, Red Grange
Hockey	Bobby Orr, Eddie Shore
<u>TEAMS</u>	***My very favorites were those I coached, after them…***
Baseball	Yankees, Red Sox (as a youngster, the Boston Braves)
Basketball	Boston Celtics
Football	Notre Dame
Pets	Duke, Duchess & Cochise. Honorable Mention: Dolly & Saysha
Hockey	Boston Bruins
Pizza	Cape Cod in Brockton, Venetian in Taunton
Onion Soup	Red Coach Grille in Framingham, Old Salt in Hampton.
Clam Chowder	Farr's & Gally Hatch in Hampton
Corn Chowder	Gally Hatch in Hampton and Jean's home made.

Prime Rib	Old Salt in Hampton
Non-Pizza Restaurants	Old Salt in Hampton (Prime Rib), Christos in Brockton (for all around food and best prices.)
Friends –As a Youth	Dino Bertelli & Bob Pratti, (killed on D-Day in France) Also all of my ball playing pals in the Stanley area.
Friends - Adult	Warren Meacham and all my playing and coaching colleagues.
Fans & Loyal Supporters	"The Folloni Team", David 'Coontail' Freeman, Peter Murby (# 1 fan from his wheelchair) Warren Meacham. Bill Prophett
All Time All Place Food	Pizza, My Mom's Torta & Spaghetti & Meatballs, Veal Parmigiana, Prime Rib, Jean's home cooking
Desserts	Mama Mark's & Jeans Muffins, cakes & cookies
Italian Restaurants	The Venetian, Weymouth, The Italian Kitchen, Campello
Asian Cooking	Ocean Wok, Hampton Beach, Thuy Vo Eclectic, Oakland
Fast Food	Farr's Hampton Beach & Boston Market
Snack Food	Cheeze-Its, Cape Cod Potato Chips
Politician	John F. Kennedy, Dave Flynn
Doctor	Dr. Charles Ferguson, Dr. Hector Douglas, Dr. Herb Cohen
Nurse	Leslie Taylor & "Sue" The Rejuevenator
Beverage	My own 'Dad's Delight' concoction, with cranberry, lemon, raspberry, orange grape, apple, pineapple juices & cherry cider!

My preferred sound: Roberto – One half of "The Fabulous Cassottos"

The "Electric Bubble Gums" (Not to be confused with Glenn Miller or Harry James)

4th Quarter

TWILIGHT YEARS
'Crunch Time'

*"Your goal in life should be to never retire,
but always have the option to."*
T. Hayes

"Nobody loves life like him who is growing old."
Sophocles

Passing the torch that burns so intensely

My (Near) Last Hurrah
Severely Injured and Disabled List

There comes a time in life when *The Guy Up There* calls your number. Some are called early. Some of the lucky ones get to enjoy a few extra years with their families and their friends on the golf course. Even though I had just turned 79, I counted myself firmly in the latter group, especially in that I felt about as healthy as I did at a vigorous age 59.

Helen, Larry Jr. & I were all born in November. Here we celebrate our birthdays in the fall of '98.

I was just stunned, therefore, when my physician Dr. Ades informed me in early November 1998 that I was diagnosed as carrying a malignant cancer in my colon. It was just like being hit with a bruising tackle by Lawrence Taylor *and* Sam Huff, just as I was vulnerable after releasing a pass to a teammate.

I had lived a very active athletic life and never had any real serious physical problems other than a few accidents, the late onset of arthritis and my plaguing coughing following occasional sinusitis and bronchitis attacks. This gave me the complacent feeling that I would go on to live **healthy** for another 15 to 20 years or more. After all, my Dad lived to the ripe old age of 93, and I think I took as good a care of my body as most anyone does.

How old would you be if you didn't know how old you was?
-Satchel Paige

My life as I had expected it to unfold, however, came to a screeching halt that week. Since I soon ended up in a "coma" for about three months and I remember little, if anything that happened during that time, I will try to recall my stupendous fall and miraculous (partial) recovery with the help of reminders from my family.

I am not a doctor and therefore do not know the technical definition of the word "coma", nor do I know if my condition technically fits within that definition. For ease of reference, I refer in this book to the word "coma" as meaning that although I am told I was at the time experiencing pain, agony, etc. and was able to motion at times to my family, I thankfully have little, if any, recollection of what occurred. (I am told that perhaps I suffer from post-trauma memory loss.) Whatever you want to call it, it was a harrowing three months of near death, a time I am happy to not recall. It is bad enough that I remember the excruciating recovery period.

On December 7, 1998 fittingly, "Pearl Harbor Day", I was admitted to a New Hampshire Hospital for what was supposed to have been routine surgery and also supposed to have me be well enough to even be back on a golf course in 10 days. The results instead were disastrous.

The operation at first seemed to have turned out fine. The doctors removed about 6 inches of my colon, and told me that all of the cancer appeared to have been removed with it. Within a day after surgery I was feeling pretty good, and was even able to follow nurses' instructions by walking up and down the corridor. After a few days, however, peritonitis, a syndrome marked by severe infection and body temperature fluctuations, set in. Apparently the doctor's stitches had detached causing the lethal contamination. My family tells me that I was aware between operations of the need to go back for the second surgery. For the next several days, I languished in severe pain, variously slipping in and out of consciousness.

Unknown to me at the time, the surgeon who performed the first operation took off for California the next day, leaving instructions that he was not to be contacted for any reason. Had I known that he would be leaving, there is no way that I would have consented to have him perform any surgery on me.

After the peritonitis set in, I was treated by another surgeon, who was foisted upon my family and me in my surgeon's absence. With my condition rapidly and critically deteriorating, we were presented with little remaining choice. Little did I know that this second surgeon was not only not present during my first operation as was promised by my first surgeon, but he also was apparently not competent to properly treat my conditions.

After the second operation, it was, to say the least, touch and go for the next few days. Finally, my oldest son, Larry and my daughter Jean took over and Larry wisely insisted that I be transferred to Massachusetts General Hospital. On December 20, 1998 I was transferred to (MGH) by the emergency medi-vac helicopter. My two weeks of torture at this NH Hospital were over. Thanks to the nick of time intervention by my kids, my life wasn't.

Fortunately for me I was placed in the hands of Dr. Charles Ferguson and his staff at MGH. He informed my son Larry that there was no time to take any X-rays or do any other diagnostic tests on me. I'm told that he said, *"This man is at death's door. He needs emergency surgery right away to have any chance at survival, we don't have time for any preliminaries."* Without any further hesitation, he and his great team immediately began their surgery and lifesaving work.

The MGH rooftop heliport, which received me just in time for Dr. Charles Ferguson (right, in a rare at-ease moment) and his team to save my life. Storrow Drive and the Charles River are to the left of and below the heliport.

After this surgery the seemingly unending precariously high fevers alternating with chills from dramatic temperature drops was beyond horrible. The massive infections that permeated my body were devastating. Doctors tell me that when things go so bad that a human being can no longer tolerate it, that some internal mechanism kicks in to help erase at least from memory, if not from experience, the worst of it. I know that I was out of conscious touch with the outside world a lot. If what I remember wasn't the worst of my suffering, I'm glad that I don't know what was.

For the ensuing three months, my life was hanging on by a thread. (Actually by many suture threads and many tubes.) Each of my major organs and vital signs had in turn failed or almost failed, and required artificial means to support them while nature brought them back into service. MGH intensive care staff played the ultimate juggling game: monitoring all of my bodily functions second by second to keep them in balance as they pinpointed the infection types and defeated them, and identified system weaknesses and bolstered them. Often when they had to concentrate all of their efforts to save my kidneys, liver, lungs, or heart, the strength of one or more of the other organs would falter to dangerous levels. The MGH staff played this precarious game without error for minutes, hours, days, weeks and months on end.

My body had a constant input of *dozens* of tubes and probes to keep my life force supported. (Some gruesome photos from that time and my lasting scars give testimony to this.) I underwent countless "invasive procedures" and numerous more trips to the operating room.

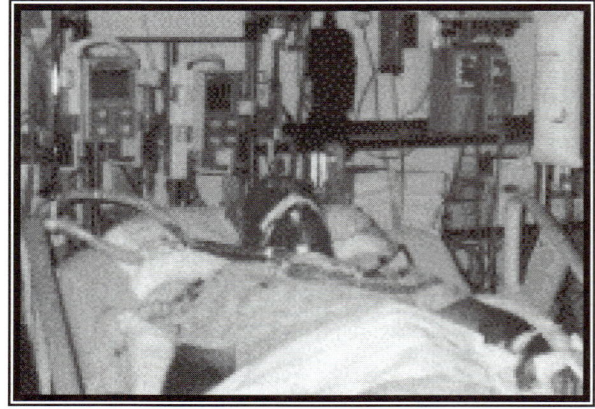

I had many close calls as an athlete and a coach, but this was the ultimate cliffhanger for me, and more poignantly so for my family and the MGH staff, who were right with me through the knockdown drag-out fight.

Rocky Marciano had an indomitable will that powered him to a 49-0 record. Muhummad Ali liked to talk about how he somehow managed to stay on his feet when Frazier blasted him temporarily into *'the halfway room'*; *"full of monsters and swirling lights"*. I honestly don't know whether or not my ingrained will helped me through this harrowing ordeal, or if I was just plain physically strong, or lucky, or had better prayers and people and science on my side, or all or none of the above. All I know is that I'm grateful to God to be here.

Certainly without the skill and dedication of Dr. Ferguson and his staff I never would have pulled through. I finally showed my first signs of recovery when I came out of my coma around the first week in March, 1999. All through my long battle for life at MGH, my family, relatives, and friends maintained a constant vigil over me. I know that it was a very difficult time for my family, who had to commute 100 miles from New Hampshire on a daily basis, and who had to endure the day by day uncertainty as to whether I would live or die.

There was at least one 'lighter side' moment amidst all of this. During the early weeks of my stay at MGH my poor wife Helen was at her wit's end trying to comprehend what was happening to me. In one conference with Dr. Ferguson she told him: "I don't understand how this can be happening to my strong, healthy and active husband. He never drank booze, never smoked and never caroused."
Dr. Ferguson deadpanned, ***"He didn't know what he was missing."***

Helen visited me and stayed by my side every day. When nurses or doctors needed to treat me, she would often walk around and do her favorite thing, which was to talk with people. My son Bob tells me that one day after Helen had been on her rounds for awhile, he found her talking with two young African American sisters in a room where he had seen the two crying earlier that day while going through grief counseling. The sisters had just made the decision that that night they would have the life support taken off their mom, who would therefore only have a few hours to live. Putting his head inside the door, my son told the ladies that he knew that they were having a tough day, and wondered if they wanted to be left alone. They replied that quite to the contrary, by telling her life story and giving such a touching mother's perspective on the here and hereafter, that Helen had snapped them out of their deep grief. They said that Helen was a wonderful person who had reminded them of their mom, and got them thinking about the beauty and fullness in the life on earth that their mother was about to complete, and that Helen had thereby helped bring them peace. Everyone talked for a short while longer, then the two sisters gave Helen a big hug and Helen returned to visit me.

Thanks to the generosity of our dear relatives and friends, the burden on my family was similarly made bearable. The family of my wife's best friend of many years, Zartar Minassian, made one big contribution by coming to the rescue of my travel weary clan. When Zartar became aware of our predicament, she immediately contacted her daughter Becky, who owned a rental apartment just across the street from the MGH.

Becky made her apartment available to our family to stay for months on end. When my sons Larry, Jr. and Jimmy offered to pay her for it, she refused to accept. She related to my kids that when she and Ricky were children, Helen and Larry had let their family stay in one of their apartments in Bridgewater at low and no rent as needed to help them get on their feet. She said: "It is only fair that we return your kindness to us in your time of need." I shall never forget these words and gestures from Becky and the Minassians. That's what I call real family.

The next few weeks of my stay at the MGH were even more grueling for me, as I was then much more alert. I was being fed by a tube in my stomach, and had to breath through a tube in my throat. Although actually emaciated of muscle and fat, until they took me off certain medications, I was unnaturally bloated with the fluids I retained. Although less so than before, I was still 'plumbed and wired' from head to toe, and practically immobile. I couldn't move my legs and could not roll over on my side. For a guy who spent the last 75^+ years in almost constant motion and limelight, this was an attention getting predicament that I would have much wished to do without.

My lips and mouth were constantly dry and I kept craving for ice chips or water for relief. I can remember *begging* for some orange juice or a popsicle. I wasn't allowed to take any food or drink from my mouth, as they feared that it would go into my lungs and bring on another attack of pneumonia. During the preceding months I was hit with one bronchial pneumonia attack and another such attack then would likely have been fatal.

All through my days at MGH, I had many of my relatives and friends visiting me and praying for my recovery. Among the many visitors were my golfing buddies, Bill Snow, Hank Richardson, Herk Phylides, and Bob Shaw; Donnie Strong of the 1956 State Champs; and my ever-loyal coaching assistants and boyhood pals, Joe Lazaro and Hank Pearson and his friend Harry Sirinossian.

All of my and Helen's surviving brothers and sisters, Mike, Johnny and Angie on my side, and Paul, Teresa, Eddie and Jackie on her side, were there with their encouragement and support. My many nieces and nephews; including the Filippetti kids, Louie, Mary, Rosalie, Helen, Frances, Nancy, and Richard came by, as did Paul's wife Francis and daughter Bonnie, Jackie Mark and his family, the Quattrocchi clan of Nancy, Donna, Pamela, Paula and Diane, and the Maiocco's, Tony, Steven, Lisa and Leslie. Nancy and Bonnie visited quite often. I'm sure that there were many others, but I was either too out of it or too stressed to remember them in particular. In any case, with the positive results, I take it that all those who I know and love were there in flesh and or spirit, and I'm thankful for that.

I'm also told that my wife Helen met Cardinal Law of Boston in the MGH foyer one day, and prevailed upon him to say a special (and apparently effective) prayer of intercession on my behalf.

Speaking of blessings, I understand that shortly after my arrival at MGH my son-in-law Kevin Leen's family hosted a very welcoming and comforting Christmas dinner at their Woburn home for most of my family. It's little wonder that Taylor and Cammy are turning out to be such little wonders with the familial background that they have. The Leens have always been great to our entire family. Since they also have a home in Seabrook Beach, just south of Hampton Beach, their helpfulness during my and Helen's health problems have extended to extra child care and countless other thoughtful little gestures year round throughout the recent years. We count ourselves very fortunate and enriched in our relationship with the Leens.

Katherine, Joe, Kevin & Mrs. Isabelle Leen, Michael with Isabella, Martha, and Mark Leen with Cammy, Mark's wife Anthonette, Jean Leen, Helen & Michael Folloni, Anne, Taylor and Mary Leen. James Folloni photo.

Helen with Katherine Leen

It was not until months after admittance to MGH that I became fully aware of my surroundings. I vaguely remember the visit of my niece, Mary (Filippetti) Markey and her sisters Helen and Rosalie. I recall Mary trying to converse with me and getting me to nod yes or no, which in addition to some 'eye expressions' and the electronic vital sign monitors, were about the extent of my communicating ability.

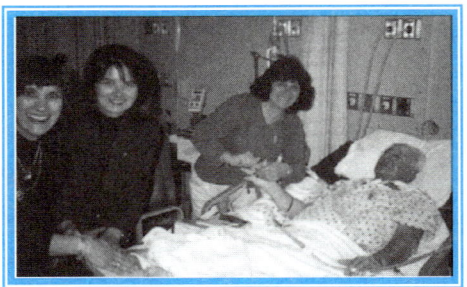

I'm told that the family had been speaking to me for months, but I have no recollection of this. I finally remember awareness of my son Jimmy telling me his view of my ordeal and informing me of the role that Larry Jr. had played in saving my life by his insistence to have me transferred to MGH by helicopter. Since a breathing tube had been down my throat for months on end, and my arms and hands were still laden with probes and monitors, I could not yet reply except by facial gestures.

Eventually I was able to communicate, first in writing and then, with painful rehabilitation, with speech. My first written communication to my family members was simply: **"Thanks for all your support, which I shall never forget."** They said that in reading this it made them feel about me like the disciples did about seeing Lazarus having returned from the dead. They now treasure copies of the note scratched on an envelope as a miracle response to their ardent prayers.

One very noteworthy incident occurred shortly after. I was having an exceptionally tough week when Jackie Mark came to visit me. Jackie is a disabled Korean War Veteran, who had gone through Hell and Back from his war injuries and later from an extremely severe and debilitating automobile accident.

Jackie was alone with me in that hospital room and I was really down in the dumps. I asked him sincerely if he ever thought of calling in the famous 'assisted suicide' practitioner Dr. "K" while he was going through his ordeals. Without any hesitation, Jackie shot back, *"NEVER! - LIFE IS TOO PRECIOUS TO EVEN THINK ABOUT THAT!"* I shall never forget his answer, or how it motivated me. From that day on I faced my struggles, no matter how tough, with a renewed will to live.

Words can hardly express how wonderful the nurses and other support staff members at MGH were during my trials. They were all truly angels on earth, doing far more than duty might be expected to call. They did all that they could to lessen my pain and make me comfortable. I shall be forever grateful to them for their efforts on behalf of other desperately needy people and me who were lucky enough to be under their care. Since I was only vaguely in touch with my surroundings for the intensive care portion of this help, I don't recall particulars of the staff there.

My family members have unending praise for the kind and competent efforts of many of those phenomenal work-a-day heroes and heroines. In intensive care a dynamic and colorful professional jazz and opera singer / nurse named 'Diamond' highlighted the entire staff's above & beyond the call service by singing an Italian song for me to celebrate my graduation from there.

My family tells me that during my time in IC, they shared many hours, days and weeks in the IC family waiting room with the Constanza's, a Sicilian fishing family out of Gloucester. Their dad was apparently going through something similar to me, and they were of great company and comfort to my wife and kids. *Those who suffer together, buffer together. (And those who pray together, stay together!)*

The entire family kept vigil while I was at MGH

I couldn't join James, Robert, Helen and Michael for the Christmas of 1999, but they went out to Helen and my favorite posing spot by Boar's Head Hampton Beach to have a photo taken for me.

In Ellison 7, the stop off between intensive care and rehab, I remember two nurses named Cathy who were among the super staff.

Another among those who were particularly helpful to me, who to this day I hold in great esteem, is a physical therapist named Leslie Taylor. Leslie, a pretty young woman who was really dedicated to her work, went to extremes to help get me back on track. Her father was a surgeon in Florida and she had hopes of continuing her education to follow in his footsteps.

Supported and sustained for the long run by Angels Leslie & Helen

Leslie was great for my morale, as well as in helping to get me back on track physically. Even after I was transferred to the Spaulding Rehab Center next to the new (Boston Garden) Fleet Center, she came to visit me every week. On one of those visits she informed me that she was going to London, England for a family vacation in April and that while there she was going to run in the gruelling 26 mile marathon and dedicate the run to me to get well.

To my pleasant surprise when she returned a few weeks later she had had some pictures taken of her vacation. The one picture that I loved showed Leslie after crossing the finish line. On the back of her sweatshirt was emblazed the words "For Larry". She told me that she had many cheers from the spectators who chanted **"Do It for Larry" & "Run for Larry"**. As they say on the other side of the pond, *"Fancy that!"* How nice it is to have such angels as Leslie walking (& running) among us!

The last communication I have had from Leslie came just before the Christmas, 1999 holiday, she informed me that she was back in medical school to pursue her dream of becoming a Doctor. I can only hope that a word or two of encouragement from me may have even begun to return the favor of her helping me to get re-dedicated to fulfill my destiny. May God Bless you and help you in all of your endeavors, Leslie. I shall never forget your kindness and help to me during my early convalescing days.

Here's part of the text of Leslie's letter to me:

> "Enclosed you will find a picture that is endearing to me...It was taken after I finished the London Marathon. The vision of all we put you through to save your life this past year at MGH kept me going all the way to the finish line. I never would have made it without you having inspired me!
>
> Everytime I was feeling like I had to stop, someone in the crowd yelled, "Do it for Larry!", and I seemed to get a burst of energy. It was an awesome experience and has become a very important accomplishment for me. Thanks to your inspiration, I have realized that if you work hard enough you can do anything you set your mind to.
>
> Thank You!!!" – Leslie

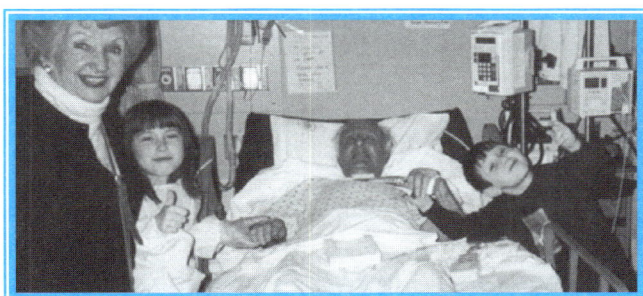 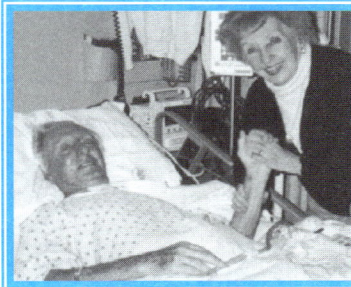

Larry's greatest comeback coming begins with assists from Helen Taylor & Cammy.

There is one other Physical Therapist who stands out to me. I believe that her name was Sue, although I grew to calling her **"The Terminator"** due to the vigorous workouts she pushed me to perform. She was the one who first got me to sit up. She was relentless in her efforts to get me to progress. Though she was petite, about 5' 2" and about 110 lbs., she was able to lift me up to a sitting position and maneuver me into a chair. It usually took 2 or 3 other nursing assistants to accomplish what she did by herself. Indeed, I recall one day when 3 aides were trying to get me out of bed and into the chair beside my bed. Halfway through the transfer, one of them, a 6-foot 220-pound trainee, lost his grasp on me and let me fall to the floor, causing me great pain.

It was the usual procedure to sit me up daily for about 10 to 15 minutes. One day "The Terminator" left me sitting in the chair for about an hour and I begged her to get me back in bed. She refused saying that it was time for me to get moving out of the bed. At the time my back was aching so much that I was very angry with her. The next day when she returned to give me more therapy I yelled out, "Here comes The Terminator, get her out of here!" A few days went by and when she finally returned, I apologized to her. I well realized that the reason she was working me so hard was for my benefit. I now fondly call Sue *"The Reinitiator"*.

After a few weeks of therapy at MGH, I was getting restless and looking forward to going on to the next step of my Rehab. It was hard to find a room at a Rehab center that would be convenient for my family to travel back and forth to from New Hampshire.

Finally, Jackie Mark made a few phone calls to friends of his and, within a week, I was transferred to the Spaulding Rehab Center, which is located in back of the old Boston Garden, the scene of many happier days with our Champion Basketball teams of 1956, 1960, and 1961.

How ironical that in 1999, I would be back at this site being carried in on a stretcher, when back in 1956, '60 and '61 I was being carried off the Boston Garden floor on the shoulders of my exuberant players.

I spent the next two months at Spaulding going through an intensive Rehab program. The process was slow, tedious and painful. Most of the nurses and staff were very good, a few were fair, and about 10 % didn't belong in Rehab work.

The most difficult time that I had was the transformation of my diet. I had to go from taking nourishment intravenously or through a tube in my stomach, to accepting liquids and purees by mouth. Although I was glad to get off the tube, I had difficulty swallowing anything, especially medication pills. I would gag at the feel of any solid items in my throat (up to this point I was given the medication via tubes). After weeks of retraining for the intake of food, little by little my appetite started to return. The baby food that I was allowed to take was not very appetizing; it was hospital food at its worst. I used to call it "PIG SLOP".

Pre-op Be-bop, 12/01/98

Somehow I managed to survive all of this, and on May 15, 1999, I was discharged from Spaulding. It was an especially happy occasion for me as it was also the day of my loving granddaughter Taylor's long awaited first communion.

Before I went into my first operation in early December of 1998, Taylor showed off a Christmas gift dress. I could easily hoist her up then, but never again after my surgery.

When I was finally well enough to talk with her around early April, I promised Taylor that I would push through my hospital rehab and be home for this important event. It was not easy going, but with all my guardian angels and a bit of grit I did just make it! We arrived at 13 Ross Ave. Hampton Beach at about 1:00 p.m., the same moment that Taylor was receiving her first communion.

1st Communion 1st Day Back Home New lives begin with beloved kin. 05/15/99

About an hour later, Taylor came back to the house all dolled up in her lovely white dress. It was a touching and unforgettable reunion and tears welled up in my eyes as she wrapped her little arms around me with a hug and kiss, exclaiming:

"Papa I Love You very much!"

Then my rising star "Champ" Cammy came in and ran over to embrace me and make my day complete. My situation was still grave, but there was 'Joy in Mudville' that day. And these two grandchildren gave me all the impetus that I needed to get back up to bat, even though I had been demoted to the minor leagues of self-sufficiency.

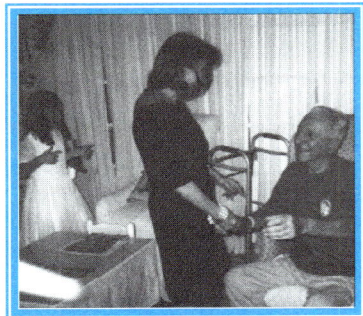

Taylor, Jean, Helen and Jean's Godmother Angie gave me warm homecoming greetings. As tough as things had been to get to this landmark point, everyone's really hard work had hardly just begun.

There were many tough days yet ahead. I still couldn't walk without help, and a deep and stubborn open sore that developed on my achilles while I was bedridden needed state of the art wound regeneration therapy. Physical Therapists and Home Health Aides came in three times a week as did Home Care Nurses. This went on for several months.

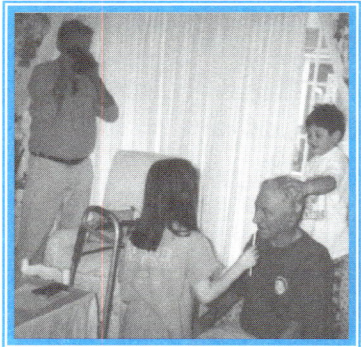  

I had lots of bad days, but not too many 'bad hair days' thanks to all the family's help!

"Arriving at one goal is the starting point to the other."
-John Dewey

My sons Bobby and Larry gave me daily physical workouts to help get me back to walking again. Everyone participated in the often-unpleasant details of keeping me nourished and clean.

And thanks to the ever-hard work of my daughter Jean and my lovely wife Helen, I eventually started to get my appetite back. The irresistible attraction of Jean's cooking was finally able to overcome the seemingly immovable objections of my devastated digestive track: Just before my 80th birthday on November 5, 1999, the long awaited day came when I was able to ask her for seconds!

After a joyful (re)birthday celebration that included Taylor, Cammy, Helen, Michael, his sweetheart Thuy Vo and everybody's favorite SAYSHA the Yorkie, it then came time for me to go back to Dr. Ferguson for the operation to have my external bag removed and reverse the Colostomy. On November 10, 1999, 11 months After my first operation that went horribly wrong, I went back for this next corrective surgery.

This operation lasted about 4 hours and when I woke up Dr. Ferguson was at my side to inform me that operation went well. I spent the next two weeks in the hospital and the pain was excruciating. I again had a lack of appetite and had to start my Rehab once again. Within just two months, however, Jean's cooking once again enticed my appetite back and I regained enough strength and energy to get back to the computer to try to finish "MY WAY".

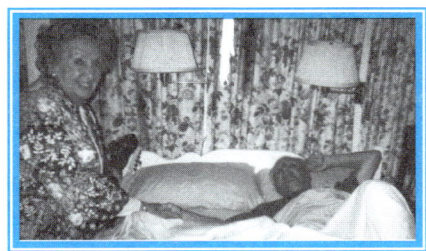

My son Jimmy says that on November 5, 1998 I was a 79-year-old with the body of a 58-year-old. And he says that just months later I looked like a 99-year-old! Helen and the kids nursed me back as lovingly as anyone could, but despite our best efforts, I often seem to be slipping downhill my uphill struggle.

Between the third and the fourth year after the operation (Dec. 2001 – Dec. 2002), my family rushed me to the hospital once a month on average for heart, kidney and breathing problems related to the horrible stress that the trauma of the previous few years put on them. Overall weakening of the system also made me more susceptible to diabetes, which creeped in. I no longer could aspire to winning seniors golf championships or to living to be 100, but I can still find purpose and satisfaction in life.

Watching the kids grow up is a great blessing. Scottie, Michael, Jennifer & Victoria Dent have been entertaining visitors to Hampton. I fondly remember when their cousins Taylor and Cammy visited them in Chicago

With my miraculous survival and my mega roller coaster ride to partial recovery, the Guy Upstairs gave me the opportunity and the time to reflect upon 'The Good, The Bad and The Ugly' of my life.

And I decided to act on one big lesson I learned from my buddy, Ted Williams: I want to remember the GOOD things, and have them ingrained in my mind and body forever. And I want to forget The BAD and UGLY things from the past and eradicate them from contaminating my mind and body.

I hope for many more relatively happy and productive days, which will be even more so if I can follow Ted Williams' philosophy. In any case, to the extent that I can abide by this, it will help me to return to the Ultimate Clubhouse in PEACE TRANQUILITY AND HAPPINESS when **The Manager Of All** finally pulls me from the game of life.

ANOTHER SETBACK FOR THE FOLLONI TEAM
'Knocked Down'

From the spring of 2000 to the summer of 2001 I took another long hiatus from the My-Way story. The Reason? The love of my life, my wife Helen, suffered a terrible stroke in March, 2000 around the day of my late Mom's birthday. Maybe my saintly mom was looking over us in a way, because Helen miraculously survived to celebrate *her own* 80th birthday with us on November 7, 2002. Thanks to somebody up there, the horrible events of that spring didn't completely rob us of our last somehow fulfilling, albeit challenging years together.

Just before this catastrophe, I was finally beginning to get back on my feet to begin to once again try to enjoy life with my wonderful wife and BOOM! All of a sudden the Helen of old was gone, never to make the recovery that we prayed for.

Of course, 15 years previously Helen had her first stroke. She survived that one pretty well, however and regained her speech within a few days. She didn't suffer any paralysis then and she managed to return to a pretty normal life. Though Helen would often repeat her stories, she still had her gift for storytelling to entertain everyone. (One of her favorites was of her Dad, a ship engineer, as *"he saw the Titanic all lit up like a Christmas tree, passing his boat while on its fateful voyage..."*) Although Helen never came back to 100%, she did live a quality, *'with it'* life and continued to contribute to and enjoy the Folloni Family life.

Helen 1999

March 15, 2000 was the beginning of the near end for Helen. I was sitting on my chair in the living room about 9am reading the morning paper, when Helen suddenly appeared in the room in a daze. She tried to speak to me but the words wouldn't come out. I called my daughter Jean on her cell phone to come home quickly. I'll never forget how Helen embraced me as we waited for Jean to take her to the hospital. By the way that Helen hugged and held me, I knew that something was terribly wrong and that she knew it too. She was admitted to a local Hospital for a couple of days and then released, unfortunately, too prematurely, without proper diagnosis and treatment.

For the next week, Helen had severe headaches and was not her normal self. On March 17, St. Patrick's Day, Larry and Bobby even brought Helen to an emergency room in Boston, but she was again sent home prematurely.

On Thursday, March 23, Helen and I went for a long walk up on the boardwalk of Hampton Beach. My heel had finally healed to where I could walk with a limp and spring of the year had come with the new spring in my step. Helen and I were enjoying ever longer daily walks and renewed our hope of my possibly getting back out on the dance floor with Helen by summer. How would I have known that this would be my last chance to walk side by side, hand in hand with Helen? Oh how I miss this simple pleasure.

The very next morning, Helen woke up at about 6am, went into the living room and saw her grandson, Cammy, watching television. She asked him why he was up so early. She then returned to the bedroom and told me that Cammy was up watching TV. Those were the last words that I heard from her. At approximately 9am, my daughter Jean woke me up to inform me that Helen came out of the bathroom acting very strangely. Bobby and Jean helped carry her to my bedroom where she collapsed in the chair and began to go into convulsions. Bobby called 911 immediately. The efficient EMT's arrived in minutes and rushed Helen to the closest NH hospital, the same one which initially treated Helen nine days before. Over the next two days Helen was beginning to respond, but on the third day she suffered a major setback.

There are two types of stroke someone can suffer. The course of treatment for each type of stroke is radically different. Unfortunately, Helen's condition was misdiagnosed and treated in a manner that increased, rather than stopped, the damage done to her brain. Helen's condition went from bad to worse, which prompted the family to once again look to Massachusetts General Hospital to attempt to save her life. So the family had her rushed via ambulance to Mass General Hospital (MGH) in Boston. Immediately upon Helen's arrival at MGH, the team of neuroligists, neuro-radiologists and neuro-surgeons went to work. She was given a series of thorough tests, which indicated a hemorrhagic stroke caused by a ruptured aneurysm.

On Friday evening, Dr. Bob S. Carter and Dr. Lee Schwamm came out to the waiting room to report the findings. The news was not very encouraging. They informed us of the ruptured aneurysm and associated catastrophic bleeding that was revealed by the tests. They then said that her only hope of survival was to operate immediately. They said there would be no guarantees that she would survive the delicate operation. If we did not proceed with the operation, however, they doubted that Helen would have lived another 24 hours.

I was faced with the most important decision of my life. After a soul-searching discussion with the family, we decided to give her the only chance that she had to survive. With tears streaming down my face I signed the release for Dr. Carter to proceed with the operation.

Rather than triumphant, my first return to the MGH walking by myself and dressed normally was instead the occasion of tragedy and decision

"I did what I had to do and saw it through, without exemption" -*My Way*

Dr. Carter and his team went to the operating room close to midnight and the surgery went on for about 6 hours. Following the operation, our heroic Dr. Carter told us that the operation went very well and that he was optimistic that Helen would survive. Doctor Carter's team removed a 3" by 4" portion of her skull and placed it in her torso to keep it viable so that it could be replaced at a future date. Doctor Carter informed us that neuro-radiologist Doctor Reinking was about to begin an immediate follow-up operation as a preventive measure to guard against future strokes. This operation took another six hours to complete. The next few days would be critical.

Bobby and Larry maintained a constant 24-hour vigil and Jean and I made the daily trips from Hampton to be at her bedside. With each passing day we saw hope for Helen's recovery. She could not respond vocally and the right side of her body was completely paralyzed. Her only significant sign of life was that she maintained a firm grip with her left hand. After about 10 days in the intensive care room she was transferred to the Ellison Wing.

While Helen was in the Ellison Wing of MGH, Debbie flew in from Chicago with her two young children and Jimmy and Michael came in from Oakland. Upon seeing her mother for the first time all wired up and filled with tubes and with a major indentation where her skull was removed, Debbie became hysterical. We had all we could handle in trying to calm her down.

We then had a family conference with a neurologist regarding Helen's status. We asked him for an honest prognosis of Helen's future. The Folloni Team was looking for another miracle to follow the partial recovery that I had made from my near fatal disaster of the preceding year. Alas, the prognosis as laid out by this doctor was not the message that we wanted to hear. As tears streamed down all of our faces, we listened as he gave us a tale of gloom. His opinion was that Helen would likely make it out of MGH, but for the rest of her life she would not be able to walk, talk, feed herself or even be hand fed, or do much of anything at all other than survive.

We then dutifully prepared for the worst-case scenario, while never letting go of the hope that she would recover more completely. We continued to maintain our daily vigil at Helen's bedside. Thankfully, with each passing day, we saw some faint signs of response from Helen. All of her children and grandchildren stayed with her for long periods of time. Debbie's daughter Victoria Helen, then just three, sat patiently at Helen's side, constantly holding her hand, Helen's hand squeezes being her only means of communication. After a week or so, it came time for Debbie to leave for Chicago. As Debbie was going through her emotional and impassioned goodbye to her mother, Helen *miraculously* lifted her left arm, raised her body and semi-embraced her! In her motherly compassion, Helen just couldn't stand to see how hurt her child was at seeing her condition and she somehow willed her way to overcome her paralysis to thrust herself upwards to her daughter.

Our joy was unbridled at seeing Helen respond to us after all of the dire predictions that she'd never be able to. She was understandably out of it for most of her time at MGH, but she did respond enough to lift the spirits of her family.

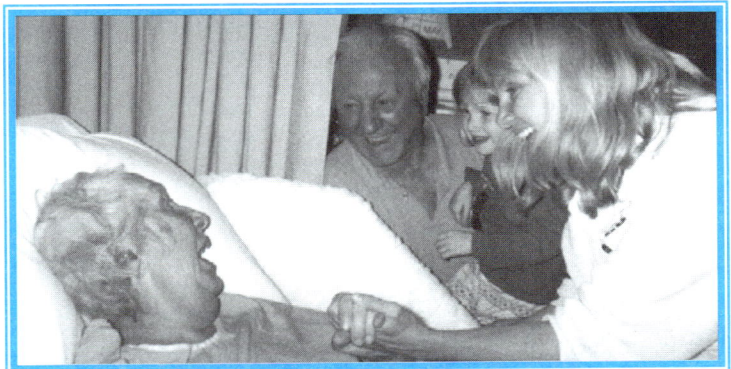

This was the first encouraging response sign we had seen from Helen. Most of the family was present to witness this truly extraordinary event, which lifted our spirits. With rekindled hope to match our faith and Helen's Love, we then set about the quest to find her housing and rehabilitation outside of MGH. Helen did make it out of MGH and with time and our care and nurturing, she has been able to have some limited participation in family life. Unfortunately, though, she was incapacitated to a devastating extent and her and our family's quality of life has suffered horrendously ever since.

I'm told that Debbie had a similar emotional outburst when she first saw me in the same intensive care ward two years prior. She was at that time so weepy and vocal that the intensive care staff asked my other kids to remove her and to not let her back into the ICU until she gained her composure. Before she left, however, Debbie successfully demonstrated the power of passion. I'm told that her pleadings somehow induced me to show the first sign of life in weeks, as I ever so briefly opened my eyes and clutched her hand before I slipped out of it again. This again happened in front of several of my other children and was enough to assure them and the rest of my family that I had a real chance to come through. I thank God that Helen and I have been so tremendously blessed with such exceptionally loving children and that together we somehow found the will and the ways to continue together for so long!

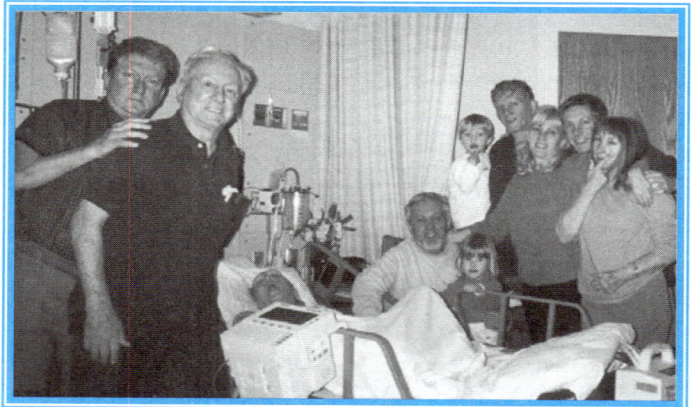

The entire family pulled together and was as positive as possible to help set the atmosphere for a miracle recovery.

Helen was out of it for most of our vigils at the MGH Intensive Care Unit and the Ellison ward.

Helen's stay at MGH's Ellison Wing lasted only about 10 days and then she was transferred to a rehabilitation facility. Helen was evaluated by a representative from Spaulding, one of the preeminent rehabilitation facilities in the area, but she was not accepted into the program because the representative felt that she was not ready for skilled care. This was another emotional setback for the family. Helen was also rejected by another Rehab center before finally the Whittier Rehab Center in Haverhill accepted her. Her stay at Whittier lasted about two weeks and then that facility similarly concluded that she did not, at this time, appear qualified for skilled care. Though they were not able to keep Helen, the facilities at Whittier were top notch and the staff treated her with great respect and care.

We've never given up trying to get help for Helen to regain basic functions and to become more interactive. For example: During the year following her surgery, the doctors and therapists continually told us that we should accept the fact that Helen would never be able to take any food or liquid orally. My son, Robert, however, found a speech language pathologist, Elizabeth Lee-Hood Ahmad, at MGH who was smart enough to recommend that Helen should be given swallow tests to see if she could eat. We persistently promoted this idea until Helen was able to take and pass the test. We got Helen off of the feeding tube and now, with assistance, she can at least eat somewhat normal food, ground up like baby food, one of her few remaining pleasures.

Dance entertainment provided by Michael Dent and Oliver (Twist-ing) Spratt

Jimmy, Scottie, Jean Taylor, Larry Jr & I enjoy a rare moment with Helen back at home.

Helen, Debbie Victoria, Bobby and I are happy to be together on Christmas, 2000

Bob shows off handicraft made by Helen during better days.

ITALIAN SERENADERS
'Down But Not Out'

One very exciting event happened during Helen's stay at Whittier. A group of singers from the north shore called 'The Italian Serenaders' had come to visit one of their members who was a patient across the hall from Helen's room. They were gaily dressed in colorful Italian costumes and with one of them playing the accordion they belted out many of Helen's favorite Italian songs. Upon hearing the lovely tunes we went over and I asked them if they would be kind enough to come in to serenade Helen.

Back in 1979, when we went to visit Bobby in Rome, one of the highlights of our trip was an excursion to The Isle of Capri. On the boat ride from that Isle back to Sorento, we encountered a group of Italians who were having a gala reunion of their war days. Among the group was a captain, with a beautiful singing voice, who singled out Helen to serenade her with the beautiful Italian Ballad, "Parla mi d'amore Mariu." This event was a lasting memory for Helen and she always treasured those glorious moments.

When the Serenaders came into Helen's room and lined up around her bed, Helen had her eyes closed and was unresponsive while they sang their first song. They asked me if she had a favorite song and I requested: *"Parla mi d'amore Mariu"*. As soon as they began singing this lovely ballad, Helen's eyes opened and she began smiling as tears streamed down her face. It was a real touching moment for all of us as we tried to stem the flow of tears of happiness at Helen's remarkable response. The moment was all the more poignant given Helen's inability to speak and the translation of the song title: *"Speak to Me of Love…"*

The Serenaders went on to sing many more of Helen's favorites and when they concluded some 20 minutes later, I asked if I could contribute something to their group. I shall never forget the immediate response from one of the group's members: *"We've been repaid a thousand-fold by seeing the response that came from your precious wife. That's reward enough."*

THE SEACOAST / HAVEN HEALTH CENTER

Helen's "Yahoo" custom handicap van in front of Haven Health Center.

Following her two-week stay at Whittier, it came time to move Helen on to the Seacoast Health Center, to be near the family and to get a high quality care for her almost total physical dependencies. The move was made on May 18, 2000.

At the Seacoast Health Center (SHC) Helen has received the best care that could be expected. I could never say enough about the positive relations and incidents involving her stay there, but I will note just a few.

The director at the time, Mark Durant, was very cordial and helpful to us in making this transition. He was very caring, considerate and efficient in his daily work of running the complexities of this Health Center. His assistant, Dennis Donovan *(right)* recently became the Director and is also doing a very good job. Dr. Peter Dicks and his medical assistant, Corey, have also been very helpful to us. The facility has also recently changed ownership, but their service has remained excellent.

The Center stays well staffed and everyone, including the top nurses, assistants, orderlies, therapists and the maintenance staff, has done an excellent job in caring for Helen. As devastatingly disabled as Helen has been, she has always related very well with the entire staff. It's amazing to see the true affection that so many of the staff and other residents there have developed for Helen. Of course Helen can be fairly easy to appreciate. Despite being in worse condition than almost everyone there, every time that anyone comes into her sight, she greets them warmly, with her face lit up with a glowing smile and gleaming eyes. The little she has she uses well.

One nurse to whom Helen has been particularly responsive is Debbie on the evening shift. After Debbie completes her duties in the skilled nursing wing, she often spends extra time with Helen on many an otherwise lonely night for Helen. Helen shows her appreciation by the ***extra special*** smile that comes over her face every time that Debbie comes into her room. Some others worthy of note for their dedicated and kind care include Laurie, Carol, Rita, Priscilla & Geneva Cogger, the Recreation Director.

Helen & Bella Fortin, June 2003

In 2002, Helen moved from one side of the west wing to the other, where she was lucky enough to be roomed with Bella Fortin, a 93-year young and vivacious woman who is great therapy and a great friend for her. Among the very helpful staff on that side have been the night crew, including Sandy, Marcia, Kevin, Bob, Angie, Kim, Cheryl, Karen, John, Beth, Elena, Ginny, Addy, Robin, Jeff, Collins and Chris and day crew including Wade, Ruth, Jane, Jennifer, Miriam, Sherry, Donna. Geneva, Chalaigne, Laurie, Marlene, Carol, Priscilla, Rita, Norlita and Christine.

Helen has gone through a lot over the past few years. On June 22, 2000, she went back to MGH to have Dr. Carter replace her skull bone that had been removed on April 1st during the initial brain surgery. Helen remained at MGH for a couple of days, then returned to the Seacoast Health Center.

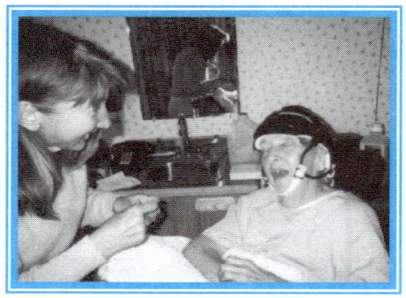

Jean humoring protection-helmeted Helen

Night after night for the longest time, I would be crying as I walked from Helen's nursing home room back to my car. I would keep looking up at the stars in the sky and saying to God, *"WHY-WHY-WHY did this have to happen to Helen?"*

Helen didn't deserve to be stricken in this manner. She was always so kind and considerate to everyone. It mattered not who they were or where they came from or what they looked like. She treated all with respect and kindness far above and beyond the norm. Helen is one of those rare individuals who was loved by all. There were many times when Helen would stop by a couple of disadvantaged youngsters and hand them a dollar. Many a time when she spotted some destitute lady or man on the street, she would place some money near them, but without them noticing. Then so as not to embarrass them, she would say, "Excuse me, I just found this money here. No one else is around, so it must be yours." She would always make donations to the blind children mission and get prayers from them for her family. Through her example, Helen instilled a sense of charity in her children, so her legacy of good deeds is still going strong. Although it hurt her to give leave of her kids out of the nest when they left for college or work, if they were off to do good, they had her complete blessing.

One very humorous charitable incident came about on one of our visits to California. While travelling after Jimmy's graduation from Stanford in 1983, we made a stop at Carmel on the way towards Santa Barbara. As we pulled up to a parking spot, a shabbily dressed man approached our car and begged for a handout. He was obviously a down-and-outer seeking some money for drugs or alcohol.

He said to Helen "Excuse me m'am, but I haven't had a bath for a week, can you help me out with some money to buy a bar of soap?" Well Helen, believing that he really just wanted to get clean, responded, *"I have just what you need."* As the bum eagerly looked on, Helen reached into her pocketbook, pulled out *a bar of soap* and handed it to him with an innocent and sincere smile! The befuddled beggar was flabbergasted! He said, *"Uh, oh, thank you,"* and turned away before slamming the soap on the street and staggering south swearing unclean words.

Our entire family has been very supportive to Helen during these very difficult years. Granddaughter Taylor Rose and son Bobby have the knack of getting the greatest responses from Helen.

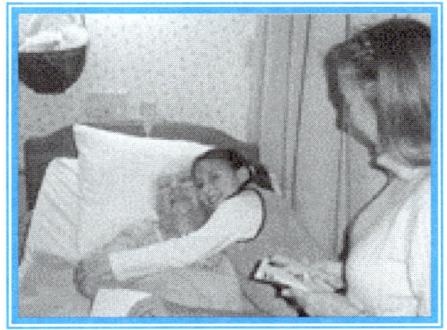

Jean and her daughter Taylor Rose are the ultimate in true loving caregivers for Helen.

Bobby dedicates a lot of time to helping Helen with physical movement and has been the catalyst in trying to get her to talk again. In 2001 he actually had her, on one or two occasions, counting up to 10 and perceptively calling out the days of the week and the months of the year. Some days of course are better than are others. Lately, it seems that Helen has just about given up on her struggle to communicate with words.

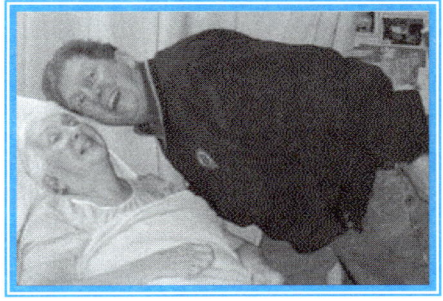

For the first several months of Helen's stay at Seacoast, we were unable to bring her home. Instead we visited Helen daily and tried to stagger our arrivals so that she would have company throughout the day as often as possible.

Due to her hearing problems, it was often very difficult for us to know if she could hear us when we talked. At first she wouldn't respond unless she was actually looking at us. After a year or so, we noticed that she began responding to sounds even without eye contact. I installed an audio link hearing device in her room and she appears to be responding to some of our messages. We believe that she understands many things that we say to her or present her with. She will sometimes obsessively interact with old family photos, magazine pictures and dolls for hours on end, but if anyone addresses her, she generally stays attentive to them until they leave her sight. As time progresses, so does her apparent recognition of portions of certain photo albums we place before her and old movies, music and some of our old favorite TV shows that daughter Jean puts on for her and to see.

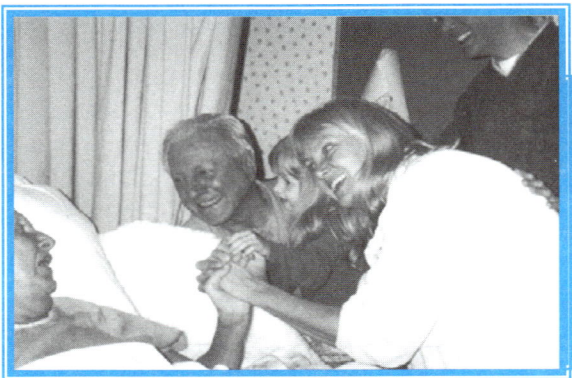

The professional caregivers have many helpful resources that are worthwhile to make use of, but there is nothing like the understanding eye contact and touch of one family member to another. This is especially true of child to mother or husband to wife.

Early in her stay, we brought in the portable electronic piano that Larry Jr purchased for her shortly before the stroke. Little by little, she responded to this and other stimuli. On occasion, she actually played the scale. We always hope that she will regain some of her self-taught mastery of playing the piano.

Before Helen was able to visit home, Jean remained the stalwart of the family with her daily visits and on many occasions she brought along our grandchildren, Taylor and Cammy. Taylor is great therapy for her grandmother, who just loves her warm and enthusiastic company. As Cammy grows older, he too is interacting more with her.

Debbie and her family came in from Chicago in August of 2000. Helen was thrilled at seeing Debbie and Debbie's children, Victoria and Scott. It was so heart warming, watching little Victoria holding her grandmother's hand and trying to talk to her.

During Debbie's first visit after Helen moved into the nursing home, we hired a commercial wheelchair van and driver to transport Helen in her wheelchair back to Ross Avenue for her first trip home since her stroke back on March 24th. She spent nearly the whole day with us. We took her for a stroll down the boardwalk of Hampton Beach and stopped off at the band stand, hoping that she would recall many pleasant memories of the many days and nights we had spent there over the past 30 years.

We all had a very emotional day as Helen was taken from room to room back at the cottage. Helen was awe struck at seeing her old surroundings and I am sure that she was happy to see that her home was just the way she had left it.

They say that all good things must come to an end and Helen's visit home ended at about about 5pm when the van returned to pick her up. It was a heart-breaking experience for us to watch as they loaded Helen into the vehicle. As I stood by the door watching the driver strap Helen in to secure her, I couldn't restrain my emotions any longer. It was a horribly cruel sight for all of us to see Helen shackled like this and carted away from home. Tears came streaming down my cheeks as I waved goodbye to her. You will never know how much it hurt every one of us to watch that scene. As the van pulled away, I went back into the house, sat in my lounge chair and cried myself to sleep. Others in the family, I'm told, did the same.

Some of our relatives made long trips to visit Helen during her first months at SHC. My sister Angie made several visits. During her last visit, she came along with our niece, Helen Preti Wallace, who is my sister Virginia's daughter and my wife's namesake and Godchild.

Helen, who came all the way from the state of Virginia (that my sister was named after), carried a beautiful bouquet of flowers into my wife's room and she was rewarded with a big warm smile of recognition.

There was also a pleasant surprise visit later that summer by Helen's sister Teresa and two of her daughters, Nancy and Pamela. This was the best therapeutic medicine Helen had in a long time. On that day we had a large family gathering with most of my children and grandchildren present spending the afternoon with Helen at the Seacoast Health Center.

This was Helen's most responsive day yet since her stroke back in March. She was so happy to see us all together. Teresa was disappointed to see how impaired Helen had become and felt bad that Helen didn't seem to recognize her. After Helen watched Teresa's repeated expressions of dismay that afternoon, she finally found a way to summon up a rare verbal message. She looked at Teresa, Nancy and Pamela and actually said, loudly and clearly the word *"Quattrocchi,"* which is Teresa's married name.

In more recent times, with "Doctor Donna" Spratt having presented my son James with a beautiful baby girl, 'Ava Grace'; they too make frequent trips up from Pittsburgh to brighten Helen's and my days.

Michael, his lovely sweetheart Thuy and their adorable 'Mity Mite' Yorkies Dolly & Saysha, also visit us from California at least a couple of times a year.

Jean has done wonders in working with the Seacoast/Haven staff to make life more interesting for Helen. A grade-school class at Sacred Heart School in Hampton has made Helen their "Adopted Grandmother" for each of the last two years. They give her hand made cards with personalized messages and they stop in to visit! Helen treasures these notes and interactions. It's interesting how many cute and intimate sentiments that the children convey. Always a life of the party, one year, with the help of Jean, Helen won the Halloween Costume contest!

Helen still clowns around from time to time! Even in her predicament, she still seems to know that life is what you make it and she tries to remain upbeat.

For her loving spirit and attitude that keeps her in it,
I consider Helen to be my ALL TIME CHAMPION OF CHAMPIONS!

At this writing in mid 2003, Helen is still dependent on others for virtually all of her bodily needs, being paralyzed completely on one side and partially on the other. She is wheelchair or bed bound and is not able to talk except that she does try to get words out and occasionally we can understand her utterances. During the Valentine week this year she surprised us by clearly mouthing: *"I love chocolate!"*

For the first 12 months after her surgery she was fed through a tube in her stomach. In mid 2001, she made a great achievement and started taking hand fed food by mouth. Once in awhile she can even feed herself a little if food is place within reach of her left arm, her only functioning limb. She can only drink thickened fluids that are spoon-fed to her. It's very discouraging for all of us to watch her struggle in vain everyday to try to regain her speech and other physical capabilities.

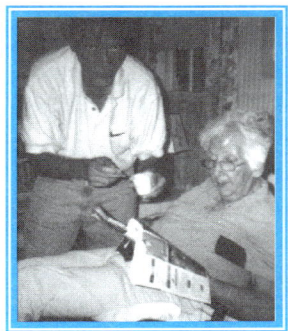

Larry Jr. and Bob have volunteered to stay close and have sacrificed their other activities to spend time daily helping with Helen's care and transportation. Larry has logged countless hours at her bedside and sometimes even peeks in after midnight to make sure that she is OK. Bobby's devoted efforts are relentless, taking on the mantel of driver, medical & social services advocate and amateur speech and physical therapist.

Jean makes countless thoughtful contributions to Helen's well-being. She tries to make sure that Helen is always treated with dignity and made to look and feel 'special' and wanted. For example, Jean keeps Helen's room tastefully decorated with photos and artistic reminders of the family. Jean also usually stops by Haven in the early morning and lays out appropriate outfits and puts make-up on Helen. The two often go to the mall where Helen gets her hair done and where she and Jean can relive treasured moments of the past, albeit in an extremely different way. The results of everybody's extra attention show in Helen's occasional warm smiles and eye communications.

"The supreme happiness in life is the conviction that we are loved."
-Victor Hugo

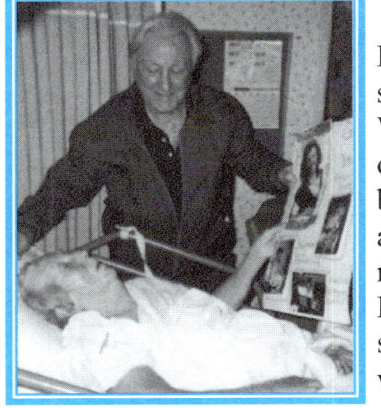

It is hard to describe how much of a strain the difficult situations of Helen and me have placed on the family. We sold some property to help pay for a specially outfitted handicap van with "Yahoo" license plates to bring Helen back and forth to home, which the kids and I do faithfully every day. We also had a motorized lift installed in the back of the home to get Helen up and down for access to the living areas. (My sons Larry and Bobby actually carried her and her wheelchair up and down the stairs before that.)

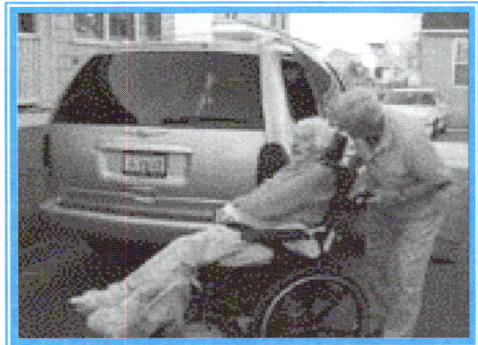

I doubt that many people in Helen's condition anywhere get the kind of unwavering attention and treatment that our family gladly gives to her. Then again I doubt that too many mothers anywhere gave as much to their families as Helen did over the years. We don't of course, do anything just so as to compare ourselves to others.

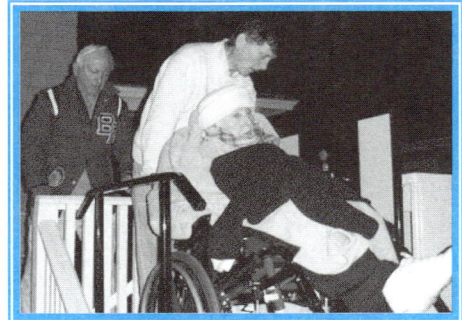

There can never be satisfaction with that attitude. We only do what Helen deserves and what we believe to be right. We take our satisfaction from that as best we can. Between taking care of Helen and bringing me to doctor's appointments and other related errands a few times a week, it is very difficult for my kids to attend to their work and lives outside of our 'Folloni-Team' family circle. Somehow they persevere. I keep needling my kids out of habit, I suppose, but really I treasure every second with them and everything about them. We have our share of friction, but I would do anything in the world for them and they keep doing everything in the world for Helen & me in our twilight years.

The sad reality has been that despite the best efforts of the family and of the Haven Nursing Home staff, Helen spends most of her time languishing helplessly in her bed or in her wheelchair. Still, we thank God for what we have been able to share.

Johnnie, Angie & Mike

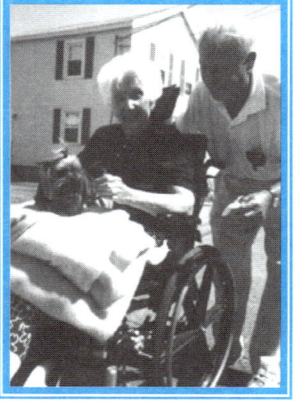

Helen's best friend Zartar

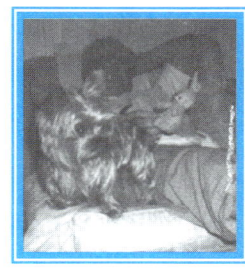
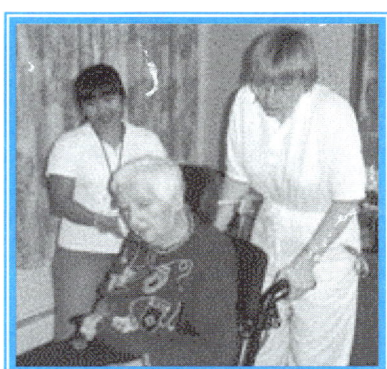

Bobby, Helen & Thuy yuk it up.

Helen & Larry and Helen & sister Teresa in better days

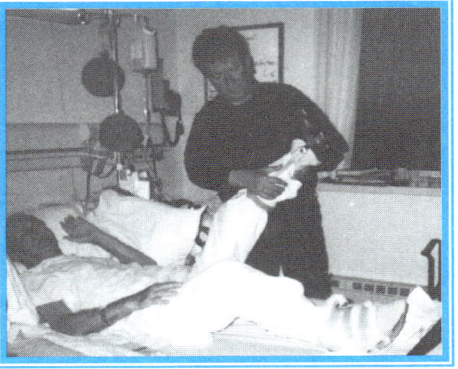

One Christmas holiday evening in 2001, as most of the family was gathered listening to Carols, Helen suddenly began singing along with the song Silent Night! She did a 'solo', clearly singing just about all of the lyrics. We were all truly amazed and overjoyed at Helen's spontaneous electrifying performance, which we fortunately were able to capture on videotape. The family broke out in a big applause when she finished. Since Helen had spoken very few words or phrases since her stroke, we felt as if this were a Christmas miracle.

Over and over again through this narrative, you've seen references to the Folloni Team's ardent faith that a miracle would hold forth. Helen was at death's door, but through the miracles of modern medicine, and the miracle inducing power of a loving family's faith, she has somehow made it through to present an even more powerful testimony to the power of Love. Year after year, we did what we could to make sure that our children's dream's came true on Christmas day. This was to them evidence of living the right way. As if to prove that their memories did not lie, Helen once again resurrected, to sing us Silent Night.

HAND ME DOWN FAMILY TRAITS

In our family backgrounds we all have some traits, genetic and learned, that carry on from generation to generation. Some are good, some are not so much so. As related to the Lombardi / Folloni clan, the trait that I am most proud of is that of charity and compassion for our fellow men and women.

On the not so good side, those of you who know me may not be too surprised that according to my oldest sister Virginia, our family has a very temperamental side. My Dad was a very abrasive and always complaining perfectionist. My poor Mom was usually the recipient of his rants and raves that many times were very trivial in nature, but which would too often escalate to the point where it adversely affected the entire family. When my Dad went on one of his abusive tirades, my saintly Mom would usually head for the bedroom and kneel and say a prayer that dad be forgiven Dad for his outbursts. This at least stopped the pernicious incident at hand.

An incident that remains in my memory occurred one day when my brother Mike came home from work for his daily lunch. We were all seated at the kitchen table when Dad started out with one of his nasty, trivial complaints about the soup that Mom had prepared. As usual, he loudly berated Mom saying there was not enough salt or pepper in the soup or that it was cold, etc. It was always something trivial.

Well on this particular day my brother Mike finally became fed up with Dad's complaining and yelling. When Dad got started, Mike got up from his chair, opened the window and yelled back at Dad. "OK you don't like the soup so out it goes!" as he fired it out the window. My Dad was so stunned by Mike's action that he never opened his mouth again for sometime. He got the message and from then on he was pretty docile and quiet during dinnertime.

Being an Italian or an anything else is no excuse for being abusive and nagging. We are all responsible for our actions and we will all reap what we sow.

"And in the end, the Love we take, is equal to the Love we make."
-The last lyric on the last song written by the Beatles.

This trait of being a perfectionist and complaining has drifted down to me and in turn I can see the same traits on occasion in some of my children. It's not that we complain with an intention to hurt anyone. Just the opposite, our complaints are directed mostly to correct some inequity and try to make things better for all. I can cite many examples of my many complaints that have resulted in improvements in Schoolboy Sports, highway safety and other areas that affect all citizens in our daily living. I think that my record shows that many good things have come about due to my complaining how things were in conjunction with a plan to improve and my hard work to overcome obstacles that stood in the way of progress. More often than not, in the end my way turned out to be the best way for all of us involved.

Despite the good that can came from seeing wrong and working to overcome it, I would be highly remiss if I failed to apologize to all who we Folloni's (especially me) offended, and / or rendered unwilling to continue with efforts to fix ills because of our headstrong pushes for change. To the extent that our quests for improvement stifled others participation in it, I, and I'd guess we, are truly sorry.

> *Some see things as they are and say, "Why"?*
> *Others see things as they could be and say, "Why not?"*
> -Robert F. Kennedy (Father of son Michael's Harvard Classmate, environmental activist R.F.K. Jr.)

Probably my greatest regret in life is that sometimes my attempts at encouraging my children and others to excellence via chastening were OVER exuberant, and therefore had a counter effect of not instilling the confidence that they needed to accomplish what I knew that they could. There is no defending the indefensible.

The fact that some Folloni's sometimes let too much 'heat' get in the way of the light we had to share often cast us in a bad light with others. The worst part about this occasional failing on our behalf is that it hampered joint moves to improve. I am well aware that I personally have not been the most popular guy on the block due to my sometimes overly abrasive and frank manner. Hopefully there is sufficient redeeming benefit in that there are few people who are more charitable and compassionate to their fellowman than are the Folloni's. As I have stated before, even though we are hard-core on the outside, on the inside we all melt like butter on a hot stove when we see the need to help out others in need of help. In the long run, I hope that our clan soon evolves past our tough exterior to a firm but soft approach to helpfulness, so that we can be both charitable and palatably effective along our way as being agents of change. We still, of course need to focus first on our own success to have something to share. Niece Linda Balboni Bardoff and my beautiful Helen would want it no other way.

> *"There is no way to Peace, Peace is the Way."*
> -Lao Sze

WHY DID I CHOOSE TO BECOME A COACH?

That's an easy question to answer. As a youngster I had a passion for sports. While growing up and playing games in the vacant fields and sandlots of Stanley, I had so much fun playing sports that I vowed to come back someday to impart my God-given athletic skills and knowledge to others. I wanted to teach and coach youngsters so that they could enjoy their youth just as I had.

If these youngsters only had 1/10th fun that I had as a youth they would likely have had a great childhood. Kids are kids for such a short time. They should all *(boys and girls)* be given the opportunity to enjoy those days with fond remembrances.

WHY ARE SPORTS SO IMPORTANT?

Yes sports are only games, but these games are a healthy avenue of training for our youth. Within the bounds of sports, children's coaches teach them to follow society's rules and regulations as a means of achieving individual and group goals. Cooperation, individual responsibility training, dedication, expectation of intrinsic rewards for achievement, team spirit and so many other good things are also imparted. These lessons will carry on through adulthood to help kids to become first class citizens in our society. These are all truisms to many. The unfortunate truth is that these simple concepts are foreign to more youth than they are familiar to. We must, as an advancing society, continue to spread the positive values that we've been able to aspire to in this land of the free. Sports is not our only hope by any means, but it is certainly an effective means for many. COMMON SENSE IS NOT A COMMON THING, and I sense that society-wide, sport and healthy recreation is still not quite a common enough thing for our youth.

HOW I WOULD LIKE TO BE REMEMBERED

I'd like to be remembered as an aggressive determined guy who fought fiercely to to establish and sustain athletic and recreation programs for the kids in Bridgewater & Raynham and throughout the State. I would like it to be remembered that I did things *"My Way"* because I believed that *"My Way"* was the right way for kids.

My recommendations to kids are that they live a clean life, and that they

- Be loyal to their God.
- Be loyal to their Parents, who raised and weaned them.
- Be loyal to their Coaches and Teachers, who teach them important life lessons.
- Be loyal to their teammates and classmates their most precious friends.
- Be loyal to their fans that are there to support them.
- Be compassionate and charitable to their fellow man.
- And finally, that each and every one be loyal to him or herself.

A MAN'S WEALTH IS DETERMINED BY HIS ACCOMPLISHMENTS - NOT BY THE MONEY HE ACCUMULATES

This quote brings to light a chat that I had at the recent High School **Super Bowl** game between B-R and Everett at the Boston University Field. At half time, while seated in the Case Lounge, I was chatting with Bill Gaine, the MIAA Rep. and Eddie Burns, the coach's Rep. on the Super Bowl Committee. The conversation got around to our battles back in the early 70's to get this Super Bowl extravaganza started. I made a joking comment that if I had a dime for every mile and every hour that I'd put in to assist Mauve Pave, Billy Abramson, Bob McIntyre and Eddie Schluntz in their proposal to get this Super Bowl Playoff approved by the Headmasters, that I'd now be a rich man.

Bill Gaine shot back quickly, *"Larry you **are** a rich man, you are the richest man in the State for what you have accomplished by your dedicated work"*. Eddie Burns then joined in and said, *"Larry you are very rich, look down there at those kids playing their hearts out and the thousands of spectators out there enjoying this great game, thanks to your foresight and hard work."* This was extremely gracious and generous of two men who in many ways were as responsible as me for progress in state schoolboy athletics, but it did ring true, and therefore fitting and satisfying.

As I drove home to Hampton Beach, New Hampshire after the game I began to reflect upon the many good things that have happened in my lifetime. When I hear reports of my former athletes turning out to be great citizens and parents, I indeed feel like a rich man to have made even a small impact in their lives. Not too many corporate chiefs can have the joy of knowing on such a personal level the impact of their life's work. How much is that worth? At my age the money matters little. The joy of my memories and the feeling of fulfillment through the good works of 'my kids' is immeasurable.

I've loved my own children, yet it is true that I loved all of the sporting youth in our town and in the state that I was lucky enough to be able to serve. I think in the end that my love didn't have to go to one group or the other. *Just as they say that God gives you no tribulation that you can't handle with His help, so it is that He gives no inspiration that can't be totally fulfilled. The game of life can indeed be Win-Win!*

Even though I've nearly reached the pauper stage financially due to expenses for the recent medical misfortunes of my lovely wife and myself, *I still feel like a billionaire for the things that I have taken part in to make the world a better place for our youngsters.*

Closing Thoughts

I have been fortunate indeed to have lived through the period (1919 to 2003 and counting) of the greatest evolution, expansion, growth, and progress ever in the history of our civilization in the fields of Sports, Medicine and Technology. I only hope and pray that our morals and values can keep up with and exceed the advances in these other areas. With a few severe exceptions, based upon my being the recipient of the absolutely phenomenal life saving, extending and enhancing care of today's medical profession, I can see that the progress in science *can* be matched by the progress in dedication to caring by our leading health professionals. Few can appreciate these heroes of our time until confronted with having to be taken care of by the likes of them. If today's youth can go forth in many fields to match the goodness and greatness of the best of our health care givers today, I think that we can be all right as a species. It won't, however, be at all easy. That's why we adults must do all that we can to impart wisdom and confidence to our youth.

We have progressed in just about everything except in that nations and religions are still not at peace with each other and in how greed sometimes overtakes the greater good that can be achieved by cooperative effort. We still have not, as a species, learned to live without war against each other **and without taking from ourselves by unjustly taking from another.** Sad to say, right here in our own country there still exists racism, jealously, harassment, discrimination, hatred & terrorist activity.

Why can't we live in peace and learn to settle our disputes and differences on places like the Athletic Fields, Basketball Courts and Arts Centers?

Jews, Muslims, Christians, Buddists, Hindu's and most of the rest, all know that *"those who pray together, stay together".* The problem is that between (and sometimes within) different sects, a very small percentage of the total population believe in the same rigid ways of seeing things. Perhaps just as 'ping pong diplomacy' helped open the door of communication and relations between the US and China 30 years ago, now, more than ever, we need to adopt a more 'neutral' and encompassing concept to bring us to mutually acceptable and beneficial prayer:

"Those who PLAY together, stay together."

I love my country and I am very grateful to my parents for having the foresight and for making the sacrifices to make the move from the 'Old Country' to come to America, the land of opportunity and freedom. Their move is the best thing that ever happened to our extended family. And most everyone in this country today has, in many ways, a similar background of one generation having sacrificed to pave the way for them. Our forebears gave their all to give us the opportunity to be born in the USA where we can live a happy life, free from despots and dictators. We must be aware of history so as to repeat the good of it, and avoid some of the unnecessary terrors that life can hold.

Now as I reach the end of my journey, I've been fortunate enough to have the opportunity to review key points of my life through the medium of writing these memoirs. With each review of my notes and quotes herein, I find myself in awe that with the help of my son Michael and others, I was able to compose such a meaningful and to me, at least, heart-warming story. Each time I read the funny stories I chuckle and laugh out loud. No matter how many times I reread the sad things that happened in my life, the tears still flow. I have to believe that in many ways this story of an early 20th century immigrant's life must mirror those of my contemporaries of *"the greatest generation"*. Writing these memoirs has been a very gratifying process that I recommend that others endeavor. The changes that our children and we have lived through encompass more than in any other epic in the history of humankind. And in our fast expanding yet closer knit world, both our challenges and our opportunities going forth are greater than ever.

"It is my fervent wish that you have enjoyed reading this book as much as I have enjoyed writing about **"*My Way*"**. In the end, the beauty of life is far richer than words can explain. Each of us has only our own little window on the grand scheme of things and our own unique part to play in helping things to unfold for the best. I pray that in some way my stories can serve to help you to renew your quest to do things in *Your Own Special God Given Way as best you understand it*. As my mentor Jim Buckley would say, in the end all that we can do, moment after moment, is to try our best, and then let God do the rest.

Hopefully for the better overall,
albeit sometimes for worse
when I acted small,
I'm satisfied to say
that everyday
I tried the best that I could
to do as I should
by doing things MY WAY.

Yes it was My Way.

"My Way"

And now, the end is near,
And so I face the final curtain.
My friends, I'll say it clear,
I'll state my case, of which I'm certain.
I've lived a life that's full,
I've traveled each and every highway,
And more, much more than this,
I DID IT MY WAY

Regrets I've had a few,
But then again, too few to mention.
I did what I had to do,
And saw it through, without exemption.
I planned each chartered course,
Each careful step along the byway.
But more, much more than this,
I DID IT MY WAY

Yes, there were times,
I'm sure you knew,
When I bit off more than I could chew,
But through it all, when there was doubt,
I ate it up, and spit it out.
I faced it all, and I stood tall,
AND DID IT MY WAY

I've loved, and laughed and cried,
And had my fill, my share of losing,
And now, as tears subside,
I find it all so amusing.
To think, I did all that,
And may I say, not in a shy way,
Oh no, Oh no not me,
I DID IT MY WAY

For what is a man, What has he got?
If not himself,
Then he has got to say the things
He truly feels,
And not the words of one who kneels.
The record shows,
I took the blows,
AND DID IT MY WAY.

YES, IT WAS MY WAY!

BRIDGEWATER-RAYNHAM SCHOOL'S FIRST ATHLETIC DIRECTOR
BRIDGEWATER (1952 – 1961)
BRIDGEWATER-RAYNHAM (1961 – 1983)

A message from "The Old Coach" Larry Folloni:

"To all the athletes who walk through this sports complex…

Be loyal to your God, your parents, your country,
your coaches and teachers, your teammates and
classmates, your fellow man, and to yourself.

Have fun—play hard, play fair.

Do your best and let God do the rest.

If you win, enjoy. If you lose,
be gracious and congratulate the winner.

Be compassionate and charitable to others."

Postscript

It's been said that great success can come from being able to find something that works, then replicating it. There is no shame in simply finding something good that someone else has done to replicate. I find it more fun to find something good and then *'break the mold'* to create something even more worthwhile to replicate. This creative process is an entirely individual yet God inspired endeavor. I support your efforts at recognizing and affirming your life's goals, in giving thanks for the inspiration and help pursuant and in taking action to fulfill them. *Let's Go!*

Helen looking out towards Legion Field from the porch of our 91 Bedford St. Home

As bad as things sometimes seem, as I contemplate Legion Field, I must admit that the future, for those astute enough to observe, watch, listen & learn and who are willing to apply concomitant foresight, logic, anticipation and action, looks pretty much like my past, which was pretty good. Indeed.

1st Overtime

COACHING TIPS
&
ALL TIME ALL STARS

Bonus Shots

"Now everybody pair up in threes."
Yogi Berra, coaching at a training camp

Coach Robert Folloni with his Overseas School of Rome Team, 1979

BONUS SHOTS

- Excerpts from the Old Coach's Upcoming Book
  "How to Become A Successful Basketball Coach"

- Comparison of Basketball in the '30's, '40's & 50's to the Present Era

- Some of My Favorite Coaching Colleagues

- My All Time All Star Teams

- "The Best of the Best--My All Time All Star Players"

- Achievements of Some Former Pupils

- Old Timer All Stars

- Events, Games and Teams I remember and "The one's who got away"

- My Best Comeback Teams

- Our Best Comeback Games

EXCERPTS FROM THE OLD COACH'S UPCOMING BOOK:

"How to Become A Successful Basketball Coach"

Many times including at Coaches Clinics and Conferences, I have been asked by my colleagues for tips on what led to the great success of our Basketball Teams. I will try here to share a few pointers and my philosophy on developing a high quality basketball program for the kids. Let me say in general, that no matter the organizational structure, the key nexus is that between the mentor and the student. A Good Teacher **can** be a Good Coach. A Good Coach **must** be a Good Teacher.

First and foremost, build a good Foundation

"A successful man is one who can lay a firm foundation with the bricks that others throw at him."
— Rabbi Sidney Greenberg

I started the kids out in our programs at a tender age. I had a ball in the hands of my own children while they were still in their baby crib! I don't believe in subjecting youngsters to any activity that will be a danger to their future physical or mental health, however I am a firm believer that all youngsters should start early to build their bodies to the maximum of their talents.

I organized the multiple stage Biddy League and Little League Programs in our town when I first arrived there to begin my teaching and coaching career in 1950. From these grade school programs the kids went on to various Junior High School programs, then to the Jayvee level before they reached the Varsity.

At all levels, we had a *No Cut Policy*. All of our Coaches were instructed to never release any youngsters. There are many *'Late Bloomers'* who are awkward as youngsters, and then as they mature they blossom into stars. The primary goal of our youth programs was to create an atmosphere where the youngsters had fun and enjoyment while learning basic rules, coordination and athletic habits.

Our Farm System became the envy of Coaches throughout the State. The results of implementing this extensive system were quite evident with the Three State Championship Teams that we had in close succession as soon as our first groups of youth graduated from all the levels in the late '50's and early '60's. Our town's teams and individual athletes continue to dominate in the state in part because my successors, many of who went through the programs since childhood themselves, have done a superlative job in carrying on and improving the programs.

To select my teams I would give all participants a basic physical fitness test that I designed to find their natural talents. These tests consisted of jumping, agility, and split-vision abilities. I found that the results of these tests were 99% accurate in selecting the top future players. (See the coming complete coaching guide book for details.)

"We are told that talent creates its own opportunities. But it sometimes seems that intense desire creates not only its own opportunities, but its own talents."
Eric Hoffer, American Philosopher, (1902 – 1983)

Another simple part of the evaluation process was having the players fill out a questionnaire to indicate their Name, Address, Phone Number, Age, Athletic background, etc., and asking them to write a short paragraph to explain why they were coming out for the sport. This helped me to *see how much desire they have to do whatever it takes* to make the team and how good they were at following instructions. Watching their response to this unconventional challenge also often gave me information and insights to assist later in motivating individuals.

Also of course, it is foundational that the kids have proper equipment and uniforms for their safety as well as for self-esteem and team identity building.

BE AN 'OWL & L': OBSERVE, WATCH, LISTEN & LEARN

*The wise old owl sat in an oak
The more he saw the less he spoke
The less he spoke the more he heard
Why can't we be like that old bird?*

Don't be afraid to be an *'OWL'*. Humble yourself. Observe-Watch-Listen & Learn: From your Assistant Coaches, your players and anyone else who might give you valuable insight to any problems, or any tips to improve your coaching.

You'll remember from the *'Team Rebuilding Years'* section how by being an *'OWL'* at a scrimmage where the Jayvees completely disassembled my Varsity, I developed *'The Folloni Special Press'*, which later raised havoc with all of our opponents and was a major factor in our championship runs.

And how I related in the *'Perfect Practice Makes Perfect'* section how Ted Williams, the greatest hitter in the history of baseball, asked me, a mere High School Coach, for some tips on hitting. Ted's being an *'OWL'*, always trying to learn something new from any source, certainly contributed to his greatness.

Ted reinforced in me that we can and should glean any bit of help from any source. The principle of *OWL learning* of course also yields very powerful results when applied in the midst of great successes. You'll recall how after he hit a great golf shot Ted stayed in place to practice the successful swing. And that his answer to my *'OWL'* inspired question was, *"LARRY, WHENEVER I DO SOMETHING RIGHT, I WANT TO REMEMBER WHAT I DID AND PRACTICE THAT, WHEN I DO SOMETHING WRONG I WANT TO FORGET IT IMMEDIATELY AND GO BACK TO PRACTICE WHAT I DID THAT WAS SUCCESSFUL."* I've always tried to remember and use this tremendous tip in my coaching, and it has paid *enormous* dividends.

The moral of the above examples is that you can learn from anyone if you use the *OWL* principles. There is nary a person too humble or too exalted to have something to teach. You are never too young or too old to learn. The learning process starts the day you are born and continues until the day you die.

Seek out those who have succeeded before you and ask them their advice. Most will be happy to share their wisdom. Indeed most people enjoy sharing the secrets of their success. It is reaffirming to them and by helping others improve it makes their world a better place. The ancient Greek axiom: *"If I stand taller than others it is because I have stood on the shoulders of giants."* applies to the shoulders of Jayvee Juniors *as well as* to those of Major League Legends.

BE POSITIVE, NOT NEGATIVE

Being positive will add to your success. Negativity ends in failure.

Dwell and work on the good. Acknowledge the bad or defeat as something that you don't want to repeat, then forget it. Don't dwell on past mistakes. The time and energy wasted on that could be far more profitably invested in identifying and practicing the good. Another way to look at this is that we should often try to count our blessings so that we can build upon or *appreciate* them. This advice may seem simple and trite, but the simple truth is that it works. The 1944 song *'Mister In-Between'* by Johnny Mercer lifted our country's spirits for the final push to win WWII, and helped give us the momentum to power the post war booms that we've enjoyed. This popular song, which was also recorded at different times by many others, including Frank Sinatra, Bing Crosby and the Andrews Sisters says:

"You've got to accentuate the positive
Eliminate the negative
Latch on to the affirmative (and)
Don't mess with Mister In-Between!"

My son the salesman moves much more product than the next best in his field. He does this in part because at every opportunity he is far more positive in his attitude and expressions than the next guy. He doesn't encumber his prospective customers with reasons *'why not'*, but keeps them focussed on *'why it is so'* that his product is of great benefit to them.

This advice also works wonders in motivating kids of all ages. Remember how my greatest boss Mr. Serge Bernard would 'catch me doing something right' and praise me on that before mentioning what the problem was that we were going to overcome together? And then he'd reinforce my ability to do my part by engaging me in a refocused productive task. No extraneous chatter went in-between, Mister. Serge was a great teacher. So as a coach, if the kid can't master a move, bring him back to the foundational skill for that move to that he had mastered, reengage him in drills on that with attendant praise for doing that right. With confidence restored, he'll be ready for more task learning and appropriate repetitive drills to establish and reinforce it.

NEVER CRITICIZE A PLAYER DURING A GAME OR IN PUBLIC

"You can't let praise or criticism get to you.
It's a weakness to get caught up in either one."
-Legendary UCLA Basketball Coach John Wooden

He's right of course, and I have more thoughts on putting both praise and criticism into proper perspective and utilization. If something truly needs to be criticized, *the Coach must carefully control when and how valid criticism will take place, or there is no way that it can be constructive.* Save your criticism for practice sessions or talk to the player individually at the proper time and place to discuss and correct mistakes. This simply goes back to eliminating unnecessary or perceived negatives. **Hu**miliating someone in front of others is a **H**u**g**e negative that comes from a coach's ignorant **Hu**bris and that can do little but **Hu**rt the victim's motivation to ***hustle*** *for you.* Of course it can motivate him to **Hu**rl away his sporting career with you! **H**ighly **U**nnecessary.

REMEMBER TO PRAISE PLAYERS WHEN WARRANTED

A word of praise will do more good than a million of criticism.

Praise should be used before and after constructive criticism, especially during the long trust building stages of the Coach-Player relationship. A coach should show the youngster what he did right; what the point of departure from being right was; and what the correct course is to the winning end. Show them by your every gesture and the inflexion of your voice that you are confident that they can pass muster to master the task at hand. **Students and Players love to perform for Teachers and Coaches who show faith in them.**

Praise by itself without any criticism, of course is great. After each game, for example, we always ceremoniously called out the player who had the most steals and gave him the "Hawk" award. Similarly the player with the most rebounds got the "Bear" award. Other awards for most assists, hustle, etc., were also often awarded.

Of course false praise won't work. Kids can pick up a phoney manipulator a mile away. The Coach must truly attend to **O**bserving the basics of what the player is doing, and provide detailed and accurate feedback to help establish and reinforce the youngster's own skills at self-assessment. When a great deal of trust is achieved over time, then you can be a little less vigilant to the need for praise before every critique. *Don't, however, **ever** take it for granted that any kid has gained enough confidence to take little but criticism, even if it is meant to be 'constructive'!* Life and sports can be tough, and all of our spirits need to be lifted a little everyday. The upbeat ambience created by a few *true* compliments can pervade the atmosphere of a gymnasium and inspire teammates to boost one another towards greatness.

HAVE A NO CUT POLICY
(EXCEPT FOR VERY SERIOUS DISCIPLINE PROBLEMS)

Guard well your spare moments. They are like uncut diamonds.
Discard them and their value will never be known.
Improve them and they will become the brightest gems in a useful life.
　　　　　　　　　　-Ralph Waldo Emerson

Emerson spoke of guarding spare moments, I speak of the momentous potential of spare guards, (and forwards and centers) who may some day become stars. Never, ever, cut any players for lack of ability or size. Some kids are late bloomers and when they mature they may turn out to be real stars. For example, Stan Smudin was a gangling 6' 4" kid who was very awkward and didn't start playing Basketball until he was a Junior in High School. I turned him over to my Jayvee Coach, Bernie Chestna with instructions to play Stan as much as possible and work on his agility and rebounding. By the time Stan became a Senior he was ready to become our starting center and was a great cog in our winning the Massachusetts State Championship in 1956. Also remember a guy named Michael Jordan. Do you know that he was cut from his Jayvee team while in High School? Also cut from secondary school hoop programs were Bill Russell and Bob Cousy! Imagine if these three of the greatest-all-time players didn't have such great determination and practice ethics and self-confidence? They may have been discouraged from continuing basketball. Only their opponents would have been happy about that. My son Robert was a grade school physical education teacher for the now famous Kobe Bryant at the American Overseas School of Rome. Imagine if Bobby had had the shortsightedness or the disposition to make the gym an unpleasant or unwelcome place for this youngster? *(Then again, maybe that was one time Bob really could have helped the Celtics!?)*

Remember the story of when I was unceremoniously cut from my Jr. Legion Team before even trying because the Coach thought I was a *'WOP'* who needed to eat more spaghetti to grow first? I was disappointed, **hu**rt and **hu**miliated. Luckily it didn't discourage me forever, and it did help to motivate me to come back and give a 'WALLOP OF A WHIPPING' to that Coach's teams in later years.

All kids deserve an opportunity to play and be a part of a team. If varsity player's talents are limited then let him play on the Junior Varsity level *or **create** another level for them to have fun and be prepared to bloom later in life*. She or he will eventually find the way to become a star in their own right.

ACTUAL PRACTICE PRINCIPLES AND TIPS

"When a man says he approves of something in principle,
it means he hasn't the slightest intention of carrying it out in practice."
- Otto von Bismarck

Work on the basic fundamentals of the game. Focus predominately on these essentials, and secondarily on plays and other complex schemes. Make the basics 2nd nature to the players, and then the learning and execution of more advanced methods, and their application under game conditions can and will flow far more seamlessly. Even when our best teams were well along the road to Championships, we still started every practice with 1/2 hour or so of various **basic drills**. Here are a few conceptual items to cover to help keep the drills productive and focussed:

- ◆ PASSING: Stress the accuracy and crispness of passes. When I say accurate, I mean get the ball to your teammate in the exact spot that he will be shooting or passing from. If he has to move right or left or up or down to receive the ball, it can throw off his natural motion and that fraction of a second lost may give the defense the chance to hamper the play or otherwise cost a chance to score. Remember Larry Bird, the Boston Celtics Great. He was a master at deception but his passes were *ALWAYS PRECISELY ON TARGET* so that his teammates didn't have to break their rhythm in preparing to shoot. Jason Kidd is the same. By keeping his delivery in sync with his teammate's location and ability range, the receiver is able to smoothly finish off in a way that he is comfortable with. For a successful pass it takes two to tango, the passer and his teammate the receiver. The receiver must at all times have a hand up to show the exact target to be hit by the passer. In all of our drills this is emphasized. The receiver must also come hard, fast and with good timing to meet the ball. (The 'fast break' and 'back-door' passes are two exceptions to 'meeting the ball'.)

- ◆ DRIBBLING: In order to maintain full control of the ball push it down with your finger tips, not with the palm of your hands. Your fingers are the eyes. Keep your head up. Never look down at the ball. Let your fingers do the watching. Use your body to protect the ball at all times. Whenever possible while practicing on your own, dribble two balls at a time. Dribbling one will seem easy after this. Rarely should you dribble when you have a teammate open ahead of you, unless you are making a *quick* maneuver to clearly get your teammate into even better position for an easy shot. In clinics I participated in with Red Auerbach at the Boston Garden, he too had the pet peeve that one should avoid dribbling forward when a good pass is possible. One great team drill I employed to encourage passing was fast breaking with a deflated ball!

♦ REBOUNDING: Teach your players the proper way to **block out**. This is a forgotten art on playgrounds these days. Teach all players, short and tall how to properly use their arms and their butt to keep their opponents out of likely rebounding position.

(I called the butt 'the Professor', to emphasize the importance of its use in teaching the opposition a lesson in court and board control. Here Steve Pivacek of our 1961 State Champions effective keeps bigger opponents at bay with his professor.)

When an opponent shoots for the basket, don't watch the ball in flight, use your split vision for that. Do follow the shooter or the man you are guarding and use your quick foot movement and bent leg & torso positioning for strong self–balance and your fixed extended elbows & 'Professor' to keep him as far away from the hoop as possible. *Awareness, balance and positioning are the keys to rebounding.* Don't just move towards the hoop at the shot. Use the time of the ball in flight to **establish your optimum position** between the goal and the person that you are guarding. Coaches should walk through lessons with players using line props to demonstrate critical angle sets to impress upon all the importance of creating them.

A. The further away from the likely landing area of a shot the opposition is held, the exponentially larger the area that you control.

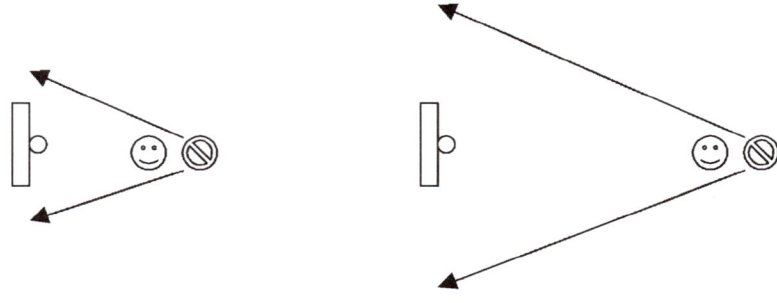

B. *More importantly, the closer you are to the person you are blocking out, the longer you delay his movement and the greater the size of the area that you own.*

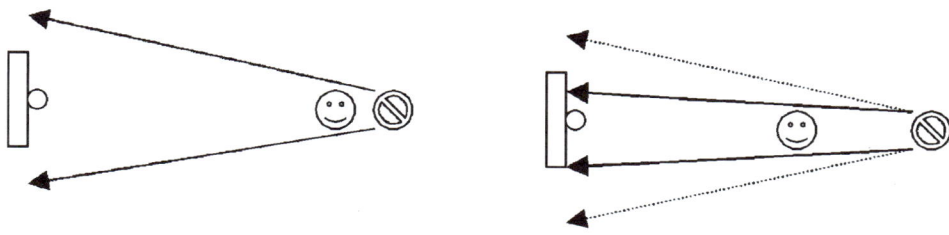

So the further away from the hoop that you can position your opponent, and the closer you can get to him while staying between him and the basket, the higher the likelihood that you'll get the rebound. Teaching a player to grow 6 inches is very difficult to do but a coach can 'elevate' his players closer to the rim with jumping and conditioning exercises specifically incorporated into fun basketball drills and competitive contests. (Contests can make hard work become fun during practices.)

Size, strength and weight training help in rebounding, but balance, technique and awareness of court positioning and likely rebound direction matter more. Mix that all with desire and you've got a Dennis Rodman, Bill Russell, Charles Barkley, or Jason Kidd-like boards master. Note that none of these dominant NBA rebounders were usually the tallest on the court, and that Kidd was usually the shortest.

- FAKING: FAKE! FAKE! FAKE! I can't over stress the importance of good faking. Unless you have an uncontested play, always, every time you get the ball, make a fake to throw the defense off. Make the defensive man commit himself, and then you will be free to maneuver. The offensive player has the tremendous advantage of knowing what he or she wants to do, while the defender must react to what is seen. If the defender finally gets wise to your faking patterns, then you can fake the fake and go strong straight. Faking (and crucial communication between teammates) also extends to **eye movement**. Don't telegraph your passes. Look one way and pass another, once again using that crucial peripheral vision. (As with all of these areas, specific drills can be designed to train and perfect the right responses.)

- RUNNING and JUMPING: Get your players in condition to last the rigors of a hard fought contest and still have the stamina to survive the last few minutes of the game. They also need to be in good enough shape to make it through the entire season. When I say running drills, I don't mean just running up and down the floor. Why not save time and player boredom by incorporating running into learning drills that will in turn be incorporated into your game plan? You can condition your players with Fast Break Drills with a Basketball just as well as if you just run them up and down the floor without any other goal in mind. Leg strength exercises and distance running endurance regimens for the off season can be programmed.

◆ DEFENSE: Good defense is the *Key* to any successful team. On my pressing teams our best offense was generated by our defense! Teach your pupils how to crouch properly in order to keep their balance. Teach them to shift their weight on either foot as needed. Side-to-side shuffling drills are useful here.

Good quick hands play an important part in good defense. Once again, drills for properly stabbing and swiping without reaching or leaning in, while keeping balance and control can be devised and practiced. Teach your players to come in under the arms when trying to steal the ball.

Stay under control and don't be fooled by a fake. *Keep one eye on your opponent's naval. That is the key as to where he is going.* The body won't move if the navel doesn't.

Teach the kids to overplay the offense to their weakness. 99% of High School Students cannot move equally well with the ball to their weak hand side as they can to their strong hand side. So if a player is right-handed, his defender should park himself exaggeratedly on his right to force him to make the unnatural move left. Even if beaten to the weak side, teammates can help out, and the offensive player is far more likely to make a bad shot or pass from this unaccustomed position. When overplayed, many offensive players will feign to their weak side and then go right back to their strong side. This tactic should be carefully practiced and monitored to make sure that the defender doesn't bite on feigned fakes. Defenders must make an offensive player PROVE that he can be consistently effective to his weak side. A side benefit of practicing overplaying defense is that your own players on the practice squads get more accustomed to going to their weak side.

On defense as on offense, **THE CARDINAL RULE OF BASKETBALL** is to *Never take your eye off the ball.* If you are in a man-to-man defense and not denying the closest pass, you may want to make a triangle pointing to the ball and your man ('ball-you-man'). There are certain complexities to these concepts that I'll reserve for the next book. Basketball is both a simple, yet intricate game.

There is no shortcut. Good defense is hard work. It is smart work. It provides however great rewards. It leads to steals, bad shots, fast breaks and frustration of the opponent. Commend your defensive successes whenever possible.

- ANTICIPATION and SPLIT VISION: I really don't know exactly how you teach these skills. I guess they are natural instincts, but I am convinced they can be improved with imbedded *AWARENESS of their importance* and constant practice. One of the slowest players I ever had play for me became one of my best anticipators in the Folloni Special Press because we worked on this with the Press Drills that I had developed.

- TRICKS AND SCHEMES TO PRESS ON & PROSPER: Being only 5' 7" tall and a fly weight, I had to scheme up a few tricks as a player in order to survive the competition inherent in all sports. As with all sports my knowledge of the rules of basketball allowed me to have a great advantage over players who did not fully know them.

Then there was just heads-up, clever play. I would actually hide myself behind an opponent while he was waiting to take a pass inbound from his teammate and at the last instant I would anticipate the pass and break in front of him for the steal.

I taught my kids how to build a two-man trap around an opponent with the ball. We'd drill them to get into a predatory position, and to pounce in unison at the right moment setting and balancing their bodies to 'cage' the victim with synchronized frantic arm waving high and low, and measured jabs and swipes at the ball. This in an of itself yielded many steals, but it was the second wave of defenders perfectly positioned in waiting behind the apparently open teammates of the victim who typically sprang forward as drilled for the steal. If by some miracle the opponents survived the first wave, our temporarily beaten players were trained to revolve around to cover the next apparently open guy. Meanwhile one of the two on trap had been trained to anticipate the almost inevitable eventual interception and had already sprung free to the hoop for the pass and lay-up. Every Folloni press maneuver and response was drilled until the reaction was automatic and every conversion was quick and deadly effective. In this case we broke it down into very specific and coordinated "Recovery, Intercept and 'Break to the Hoop' drills.

Many coaches these days have abandoned the press because they think that it doesn't work. I've got news for them, it still does, and at every level. The problem is that the coaches don't take the time to properly learn and teach it. My successor Larry Fisher did. And combined with his own ideas, skills and dedication (and some great student-athletes who were attracted to our town), he has made his basketball teams perennial league and state champs or contenders.

In the *'Go to College'* section of this book I related how while playing for BU in a showdown game against Harvard to determine who'd qualify for the NCAA tournament, I learned a great trick from Saul Mariaschin, their star guard who went on to play professional basketball.

I had gone on a 9-point scoring spree and Harvard's coach called a time out and assigned Saul to stick with me like glue, which he did by *actually grabbing my trunks and holding on to them* so that I couldn't get away from him. I kept complaining to the officials, but to no avail. He shut me out from any more scoring and Harvard went on to defeat us.

As a coach I'd teach my most athletic short player to line up behind the foul shooter to silently spook him. Then when the ball was in the air, I'd have my guy loop around the key and come up between the baseline and the opposing big men, who by that time would be coming down with any rebound and concentrating on our big guy who was on his back. Our little guy would be waiting beneath, with arm stiff and straight up ready to easily scoop the ball from the bottom. Once again this was drilled, effective and demoralizing to the opponents.

I'd tell you many more tricks, but then I might have to make you swear to keep the secret. Unless, of course, you buy my entire forthcoming book which details many tricks and hundreds of other Successful Coaching Practices.

PLANNING PRACTICE AND GAME SCHEDULES

"Fill the unforgiving minute with 60 seconds worth of distance run."
-Rudyard Kipling (1865-1910)

Plan your schedules in advance. Set time limits for each drill and stick to it. You may have to make revisions from time to time to correct problems that may arise but for the most part stick to your scheduled time limits. The kids need order and organization in their life, and their busy parents also need to plan. Respect them and they'll respect you. Set a good example. Also if everyone knows how much time the practice lasts, they know they have to make the best of every minute.

TEACHING AND COACHING

Get down to the level of the pupils.

This is so important. I don't care how knowledgeable or how proficient your are in the sport, if you cannot convey your knowledge to the pupil, all the teaching is to no avail.

I will cite you an example of this theory. One of our Coaches we hired at the new B-R Regional High School was a young man who was very talented and very knowledgeable of his sport. He had been a capable assistant at Boston University and later coached at a High School. His problem was very simple. He was trying to teach High School pupils and using terminology that even many College pupils would have trouble relating to. The results were quite evident as his teams floundered for a few years until he finally gave up in frustration. He later went on to become a very successful administrator in another school system.

On the other hand, the students need to be challenged. Remember, we're trying to develop well rounded 'STUDENT-Athletes' who'll be prepared for everything that life throws at them. *(Why else would I quote - Otto von Bismarck and Rudyard Kipling in my coaching section?)*

DRILLS

*Draw up your drills on the basis of what they will do
to enhance your style of play in a game.*

Don't have drills for the sake of drill, but be creative and draw up drills that will actually be of help in game situations. The best thing that ever helped me in my career was the night that I was inspired enough by the Jayvee's inspired practice success against my varsity to stay awake to draw up my drills for *the Folloni Special Press*. We worked feverishly every day at practice on these drills and they really paid off, as the repetitions became instinctive reactions during games.

Here's one important tip on how to implement drills or set plays:

I.   EXPLAIN THE DRILL OR PLAY
II.   DEMONSTRATE BY WALKING THROUGH THE DRILL OR PLAY
III.   GO SEMI--SPEED WITH THE DRILL
IV.   THEN GO FULL SPEED WITH THE DRILL
V.   AND REPEAT THE DRILL OVER AND OVER UNTIL IT BECOMES INSTINCTIVE REACTION.

I learned this valuable lesson early in my coaching career, while an assistant football coach at Dighton High School under Coach Leo DeMarco, a Fordham football star. Coach DeMarco had very few set plays, but he was a stickler on fundamentals and on the walk through method as explained above.

SET PLAYS

Don't spend too much time in practice on set plays.

This is especially true at the High School level where probably less than 10% of the time in a game is actually involved with set plays. Why give up valuable practice time on 10% of your game? Why not devote 90% of your time to fundamentals and to the drills that will actually help you in game situations?

Said the late Lenny Dempsey of Medford, coach of New England Champion Malden Catholic, Europe Military Men's League Champs and DODDS American Schools in Italy League Champs: ***"I NEVER drew and X or an O. The ONLY statistic I ever kept was how many shots we were able to take. If we took 90 shots or more, I knew we would win."*** Lenny was a successful believer in 4 quarters of the exciting brand of multi-player trapping defense and fast breaking, and likewise, made wise use of his practice time on fundamentals.

DON'T OVER PRACTICE

"You get the team ready in training camp,
and you keep the practices after that short and brisk.
You try to keep your players fresh and mentally ready to go."
-Red Auerbach

I don't mean don't practice a lot, because repetition of practice is what makes a player. What I mean by over practice is DON'T BURN OUT YOUR TEAM IN PRACTICE, ESPECIALLY THE DAY BEFORE A GAME, AND PARTICULARLY DURING TOURNAMENT TIME. SAVE THE PLAYER'S ENERGY FOR GAMES. Adhering to this is one of the reasons for our great success in Tournament play. The time to really over work is during the first 3 weeks of practice when you really work your players on fundamentals and conditioning. The key to a successful season depends so much on those first 3 weeks of practice, and on encouraging off-season conditioning.

MAKE NOTES CONSTANTLY

Whenever and wherever you are, when you think of an idea or a scheme that will be of help to your team, write a note to yourself immediately. Don't wait, you may forget the idea and it will be gone forever. Some of my best schemes and ideas have come to me while lying in bed. That is why I have a pen and pad on the night table and I have trained myself to record the ideas, then forget about them and fall back to sleep, confident that I'll plug them into my system come morning.

MOTIVATE

Learn to motivate to get the most out of the talent that is available.

A little humor and a little Knute Rockne style exhortations both have their place. You must truthfully review what is transpiring to let your players know that you are on the same page with their feelings and impressions, then remind them of what they have done and can do right, and paint the **accurately feasible** *'from zero to hero step-by-step winning scenario'*. Make small objectives pursuant to the goal, and build confidence with achieving these realistic incremental steps, counting successes at each stage on the way. If the kids know that you care about them, that you are always there for them and that you'll accept them even if you refuse to accept their mistakes, because you have conveyed trust in a successful future for them, they will be motivated to generate wins.

Speaking of motivating reminds me of one of my ploys that I used on officials. During the half time of one of our games, our locker room was located next door to their quarters, well within earshot of my half time pep talk to our team. My last words to my players, good loud and clear so that the officials next door could hear was, "Boys the Officials are doing a great job. Let's go back out there and do likewise." Come the second half we had gained two more players for our team! Conversely, if our team is way ahead in a game, I might go off on an official to get his attention to make an especially strong point. I've even done it to the extent to where I'd get thrown out of the game. Why? I couldn't get the same important point across too emphatically in a closely contested game where I might risk ejection or hard feelings on the spot. I'd rather that the official who I'll see in a later important game gets to feeling sorry for booting me when things cool down, but remembers my point, and maybe even feels he owes me one for booting me when the game wasn't even on the line.

The greatest success in basketball and in life goes to those who have a clear vision of what they want, and a highly developed desire to get it. Spud Webb, the 5'6" pro phenom of the '80's, was once asked why he often drove right down the lane that was so crowded with giant opponents. His answer was:

"Because that's where the goal is!"

Of course ambitious kids need to have their motivation nurtured with good guidance from their teachers and coaches. Note what renowned lousy team player Willy Sutton said when asked why he robbed banks:

"Because that's where the money is!"

LEARN TO RELAX

"Only the organized can loaf with Peace of Mind"

I know it is not easy to relax in the heat of a closely contested ball game and I was probably guiltier than anyone was because I was so hyper during many phases of my career. Later in my coaching days I learned to control my emotions and was actually a better coach and made much better decisions at crucial times. I employed several techniques for this, some were as simple as quite prayer before the game in my office and others were as innovative as using a tape recorder to record my concerns during game action. This got the pressure off my chest and into the 1st stage of a system to where I could work with it. (It was also a way for me to make notes constantly, as recommended above.)

Remember it is still only a game. And whether we win or lose, tomorrow the sun will rise again. So take the time to take the wife out to dinner and RELAX.

USE OF STRATEGY – KEEP ABREAST OF THE TIMES

*Don't be afraid to change your tactics if the need arises.
Be ahead of the times, always stay at least one step ahead of your opponent.*

As game situations change you may need to change your strategy. One example of strategy that paid off for us came during the finals of the 1960 Championship game at the Boston Garden. We were matched to play Marshfield High School, who we had defeated twice earlier in the season in real close encounters. One was an overtime win, when Dave Messaline scored the winning hoop on a break away after a steal. The other game we won by a couple of points in regulation. Their All-Scholastic star Eddie Fonseca had scored about 30 points in each game. As I explained in detail in the 'Glory Days' section, by watching movies of Fonseca I spotted a weakness that when explained to our guard Paul Pallatroni, allowed him to hold Fonseca scoring and Marshfield down to assure us the Championship.

In 1961 Weston High School, our opponent during the championship game at the Boston Garden, had scouted us real well and they were concentrating on packing the defense in the key to stop our two key pivot men Steve "Froggy" Prophett and Steve "Checkers" Pivacek. We called a time out and Checkers said, "Coach they're playing Froggy and me real close in the pivot area and follow us wherever we go."

I immediately instructed the two Steves to move out to the sidelines. The bait worked. With the opponent's two big men following the two Steves out of the pivot area it opened up the lane for our back court men, Paul Pallatroni, Dave Messaline and Larry Folloni, Jr. They took turns going one on one with their defensive opponents and driving down the middle of the lane, which was then wide open. Paul Pallatroni had a field day. When he didn't score on his drives, he was fouled on his way in to the hoop. Just coincidentally Paul was a $90\%^+$ shooter from the free throw line.

The strategy worked to a 'T' and we won our 2nd consecutive State Championship quite handily. This strategy would have been to no avail, however, if our talented back court men had not been drilled through the farm system in their fundamentals of dribbling and driving to the hoop. Without these fundamentals, all the strategy and set plays in the world would be fruitless.

GOALS AND PHILOSOPHY

Foster teamwork at all times.

If you want to be a winner in basketball it must be:

ALL FOR ONE AND ONE FOR ALL

The epitome of this was my 'Dream-Teamwork' Championship Game of 1956 against Wayland, where all five of our starting players scored in double figures.

Of course the limit of this is that you never compromise the health, safety or morals of any player for the good of the rest. In all things do what is in the best interests of the future of the kids.

> *REMEMBER THAT THINGS DON'T JUST HAPPEN,*
> *YOU HELP MAKE THEM HAPPEN.*

A SAMPLING OF COACH FOLLONI'S BASKETBALL DRILLS
(See the coming complete coaching guide book for details.)

The Star Drill: This drill received rave accolades from the coaches who attended the State Tournament games at the Boston Garden. This was one of the classier pre-game warm-up drills that announced to all that your team was well trained and disciplined. It stressed passing accuracy, alertness, and team coordination. John Killilea of Silver Lake and Melrose High Schools, and later of the Milwaukee Bucks Professional basketball team under coach Don Nelson, utilized this drill to great effectiveness and acclaim.

The Folloni Special Press Drills: Thanks to that gang of Jayvees who gave me the idea to develop these press drills.

Fast Break Drills:- (Look down the floor first) These fast break drills were right from Frank Keany's "Firehouse" Rhode Island great teams and Red Auerbach's Celtics fast breaking teams.

Fake & Shooting Drills: When you think you have faked enough, fake again. Let's face it. What is more fun that shooting? Good drills and shooting contests make it even more fun. There should be A BALL for EVERY KID, both at practices and at home. Instill in the players that it is worse to practice 'lazy shooting' than to practice shooting at all. Shooting drills should be fast and simulate game speed and pressure. 10 minutes of fast paced shooting drills will be better than 30 minutes of 'shooting around'. (There are mechanics of shooting also. THESE should NOT be taught at a fast pace.) Contrary to the more rigid Europeans and International players, Americans allow for more flexibility in shooting styles. I agree with the American style, but please do not avoid teaching the mechanics, including concentration, eye-rim contact, arm, ball and finger position, follow through, arc, and the use of the legs and body in balance, direction, rhythm and power of the shot. Foul shots must be practiced each day, and often under simulated pressure. Oh yes, let us include the 'forgotten art' of following one's own shot for second and third chances. Not all other sports allow you to hustle your way into an instant 'Mulligan'. Mulligans are constantly right there for the taking. You just have to want them.

Rebound Drills: With the right attitude and training any player can become at least 'the Garbage Man' if not the 'Chairman of the Boards'

Intercept Drills: My Assistant Coach Jim Swan thought that these drills were crazy but after becoming a head coach he realized their true value and worth

Steal The Ball Drills: Dave Messaline was a master at this drill, as was my entire backcourt in my 1967 team. They used it countless times in games to steal the ball from unsuspecting opponents.

Defensive Drills: We called them the "Defensive Dogs".

Foul Shooting Drill combined with our Press: This is one of our most important drills that we used faithfully at the end of every practice. It not only helped our foul shooting percentage go up but it was the catalyst for the start of our Special Press.

Health allowing, I hope to collaborate with my son Coach Bob Folloni on a full length fully illustrated basketball coaching manual and video. Watch for it!

Son's Michael and Robert with Red Auerbach and defensive dogs Saysha & Dolly.

COMPARISON OF BASKETBALL IN THE '30'S, '40'S & 50'S TO THE PRESENT ERA

I've been asked by my friend Donny Strong, #23, of the 1956 Championship Team, to compare the game of basketball as it was back in the 30's, 40's and 50's to how it is played today, and to give a brief history of the State Secondary School Tournaments.

Let me begin with my introduction to the game back in 1935 when my High School Coach, Lester Lane talked me into coming out for the School Basketball Team. Prior to this my only experience with the game was when we took a medal rim from an old wine barrel and nailed it on to an electric light pole to use as a hoop to shoot baskets with a makeshift ball.

The game has come a long way from the day that Canadian born Physical Education Teacher and Minister James Naismith installed the first peach basket hoops at the YMCA in Springfield, MA in 1891. His original game had only 13 rules, including:

> "If either side makes three consecutive fouls
> it shall count as a goal for the opponents.
> (Consecutive means without the opponents in the meantime making a foul)."

I don't know whether or not this was the original anti- "hac a shac" rule. When I played my first organized game of basketball in High School we used the rule of having a jump ball at center court after every basket. In my senior year 1937, I went through the transition of this game from the jump ball after every basket to taking the ball out of bounds after each basket. I must admit that this one rule change alone has been the greatest boon to the present day game of basketball.

Not only did this give the smaller players a more equal opportunity to compete but it also speeded up the play and created greater spectator interest. Prior to this rule change, the game of basketball was monopolized by tall players and relegated to having a big center to control the tap to some tall forwards and to go on with set plays from the jump ball. This jump ball process was dull and boring to fans and players.

The enthusiasm and popularity of the game was never more evident than with the 'March Madness' that grew at the end of each Basketball season with High School and College Tournaments springing up all over the Country. My own Tournament experiences started with the Old South Shore H.S. Tourney. Our team won the Championship in 1936 and in 1937 we were the finalist, losing to the Class "A"

Attleboro team by a 'high' score of 24 to 22. In those days, games were low scoring affairs. It was a rarity for a team to score more than 20 points in a game.

All sports suffered during WWII, but soon after those War Years, in the late 40's the game really began to flourish. Outdoor basketball courts sprung up all over. They became a haven for kids from the affluent suburbs as well as for under privileged children in the cities. The ghetto's of the '50's and '60's became the breeding grounds for the basketball stars of the future. 'One on one' and 'three on three' games were prevalent anywhere that limited playground space would allow.

With the end of the War, new gymnasiums were being built all over the country and the popularity of the game increased a thousand-fold with both the players and spectators. In Colleges the NIT Basketball Tournament was the center of national attention at the end of each season. In the '50's, the NCAA Basketball Tournament took over prominence as it had by then grown to its present 64 team extravaganza.

In Massachusetts High School competition the Old South Shore Tournament was played in the YMCA 'Bandbox', which had a circular track around the mezzanine level of the gym that took the shooting corners out of the playing area. We went from this regional Tournament on to the State Tournament, which had its beginning when **Henry McCarthy** founded it

After a few years of playing the Tech Tourney in the MIT Gym (The name *'Tech'* Tourney came from the Massachusetts Institute of TECHNOLOGY!), the Tournament became so popular that it was transferred to the old Boston Garden. I have many fond memories from while I was still a student at BU, of taking in the High School Tournament games with teams from Durfee, New Bedford, Brockton, Somerville, and Quincy to name a few of the outstanding teams of the '40's.

Sellout crowds of 13,909 were the rule at these highly contested games. The enthusiasm and gaiety of the players and spectators was mind-boggling. The Bands blaring, the crowds yelling and the confetti blowing down from the balconies like a Northeast Blizzard it was an electrifying spectacle to behold.

I become an active participant in this great tournament during the '50's. Following my graduation from Boston University I started my Coaching career and became very active in the State High School Athletic Planning Activities. This popular State Tournament had grown from its original 8 teams by invitation only, with One Class made up of the larger High Schools in the State, to where it added more teams and a Class B Tournament to the fanfare.

This went along for several years until I finally convinced the State Principals Association that the smaller schools should be given the opportunity to play in the

State Tournament in their own class. This was over the objections of the Original Director, Henry McCarthy who steadfastly insisted that the Tournament be held exclusively for the larger schools. My crusade for equality for the smaller schools paid off for us later in the 50's as our Bridgewater High Teams enjoyed the success of winning three State Championships in five years.

An ironical twist to Henry McCarthy's objections to the smaller schools becoming involved in this great tournament came about several years later. Henry's son became the Basketball Coach at Chelmsford High School and his Class C team was the winner of that division one year in the early 60's. At the end of this cherished triumph by his son's team, Henry, Sr. proudly boasted to the press that watching his son come away with the Class C State Championship was one of the greatest thrills of his life. If I had not fought so hard to have the smaller schools added to this great tournament, Henry Sr. would never have experienced this great thrill. Like some before and many after him who gave much to the game in Massachusetts, Henry deserved to gain some added satisfaction in spite of some regrettable decisions earlier in his career.

Much to the pleasure of the spectators it was also in the '50's that the game was changing from low scoring defensive events to high scoring fast breaking games. With the more free-wheeling fast breaking styles came the onset of one hand shooters, the twisting turn around shots, the dunk shots, the more complex zone and man to man switching defenses, the pressing defenses, the three point shots, etc.

Among the more revolutionary rule changes were the 3-second rule, which kept big men from so dominating the key, and allowed all 10 men on the court to be more involved in the game and the 24-second rule, which prevented the boring slow-down offenses. Both rules sped up the game and forced all players to become more proficient at the most exciting part of the game: ***SCORING!***

Here's some of my impressions about some of the changes that have evolved over the years in the game of Basketball:

THE ONE HAND SHOT: When I first started playing this game in the early '30's, if anyone took a one hand shot he was promptly taken out of the game and censured by the Coach. It was all 'Two Handed Set Shots' in those days. My son Larry tells me that it was "Hank Luisetti" of Stanford University who was responsible for the acceptance of the now very popular and very exciting 'One-Hand Shot'. Luisetti changed the sport when he introduced his one-handed shot at New York's Madison Square Garden during a Dec. 30, 1936 game against Long Island University. It makes a lot of sense in today's fast pace game to be able to get the one hand shot off a fraction of a second sooner to avoid having it blocked. A one-hand shot is also more accurate if done correctly with the wrist and pointing fingers, as there are fewer mechanics to go wrong with one hand than there are with two.

TWISTING TURN AROUND SHOTS: Today's players must out of necessity be adept at faking, dribbling, and handling the ball in such a manner as to outfox the defense with sophisticated moves such as the quick twisting turn around shot. Of course no matter how athletic a player is, the basic tenents of body balance, shot selection and practice makes this work reasonably consistently or not.

FOUL SHOTS: Here again we go back to the '30's when the underhand and two hand foul shot were in vogue. Nowadays you very seldom see anyone using the under hand or the two hand shots. Wilt Chamberlain had great success with the underhand foul shot, as did Rick Barry. I've found it a good starter for smaller pre-teens who cannot yet reach the hoop overhand. I thought that Shaq O'Neil should try it to help him put an end to the 'Hack-A-Shac' defenses that exploited his weakness from the line. He, finally, however, just put in good old fashioned long and hard practice to mightily improve this area of his game and his related all around effectiveness. By the way, Shac's little dog is named "Brick"!

THE DUNK SHOT: Although the 'Slam' gets a lot of ohh's and ahh's from crowds, my impressions of it from a coaching viewpoint are on the negative side. To me it is nothing more than *'Hot-Dogging'* by the modern spoiled players looking for attention. I suppose it can have some intimidation or rally building value, but still in my mind nothing takes the place of a strong and sure conventional lay-up shot. Maybe it's the difference between how Jerry Rice and Terrell Owens make a touchdown. Are Rice or his team any the less for being swift, sure and matter of fact in putting up the points without drawing the ire of those who've been shown up? Then again, with these huge athletic guys of today on defense playing 'above the rim', maybe sometimes a dunk is the only way to be sure that the points are delivered without deflection.

THE FAST BREAKING GAME: The Fast Breaking game as was sensationalized in the '40's by Coach Keaney and his Rhode Island State College Team and was perfected by Red Auerbach and his Boston Celtics is the epitome of Basketball at its best. It is crowd pleasing as well as creative to an excellent offense. The fast breaking teams must be always on the alert and be able to anticipate the change over from defense to offense.

THE PRESSING GAME: The best teams in Basketball today are the teams that can press at opportune times in a game. It can be particularly successful at the High School and College levels. As Rick Pitino found out, at the professional level it is more difficult to successfully carry out an organized press due to the fact that the

Pro's are so masterful of their basic skills and can therefore handle the press with more ease.

As I found out early in my coaching career, most High School teams will buckle under a good pressing team. As I have explained elsewhere, I came up with the Famous Folloni Special Press from watching my Jayvee players devastate my Varsity with Helter-Skelter play during a scrimmage. I then devised some drills and 'rules of engagement' that would give my players the instinctive moves and reactions necessary to carry out the press in game situations. Not only did the press demoralize the opponent's offense but also it created a great offensive weapon for us. Remember the best offense starts with a good defense.

THE 3-POINT SHOT: The arrival of the three point shot was a change in the game that nearly rivals the effect that came about in the '30's with the elimination of the Jump Ball after each basket. This really emphasized the role of the shooter, big or small, and opened up the middle even more for driving and a myriad of other exciting plays. The three point shot certainly has put a new dimension in the game. I am also in favor of this change as it has given a team the opportunity to come back quickly in an otherwise not so closely contested game. In many respects it has improved the game from a spectator point of view.

ZONE DEFENSES VS MAN TO MAN DEFENSE: Back in the early days of Basketball the zone defenses were predominant due to the lack of playing space of the many small gyms that were available at the time. With the building of many new large gyms in the '40's and '50's the pendulum swung over to the Man to Man Defenses and the Presses.

The Pros outlawed the Zone Defense with good reason: it detracts from the entertaining aspect of scoring. I understand, however, that there is a move on to allow a modified Zone Defense to take away some of the great advantage of the big men playing pro ball. It is my firm conviction that the only way to play the game of Basketball is by playing Man to Man. An exception of course is the use of the 'Trap' in the Press. We would keep teams on their toes by mixing in a 1-2-2 zone and trapping zones. On rare occasions we would use a box-and-one to shake up a high scoring opponent. The bottom line of our defenses was to cause confusion and frustrate planned offenses.

ATTITUDES: I will agree that the present day players are far superior in their achievements than the players of my days. Modern day players however, do too much hot-dogging and showboating. Basketball has become too much of an individual game and not the team play game that it should be.

The reason that the present day players achieve more is because of the better equipment, facilities, nutrition and training. Due to our stronger modern day economies and the delayed entrance of kids into the workforce, kids have more leisure time to specialize than we did as youth. People are just plain bigger now and there is a larger pool of players to select from. I don't believe that today's athletes are inherently better players. A good player of the 1930 era would be just as good or better than today's if given the same playing equipment and conditions.

We played the game because we loved it, not for the money or to show-boat. We conditioned ourselves by hard work and by doing the family chores and jobs. Today's players have to go to the weight room to condition themselves or take steroids to increase their physical strength. In the Professional Game they play for the money and not so much for the sport as was the case in earlier days. It makes me sick to see the prima-donna's of today who don't play their heart out because they are mad at a management decision or they want to get traded.

And as the former Celtics great John Havlicek recently stated,

"TO PLAY THE GAME OF BASKETBALL IS A PRIVILEDGE NOT A RIGHT."

SOME OF MY FAVORITE COACHING COLLEAGUES

The coaching fraternity is much like a family. You may at times have your fierce competitions and differences of views but over the long haul the brotherly colleagial instinct prevails.

I rate and judge the coaches who work with me by their relationships with the students and by their performances in these areas:

1. Honesty
2. Trustworthiness
3. Loyalty
4. Performance and most important,
5. Dedication

I don't use wins and losses as the main criteria. Too many coaches, myself included, have been unjustly fired because of their team's records. This is totally unacceptable. The overall average won-loss record in all sports forever is .500. This does not mean that 1/2 of the Coaches and competitors are less than worthy. Teaching and Coaching go hand in hand. One must be a good Teacher in order to be a good Coach. His/her primary goal and main concern is the health, safety, and welfare of the athlete at all times and to train and discipline the pupils to become good healthy citizens of our society. That's why I say:

"Have Fun, Play Hard, Play Fair. Do Your Best and let God do the Rest!"
"If you win enjoy, if you lose, be gracious and congratulate the winner."

With apologies to those who belong here who I've overlooked, here's mention of some of my favorite coaching colleagues from over the years.

Three at the top of my list have to be John Henry "Hank" Pearson, Joe Lazaro and Larry Fisher. Joe and Hank were my childhood teammates on local youth and semipro baseball teams, and they became very instrumental in my eventual success in the athletic world.

When 6'4" Hank was the first baseman target for our semipro teams, very few balls ever got by him. He was an aggressive, self-critical type of a ballplayer, who would curse himself anytime that he failed to make a hit. You never knew when his temper would flare up but he was a great team player and wanted to win in the worst way. Hank never took things out on his players or teammates the way he did on himself.

And of course he made very few mistakes of his own during his coaching career to get mad at himself over.

 Following his graduation from college, Hank played professional baseball with the Brooklyn Dodgers farm teams in Olean, Trenton, and Newport News before going on to his very successful teaching and coaching career.

Hank started out at a school in Alexandria, Virginia for a couple years then moved on up to teach in Braintree, MA and to coach their baseball, basketball, and football teams. While he worked there under Head Basketball Coach Fred Herget, one of Hank's players was Jimmy Calhoon, the renowned coach of the NCAA Champion University of Connecticut basketball team. Hank was also an assistant to Head Football Coach Rigo Latanzi.

After about 8 years at Braintree, Hank applied for the Baseball Coaching position that was to open with the new Regional School. Superintendent Serge Bernard submitted his application to me. Following our interview we hired him to become our baseball coach for the next 22 years until his retirement in 1982.

Coach Pearson turned out to be the most loyal and devoted coach that ever served under my direction. He was very popular with his biology students and with all the athletes that played for him. He was a truly excellent coach who's teams won many league titles and two District and State Championships.

Following his retirement he was inducted into the **State Coaches Baseball Hall of Fame**. *Some of his protégés who went on to play professional baseball included:*

 Phenom Glenn Tufts, who was the Cleveland Indians first round pick in the 1973 draft. Glen was seriously injured in a car accident, which cut short what would almost certainly have been a stellar pro career. He went on to Coach at Bridgewater State College from 1986–'93, compiling a fabulous 192-72-1 record. (Glenn is the nephew of our Track Coach Larry Tufts and the step-son of Bobby Fernandes, my captain of the 1956 Championship Basketball Team.) Glenn is now a scout for the San Francisco Giants and runs a very successful summer baseball camp at Legion Field.

- *Fireballer Richie Dubee, who was drafted to play professional baseball and after years in association with the big leagues was for a short time the acting manager of the Florida Marlins. He was the pitching coach for the Marlins when they won the World Series.*

- *Mickey Pina, who had a short stay with the Boston Red Sox playing with the AAA Pawtucket Red Sox.*

- *George Stanley and Sam Leclair were drafted and played minor leaguer ball.*

- *Rick Smith, a 1972 graduate, was taken in the fifth round of the annual amateur baseball draft by the St. Louis Cardinals. Rick went on the Coach BSC baseball, where he eclisped the all time win record previously held by Glen Tufts!*

- *Andy McCormick who played in the late 80's, early 90's for B-R and went on play in the Chicago White Sox minor league system.*

- *Brian Warren was drafted by the Detroit Tigers organization in 1990. He pitched in AAA for the Reds, the Rangers and the Tigers then went on to star in Japan's major league for the Chiba Lotte Marines. There in 1999 he had 30 saves, a 1.86 E.R.A, winning 'Fireman of the Year' plus being chosen for the same All-Star Team as Seattle Marina star "Ichiro", playing against NY Yankee star Matsui on the opposing All-Star Team. During the season Brian pitched to both of these great players, holding Ichiro to one hit in six at bats. After several years in Japan Brian returned north to play in the Mexico Major League and then went back to play in Korea.*

Brian in AAA

Who knows where Brian's interesting baseball career will take him next? Brian is the son of our Freshman Basketball Coach Ricky Warren.

Hank and other BRRHS baseball coaches after him can also thank their feeder system. In particular, Al Warren, dad of Ricky and Grandfather of Brian, along with Tom Conn, have put in 40 to 50 years of coaching and managing Little League and American Legion Baseball (for Bridgewater and area towns).

"Great Going Coach!" Coach Tom Conn & the old Coach greet each other in 2003

In more recent years they have been Legion Representatives and have passed the coaching duties to Tim Fitzgibbons, who's endless hours of commitment have produced many fine young ballplayers. The unselfish guidance of these three men, along with assistant Mickey Pina, has been great for the town's youth and Bridgewater baseball.

Tim Fitzgibbons watching his proteges in the '03 finals.

The efforts of these men and so many other volunteers have helped to continue to make our high school a baseball powerhouse in Coach Hank Pearson's winning tradition. All of Coach Pearson's athletes left his fields far the richer for having had the experience of playing for this good-humored down to earth Coaching Giant.

Lincoln AA Baseball Team, 1946

Back Row, l-r: Tony Domingos -Mgr., Charlie ('Herc') Balboni -C, Elmer Balboni –I, Roscoe Turner –I, Mickey Ferioli –O, John Zenavich –I, Eddie Snarski –3B, "Bo" Ferioli –O, 'Ney' Chiocca –I, **Larry Folloni** –2B, John Roderick –SS, 'Shine' Moruzzi –P, Mike Folloni, Mgr.

Front Row l-r: Johnny Flynn –C, **Joe Lazaro** –O, Dino Bertelli –P, Aldo Ferrarie –Bat boy, Bill Ferrara –1B, **Hank Pearson**-1B

All of these pros and thousands of other successful youngsters were also greatly influenced by Joe Lazaro who grew up with me near the Stanley area where we played ball together for many years. Joe never completed his High School education, as he had to go out to work to help with the support of his parents and brother and sisters. This lack of formal education is the only thing that kept him from becoming a great head coach.

Nonetheless, Joe accomplished much for the kids of town during the 41 years after WWII. And he became one of my most trusted and helpful assistants throughout my career and in developing the Athletic and Recreation Programs we started in the town of Bridgewater. Joe passed away on May 21, 2001.

After our youth league adventures, including my 'Stanley Steamers' against his 'High Street Tigers', and our exploits with the youth K. of C. teams, Joe and I went on to become teammates at the High School level under Coach Lester Lane.

We then went on to semi-pro ball with the 49ers and the Lincoln AA both before and after WWII. Joe was the center fielder on our team and he covered the expansive area with ease, 'a la Joe DiMaggio.' *(Joe L. even looked a lot like Joe. D!)* I'll never forget Joe's valiant efforts during the Boston Globe dubbed 'Little World Series' that we played against Rocky Marciano's St. Coleman's of Brockton in 1946.

When I returned to Bridgewater to take over the Athletic Program in 1950, once again it was my Old Buddy Joe who became my invaluable assistant in starting all the recreational and athletic programs. After the townsfolk chipped in with cash, Joe and I started the ball rolling with the Biddy League Basketball Program. Then we organized the Baseball Program which started with the Mighty Mites and then on to the Little League Teams, expanding to adult recreation and games with the state farm prison.

Joe took over as the maintenance man at Legion Field and did an excellent job in manicuring and maintaining the fields as the best around. With the strong subscription to our early recreation programs, we had to first install the Mighty Mites and Little League Baseball Fields at the corners of the football field. At the end of each baseball season Joe would patiently restore the worn baseball paths back to football playing conditions. Joe would never complain, he'd just serve the youth and the town.

In forming our advanced youth leagues I constantly turned to Joe for advice and help. Joe not only took care of the fields and gym equipment, but he very willingly acted as an official at the games and coached all the youngsters, from all age groups and from all teams. Joe always found time to hit some grounders to the kids, or to simply extend a helping hand and a warm smile. Joe also stood in as a counselor and gave fatherly assistance to any youngster who may have been troubled by problems at home. Joe's contributions didn't stop with the recreation leagues. He became my volunteer unpaid assistant coach for the Championship High School teams and later served as an assistant coach at the State College.

Typical of Joe's scouting of talent pursuant to developing it to its maximum was the day that he came to inform me of the rising future athletic great, Eddie Amaral, who later died at an early age of prostate cancer. Joe said, "LARRY, WE HAVE A REAL JEWEL IN THE MAKING, EDDIE IS GOING TO BE A GREAT ONE." How could Eddie miss, having been raised by two wonderful parents, and helped along by townsfolk the likes of Joe in the way I'm sure that God intended.

Following our first State Basketball Championship Season in 1956, we had a team photo taken with all the players and coaches. One of our administrators objected to Joe appearing in the photo since he was not a paid coach. I was furious and made my feelings known. Joe was just as much a part of this Championship effort as anyone of us and I insisted that he be included in the official team photo, even if it meant that I would be fired for doing so. After many hassles, I finally won out and the powers in authority granted my wish to rightfully include Joe where he belonged in the official Championship Team picture.

Joe continued on with his volunteer coaching work right up to his retirement. It was largely through his dedicated planning and work that the Legion Field was expanded to include many more ball sport and Little League Fields, one of them appropriately named in his honor.

Although Joe never married or had children of his own, he really adopted all the youngsters in our town. It has been said: *"WEALTH IS MEASURED BY THE NUMBER OF FRIENDS THAT ONE HAS ACCUMULATED OVER THE YEARS."* **BY THIS YARDSTICK, HUMBLE JOE HAS TO HAVE BEEN THE RICHEST GUY IN BRIDGEWATER.**

Left to Right: Larry Folloni, Athletic Director, Billy Sullivan, Freshman Coach, Hank Woronicz, Head F Coach, Moe Rucker, Faculty Manager, and Charlie Varney, Assistant Coach. Good men, all.

Some others that worked in my program at the old Bridgewater High School included Football Coach Henry Woronicz, the Boston College star who caught the winning touchdown pass from 'Chucking' Charlie O'Rourke in the Sugar Bowl Game against Tennessee. Doug Flutie was not the first B.C. Alum to captivate the nation with Florida bowl game heroics! Bernie Chestna served as Henry's capable assistant coach and Billy Sullivan was the Freshman Coach.

Charlie Varney, Coach Woronicz's, brother in law, succeeded him as the Football Coach in the middle '50's. Charlie and Henry married the very pretty Mitchell sisters, who came from the athletic Mitchell family of Middleboro. One of the Mitchell brothers was killed during WWII and in his honor they named the Middleboro semi-pro athletic teams the "Mitchell Athletic Association."

When we moved over to the Regional school with the town of Raynham we started out with an initial coaching staff of six coaches covering four boys sports and one girl's sport. We built up our athletic programs to the point when I retired when we had 42 teams, with 48 coaches. I can't readily remember all of the 100$^+$ coaches that worked under me at the Regional School, nor can I do justice to all who I can remember, but here's a mention of some, beginning with Football:

l-r: Hank Walmsley, Charlie Varney, Stan Sikorsky, Dot Moore, Larry Folloni, Bernie Chestna and Moe Rucker. 1961, BHS.

Lennie Hill, a BU star, who had a brilliant mind and really knew his sport, was the first Head Coach at B-R. Coach Hill was the person who sketched out the original *'Trojan'* Emblem Logo that all of our sports teams have worn so proudly and successfully over the decades.

Jim Harrington succeeded Lennie Hill, and stayed for a few years. In the late 60's Jim Kelley, a friend of mine and the Athletic Director from Mansfield, called me to recommend his son-in-law Jack Parker for the head-coaching job. After reviewing all of the candidates, I recommended Jack for the job. Coach Parker took over in the late '60's and within a few years he turned the program around to become a winner. After a couple of successful years of coaching, Mr. Parker went into administration work at B-R. His replacement as football coach was one of our former star players, Tim Driscoll, who led the state in scoring as a senior. Tim went on to star in college then returned to his high school alma mater to take over the head-coaching job during the early 70's.

During the next few years, the Football program went back downhill. Its demise was not the fault of Coach Driscoll. We were in the very highly competitive Old Colony League and we just didn't have the talent or foundation to win against the other schools. We went through a trying period and at one time even contemplated withdrawing from the league. Tim Driscoll left teaching and went on to a very successful career in the financial field. He is now a vice-president of I.D.S., a part of the American Express Corporation. The Football program was once again turned around when we hired Paul Urban, a very successful coach in the area. With the addition of an excellent weight-training program that was initiated by Superintendent Ed Denton, we were then able to compete on a very favorable basis with our opponents in the OCL.

In 1982 Paul Urban retired from his coaching duties and was succeeded by Coach Almeida, another very accomplished coach in the area. Coach Almeida had several very successful years into the '90's when upon his retirement another one of our former star athletes, Danny Buron, after a fine career at Holy Cross, took over as the new Head Football Coach. Danny had great success in bringing the B-R football program up to top flight Division One Championship caliber. B-R went to the Super Bowl many times in the 90's, and we've won far more than our share. Danny's 1998 team won the Division One State Superbowl Championship when they defeated mighty Brockton High School, coached by Armand Columbo, the winningist coach in the state. Armand was the brother-in-law of Rocky Marciano, and although very proud of him, Armand perhaps had some mixed feelings in that the budding Chicago Bear star Marc Columbo was playing high school ball at Bridgewater instead of with Armand's team in Brockton!

Upon my retirement in 1983, I recommended Paul Urban to succeed me as Director of Athletics, and he was so appointed and has done an admirable job in continuing our fine Athletic Program. Upon Paul's retirement, Bill Walker took over the Athletic program and he remains there doing a fine job to this day.

The Basketball Coaches began with Len Hill taking over for one year as a fill in after my first retirement from coaching. He was followed by Donald Prohovich, a former star at Holy Cross, who played on their NCAA Championship team along with Tommy Heinson, and Togo Palazzi. Don was also selected as an All-American baseball player while at Holy Cross and went on to play several years of professional baseball. Don coached well for two years then left to take over the Athletic Director's position at Waltham High School.

Upon my final retirement from coaching I turned the reigns of Head Basketball Coach over to Steve Sarantopoulis and my Assistant Larry Fisher. Steve had been a great star for our neighbor Brockton High School and had set the Schoolboy State Tournament scoring record at the Boston Garden when he scored a phenomenal 51 points.

Steve was also a Providence College player where he was a teammate of Jimmy Walker and Ray Flynn. Walker was an All American College player who later starred with the Detroit Pistons in the NBA. Ray Flynn went on to become Mayor of Boston. Steve coached his teams more in the traditional Providence College slow down patterns, using set plays for his offense and zone defenses. This was a departure from the style that I had used with my fast breaking offense and the Folloni Special Pressing Defense during my coaching career.

Steve was very successful with his teams over the next 15 years. His teams overall were well above the .500 mark, and they won one Old Colony League Championship in the middle 80's. Before going on to be a successful school administrator, Steve passed much of his coaching know-how along with the head coaching duties to our mutual Assistant Coach, Larry Fisher.

The Larry Fisher coaching era took on a new look. He immediately returned to the "Folloni Special Pressing Defenses and the Fast-Breaking style of basketball that he learned while serving as my Assistant Coach back in the '60's. Very quickly the B-R Basketball teams became the scourges of the tough OCL. Throughout the '90's B-R dominated the League and they qualified for State Tournament play nearly every year under Coach Fisher's leadership. In 1998 after his team won the League title and the South Regional Championship and finally lost out in the finals for the State Championship, I had sent him this note congratulating him on his success:

April 24, 1998

Hi Larry,

We just got back from Florida and while catching up on some of the news back in New England I heard about your success this past year with the B-R Basketball Team. I was so thrilled, proud, and happy for you for your great achievements. And to crown it all off the naming of you as coach of the year by the Officials. A well deserved honor to a great guy. CONGRATULATIONS!

This news brought back many nostalgic memories for me of our coaching days back in the 50's and 60's. When I last met you at the Wedding reception for my niece Kristin Morast you revealed that you had dug out all of the old Basketball Drills that we used back in the 60's. I just knew then that it would only be a matter of time before your teams would reach the heights that you have carried them to.

Really, Larry, I felt proud and flattered to think that anyone would consider using my hard-earned knowledge that took me years to develop.

I can still recall how Jim Swan used to scratch his head and wonder what we were doing with all of the crazy drills that we used. Well as you were smart enough to absorb and learn, these drills did pay off with pretty good results. As you well know we managed to beat many teams that we played who had much more talent than we did. We had no business beating them but due to the instinctive reactions that our kids developed from these drills, they prevailed.

Larry I am enclosing a couple of clippings that you may enjoy reading. One is about the Old Coach and his Golf Machine. The other is a copy of a little note that Rick Pitino wrote on the cover of my testimonial booklet. I had a nice chat with him last November at the Boston University Basketball Tip off Dinner.

During our chat I mentioned to the Celtic's Coach that he wasn't even born when I first developed our Press and that I was very impressed with his success with his Press. I told him that over the past 40 years I had not seen any team even come close to emulating our pressing trapping defense, until I observed his Kentucky team in action. He got a big kick out of my remarks as we compared notes on our trapping and pressing tactics, which are so similar.

Larry, that's enough of my personal nostalgia. This letter was intended to congratulate you on a job well done and to wish you continued success. Give my best to your lovely wife, Sue, and to the rest of the gang at B-R.

Sincerely,

Larry Folloni, The Old Coach… Keep on Pressing.

A short time later I received the following note from the always-gracious Coach Fisher:

5/13/98

Dear Laray:

I can't thank you enough for your kind and thoughtful letter. It means so much coming from you. This past year we were fortunate to win 20 games. We used your press for most of every game. We were losing in the second half in most of these games and as you know, how the press will wear down a team especially at the end of a game. I have enclosed the original copy of your drills and press strategies. I have made copies and use them in my practices. It is great to see Rick Pitino use the press at the professional level.

I can remember you showing me your golf machine. I marveled at the creativity of your ideas. My wife Sue and I have joined Franklin C.C. We love to play other courses and would like to play this summer with you at Portsmouth.

I hope your family is doing well and I will definitely call you this summer.

Thank you again

Larry Tuck

Larry Fisher is a soft spoken, unpretentious and very calm, cool and collected coach. I'm sure that his athletes were able to take away many valuable life lessons from exposure to this slight of physical stature, giant of a man, who in "Teddy Rooseveltesque" winning form, *"spoke softly and carried a big trick"*.

Two members of my physical education staff who also did an excellent job of coaching were Stan "Bunky" Holmes and George Pacheco. 'Bunky' Coached the Wrestling Team and was an assistant in both Football and Baseball. His wrestlers won many individual championships. Neil Zonferelli won the State and New England championships and was inducted into the UNH Hall of Fame. Heavyweight Lee Beane was 2 time State & New England champ and 6th in the High School Nationals. Toby Wyman was also a state champ. And with all his tremendous success, Bunky Holmes was recently named to the National Wrestling Coaches Hall of Fame. Bunky took over the Head Coaching job in Baseball when Coach Pearson retired in 1982. B-R graduate George Pacheco was the Boys Soccer Track Coach for many years, compiling excellent career records in both.

For many years at BHS and BRRHS Larry Tufts was the very caring, dedicated and effective Boy's Track and Cross-Country Coach. Coach Tufts had a quiet but powerful way of encouraging and challenging the kids to push them on to ever improving personal performances, while keeping them ever mindful that they were part of a (usually quite successful) team. Coach Tufts (who is Glen Tufts' uncle) has many record holders, champions and championship teams that developed under his training.

Billy Crane was the Ice Hockey Coach who also dedicated himself for more than 20 years as an Assistant Soccer Coach. He was recently honored for his unselfish dedication by being selected by the State Coaches Association as the 'Assistant Coach of the Year'.

B-R was blessed to have had many other fine assistant Coaches on our staff. Others from the early 60's that I recall were Bernie Gilmetti, Eddie Cassabian, Jeff Fanning, Bill Creighton, Jack Cullen, Jim Swan and Al Roy.

Coach Gilmetti coached the freshmen football and basketball teams in the early 60's before moving on to become the Athletic Director at the Mass Maritime College. He was a tough but well liked Coach, and a real good guy. Jeff Fanning went on to become a School Superintendent. Ed Cassabian coached football for a few years then became Chairman of our English Department and finally tied up with our girls coach, Joan Ando Cassabian in a happy marriage. Joan and Ed have been great supporters and boosters of mine over the years. Jack Cullen was a young spirited assistant football coach who put up with no shenanigans. Jack went to Northern New England to continue his teaching and coaching career. Al Roy a product of Luke Urban's Fall River Basketball Teams, and an assistant basketball coach in the early 60's was a very good basketball player. Jim Swan was also a great player, and a high-energy hoop fanatic and freshman and JV coach who was liked by most. When Paul Moscardelli, a warm and friendly teacher, our tennis coach and an enthusiastic BR sports supporter got together with Steve Sarantopoulis, Jim Swan and Al Roy on the hoop court, few adult teams in New England could compete with them.

As my assistant basketball coach for a couple of years, Jim Swan was fascinated but at times not fully impressed by the basketball drills that I had devised. Many years later he confided to me that when he first watched my drills he thought they were crazy, but after seeing the results he became convinced that they were indeed very productive. Later when he became the head basketball coach at the Plymouth South High School, he came back asking me for these drills.

Steve Heaslip gave a lot of guidance to all of our athletes, and served as our soccer coach and a social studies teacher. Like Paul Moscardelli, Steve was a popular but tough teacher who was also dedicated to working with our athletes. A favorite instructor, advisor and supporter for several of my children, Steve Heaslip is now the Principal at BRRHS.

In addition to the many dedicated coaches of the boys sports, we have been blessed with some real excellent and dedicated girls coaches. The first one that comes to my mind is Miss Dorothy Moore who coached all of the girls sports teams and was the Cheerleader Advisor at the Bridgewater High School during its 9 years of existence prior to our going into a Regional District with Raynham.

One of BR's many girl's championship teams

1st. Row: Susan Gibb, Faith Ghelfi, Ann Britton (Co-Capt.), Joan Rosa, Margaret Dowling, Elizabeth Hess, Annett Chouinard,

2nd Row: Linda Grubis, Coach, Paula Baran, Mary Dowd, Marie Champagne, Jane Wood, Kathy Malood, Cheryl Miller, Diane Nicol (Coach)

3rd Row: Darcy Britton, Mary White, Patricia Rich, Carol Galante, Donna LeClair, Cathy Armour, Janice Cipriano

4th Row: Marilyn Bouldry, Marion Mathews, Elaine Souza, Donna Sanville, Janet March, Deborah Parsons, Donna LeClair. Missing from picture: Co-captain, Karen Costa, Susan buckley, Ann Dowd, Leslie Kiernan, Nancy Keith, S. Cassani

At the regional school Mary Ann Silva, Joan Ando Cassabian and Cheryl Farrington coached the Girls Sports. Judy Sullivan, who was with us for a couple of years, went on to become the Girls Athletic Director at the University of Massachusetts in Dartmouth.

Two of our Student Trainee Teachers from the College have also gone on to great accomplishments in the athletic and education field. 'Dee Dee' Abenater became one of the most successful College Girls Coaches in the State. She recently was appointed to be the Head Softball Coach for a Division 1 Univ. of California school. Rena Shea went on to coach at Rockland High School and was one of the first activists who fought for equal pay for Girls Sports Coaches. She later went on to become a Superintendent of Schools where I trust her pay was justifiably commensurate with her many talents.

With the rapidly increasing participation of girls in all sports after Title IX implementation it became increasingly difficult to find enough female coaches to carry on the girls sports. At times we had to dip into the male population to secure capable coaches for the girl's. Two of our most successful in this group were John Heslin and Gerry Cunniff. Coach Heslin has been with the Girls Soccer program since the early '70's and has had great success with his teams, and in grooming several individuals for intercollegiate play. Now in his 70's Coach Heslin is still going strong.

Gerry Cunniff took over the girls Basketball program in the early '80's and has developed many championship teams. One of his teams in the '90's went on to win the Division One State Championship with a 25 and 0 record! This is the best ever record for a B-R basketball team. Coach Cunniff has a remarkable record of over 400 victories and counting. Kris Morast, (my sister Virginia's grandchild, Francis and Jack Morast' daughter) was one of the stars of this team who dazzled everyone at the Boston Garden with her behind the back passes and spectacular all around play. She made the State All-Scholastic Team and later went on to be a star with the Stonehill College team. Kris was honored as a Stonehill College Hall of Fame inductee in May of 2003.

Among my other favorite coaches, I can't forget some of my former pupils who went through our various Youth and High School Athletic Programs.

The first one on the list has to be my son Bobby. As a member of the high school basketball team, he scored over 1,000 points and was selected for All-Scholastic honors. After graduating from Bridgewater State College, Bobby took a teaching and coaching position at the Overseas School of Rome in Italy, from 1977 to 1989.

Some of his students included the children of former NBA players (playing in the Italian pro league) including George Gervin (Spurs), Willie Sojourner (Nets), Larry Wright (NBA Champion Bullets), and Joe 'Jelly Bean' Bryant (76ers and San

Diego Clippers). Bob also taught the children of: actress Claudia Cardinale, the Peroni Family (of Peroni Beer), the Butoni's (of Barrilla Pasta) and Corrine Clery ('James Bond Girl' from the movie 'Moonraker').

Bob had a great deal of success in coaching AOSR High School Basketball with Six Finalists along with two Soccer Championships in the DODDS (Department of Defense Dependent Schools) American Schools in Italy League. His soccer team came in 6th place out of 16 international teams in a world High School tournament in Mexico City. He was Athletic Director of the school from 1985-1989. I am very proud of his accomplishments. Bob's most notable achievement to me was when he called home one Christmas from Rome to inform us that he wouldn't be able to send any gifts home that year. He said that he had donated his extra coaching income to the survivors of the Volcano that erupted in a poor suburb of Naples. (This, you'll remember, is the same area where several thieves accosted and robbed us during our Italian vacation.) My wife Helen and I told Bobby that by this gift he had given us the greatest Christmas gift possible.

Ricky Warren, who is now Coach Fisher's very successful Freshman Basketball Coach and scout, is another of my favorites. Having passed every level from our Farm System through Varsity Programs as a player, he had first hand knowledge of what it takes to make a winner. Ricky has also been an effective volunteer contributor in carrying on various echelons of the Athletic Programs in Bridgewater.

There's a bittersweet story behind Ricky's success. During his Senior year when he was to be a starting guard on our Basketball Team, he was involved in a situation that resulted in his suspension from play. This was costly to us, as Ricky was an extremely quick, smart and agile athlete who teamed up with other similar athletes on that squad to terrorize many an opponent. This was a team packed with short players, but when operating on all cylinders it had more than enough horsepower to match up with anyone in our class. If Ricky could have played the whole year we would have had an excellent opportunity for another State Championship.

Of course the biggest price for all this was paid by Ricky himself, who had the weight of the world placed on his narrow shoulders. You see the suspension was meted out because Ricky fathered a child out of wedlock with his teenage girlfriend. In those days this was considered a sacrilegious offense and right after the fall football season (Ricky was our quarterback) our morally self-righteous School Committee banned him from participation in all future Sports. Can you imagine that harsh a penalty in today's day and age?

Ricky's life was very wrapped up in sports and following this suspension he was so disappointed, distraught, distracted and discouraged that he left school during his senior year. He went to work for a few years to support his offspring. With encouragement from his friends and counseling by me and others he found the determination within himself to go back to school to get his High School Diploma and a few years later to go on to get a College education. I am very happy to say that he is now a model citizen doing an excellent job in the teaching and coaching profession.

"Tough times do not last. Tough people do."

Another one of our pupils who went through our **'Toddler to Terrific'** Athletic Programs is Michael Perry. Michael is a quiet reserved type of fellow, similar in disposition to Larry Fisher and in physical size to Larry and myself. Although he was not hefty, he was a pretty good athlete and very teachable, thanks, I'm sure to his Dad who was a former standout athlete and a very competent and dedicated coaching volunteer in town.

Michael is now teaching Physical Education in the Bridgewater School System and coaching the Basketball team at Cardinal Spellman High School in Brockton. He has had a great deal of success with his Teams and was selected for 'Coach of the Year' honors when his team won the Class "C" State Championship.

Eddie Amaral, who coached at Cardinal Spellman and later at Hanover High School passed on to heaven at the young age of 44. He, along with Jerry Buckley and Bobby St. Pierre, were members of our undefeated Junior High Basketball team. These three left our Farm System after the Junior High School years and attended Cardinal Spellman Catholic School where they went on to win the State Catholic Schools Championship. If they had stayed at our school in Bridgewater, along with Steve Prophett and my son Larry Jr., we would have been the odds on favorite to win our Third and fourth straight State Championships.

At the time I was very disappointed that these players were recruited away from us. As I look back upon this move now, however, I'm convinced that these boys and their families made the right decision. They received an excellent education and they all went on to become very successful and contributing citizens in our society, which is what we teachers, coaches and town administrators really wanted.

My All Time All Star Teams

Choosing my *'All Time All Star Team'* from my players has to be one of the most difficult tasks of my career as a coach. When I was asked to make this selection I was very reluctant to do so, as I didn't want to neglect or forget any deserving athlete, and I know that at least some who have been named are modest about their accomplishments as compared to those of their peers. I have always stated that any youngster who pulls on a pair of sneakers, put on a pair of shorts, and runs up and down the basketball court, is in my mind an 'All Star'.

Now that I've been retired for several decades I hope you'll forgive me if I've omitted anyone in my selections as I try to remember the "Best of the Best". To be little fairer I will break it down into different eras of my coaching career.

First Coaching Job at Dighton High, The late 40's

Jimmy Dutra
Bob Smith
Bobby Booth
Edgar Standring
John Dutra (Killed in Korean War)
Billy Baxter-Greene (Deceased)
Karl Spratt (Deceased)
George Dutra (Deceased)

Best 6th men: Eddie Rose & Dick Barry

Bridgewater High School, the early 50's

Bob Seaver
Don Pittsley
Stan Smudin
*Ronnie Hogg
Lou Filippetti
Bob Fernandes
*Ed Denton
**6th men: Dick Cornwall & Donnie Strong

- Were it not for devastating knee injuries they suffered during the football season, Ed Denton and Ronnie Hogg would most definitely be listed in the top echelon. Both of them missed most of their senior years' playing time and they never did reach their full potential due to these injuries. Both of them, through sheer grit and determination came back before the end of the year, playing on a leg and a half, to contribute greatly to the success of their teams.

**Dick Cornwall with his great outside shooting, filled in admirably when Ronnie Hogg was injured.

**Donnie Strong came through for us in many clutch situations. Most notably in the Wrentham game when he pulled us through in a great overtime victory. Also in the Oak Bluffs State Tournament quarter-final game, he made the clutch rebound and a great fake and pass to Captain Bob Fernandes to seal the win, which eventually sent us to the Boston Garden on our way to our First State Championship.

BRIDGEWATER HIGH SCHOOL, THE EARLY 60'S

Mike Crowley   Paul Pallatroni
Steve Pivacek   Steve Prophett (Deceased)
Dave Messaline
Best 6th men: Shawn Burke, Artie Hoke and Larry Folloni Jr.

BRIDGEWATER-RAYNHAM REGIONAL SCHOOL, THE EARLY 60'S ERA, UNDER COACHES LENNIE HILL AND COACH DON PROHOVICH:

Tom Keith   Larry Folloni, Jr.
Stan Holmes   Steve Prophett (Deceased)
Danny Ryan   6th men: Ed Sherman & Joe Hirst

BRIDGEWATER RAYNHAM REGIONAL SCHOOL, MIDDLE 60'S ERA

Barney Ross   Bob Folloni
Frank Barstow   Bob Morgan   Dave Alden
6th men: Mike Tokarsky & Ronnie Dziergowski

MOST UNDERRATED PLAYERS WHO CONTRIBUTED A GREAT DEAL

Doug Wiggins (Deceased)   Allan Poole (The Charles Barkley type) (Deceased)

"THE BEST OF THE BEST—MY ALL TIME ALL STARS"

They were all great dribblers, great at driving to the hoop, great shooters and rebounders and deceptive fakers. They passed with good split vision, were excellent playmakers and defenders and very coachable. The main criteria for my selections, however, were threefold: They were chosen on the basis of their:

Dedication, Team work, and Production under fire.

The top eight in no particular order:

- **LOU FILIPPETTI**
- **BOB FOLLONI**
- **STEVE PIVACEK**
- **BARNEY ROSS**
- **DON PITTSLEY**
- **PAUL PALLATRONI**
- **STEVE PROPHETT**
- **MIKEY CROWLEY**

Note: Larry Folloni Jr., who was an ace shooter and defender as a sophmore for the 1961 State Championship Team, and a premier player and eventual team captain did not make the all time list. This is for the simple fact that during his 4 year stint in High School he was not quite as good as the 'Magnificent 8' listed above. I never showed favoritism to my sons on the court and I don't here. (Although I know that some of his peers made it extra hard on Larry Jr. in the classroom and on the playing fields because they imagined favoritism and that he excelled against these added odds.) It should be noted that due to the fact that he was and is a genius, Larry Jr. started grade school and finished High School at a younger age than most of his peers. Had he been able to compete at the same age as his peers, Larry almost certainly would have headlined this list of my *'All Time Bridgewater and B-R Regional School Basketball All Stars'*. In subsequent post scholastic competition against many of these top all stars, Larry proved to be their match and then some.

 Lou Filippetti

…was a true team player, very deceptive with great driving ability. He was the backcourt leader of the team who set them in action. Lou was selected for The Boston Garden All Tournament Team and on many media All Scholastic Teams.

 Donnie Pittsley

…was one of our best outside shooters, great at faking and driving to the hoop, and adjusting to changing game situations. Donnie was also selected to the Boston Garden All Tournament Team.

Bob Folloni

Bob ('Slim') led B-R in scoring, assists, and steals. He also got more than his share of rebounds. He was always after the ball. In four years he scored 1,113 points including (405) in his senior year. While a starter as a sophomore, he often asked to be removed from play so that a senior could participate.

  Paul Pallatroni

Cool hand Luke...Best foul shooter ever...Played like Bob Cousy... Great dribbler and passer... Good Split vision... Could drive with either hand... Great on defense. In the Marshfield game for the State Championship at the Boston Garden I gave Paul the job to defend their star who was averaging about 30 points per game. Paul held him to one basket for the first 3 periods as we built up a nice lead to go on to win the state championship... Selected to the Boston Garden All Tournament Team and to many Media All Star Teams.

  Steve Pivacek

Great driving from the base line...Great rebounder...In spite of a dislocated shoulder in the State Championship final game against Weston at the Boston Garden, Steve was a very vital cog in our victory....Excellent pupil.... easy to coach....Always gave his best in practice, in games, and in the class room.... Selected to Boston Garden All Star Team and local media All Star Teams.

  Steve Prophett

The last of the "P" trio who produced so much for our Championship team...."Froggy" (as he was affectionately named) would go through a stone wall to help his team... He had great jumping ability and was a great rebounder.... Member of the 1000 plus club in scoring during his high school career.... Always hustling.... Really dedicated to the game and loyal to his teammates.... Selected to Boston Garden All Star Team and all of the media All Star Teams.

Barney Ross

Worked real hard... had great hustle... great driving ability... good rebounder.... He was a John Havlicek type player... wherever the ball was on the court you would find Barney there battling for it.... Member of the 1000 point club. Selected to Enterprise All Scholastic Team, excelled at college level.

 MIKEY CROWLEY

Great penetrator to the hoop or to dish off to an open teammate... Scrappy defender.. Classic floor general... perfect split vision... Winning instinct. Like the rest, a true Champion! Best pound for pound athlete ever.

MY BEST COME BACK TEAMS

The 1957 & 1968 Teams

The 1957 Team which followed the '56 Champs was not expected to do much due to our loss by graduation of our stellar players, but they surprised everyone, including myself, by coming on to again qualify for the State Tournament.

The 1968 Team, my last year of coaching before my final retirement, was perhaps the greatest and the most satisfying coaching achievement of my career. From the previous year's State Tournament Team, we had lost 7 of our 8 leading players to graduation and were picked to finish last in our League. With only Captain Frank Barstow and a gang of inexperienced players from Coach Larry Fisher's jayvee team returning, we lacked the experience and manpower to compete in the tough Old Colony League.

We started out the year losing 7 out of our first 8 games. The kids never gave up and worked hard in practice to overcome their inexperience. By the middle of the season we finally started to click and we went on to win 7 out of the last 8 league games to finish with a 13-7 record and just missed out qualifying for the State Tournament by one game. Had we just started our winning run a game earlier, I'm sure these kids would have made quite a mark in the State Tourney. This team gave me the most thrills and surprises of any of the many teams that I have coached over the years.

B-R's IMPOSSIBLE DREAM

by Ron Ticchi

"It's a dream come true — an impossible dream. For a team that was picked to finish in the cellar, these boys surprised everyone, including myself."

These were the words of Mr. Larry Folloni, Athletic Director and head Basketball Coach here at B.R. when asked about this years basketball team.

B.-R.'s hoop prospects this year were very dim indeed. Only one of last year's eight top men was back and the remainder of the team did not have much experience. In the first game of the year, B.-R. was defeated by South Shore League Champion East Bridgewater while the second game was lost to Abington.

But these two early losses did not dampen the boy's spirits. Through lots of hard work and determination, the team came back to win several games. By the time the season was over, they had compiled a 13-7 record, one game short of qualifying for the Tech and had finished in 3rd place in the O.C.L.

In the last game of the year, at Whitman-Hanson, our boys really showed what they could do. In just 2½ periods Bob Morgan scored 32 points and Frank Barstow and Doug Wiggin 18 each. With a 30 point lead, Coach Folloni took out starting five and gave the second and third teams some valuable experience.

"I'm very proud of this team," said Mr. Folloni, "They've given me a great many surprises and thrills." In speaking of the individual players, the coach made these comments. "Frank Barstow was just great. He did a tremendous job in all departments. Doug Wiggin was a pleasant surprise. He was excellent on defense and was a fine shooter. Tony Belloli was another surprise. He did a lot of rebounding for us and after getting some experience he developed into a fine ball player."

The other two starters, Bob Morgan and Dick Fillipetti, have been elected co-captains for next season. Also deserving of credit are seniors Lou Resmini, Wes Morris, and Bruce Maclay; Juniors Paul Yanuskiewicz, Scott Donaldson, Glenn Meixner, and Ronnie Cogliano; and sophomore Peter Daley.

When asked about next year's prospects, Mr. Folloni said, "We'll be in the same boat as this year. We'll have to start from scratch and really work hard. But who knows, with a little luck and determination, we may just realize another "Im-

THE BEST COME BACK GAMES

The Cohasset game in 1954 & the Holbrook game in 1957:

In the Cohasset game we were down by 23 points after the first period. We came back in the second period with *"The Special Press"* and ended the first half with a 3-point lead, going on to win the game handily.

The Holbrook game is best told by Donnie Strong's "Rebounds of the Past", which is in the archives section.

There were a couple of our games in which our teams were ahead by 20 or more points early in the first quarter, *and our opposition made great comebacks to beat us,* **yet I can still remember these games in a positive light!**

For a perspective on this, let me first relate a story of a humiliating defeat of one of my teams *at the hands of a new coach* of Holbrook H.S. This neophyte kept his starters in through every minute of the 4 quarters and encouraged them to run up a score of over 100 points to our 55. After seeing the destructive effects on our boys of this completely unnecessary and cruel thrashing, *I vowed that I would never allow any of my teams to embarrass any opponent.* I did this both for the opponent, as well as for my boys, to teach them that kicking a guy when he is down is never a real victory.

My 1967 team of overachieving scrappers was among the best I ever had at ferociously implementing my press from the opening tip-off. Many a game they had in the bag before the competition woke up and knew what had hit them. In many of these games, where the score was quickly in the range of 25 – 3 or so, I called off my starters and put in my subs, both to give my subs some experience, and so as not to embarrass the other team. In a few of these instances, the opponents starters were able to take advantage of the mismatch, and get back into the game, and in a couple instances, when our starters got back in, they could never regain the momentum and we ended up losing.

In retrospect, none of these losses ever cost us an opportunity at getting into the state tournament, and I firmly believe that the overall lessons learned by all involved were well worth the 'L'.

No evil is without its compensation. The less money, the less trouble, the less favor, the less envy. Even in those cases which puts us out of our wits, it is not the loss itself, but the estimate of the loss that troubles us.
Seneca, 6 – 4 B.C.

On the other hand it is said, and I can't wholehearted disagree, that:

"Some people are good losers, and others can't act."

Therefore I fully praise the discipline and determination to be winners that created:

BRIDGEWATER AND BRIDGEWATER-RAYNHAM'S 'PURE SHOOTERS'

These are the 'sharpshooters', the 'guns for hire' the smooth as silk soft touch **'all net'** swishers that can put up points in a seemingly effortless manner. All players can improve their shooting with good practice, but others also have a natural born talent to go along with their practiced desire to put up the two's and the three's that count: Here are some of BHS and B-R's best at this skill:

Melvin Crest:	One of the very best in practices
Don Pittsley:	Made about 70 straight free throws in the men's league
Tommy Keith:	Played at Bridgewater State College.
Danny Ryan:	Just 17 years old, he missed eligibility his senior year due to a transfer technicality. Went on to shoot the lights out at Bridgewater State College. He now is the High School Basketball coach at East Bridgewater High School.
Frank Barstow:	'Bunky' Barstow was a smooth shooting big man who, like a good wine kept improving with age. He became the high scorer for his Salem State College team.
Don Prohovich Jr.:	Played baseball at Stonehill and now takes aim with his drill for his dental practice.
Bobby Doyle:	Defended our country in Vietnam in the Marine Corps. Very sharp on defense for BRRHS too!
Bobby Morgan:	Working for law enforcement now. Short but sweet shooter.
Michael Perry:	More about Michael later.
John Frost:	Late 70's, just after my time. Great soft touch shooter, several 30+ point games.
Tim Bollin:	6' 7" forward. Received basketball scholarship to Division I Colgate. His team made NCAA tournament in the early 90's and were defeated by Kansas.
The Quimbly Twins:	Keith and Kyle: Took the Trojans to 1999 Division I Finals at the Fleet Center. Received scholarships to Stonehill. Kyle became team captain.
Matt Cahill:	3 point wizard from 'Way Downtown'. (More on Matt in Archives)

Joe Rich: Scored over 1000 points. Played football at Northeastern. Now in law enforcement. Once a shooter, always a shooter!

Mike Rich: Made 9 three pointers in ONE HALF!

There are other players who had a **_knack for the hoop_** and would always find a way to put points on the board. Baseball players Richie Dubee and Glenn Tufts were pretty good at this. So were Steve Arrighi, Mike Lyford, Tommy Balboni, Billy Kairit, Danny Buron, and Jim Waterman.

I apologize for the players I left out of these two categories. I'm sure that I missed quite a few.

In the 'Archives' that follow, you'll find a not complete, but fairly broad group of summaries of Bridgewater and Bridgewater Raynham Regional High School Sports History Highlights categories, along with some anecdotal reviews of some of our stars of the 20th Century.

As a teaser of the eclectic information in the archives, here's the list of the top first round picks in the 1973 Major League Baseball Draft:

1. David Clyde   Rangers
2. John Stearns   Phillies
3. Robin Yount   Brewers
4. Dave Winfield   Padres
5. Glenn Tufts   Indians
6. Johnnie LeMaster Giants

A couple of all stars and a good active player are on that list.

By the way, Steve Balboni was stranded for some time at the Yankee's minor league affiliate Columbus Clippers Club because Dave Winfield and Reggie Jackson in their primes were holding the first base and DH chores for the parent club.

2nd Overtime

ARCHIVES

PICK & CHOOSE WHAT'S OF INTEREST TO YOU!

- *More Bridgewater & B'wtr Raynham Sports History Highlights*
- *Recollections of Stanley, Old Time Games & Sacco & Vanzetti*
- *Family Athletic Connections & 1st Edition of Photo Album*
- *Testimonials, Awards, Fortune, Observations & Innovations*
- *A Few More of My Favorite and not so Favorite Things*
- *Parting Thoughts…Wait Until Next Year*
- *Do as I say -- "My Way or the Highway"*

"The road to success runs uphill,
so don't expect to break any speed records."
Edmond Burke

More Bridgewater & B'water Raynham Sports History Highlights

BASKETBALL ALL STARS & NOTABLES

The 1920 era under Coach Herb Archibald

Mickey Cochrane
Harold Goodnough
Jib Belmore
Frank Emalovich
Jack Waite
Inky Kilbridge

John Buckley
Jerry O'Donnell
Frank Sadowski
Art Pratt Sr.
Mickey Costa
Harold Hunt

The late 20's and early 30's era under Coach Lester Lane

Bud Case
Bob McNeeland
Earl Jackson
Ed Shally
Joe Jozack
Eddie Stewart
Bob Jackson
Lou Buron

Archie Smith
John Spirida
Paul Anacki
Pete Zion
Joseph Yuknis
'Soup' Kidney
Tom Tinsley
John Selivonehik

The middle 30's era under Coach Lester Lane

Alec Dziergowski
Bois Twins, Teddy & Wilfred
Nelson Houlberg
Jack Tobin
Fred Kondrotes

Bill "Biscuits" Rubeski
Doctor Charlie Resevich
Arthur Pratt
Larry Folloni Sr.

The 40's era under Coaches Lester Lane, Joe Teeling, & Knute Anderson

Pat Jantamaso
Bobby Clark
Roddy Prophett
David Balboni
Richard Enos
Billy Case
John Colby

Eddie Denton
Dick Bradley
John Sadek
Harold Thompson
George Mandeville
Richard Akeke
Bobby Bois

The 50's & 60's era under Coach Larry Folloni, Lennie Hill and Don Prohovich

Listed in the end of my Coaching Section, "1st Overtime"

NOTE: I can't really do justice to properly naming all of the top players from the Sarantopoulos and Fisher Coaching eras. My apologies to those who I omit here.

The 70's era under Coach Steve Sarantopoulos

Michael Lyford	Billy Kairit	Michael Perry
Paul Revil	Richard Dubee	Glen Tufts
Jim McDonald	Don Prohovich, Jr.	Jimmy Keif
James Folloni	Michael Parker	Danny Buron
Bob McGovern		

The 80's and '90's era under Coach Larry Fisher

John Frost	Tim Bollin
Keith Quimby	Kyle Quimby
Jim Waterman	Mike Rich
Marc Columbo	Joe Rich

Although due to my wife's and my poor health I have not been able to come out to see him, many people say that Matt Cahill is perhaps the best pure shooter and possibly the best basketball player overall to have ever come out of Bridgewater. *Matt Cahill*

Matt, currently a 6 foot 3 shooting guard for Saint Anselm College, had a monster senior season at Bridgewater-Raynham. He averaged 29.0 points, 7.0 rebounds, and 6.0 assists per game en route to selections on the Boston Globe Super Team, Boston Herald All-Scholastic, and his second straight Old Colony League MVP honor. Cahill finished with 1,322 points, played in the Hoop Mountain All-State Game for seniors and was a McDonald's All-American Nominee.

SOME STAR FOOTBALL PLAYERS & TEAMS FROM THE BRRHS ERA

Artie Hoke was a super running back at BHS and at B-R. He was a Jim Brown type power runner, and great all-around athlete. Artie went on to work in Social Services being of great help to people in the Brockton area.

Tim Driscoll led the state in scoring as a senior. Tim went on to star in college then returned to his high school alma mater to take over the head-coaching job during the early 70's.

Peter Daley closely followed Tim's statewide dominance as a running back for B-R. He was an unstoppable great runner and one of the highest scorers in all New England. Graduating in 1970, Peter went to Harvard on scholarship where on his first play he ran for 70-yard touchdown. On the second play, he broke his leg, which ended his college-playing career. I believe that Peter also went into social services in CA.

Doug Bissette played for the 1998 B-R Superbowl Champion Football Team. He was the all time leading scorer at B-R. He had a great career at Boston College, starting at defensive safety for some very successful Eagles teams.

Dan Collins of Raynham played a few years earlier at B-R, had a successful career at offensive tackle at Boston College, and was drafted by the Dallas Cowboys. He had successful tryouts with both the Cowboys and Seattle Seahawks and probably would have made one of these NFL rosters had he not had a serious injury, which forced him to end his football career early on.

Marc Columbo who also starred in basketball, made his biggest mark in football. He was an Honor Roll student at BR, and involved in community service projects at his church. Marc starred at Boston College, and went on to become a starter as a rookie for the Chicago Bears in 2002.

TEAM FOOTBALL

Coach Dan Buron's teams have won two Super Bowls; They once won five outright league championships in six years, and Dan is still racking up records.

MASSACHUSETTS STATE SUPERBOWL TEAMS FROM B-R

1985   Div. 2 - Xaverian 14, Bridgewater-Raynham 13
1991   Div. 1B - Waltham 21, Bridgewater-Raynham 20
1996   Div. 1A - Brockton 32, Bridgewater-Raynham 20
1997   Div. 1B - Everett 21, Bridgewater-Raynham 0
1998   Div. 1 - Bridgewater-Raynham 20, Brockton 12
2000   Div. 1 - Bridgewater-Raynham 7, Waltham 0
2001   (First season of MIAA playoffs) Div. 1 - Everett 8, Bridgewater-Raynham 7

More Team and Individual Champions from the BRRHS Era

WRESTLING

Lee Beane: 2x state & NE Champ, 6th in High School Nationals - Heavyweight

Neil Zonfrelli: 2x MA State Champion State Champs UNH Hall of Fame

Toby Wyman: State Champ

GOLF

Larry Folloni Jr.: See Chapter on 'Chips off the Old Block"
Kevin Flynn: State Champ 1983

GIRLS BASKETBALL

Kristin Morast: '90 25-0 State Champs –all scholastic Stonehill Hall of Fame
Jennifer Mead: '90 Co-Captain. PC College, then woman's Pro Soccer.
Kim Morast '03 OCL Champs Captain OCL MVP – All Scholastic

SOCCER

Philip Sheridan, *Most Career Goals Scored in the entire country – 6th All Time!!*

1963	213, Sean Shapert, Moon (Coraopolis, Pa.), 1981-1984	
1964	208, Troy Snyder, Fleetwood (Fleetwood, Pa.), 1980-1983	
1965	203, David Russell, Weatherly (Pa.), 1999-2002	
1966	192, Craig Turley, Diamond Bar (Diamond Bar, Calif.), 1984-1987	
1967	176, Aaron Beth, Marshall County (Benton, Ky.), 1983-1986	
1968	*174, Philip Sheridan, Bridgewater-Raynham , 1983-1986*	

Ann Moniz Bridgewater-Raynaham: Was a four-year member of Coach John Heslin's squad. Third in OCL scoring in '01. OCL All Star...Her Spirit of Massachusetts club team traveled to the 2001 State Cup semi-finals.

Holly Laubinger: Going to Fordam, Boston Globe's 2002 PLAYER OF THE YEAR. OCL leading scorer for three consecutive seasons. League MVP two seasons. Holly holds the school (female) record for career points with 74 goals and 39 assists. Behind her leadership as captain, B-R won the MIAA Div. 1 south title in '02. All-State Div. I All-Star. Holly was the leading scorer for a non-school traveling team that won a high level international tournament last year in Denmark.

FIELD HOCKEY

Chrissy Hall, Career assists leader at BRRHS. two-time league all-star. She participated in the National Futures Program and the 2000 Bay State Games and the 1999 Jr. Olympics. Went to Yale.

BASKETBALL CAPTAINS COACH LARRY FOLLONI ERA

BRIDGEWATER HIGH SCHOOL

1953	Edwin Denton
1954	Robert Seaver
1955	Herman Fries
1956	Robert Fernandes
1957	Richard Cornwell
1958	Peter DeVeber & Anthony Ghelfi
2002	Robert Bumpus & Robert Ghelfi
2003	Michael Crowley
2004	Shawn Burke-David Messaline-Paul Pallatroni-Steven Pivacek & Steve Prophett

BRIDGEWATER-RAYNHAM HIGH SCHOOL

1962	Steve Prophett
1963	Larry Folloni, Jr.
1964	Thomas Keith
1965	Ronald Dziergowski & Barney Ross
1966	Michael Valeri
1967	Robert Folloni, Tommy Balboni and Mike Tokarsky
1968	Frank Barstow
1969	Richard Filippetti & Robert Morgan

Special Commendation for the many Volunteers with the 'Farm Systems', without who, these All-Stars might have been Also-Rans.

A great representative of this large group is Mr. Bob Stearns, whose complete dedication to improving the sporting lives of our youngsters has been Sterling.

ACHIEVEMENTS OF SOME OF MY FORMER PUPILS

As stated earlier, my prime goal in teaching and coaching was to try to make good constructive citizens out of our youngsters. Many of these children were just run of the mill athletes. Although none of them may have been endowed with Michael Jordan's or Larry Bird's talents, to me, any youngster who gave an effort and who tried their best to contribute to the fun and enjoyment of team play was an All-Star.

I will try to list only a few of the sporting youngsters and coaching associates from my era and the areas where they have achieved. *It's folly in a way to even attempt this, so please accept my apologies it I didn't include you.* I coached and directed programs for over 10,000 kids during my career, so ***I'm only including the 1st 1% or so here*** that come to my mind at the moment. I know that there are many, many, more success stories from many other of my favorite students that I am not aware of or that just didn't come immediately to mind. I would be thrilled to hear from any of you who I haven't kept in touch with, and I'll be sure to include you in the 2nd 'unabridged' edition of ***'My Way'***. Note that updated versions of the book will be coming out periodically on CD – Be sure to submit your input for inclusion.

ADMINISTRATIVE WORK:

Ed Denton,	Superintendent, BRRHS and Paso Robles, CA
Charlie Costa	Superintendent of Schools in Illinois
George Guasconi	Asst. Supt. Bridgewater.
Billy Sullivan, (coach)	Superintendent of Schools, Raynham
Bernie Gimletti, (coach)	Director Of Athletics, Mass Maritime Academy
Lennie Hill, (coach),	Supt of Schools, Medfield, Academic All American at BU
Rena Shea, (coach)	Supt. Of Schools, Rockland & W. Bridgewater
Judy Sullivan, (coach)	Girls Athletic Director, U. Mass
Jeff Fanning (coach)	Superintendent of Schools, Stoughton
Don Prohovich (coach)	Athletic Director, Waltham
Chet Millett (boss)	Supt. of Schools, Abington, Principal, Raynham
Raymond Calabresse	Administrative work.
Robert Tartufo (coach)	Director of P.E., Raynham

H.S. COACHING

Eddie Amaral	Led Cardinal Spellman to many championships (Basketball Coaches Hall of Fame)		
Michael Perry	State Basketball Coach of the Year 2001.		
Stan Holmes: "Bunky"	Built B-R wrestling program to become one of the best (State of MA & USA Hall of Fame Coach!)		
Ricky Warren	Bob Folloni	Gordon Ross	Jack Levy
Danny Buron	Future Hall of Fame(s) lock		
Danny Ryan	Dave Driscoll		Tim Driscoll

TEACHING

Ronnie Dziergowski (also a sports writer for The Enterprise)
John Andre   Philip Prophett   Bobby Morgan   Danny Ryan
Michael DeGregory   Andy Fruzzetti

LEGAL FIELD

Bobby and Richard Clark followed in the footsteps of their Dad, Judge Robert Clark, one of the greatest trial lawyers in MA
Bobby Seaver   Steve Marzelli   Pete Matheson
Wesley Morris (Wesley has been an ongoing help in family legal matters.)
Robert Karnes (Well known varied practice including 'entertainment law' representing 'The Fabulous Cassottos')
Larry DiNardo   Debbie (Folloni) Dent
William Carpenter, Successful Attorney & State Supreme Court Justice

MEDICAL & SCIENTIFIC FIELD

David Mulligan Head of the State of Mass Department of Health
Larry Folloni, Jr. World leader in Chemical QA & QC for Computers
Wm. Devine, Jay Gauthier & Kenny Amaral, Pharmacists

POLITICS

The Flynn Brothers, David and Peter. **Dave**, a fine golfer and a veteran 'Pol' of many years, is still the State Representative for our Bridgewater District. **Peter** was also the State Representative for many years and then became the Sheriff of Plymouth County.
Allen Chiocca, former State Representative and now Selectman in Bridgewater.

POLICE AND FIRE PROTECTION WORK

William Ferioli	Chief of Police, Town of Bridgewater
Roddy Walsh	Fire Chief, Town of Bridgewater
Karl Spratt,	Chief of Police Town of Dighton
Bobby Fernandes Sr.	Mass State Police
Jimmy Buckley,	Police Sergeant, East Bridgewater
Billy Nicholas,	Police Sargent, Bridgewater
Bobby Fernandes, Jr.	Police Dept. Bridgewater
Robert Bois	Police Dept. Bridgewater

ATHLETIC FIELD

Ronnie Hogg	Professional Baseball Player
John Spirida Sr.	Pro Football Player Washington Redskins (Barney Ross's Dad)
Glenn Tufts,	Professional Baseball Player, now a scout for S.F. Giants.
Richard Dubee	Pro Baseball Player & semi-pro Manager - Coached FL. Marlins.
John Scheffler	Golf Pro
Rick Smith	Pro Baseball Player, Coached BSC to Div. III World Series wins
Brian Warren	Professional Baseball Player

Peter DeVeber	Public Relations Manager for boxing champion, Marvin Hagler.
Donnie Pittsley	Well known Basketball Referee.
Richard Filippetti	Basketball Referee and Baseball Umpire.
Louis Filippetti,	Basketball Referee and Baseball Umpire, President, Intl. Association of Approved Basketball Officials; C.B.O.A.
Marc Columbo	Professional Football Player
Mickey Pena	Professional Baseball Player
George Stanley	Professional Baseball Player
Sam Leclair	Professional Baseball Player

SECURITIES / STOCK MARKET FIELD

Dave Messaline	Very successful stock broker and Vice President of Tucker & Anthony, National StockBrokers
Steve Pivacek,	Also a very successful stock broker in Connecticut.
Tim Driscoll,	Vice-President of I D S Financial Services Co.
Henry Cormier Jr.	I D S Financial Services Executive

BUSINESS FIELD

Stan Smudin,	Retail store owner.
Donald Gotchalk	Owner of Fashion Clothing Store
Alan "Skippy" Poole	Farming
Mike Tokarsky,	Graduate of West Point Military Academy, Executive Officer for Ford Motor Company in Michigan.
Steve Bernard	Founder and Former Owner Cape Cod Potato Chip Co.
John Cirelli	Cirelli Food Services
Jim & Mike Folloni	Light Energy Corporation
Kenneth Rezendes	Very successful in the construction business. Philantrophist who donated Athletic Fields for the youngsters in Berkley, MA.
Ralph Sherman	Owner, Village General Store in Martha's Vineyard

SOCIAL SERVICES FIELD

Jerry Buckley   Artie Hoke,   Peter Daly

MEDIA FIELD

Joe O'Brien,	My Student Manager of the Basketball Team and the first 'PR' man on my staff when we started the Recreation Program in the early 50's in Bridgewater. Joe went on to the Enterprise Staff and rose to become Editor in Chief.
Paul O'Brien	Sports writer and P-R man for all Bridgewater
Ron Ticchi	Excellent sports writer for our teams. I'm sure he went on to success in this or related field.
Mike Valeri	Free-lance photo-journalist. Expert in sports
Ed Querzoli	Editor, Quincy Patriot Ledger

SERVICE OF OUR COUNTRY Too many to mention, but here are a few that come to mind. If you know of any others, please let me know and I will add them in the next edition

Donnie Strong, A Naval Reserve Aviator who served on board the U.S.S. "Wasp" & "Intrepid". Dieter Stark-Strong still photographs war cemeteries & memorials for veterans.

Richard Balboni, Marine. Only member of his platoon to leave Vietnam alive. Richard was left wounded on the battlefield for many hours before the medics team rescued him.

Peter Jackson, Air Corps Pilot, Distinguished Service in the Army Air Corps.

Richard McFadden, U.S.Navy. His C.O. sent me a letter explaining Richard's distinguished service and thanking me for having assisted in his maturation process.

Vietnam Vets

Eddie 'Bubba' Gibbs	Ralph Bradley	John McKinnon
Charles 'Chuck' McKinnon	Kevin Choicca	Carl Soderbom
Richard Lankalis	Bobby E. Doyle	Robert Doyle
Joseph Ouellette	Robert Bois	Richard Legan
John Nelson	Nick Douzanis	

Robert Baker (in Korea during Vietnam era)

THOSE WHO MADE THE SUPREME SACRIFICE IN THE SERVICE OF OUR COUNTRY

WORLD WAR II

Alfred P. Bertelli	Manual G. Riberio
Joseph Chestnut	Howard A. Goff
Robert Pratti	Kenneth J. Harding
Mario A. Chiocca	Robert A. Pierpont
Michael J. Curley, Jr.	Quintin L. Dunn
Kenneth J. Harding	Joseph E. Lynch, Jr.
Albert A. Enos	John M. Pierpont
Anthony F. Souza	Paul R. Stubbs
Raymond J. Mason	Robert A. Silva
Thomas P. Buckley	John A. McNeeland

KOREA

Roger M. Tansey   Johnny Dutra (From Dighton H.S.)

VIETNAM

Lawrence F. Beals	Lawrence K. Dowd
Walter J. Kacsock Jr.	Glenn A. Menowsky
Robert E. Morris Jr.	Bruce E. Johnston III
Theodore F. Johnson	

A Reminder Of Some Of The Other Deceased Members of Our Teams

Eddie Amaral
Billy Baxter-Green
Doug Bromley
Bruce Crest
Keith Deane
Mike Lyford
George Dutra
Paul Pallatroni

Steve Prophett
Karl Spratt
Charles "Chuck" Thibault
Connie Thibault
Doug Wiggins
Paul Pallatroni
Victor Bissonette
Bubba Gibbs

I am so proud of the achievements of my former pupils.
To all of them, my congratulations for a job well-done.

Following is the text of the bronze plaque on the memorial in front of the Bridgewater Raynham Regional High School. The BRRHS class of 1971 donated the original memorial. My son Michael, inspired by discussions with our mutual mentor, Jim Buckley, wrote these words in 1971:

> IN MEMORY AND HONOR OF THOSE BRIDGEWATER-RAYNHAM STUDENTS WHO LOST THEIR LIVES IN VIETNAM AND FOR OUR OTHER CLASSMATES NOW DECEASED. MAY THEIR EXAMPLES OF CHARACTER AND LEADERSHIP HELP GUIDE US TOWARDS A NEW WAY OF PEACE.

Misc. Memorable Events Teams & Individuals from my Coaching Days

The Ones That Got Away

What If ??? Eddie Amaral, Jerry Buckley and Bobby St. Pierre had not left us (after our 8th grade team's undefeated year), to go to Cardinal Spellman for their High School Education. Just think of this trio, along with Steve Prophett and Larry Folloni, Jr. We would have been odds on favorite to go on to win our 3rd and 4th straight State Championship. They led Cardinal Spellman on to the finals of the Catholic Schools New England Championship. As disappointed as I was when we lost them, now as I look back, I know that their parents did make the right decision to send them to the parochial school. They all turned out to be great successful citizens of our society, which is the primary goal that we seek.

More 'Bests'

Best Student Boosters:	David "Coontail" Freeman & wheelchair-bound Peter Murby
Best Adult Boosters:	Jim Buckley, Paul Anacki, Bill Prophett & Warren Meacham, Gino Guasconi
Best Little Man:	"Pound for Pound" 5' 5" 3-sport star Mikey Crowley
Best Big Man:	Stan Smudin @ 6' 4" & Frank Barstow @ 6'4"
Toughest Opponents:	Mayflower League: East & West Bridgewater Old Colony League: Plymouth & Silver Lake
Best Opponent Coaches:	Hank Rogers, Plymouth; Joe Morey, East B'water; Dick Morey, Abington; Val Muscato, Oliver Ames;
Best Coaches Other Leagues:	Leo Miller, Nauset; Mel Wenner, Belmont; John Certuse, Foxboro, John Killelea, Silver Lake, Melrose

Almost all of our best players came up through our excellent farm system, with the help of many parents and other volunteers

Some Scary Stories

Lead Paint – Albert Bengston

This happened one day during my first year as Supervisor of Physical Education in the Bridgewater Schools. I had just given one of the elementary school teachers a lesson on conducting a physical education class when someone came barging into the classroom yelling for help for a youngster in the next door classroom who had passed out.

I rushed into the room to see Albert Bengston stretched out on the floor with his skin turning blue. I immediately proceeded to administer C. P. R. After working on him for several minutes, Albert began to breathe. We immediately rushed him to the hospital where the medical team took over to rehabilitate him. His recovery was complete in a few days.

Upon investigating the cause of his illness it was found that Albert had been chewing on a colored crayon and the lead paint from it had poisoned him and nearly caused his death.

The doctor that treated Albert later congratulated me for my informed and decisive action, and told me that my quick action in reviving Albert saved his life.

Lead Shot – "Skipper" Doyle

As part of a physical education class one day in the '60's we were having track & field event practice on the Legion Field. Roddy Walsh, our Football QB, and a pretty darn good one, tossed a shot put that accidentally slipped out of his hand and landed squarely on the forehead of "Skipper Doyle". The force of the shot put opened "Skipper's scalp to the bone. I immediately ripped off my undershirt and wrapped it around his forehead to close the wound and stop the bleeding.

We rushed "Skipper" to the hospital where his life was saved by the medical staff. It was a scary moment. When I first saw the open wound, I thought for sure that would have killed him. Fortunately, "Skipper" came out of this accident to make a complete recovery. I promptly sent a letter to the town officials praising the EMT's who so skillfully responded.

Well Led – Roddy Walsh

Roddy went on to become Bridgewater's Fire Chief, from which position he now oversees coordination of activities with EMT's to save lives and to effectively help other emergency situations on a day to day basis. Roddy knows how to get and keep things on track.

Here's a Draft of Donny Strong's excellent article called "Rebounds of the Past", which includes a chronicle of one of our greatest comeback games.

"Rebounds of the Past"

BHS "Hoop Remembrances" from Don Strong, '57

Well, Coach, we're "back on the court", nearly half a century after that Wondrous, amazing 1956 season, and the winning year after that surprised A hell of a lot of people! I hope these anecdotes can find a spot in your "My Way" roster. Okay, let's tap-off...

1st Quarter --

My first meeting with you took place in late fall 1953 when my folks Moved to Bridgewater... It was a Saturday afternoon, we were unpacking Stuff at the cozy little 36 Main St. home you rented to us, when Landlord Folloni showed-up and introduced himself to the "Strong Kids"... I was a Little chubby then, but you asked if I liked sports, especially basketball.. Unfortunately, my only hoop experiences at that time were "shooting around In my Manchester, NH grammar school yard". You gave me a quick look and said I should probably build-up my body, 'cause you were seeking new Young talent....Few weeks later, after a big storm knocked down several tree limbs in your property, you handed me an axe and suggested that I go out and chop a few things...I did, and by Spring, with a few more of your Body-building tips & exercises, I lost several pounds and could actually jump up and brush the rim with my fingers...(I don't know if you recall this, Coach, but during practices I could almost always "box-out" Stan Smudin and rebound).

Of course, there were other key sporting moments during my Freshman and sophomore years, thanks to you....The most important of which was the Essence of "Teamwork"... We spent hours 'n hours learning how to set picks, screens and pass the ball (remember those little round groups of four or five players, one in the middle on defense, that passed left, right, both hands, & bounce passes?)...One fundamental I particularly absorbed was your insistence that "you must give at least one FAKE before every pass or shot!" Lotta guys in my class used to smirk at you when you demonstrated that rule, perhaps because they never fully understood or realized the importance of ball fakes – to launch a shot or pass when tightly-defended, or to open-up your opponent's defense! Well, I took a lot of "good-natured Trash-talking" due to my constant faking, but it all paid-off (for me & the

Team, at least) in an important future playoff-game...

2nd Quarter –

which came in the '56 Tech Tourney against Oak Bluffs...I believe the game was played in Wareham and we really had a tough team against us...The scoring was low, defense great on both sides but a lot of fouls were being called....That led you to put me in for either Smudin or Hoag late in the fourth quarter; we were either down or up by just one or two points. "Okay, Donnie", you said, slapping my butt, "you can do it"...

"Do IT"...What was "IT?" What did you mean? What was I supposed to DO? All those things were going through my mind as Oak Bluff took the ball out underneath our basket. They made the inbound pass and Lou Fillipetti stole it and broke off down court...He was on the right, driving for a layup & possibly a foul from one of the two opposing players covering him...I was on the left when Louie stole the ball and automatically (thanks to your coaching) ran down to the hoop...Well, Louie drove hard but missed the layup (no foul called) and the ball came off the other side of the board, where, ta-ta, I was (following your practice rule of "always following up your teammate's shot). I leaped between two Oak Bluff guys (who probably never expected another Trojan to be there on such a fast steal), grabbed the ball, dribbled twice, got covered quickly by those two players, then made two fake passes to Cornwall or Pittsley (can't remember who exactly) near half-court, which took one guy off me, and allowed me to see Bobbie Fernandez cutting across the middle to the hoop. I threw him the ball, he scored, they called time-out, you slapped me on the butt again (with a smile) and, obviously, we won the game! Coming back home that night in the bus, it finally dawned on me that I did "do IT"..."It" was remembering two key fundamentals, a) always following your teammate's shot, and, b) always throwing a fake or two!

You know, Coach, I guess I was your 7th or 8th player on that championship team...I never scored much, but it always seems that whenever you put me in (discounting blow-out games against Plainville or Wrentham or Norton), perhaps it was because I had always paid attention to your "fundamentals" and you could always (I hope) count on me. And those important "hoop lessons" stayed with me for a long, long career....

3rd quarter –

Another warm memory stems from my senior year (the 56-57 season). On the heels of such a fabulous "Championship Year", our team (minus the five great starters of '56) was not expected to be more than "another break-even squad"....We had really only one shooter, Dickie Cornwall, but he was great! Tony Ghelfi had some nice moves but he was still only a junior..Senior players? Well, there was Pete Flynn (good footballer, but not much more than a 3-4pt. & couple rebounds per game forward), Jimmy Buckley (an "Ace" pitcher but no better than Flynn) and me...Now, coach, please don't misinterpret the following self-analysis as an "egotistical" review...but at only 6' I could outrebound most guys in the league (except for those two 6-5 West Bridgewater players) and I did average over 10 pts. per game....So, basically, that was our team --- A great shooter, an excellent rebounder, a bunch of average players, and a super coach, who knew how, physically & psychologically to inspire or "influence" his squad. The word "influence" leads us to the "fourth quarter" and the story of an important game that we lost by four points but "won" by "teamwork", "team spirit" & just plain old "hustle"....

4th Quarter –

Towards the end of the regular season, the '57 team was tied for 2nd place in the league with East Bridgewater (Westies were first with a powerful offense) when we had crucial game with Holbrook, whom we had beaten earlier on their court. Cornwall was among the league leaders in scoring at that time and, you may not remember this, coach, some of the guys on the team were getting a bit "ticked-off" that he was taking about 75% of the shots each game. And this not-so-secret attitude was also affecting our defense. In short, Coach, we were ALL to blame for what was to happen in The first half vs. Holbrook. We got blown-out....We took terrible shots, played terrible "D" (never hustled) and came to the locker room at halftime down by 22 points. I'll never forget that night...We're slumping against the lockers, waiting for you to come in. Bernie Chestna is staring at the floor, nobody is talking....The door opens, you come in, look around the room, walk to the back, shake your head and then say, in disgust, "In all my coaching days I've never witnessed such a pitiful performance by a Bridgewater team....No teamwork, no defense, no hustle, and, worst of all, no respect for your school or the game." Then you walked to the door, paused momentarily and declared, "If this is the way you want it, gentlemen, then the season is officially over. I'm out of here." Wheeewwwwww, what a statement! We looked at each other for a few minutes, then somebody (I don't know who) slammed his locker and shouted, "we're bullshit"...We went back out onto the court feeling totally humiliated and embarrassed...You huddled us at the bench...We put our hands together...And silently resolved to play worthy of a defending champion.

-4

What took place? I'm sure you know, coach... We burned-up the floor, full-court "Folloni-pressing" and coming back, with super aggressive defense (though getting lots of fouls called), to within two or three points with a minute to go. The crowd was going nuts, standing on the bleachers & shouting "Go, go, go, Trojans!", the cheerleaders were screaming & crying at the same time, and you were slapping butts and shouting encouragement! But, unfortunately, couple of our key guys fouled out (I think it was DeVeber & Ghelfi) and we were so "drained" from the amazing comeback that we couldn't pull off the win. Again, however, we did "win"... We proved to ourselves that we had the "pride" and "desire" to be a "winner", to play at our very best (I often think we probably could even have defeated West Bridgewater with that performance)... And, above all, it was your "psychological" leadership that triggered it! A week or two later, just before the first game of the Tech Tourney, we held a special "hoop honor ceremony" in the gym, attending by the whole school. You introduced each player and, despite the fact that we had already won 11 games (at least four or five more than the Enterprise had predicted), you reminded the student body of our dramatic comeback against Holbrook. I'll never forget that.. Nor will I ever forget a "personal triumph" (Hey, every player has to have at least one game in his HS "Hall of Fame"..... For me it was an overtime contest....)

OT –

A week after (I think) that Holbrook game, you were very concerned that we might not qualify for the Tech Tourney. At that time we had lost both games to East & West Bridgewater, and were in third place with just eight wins. We needed nine to qualify and the next game was away vs. Wrentham, which was playing better as the season progressed. However, at this time, the school paper (The Periscope) had selected four senior editors to attend a special WHDH broadcast in Boston on that Friday game afternoon. I was one of them... And, I really wanted to take part in that trip. Well, a snow storm was predicted for early evening (not enough to cancel the game) and you were very concerned that, given the heavy evening traffic and possible snow, I might not make it back in time for that game. I remember you calling me down to your closet-like little office and asking me to forgoe the Boston trip for the team. I always thought of myself as a "Team Player", Coach, but this WHDH appearance was a once-in-a-lifetime Dream event for a high school senior... So, I just said "Don't worry, Coach, I'll be there".

Five hours later, after the WHDH show finished, we (Vera Litzen, Ellen McNeilly, Pete Jackson and I) were stuck in the snow on Rte. 28 heading south of Boston. It was already 6 p.m. (the JV's were playing in Wrentham) and we were still 25 miles away from BHS, where Vera's mother was waiting to drive us to Wrentham. Finally, we reached the HS at 7:30 p.m. and jumped into Mrs. Litzen's car. She had already put Vera's cheerleading outfit and my uniform bag (which you gave to her) in the car... but she looked out the window and said "I don't think you're gonna make it kids"... I remember saying, "Hey, Mrs. Litzen, I gotta be there... Coach'll Never forgive me"... So, she drove off.. We arrived at the old Wrentham gym (was it inside the school or the town hall?) and I jumped out of the car even before she stopped it at the curb. It was around 8:30 p.m.. Entering the gym, I was so nervous, I rushed right to the end of the bench and sat there (with my suit and overcoat on), hoping not to offend you... You glanced at me, gave a quick smile and pointed to the locker room... Flynn lifted me off the bench and gave me a push to the room. I changed quickly, but not in time to play in the first half, which ended with us down about five or six points...

In the second half, we hung close to Wrentham and at the buzzer we were Tied. I think that because Wrentham was playing a very tight zone and their Gym was so small that Dick Cornwall really couldn't get his shots off and that is one reason the score was so low... In the huddle you decided to change the offense, and go inside to our "Big Guys" (me & deVeber). Tell you the truth, Coach, that surprised the hell out of me, and I got a nervous Feeling... Anyways, to make a long story short, we only got four or five shots off in OT, three by me... My first was a running sort of hook that bounced around and plopped in... The second was my strong drive to the right for another score.. And the third rolled-out but I got fouled and made one of two free-throws. Only five points! But that's all our whole team scored... Wrentham scored just four. We won. We qualified for the Tech. You gave me a little hug in the bus, and I was in "7th Heaven" for the whole Coming week.

Well, Coach, that's it for now... I have other memories of my BHS days and our relationship (i.e., that horrible evening before game-time when [   ] [   ] went berserk against you, and many other incidents), which not only greatly influenced the way I continued to play ball (at BU, in the service, the Eastern League when I was at NAS Quonset Pt., two years in Europe, etc.etc.) and conducted myself in sports. In the past fifty years, I've Had and dealt with dozens of coaches... You top the list!   Thanks, #23.

GIVING A STUDENT A SECOND CHANCE IN LIFE
"Rebounds for the Future"

A young man who I'll call Joseph Riggus was the oldest of about 10 children in his family. His father was an alcoholic who constantly physically abused his mother and the kids. During one stretch of a few days when Joe didn't come to school or practice, I wondered what had happened to him.

Finally one day, Joe arrived at school sporting a couple of black eyes. I called him into my office and tried to find out what had happened to him. After some probing, he reluctantly revealed to me that his father went on a drunken spree and beat up on his mother. Joe had intervened and begged his father to hit him instead his mother. The drunken father obliged by beating Joe up and giving him the black eyes.

It was sometime later that I had to discipline this boy because he broke a standing rule of all players that they were not to interfere in anyway, with the girl's basketball practices. The girl's coach had informed me that he had broken this rule and I had to suspend him from the team for the game that night.

On the night of the game I was standing at the entrance of the basketball gym when out of the blue, Joe came up behind me and delivered a hearty stinging blow to the back of my head. I was stunned to say the least. The policeman on duty immediately took over and hustled him off to the station to charge him with assault and battery.

A few days later I had to appear as a witness in court on Joe's case. After the assault and battery charges were read, the judge invited me to his chambers for a private conference and asked me what I would like to have handed out for a sentence. I explained to the Judge Joe's family background and the home pressures that had built up in him that caused his outburst at me. I asked the judge to be lenient with Joe and give him another chance.

Following my advice, the Judge placed Joe on probation for 1 year, telling him: "I was prepared to sentence you to the reformatory school for your vicious assault against your coach. Thanks to your coach's compassion, I'm giving you this second chance."

Joe became Captain of his football team, graduated from High School and joined the Navy. A few years later I received a glowing letter from his commanding officer to tell me of this boy's high caliber of service to his country. The C.O. let me know that Joe had often related how I took him under my wing with my pleadings with the judge to give him a second chance and after, and that Joe was truly eternally thankful to me for helping him to rebound to achieve his positive goals.

RECOLLECTIONS OF STANLEY
SERIOUS OLD TIME GAMES

PRANKS AND MISCHIEF AS TEENAGERS

In this book I relate some tales of wayward youth. Lest one think that I have a 'Holier than Thou' attitude, it's only fair that I fess-up to some of my own youthful hijinks. You've heard the song *"Angels we have heard on High",* but we were no angels growing up. Of major importance regarding youthful transgressions in most cases, are not so much the actions of the youths, as are the precurser (and post-cursing?) actions of the adults who they look up to. Are wayward kids going to be simply punished and/or otherwise neglected? *Or will adult's efforts be invested in working to help them to redeem and reshape their own futures?* Kids have to test their limits to help them to decide what to commit their caring to as adults.

"During the first period of a man's life the greatest danger is: not to take the risk.
S.A. Kierkegaard

In this process it's natural that they stray a bit out of bounds on occasion. Kids need caring adults to correct, support and sustain them pursuant to a more generative direction. Only with help was I lucky enough to have made it past these challenging adolescent years for the better. I can only hope that I continued the tradition by helping a few others in my small way over the years.

I'm brought to this topic because last night my grandchildren celebrated Halloween and it rekindled memories of how we celebrated the *'Trick or Treat'* night and other thrill seeking occasions when we were teens. As I reflect back on some of the pranks we pulled, the transgressions of many of today's youngsters seem far less destructive than ours were. And where today's are more destructive, such as the tragedy at Columbine High School, to me the fault lies mostly with the parents who failed to properly guide and supervise them from the beginning. If only those children had had the opportunity to gain better self-esteem by having learned to skillfully wield a tennis racket or a baseball bat or other constructive avocation in competition, instead of a rifle in desperation.

Back to our 'less than angelic' activities as teens: Well of course there was the ritual **tipping over of the railroad crossing tender's outhouse**, preferably while he occupied it! Another of our favorites was to tie an iron weight onto a rope and hang it on a neighbor's door or under a window. Then we would attach the weight to a long rope and from across the street we would pull on it to create a pendulum effect that pounded the door on every swing. The repetitive ruckus was easily enough to raise the ire of the occupants.

Another more regretful escapade was more on the vandalism side and if we had done it today it would have landed us in jail as arsonists. One night two of the older boys enticed me to go along with them to an old abandoned hay barn. I was really just an innocent bystander as I watched them set the hay on fire. My innocence notwithstanding, if we had been caught, I would have been just as guilty under the law as the two who set it. Fortunately, the firemen quickly extinguished the flames and saved the building. A side note: That old barn was later renovated and became the home of the 49ers Club.

Another favorite ritual that occurred on Halloween night or the night before the 4th of July was to set fire to one of the abandoned freight cars that were parked on the old Branch Tracks across from the Stanley Works Company Field. Again this was a prank then and would be a significant crime today.

Intermingled with all of the more constructive games we played as youngsters, were the more dangerous 'Rock Fights' we held, and other petty vandalism we did. We were not angels. Fortunately we had family, neighborhood, school and eventually recreation support systems to eventually get us flying right.

"Judge not, and ye shall not be judged; condemn not, and ye shall not be condemned, forgive, and ye shall be forgiven"
-Luke 6:37

NEIGHBORS IN STANLEY BETWEEN WWI & WWII

Starting at the foot of Wall Street we had the Resmini family living in the three decker over looking the Town River. (I believe that this is the home that Lena Cassani said was converted to a hospital during the 1918 Diphtheria Outbreak.) The parents were named Genaro (we called him Genny) and his wife Tranquila, (who was the village Midwife who delivered my sister Angie and me.)

Genny was one of the three Resmini brothers who lived in Stanley. They were related to the Folloni family via marriage. My father's sister Louise married Louis Resmini. The other Resmini brother was named John. Genny's family consisted of 3 girls, Mary, Esther, and Mina, and a son Peter, who was a scrawny little fellow. Next door lived the Giovanni Family and son "Skinny" Giovanni, a tall slender kid, who played first base on our ball team. Skinny had two sisters, Dena and Alice.

Moving on up the same side of Wall Street were the Alberghini's. Enio Albreghini was a quiet kid, who turned out to be an excellent bowler. Enio had two sisters, Olga and Anita. Living in the other side of the same duplex was the Tassinari Family consisting of two girls Laura and Mary and their stocky brother Leonard "Mutt" Tassinari.

Across the street we had the Cassiani family. Actually they lived on High Street at the foot of Wall Street next to the river. The Cassiani family had 4 boys. Nato was the oldest, next was Quinto, followed by Vinnie, the guy who would come into play as the hero in my previously mentioned near drowning incident. The youngest boy in the family was Renaldo, nicknamed "Tack" due to his small stature. There were three sisters, Carmon, Eleanor, Lillian, and Mary.

Coming back to Wall Street, on the east side of the street, was the Filippini household. Tozi was the oldest, followed by Bobby and Nello. They had 2 sisters, Nora and Nina. In the same duplex lived the Rubelli family. Gus Rubelli was the oldest boy followed by three girls, Teccla, Miranda, and Nini.

Next door was the Moruzzi family. Joe, the oldest, was a professional boxer. Danny, John, Andrew, and Alphonse, ("Shine") followed him in order. That was the nickname we gave him because he really did shine as a pitcher on our baseball team. They had three sisters, Faustina, who married Tom Magistrate, Margaret, who married Ernest Molla and Rose.

The next house was the home of the Chiocca family. I have been told that somewhere back in the family tree the Chioccas' were supposed to be related to the Lombardi's (on my mother's side of the family) back in Italy. The Chioccas' were a large family; Albert was the oldest, followed by Jimmy, Mario, (who was killed in Germany during World War II), Eddie, and Ernest, "Ney" the youngest. The three sisters were named Mary, Angie, Primely, and Della.

The only non-Italians in Stanley occupied the next two houses. The Meheen Family, much older than our age group, consisted of Connie and his brother Jim and their two elder spinster sisters, Bridget and Annie.

Many were the mornings when Jim would awaken us early as he was passing our house on his way to his job as a Railroad crossing tender. As he passed Jim would be cursing loud and clear that Annie had burned his toast or about some other trivial but overblown home encounter. One of the mischievous activities our gang pursued was the ritual of tipping over Jim Meehan's outhouse, which was located directly across from his railroad crossing shed. No wonder he was in a foul mood when he got home!

Next to the Meehan's was the Martin house, which was located next to the Folloni home. In the Martin household were sisters Mary and Beatrice and brothers Joe and Ralph. Ralph later became a principal at the Framingham High School and the Assistant Director of the State Principals Association. When I became the Chairman of the State Rules Committee, Ralph and I had many meetings together.

Across the street again we came to the Resmini Family, who were cousins of our cousins who lived on Bolton Place. There in a duplex home was a large contingent of the John "Minasse" Resmini Clan. "Minasse" as we nicknamed him, had three sets of families. One family, the Resminis', from his first wife who died at a very young age and the "Matties" who he later married, taking in her whole family to live with him. The third set came from his second marriage to Mrs. Mattie, who also had a split family with a deceased spouse. The third set made a total of 10 children in the family who all got along as one happy family.

The John Resmini family consisted of Tim, Mike, Louise, Molly, and Tina. The Matties' family consisted of Irene, Louie and Peter. They were a happy large family and at one time they ran a small Mom and Pop Store that was adjacent to their home. In the upstairs apartment lived the Ferrari family, John and Lena, with children Marissa, Louise, Aldo and John.

At the rear of the Resmini home was another house where the Querzoli family lived. They too ran a Mom and Pop store for many years. Oreste and Carmen raised their family of Albert, Edward, (who became the Editor of the Quincy Patriot Ledger newspaper) and Nancy.

Next door to the Resminis' came the Donati Family. The patriarch of the family was named "Gildo", who was a constant visitor and companion to my Dad. I believe his wife's name was Victoria. They had four children, sons Elmer and Peter and daughters, Inez, (who married "Digger" Campbell) and Jenny, who married a nice Jewish fellow from New York City. They returned every summer for vacations at the family homestead. I remember that on each visit he would treat all the kids in Stanley to ice creams.

Elmer Donati married a girl from Plymouth named Eleanor and they built a home on a vacant lot next to the family homestead. I still recall as a youngster of about 10 years old, the day that they broke ground to build, as I was the one they selected to dig the first shovel of dirt for the new foundation.

The last house on Wall Street before the railroad tracks belonged to the Balboni Family. Aristus was a barber. He and his wife, Albina raised a large family consisting of sons, Peter, Preston, Jake, Elmer, (who was to become my brother-in-law), and Charlie. The daughters were named Margaret, Rose, Mary, and Alice.

Across the Railroad tracks the first house on the right belonged to the Campanini Family, with son Romeo "Roach", and daughters Tina and Irene. Next to them came the Abati Family consisting of the girls, Jennie, Mary, and Fifi. The boys were Erminio, ("Bo") and Patrick.

The next house, a duplex, belonged to one of the local Molla families. Teresa and her son Tony and his wife Edith lived in the other side of the duplex.

Going on further north about 1/4 of a mile was the Perry complex. Jesse Perry lived in the house and adjacent to it he had a used car dealership. It later became known as Perry's Junk Yard. Ralph Balboni lived in an adjoining apartment.

The next house North of the junkyard was the home of Ernest and Margaret Molla and their two children, Ernest Jr. and Margaret.

Back to the West side of Wall Street just over the Railroad tracks we came to the Cassiani home. Sylvio and his wife raised a family of 3 girls and a boy on their farmhouse. The Stanley Works sold them the large 'Company Field' tract of land across the street. This was the field that was used by Tim Madden for cultivating his annual hay crops that I mentioned elsewhere in my story. It was the scene of many incidents in our growing childhood days.

Up to the next house that was located across the street from Perry's JunkYard was the Victor Martelli Family, consisting of 2 girls and 2 boys. I well remember Victor, as he was a real good left-handed Bocce player who played many a game on my Dad's home-built Courts. I guess that my Dad was a community recreation activity director in his own right!

Next on the left of Wall Street was the Oreste Bresciani family homestead. The oldest daughter was named Josephine, who was a real toughie and acted the part of a male on many occasions. Josephine and her brothers Quarino and Albert were the bulwarks in maintaining the family chicken farm. Twin brothers Fatty & Skinny, also lived there. This farm has since been converted to a huge housing development. The last house up on Wall Street was a newer home built by son Quarino.

Up on Oak Street were the Ventura Farm and the Munise Farm. Manuel Munise was our milkman. His sons were Manual and Joseph, and Beatrice and Malina were his daughters. Then came Joe Poleti and his animal farm. The Duponts lived next to the farm. (The Rockefellers and the Vanderbuilts were nowhere to be seen.) Up the Street was the Piscatori and Paleti household which included Harry, Gene, and Albert Piscatori. George Paleti, my ball playing buddy, also lived with his family in separate quarters of this household.

Back to Bolton Place, which was diagonally across the street from our home. It started with the Ferioli household. Martini and Edvega had a family of six, including four boys, Mario, Frank, Aldo, and William. The two girls were Mary and her sister Alice, who later married Paul Pallatroni Sr. and moved in to the next apartment.

Located in the same duplex was the Bertelli family, with sons Dino and Alfred. Alfred was killed in World War II. They had 2 daughters, Caroline and Mary. Next came the Guasconi family with sons Albert and Eugene (Gino) and daughters, Katherine and Mary.

After that came the Vincento and Gousta Rego family with son Peter, and in the next house lived Victor and Eva "Sala" Resmini with son Renaldo and daughter, Eleanor. Their grandmother named Nonni also lived here.

Then came the Louis & Louise Resmini (my dad's sister) family with their brood. Starting with Gelmedia (my godmother and still living at the age of 94 at this writing), Mary Ralli, Emma Messaline, Alice Ferioli, Dorothy Pratti, and Ilene. Their sons were Primo (who married his neighbor Annie Pratti), Raymond and Louis.

Living in the last house on the street was the Pratti family; Charlie and Delchesia were the parents of Sandy, Harold, Robert, Nello, Raleigh, and daughter Anne.

Back up Bolton Place was the Santelli Complex. I don't recall the parent's names. Their children were Alexander, Minnie Valeri, Peary Gabriel, Malina Valeri, and

Anne Cassiani. (They all lived in adjoining homes in the Santelli Complex and since there was no telephone system in those days they all opened their windows and bellowed their daily news gossip loud enough for all of Stanley to hear.) The only outsider from the Santilli family living in their complex was the Ticchi family. The Ticchi children were sons Andrew, Sam, Albert, and James. The daughters were Julia and Helen.

One family I almost forgot was the Mike Azack Family who lived way up in Bolton Place about a half mile from the Pratti's home. It was a narrow cart part that led up to their home in the middle of nowhere. Daughters Delia and Emily lived there along with a caretaker called Jessie. At one time my brother Al suggested that we purchase this property along with the Heywood property and home up on East Street, on the West Bridgewater line. That would have given us the property rights to land that now could be worth big dollars to developers. We should have listened to Al. We could have purchased this property for a song.

WANT BUS IN RAIN—A protest movement over the lack of a bus to carry Bridgewater high school and junior high pupils a mile and a half to classes, resulted in what school officials believe is a strike. Students want busses, even if only on rainy days. Angela Folloni and Charles Balboni (above) agree.

Angie Folloni with her future brother-in-law and neighbor, Charlie Balboni, shown here in support of busses from outlying areas to school, "even if only on rainy days."

Their 'move to improve' looks to be pretty innocent and progressive, although it says "school officials believe that their protest movement is a strike". The paper's headline seems to agree.

Sometimes a little civil noise has to be made to get the attention required to begin the process of making progressive institutional changes.

GAMES WE PLAYED DURING OUR PRE-TEEN YEARS

PADDLE BASEBALL: This was a game we played using two paddles we carved out of the end of grape boxes that my Dad had emptied to make wine. With two paddles and a rubber ball we devised our own rules to play and get a good workout.

DUCK ON THE ROCK: (See Chapter on Family Roots)

KICK THE CAN: This game was in some respects similar to the game of DUCK ON THE ROCK. The "IT" player would place a CAN in a circle about a yard in diameter. The other players would then seek hiding places in the area. Ideal hiding places would be behind a barn or outhouse, down an embankment, behind a tree, etc. The "IT" player would count up to 10 or 20 to give the other players a chance to find a hiding place. The "IT" player had to cover his eyes or turn his back to give the other players a chance to hide. Once the count was up, the "IT" player would then try to locate any of the hidden players. If he found one he would have to identify him, tag him and run back to the circle where the can was located and tag the can before the found player could reach the can. If he legally got back to his can the player he identified and tagged would then become "IT".

Remember that the can would always have to be in the circle before the "IT" player could seek out another player who is in hiding. In the meantime while the "IT" player was seeking someone in hiding, anyone of the other players could come out of hiding and run to the circle and KICK THE CAN to protect the other players. Once the can was kicked out of the circle, the "IT" player then would have to retrieve the can and return it to the circle before he could seek out another player.

PEG: The equipment used to play PEG was very simple, as follows: two paddles made out of the ends of grape boxes and a peg about 4 inches long and 1 inch in diameter. The ends of the peg were carved to a point on each end. Goals were set up similar to a complete baseball diamond or, for close quarters play, using just two bases of the diamond.

The player at bat would put his peg down at home plate and hit down on the end of it with his paddle to get it airborne. Once airborne the player all in one motion would attempt to hit his peg as far as possible, then take off for first base. The rules are the same as in baseball. The only difference being that you are using the paddle and peg instead of a bat and ball.

BUCK BUCK: Two teams are selected. The number of players on each team could be from 6 on each side, on up to as many players available. The more players, the longer the buck and longer leaps were needed. A coin was tossed to decide which team would begin by making the BUCK and which team would be first to leap.

The 'Buck' was made by one player from the 'down' team lining up bent over with his backside against a wall. If the game was played at night the backstop would be an electric pole with a streetlight that would illuminate the game. The next player on his team would then line up next to the post player by bending at the waist and placing his head up against the side of his teammates butt, and forming a sturdy connection to his teammate with his shoulder. Each succeeding player would then line up in the same way with the player in front of him. When the Buck was formed the other team would then begin leaping. Usually the most agile players jumped first in order to leap as far up on the Buck as possible to make room for the other players who would follow to make successive leaps on to the Buck. If any of the players on the leaping team should fall off of the Buck or touch the ground with their feet or any part of their body, then that team would be out and would then take the Buck position, and the other team would become the leapers. Of course there was a code of fairness adopted by the 'down' team, who could not shift around unduly to rock the top guys off.

Once all the players from the leaping side completed their leaps successfully on the Buck then the last leaper would place his hand up showing the post player how many fingers he had up and would yell out, *"BUCK BUCK HOW MANY FINGERS DO I HAVE UP?* Which showed a random number that the lead leaper chose. Then the captain of the team that was down (someone other than the post-man) would have to guess the correct number of fingers up. If he made the correct guess, then his team then became the leapers and the game repeated as explained above. If at any time during the process of leaping and before the captain made his guess on the number of fingers, the buck should collapse from the weight of the leaping team (which did happen quite frequently) the down team would continue as the Buck and the game again repeated.

HORSE AND RIDER: Teams were made up of two players each with one player mounting his partner piggyback. When all of the teams were mounted the signal was given to start. The rider of each team tried to dismount any of the other riders. Once any part of a rider's body touched the ground then that team was eliminated from the contest. The take down battle continued until only one team remained intact and they became the *WINNER AND CHAMPIONS FOR THE DAY.*

CRICKET (Stanley Style): We made up our own version of Cricket. We lined up two tin cans with a cross stick on top of them. Another set of two cans would be placed about 60 feet away with a small hole made in front of each set of cans, which we called the goals. The number of players on each team could range from one or two up to 3 or 4 depending upon the playing area available. The players at the goals would have a bat.

The opponents would be the field team and one of the field team players would pitch the ball from behind one of the goals. The pitcher would try to knock the stick off of the can at the goal 60 feet away. When the pitch is made, the player at bat attempts to hit the ball as in baseball. If he hits the ball he then would run to the other goal and he and his teammate would keep on exchanging places and touching the hole in front of their cans until the opponents could retrieve the ball and try to knock the sticks off the cans. Anytime that the stick is knocked off of the can while the opponents bat is out of the hole that is an out for the team at bat. The number of exchanges made from each goal counts the runs. The rules of baseball apply other than rules listed above.

"STINKOS"

The Jenkins Leather Board Plant abutted the Stanley residential section. It was on the Town River, which it used to dump the leather board waste materials. For awhile this area of the river was our favorite swimming hole on the hot summer days, however when waste dumping became more prevalent around the '30's, the swimming had to cease. Not only did it take away our summer recreation area but also on hot humid days and nights, the unbearably horrendous smell of this waste would permeate throughout the whole Stanley area.

The local residents complained vigorously about the stench, but to no avail. This "Stinko Scenario" went on and on for many years before the town officials finally put a stop into the dumping of the waste into the river. We residents of Stanley, who were the primary victims of this pollution, were also stigmatized by some in town as "Stinkos" because we lived there.

How wonderful that this area is now being converted back to a more pristine recreation park for all of the people of town and the area to use. I'm so glad that we are making progress by going back, in a manner, to *some* of the old ways.

A section of the old Stanley Ironworks property is in the process of being converted into a Park. The park will be a joint effort of the Bridgewater Conservation, Historical and Recreation Commissions, directing donations of time and funds from various state and local agencies and private contributors to create a beautiful town park.

Contributions for development of the park can be made care of: The Natural Resources Trust of Bridgewater. P.O. Box 15, Bridgewater, MA 02324

SACCO & VANZETTI

Many have heard of the Sacco & Vanzetti Trial. Yet few realize that the town of Bridgewater was intricately involved in this historic drama. The attempted robbery of the L.Q. White Shoe Factory in town that was a key factor in this world famous case, happened on Christmas eve of 1919, six weeks after my birth.

Nicola Sacco and Bartolomeo Vanzetti, two south shore area Italian immigrant anarchists, were convicted and executed in 1927 for the murder of two guards during the 1920 robbery of the payroll of the Slater and Morrill Shoe Factories in So. Braintree. This 'trial of the century' is highly controversial to this day and many books and treatises have been written about it. Many believe that these two were found guilty and punished because of their ethnicity and political beliefs. Other credible accounts indicate that Sacco was really guilty and Vanzetti wasn't. Maybe one or both were guilty or innocent no matter how tainted the judicial process may have been. Whatever the truth, they may never have gone to trial for the capital crime had Bridgewater Police Chief Michael Stewart, who was investigating anarchists during that 'red scare' era, not noticed the similarity between it and the similar Christmas eve robbery in Bridgewater.

Chief Stewart set up a trap at an Elm Square address where a stolen Buick presumably involved in the Braintree murder was being repaired. Under a prearranged plan, the wife of the repair shop owner called police when Sacco and Vanzetti and two other anarchists arrived. The group suddenly left after seeing that the cars plates were out of date. Sacco & Vanzetti were quickly arrested on a streetcar in Campello. Their two cohorts, who had solid alibis for the murder day, were released.

Sacco & Vanzetti repeatedly lied during purportedly slanted police questioning, presumably out of fear that their anarchist ties would taint them. Since Sacco was at work the day of the Bridgewater crime, and the self-employed fish dealer Vanzetti couldn't establish a strong alibi, he was convicted of that attempted robbery and murder and given substantial jail time. This conviction was used as a basis to bring both of them to trial for the Braintree robbery, which happened on a day that Sacco was off from his work at a Boston Shoe Factory. Witnesses from the area appeared for both the prosecution and the defense at both trials, variously placing the men near the scenes of the crime, or with alibis. A railroad crossing gate tender testified to seeing Vanzetti get out of the passenger side of the front seat of a Buick at the Matfield crossing just north of Stanley several hours after the killings.

Of particular note to this story is that on many occasions growing up I heard hush toned rumors that Vanzetti, the fish peddler from Plymouth, sometimes visited the area. It's pretty certain that Vanzetti peddled both eels and anarchist propaganda in Bridgewater and environs. Beyond that, I don't know what, if any acquaintances or business dealings he may have had in Stanley. I never pursued any details of any possible Sacco and Vanzetti 'Stanley connection'.

I wonder if the reluctance of the adults of that time to discuss the matter was related to a fear of being singled out as a troublemaker by the authorities of that 'red scare' era. Or maybe it was out of the difficulty they must have had resolving a conflict in their feelings about them. On the one hand Sacco & Vanzetti were considered folk heroes and martyrs for being accused and punished based on their ethnicity. On the other hand, the hard working upwardly aspiring Italian-AMERICANS in Stanley scorned their anarchist beliefs.

Bartolomeo Vanzetti & Nicola Sacco, circa 1920

It would be interesting to hear if any of the remaining old timers from Stanley have any recollection of stories of these events of eight decades ago. In any case, anarchy was the furthest thing from the minds of Stanley youth as we were as organized as we could be with our games and our dreams for a better future of our own creation in this great land.

NOTE

For whatever its worth, on August 23, 1977, fifty years to the day of the executions of Sacco and Vanzetti, Michael S. Dukakis, Governor of Massachusetts, issued a proclamation that concluded with the words:

"Therefore, I, Michael S. Dukakis, Governor of the Commonwealth of Massachusetts ... hereby proclaim Tuesday, August 23, 1977, "NICOLA SACCO AND BARTOLOMEO VANZETTI MEMORIAL DAY"; and declare, further, that any stigma and disgrace should be forever removed from the names of Nicola Sacco and Bartolomeo Vanzetti, from the names of their families and descendants, and so ... call upon all the people of Massachusetts to pause in their daily endeavors to reflect upon these tragic events, and draw from their historic lessons the resolve to prevent the forces of intolerance, fear, and hatred from ever again uniting to overcome the rationality, wisdom, and fairness to which our legal system aspires."

They weren't pardoned. That would have been a declaration that they definitely had been guilty. They were, in a manner of speaking, apologized to.

Family Athletic Conquests & Connections
& 1ˢᵗ Edition of the Extended Family Photo Album

"From a single acorn, a thousand forests grow."

FOLLONI TEAM PATRIACH GIOVANNI 'JOHN' FOLLONI (NONO)
pulled himself up by more than just his bootstraps.
Shown here doing a septuagenarian pull-up* on his grape vine trellis
above his old Bocce Ball Courts on Wall St. in Stanley. Caesar Filippetti watches.
[You should have seen him do octogenarian dancing, balancing a half-filled beer glass on his head!]

"It is a classic immigrant story - one generation paving the road of success for the next."
Brian McGrory, Boston Globe feature columnist on another family's story

At the turn of the 20th century my dad, John Folloni and his wife Mary "Lombardi" Folloni decided to leave the peasant life of the old country in Italy to come to America, the land of the free and the home of the brave. It was a courageous move on their part to have my dad leave my mom and their newborn daughter Virginia back in Italy to come over to America to seek the benefits of this new country for his growing family to come.

Actually, my dad came over alone at first and worked himself to the bone as a labourer building the railroad lines from Canada to the eastern borders of New England and New York. He earned all of 50 cents a day for this work. Out of this meagre stipend, he managed to save enough to later send for his wife, my mother and my oldest sister Virginia to come over to America. This great move by my parents gave us the opportunity to enjoy the freedom, the educational opportunities and the wealth of this great young nation.

Dad and mom had (7) children, Virginia, Michael, Albert, Larry. Angie, and Johnny. (Their second son, also named Albert, died at age 3.) My parents and siblings worked so hard at just surviving that it is amazing to see how far their descendants have prospered and been able to excel in 'non-survival' endeavours such as athletics. Its not that they weren't gifted in the arts or athletics, or that they didn't enjoy athletics and recreation, its just that *'the right thing'* that they knew they had to do was to set the foundation for the future of their present family and their offspring.

Our family is no more special than any other who inhabited and developed this great land. I believe, however, that it is at least an exemplary story of our times and quite positively so. So let me try to relate a bit about the Athletic Conquests and Connections of this extended "Folloni Team".

I guess we could start with my Dad who was a champ "Bocce Player". For those of you not familiar with the game, it is very similar to 'lawn bowling', where players score by bowling their ball closest to the target ball. Unlike standard bowling of today, strategy as well as athletic prowess is involved, as players can play both offense and defense at the same time, with the option of hitting the opponents' balls out of scoring range. Dad built his own "Bocce Court" next to our family store in the little Italy Stanley area where weekly tournaments were held.

From here on we go to my oldest brother, Mike, who was a bowling star in his own right and the winner of many bowling championships. He once bowled a 193 score in candlepins to win a coveted $5,000.00 prize. He used the money to build a swimming pool in his back yard for family workouts and recreation. At the age of 87, he still plays golf 3 or 4 times per week and is still winning tournaments. I shot my age at 77 and get this, Mike just shot his age when he scored an 87! Remarkable!

My brother Al was not too athletically inclined, but he was a great businessman and innovator. He became the personal business manager of the one and only undefeated heavyweight boxing championship of the World, "Rocky Marciano".

Next in line came me, Larry Folloni. My first venture into the Athletic Field came about when as a 10-year-old youngster; I organised and coached my first team, "The Stanley Steamers". We went out and collected junk items such as old lead and copper pipes, rags and newspapers to sell to the Junkman. The money we earned we used to buy our first uniforms for the baseball team. We proudly wore these bright yellow and blue jerseys with the words "Stanley Steamers" blazoned on the chest. The rest of my story is told in this book.

My kids dislike that I talk about their athletic accomplishments to others. I certainly never gave them glowing accolades while they were achieving them, as I always wanted them to aspire to even greater heights. To the extent that I failed to impart confidence in them with this tact, I failed, but let me try redressing this a bit as I'm able to, and continue with the expository nature of this commentary, with the succeeding:

CHIPS OFF THE OLD COACH'S BLOCK

Larry Jr. not only was the top academic student in his class but a super athlete.

He was the leading hitter and pitcher on his little league baseball team. As a 10-year-old he pitched a No Hit-No Run game. He was captain and star on his high school basketball team, which would most likely have been state champs except for the transfer of 3 stars from his Jr. H.S. class. In adult leagues he outscored many of my 'all time all stars'. Larry was the leading scorer on his Biddy League basketball team and the statistical leader in most categories on his biddy league and little league baseball teams. In reviewing old playground league records I see that in many years and for many categories (hits, runs, homeruns, etc.), Larry Jr. actually led the league. At the end of season, however, trophies in all but one category were awarded to others so as not to hint at favouritism, to instil team spirit, and to 'share the wealth'. I'd guess that this was an ambivalent pill for Larry to swallow as a youngster. I don't know how those days contributed to the merit-based, yet benevolent views on life that he holds as an adult.

Larry Jr's greatest athletic accomplishments came on the Golf Course. He was the only player in history to win the Brockton City Junior Golf Tournament for three consecutive years. He won the prestigious Hearst State Junior Golf Tournament. At the age of 18 he had the lowest competitive round of golf in New England when he shot a club record 6 under par of 66. At the age of 18 he was the Brockton Country Club Champion. Larry went on to become one of the most successful computer chip Chemical Engineers in the country.

My son Bobby's athletic heroics were mostly in basketball, and have been mentioned previously. Some of his greatest performances, however, have been made in what might be called the amateur entertainment field. Bob is a humorous delight to have around, and the life of many a party.

Son Michael was Captain of his cross-country team and won many trophies while setting many enduring course records in long distance runs across the State. During one of his meets when he was coming down with a flu, he stumbled and fell about 20 yards short of the finish line. With grit and determination he clawed and crawled the last 20 yards to do the best that he could, which is all that we can ever ask of anyone. Michael missed his senior year of competition due to a back injury, but he finished 6th in a New England Invitational meet at Franklin Park in his last race as a junior. Michael went on to Harvard University where he was a roommate of All-American football player #87 Pat McInally, ultra marathoner 'Moonshine' Jim Brynteson, John "Doctor Wagstaff" Forman and the Quinntessential intramural athlete, official and author, Don Hirsohn.

My two daughters, Jean and Debbie were married to Kevin Leen and Tom Dent, respectively, who were both very good athletes in their younger days. Debbie was an excellent tennis player in high school and showed great promise as a basketball player until a knee injury cut short that endeavour. Jean was a very good field hockey player under Ms. Joan "Ando" Cassabian. She has been limited in athletic range as a young adult with the early onset of arthritis. She still manages to often jog distances with her friends and daughter. Both my girls did more than respectably in high school girl's sports and their kids are really shining stars!

Jean and Kevin's daughter Taylor is a premier dance troupe performer and an enthusiastic surfer under the kind tutelage of a friend and former olympic surfing coach Kevin Grondin. Taylor also skis and is a fine basketball and softball player. She recently won the female division (2nd overall for her pre-teen age group) in a Rye, NH 5K running race. Whatever she dedicates herself to, with her skill, mental acuity and determination, Taylor will succeed in. *Taylor's early dance moves.*

Fashionable, friendly Taylor-a great catch!

Their son, "Hammerin' Cameron Hank" is a fierce and capable competitor in all-major sports. He is a great contact hitter in baseball, a hard working and effective scorer in basketball, a top notch QB and receiver in NFL sponsored flag football, and a vicious scorer and stalwart goalie in soccer. Cam's father Kevin is a great all around athlete and an avid, long-ball hitting golfer. Kevin nurtures Cammy's enthusiasm for sports and learning, and the ambience of our sporting household is not lost on him. Watch for Cameron Leen!

Debbie and Tom's children are naturally very good athletes and great sports. Jenny and Michael lead the Dent ski & song & dance team that visits us in New Hampshire every winter. In diminutive Victoria's 1st year as a soccer play she was notorious for being able to weave in and out of traffic with the ball, and for having a knack of emerging from clusters with the ball. They knick-named her: "Here comes Vickie!" In Scottie's 1st ever organized basketball game at age 5, he scored 10 of his team's 12 points on 5 of 6 shooting! Thomas Scott <u>Lawrence</u> Dent has also already scored several 'hat tricks' in his 1st year of youth soccer!

Jennifer, Victoria, Michael and Scott.

Tom is an avid skier and sailer, a pretty good golfer, and was a champ wrestler in his school days. Besides his exploits as a great trial lawyer, one of his major claims to fame was:

Tom Dent's Hole In One
(And One Of All)

An Ace's Ace (and covering every base) Day

A very unusual event happened over Labor Day weekend, 1998. My son-in-law Tom Dent and my daughter Debbie came in from Chicago for the christening of their new baby boy Thomas Scott Dent Jr. The day before the christening, Sat., Aug. 30, I took Tom out to the Portsmouth Country Club for a round of golf. We had a foursome made up of Tom, Frank Pickard, Bill Snow, and myself.

Since he is a corporate lawyer for a large law firm in Chicago, he has very little time to spend on the golf courses, and this was only his 6th round that year.

Not only did Tom make his first Hole-in-One on the 16th hole, but he also came within a hair of having two holes in one within the space of 4 playing holes. According to other players by the green, Tom's tee shot on the 13th hole rolled right over the edge of the cup and nearly dropped in.

Interestingly, Tom had every number from 1 to 7 on his scorecard, and on the last 7 holes he had the numbers 1 through 6! On the difficult 18th hole he made about a 7-foot putt for a birdie to complete his most unusual round. I'm sure that he was not trying for a '7' on that hole to complete the flush.

Jimmy, my youngest, was also a star on the basketball team and the Captain of his golf team. One of his claims to fame (in addition to his Ty Cobb / Ted Williams connection as explained earlier) was that in the first week of his senior year, he and a high school senior named Patrick Ewing were both Bay State "Players of the Week" in their respective divisions. His and Donna's daughter Ava Grace, though only a year old, is definitely breaking the mold in terms of published expected behaviours from her age group.

Next came my younger brother Johnny, who played baseball for the local High School Team then went on to join the Army Air Force to become a Colonel. I see from the internet that along the road to success, one of his son's competes well in non standard up-hill races and I hear from him that his grandchildren are great sports enthusiasts and are great basketball players.

My younger sister Angela was a "Rosie the Riveter" building ships at the Quincy Shipyard for the War effort. She married Elmer Balboni, whose nephew was Steve "Bye Bye" Balboni the very successful major league baseball player who I've mentioned earlier. Angie and her husband Elmer were avid golfers. They are the only husband and wife team to each have a hole-in-one at the prestigious Manchester Country Club.

Last on the list is my oldest sister, Virginia, who was married to Caesar Filippetti. They were the proud parents of 5 daughters and 2 sons who grew up close to my family and have remained very close. Sports have filled a very important role in lives of the Filippetti Family. In so many ways they have fulfilled the aspirations of their mother and grandfather and for their kids, their grandmother and great-grandfather (soon to be great-great grandfather for the hopefully durable 'Durham' generation.) According to Rosalie, The competitive nature of 'the games' was imbued in their family in part due to the size of their family: They all wanted to be 'seen' and to be the best. Their parent's greatest joy was to watch them grow intellectually, but their pride in their children's sports accomplishments would not be denied either!!

Their oldest daughter Mary played basketball and volleyball at St. Patricks High School and was a cheerleader at Stonehill College. She married Stephen Markey who became a very successful lawyer. They are the parents of five children. Her oldest daughter, Lisa married Bill Zolga, who was a star Basketball player for Stonehill College. He then played professional basketball in the European League with a German and a Belgian Team. Bill was named to the Stonehill College Athletic Hall of Fame. Steve and Mary's children and grandchildren are star athletes in baseball, basketball, soccer and lacrosse.

Next came son Lou, who like his sisters, started his athletic career with our early town playground programs of the early '50's. Lou was an all-scholastic basketball player on the 1956 State Championship Team at Bridgewater, and went on to star at Stonehill College. An insurance industry executive by original trade, he later become a renowned referee in Basketball and Umpire in Baseball. Lou has been one of the top Officials in the Country and was at one time elected to become president of the Eastern Board of Basketball Officials. Lou was honored by the IAABO with a lifetime achievement award in Atlanta, on April 25, 2003. Lou's daughter, Terri, a top volleyball player at Stonehill is married to **Karim Garcia**, now playing for the Cleveland Indians professional baseball team.

Notice how the 'rocks' of yore evolved into so much success at **Stone**hill?

Virginia's daughter Rosalie married Tony Ghelfi, a three-sport star at Bridgewater, who turned to golfing after his school athletic days and became a 2 handicapper. Tony, by the way, grew up on High St., just a few hundred yards above Stanley and a few hundred more below his future 'Italian Queen' of a wife, Rosalie.

Their oldest son Scott was a top distance runner at Falmouth High School where he was captain of the Cross Country and Winter and Spring track teams, leading them to 3 state titles in the early '80's. He went on to the University of New Hampshire to continue his athletic feats. Scott is now involved as a coach in several youth sports for many age levels.

Their son Christopher was also a track ace at Falmouth High and finished 3rd in the State Freshman race before going on to star on the repeat State Title team. Chris is now a veteran actor on Broadway.

Chris Ghelfi (center) hosts l-r Michael Folloni, his dad Tony, James Folloni, Donna Spratt, his mom Rosalie and Thuy Vo between his Broadway touring performances as a star of 'Saturday Night Fever'. San Francisco, 2001

Rosalie and Tony's son Michael is probably the most accomplished athlete in their family. He was arguably the best golfer in the State in his senior year of High School. He was a star at Providence College where he was selected as athlete of the year in 1989. He has won many titles, including the Big East Championship. He also qualified for the NCAA tournament in his junior and senior years when he got to compete against the likes of Phil Mickelson, the noted Pro golfer. He is currently golf pro at the Ballymeade Country Club. Michael has won many golf tournaments over the years. Rosalie and Tony's grandchildren are now making their marks in the athletic fields. Their son Scott's son Durham leads the way as a star on several teams. He is a top baseball & soccer player, but hockey is where he is currently making his mark playing for Falmouth and a AAA team (top level youth hockey) in Bridgewater where he is proving to be one of New England's best players in his young age group. Can you imagine how far sports and our way of living have progressed? As long as the kid's can achieve, but also just be kids, we're going along the right way.

Next comes Virginia's daughter Helen, my loving Godchild. She was a cheerleader in high school and played on the field hockey, basketball, and softball teams. Her son Todd was a select soccer team player as well as a star baseball player on his school team. He is a devoted father who instills the love of sports in each of his four children, all of whom play soccer, and two of them also play golf. Todd is also a wonderful volunteer with the Recreational League: he coaches two teams, assistant coaches another, and became the President of the League in 2003. Todd is now a partner in a prestigious Norfolk, VA law firm. Helen's daughter Monique played softball and basketball and is now coaching youth teams. Her children are also now beginning to make their major marks in the athletic field. Helen now plays tennis and golf, and she and Ed have great fun and have lots of friends from these activities.

Next comes Frances who was a varsity cheerleader for Bridgewater-Raynham Regional High School and graduated from Bridgewater State College. She became a Reading teacher for the Bridgewater Public School System and has worked at the Williams Middle School for over thirty years. Frances married Jack Morast, a native of Kansas City, Mo. Fran and Jack are the parents of 4 daughters and 1 son.

Their son John followed in his father's footsteps and works for the U.S. Postal Service in Randolph, MA. The daughters have been sports stars on their early path in life.

Their oldest daughter Kristen was an all-scholastic basketball player on the Bridgewater-Raynham Team that won the Class A State Championship in 1990. She dazzled the crowd at the Boston Garden with her behind the back passes 'a-la-Bob Cousy' and her all around play. Her team was the only undefeated team in the history of BRRHS. They finished that year with a 25 and 0 record. Kris later attended Stonehill College on a full basketball scholarship, where she also was a star on the Lady Chieftains Women's Basketball team for four years. Kristen is now married to Georgetown University Women's Basketball Assistant Coach Robert Clark and is the proud mother of Alyssa. (Attention WNBA scouts!) Kristen is a Reading Specialist in Baltimore, Maryland. Every year Kristen and a former Stonehill basketball teammate run the Elite Basketball Camp for girls in grades 2-8. Kristen was inducted into the Stonehill College Athletic Hall of Fame in May of 2003. They should make Nono, (Summa Cum Laude in the "School of Arduous Endeavours" = "Hard Knocks & Rocky Road U.") an honorary degree recipient. He sure bequeathed a lot to Stonehill.

Frances and Jack's middle two daughters, Kerry and Karla were cheerleaders for the B-R Regional High School football and basketball teams. Their cheerleading squads won numerous cheerleading competitions.

Their youngest daughter Kimberly is presently a senior at B-R Regional High School. Following in the footsteps of her older sister Kristen, Kimberly is also a star varsity soccer and basketball player for BRRHS. Kimberly was captain in her senior year at B-R where she has been the star since her freshman year. She was again selected for All Scholastic honors and she was named as the O.C.L. M V P of the year in 2003. She is planning to attend (let's guess?) Stonehill College next fall on a basketball scholarship.

Nancy was the sixth member of the Filippetti clan. She also played field hockey, basketball and softball and was an enthusiastic cheerleader. Nancy has six children, all of whom have been participants in high school or other recreation team sponsored sports activities. Her two oldest children, Scott and Lisa are now successful business people. Her youngest children are just starting to play sports, but show great promise in baseball, basketball and soccer. Two of Nancy's daughters followed in their mother's footsteps in becoming B-R cheerleaders.

Virginia's 7th and youngest child was Richard. Richard was a co-captain and an excellent basketball player for B-R. He went on to Worcester Polytechnical Institute and married a nice girl from the Cape. They now live in Shrewsbury, MA with their 3 children, Richard, Gregg and Katelyn, whose athletic exploits I've not yet heard about.

There in a nutshell are some of the Folloni Athletic Connections. I'm sure that we will be hearing more from the Folloni Clan as the children and grandchildren continue to carry on our Athletic Traditions.

Oh yes, there are many more offshoots to this athletic and immigrant's story than one might ever know or expect. Note, for example, the following excerpts from recent email correspondence between my cousin Adolf 'Bing' Folloni's son Danny and my son Michael, who found Danny through the internet:

1st reply

"Yes Michael I am the Dan (Danny) Folloni of Bridgewater MA. I hope that all is well with your Dad and family. Your dad was like an Uncle to me growing up he gave me my first summer intern job in 1967 at the Independent Nail Company (my Father "Bing" worked with your dad along with Hugo Baroni in those days) it was a learning experience which I will always remember. [Ed. Note – Danny was referring to my brother Michael Folloni here.]

I graduated from Northeastern University in 1975 majoring in MIS, Management Information Services now known as ITD, Information Technology Division in 1975. I reside in Marshfield Ma. with my lovely wife Jeanne since 1972 we just celebrated our 30th wedding anniversary October 21st 2002. We have 3 children Jacqueline 28, graduated from UMASS Dartmouth and lives a few miles down the road in Brant Rock Ma. Joseph 22 is attending Bridgewater State College majoring in Criminal Justice class of 2004 and Jessica 21 who is a part time student at BSC.

Since October of 1983 I've been employed by the Commonwealth of Massachusetts Information Technology Division under Administration and Finance my responsibilities are managing the Local Area Networks and Desktop Services for 14 state agencies including the Governors office staff at the State House in Boston. My wife and I vacation and spend the Summer and Fall weekends in Bethlehem New Hampshire a nice quite town in the sticks of NH. I enjoy all sports on TV take in a couple of movies a year, attend baseball, basketball, football and hockey games but most of all I enjoy walking the beaches of Marshfield and Duxbury with my wife and dog Samantha, we also have a cat named Whiskers.

Well that's it in a nutshell Oh, I almost forgot I do landscaping and gardening at my home and like all Italians I do have a green thumb. Say hello to all."

Dan Folloni

2nd Reply

"Mike, well now that I know its Mr. Basketball Larry Folloni I must mention your Dad taught me a lot about the game of basketball growing up in Bridgewater. During my four years at BR just watching him coach all you guys at practice and games meant a lot to me. When my son Joe started dribbling a basketball I knew he was born to play the game (yes one more Folloni on the basketball court). I would work with Joe especially using both his hands when dribbling, passing and shooting the ball. Joe worked hard at his game your dad and my son Joe would share letters on his awards he attained winning Elks and K of C free throw shootouts. Joe never made it to the Elks finals held in Indiana missing it by one free throw in three overtimes in his last year of eligibility, however, he did make it to

the finals, representing the Marshfield K of C held in Springfield, Ma. at the Hall of Fame, coming home victorious that year. The number one achievement in Joe's basketball career was when he was named Captain of his High School Team 98-99 we were so happy for him. All my children were involved in town sports soccer, basketball, football, baseball and softball it was a fun ride for all of us.

As for myself I was involved in basketball programs in the South Shore for 13 years. Marshfield and 5 surrounding towns formed the South Shore Youth Basketball League in 1989 which now has ballooned into 13 towns 6th, 7th and 8th grade levels broken down by A and B traveling teams 26 in total along with a girls league formed in 1994. In 1995 I formed a traveling league for 4th and 5th grade boys named Boys Youth Traveling Basketball League the 10 towns involved would travel to Marshfield the Marshfield parents loved it where they would only travel to the Marshfield gym every Saturday December through March Madness Playoffs. My wife and daughters were involved as the organizers of all the games keeping score and running the refreshment stands at the gym."

Dan Folloni

WOW! All these sporting connections and career success from Danny. And his sister Elizabeth is one of the most loving and beloved teachers to ever have served in Bridgewater. To think that both of them and all that they've contributed would not have come about except from "a single acorn" of a stop-off home made in America for their dad by my dad! Of course there were some hard knocks on a home-made bocce ball court during the Depression, but its within such tight community based recreation situations with understanding adult support is where youth best play out its flings and swings.

FAMILY ALBUM
1ST EDITION

Some of Filippetti family, C.1950

Some Filippetti grandchildren, C.2000

Mary & Steve Markey

Lou & Laurie Filippetti

Lou with grown kids

Helen Filippetti Preti-Wallace Family
Top: Todd Preti, Tricia Preti, Lauren Jones, Helen Preti, Ed Wallace and Monique Jones.
Middle: Sarah Jones & Taylor Jones
Bottom: Brent Preti, Merrick Preti, Megan Preti, Emily Preti and Michelle Jones

Nancy and family

Rosalie in High School

School kid Francis

Aunt Angie & Lou

Marie Falloni McClure's wedding

Helen Folloni & namesake God daughter Helen Filippetti Preti-Wallace in 1999.

Barbara Falloni, High School

Some Folloni & Filippetti relatives, 2002

Left: Richard Balboni's Daughter Wendy with cousin Steve.
Right: Angie & Elmer With daughter Linda Bardorf's family.

Son Michael visiting the home of Helen's mother, Mama Mark in Ireland. Mama was sent by herself from Ireland at age 8 to live with her aunt in Cambridge. Original house had thatched roof.

Helen with brother Paul Mark and Nancy Quatrocchi? Nelly top right of photo?

Bathing beauties Helen and sister Agnes at Old Orchid Beach in Maine

Nancy Quatrocchi High School

Agnes & Nick Maiocco's boys Stephen, Anthony & Michael Before Lisa & Leslie's arrival

Top: Caitlin, Jennifer & Jaclyn
Bottom: Kathy & Jackie Mark
Left: Christopher Mark, High School
All Beautiful Mark people!

TED WILLIAMS RED LETTER DAY – JEAN MARIE FOLLONI LEEN

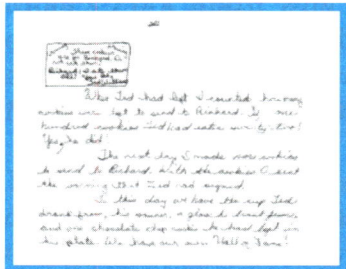
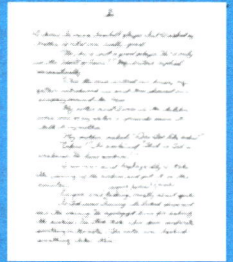
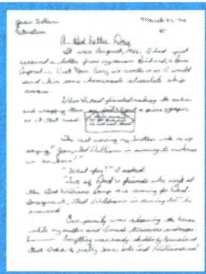

8th grader Jean's report on her 'Red Letter Day'. A copy of this text is on the next page.

Not to take anything away from Ted Williams, my and every American's Hero in WWII and on the playing fields, but the man to left who Ted so graciously wrote to is THE prototypical true American Hero. Unassuming, humble, happy to be alive, and to bring simple joy into the lives of those around him: Richard Balboni. A credit to his 1st USA generation parents, a credit to us all. Richard was the only member of his platoon to leave Vietnam alive. Hurt, but not bitter, Richard said of his pre-teen Vietcong Captee's: "I didn't know whether I should shoot them or spank them." Angie & Elmer were great successes in raising Linda & Richard.

Richard's reply to Jean's cookie care package and letter and Ted William's note:

"Hi Jean! Well, I am writing to thank you for the cookies. Boy, were they delicious, you're a great cook. Boy, I couldn't believe it when I got them. I ate them all in about a half hour.* They were just great. Thanks a lot. Boy, I must be pretty special if you wouldn't let anybody eat any, not even Ted Williams! I really appreciate it an awful lot.

Well, you will be going back to school pretty soon. I bet you will be glad to get back. What grade will you be in?

Well, there isn't much to say. So I will go for now. Say hi to every one for me. Thanks again for the cookies. Your cousin, Richard."

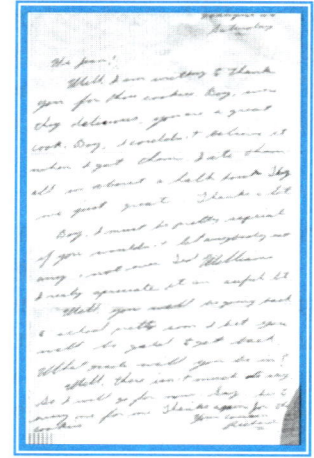

*Ties all time record for chowing Jean's cookies. Ted Williams, 1966, Cam Leen, 2003.

March 23, 1968   Literature 8T

A Red Letter Day

It was August, 1966. I had just received a letter from my cousin Richard, a Lance Corporal in Vietnam. Every six months or so I would send him some homemade chocolate chip cookies.

When I had finished making the cookies and wrapping them in foil, I put a piece of paper on it that read:

> Warning Warning
> These cookies are for Richard.
> Do not eat them."

The next morning my brother woke me up saying, "Jean, Ted Williams is coming to our house in an hour!"

"What for?" I asked.

"Two of Dad's friends who work at the Ted Williams Camp are coming for Dad. Imagine it, Ted Williams is coming too!" he answered.

Our family was cleaning the house while my mother and I made turnovers and coffee. Everything was ready. Suddenly, I remembered that I didn't really know who Ted Williams was! I knew he was a baseball player but I asked my brother if Ted was really good.

"No, he's not a good player. He's only in the Hall of Fame!" My brother replied sarcastically.

When the men entered our house, my father introduced us and then showed our company around the house.

My mother and I were in the kitchen when one of my father's friends came to talk to my mother. My mother asked, "Does Ted like cookies?"

"Cookies!" he exclaimed. "That is Ted's weakness. He loves cookies!"

I ran over and haphazardly I took the warning off the cookies and put it on the counter.

Everyone was talking, mostly almost sports.

As Ted was leaving he looked down and saw the warning. He apologized to me for eating the cookies. He then took his pen and wrote something on the note. The note now looked something like this:

> Richard: I ate them all. Your pal,
>   Ted Williams

When Ted had left I counted how many cookies were left to send to Richard. Of one hundred cookies Ted had eaten seventy-two! Yes, he did!

The next day I made more cookies to send to Richard. With the cookies I sent the warning that Ted had signed.

To this day we have the cup Ted drank from, his saucer, a glass he drank from, and one chocolate chip cookie he had left in his plate. We have our own Hall of Fame!

Jean is our all time, every day heroine for her unflagging style in family service.

My Awards, Testimonials, Innovations & Observations

AWARDS & TESTIMONIALS

> **Introduction Speech by David Messaline (Captain of the 1961 State Basketball Championship Team) to present his coach Larry Folloni for into the *Massachusetts State Basketball Coaches Hall of Fame*, @ W.P.I in Worcester, MA, September 27, 1980.**

At 7:30 p.m. this evening I was standing with Joe Amorosino, and Joe said two things, "Relax and say a lot of nice things about your coach". Standing along side of Joe and myself was Ronnie Perry's All-Scholastic (6' 8") Ron Teixeira and I knew at that moment that Larry Folloni must be the greatest coach in the world because he used to call me his "power forward."

Ladies and gentlemen it is with distinct pleasure and honor to be before you tonight to present to you a man who has had more influence over my life during my formative years, with the exception of my mother and father, that any other person. If ever a man was deserving of the recognition that this award stands for, my former coach is surely the most deserving of this honor. I can honestly say without exaggeration that no man in this state that I am aware of has given more of himself during the past thirty-five years in the interest of inter-scholastic athletics.

I am not going into the statistics of his athletic achievements, as they are in booklet form and well documented, but I would like to take a few seconds to delve into the man himself. I have know Coach for as long time: as a nine year old boy I played on the little league team that he coached: ten, eleven, and twelve years old I played on an intramural basketball league that he organized. From twelve years old to fourteen or fifteen, I was a paid supervisor during a summer recreational program that he formed. As a freshman I played on his varsity basketball team.

Larry was a supreme tactician; a fundamentalist and disciplinarian, all rolled into one. He never took anything for granted. He taught us to walk before we ran. We were constantly drilled in the basic fundamentals. His practices were run with the precision of a fine tuned watch. No wasted time, every drill had a meaning. Any drill he designed was for the expressed purpose of being used in a game. Teamwork was his hallmark, always was, and always will be. No player on his championship teams was head and shoulders above any one else. Everyone scored in double figures. Everyone helped each other out on defense. And no one dribbled the ball that he caught, if a pass would suffice better. Larry was also a firm believer in Red Auerbach's theory that a good DEFENSE was your best OFFENSE. The pressing defense that was the hallmark of his teams was practice, practice, and more practice. The pressing defense that all of his teams were famous for was not something "Helter Skelter". His press was designed, planned, and drilled into us so thoroughly, that it was automatic come game time.

I debated whether I was going to use this last bit of information. My wife said I shouldn't, but I will. I am sure that everyone here has had an experience in life that some person has left an indelible mark on our life and in many instances changes it. My experience occurred March of 1960. It was my junior year. There were four juniors and one senior on our basketball team. We had made the finals for the State Tourney. We were in the dressing room at the Boston Garden prior to the game and everybody was obviously nervous, but there was something wrong with our Coach. We could all sense it, but we couldn't put our fingers on it, and finally it came out...Larry's father was very, very sick and he was on his deathbed. Coach told us he was going to go through a very difficult period during the game and he wanted us to dedicate ourselves during that game, and say a prayer for his father. Very emotionally, he left the locker room in tears. We played four periods like possessed "DEMONS", and we won the game. I don't remember who we played, I don't remember the score, I don't remember how well I played, but *I do remember that after the a few minutes of celebration at the end of the game, we all went to the center court of the Boston Garden, all the players, managers and cheerleaders, and we knelt down right in the middle of the basketball court to thank God, and we cried.*

This extraordinary man before you tonight, through his example has taught us qualities that I'll never forget. Hard work, dedication, perseverance, teamwork and respect for one another, and above all, "he made us win and made us enjoy winning."

"On behalf of all the players who have been fortunate to have benefited by your teaching and coaching, I deem it of the highest honor and privilege, and it is with pride that I present you Coach Larry Folloni for Induction into the Massachusetts State Basketball Coaches Hall of Fame."

Hall of Fame

Coaches Ron Perry, Tom Keough, Bill Summers & Larry Folloni

> **EXCERPTS FROM BASKETBALL COACHES HALL OF FAME INDUCTION SPEECH BY LARRY FOLLONI @ W.P.I in Worcester, MA September 29, 1980.**

…If you will bear with me I would like to pass along a short message to all of you coaches, particularly you younger coaches just starting out.

"WHEN THINGS GO WRONG AS THEY SOMETIMES DO (especially in this crazy game of "Roundball") DON'T DESPAIR, DON'T LET IT GET YOU DOWN"

I know it is not an easy thing to do after you lose a tough ball game, because I have experienced the "AGONY OF DEFEAT" many times and it did get me down. Now as I look back, I say to myself and I say to you, if you lose a game, SO WHAT? THE WORLD WILL NOT COME TO AND END. TOMORROW THE SUN WILL RISE AND SET, AND THE NEXT DAY IT WILL RISE AGAIN IN THE MORNING AND SET AGAIN IN THE EVENING. (If you don't believe it, get up tomorrow morning about 6am and see for yourself.)

As I look back on my career, I can't help but think that two of the best breaks in my life came about after incidents that at the time seemed to me to be great tragedies. I was fired from my job at the shoe factory and made up my mind to go back to college. And 10 years later I was fired from my first teaching and coaching job…

…There I was with a wife and two young children to support, and no job. I was really down, but this turned out to the SECOND BIG BREAK OF MY LIFE. Thanks to the Veterans G.I. Bill I was able to go back to my Alma Mater, Boston University, to work for my Master's Degree and fortunately, the next year I was lucky enough to land the job in Bridgewater, I'm sure that all of you know the rest of the story.

To end this message to you coaches -- and I say this from my experiences over the past 40 years. I would like to ask all of you to do yourselves a favor before it is too late. *"ENJOY YOUR FAMILIES EVERY DAY".* Our time with our loved ones is too short and too precious to allow even a singe day to go by without some expression of love and enjoyment with them. I know that in this day and age that it may not always be possible, but please do try to PLACE YOUR PRIORITIES WHERE THEY BELONG."

FIRST AND FOREMOST	*YOUR FAMILY*
SECOND	*YOUR GOD AND YOUR RELIGION*
AND LAST	*YOUR WORK AND YOUR RECREATION*

*IF YOU FOLLOW THESE PRIORITIES
YOU CAN'T HELP BUT BE A SUCCESS IN LIFE!*

What I have to say for the next few minutes was not planned as part of my original speech. During this past week I had the unpleasant task of attending the funeral services for one of my former youngsters who died a tragic death while playing in an athletic contest. He was not really one of my flesh and blood youngsters, but one of my many adopted youngsters who had gone through the many recreation programs for which I am being honored here tonight. He participated in The Mighty Mites, The Biddy League, The Little League, The Junior High School Programs, and finally in the High School Athletic Programs. To me he is symbolic of what life is all about for those of us who have chosen the teaching and coaching profession. "Doug" was a mediocre basketball player, who played not on one of my championship teams, but rather on one of my 'mediocre' ones. He was a pretty good, but not a "SUPER ATHLETE." HE SURE WAS, HOWEVER, ONE SUPER KID who became a wonderful young man."

I'd like to accept this Award tonight not only because I was lucky enough to have some winning Championship Teams, BUT ALSO ON BEHALF OF THE MANY MEDIOCRE ATHLETES, THE SUPER KIDS, LIKE DOUGIE BROMLEY WHO I'VE COACHED. Only thusly will I feel that I have earned to have my name inscribed on this Hall of Fame Plaque along with the many other deserving Coaches who have preceded me.

MY THANKS TO ALL OF YOU WHO HAVE MADE THIS A NIGHT THAT I SHALL NEVER FORGET.

I will close this treasured night with a quote by my son,

"WHEN LOVE MEETS A MOMENT IN DESTINY
...IT CREATES FULFILLMENT."

MAY GOD BLESS ALL OF YOU.

David Messaline and The Young Old Coach

My Way

> **Introduction letter submitted via mail from out of state business trip by Larry Folloni Jr. (Captain of the 1963 BRRHS Team) on the occasion of his Dad's *Retirement Banquet.***

WORLD'S GREATEST COACH

5/22/83

To the average passerby, he was just some crazy kid and a couple of trash cans. But to that crazy kid, those trash cans were Jerry West and Elgin Baylor. And when stacked one on top of the other, a nightmarish shot-eating dragon (a/k/a Wilt Chamberlain) guarding fabulous hoop treasures. Everyday I'd race home from school, swap my books for a basketball, set the cans up in our driveway, and proceed to single-handedly destroy the hated Lakers . . . wizardly sun-scraping a swisher over the Stilt (or when I felt cocky, flying like Superman and throwing down an "eat-your-heart-out-Dr. J 9'3 1/4" white lightning slammer jammer in his fearsome face). Most boys dreamed of growing up to play for the Celtics or UCLA. But I had even grander ambitions. I was gonna star for "The Mighty Trojans" and THE WORLD'S GREATEST COACH!

When knowledgeable sports buffs talk great basketball coaches, legends like Red Auerbach, John Wooden, and Ron Perry usually pop up -- and well they should. With all due respect to their coaching masterpieces, these remarkable "artists" had a pretty impressive "paintbrush": namely All-Universe players like Cousy, Russell, Havlicek, Bird, Jabbar, Walton, Johnson, and the two Ronnies. Well it was our town's fantastic luck to have a high school coach who could sell the Devil a pair of long johns and outhit Ted Williams with a toothpick. And take a bunch of average-ability farm boys not tall enough to dunk a donut; arm them only with a tricky dribble, "Annie Oakley" jump shot, brilliant strategy, belief in themselves – and each other, and slings (cleverly disguised as jockstraps); then send them out to slay the basketball Goliaths and capture an incredible three state championships!

Amazingly, winning didn't even seem uppermost in The Coach's mind. Every kid who came out for the team automatically made the cut; everyone got a chance to play and contribute. There were no individual heroes. Just a "Sonny, a Mike, a Paul, a Dave, and "the Frog" -- dots connected by The Coach's magic pencil to form a shining 5-pointed star. You practiced hard, you learned, you did your very best on the court as well as in the classroom and at home ("A" report cards, making your own bed so a busy Mom wouldn't have to, and Mass each morning were every bit as important as scoring "triple-doubles"), you were a good sport in victory -- and defeat, and you had fun. Do these things and success sort of just happens . . . a valuable lesson we've carried through the BIG GAME of life.

As the young son of an immigrant woodchopper, The Coach was an outstanding 3-sport athlete -- setting records that like Wilt's 100 points and Aaron's 755 homers may last forever. (Even today while his contemporaries play checkers and watch Lawrence Welk, this ageless wonder can still dazzle high school hotshots in a game of H-o-r-s-e or Hustle and give Old Man Par a good whipping.) His stint as a bomber navigator/pilot helping Uncle Sam whip Hitler earned a free ticket to college and a "phys-ed" degree. A tragic injury which cut short a promising future in pro baseball can now be looked upon as a blessing when you consider the marvelous career it subsequently launched. For as an adult he's designed, built-- with a great deal of help from the likes of a super guy named Joe, and managed one of the finest community sports programs in the country. Not content to sit on his "Basketball Hall of Fame" laurels, The Coach has also won the prestigious "Athletic Director of the Year" award, run several highly acclaimed state tournaments, and (as Chairman of the rules committee) played a key role in writing the Ten Commandments of interscholastic competition. If they ever establish a Nobel Prize for Sports, the Coach better start rehearsing his acceptance speech . . . and pounding the typewriter for that autobiographical Great American Dream.

Over the years I've gotten to know The Coach pretty well. He's married to a beautiful lady who could win a few titles of her own ("World's Greatest Wife & Mother" for starters). His children have graduated with top honors from the Harvards and Stanfords and are now successful business executives, lawyers, and scientists. One son sacrificed fame and fortune to teach and inspire hope in the ghettos and migrant labor camps. His daughters make Charlie's Angels look like the Three Stooges. And just like in the movies, the torch has been passed to the next generation. Because much to his Father's delight, another son – a former high school "All Scholastic" -- is a terrific basketball coach in his own right. The coach's philosophy is simple: God, family, and your profession in that order. He led by example, a nice guy who finished first. With his tremendous talent and determination, I'm sure he could have been President or a billionaire (but I know a town that's glad he isn't). And all his glittering athletic achievements notwithstanding, I'm personally proudest of him for the numerous acts of kindness he's shown to the poor, sick, handicapped, elderly -- especially his own greatly loved and admired high school coach, and life's underdogs in general.

Tomorrow night athletes, fans family, friends, and a grateful community will pay tribute to The coach for his awesome contributions and unbelievable accomplishments . . . and the priceless memories. (A social satirist once predicted that everyone will be famous for 10 seconds, Thanks to The Coach we'll always be #1, we'll always be "Champs," we'll always be famous -- how sweet it is!!!) And speaking of memories, I'd like to suggest a gift that will be remembered and cherished long after the customary retirement gold watch, TV set, or golf clubs are in the junk heap. A few years ago, the local high school gym was dedicated in honor of another wonderful man – for whom (along with a school board member and original superintendent primarily responsible for its creation and excellence) the whole school probably should be named. I think this would be a most appropriate time to switch some plaques around and bestow honors in their proper place. Considering all the trophies The Coach has given the town, the town can now return the favor with an eternal trophy. For just as Yankee Stadium is "The House That Ruth Built", the magnificent Bridgewater-Raynham Regional High School Gymnasium should become a monument to THE WORLD'S GREATEST COACH: LARRY FOLLONI. Congratulations, Dad!

Larry Jr.

Photo Album from BU Hall of Fame Induction Banquet, May 2, 1992

Helen & me, Larry Jr. w/ cousins Francis & Nancy

Special surprise salute included in BU Hall of Fame booklet by my children

Relevant caricature commissioned by son Larry.

Taylor shares Papa's joy.

Inducted along side of Helen & Boston Bruin and US Olympic champion Dave Silk

Mike to Helen: "They did it!"

Seamus & Larry: "He did it!"

"Thanks & Glory be to God!"

"This is fulfilling and fun!!"

Godmother Linda with James Folloni

Larry Jr. with Francis & Jack Morast

"Well you know, when Love meets a moment in Destiny, you can expect these satisfying results" "I see." "Yes!"

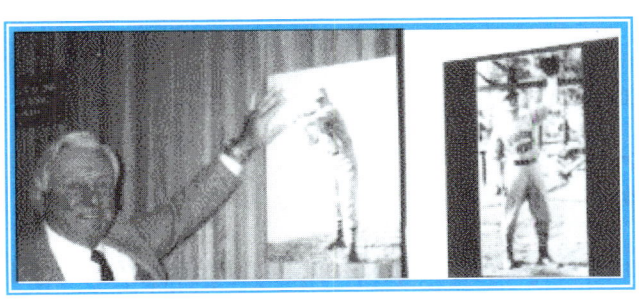

THE GREATEST FORTUNE AND LOVE OF MY LIFE, MY WIFE
Helen Mary Louise Mark Folloni

THE BEST THING THAT EVER HAPPENED TO ME WAS TO MEET AND MARRY MY BEAUTIFUL WIFE, 'HOLLYWOOD" HELEN'

Helen gave me six beautiful children who in turn gave us five grandchildren to enjoy. Helen practically raised our six children all by herself since I was usually too busy with my work schedule to devote as much time as we would all have liked to my growing family. Not being able to spend more time with my children during their formative years is one of my major regrets in life. I hope I can be worthy of my extra good fortune to now have some time to try to make up for this loss by enjoying my grandchildren.

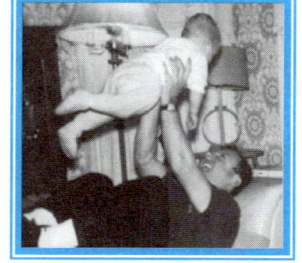

Helen was enormously intelligent, super caring and very humorous. She was my original 'spell checker', who typically did a better job than our computers of today. Although quite capable, she never went to college or had a 'career'. As did most in her age group, she went to work right out of high school in support of the war effort, before marrying a GI. She became a Professional Mother and super supportive wife. I'm sure that at times she felt a bit trapped by having to manage our busy household with limited resources, but she was a genius at doing the best for her family with what she had. She made sure that each and every child was well dressed, well educated, well liked, well on their unique way and that they each knew that they were very well loved.

Though working from dawn to far past dusk, Helen somehow found time to meticulously make extensive and well-labeled scrapbooks on each of her kids and me, which became the source of much material for this book. The touching notes that she'd pen in her perfect writing on the bottoms and back of photos and clippings are family treasures today. Rummaging through old books, my son Bob came across a rare gift that Helen gave herself, a caricature book about her childhood neighborhood by Harvard Square in Cambridge. Therein was found the following she wrote on the celebration of her mother's birthday in 1977:

'Our family home was across the street and my friends and I and sisters and brothers used to climb the tree in the same spot.'

I will always cherish my home in Cambridge. I attended St. Paul's School in blocks away from my home and we had a happy life there."

∞∞∞∞∞∞∞∞∞∞∞∞∞∞∞∞∞∞∞∞∞∞∞∞∞∞∞∞∞∞∞∞∞∞

"This book ('The Beard and the Braid, Drawings of Cambridge' by Barbara Westman) is the property of Helen Folloni and is valuable to her, as she was born on De Wolfe Place, Harvard Square on November 7, 1922. Her dad, James Morgan Mark, was Chief Engineer of Harvard College. Her earliest memories of Harvard College were at her Dad's blackboard, where he did his Algebra equations, and she wrote her numbers.

The Mark Homestead was taken over, as were the entire block of houses, by Harvard, and here Harvard built new dormitories facing the Charles River and the footbridge. In this general area Helen had experienced a very happy childhood, and this illustrated book is a pleasant reminder of familiar places of her childhood.

The special area of the 'block' where the Marks resided before Harvard took over all homes by eminent domain, was situated on Copperthwaite St. on one end, and the Memorial Drive, on the Charles River side. What I, Helen Mary Mark, recall of this block was that I was between 6 to 8 years of age, and I was proclaimed the 'Official' story-teller for the neighborhood. I would walk around the large block several times a day with an audience of 3 to 5 friends, sisters & brothers too, and spin many tall tales to the delight of my audience. Later on when we moved to Arlington when I was 11 years of age, I started writing poetry that was published, and won many prizes for my mother by the gentle art of poetry. I branched out to writing plays and staging them in friend's basements. I wrote words and music. Later in High School I won several essay contests, and one was for the American Legion. I won a blue ribbon. I wrote on "What it means to be an American." My high school pals all were victims of my pen, and they cajoled me into writing stories about them, which became a favorite pastime of mine, and were really loved by them. Did I have a talent or not? I would like to think so. However, it lies dormant now, awaiting the right moment to strike again.

A magical day of sons Robert & Larry being led around to her childhood homes in Cambridge and Arlington by Helen was capped off by the amazing serendipitous meeting on Mass. Ave by Arlington's City Hall with Helen's sister Mary's daughter Marilyn Cullen! They found four of her family's homes that day, and got gracious tours and gifts from two present day residents. Marilyn's mom Mary is my son Michael's Godmother, who always taught him to trust in the spirit. Like Linda Balboni Bardorf, she loved Mother Teresa. I was in Spaulding Rehab. Center that day. Our guardian angels were on double duty!

Here they are! God's great gifts to the Bay State. Milly (Gallagher) Mark, Mama Mark, Teresa (Quatrocchi) Mark, Mary (Cullen) Mark, and Helen Mary Louise (Folloni) Mark!!!

Helen in front of one of her childhood homes in Cambridge, MA.

Note Harvard's Lowell House in the background, the eventual home of our son Michael during his undergraduate years at Harvard. Helen's brains & heart are a good part of what got & kept Michael there.

MY GREATEST TESTIMONIAL, MY FAMILY
SOME OF MY FAMILY'S ACCOMPLISHMENTS
AND THEIR CHARITABLENESS

"Let another man praise thee, and not thine own mouth."
Proverbs, 27:2

Helen and I raised our kids to try to do their best for themselves so that they would have something to generously share with others less fortunate. My kids weren't, of course, angels all of the time. Indeed some had more than their share of peccadilloes. We've stood by them throughout the good times and bad though, and I think that these 'works in progress' are now looking pretty good. Naturally, however, a dad is not going to sing anything but the praises of his brood to the rest of the world. As in sports, our kids were never overly praised or taught that they were special in any other sense than the fact that God made each of us to be special, and that our job is to "aspire to respire inspiration" to fulfill all that we can become. Helen and I simply expected our children to excel in academics, athletics and citizenship. I've never gloated to my kids about their achievements and good works, but please excuse an old man for gaining some satisfaction from reliving some of the good things that his kids have done as representatives of their religious and lay teachers, their parents and their forebears.

Keeping in mind the biblical exhortation that all of the good works in the world are nothing without love, I think I can say that many of the actions of my kids are at least exemplary. And to the extent that these works were done in that spirit, they have been accomplished without self-righteousness and with a true sense of enjoyment. These 'charitable acts' have not been of self-sacrifice so much as they have been of self-affirmation. My children would be the first to assert that their efforts have been richly rewarding to them, and I share their stories to share the wealth.

My 1st son Larry Jr. was and always will be "Number One". He was President of the National Honor Society, then went on to one of the most acclaimed technical colleges where he made high honors en route to becoming a Chemical Engineer. After graduating, this Mensa Member son went to work for a prestigious pharmaceutical firm and years later to perhaps the world's leading computer manufacturing company, where he rose to become one of their top research scientists and a top notch **chip engineer**. [It's interesting to note that his grandfather James Morgan Mark was a leading **ship engineer**, who went on to become Chief Plant Engineer at Harvard.]

Helen Mark Folloni & chip off the block Larry Jr. peer through the porthole to the future

Many computer industry groups and authorities have acknowledged Larry's outstanding contributions as a world-leading expert in his field. Not only was Larry Jr. a top student and chemist, he was also blessed with great athletic talent. Some of his athletic feats have been noted elsewhere in these memoirs.

Larry Jr. is a consistent and very generous anonymous donor to many charities, typically for the benefit of poor and sick children. He has also played 'Santa' year after year for his younger brothers and sisters, for random people in need and over the past few years for his mom and dad. As a teenager he bought our kids a swing set, a pool table, their first skateboard, bike, Barbie doll etc. These gifts came out of his hard-earned pay from work at caddying, the brickyard and the auto wash. When I was busy with my career and extra jobs, Larry Jr. often stepped in as an additional father figure for his younger siblings, and they still look to him for support and guidance. He is a genius at recognizing the gifts of those around him and at creatively encouraging people to make maximum use of them. Larry has always been one to step in and fight against any odds for an underdog, especially one who he thought was being unfairly taken advantage of.

My second son Bobby, though not as brilliant a student as his older brother, did well enough to get undergraduate and graduate degrees. As noted earlier, Bobby was a terrific basketball player. He graduated from Bridgewater State College and then went overseas to Italy to become a very successful Basketball and Soccer Coach at the Overseas School of Rome. He earned a Masters degree in Business (MSBA) attending evening school at Boston University's overseas program in Rome. After 12 years of coaching and teaching there and two years working for an Italian seafood company as a buyer Bobby returned to the States to be near his family. He was a salesman in California for Foundation Health, Healthnet and in the energy field. He is now a very successful independent sales representative, most recently with Circus Man and JBM.

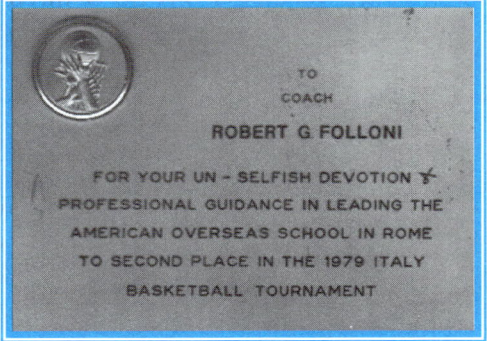

Bob with his '89 soccer team that finished 6th in international competition in Mexico City.

"He seems about as Italian as you can get. And it's more than just the name. His favorite pizza is mascarpone con asparagini, his favorite pasta, penne all'arrabbiata, and his favorite beer Nastro Azzurro. His favorite pastime seems to be swapping carabinieri jokes with the Roman bus drivers in the local dialect. But make no mistake about it. In spite of his charming Italian airs, he's as American as his New England Yankee stock, the American-invented sport he likes best – basketball – and a close second to pasta, as a decent way to begin a meal, in his opinion, is Boston baked beans with Louisiana hot sauce. He's a veteran on OSR's faculty now. He's coached long series of championship or near-championship basketball teams and has recently taken to directing the soccer squad as well. As Athletic Director, he's one of OSR's most familiar faces and busiest talents. The yearbook staff is proud to dedicate Tabularium '87 to Coach Bob Folloni"

*Bobby was very popular as a coach & AD at the AOSR, and was appreciated throughout the American Schools in Italy Leageue, who gave him this plaque: "To the man who taught us what it means **Never to Quit**. ROBERT "BOBBY" FOLLONI - In grateful appreciation for this outstanding, unselfish service, dedication and friendship (1978-'89) From the players and coaches of the ASIL.*

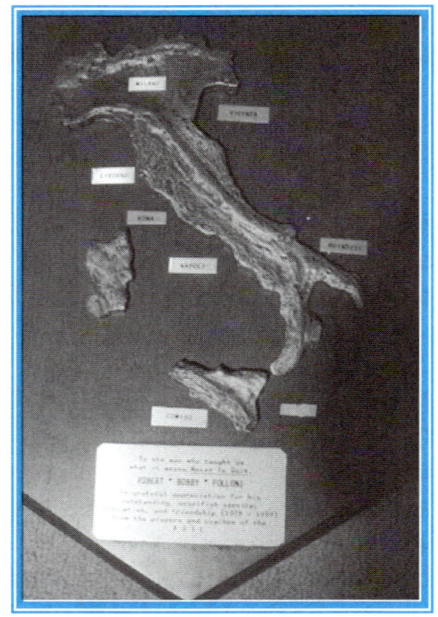

Bobby has a heart as big as any one person can carry. He is extraordinarily loved by most all who he meets for his warm humor and open spirit. Year in and year out he demonstrates that he would give his last morsel to help another. Larry Jr. says if he ever had to go to war, be it against oppression or for need, that Bobby is the one who he would want at his side. Bobby has fought fiercely with the health services establishment as an advocate for Helen and me during many dependent hours of our latter years. Whenever a sibling needed a helping hand financially or with physical labor, Bob would be there without a doubt or a thought of self-benefit. Bob is one of the hardest working yet most fun loving and generous persons you'll ever meet. He's also the family's leading procurer of useful gizmos.

Mark Andreoli of Italy & MA

Slim and Betty

The Fabulous Cassotto's

Bob, Dad and Johnnie Most, 1967. "Havlicek Stole the ball!!!"

Bob and Larry tend to their beloved mom during her darkest hours.

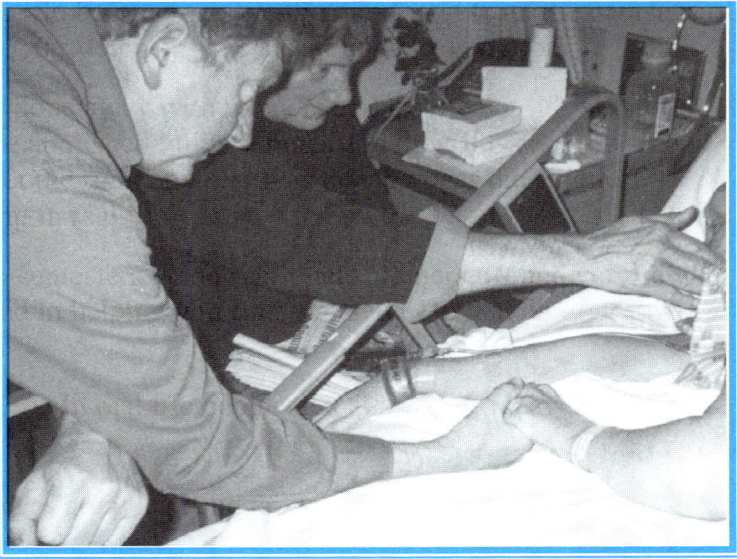

Next came Michael, a born leader who was President of his High School Class. Mike was a dedicated and accomplished athlete who continued his long distance running winning ways until a chronic back injury sidelined him in his late 20's.

While still in High School Michael was the Youth and Chairman of the 'Hike for Hunger' led by the St. Thomas Aquinas and other area church civic groups. This raised over One Hundred Thousand Dollars locally to contribute to self-help development programs for the poor and needy of our area and abroad. When Mike went off to Harvard, his sister Deborah took over as the Youth Director of the 'Walk for Development' to continue this community wide charitable effort.

Michael ended up serving on the Executive Board of the American Freedom from Hunger Foundation and the U.S. Committee on Refugees. After his sophomore year at Harvard University he took a leave of absence to go down to Guatemala. There he contributed his time and skills to start a recreation program (sound familiar?) in collaboration with the Catholic mission in the predominately Mayan Indian village of San Lucas Toliman on beautiful volcano-laced Lake Atitlan.

The Rev. Mr. David Mayhew of Bridgewater and the Heifer Project International, made the initial arrangements for Mike to go to Guatemala. David Chuckran and Mary Ellen Shea of Bridgewater also spent time as volunteers at San Lucas, where the both represented our town, and helped to distribute funds raised by its good citizens and civic groups. The idea behind Heifer Project is that after livestock and training on how to care for the animals are that are supplied to one poor

family, that they, and then each succeeding recipient in turn, donates a first born animal to another deserving neighbor. The Indian girls pictured above with Mike and to the left with a gift were poster children for Heifer Project, under the slogan: *"Love is here to stay!"* These children and Michael became close companions during his stay there.

The Guatemalans were plagued with many health problems due in part to the lack of a sanitary water supply. Michael worked in support of several other Ivy League volunteers including Richard Raines, now the President of *Carfax*, and project Director Bruce Clemens, to help establish an organization to build potable water systems with and for the people. This group, Aqua del Pueblo, (The People's Water) still thrives 30 years later under local management.

Richard Raines in 1974

Old method of transporting water for all domestic uses.

To this day Michael still meets immigrants from Guatemala in California whose families have benefited from this program and also still meets government officials from Latin America who are familiar with and appreciative of Aqua del Pueblo.

Michael and his cohorts suffered many bouts of dysentery and some lingering intestinal parasites from their efforts, but he says this is easily forgotten, while the heartfelt love and thanks of the many Guatemalans, and the satisfaction of working with such fine people in a good cause will never be.

Michael also credits the poor but enthusiastic and patient Indian and mestitzo children with teaching him the Spanish language that has helped him so much in his later career as a renewable energy resource developer in Mexico and CA.

His Harvard classmates at graduation gave Michael special recognition for his work in Guatemala, as a Big Brother in Roxbury, and for his volunteerism at school when they awarded him the prestigious **Ames Award for 'Character & Leadership'**. After college Michael worked as a special legal services program for migrant farmworkers in PA as promoted by the saintly Mary Ellen Beaver who continues this work this day. This work, with young activist attorney Justina Wasicek, gained AFSC congressional study group accolades unique effectiveness. Mike went on to work in the energy conservation and clean energy resource development field.

Then along came Jeannie, the first girl member of the Folloni Team, who like Bob, graduated from Bridgewater State. In high school she was a stalwart participant in the 'Project SOUL' community volunteer program to help disadvantaged youth. Jean is a Gem! Not only is she a beauty like her mom but her work as the chief caretaker for many years for her parents freed up her siblings to pursue their careers. I don't know how we all would have survived and prospered without her helping hand.

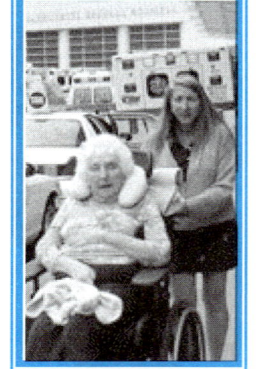

Along with helping her parents here at Hampton Beach, Jean is now a handicap-van-driver-daughter and a 'soccer-surfing-baseball-softball-basketball-dance&ski-club-camp-sleepover-mall-runner-car chauffeur Mom, for her and her husband Kevin's two beautiful children Taylor and Cameron. Jean is a great cook and homemaker who does an excellent job at landscaping and remodeling around our home. If it is true, as I believe, that charity begins at home, then Jean is certainly the most unsung and most charitable of us all.

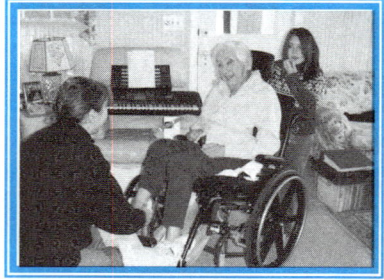

Jean has cared day in and day out for us for decades, and is the sweetest and kindest of persons when it comes to remembering and celebrating special events for her parents, siblings, husband, children, church and friends. There is nothing, of course, that Jean wouldn't do for her Taylor and Cameron. And she does everything with a warm wit and humor.

Mother Teresa once said that we cannot do great things in this world, only small things with great love. Besides her mother Helen, I've never met anyone who embodies this concept more than Jean does.

Next came our fiery 'blond bomb-shell', Debbie, who was always the independent one. She showed this trait from the first day that her mother took her to kindergarten when she asked Helen to not come in to school with her as she wanted to do it on her own. She didn't want to have her classmates see her being led by her mother holding her hand.

Debbie graduated from Stanford University and then went on to Georgetown Law School where she made the Law Review on her way to become a successful lawyer. How she chose to become a lawyer is a story in itself. While shopping with her mother in Boston one day, a thief grabbed her handbag and ran off with it. The thief was later apprehended and Debbie had to appear as a witness when he was arraigned in court. The thief was released when the prosecutor botched his presentation. Debbie was so infuriated that she then and there made up her mind that she would become a lawyer to see that better justice was done.

Debbie not only took over for Michael in running the local charity drives, but she also became a great philanthropist for family needs. Like some of her predecessors she sometimes comes off with a hard shell, but in actuality she is the softest and perhaps the most feeling of them all. She was a brilliantly successful labor attorney for a major D.C. and Chicago firm. Ironically, while there she ended up representing a group of farmers in a case instigated years earlier by her legal services outreach worker brother Michael against these farmers on behalf of the farm-workers that he represented! Although ostensibly on different sides of the battle, it was Debbie who ended up negotiating a deal that brought satisfaction to both sides! Yes, it's a very small world after all. And with the right approach, everyone can be considered winners.

The last member of the Folloni team, who arrived shortly after our 3rd State Championship in March of 1961, was James Mark Folloni. Although somewhat spoiled by his mom and siblings and especially by Jean as the baby of the family, he ended up with no less of a heart than any of them have. When James was only about 8 years old he trudged the entire 25 mile 'Hike for Hunger' route with his brother and sisters, singing all the way through blisters and cramps that would have sidelined most children. He holds the family little league home run hitting title, and was a very good student, athlete, debater and writer. Young James kept extensive notebooks full of news about and correspondences with his siblings, and was a prolific and thoughtful letter to the editor writer. He could still write professionally if he decides to.

James and I had a fortunate thrill together on the one-day that we attended a Met's game in Shea stadium. As fortune would have it, that was the game when Bob Seaver tossed his 20 strikeout game! Jimmy is a charmer and a charm.

Like his sister Debbie, Jimmy also graduated from Stanford University where he successfully managed the student run café. Jimmy is a whiz with the computer and did very well giving all of us advice on working the stock market. He is the most meticulous and accounting oriented of the kids, but he has never left out of the bottom line equations the importance of helping family and other deserving individuals and charities. Jimmy worked year after year with little or no compensation doing the books and taxes for Michael's many businesses and non-profit endeavors, and he selflessly loaned cash on top of that to sustain them when needed. James has also set up trusts for his nephews and nieces, and can often be counted upon for level headed and carefully thought out creative approaches to family problems. James has travelled more places throughout the world than most people, often on business but I think mostly for fun (great idea!). He has written "James' Guide to London" and may someday write a book on his travels. No matter where on the globe he is, he never misses coming to visit his mom and dad at their birthdays and on major holidays. While there, he exhibits the patience of Jove in dutifully dealing with computer issues with his somewhat cantankerous task-master of a Dad. James can be sensible and generous and he'll at times act contrary what he knows others might deem as 'sound business judgement' to be extra generous. I think that this tact, so long as it comes from love in heart, will beat the market in the long run!

To keep the ball rolling, let me introduce my grandchildren. Jean's daughter Taylor is our first grandchild and what a beautiful person she is. Taylor was extremely loveable from the first day that I cuddled her in my arms and sang her to sleep with the Italian song that my mom sang to me as a baby, *"Cara Mia Bella Bambina"*. Taylor is very charismatic, intelligent and athletically inclined. I have a confession to make about Taylor: When she was born on Fathers Day in 1990, I was very disappointed that she was not a boy. ***Now watching her develop into a wonderful lovable little girl and young lady, I wouldn't trade her for all the boys in the world.*** Taylor gets the best response of anyone from her ill grandmother, who always lights up with her Hollywood Helen smile any time that she approaches her. Never a night goes by that she doesn't come over to me and give me a hug and kiss and say, "Papa I love you very much". She does the same for her Grandmother. She makes each of our days complete, without fail. I pray that whatever the world may bring her, that she will forever keep her warm enthusiastic response to life. I know that with that attitude, the world will tend to bring her very well deserved good things indeed.

My son-in-law Kevin, is really a great guy. I can't imagine any father being more attentive to his children than Kevin is. Kevin has also been very tolerant of Jean's commitment to care for her parents, and a good 'behind the scenes' supporter of our entire household. In the 25 or so years that I've known him, I haven't seen him raise his voice or his temper a single time. He has made sure that my two precious first grandchildren are raised in a safe, secure, progressive, serious but not rigid, loving home and school environment.

Our next grandchild is Jean's son Cameron, who is growing like a weed. He too is very bright and very athletically inclined with a great passion for sports. **'Hammerin' Cameron'** hit a grand slam in a fast pitch league game the other night to establish a revised nickname of **"Slammin Cammeron"**. As he matures Cammy is beginning to show the athletic competitiveness of his Grandfather. Cammy hates to lose and he is constantly outdoors, practicing basketball, baseball, football, hockey and soccer. He is and will continue to be a great athlete. More importantly, Cammy is an excellent student who is constantly reading, although he is still inclined to watching some cartoons, 'The Three Stooges' and sports on T.V.

Cam's dad Kevin is great in immersing himself in Cam's athletic world. Kevin coaches, keeps score, and / or attends all of Cammy's many games, and along with Jean, makes sure that he has every opportunity to participate in a variety of games and venues. In an end of year participation proclamation, Cammy's 4th grade class said of him:

CAM LEEN "Smart, athletic, kind, sporty type, really likes baseball, serious, nice funny, cool, friendly, helpful, caring, loyal, good student, good friend, takes school work seriously."

The Love of my son Michael's life since the early '80's has been Thu Thuy Ti Vo. Thuy has been a very loyal and loving companion for my son. Her family treats Michael like one of theirs, and he happily reciprocates. Michael is "Uncle Mike" to Thuy's nephew & niece Alex and Wendy, who he thinks the world of. Alex's wife Michelle and their kids Xanders & Song, along with Hung & Josie Van, and Rose & Phi Yen Vo also call him "Uncle". Thuy, is 'Auntie Thuy' to my grandchildren.

Debbie's first born is Vicky Helen Marie Dent, who is a chip off the 'young' block. She reminds me so much of Debbie when she was a little girl that age. Along with her dirty blond hair, she looks like her mom and is very wiry and active. She also already has her mother's independent traits.

Debbie's son Scotty was next to arrive on the scene a year after Vicky. Scotty is a 'rough and tumble' rugged sort of a guy, just like his dad, Tom. Even at this young age Scotty shows signs of becoming a very good athlete. I just hope he turns out to have a good portion of the athletic skills and professional know-how of his parents.

I would also like to acknowledge Debbie's two stepchildren, Jenny and Michael, who are Tom's children by his first marriage. Jenny and Michael spend much time with Debbie and Tom and Vicky and Scotty and they always come up to visit with us during the Christmas vacation and during the summer season. Jenny and Michael are both intelligent, well mannered, lovable and athletically inclined. Jenny and Taylor Rose's periodic song and dance choreographs are treasured memories for the entire family. Their 'Mumbo #5' act of around 2000 was also a hit for all at home, as well as for the adults at a talent show at a pizza bar on the Hampton strand.

James and Donna brought us our fifth grandchild, Ava Grace Folloni, on April, 17, 2002. Looking at Ava I see so much of all of my other children as babies. She is also precocious like them. I just got word that this week, at age 13 months, she managed to climb out of her crib, and lower herself several body lengths down to the floor without being phased. She then calmly walked into the next room to greet her astounded parents! Her older brother Oliver Spratt is Donna's son by a previous marriage. Oliver also visits us in New Hampshire every few months. We are amazed by his dance moves and his clever ways of adapting to the world. We delight in watching him grow up into a fine young man and a great older brother for Ava Grace. Like Jennifer and Michael Dent, we happily welcome Oliver as a member of our family.

We are extremely pleased that Donna and James got together. Donna is very intelligent, charming, hardworking and helpful to everyone. As I write she is completing her internship as an anesthesiologist at the Univ. of Pittsburgh Hospital.

Our youngest and oldest children (James & Larry) and our youngest and oldest grandchildren (Ava & Taylor), pose with Jean, Helen and me on Ava's 1st Birthday, April 17, 2003.

Joker Oliver mugs with assistance from his mom Donna.

HOW FORTUNATE HELEN & I ARE TO HAVE SUCH GREAT CHILDREN, SUPER 'IN-LAWS' AND GRANDCHILDREN WHO HAVE BEEN SO CARING TO US.

OTHER *GOOD THINGS* THAT HAVE HAPPENED TO ME

Next to my loving family "The Folloni Team" I have to rate my birth family, "The John Folloni Team" and Helen's family "The Mark Clan", as being next on the list of the Good Things that happened in my life. It was the John Folloni Team that weaned and raised me through my childhood and helped get me started on my way to success. They housed us and gave crucial financial support following my army duty in the '40's and our  house fire back in the '60's. They gave me the guidance and helped with the financial wherewithal to make my real estate investments. Through thick & thin, lose and win, they were great kin.

The Mark Clan took Helen, baby Larry and me and me to live with them while I completed my studies at Boston University. Helen's brother Paul traveled over 60 miles every weekend to come down to do the electrical work to restore our home following our fire. The Mark's were great hosts to us during many a happy and memorable family event, and wonderful in visiting during our sick days. Paul's daughter Bonnie, Teresa's Diane, and Mary's Carole Ann have been a great God children for Helen, and Agnes' Anthony has been a loyal and entertaining visitor throughout the years.

WE HAVE BEEN SO FORTUNATE AND BLESSED TO HAVE TWO SUCH WONDERFUL FAMILIES TO GIVE US THE SUPPORT AND LOVE THROUGHOUT OUR LIFETIME.

Another miracle of our age that I've been fortunate enough to get good use of in my waning years is the computer! My son Larry bought me my first about six years ago, and with Bobby's help we've upgraded a few times since then to be able to write this book and so that I could carry on a number of 'concerned citizen' campaigns as health allowed. I am amazed at what this mind-boggling equipment has done to improve our world and my life. The possibilities that they open are limitless. I enjoy learning something new on them everyday. Computers have been of great help in running my real estate dealings until health problems intervened, and the internet has been both fun and informative, and a lifeline into the outside world for a now pretty much shut in guy. I appreciate the assistance that I received from sons Jimmy and Michael to learn the intricacies of operating the computer.

If I may say not in a shy way, if our generation had had the benefits of computers, we would probably by now have solved the world's energy and pollution problems, and we'd all be flying around in auto guided personal planes. Then again, it took our generation to set the stage for the Bill Gates, Larry Ellison and Larry Jr.'s generation to bring this gift to the next generation to help them to solve problems for theirs and subsequent generations. If we can give today's children the good foundation of values on the playing fields, hopefully they'll use all the wondrous technology for good.

Larry Jr., seeking more advances to benefit future sporting generations

Steve Prisco wallops a double off the wall in the 9th inning of the 2003 EMA finals

BRRHS coach John Kearney preparing his kids to carry themselves as champions in the game of life

THE OLD COACH'S OBSERVATIONS
AND SOME ON & OFF THE FIELD CONTRIBUTIONS

They said it couldn't be done
I said it could be and it was

I will try to cite some examples where my ideas and innovations that once appeared to be fantasy tales have now been brought into being and are in some cases now taken for granted as part of our everyday lifestyles. I'm happy and proud that my innovations in recreation and sports programs have done so much for student athletes in my town and state, and I'm glad that some of my public safety initiatives have carried. There's a whole series of my other ideas for inventions that I never made a penny from, however, because I didn't follow through on them. And since I didn't, the world had to wait a little longer to benefit from them. Let this be a lesson to young readers. I can't say that I'm sorry I dedicated my career to student sports, but I do wish I'd found the time to completely see through a few more commercial ideas.

Many people have many great ideas. The difference between great innovators and the common man is that the greats take concerted action on their ideas. If you can bat 30% (.300) in baseball you're considered a great. If you can be about .3% (.003) successful in faithfully being true to your self's inspirations by carrying those ideas through to fruition and if you can show appreciation to others who help where credit is due, then you'll likely be very successful indeed in this great land of opportunity.

"Great discoveries and improvements invariably involve the cooperation of many minds. I may be given credit for having blazed the rail but when I look at the subsequent developments I feel the credit is due to others rather than to myself."
-Alexander Graham Bell

How did I succeed where I did? By using my "**O W L & L** and **FLAP-A**" approach. Are you ready for a Coach Folloni secret and *axiom*?

F	Foresight	O	Observe
L	Logic	W	Watch
A	Anticipation	L	Listen
P	Planning		
&	*then take*	&	
A	Action	L	Learn

Want to soar above the common?
*First be an **OWL** to Learn.*
*Then **FLAP** to Action.*

I think that my life's story has proved both the efficacy of following the *"O W L & L and FLAP-A"* way and the frustration of failing to.

Being a guy who was always very innovative, creative and impatient, and wanting to get things done in a hurry and efficiently, I came up with many ideas and schemes and a few inventions. I rarely brought them to fruition and profit, but they were of my early inspiration. My advice to you is to learn to listen to your inspiration, and to act upon it, as Mike Tyson would say, "With vicious intent to vital locations!" *OF COURSE ONE OF THE 'VITAL LOCATIONS' IS GETTING & MAINTAINING LEGAL PROTECTION FOR YOUR IDEAS, AND ANOTHER IS GAINING THE KNOWHOW TO DEVELOP YOUR IDEAS INTO A PRODUCT. A THIRD IS LEARNING HOW TO BRING IT IN TO THE MARKETPLACE.* **So go to college and get some knowledge! And get a mentor, for what they're sent for.** For whatever it may be worth, here are some of my inspirations, though not all personal innovations and inventions.

> *"I haven't failed, I've just found 10,000 ways that won't work."*
> -Thomas Alva Edison (1847-1931)

Clock Radio: One of my first ideas that turned out to be a very lucrative invention for someone else is the Clock Radio. Back in the early '30's and '40's I had this idea of waking up to music in my ears. Instead of pursuing it on my own, I leaked out the idea to a chief design engineer at Philco Radio. He immediately grasped its importance and the company proceeded to come up with the Clock Radio.

This innovation was the forerunner of the many uses of an alarm to set off or open up the circuitry of stoves, microwaves, TV's security systems, and many other electrical instruments that needed a timing device to set them off.

Batting Tee: In the early '50's while my youngsters were at the ball playing age, I rigged up a baseball batting tee at our family home at 36 Main Street, in Bridgewater, MA. I also I rigged up a ball with a screw attached to it and hung it from a clothesline. My youngsters spent many hours at hitting this ball and sharpening their hitting skills.

Bab-A-Loon: Also in the '50's I got the idea for the *'Bab-A-Loon'*. I had the bladder of an old cage ball inflated and left it out for the children to play with. They all had a great time rolling on this ball and I felt if we could put a handle on it to help control it, that it would be a great toy for children. Sure enough within a few years this idea appeared in a toy magazine and it became one of the most popular play toys of the year.

Match Book Toothpick: A novelty idea with potential for dental use is the Match-Book Toothpick. This is rather like a portable dental floss. No more details as I might just follow through on this yet…

Golf Machine Exerciser: In the late 50's I came up with my **Golf Machine** invention and my ideas on **Year-round Daylight Savings Time.** Several stories about these two items appeared in newspapers. How I wish that I had developed the golf machine!

Luggage on Wheels: My brother Al arranged a meeting in the Empire State Building in NYC with the CEO of a company that patented inventions and ideas. The meeting was to discuss the possibilities of my Golf Exercise Machine that I had constructed. In order to transport my bulky machine more easily, I attached a pair of old roller skates to the bottom of it.

I wheeled the Golf Machine down Times Square and up to the 77th floor of the Empire State Building. As I wheeled my pride and joy invention into his plush office the CEO said, "Hey that's a great idea to have those wheels to transport your heavy machine". I then answered back, "Yes, wouldn't this be a great way for people traveling with luggage to have their suitcases on wheels." That was a mistake, because he immediately seized upon the idea himself and you now know the value of this means of baggage movement. This is just another case of my stupidity in revealing my ideas to strangers instead of my pursuing them on my own to fruition and riches.

"Dad's Delight": Here's another one of my ideas that have turned out to be a very profitable spin-off to a very lucrative enterprise. I paid a visit to the Cranberry Headquarters in my neighboring town of Hanson during the early '60's and had a conference with the President. During our conversation I revealed to him the various Cranberry concoctions that I had created. The concoction was as follows: Mix of Cranberry Juice with, Lemon Juice, Orange Juice, Grape Juice, Apple Juice, Pineapple Juice and some of "Mr. McRae's" delicious home-made Cherry Cider. I called this concoction: "Dad's Delight".

They immediately copied my idea and I'm sure you know the rest of the story of the many mixed fruit drinks now on the market. These were virtually non-existent when I retired from teaching & coaching. I should have hired my brother Al as a full time manager for a second, more profit making career after 'retirement'!

"A rope you dope": First come, first serve is a good concept that wasn't used in banks & post offices with multiple service windows. Inevitably, some would choose the slow line, and wait unfairly. I promoted using a rope system for fairness.

Cam Tay: The following is a game which I named **"CamTay"** after my grandchildren, Cameron and Taylor, who gave me the idea as I watched them toss the metal covers from the frozen juice containers. When we were youngsters growing up one of our favorite pastimes was the tossing of Baseball Cards that were enclosed in the gum wrappers to a wall or a line. The card nearest the goal would win all the other cards that were tossed.

With the memories of my baseball card throwing contests, I had the brainstorm of putting the pictures of Athletes on the metal covers with information similar to the information on the Baseball Cards. Then the youngsters could play the same games that we played with our Baseball Cards and make collections similar to the Baseball Collections of today. They would be much more durable than the cardboard Baseball Cards and could stack up very neatly in a box similar to the cylindrical Cheese-Um Potato Chip Containers for neat storage. (Plus the Cheese-Um Box could serve as the goal in the **CamTay** tossing game.)

Just think what a great selling attraction that the juice companies would have in advertising their products with Athletic Heroes on their metal Covers. Every All-American youngster would crave for the opportunity to collect the covers of their Athletic Heroes. Not long after this, my grandson Cammy became enthralled with the 'Pokeyman' game cards and disks. Trust me this idea is going to happen some day soon. I think I'll have my son Michael contact sports and game entrepreneur Pat McInally about this before you do!

Doctor Folloni's Excelsior: Here is another great idea waiting for someone to capitalize on: Living along the ocean, whenever I come up with a bruise or a cut, my first medication is to take a dip in mother nature's bath. Believe me, with all of the mineral salts, it is the best medication in the world and it is very, economical. Why not bottle this ocean water, (taking out the impurities first) and sell it with fancy advertising and branding. With proper marketing, someone could help many ailing people and get rich on this idea.

Some ideas of mine that have stuck, thanks largely to the fact that I proposed and implemented them in conjunction with the very public-good minded officers and volunteers of the MIAA, include state scholastic athlete rules and tournament guideline revisions. I also think that my 'Folloni Special Press' has somehow managed to permeate into basketball lore and fact.

Last but not least, "The Locater" - Another of my 'pipe dreams' is a magnetic, radio or sonic wave and/or electronic 'finder' with audio and/or global positioning feedback for (temporarily) lost keys, eyeglasses, hearing aids, remote controls, pets, kids etc. Each could be micro engineered with a personalized ownership stamp. Consumers could buy dozens of these personalize tiny attachable devices, each equipped with a different sub-codes associated with their various lose-able devices. Don't think it will happen? Just watch (or OWL & L, then FLAP & A) and see.

A FEW OF MY FAVORITE AND NOT SO FAVORITE THINGS

Training Table –
My Favorite Home Cooked Meals and Restaurants

Since eating is probably one of our most favorite pastimes, let me reveal some of my favorite home cooked meals as prepared by my Mom, my wife Helen, my daughter Jean and myself. I'll also list my favorite restaurants and the delicious meals and drinks they served.

MY MOTHER'S COOKING

Let me start with the home cooked meals that were concocted by my Mom. At the top of the list is the delicious **Torta** that she made. Since my Mom was a devoted Catholic and we never had meat on Friday, this was our end of week Special. Her Torta was made of leaks, potatoes, onions, and a mixture of Italian cheeses and spices. The ingredients were then placed in an Italian piecrust and baked in the oven. Oh how I long for those delicious Tortas! My sisters Virginia and Angie remembered the recipe and on many happy occasions they were kind enough to send me some helpings of them.

Next on the list and a close second to the Tortas were my Mom's delicious *spinach and cheese Raviolis & Tortellinis*. I never was one to cherish spinach or any other boiled vegetables but the way that my mother blended the spinach with the Italian cheeses and spices made for a wonderful tasting meal. The Raviolis and Tortellinis were usually served with a tasty Italian sauce or in my mother's delicious 'from scratch' chicken broth. I understand that Preston Balboni's son Tommy, one of the stars from our 1966-67 teams, continues this wonderful Stanley tradition by preparing thousands of these delightful delicacies for family and friends every Thanksgiving weekend.

Another favorite was the various *Rice Puddings* that Mom created. One of them had a mixture of Italian Cheeses, eggs, milk and spices baked in the oven. A takeoff of this creation was her unique *Risotto and Peas*. This dream food consisted of the above items plus a spaghetti sauce mixed with rice then baked in the oven. Occasionally, if it were not a Friday or another fast day, she would add some Italian sausages or veal to this specialty. She often cooked it in an 'Angel Food' cake mold. And Oh, how heavenly it was!

Mom was also noted for her *Polpetti*. They were created from ground hamburg, eggs, breadcrumbs and a mixture of Italian spices. (MacDonald's, Wendy's, and Burger King take note.) You have never tasted a great Hamburger until you have tasted one of Mom's delicious Polpetti.

Mom's *Pork Roast with Roasted Potatoes* was also out of this world. Turkey dinners were few and far between but since we had many chickens in our barn, we did have many a roasted *chicken dinner* with all the trimmings. And of course my Mom's *Home Made Soups* really hit the spot on the cold winter days.

These are just a few of the many scrumptious home cooked meals that my mother created. As I think back to those early days, I often wonder how my poor mother managed to cook for our large family of six children along with many live in boarders and still put in time working in our family Mom and Pop store. We never lacked for food, or for the tender Love that went into it.

HOLLYWOOD HELEN'S HOME-COOKED MEALS

Next on the list of *'finding my heart through my tummy'* are my wife Helen's kitchen creations. Let's begin with my number one favorite, Helen's delicious *Turkey or Chicken Casserole Pie*. She came up with her own special sauce, which included some potatoes, peas, carrots, cream and an assortment of Italian cheeses, she then added a crust to the top and baked it in the oven. You have never tasted anything so satisfying in your life. Even the leftovers (of which there were very few) when reheated were just as good in the days that followed.

Helen's full course *Turkey Dinners with all the trimmings* for Thanksgiving and Christmas were more than the frosting on the cake to make our Holidays complete. Of course she always added her famous *'Tomato Soup Cake'* for desert. Yum, Yum, Yummy -- was that cake ever tasty!

Another of her favorites was the *Krakus Ham Dinners* that she created for Easter Sunday. She added a mixture of pineapples with cinnamon topping, which really added to the sweet flavor. She would complement the main dish with a scrumptious serving of *Escalloped Potatoes* that was *beyond* out of this world. To add to the flavor of these potatoes, she would add a touch of sautéed onions and loads of, you guessed it, Italian cheeses.

When Helen and I were first courting, her divine Mother wanted to make her Italian boyfriend feel welcome, so she prepared spaghetti for me one evening. It was all I could do to keep my composure as she proudly served us a can of warmed up tomato soup over the soggy noodles! Even though Helen came from Irish and English parentage, she soon learned to make *the best Italian Spaghetti Sauce* of any of my Italian families. To this day I still crave for her home made Italian Sauce on my pasta.

Baseball Hall of Famer Larry Doby, who passed away in June, 2003, just days before this book went to press, can attest to Helen's pasta cooking skills. Larry was the first black player in the American League. He joined the Cleveland Indians in July of 1947, three months after Jackie Robinson entered the national league with the Brooklyn Dodgers. Larry was an all-star center fielder from 1949 – 1959 and the 2nd Black Major League Manager (1978 Chicago White Sox). In the early 70's, Bridgewater had a very rich crop of young baseball players, including Glenn Tufts, Rich Dubee and Cardinal Spellman's Charlie Simonds. One spring day around that time Larry Doby came to Bridgewater on a scouting mission. He came to dinner at our home where we shared old memories of baseball. Larry Dobey simply loved Helen's spaghetti and meatballs. *Larry Doby*

Larry graced the same 'guest of honor' chair in our kitchen as did Rocky Marciano, Ted Williams, Ricky Warren and David Freeman.

Helen could also make *homemade soups* to match the best. Her nice thick vegetable soups hit the spot on cold winter nights. She would add all kinds of vegetables then she would strain them, as she knew that I didn't like any boiled vegetables other than peas, carrots, and potatoes. After carefully straining all of the vegetables she used the nice thick soup and cooked up some ditalini pasta and meatballs, then added some nice corn bread or hot rolls to complete a fantastic meal. Her *Swedish Meatballs* were also scrumptious.

Oh I almost forgot how Helen carried on the tradition of *Mama Mark's Delicious Home Made Muffins.* Her muffins contained any of the following on any given morning: Cranberries, Blueberries, Pineapples, Apples Cinnamon, or just the plain excellent moist delicate and buttery muffins. Mmm mmm mmm!

Also her *deserts* were something to behold. In addition to her well-known *Tomato Soup Cake*, add her Lemon Meringue Pies, Banana Bread, Butterscotch & Rice Puddings, and Brownies to name a few. Helen had a special craving for sweets, because she was such a sweet lady.

JEAN THE QUEEN'S HOME-COOKED MEALS

For the last 15 years or so my daughter Jeannie has taken over the chores of making the Home Cooked Meals. She has done an excellent job of carrying on the traditions of Mama Mark and her mother Helen's fine offerings.

One of Jean's Trademarks is the *breakfasts* that she cooks up to get all off to a great new beginning. These included *Mama Mark's famous Muffins* and *Jeannie's Special French Toast, Cinnamon Rolls and pancakes*. The nutritionists may frown on dessert for breakfast, but they haven't tried Jeannie's.

Jean can whip up a *grilled cheese or tuna, or crab sandwich* on an English Muffin, in a jiffy and they are very tasty too.

Her *Salads* are a good match to Christo's famous Salads. The one special item that Jean puts out has to be her Friday night *Perfect Pizza*. No one can approach the taste of her Pizzas, with a real good blend of different cheeses, sautéed onions, and her own spiced sauce. We all really look forward to Friday nights.

Another tasty dish of Jean's is her *Shrimp dinner with rice or a shrimp, bacon, and cheese on an English Muffin baked* in the oven. She can make up the best tasting potatoes, be they mashed, escalloped or twice baked. They are all delicious.

She can cook up a real tasty *Chicken or Ham dinner* with all the fixings and stuffing to go with it. Her *Drumsticks* are out of this world. Jean's Soups, Vegetable or Mexican are a real treat on any cold night. Jean is always handy with *snacks* for her children and any of us who happen to be around in between meals. Last but not least, Jean can cook up *the most luscious tasting deserts* for any occasion. Her butterscotch puddings, myriad cakes and cookies with creative stuffings and toppings, the jelly rolled cake and countless more are the only rivals I've seen to the Cinnamon Apple Pie a la mode with glazed sugar crust that I enjoyed during WWII at a restaurant in New Orleans, Louisiana.

I am very grateful and thankful that we have **"Jeannie Pie"** around to take over, especially since Helen became physically incapacitated.

FAVORITE PIZZA PLACES

As much as I appreciated all the home cooked meals of Mom, Helen, & Jean, there were many times that we went to Restaurants to enjoy an afternoon or night out.

To this day a good Pizza is still my number one treat. My first favorite Pizza place is the *Cape Cod Pizza House* in Campello. I consider myself a Pizza connoisseur. I have tasted Pizzas across the entire USA including California, Chicago, Illinois, Texas, New Orleans, LA, all of Florida, Washington, DC, New York and all of New England (and throughout Italy) and I can go out on a limb to unequivocally state that *the Cape Cod Pizzas are the best in the whole USA and the World.*

The onion Pizza at the Cape Cod is really scrumptious. Their flavor comes the nearest to the taste of my mom's home cooked Torta. By the way, I recently saw the Phantom Gourmet TV Show rate the best Pizza in New England. They put Regina's in the North End of Boston at #1 and the Cape Cod in Brockton at #2. I stongly suggest that they reverse that rating and place Cape Cod where they belong at # 1.

The next one that comes to mind is the *Gondola* Restaurant, in Taunton, MA. Every Friday evening we would bundle up all the children and head for this quaint spot on the lake. I can still recall how we passed the time waiting for our Pizzas there. The children and I would take the Salt and Pepper shakers and slide them across the table to see who could get them the closest to the edge of the table without falling off. Of course there were many misses and the shakers did sometimes go off the deep end of the tables much to Helen's consternation. We all had a blast though and to this day the kids love to engage in friendly and frivolous impromptu competitions with their friends and family.

After about 15 minutes the delicious Pizzas finally were served. What a treat! My special favorite was, of course, the Onion Pizza.

A few other Pizza places worthy of commendation include: *Christos* in Brockton, *Mina Resmini's* place in Middleboro, the *Venetian* in Weymouth, and *J's Flying Pizza* and *Anthony's Charcoal Pit* in Bridgewater. Also *Kelley's* of East Boston, which was rated by Eddie Andelman as the best Pizza around. Despite the high rating given it by some of my kid's, I leave the over-rated Regina's off my list altogether.

Speaking of bests in food & sports, my favorite sports talk show host is Eddie Andelman on 1510, and my favorite food show is the Phantom Gourmet with Eddie's sons. Eddie's annual "Hot Dog Safari" charitable event for Cystic Fibrosis & the Joey Fund really puts him at the top of my all around all-star list.

Favorite Restaurants, Meals and Drinks

My number one restaurant is *The Old Salt* in Hampton Beach. A disastrous fire around 1990 destroyed their beach site, and they have relocated to the crossroads at Hampton Center. The Old Salt meals are excellent. The portions were extra large and tasty. The Chef always did an excellent job and the prices were very economical and well below those of other area restaurants. My favorite there is their extra large portion *Prime Rib*. It was too much for me to consume in one sitting, so I always took the leftovers home in a doggie bag. Their soups were delicious, particularly the *Onion Soup* and the *Corn Chowder*.

My next favorite is *Christos Restaurant* in Brockton, which is noted for their *famous Greek Salads*. My favorite meal here is their *Pork Tenderloin*. Again here at Christos the portions are large and tasty and the prices very reasonable, especially the daytime dinners up to 3pm, which when I could travel there until recently went for between $4.00 and $6.00 for full courses. It is the favorite eating-place for Senior Citizens in the Brockton area. I'm notoriously picky, but I can honestly say that I have never had a bad meal at Christos.

Now I move on to my favorite Italian Restaurants. The *Venetian* at Jackson Square in Weymouth had the best *Veal Parmigiana and Raviolis,* with my kind of Sauce. They also had pretty good *Pizza*. After some of our memorable Boston Garden Championship games we would caravan the busses directly to *The Venetion* for our celebration feasts!

The Italian Kitchen in Campello has by far the best *Spaghetti Sauce* of any Italian Restaurant that I have patronized. I just love their *Raviolis and Meatball and Sausage meals.*

Now I continue to a few of my other favorite Restaurants. Following our Athletic Directors meetings we would go to the *Red Coach Grille* in Framingham. My favorite here was their *Prime Rib* and their delicious *Onion Soup*.

Let me include my favorite Onion Soup Restaurants: *The Red Coach Grille* in Framingham, *Harvey's* Restaurant in Boston, and the *Old Salt* and *Galley Hatch* in Hampton. Naturally I always ordered my Onion Soups *'My Way':* Without croutons or bread in the bowl, strained a la Helen with little or no onion pieces, serving mostly the broth from the cooked onions. Then add Mozzarella or an imported Swiss Cheese melted on top with a good side of Parmesan Cheese for me to add to thicken it. WOW!

My favorite soups are Onion Soup, Clam Chowder, a good thick Vegetable Soup (with the vegetables strained and cooked with ditalini and parmesan cheese), Corn Chowder and hot Mexican Soup a la Jeannie.

The best Clam Chowder Restaurants are. *The Parker House* in Boston, followed by *Farr's* and the *Galley Hatch* in Hampton.

For *Lobsters and Lobster Rolls* the best are *Manny's* in Seabrook, and *Al's Seafood* in Hampton, N.H. Also the *Old Salt, Brown's and Markey's* in Hampton Beach.

Steamed Clams and Clam Chowder a la Larry Folloni are delicacies to behold. Michael and Thuy claim that it is the best on earth.

Any good meal begins with a Salad or Soup. My choice of Soup or Salad would depend upon what the Restaurant had to offer. I have discussed the Soups above. As for the Salads let me say this. Most of the Salads that are offered in Restaurants are nothing more than grass or weeds with commercial dressings added. I hate the taste of weeds. Weeds and grass are for Cows, Sheep and Goats.

A good Salad must be prepared well in advance and left to soak up the oil and vinegar base that is so essential. My favorite Salads consist of Lettuce, Tomatoes, Cucumbers, and Red Onions. Add a few Cheese Croutons and possibly a few chunks of Ham or Salami, then a good home made Italian Dressing or French Dressing in a pinch.

Where have I found the Dressing to my taste? The first one was when my son Bob and I were invited to attend a catered affair for Italian schoolboy athletes held at the Italian - American Club in Waltham. The one thing that still remains fresh on my mind was the salad that was properly prepared in advance with it's delicious flavor that I attribute to the Italian Dressing.

The other Salad that still wets my appetite is that served at the *Rochester Country Club*, where we held our annual year-end Tournaments and meeting of the Profile Seniors Golf Association. The House Dressing concocted by the Chef was out of this world and to this day I crave it. I only wish that I could get the recipe.

Of course we must mention Christo's famous Salads and Christo's famous Salad Dressing and Feta Cheese.

Oh and let's not forget the Chinese Food. My favorites are the *Chicken Wings* and *Chicken Teriyaki* along with *Pork Fried Rice* and *Sweet and Sour Chicken and Pork And crispy Walnut Shrimp*. None other than the *Ocean Wok* on Hampton Beach fits this bill best.

For the best *Barbecued Ribs* and *Clam Chowder* go to *Farr's* in Hampton Beach.

And last but not least let's not forget the *Boston Chicken* (now Boston Market). Really for the price of $5. to $6. you get a delicious serving of Chicken Breast and good mashed potatoes along with a vegetable and corn bread.

Favorite Entertainment

Besides playing and coaching sports, my favorite entertainment is watching my grandchildren play them. Helen and I still like to go down to the Hatch Shell at Hampton Beach to listen to live concerts. I enjoy working on my book and my computer and surfing the internet more than I like watching TV. My best idle time is spent just holding hands with Helen. An occasional ballgame on TV also suits me ok, but only in the background, as I spend most of my attention on the affairs of my family. Many people have said that life around the Folloni household sometimes resembles a circus. I can't disagree, nor can I say that I regret the fun. I only wish that I had had the chance to view in person the world-famous circus act of Italy: "Circo Folloni".

FAVORITE ICE CREAM – CIRCUS MAN

Here's to the Folloni Family Favorite – Circus Man Ice Cream!

The toast of Manhattan, Circus Man President Jeff Graziano

John, Bob, Mike, Jeff

CHEF COACH

Cheeze-Its and canned tomato soup are not the limits of my own culinary capabilities. In addition to my clam chowder, I cook a popular barbeque meat mix, with onion and drippings basted diced potatoes. My garlic and Italian oil and herbs entrenched Pork Tenderloin with roasted spiced potatoes is a family favorite. My children say that the Easter 26 months after my coma when I cooked this for the family really marked my resurrection into full family life. And I'm not shy to say that my morning egg, milk, onion cheese and black pepper scramble can be a worthy counterpoint to Jean's sweet morning offerings.

And then there's my invention of Mixed Juices, *'Dad's Delight.* This concoction included: A mixture of Cranberry Juice with: Lemon Juice, Orange Juice, Grape Juice, Apple Juice, Pineapple Juice, and some of Mr. McRae's delicious home made Cherry Cider. I was creating and drinking varieties of fruit drinks long before Ocean Spray, Nantucket Nectars, Snapple, and the others came along.

I wish I could live to be 200 so that I could bring some of my innovations to mass market. Then again, maybe I can through you: If you have an inspiration, separate yourself from the crowd by seeing it through to its best conclusion. If you have many ideas, try promoting them many times until you become a professional and one or more of them generates rewards. Remember, Babe Ruth struck out more times than he hit homeruns, and all-star baseball players fail to get a hit on 7 out of 10 attempts.

We can only do great things by being committed to doing the little things that make them up. Dream as big as you can, then dedicate yourself to doing the little things that can grow into the great thing that is your life. Not only by remembering our favorite things do we feel better, but also by counting our blessings, we can multiply them.

One more thing: *Do as I say, but watch your calories and exercise them off along the way!*

3 generations of great cooks

My Pet Peeves

1) Phone systems that put you on hold for a very extended time without letting you speak with a person, with menu lists of every option except how to speak with an operator. The recordings are in 3 languages and they give you all kinds of sales pitches that you don't want to hear. The companies and organizations using these clearly think that your time is less valuable than theirs is.

2) Tele-marketers who always seem to pester you right at dinner time.

3) Drivers who park illegally on corners blocking the view of cars trying to enter from side streets. Ditto for people who grow shrubs on corners to block views.

4) Drivers who tailgate!

5) Drivers who will not allow others to exit from of side streets when traffic is heavy in their lane.

6) Drunk drivers. I AM NOT OPPOSED TO SOCIAL DRINKING IN MODERATION BUT WHEN PEOPLE MAKE LUSHES OF THEMSELVES, THEN GET BEHIND THE WHEEL IT ONLY BREWS TROUBLE AND SOME INNOCENT PERSON MAY GET KILLED. THE DRUNKS USUALLY SURVIVE.

7) Drug addicts who don't seek help: I FEEL SORRY FOR DRUG ADDICTS SINCE THEY ARE HOOKED ON AN UNCONTROLLABLE HABIT. I DESPISE, HOWEVER THE DRUG DEALERS, WHO PROFIT FROM THEIR SALES WITHOUT ANY CONCERN FOR THE SUFFERING OF THEIR CLIENTS.

8) Politicians who promise you the world to get your vote. When they are elected they fail to even respond to a simple request to make life more enjoyable for the average citizen.

9) Politicians who vote for 'Pork' projects to get your vote. They talk tax cuts but when elected they spend and waste your money on frivolous projects but won't help Disabled American Veterans or Senior citizens causes.

10) Flag wavers after 9/11 and after Wars. In 6 months or less, they forget and refuse to help the needy that they were waving the flags for in the first place.

11) Public Officials who do not protect and serve their constituents. Police scare tactics and harassment of the law-abiding citizen.

12) Smoking in public places, particularly in restaurants. CIGARETTE COMPANIES ARE NOT ALLOWED TO ADVERTISE THEIR FILTHY PRODUCT ON RADIO OR TV BUT THEY GET AROUND THIS BY HAVING TEEN IDOL SCREEN ACTORS LIGHT UP. THIS PRACTICE SHOULD BE OUTLAWED.

HELP FROM THE BENCH & SIDELINES

I know full well that I could never have achieved much without help from others. Not counting my family, teachers and coaching colleagues that I have mentioned elsewhere in my story, I would like to take this opportunity to list as many people as I can recall who have contributed to my success and achievements. Please accept my apologies both for any redundancies in this section and for any of my important friends and supporters that I may have inadvertently left off this list. Here's offering my belated and most gracious thanks to all of you.

The first person to come to my mind is Tranquilla Resmini, the Midwife who assisted in my birth.

Next is my brother Mike who rescued me from the train that was about to crush me. A half-century later he saved me again with his skillful handling of our Volvo that had a tire blow on a mountainous highway. Mike has been a real brother role model and has guided all his brothers and sisters throughout our lives.

Vinnie Cassiani risked his life to rescue me from drowning. Bystanders Mary Tassinari and Ester Resmini alerted Vinnie of my predicament.

While talking of dramatic rescues, I must list the many doctors are who worked so feverishly over me on several occasions to save my life. The first one was Dr. Hector Douglas who saved my life following a spike wound while playing baseball. Dr. Douglas was later to become the Team Physician for our Athletic Teams.

The next was when I received a wound in the service. A doctor named Bob worked on me and stood by my bedside throughout the night following a crisis that developed after a mistaken injection by a medical technician nearly killed me.

Then there was the Doctor who repaired my skull following my life threatening 'hit in the head by a pitch' baseball injury.

In my later years Dr. Charles Ferguson and his staff at the Mass General Hospital, saved my life following botched surgery by others on December 7, 1998.

More recently the medical staff at the Portsmouth Regional Hospital have taken on a good deal of the modern medicine miracle tasks to keep me alive. They include: Dr. Frank Fedele, my heart doctor, Dr. John Novello, my kidney doctor, Dr. Stephen Paul, my General Care doctor, Dr. William Berry, my vascular surgeon, Dr. Daniel Crowe, my Diabetic doctor, Dr. Miles Scheffer, my Lung doctor, and Dr. Constance Passas, my Arthritis doctor. (So far I'm doing better than Humpty

Dumpty is, and my medical team is far better than all the king's horses, and all the king's men.)

The latest additions to the above list of medical teams that are keeping me going in overtime include:

The Brigham and Women's Hospital Doctors and staff
who were so helpful during my 2003 "May Stay" at their Hospital.

Dr. Edward Bromfield, Neurologist   Keifer St. Pierre, Stroke Unit Admin.

Dr. Tammy Chang, Neurology (very helpful)   Dr. Sam Ahn, Neurology (very helpful)

Dr. Valerie Luyckz, Renal (very helpful and caring)   Dr. Galen Henderson, Chief, Stroke Unit

Hilda Torres, Mary Ann and Peggy were among the many helpful nurses.

The MGH Doctors and staff who were so helpful
during my 2003 "June Stint" at their Hospital.

Dr. Hasson Bazari, Renal   Dr. Christopher Kwolek, surgeon
RN. Greg Nazzo

Back to those who were 'lifesavers' in my career, I'll start with my first principal at Dighton High School, Dana Webber who was a kind guide for me through my first years of teaching.

To land my dream job in my home town of Bridgewater I had the help of school committee members Jim Buckley, Maurice Walsh, Gordon Hall, and Alice Holmes.

Once in the system I benefited from the leadership of principals Herb DeVeber, John McGovern, and Paul Zdanowich.

Starting from the early '50's I received much needed help to get our town's Athletic and Recreational Programs off to a great start. These largely unsung 'Sideline Helpers' included: Members of the Lions Club who came to my strong assistance after the introductory meeting when I introduced my plans for Recreation and Athletics in our town. As many names as I can recall are: First and foremost was Primo Resmini, then Gordon Hall, Maurice Walsh, Earl Jackson, William Casper, Sam Alfieri, Milt Skillings, Ralph Case, George Hogg, Bill Prophett & of course many more.

I can't forget the help from the wive's of these kind people who also contributed their time and help to all of our projects, including Marjorie Alfieri, Cissy Hogg, Eleanor Prophett, Marion Skillings, Ester Ferioli, Alice Ferioli and Mary Pallatroni

Members of our Industrial backers included: George Stone the President of the Independent Nail Company who was one of our largest benefactors, along with George & Phil Jenkins of the Jenkins Mill, Bob McIntyre of Lucy Shoe Company (Jelco Shoe), Ed McHugh of the Eastern Grain Company, and Dave Perkins of The Perkins Foundry Co.

Many of the merchants of our town also contributed: Wally Krueger of Krueger Motor Sales, Lou Berenson of Rexall Drugs Morris Gotshalk of the Fashion Clothing Store, Stanley Smudin of Smudin's Market. Bart Casey's News Stand, Sumner Paulive of The Central Square Drug Store, Ernie Saccocia of Ernie's Appliance, Al Saccocia of Saccocia Insurance Co., Richard and David Saccocia of Saccocia's Barber Shop, David Chamberlain of Cholerton Insurance Co., the Woronicz's and many, many others.

The Organizations in town that were so helpful included The K of C, The Forty-Niners, The Lincoln Club, The Polish Club, Citizen's Club, and The Veterans Club.

One of my biggest individual supporters was Judge Robert Clark who not only gave financial help but also was of great assistance and guidance to me throughout my career.

Other supporters who backed us vocally and financially all the way included: David "Coontail" Freeman, Peter Murby from his wheelchair, Warren "Red" Meacham, Jim Buckley, Paul Anacki, Fran Mansfield, Gus Lucini, and Dr Will Cohen to name a few.

Following the 10 glorious years at Bridgewater High School our town went into a partnership with Raynham to form the B-R Regional School District. There I was introduced to one of the best bosses I ever had, Serge J. Bernard, the guy who literally built the great B-R School system.

Mary & Serge Bernard after a well deserved retirement

A perfect assistant to Mr. Bernard was big hearted Chet Millett, our 'ringer'.

Bringing the B-R school system to a level envied by all in the state were the background people on the B-R school committee led by Walter Murray, Jim

Buckley, John Hickey, Doctor Edward Heywood, Shoshana Garshick, Cliff Bettencourt, Arthur Wyman and Donald Buron. The early school committee and building committee consisted of Mr. Burns, my neighbor Mr. Philip Dooley, Mr. Richard Bradley, Mr. Mason, and Mr. Ziegler

In my later years we were fortunate to have Dr. Edwin Denton to carry on the B-R traditions. Dr. Denton was my first Basketball Captain and my last Superintendent. He was the one who was the moving force in securing the financial support to build our Athletic Plant and Facilities into one of the best in the State.

At the old Bridgewater High School the custodial staff consisted of John Hall, Leon Carroll, Joe Lazaro, Louie Calabrese, and John Cabral. The cafeteria staff included the manager, Cliff Craig, Mrs. Edith Shepard, Mrs. Mildred Adams, Mrs. Lena Correia, and Mrs. Loretta Hennessey, The secretarial staff consisted of Mss Anne Norkawski and Miss Marion Sweares.

It was the custodial staff at B-R under Alec Mellin who kept our school building and grounds immaculate. His staff included John Cabral, Will Chiocca, Paul Bumpus, Frank Dutra, Paul Anacki, Angelo Mattie, and Frank Machado. Our Matron who took care of all the athletic laundry was Mrs. Agnes Yakavonis.

The Cafeteria Staff under Manager Mr. Bob Parsons included Ms. Carmalina Querzoli, Ms. Julia Scarbi, Ms. Days, Ms. Steen, Ms. O'Leary, Mrs. Helen Ghelfi, Mrs. Ann Resmini and Mrs Franklin Barney. This was the staff that help us put on our Pizza parties every Christmas and after every Basketball Reunion.

On the Political front our main supporters included: Dave Flynn, selectman and state Representative (Dean of the House, longest serving member). State Rep. Peter Flynn. Selectman Henry Cormier, one of my close friends and golfing partners, contributed much time and effort to our success. Senator Hastings Keith, Senator John Parker and Senator Edward Kirby, along with Representative Allan Chiocca and Raynham Selectman, Donald Francis were also positive supporters.

More great help came from my good friends and golfing partner Dr. Fred Meiers.

Long time friend, Harold Goodnough Coach and Boston Braves Scout and George Demers, who handled the work-study program were great supporters

And I can't forget the secretarial help I had over the years from Rita Manganaro, Betty Dowd, Viola Davis, Bonnie Murray, Grace DeMers, Janice Jones, Marie Bevis, Joan Seymour, and Ruth Alexander in the office.

Throughout my career I have had the support of many individuals who assisted me in my work with the State Athletic Administrative positions I held. Chief among them were the esteemed Dr. Bertram Holland, who was the Executive Director of the MIAA. Dick Neal took over upon Dr. Holland's retirement and for the last decade and more he has been carrying on the noble and competent traditions of Dr. Holland, and then some with a great expansion of the MIAA. Other great contributors in the MIAA office include Sherman Kinney, Bill Gaine and Ralph Martin.

Dick Neal

Along with the above named individuals from the MIAA and the 'Standing Committee on Athletics' many others assisted me in my endeavors. John Conrad, my predecessor as Director of the State Basketball Tournament was of invaluable assistance to me when I came aboard. Arrigo LaTanzi, Paul Ambler and Carl Berg were all very helpful in our rules committee work.

I cannot forget Will Cingolani, a true, trusted and loyal friend. Will was the principal at the Plymouth Carver Regional High School who was my traveling companion to all of our Standing Committee meetings. In addition to being the principal at Plymouth Carver, Will was the Commissioner of the Southeastern Mass Official's Association and did all of the assignment of officials. ***And would you believe that even now after retirement and at the age of 80 he is still assigning officials? Will represents the epitome in championing youth through education, sports and sportsmanship.***

Will along with Leo Miller, the very successful basketball coach at Nauset Regional High School and the liaison man for the State Basketball Association, were key members of our State Basketball Tournament Committee that assisted me greatly in running the State Tournament. I couldn't have done it without them.

My appreciation also goes to the many Athletic Directors from MSSADA and those from all the Coaches organizations that've been so cooperative and helpful.

In my later retirement years there were two Disabled Veterans who worked quite feverishly on my behalf to secure my benefits as a disabled American Vet. The first was Ron Reilly, the DAV field agent, who did such a great job initially in securing my benefits. The other one was Ron Currier, who is presently working to secure me additional help for my handicaps. Ron Currier is a double amputee who has what I describe as two clamps attachments for his arms. It is unbelievable what he can do with these artificial limbs. Ron is always cheerful and he never comes close to complaining about his handicap. He rather focuses his attention trying to help others who are handicapped. It's not what life gives us that counts, its what we give back to life. Ron is, of course, a champion.

I can't forget the assistance my teams received from the Media over the years. They have always been very fair and helpful to all of our Athletic Programs to give the needed publicity to encourage our youngsters in their athletic endeavors and pursuits of excellence.

I'll begin with John Sweeney, the Brockton Enterprise's local reporter for Bridgewater who covered most of our team's accomplishments. After he retired from coaching, the fabled trailblazer Lester Lane took over the local sports reporting. For the Bridgewater Independent paper, it was Pat Jantomaso on sports and Ken Moore's 'Talk of the Common' that kept the townspeople informed of what was happening in our town. Later the local "Keynote" paper with Ed Querzoli as the Editor in Chief did an excellent job in coverage of Town sports. (Ed went on to become the Editor In Chief of the prestigious Quincy Patriot Ledger.) Joe O'Brien, one of my first student managers and my recreation department publicist, went on to become the News Editor of the Brockton Enterprise.

In the Enterprise Sports Department we had Vic Dubois and Pete Farley in the early days who did such a great job in our sports coverage. Also working there as feature writers were Bob Richards, Ed Lyons, Joe Cotton and Tony Sirrico. They were followed by Nick Cafardo, Glen Farley, Frank Stoddard, Win Bates, Bob Buckley and Billy Abramson, who I believe is now, the Sports Editor. All of these guys have been super for the kids.

The ubiquitous Stanley Bauman, photographer extraordinaire, did an outstanding professional job always to chronicle the athletic and other adventures of local citizenry. I'd hardly be surprised if Stan showed up to photograph *any* event.

The Taunton Gazette had Johnny Needs as the Sports Editor. Johnny carried some excellent stories. Succeeding him were such sports writers as Paul Mosnicka, Mike Silva and Nate Thompson who have given us great coverage. These guys are all just super chroniclers of our lives and times. Like many of the others who I've mentioned in this section, they knew how to dig to the essence of stories. And, unlike some of today's writers who try to advance on the backs of those who they've trampled, these guys succeeded on the shoulders of those who they have built up.

The Boston Papers had their share of good writers who covered High School Sports. The first one I recall is Gerry Hern of the old Boston Post, Fred Foye, Bucky Yardume, Ralph Wheeler, Tim Horgan and Bob Dunbar of the Boston Herald-Traveler. The Boston Globe had such luminaries as Peter Gammons, Will McDonough, Vince Doria, Ernie Roberts, Bob Ryan, Dan Shaughnessy, Ernie Dalton, Neil Singelais, Larry Ames, and Bob Holbrook who've been kind to us.

The Quincy Ledger had Roger Barry as the feature sports writer, who gave us excellent coverage in all sports.

It is ironical and a strange coincidence that three of my favorite sports writers passed on in the past year. Fred Foye and Neil Singelais, in December of 2002 and Will McDonough on January 9th, 2003. I have no intention of comparing notes with these fine reporters any time soon.

Two other sportswriters worthy of mention for their contribution to schoolboy athletics are Marvin Pave of the Boston Globe and Billy Abramson of the Boston Herald, (now Editor of Enterprise Sports). It was these two young cub Sports Writers who called me one day and asked me to help them out in my position as Chairman of the MIAA Rules Committee. They asked me to propose the Football Playoff Tournament to the Headmasters. This proposal, after many hassles by the Headmasters, was finally adopted in the early 70's and has blossomed into a great 'Superbowl' and lead up tournament spectacle for fans and players alike.

For Radio sports coverage we start with Gill Santos, who in his early days covered the Southeastern Mass area. Next was Station WBET and Dom Valentino's Sports Show. Dom did an outstanding job in covering the Championship games at the Boston Garden, as did Don Carlson and Walt Dunbar of Station WBET.

Then with the onset and popularity of TV, we had Mike Lynch of Channel 5 carry on with his great High School "Star of the Week' show and special features to advance High School Sports.

My early playing days at the Brockton Country Club were marked by association with guys like Paul and Maynard Stetsons, Paul, The Gang Busters, and the Doc Carr Wednesday afternoon Special Gangbusters, all great men, many of whom I've talked about earlier herein.

When I retired and went up to Hampton Beach to live, I now became a member at the beautiful Portsmouth Country Club. There I was to be fortunate to meet up with some class guys like Herc Phyllides, Bill Snow, and Hank Richardson who made up our foursome for many happy years. Some other class guys that I was associated with in the Profile Seniors Golf Association are noted elsewhere in '*My Way*'. My playing partners in the PSGA Tournaments were Frank Pickard and Howard Page, two great guys. Also, Art Averill, Marty Ward, and Joe LaCroix

One of my many Golfing buddies was Bob Shaw, one of the greatest trial lawyers in New Hampshire who met an untimely death at the age of 83 after the onset of Altziemers Disease. Bob was the most generous, kind, and considerate man I ever knew on the golf course. He accomplished much in his lifetime. His generosity was out of this world.

Advice from Bill Gates that I agree with

Here's some advice Bill Gates recently dished out at a high school speech about 11 things they did not learn in school. He talks about how feel-good, politically correct teaching has created a full generation of kids with no concept of reality and how this concept set them up for failure in the real world.

BILL GATES' 11 RULES

- Life is not fair – get used to it.

- The world won't care about your self-esteem, the world will expect you to accomplish something before you feel good about yourself.

- You will not make 40 thousand dollars a year right out of high school. You won't be a vice president with a car phone, until you earn both.

- If you think your teacher is tough, wait until you get a boss. He doesn't have tenure.

- Flipping burgers is not beneath your dignity. Your grandparents had a different word for burger flipping – they called it opportunity.

- If you mess up, it's not your parents fault, so don't whine about your mistakes, learn from them.

- Before you were born your parents weren't as boring as they are now. They got that way from paying your bills, cleaning your clothes, and listening to you talk about how cool you are. So before you save the rain forest from the parasites of your parents generation, try delousing the closet in your own room.

- Your school may have done away with winners and losers, but life has not. In some schools they have abolished failing grades and they'll give you as many times as you want to get the right answer. This doesn't bear the slightest resemblance to anything in real life.

- Life is not divided into semesters. You don't get summers off and very few employers are interested in helping you find yourself. Do that on your own time.

- Television is not real life. In real life people actually have to leave the coffee shop and go to jobs.

- Be nice to nerds. Chances are you'll end up working for one.

MY FAMILY'S PETS

We had many pets, all of which were really great and worth any 'trouble' or expense they may have caused. We had many favorites, including Duke, Dutchess, Bump, Pssst, Dolly and Saysha. I won't bore the reader with all of them, but here's one story:

Cochise was a beautiful blue Russian ball of gray fluff with Mediterranean blue eyes that Jeannie fell in love with while visiting her friend Lauren Decatur. Cochise became the family favorite pet. Even grouchy me got to love him. Larry Jr. build a pet house for Cochise, complete with fotos of a pretty female cat on the wall to keep him company.

We enjoyed him for several years. Cochise loved to roam the neighborhoods (perhaps in search for the pretty kitty pictured on his wall), but he would always respond to the call that Jean invented that sounded like a high pitched 'Coo Coo Coo Coo'. One day Jean was returning from Boston on the bus, and she stopped at one of our neighbor's houses to chat. Cochise was roaming across busy Bedford St., saw Jean before Jean saw him, and ran across to meet her. Unfortunately a car struck him.

Hearing the yells of horror, I immediately went out to the side of the road where Cochise laid with the fur of his body ripped open by the impact with the car. I placed him in a box and hurried him up to the Veterinarian. Upon examination we were given the bad news that the injuries were beyond repair and that Cochise would have to be put to sleep.

Of course I was given the task of taking him up to where they put animals to sleep. I arrived at the hospital and proceeded to take the box containing Cochise for his last good bye. As I looked into the box, Cochise's eyes were wide open and the sad look in his eyes as he looked up to me brought tears to my own eyes. He looked at me as if to say, "Don't let me go". It was so sad to say goodbye to Cochise, the member of our family who I groused about admitting.

I've always let the kids have pets for just plain fun, as well as to teach them about responsibility and life. However, unfortunately we tend to far outlive our pets, and when it came down to the end of each of the family pets lives, it was me who undertook the sad final duty of bringing them to the vet for their final goodbye. I guess that is just one of the things that a parent must agree to take on to earn the prized mantel of being "Daddy".

GREAT LAST SECOND SHOTS

Pan Ho, with a little help from his friends from B.R.

Dent's Gone Wild in Panama City!!

Dolly, Tweetie, Xanders and Song On the Delta in Uncle Hung and Auntie JosieVan's boat.

THE AVA GRACE FOLLONI LOOK ALIKE CONTEST

Uncle Mike, c. 1953. Born 50 yrs B.A.G. (Before Ava Grace)

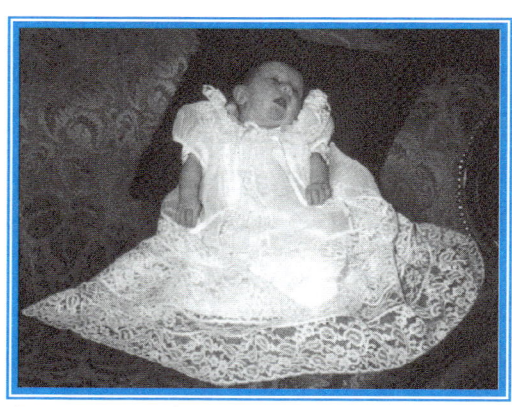

Auntie Jean, born over 40 years B.A.G

Donna Spratt & Ava Grace 'Wanna Be' c.2003

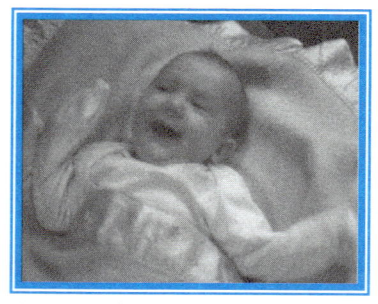

Aunt Deb, over 30 yrs. B.A.G.

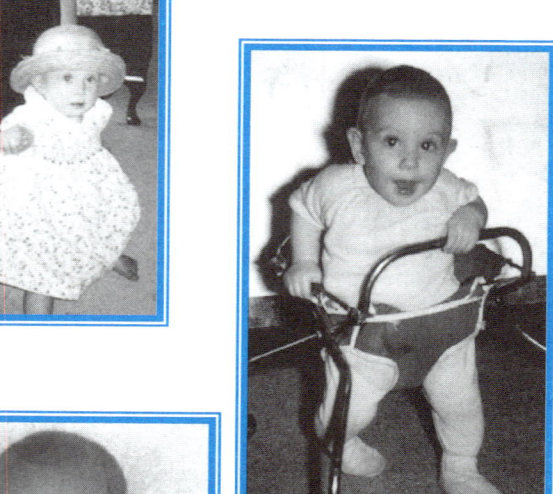

Where's Fenway? c.1963 James born 41 Yrs. B.A.G.

Donna Spratt, age 3-days

This youngster almost looks like "All of her"

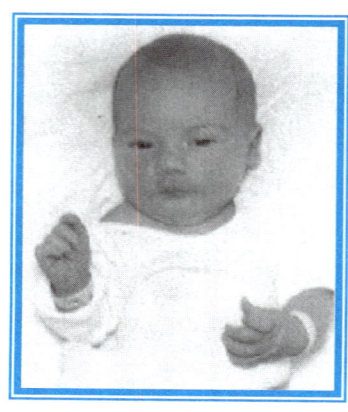

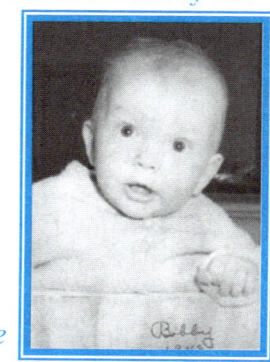

Uncle Bobby, in a daze

DO AS I SAY
Some of Dad's Favorite Sayings and Exhortations
With translations by the Folloni Team

"Common Sense is not a Common Thing"

"The Old Man Knows More than His Prayers"
I told you so. Now do as I say.

Qui dorme no piglia il pesce!
He who sleeps catches no fish. (The early bird catches the worm.)

"Don't put the cart before the horse."
1st things first

"A place for everything, and everything in its place."
Which often followed: "Who took my Pen?"

"Rise and Shine"!
" Work to be done and a War to be Won"
"Up an at 'em' atom ant!"
Good Morning

"Is Everybody Happy!!?"
Dad's warm enthusiastic exhortation upon arriving home from work
or shortly after embarking on a family ride or after his kids missed play activities due to working
thrice as long & hard on an income property project than promised.

Bunurole
Lighthearted Stanley slang warning that if one's questionable behavior persists, that it will
be rewarded with a warming of one's buns. "Keep hotdogging and I'll kick your bunurole!"

"Use Your Professor"
In basketball, the art of using one's moon
to separate the opponent from the ball you are holding or waiting to rebound.

"When the going gets tough, the tough get going."
Don't Quit

"When Preparation meets Opportunity there is Success."
When Love meets a moment in Destiny, there is fulfillment

"Natch"
Short for 'Naturally', usually used as a reply to someone mentioning that corporations or politicians
are robbing the masses, or that some dumb administrator is needlessly messing up a youth program.

"A Meal Fit for a King and a King to Eat It "
Usually said 20 minutes before 'Basta Cosi'

"Miss Jean, Mix Me A Drink"
Typically one of Dad's innovative non-alcoholic fruit mix concoctions

"Mmmm, Delicious"
After a taste of a good pizza or prime rib, or one of Jean's home cooked meals.

"Basta Cosi"
Enough Food (after a prodigious helping of same)

" Have Fun but Be Good."
While sending his youth or adult children off to any venture in the world.

"I've ain't ever lived this day before and I'm never going to live it again so I'd best enjoy it"
Don't Worry, Be Happy

"It's Gonna Be a Scorcha"
New Englandese for man will it be hot today. Followed By….

"It's Hot in Here"
Open the Windows (Don't waste money by turning on the Air Conditioning)

"Who Done It"
Usually after Dad did something offensive

"(You've Got) Bugs in the Head"
Don't worry. Be Happy.

Don't Worry, Be Happy

Or I'll swat your Bunurole!

"Let's Go" "Let's Go"
Alert Alive Awake Enthusiastic

"I Know What I'm Doing, Shut Up & Listen"
Do it My Way

"Be An OWL"
Observe, Watch, Listen

"She-He"
Early John, Paul, Ringo & George, or a Hippie of any era

"One For All and All For One"
The Team First

"Get to Work" "Get back to Work" "Time to Work" "That Works"

And of course

"My Way IS the Highway!"

Light Energy Books
(!)

My Way – the Memoirs of Coach Larry Folloni

Quick Order Form

Fax orders: (603) 926-8313. Send this form

Telephone orders: Call **1-800 425-7440** toll free.

Email orders: CoachFolloni@comcast.com

Mail orders: Coach Larry Folloni, 13 Ross Ave., Hampton Beach, N.H. 03842

Name: _____

Address: _____

City: _____ State _____ Zip _____

Telephone _____ Email _____

If a gift to a different person / address: Mail to:

Name: _____ From: _____

Address: _____

City: _____ State _____ Zip _____

A substantial portion of proceeds from sales will go to youth athletics & education.

Price per book: $19.95	Shipping & Handling for 1st book: $5.05
	Shipping & Handling for each additional book: 5¢

Circle One

1 Book Delivered	$25	5 Books Delivered	$105
2 Books Delivered	$45	10 Books Delivered	$205
3 Books Delivered	$65	20 Books Delivered	$405
4 Books Delivered	$85	**Other Quantity** ____ $____